Race and Crime

Fourth Edition

For my loving parents, Daphne and Patrick Gabbidon,
who continue to be supportive of all my endeavors.

—*SLG*

To my ancestors for paving the way.

—*HTG*

SAGE was founded in 1965 by Sara Miller McCune to support
the dissemination of usable knowledge by publishing innovative
and high-quality research and teaching content. Today, we
publish more than 850 journals, including those of more than
300 learned societies, more than 800 new books per year, and
a growing range of library products including archives, data,
case studies, reports, and video. SAGE remains majority-owned
by our founder, and after Sara's lifetime will become owned by
a charitable trust that secures our continued independence.

Los Angeles | London | New Delhi | Singapore | Washington DC

Race and Crime

Fourth Edition

Shaun L. Gabbidon
Pennsylvania State Harrisburg

Helen Taylor Greene
Texas Southern University

Los Angeles | London | New Delhi
Singapore | Washington DC

Los Angeles | London | New Delhi
Singapore | Washington DC

FOR INFORMATION:

SAGE Publications, Inc.
2455 Teller Road
Thousand Oaks, California 91320
E-mail: order@sagepub.com

SAGE Publications Ltd.
1 Oliver's Yard
55 City Road
London EC1Y 1SP
United Kingdom

SAGE Publications India Pvt. Ltd.
B 1/I 1 Mohan Cooperative Industrial Area
Mathura Road, New Delhi 110 044
India

SAGE Publications Asia-Pacific Pte. Ltd.
3 Church Street
#10-04 Samsung Hub
Singapore 049483

Printed in the United States of America

ISBN 978-1-4833-8418-4

This book is printed on acid-free paper.

Acquisitions Editor: Jerry Westby
Development Editor: Jessica Miller
Editorial Assistant: Laura Kirkhuff
Production Editor: Veronica Stapleton Hooper
Copy Editor: Diana Breti
Typesetter: C&M Digitals (P) Ltd.
Proofreader: Susan Schon
Indexer: Terri Corry
Cover Designer: Scott Van Atta
Marketing Manager: Terra Schultz

15 16 17 18 19 10 9 8 7 6 5 4 3 2 1

Brief Contents

Detailed Contents

Supplemental materials for *Race and Crime* are available
online at **study.sagepub.com/gabbidon4e.**

Preface to the Fourth Edition

"Justice is Blind" represents the basic motto and principle of our criminal justice system. It symbolizes equity in the administration of justice and represents our basic rights in a free society.

For many in the minority community, however, society is not that free and justice is far from blind. Justice in many cases has perfect 20/20 vision that distinguishes people on the basis of race, ethnicity, gender, religious beliefs and social and economic status.

—National Organization of Black
Law Enforcement Executives (2001, p. 4)

Welcome to the fourth edition of *Race and Crime*. We are excited that the first three editions were positively received by students and instructors and that—for more than a decade—this book continues to be one of the standard texts used in courses related to race, ethnicity, and crime. For this edition, we have updated each chapter and also devoted attention to the increasing societal focus on racial bias in police encounters and immigration. As in the earlier editions, we provide information on crime and justice trends in the appropriate chapters. We have also included critical thinking questions, Race and Crime in the Media Boxes, and policy-oriented Boxes in each chapter. There are also discussion questions, a listing of key Internet sites, as well as Internet Exercises at the end of each chapter. The numerous pedagogical approaches provide students with an opportunity to reflect on historical and contemporary issues and familiarize themselves with relevant information available. This edition includes coverage of several timely topics, such as biosocial theory, violent victimizations, immigrant policing, and the school-to-prison pipeline.

Race and crime is a contemporary issue in many societies where there is a diverse population and racial and ethnic minorities (Bucerius & Tonry, 2014). Since the colonial era, race and crime in America have been inextricably linked; there has been a belief that minorities, especially Blacks, are more criminal. At first, support for this belief was the result of racist ideologies that labeled minorities as both "criminal" and "inferior." More recently, support for this erroneous belief was based on the disproportionate number of racial and ethnic minorities who are arrested and imprisoned.

After the 1960s, the relationship between race and crime became more ambiguous as we learned about the role of justice practitioners and their use of discretion. Early in this century, as reported crime, arrests, and victimizations decrease, incarceration rates continue to be a concern.

The opening quotation captures the beliefs of many racial and ethnic minorities about justice in the United States in the past and present. Whites, who form the majority of the U.S. population, are less likely to believe there is discrimination in the administration of justice. Because the news media usually focus on persons who commit crimes, especially serious crimes like murder and rape, it is easy to lose sight of the fact that the majority of Americans, regardless of their race or ethnicity, are law-abiding citizens. It seems that we have just as easily lost sight of the historical context of race and crime in the United States. Why do racial minorities, most of whom are law-abiding citizens, continue to be labeled criminals? The study of race and crime has a long history in the discipline of criminology and the study of criminal justice. In the 19th century, positivist scholars (those who explained crime using biological, sociological, or psychological factors) deemed the physical characteristics of racial minorities and some White ethnics to be associated with crime (Gabbidon, 2015; Gabbidon & Taylor Greene, 2005).

Early criminology texts devoted whole chapters to race and crime that not only presented crime figures, but also sought to explain the trends related to race and crime (Gabbidon & Taylor Greene, 2001). Interestingly, contemporary criminology textbooks do not devote as much attention to race and crime as did earlier texts (Gabbidon & Taylor Greene, 2001). Even many of the early textbooks omitted many important topics like slave patrols, lynching, race riots, and legal segregation, which often resulted in socially disorganized communities. More recently, despite a strong argument for studying race and crime put forth by LaFree and Russell (1993), only a handful of comprehensive books on this topic are available (Barak, Leighton, & Cotton, 2014; Gabbidon, 2015; Glynn, 2013; Mann, 1993; Moore, 2015; Tarver, Walker, & Wallace, 2002; Walker, Spohn, & DeLone, 2012).

Most of the early scholarly research on race that is available refers primarily to Blacks. This is due, at least in part, to the fact that until recently, Blacks were the largest minority group in the United States and therefore the most visible. It is also related to the (over) representation of Blacks in official data on crime and justice. Another important factor in the focus on Blacks probably has to do with their foray into higher education, especially into the discipline of criminology. Most majority scholars were uninterested in studying race and crime. Blacks, in contrast, were interested. Throughout the 20th century, even before the emergence of Black criminologists, many Black scholars at historically Black colleges and universities were studying Black issues, including crime (Taylor Greene & Gabbidon, 2000). It is only recently that other minorities have received increased attention. At the same time, Latinos are now the largest minority group and also have more scholars interested in race, ethnicity, and crime; as a result, much more research is being published on this group. This does not mean that other racial and ethnic groups have not been subjected to differential treatment in society and the administration of justice. It means that the historical record of their experiences is less complete. Notably, although interest in Latino and Native American crime has increased, the research on Asian Americans and crime is still limited.

Despite more research, books, and government documents about race and crime, we are still unable to explain and adequately address the continuous pattern of over-representation of some minorities in arrest and victimization statistics, corrections, persons under sentence of death, and juvenile delinquency. We believe that prior attempts to make sense of the disproportionate number of minorities in the administration of justice are incomplete because they fail to consider relevant historical information.

One of our goals in writing this book was to put the study of race and crime in a more complete historical context. This remains one of our key goals in this fourth edition. Another goal is to examine several contemporary issues relevant to understanding race and crime. To achieve these goals, we utilize a limited-systems approach to examine policing, courts, sentencing, the death penalty, and corrections in the past and the present. An additional chapter examines the juvenile justice system. We include an issues approach to focus on several contemporary challenges in the study of race and crime, including hate/bias crimes, immigration and crime, racial profiling, sentencing disparities, wrongful convictions, felon disenfranchisement, disproportionate minority confinement, minority female delinquency, juveniles and life without parole, school-to-prison pipeline, and delinquency prevention. We include the major racial and ethnic groups in the United States—Asians, Blacks, Latinos/as, Native Americans, and Whites—although not as much information is available on all groups.

Various terms are used to refer to these groups. Some are the terms preferred in present-day usage, whereas others also are utilized to preserve their temporal context, especially in direct quotations. For example, you will see Blacks referred to as *Negroes, African Americans,* and *colored;* Native Americans referred to as *American Indians;* and Latinos referred to as *Hispanics.*

The book is divided into nine chapters that present historical details and contemporary information on both the administration of justice and related issues. Chapter 1 provides an overview of race and crime. It begins with a discussion of what many have referred to as the "invention of race." It also provides an overview of race and DNA databases. The remainder of the chapter highlights the historical experiences of Native Americans, African Americans, White ethnics, Latino Americans, and Asian Americans. The chapter pays particular attention to how crime has intersected with each of their experiences. Chapter 2 examines the extent of crime and victimization. It includes an overview of the history of the collection of crime data in the United States, a discussion of the limitations of crime statistics, the reported extent of crime and victimization for various racial groups, and analyses of homicide and hate crime victimization trends. Chapter 3 presents theoretical perspectives on race and crime and provides a discussion of biological, sociological, subcultural, and nontraditional theoretical perspectives, including the colonial model, counter-colonial criminology, and the recent Theory of African American Offending.

Chapters 4 through 9 examine race and several key components of the administration of justice: police, courts, sentencing, the death penalty, corrections, and juvenile justice. An overview of policing in the United States is presented in Chapter 4. Minority employment data and an analysis of the history of race and policing are also presented. Contemporary issues presented in this chapter include police bias, police militarization, racial profiling, immigration and policing, and community policing. Chapter 5 examines the history of race and the courts in America and how race impacts various facets of the American court system (i.e., bail, legal counsel, plea bargaining, etc.). A portion of the chapter also looks at the promise of drug courts.

Chapter 6 includes historical information and a comprehensive discussion of racial/ethnic disparities in sentencing. The chapter provides an overview of the sentencing process, along with a discussion of sentencing philosophies and contemporary issues related to race and sentencing. Chapter 7 examines race and the death penalty. Following an examination of the key Supreme Court death penalty cases, the chapter examines the history of the death penalty in America and also public opinion on the death penalty. Other contemporary issues discussed include the Capital Jury Project, wrongful convictions, and the death penalty moratorium movement. Chapter 8 provides a review of the history of corrections and the overrepresentation of racial minorities in jails and prisons. The chapter also examines prison gangs, explanations for racial disparities in corrections, prisoner reentry concerns, and felon disenfranchisement.

The issue of race and juvenile justice is presented in Chapter 9. The chapter presents an overview of juvenile justice in the United States and the historical context of race effects in juvenile justice, an explanation of the extent of juvenile delinquency and victimization, and a discussion of several contemporary issues, including disproportionate minority confinement, minority female delinquency, school-to-prison pipeline, life without parole, and delinquency prevention. The book ends with a concluding chapter that provides a brief reflection on the findings from the various chapters. The chapter also discusses prospects for study and the future of race and crime.

Overall, as with prior editions of the text, we envision this one as an addition to the body of knowledge in the area of race and crime. With our historical emphasis, we hope those who read this work leave with an appreciation for the similar historical experiences of most American racial and ethnic groups. We also hope that readers will see how race and ethnicity have mattered and continue to matter in the administration of justice.

❖ Supplements

An instructor teaching site at study.sagepub.com/gabbidon4e includes a test bank, PowerPoint slides, teaching tips, sample syllabi, web resources, SAGE journal articles, and more.

Student resources at study.sagepub.com/gabbidon4e include mobile-friendly quizzes and flashcards, web resources, and SAGE journal articles.

Acknowledgments

There are numerous individuals who have assisted us in the completion of this project. First, we would like to express our appreciation to our editor, Jerry Westby, for his continued support and encouragement. We especially thank Laura Kirkhuff, Veronica Hooper, Diana Breti, and the entire SAGE team for their assistance in the completion of this manuscript. We thank the following original reviewers for their constructive comments and suggestions that produced a well-received first edition: Mary Atwell, Radford University; Stephanie Bush-Baskette, Rutgers-Newark University; Charles Crawford, Western Michigan University; Alex del Carmen, University of Texas Arlington; Roland Chilton, University of Massachusetts, Amherst; Martha L. Henderson, The Citadel; D. Kall Loper, University of North Texas; Mike Males, University of California, Santa Cruz; Michael A. McMorris, Comstock Park, MI; Karen Parker, University of Delaware; Charles Reasons, Central Washington University; Katheryn Russell-Brown, University of Florida; Adina Schwartz, John Jay College of Criminal Justice; Susan F. Sharp, University of Oklahoma; Shirley Williams, New Jersey City University; Bill Wells, Southern Indiana University; and Ernest Uwazie, California State University, Sacramento.

For the second edition, we thank the following reviewers who provided great suggestions to improve the text: Tony Barringer, Florida Gulf Coast University; Dawn Beicher, Illinois State University; Lorenzo Boyd, Fayetteville State University; Roland Chilton, University of Massachusetts, Amherst; Ben Fleury-Steiner, University of Delaware; Kareem Jordan, University of Central Florida; Peter C. Kratcoski, Kent State University; Everette Penn, University of Houston, Clear Lake; Carolyn Petrosino, Bridgewater State College; Robert Sigler, University of Alabama; and Ernest Uwazie, California State University, Sacramento.

The following reviewers provided useful suggestions for the third edition: Jonathon A. Cooper, Arizona State University; Francisco J. Alatorre, Arizona State University; Tony A. Barringer, Florida Gulf Coast University; Francis M. Williams, Plymouth State University; Christine Martin, University of Illinois at Chicago; Peter C. Kratcoski, Kent State University; Stephanie R. Bush-Baskette, Rutgers University; Tara N. Tripp, Temple University; Ernest Uwazie, California State University, Sacramento; and Patricia Warren, Florida State University.

We are thankful for the comments from the following reviewers who assisted us in continuing to improve the substance of the text: Francisco J. Alatorre, New Mexico State University; Tim Berard, Kent State University; Katy Cathcart, MCJ; Matasha L. Harris, Bowie State University; Dana J. Hubbard, Cleveland State University; Chenelle A. Jones, Ohio Dominican University; Mia Ortiz, Bridgewater State University; Tim Robicheaux,

Pennsylvania State University; Ruth Thompson-Miller, University of Dayton; John R. Turner, Washington State University; Francis M. Williams, Plymouth State University.

Professor Gabbidon would like to thank his family for their continued encouragement and support. At Penn State, he would like to thank the former director of Penn State Harrisburg's School of Public Affairs, Steven Peterson, who provided the supportive environment in which this text was originally conceived and produced. During the completion of the four editions of this work, the assistance of several research assistants proved invaluable. Specifically, Nora Carerras, Nancy McGee, Patricia Patrick, Leslie Kowal, Matthew Nelson, and Grace Monjardo are acknowledged for their contributions. My son, Jini Gabbidon, is acknowledged for his efforts organizing the references into one file. Finally, Dr. Gabbidon would like to acknowledge his mentor and intellectual partner, Dr. Helen Taylor Greene, for her continued guidance and support.

Dr. Greene would like to thank her family for their continuing support and appreciation of her scholarly endeavors. She thanks Dr. Gabbidon for his contributions to the study of race and crime. She also thanks Dr. Robert D. Bullard, Dr. David N. Baker, other colleagues, and students in the Barbara Jordan–Mickey Leland School of Public Affairs at Texas Southern University, as well as colleagues elsewhere, for their support. She gives special thanks to Mr. Sean Wilson for his invaluable assistance with revisions to the fourth edition that included research and preparation of two of the Boxes for Chapters 4 and 9. She is grateful for the help of Ms. Chante Howard, who formatted several tables in Chapter 2. Finally, she thanks Mr. Carl Lucas for his encouragement, support, and understanding now that he knows who she is!

Overview of Race and Crime

CHAPTER 1

Because skin color is socially constructed, it can also be reconstructed. Thus, when the descendants of the European immigrants began to move up economically and socially, their skins apparently began to look lighter to the whites who had come to America before them. When enough of these descendants became visibly middle class, their skin was seen as fully white. The biological skin color of the second and third generations had not changed, but it was socially blanched or whitened.

—Herbert J. Gans (2005)

At a time when the United States is more diverse than ever, with the minority population topping 100 million (one in every three U.S. residents; U.S. Census Bureau, 2010), the notion of **race** seems to permeate almost every facet of American life. Certainly, one of the more highly charged aspects of the race dialogue relates to crime. Before embarking on an overview of race and crime, we must first set the parameters of the discussion, which include relevant definitions and the scope of our review. When speaking of race, it is always important to remind readers of the history of the concept and some current definitions.

The idea of race originated 5,000 years ago in India, but it was also prevalent among the Chinese, Egyptians, and Jews (Gossett, 1963). Although François Bernier (1625–1688) is usually credited with first classifying humans into distinct races, Carolus Linnaeus (1707–1778) invented the first system of categorizing plants and humans. It was, however, Johan Friedrich Blumenbach (1752–1840) who developed the first taxonomy of race. In his 1795 work, "On the Natural Variety of Mankind," Blumenbach separated the inhabitants of the earth into five races: Ethiopian (African or Negroid), Mongolian (Asian), American (Native American), Malaysian (Pacific Islander), and Caucasian (Feagin & Booher Feagin, 2012). When categorizing the fifth group, Whites, Blumenbach coined the term *Caucasian* (Feagin & Booher Feagin, 2012). Relying on Blumenbach's work, European scholars created a categorization that led to the belief that the differences among the groups were biological—and from the beginning

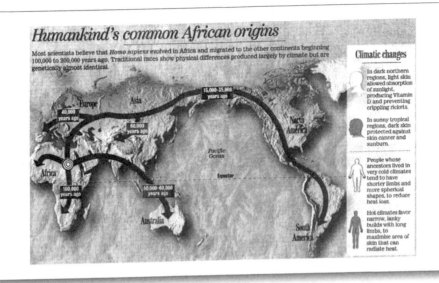

Europeans placed themselves at the apex of the racial hierarchy (Feagin & Booher Feagin, 2012). It is widely believed, however, that the biological differences among racial groups are attributable to the patterns of their migration out of Africa (Dulaney, 1879; Shane, 1999; see Figure 1.1).

Today, social scientists refer to race as a "social construct." Gallagher (1997) writes that "race and ethnicity are social constructions because their meanings are derived by focusing on arbitrary characteristics that a given society deems socially important. Race and ethnicity are social products based on cultural values; they are not scientific facts" (p. 2). Another relevant definition has been provided by Flowers (1988): "Race . . . refers to a group of persons characterized by common physical and/or biological traits that are transmitted in descent" (p. xiv). Finally, the U.S. Census Bureau (2000) has added the following:

> The concept of race . . . reflects self-identification by people according to the race or races with which they most closely identify. These categories are sociopolitical constructs and should not be interpreted as being scientific or anthropological in nature.

Thus, there is no shortage of definitions that refer to race as a social construct. Increasingly, however, some scholars—relying on scientific discoveries in the natural sciences—are beginning to challenge the notion of race as a social construct (Sesardic, 2010; J. P. Wright, 2009).

❖ Race, DNA, Criminal Justice Databases, and Civil Rights Concerns

Criminal justice investigations involving the use of DNA evidence have challenged the notion that there are no distinguishable biological differences between races. These cases have relied on DNA to identify the race of a perpetrator (D. H. Simons,

2003). In one well-known case, skeptical police investigators had a scientist conduct a sample test to illustrate support for the science behind the use of DNA to identify the race of the suspect. Specifically, the investigators sent a molecular biologist 20 DNA samples to test for racial identity; after conducting his analysis, the molecular biologist correctly identified the race of all 20 samples. He later helped investigators solve the case by identifying the offender as Black, not White, as had been previously thought (Newsome, 2007).

The general collection and use of DNA has not been without controversy. The American Civil Liberties Union (ACLU) has articulated three general concerns about forensic DNA databases. First, they believe the use of such databases can result in an invasion of medical privacy. In particular, they believe that DNA data "might be used by employers, insurers, and others for invidious genetic discrimination—against both the individual who supplied the DNA and also their immediate family members, who have similar DNA" (Schwartz, 2011, p. 1). Thus, there is concern about the Federal Bureau of Investigation's (FBI) Combined DNA Index System (CODIS). Contrary to the belief of some, the DNA information collected by the FBI does provide information on "medically relevant" genes. Second, the ACLU believes that the use of forensic DNA databases represents an invasion of bodily integrity. To collect the information for the database, officials often place a swab in a person's mouth; if the person refuses, he or she is often forced to comply. Schwartz (2011) notes that the government can get around forcibly taking the DNA by covertly taking DNA that is shed onto objects citizens have handled (e.g., soda cans). Potentially, the government could secretly seize the DNA of all Americans (p. 3). The ACLU's third concern related to DNA databases is their racially disparate impact. Here, the ACLU takes the position that because "African Americans and Hispanics are arrested, prosecuted, and convicted—often wrongly—at a far higher rate than Caucasians," they are likely to be disparately impacted by DNA databases (Schwartz, 2011). In addition to these general concerns, the ACLU is also concerned about familial DNA testing.

Familial DNA testing occurs when the DNA of the suspect is only a partial match. This can result in police questioning the immediate and extended family of the suspect, which has the potential to criminalize entire families—especially families of color (De Gruy, 2010; Schwartz, 2011). Given that people of color are more likely to be arrested and incarcerated, familial DNA testing has the potential to contribute to racial injustice in the administration of justice.

There is clearly a delicate balance that needs to be struck when collecting DNA data. In the United Kingdom, for example, there are nearly 6 million profiles in the National DNA database; these profiles are linked to the Police National Computer (PNC) that contains a multitude of information on people including name, date of birth, ethnic appearance, and geographic factors such as where the sample was taken (Maguire, McCallum, Storey, & Whitaker, 2014). Currently, in the United States, the FBI's CODIS database maintains more than 11 million profiles (FBI, 2015). Moreover, as of November 2014, the CODIS system has "produced over 266,897 hits assisting in more than 255,153 investigations" (FBI, 2015). The reality is that the successful use of DNA databases is spurring the increased use of DNA evidence in the criminal justice field—in the United States and abroad. The real challenge ahead is how to balance privacy concerns with public safety concerns (Kazemian, Pease, & Farrington, 2011; Tseloni & Pease, 2011). This precarious balance was considered in the 2013 United States Supreme Court decision in *Maryland v. King*. Box 1.1 is devoted to reviewing the case.

BOX 1.1

Maryland v. King

In the case of *Maryland v. King* (2013), the United States Supreme Court considered whether the collection of DNA from a suspect constituted an unreasonable search and seizure. The case involved Alonzo Jay King, Jr., who was arrested in 2009 on multiple charges of assault. While waiting for King's case to go to trial, the state collected a DNA sample to determine whether King had been involved in additional criminal activity. Notably, in 2008, the Maryland legislature had passed the Maryland DNA Collection Act that required law enforcement officers to take such DNA samples from persons arrested for a crime of violence or attempted violence and persons charged with burglary or attempted burglary. To protect the innocent, included in the Act was a caveat that: "a DNA sample, once taken, may not, without consent, be processed in a database before the arrestee is arraigned. In the event that the arrestee is not bound over for trial, is not convicted, has his conviction reversed on appeal, or is pardoned, the DNA sample must be destroyed" (Bower, 2013, p. 29).

King's DNA sample came back with a "hit" for a 2003 unsolved rape case. Solely on the basis of the DNA results, King was eventually charged and tried for the rape. During the trial, he pled not guilty and asked the trial court to suppress the DNA evidence because it constituted a warrantless search. While his motion to suppress was denied by the trial court, the appellate court agreed with King, stating, "the collection of King's DNA upon arrest without a warrant violated his Fourth Amendment right against unreasonable searches" (Bower, 2013, p. 29). The State of Maryland disagreed with the appellate court decision and petitioned the U.S. Supreme Court to hear the case. The case was heard by the U.S. Supreme Court on February 26, 2013 and decided on June 3, 2013. In a split decision (5–4 in favor of the state of Maryland), the majority held that "When officers make an arrest supported by probable cause to hold for a serious offense and they bring the suspect to the station to be detained in custody, taking and analyzing a cheek swab of the arrestee's DNA is, like fingerprinting and photographing, a legitimate police booking procedure that is reasonable under the Fourth Amendment" (*Maryland v. King,* 2013).

Even though the King decision was clearly controversial, every state now requires the collection of DNA samples from offenders convicted of felony offenses. There has also been support for the collection of DNA data from offenders convicted of misdemeanors (Green, 2013). In addition, because of the ongoing concerns tied to minority profiling, some observers have suggested that, though legal, the collection of offender DNA represents an unethical intrusion and will eventually—as with many crime policies—disproportionately impact minorities (Cox, 2014).

1. Do you agree with this decision and the nationwide policies that now allow the collection of DNA samples from offenders?

2. Does it matter to you whether the offense is a felony or misdemeanor?

❖ Race, Ethnicity, and the U.S. Population in 2013

Even though the debate about the existence of distinct races persists, the U.S. Census Bureau continues to track national data on race/ethnicity. In fact, the 2010 census collected these data, which became the standard practice during the first decennial census in 1790 (Humes, Jones, & Ramirez, 2011). Figure 1.2 shows the form that was used to ask questions pertaining to race and ethnicity on the 2010 census. The form

→ **NOTE: Please answer BOTH Question 5 about Hispanic origin and Question 6 about race. For this census, Hispanic origins are not races.**

5. Is this person of Hispanic, Latino, or Spanish origin?
   ☐ **No**, not of Hispanic, Latino, or Spanish origin
   ☐ Yes, Mexican, Mexican Am., Chicano
   ☐ Yes, Puerto Rican
   ☐ Yes, Cuban
   ☐ Yes, another Hispanic, Latino, or Spanish origin — *Print origin, for example Argentinean, Colombian, Dominican, Nicaraguan, Salvadoran, Spaniard, and so on.* ↘

   [ ]

6. What is this person's race? *Mark* ☒ *one or more boxes.*
   ☐ White
   ☐ Black, African Am., or Negro
   ☐ American Indian or Alaska Native — *Print name of enrolled or principal tribe.* ↘

   [ ]

   ☐ Asian Indian   ☐ Japanese   ☐ Native Hawaiian
   ☐ Chinese   ☐ Korean   ☐ Guamanian or Chamorro
   ☐ Filipino   ☐ Vietnamese   ☐ Samoan
   ☐ Other Asian — *Print race, for example,*   ☐ Other Pacific Islander — *Print race, for example, Fijian, Tongan, and so on.* ↘
   Hmong, Laotian, Thai, Pakistani, Cambodian, and so on. ↘

   [ ]

   ☐ Some other race — *Print race.* ↘

   [ ]

Figure 1.2

Reproduction of the Questions on Hispanic Origin and Race From the 2010 Census

Source: U.S. Census Bureau, 2010 Census questionnaire.

illustrates the separation of race and ethnicity. This practice dates to 1997, when the federal government mandated that "race and Hispanic origin (ethnicity) are separate and distinct concepts and that when collecting these data via self-identification, two different questions must be used" (Humes et al., 2011, p. 2).

Typically, Hispanics/Latinos are referred to as an ethnic group. The term ***ethnicity*** comes from the Greek word *ethnos,* which means "nation." Generally, ethnic groups are defined by their similar genetic inheritances or some identifiable traits visible among most members of a particular group. Ethnic groups are also generally held together by a common language, culture, group spirit (nationalism or group solidarity), or geography (most typically originate from the same region; Marger, 1997). Therefore, most scholars generally see the terms *race* and *ethnicity* as culturally relevant rather than biologically relevant.

We follow the U.S. Census Bureau racial/ethnic categories and separate the American population into five groups: Native Americans, Whites, African Americans, Hispanic/Latino Americans, and Asian Americans. We also use the definitions for each of the groups outlined in the 2010 Census. We acknowledge that there are limitations to these categories. First, these categories do not take into account the ethnic variation within each race. The most recent population estimates by race from the U.S. Census Bureau are presented in Table 1.1. Table 1.2 provides a breakdown of the U.S. population by Hispanic/Latino origin and race. As you can see, there are a number of ethnic groups within the racial classification "Hispanic or Latino Americans." This

Table 1.1

U.S. Population Estimates by Race, 2013

Racial Group	Estimate	Percentage
White	238,007,238	76.4
Black or African American	42,496,977	13.6
American Indian and Alaska Native	4,142,542	1.7
Asian	17,845,862	5.7
Native Hawaiian and other Pacific Islander	1,177,092	0.4
Some other race	16,399,187	5.3
Total Population	311,536,594	100.00

Source: U.S. Census Bureau, *2009–2013 5-Year American Community Survey.*

Table 1.2

U.S. Population Estimates by Hispanic or Latino and Race, 2013

Hispanic Group	Estimate	Percentage
Hispanic or Latino (of any race)	51,786,591	16.6
Mexican	33,392,414	10.7
Puerto Rican	4,886,378	1.6
Cuban	1,897,680	0.6
Other Hispanic or Latino	11,610,109	3.7
Not Hispanic or Latino	259,750,003	63.3
Total Population	311,536,594	100.0*

Source: U.S. Census Bureau, *2009–2013 5-Year American Community Survey.*

Note: *Total percentage slightly off due to rounding.

is true of other races as well. Another example is the category "African American/ Black." There is also ethnic diversity within this category; it often encompasses people from the Caribbean (e.g., Jamaica, Haiti), African countries, and other parts of the world. Because each of these groups has had a unique experience in America, it is, at times, presumptive for researchers to assume that the experience of one African/ Black American is representative of so many diverse groups. Nevertheless, although we are aware of the problems with these classifications, the research and data we review follow this classification approach. Second, and relatedly, with the use of the multiracial category starting in 2000, the lines between racial groups have become rather blurred. This increasing trend adds to the considerable limitations of population and crime data (this topic is discussed further in Chapter 2).

❖ Race, Ethnicity, and Population Trends

The U.S. Census Bureau provides the most recent estimates on the racial and ethnic dynamics of America. The 2013 population estimates reported more than 311 million residents in the United States. The figures also confirmed earlier estimates that the minority population had topped 100 million. The Hispanic/Latino population, as was observed in population estimates earlier in the decade, continues to be the largest minority population and now represents nearly 17% (51.7 million) of the U.S. population. Interestingly, their rise in population from 2000 to 2010 accounted for more than 50% of the increase in the U.S. population during the decade (Ennis, Rios-Vargas, & Albert, 2011). This increase in the Hispanic/Latino population is in large part a result of the increasing number of Mexicans in the United States. Specifically, relying on 2010 census data, there were approximately 11 million more persons of Mexican descent in the United States in 2010 than there were in 2000. This trend has resulted in concerns not only about immigration in general but also illegal immigration. Border states, including Arizona, Texas, and California, have especially taken notice of this trend and reacted with legislation to stem the rising number of illegal immigrants. These states and others have enacted numerous measures to restrict the benefits (e.g., medical, educational) and rights (e.g., due process) of illegal immigrants in their states (Huntington, 2004; MacDonald, 2004). Other states have followed suit, contributing to a national debate on the best way to reduce the number of illegal immigrants in the United States. Ironically, later in the chapter it will become clear that such fears are not new.

Given the rapidly changing demographics of the United States, in past years, some have called for the discontinuance of the term *minority* (Texeira, 2005). In place of *minority,* which some believe is a "term of oppression" or a term that seeks to minimize the collective aspirations of a group, the term *people of color* has been suggested (Texeira, 2005). Whatever the term to be used, if current estimates are correct, it is clear that one day racial and ethnic groups now considered to be minorities will become nearly half the U.S. population (U.S. Census Bureau, 2004). In fact, estimates are that Whites will represent only 50% of the population in 2050, with Hispanics/Latinos—whose recent population projections have slowed—still representing nearly a quarter of the population and other racial and ethnic minorities comprising the remainder of the populace (Krogstad, 2014; U.S. Census Bureau, 2004). In addition to the varying population figures, Table 1.3 provides some sociodemographic information on several racial/ethnic groups.

❖ Prejudice and Discrimination

Even with the growth in the minority population, prejudice and discrimination remain a central concern. **Prejudice** is a negative attitude toward a particular group. This is usually in the form of stereotypes that often result in people making negative

Table 1.3

Socio-Demographic Characteristics of Select Racial/Ethnic Groups, 2013

Category	White	Black/African American	Hispanic/ Latino	Asian
Education				
High school or higher	94.1%	90.3%	75.8%	95.4%
Bachelor's degree or higher	40.4%	20.5%	15.7%	60.1%
Master's degree or higher	8.6%	3.3%	3.0%	21.8%
Individuals below poverty	9.6%	27.2%	23.5%	10.5%
Unemployment rate	6.5%	13.1%	9.1%	5.2%
Median household income	$58,270	$34,598	$40,963	$67,065

Source: U.S. Department of Education. Institute of Education Sciences, National Center for Education Statistics.

generalizations about an entire group. Discrimination is the "unequal treatment of a person or persons based on group membership" (Healey, 2007, p. 20). As you can imagine, having prejudicial attitudes toward a particular group, in many instances, can lead to discriminatory actions in areas such as employment, housing, and the criminal justice system. Thus, determining whether prejudice and discrimination permeate the criminal justice system is critical to understanding the role of race in justice system outcomes.

The remainder of this chapter provides a brief historical overview of each major racial/ethnic group, highlighting the complex history of race in America and how this history is intertwined with race, crime, and the criminal justice system. Readers should keep in mind that our historical review is not meant to be comprehensive. Rather, we see our review as illustrating that concerns regarding race and crime are not new and have been the norm since distinctive racial and ethnic groups from across the globe arrived in America.

❖ Historical Antecedents of Race and Crime in America

Native Americans

Prior to the arrival of Europeans in the Americas, the native people had existed on the continent for thousands of years. It is believed that they originated from eastern Asia. More specifically, it is believed that they have been in North America for the last 30,000 years, having crossed over from Asia into America on glaciers that, due to warming trends, later melted (Polk, 2006, pp. 3–4). Over time, they built complex societies throughout the Americas. Even so, on arrival in the Americas (South America and the West Indies), it is clear from their actions that Christopher Columbus and his followers viewed the native people (then referred to as "Indians," now referred to as "Native Americans") as inferior (H. J. Clarke, 1992). The brutality that followed has been painstakingly documented by firsthand observers of the massacres (De Las Casas, 1552/1993). Sale (1990) has suggested that prior to the arrival of Europeans there were about 15 million Native Americans in North America. According to Healey (2003), nearly four centuries later, in 1890, only 250,000 remained. Today, there are slightly more than 5.1 million American Indians/Alaskan Natives in the United States. Nonetheless, considering the historical decimation of the Native American population, some criminologists have viewed their massacre as genocide (Barak, Leighton, & Cotton, 2014).

Although some have categorized all Native Americans into one group, they represent "a diverse array of nations, with major differences in population, economies, polities, language, and customs" (Feagin & Booher Feagin, 2012, p. 139). It has been noted that their societies were more advanced than those of the Europeans who colonized them. Consequently, Europeans borrowed much from Native American agriculture and pharmacology. Furthermore, some have noted that "Benjamin Franklin, Thomas Jefferson, and other colonial leaders admired and were influenced by the democratic institutions of certain indigenous nations such as the Iroquois. Even the symbol of the United States, an eagle clutching arrows, was copied from Iroquois symbols" (Feagin & Booher Feagin, 2012, p. 146).

During their initial contact with Europeans, Native Americans assisted the newcomers with advice on how to survive in their new environment. However, once colonists became comfortable with the surroundings, they began to displace, enslave, and destroy Native American societies. In time, massacres of Native Americans became commonplace throughout the colonies, but once the Constitution was ratified (with little mention of Native Americans), treaties were enacted with the aim of ending massacres and also protecting Native American lands from further pillage. But the government did not honor the treaties. Such actions were sanctioned at the highest levels, with presidents such as Andrew Jackson encouraging the defiance of Supreme Court rulings related to Native Americans. From 1790 to the mid-1800s, there were more than 300 treaties signed between Whites and Native Americans, most of which were not honored. As a result, conflicts persisted, which led to concerns regarding "criminal aggression" and the subsequent enactment of another approach: removal. Healey (2003) wrote,

> East of the Mississippi, the period of open conflict was brought to a close by the Indian Removal Act of 1830, which dictated a policy of forced emigration to the tribes. The law required all eastern tribes to move to new lands west of the Mississippi. Some of the affected tribes went without resistance, others fought, and still others fled to Canada rather than move to a new territory. (p. 190)

This infamous "Trail of Tears," as it became known, resulted in the death of thousands of Native Americans. Nearly 40 years later, in 1867, the Doolittle Committee, which was investigating several recent massacres of Native Americans, found that much of the aggression by Native Americans around that time had occurred in response to White aggression (Harjo, 2002).

The same year of this massive removal of Native Americans, the Bureau of Indian Affairs (BIA) was established to handle matters related to this population. Following the creation of the BIA, the agency had to deal with the competing aims of the federal government. On the one hand, the government created the agency to help Native Americans; on the other hand, the military had a policy of "genocidal extermination." Nearly 60 years after the creation of the BIA, the 1887 Dawes Act provided that individual families be provided with reservation lands. While well meaning, as Feagin and Booher Feagin (2012) observed, "This policy resulted in a large-scale land sale to Whites. Through means fair and foul, the remaining 140 million acres of Indian lands were further reduced to 50 million acres by the 1930s" (p. 146). In the early part of the 20th century, the government tried to assimilate Native Americans by sending them to Indian boarding schools that were Christian-based and were used to indoctrinate Native Americans into American culture. During this process, Native Americans were forced to abandon their native language and customs. The attempt to assimilate Native Americans culminated during the 1920s with the passage of the Indian Citizenship Act of 1924, which granted all Native Americans citizenship. The end of this period saw Native Americans calling for new policies, one of which came in the form of the 1934 Indian Reorganization Act. The Act, which essentially ended the Dawes Act, "Was intended to establish Indian civil and cultural rights, allow for semi-autonomous tribal governments, and foster better economic development on reservations" (Feagin & Booher Feagin, 2012, p. 147). As with all legislation, there were problems. Most notably, Native Americans saw this Act as giving too much power to the secretary of the interior. In addition, many Native Americans believed the Act violated their sovereignty, or their right to govern themselves, provided by previously enacted treaties.

The second half of the 20th century spurred more attempts by Native Americans to shed governmental control. In the early 1950s, Congress enacted legislation called *termination,* which "call[ed] for an end to the reservation system and to the special relationships between the tribes and the federal government" (Healey, 2004, p. 134). This process also negated previous treaties, a policy that was vigorously opposed by Native Americans. In addition, based on the specifics of the policy, "Tribes would no longer exist as legally recognized entities, and tribal lands and other resources would be placed in private hands" (Healey, 2004, p. 134). Because of this policy, many Native Americans moved to urban areas.

The decades following the enactment of the termination policy saw increasing opposition from Native Americans. After about 25 years, the policy was repealed. In 1975, the Indian Self-Determination and Education Assistance Act "increased aid to reservation schools and Native American students and increased the tribes' control over the administration of the reservations, from police forces to schools and road maintenance" (Healey, 2004, p. 136). This Act provides much of the basis on which many tribes now operate. Recent federal legislation has enabled some tribes to open gambling facilities on reservations, which, according to the National Indian Gaming Commission website (http://www.nigc.gov), generated more than $28 billion in revenues in 2013. Other tribes have invested in additional ways to generate revenue (e.g., tax-free cigarette sales). Native Americans' move to self-determination also has resulted in suits against the federal government seeking reparations for past broken treaties. In a similar vein, a recent article by Regan (2014) argues that there are five ways the government keeps Native Americans in poverty: Indian lands being owned and managed by the federal government, economic development being controlled by the federal government, the complex legal framework that hinders economic growth, energy regulation that makes it difficult to manage their resources, and the mismanagement of Indian assets by the government. These impediments suggest that the federal government has continued to stymie the progress of Native Americans. Despite these ongoing challenges, with 561 recognized tribes, Native Americans remain a notable presence in the United States.

African Americans

African Americans are another group that has had a long and arduous relationship with the United States. With the Native American population nearly completely decimated because of brutality, enslavement, and diseases that were brought to the Americas by the Spanish, Bartolome De Las Casas, the priest who accompanied Columbus to America, sought a way to stem their extermination.

De Las Casas's idea centered on not ending the slave system, but instead replacing the Native Americans with another labor force: Africans. Of De Las Casas's thinking, Finger (1959) wrote,

> Having heard that the Negroes of the Portuguese colonies in Africa were more robust than the natives of the West Indies Islands, he [De Las Casas] recommended that Black slaves be imported to take the place of Indians in server tasks of the plantations and mines. (p. 716)

Finger (1959) also described the results of De Las Casas's suggestion:

> A terrible traffic in human flesh ensued. Portuguese raiders carried the Africans from their homes, and English sailors conveyed them across the Atlantic. Spanish, Portuguese, and later English slave-owners worked the poor Black men as though they possessed no natural rights as human beings. (pp. 716–717)

As with the decimation of the Native American population, the slave trade involving Africans has been viewed as genocidal and referred to as the "African holocaust" (H. J. Clarke, 1992).

It is disputable as to when Africans initially arrived in the colonies. Some suggest that Africans arrived in America long before their arrival in the 1600s as indentured servants and slaves (Goodwin, 2008; Van Sertima, 1976). But the prevailing historical account describes Africans arriving in America in 1619 as a result of piracy (Higginbotham, 1996). When a slave ship carrying Africans headed to the West Indies was taken over by pirates and ran out of supplies, the pirates landed in Jamestown, Virginia, where they sold the Africans for food and supplies. It is important to note that, prior to their movement into perpetual slavery, Africans had existed much like the other citizens in the colony. Thus, from their arrival in 1619 to the 1660s, Africans were not considered slaves in colonial America; they were able to fulfill indentures and were fairly integrated into the life of the colony. After 1660, however, colonial legislation made it clear that Africans were to be considered slaves.

McIntyre (1992) believes the leaders of the colony came to a juncture where they needed to decide the best way to further the economic fortunes of its citizens, and they came up with several potential options. The first involved the continued use of the indentured servant system for Blacks and Whites. Second, the colonists, like the Spaniards earlier, thought about enslaving the Native Americans. Third, both Native Americans and Blacks could be enslaved. Fourth, the colonists could create a free labor system for Blacks, Whites, Indians, and immigrants. Eventually, they chose the fifth option: the enslavement of Blacks. McIntyre (1992) has suggested that this was the case because Whites had the option to appeal for protection from the British monarchy; in addition, they could appeal to general White public opinion. Enslaving Native Americans did not appeal to the colonists because besides feeling that they would not hold up under slave conditions, they were aware that the natives were familiar with the terrain, which would have permitted easy escape. For the next two centuries, African Americans would serve as the primary labor force keeping the Southern economy afloat.

Although much of the slave system was kept intact by "plantation justice," there was little interference in these matters from outside developing criminal justice institutions, except when slaves escaped or there was a slave revolt. In times of escapes, slave owners cooperated by enlisting **slave patrols** to ensure slaves were quickly captured and returned to their owners. Similarly, when slave revolts occurred, slave owners worked together to expeditiously bring a close to the uprisings that threatened the stability of the slave system (H. Aptheker, 1943/1993). Slave owners were so committed to quelling escapes and revolts that they enacted widespread "slave codes" to reduce their likelihood. Describing the slave codes, Russell (1998) wrote,

> Slave codes embodied the criminal law and procedure applied against enslaved Africans. The codes, which regulated slave life from cradle to grave, were virtually uniform across states—each with the overriding goal of upholding chattel slavery. The codes not only enumerated the applicable law but also prescribed the social boundaries for slaves—where they could go, what types of activity they could engage in, and what type of contracts they could enter into. Under the codes, the harshest criminal penalties were reserved for those acts that threatened the institution of slavery (e.g., the murder of someone White or a slave insurrection). The slave codes also penalized Whites who opposed slavery. (pp. 14–15)

In addition to the slave codes, Whites used psychology to keep the slave system intact. Describing the nature of this process, Claude Anderson (1994) wrote that "this process was designed to instill in Blacks strict discipline, a sense of inferiority, belief in the slave owners' superior power, acceptance of the owners' standards and a deep sense of a slave's helplessness and dependence" (p. 165). Moreover, Anderson added, "the slave owners strove to cut Blacks off from their own history, culture, language, and community, and to inculcate White society's value system" (p. 165).

Another telling dynamic during the slave era was the way in which punishment was exacted for crimes committed by African Americans in comparison with Whites. After reviewing nearly every appellate case on antebellum slavery and race relations from 1630 to 1865, A. Leon Higginbotham, the late jurist and scholar, formulated his

"Ten Precepts of American Slavery Jurisprudence" (Higginbotham, 1996; see Box 1.2). These precepts describe the foundations on which justice was distributed during this era. Most notably, to maintain the slave system, White supremacy called for little justice to be distributed to African Americans, whereas Whites were indifferent to their own criminal activity. This was most pronounced in the crime of rape. Whites might rape Black women with impunity; however, if Blacks so much as looked at White women in an unacceptable way, they were subjected to severe beatings. Table 1.4 highlights the differential punishments for African American and White crimes during the slave era.

BOX 1.2

The 10 Precepts of American Slavery Jurisprudence

1. *Inferiority:* Presume, preserve, protect, and defend the ideal of the superiority of Whites and the inferiority of Blacks.

2. *Property:* Define the slave as the master's property, maximize the master's economic interest, disregard the humanity of the slave except when it serves the master's interest, and deny slaves the fruits of their labor.

3. *Powerlessness:* Keep Blacks—whether slave or free—as powerless as possible so they will be submissive and dependent in every respect, not only to the master, but to Whites in general. Limit Blacks' accessibility to the courts and subject Blacks to an inferior system of justice with lesser rights and protections and greater punishments. Utilize violence and the powers of government to ensure the submissiveness of Blacks.

4. *Racial "purity":* Always preserve White male sexual dominance. Draw an arbitrary racial line and preserve White racial purity as thus defined. Tolerate sexual relations between White men and Black women; punish severely relations between White women and non-White men. As to children who are products of interracial sexual relations, the freedom or enslavement of the Black child is determined by the status of the mother.

5. *Manumission and free Blacks:* Limit and discourage manumission; minimize the number of free Blacks in the state. Confine free Blacks to a status as close to slavery as possible.

6. *Family:* Recognize no rights of the Black family; destroy the unity of the Black family; deny slaves the right of marriage; demean and degrade Black women, Black men, Black parents, and Black children; and then condemn them for their conduct and state of mind.

7. *Education and culture:* Deny Blacks any education, deny them knowledge of their culture, and make it a crime to teach those who are slaves how to read and write.

8. *Religion:* Recognize no rights of slaves to define or practice their own religions, choose their own religious leaders, or worship with other Blacks. Encourage them to adopt the religion of the White master, and teach them that God, who is White, will reward the slave who obeys the commands of his master here on earth. Use religion to justify the slave's status on earth.

(Continued)

(Continued)

9. *Liberty–resistance:* Limit Blacks' opportunity to resist, bear arms, rebel, or flee; curtail their freedom of movement, freedom of association, and freedom of expression. Deny Blacks the right to vote and to participate in government.

10. *By any means possible:* Support all measures, including the use of violence, that maximize the profitability of slavery and that legitimize racism. Oppose, by the use of violence if necessary, all measures that advocate the abolition of slavery or the diminution of White supremacy.

Source: Higginbotham, A. L. (1996). *Shades of freedom: Racial politics and the presumptions of the American legal process.* Oxford, UK: Oxford University Press, 195–196.

Table 1.4

Criminal Punishments by Race in Slave-Era Virginia

Crime	White Offender	Black Slave Offender
Murder (White victim) Petit treason (murder of slave owner)	Maximum penalty: death	Death
Murder (Black victim)	Rarely prosecuted	If prosecuted, whipping, hard labor, or death
Rape (White victim)	10–20 years, whipping, or death if minor victim	Death or castration (same penalty for attempted rape)
Rape (Black victim)	No crime	No crime, exile, or death (If rape of free Black women, penalty could be death)
Assault (White victim)	1–10 years (if done with intent to kill)	Whipping, exile, mutilation, or death

Source: Reprinted with permission from the *North Carolina Law Review,* Vol. 70, pp. 969, 1070 (1992).

The 1700s brought similar race and crime concerns. Some Whites, however, continued to show indifference toward their own criminal activity. Although the slave system began to expand under the encouragement of the colonial aristocracy, the slave trade began to be shunned in the international community. Subsequently, there was a movement to stop the trade, although slavery continued for those slaves already in America. Du Bois (1891) wrote about the movement to stop the slave trade as having four periods, and these were tied to large-scale efforts by Whites to circumvent the law. Du Bois wrote that there were varying levels of commitment to this initiative. The compromise of the Constitutional convention allowed the slave trade to continue until 1808; however, Du Bois's research showed that Whites never took the prohibition seriously, considering the large numbers of persons who were actively involved in trading slaves even with the threat of imprisonment.

Du Bois found that when the U.S. government signed the Treaty of Ghent in 1814, it further committed to ending the international slave trade. As a condition of this commitment, participating nations were asked to engage in searches of vessels abroad; however, the U.S. was unwilling to agree to this stipulation. Hence, many ships that flew the American flag were not American; they were slave traders who sought refuge by using the American flag. Du Bois also noted that even after the **death penalty** was instituted for slave trading, he found few instances when Whites had been convicted, much less executed, for being connected to the slave trade. In the end, this early form of White crime in America, which was particularly tied to the ruling class of slaveholders in the South, was allowed to persist because Whites were unwilling to give up the financial benefit derived from the slave trade and system (C. Anderson, 1994; E. Williams, 1944).

During the mid-1850s, there was a crisis brewing regarding slavery. Although a civil war seemed imminent, the North and South tried to delay the inevitable. Of particular concern during this period was the acquisition of territories in the southwest portion of the United States. The debate centered on which states should be slave states—if any at all. Predictably, Northerners argued to keep such states free, whereas Southerners wanted to preserve the institution of slavery, so they argued the reverse. Vigorous debate led to the well-known Compromise of 1850, which essentially gave each side a portion of what it wanted. For example, California entered the Union as a Free State, while other territories would enter the Union without mention of slavery (Franklin & Moss, 2000). One of the provisions of the Compromise led to the enactment of the Fugitive Slave Law of 1850.

A revision of the 1793 Fugitive Slave Act, the Fugitive Slave Law (or Act) of 1850 was structured to ensure the return of runaway slaves. The Act called for the appointment of numerous commissioners who were authorized to hire deputies who all could "enlist the aid of bystanders or posses to enforce the act" (Kennedy, 1997, p. 83). Furthermore, monetary incentives were tied to this process. For example, "commissioners would be paid a fee of $5 in each case in which he determined that a slave master was *not* [emphasis added] entitled to an alleged fugitive slave, and would be paid a fee of $10 in each case in which he determined that a master was entitled to the accused person" (Kennedy, 1997, pp. 83–84). Finally, to illustrate the seriousness with which the enforcement of the Act was to be taken, there was a stipulation that if a U.S. Marshall refused or neglected to execute warrants issued by commissioners he would be fined $1,000 (Kennedy, 1997). The enactment of this Act and other provisions of the Compromise still could not stop the move toward civil war. Thus, not long after the notorious 1857 Dred Scott decision that continued to increase the tensions between North and South, the country headed into the Civil War in 1861.

Following the Emancipation Proclamation in 1863, which freed the slaves in the Confederate states, and the enactment of the Thirteenth Amendment in 1865, which ended slavery throughout the United States, many African Americans chose to remain in the South. Others dreamed of migrating north and starting anew. Unfortunately, Southern landowners were unwilling to part so easily with their former free labor force. Therefore, following emancipation, they enacted the **Black codes**. These codes were an assortment of laws that targeted poor Whites and African Americans. Some scholars have argued that the laws were specifically created so that a significant number of African Americans could be returned to plantation owners through the **convict lease system** (Du Bois, 1901/2002; Myers, 1998; Oshinsky, 1996). The convict lease system allowed states to lease convict labor to private landowners. Although some poor Whites also became entangled in this legal system, most of the inmates who were leased out to Southern landowners were African Americans. Before long, whereas previously they had engaged only in trivial offenses, African Americans began to engage in more bold and brutal offenses; this development shocked Southern Whites who had created the unjust system (Du Bois, 1901/2002).

Prior to the Civil War, primarily Whites had been incarcerated in Southern penal institutions, and one product of the massive changes in the South was the increasing number of African Americans found in prisons. Following this period, along with the convict lease system, states such as Mississippi ran notorious state prisons that put the prisoners to work. Parchman Farm was one of the most infamous (Oshinsky, 1996). The Reconstruction Era also brought the formal advent of hate groups. Groups such as the Knights of White Camellia, the Constitutional Union Guards, the Pale Faces, the White Brotherhood, the Council of Safety, the '76 Association, and the infamous Knights of the Ku Klux Klan were all formed to ensure White supremacy ruled in the South following Emancipation and the passage of the Thirteenth Amendment in 1865, which officially abolished slavery. These groups wreaked havoc on African American and other citizens, who were targets of their hatred. **Lynching** became the means used to intimidate and handle those who challenged the racist White power structure (see Figure 1.3). It is generally accepted that, between 1882 and 1930, "At least three thousand Black men, women, and children were murdered by White gangs during this era of the lynch mob, and this toll does not count other racially motivated murders or Black deaths from race riots" (Beck & Tolnay, 1995, p. 121; also see Chapter 2 for lynching statistics). These indiscriminate killings of African Americans (and some Native Americans and Spanish-speaking minorities), usually by hanging, were typically carried out to avenge some unsubstantiated crime committed by an African American or other "undesirable" minority against a White person (Zangrando, 1980). In most instances, rape was alleged to justify these horrific actions.

The Ku Klux Klan emerged as the leading hate organization. In an effort to suppress African American economic equality and pride, the Klan beat African Americans for minor things, such as "Black women . . . dressing in brightly-colored clothes, and men for being impolite, talking back to Whites or failing to say 'Yes Sir'" (Katz, 1986, p. 39). In many jurisdictions, Klan activities were condoned by local law enforcement. As a result, many African Americans lost faith in the justice system and stopped reporting crimes altogether (Katz, 1986).

On the eve of the 20th century, the *Plessy v. Ferguson* (1896) "separate but equal" decision was hailed by Southern bigots. This decision was significant in that it gave Whites legal support to enforce some of their ideas concerning White supremacy and the separation of the races. Furthermore, this decision enabled law enforcement officials to take action against African Americans who sought basic services now reserved for Whites. Du Bois (1899) clearly saw the danger of state-sanctioned segregation, writing,

> [Another] cause of Negro crime is the exaggerated and unnatural separation in the South of the best classes of Whites and Blacks. A drawing of the color line, that extends to street-cars, elevators, and cemeteries, which leaves no common ground of meeting, no medium for communication, no ties of sympathy between two races who live together, and whose interests are at bottom one—such a discrimination is more than silly, it is dangerous. (p. 1357)

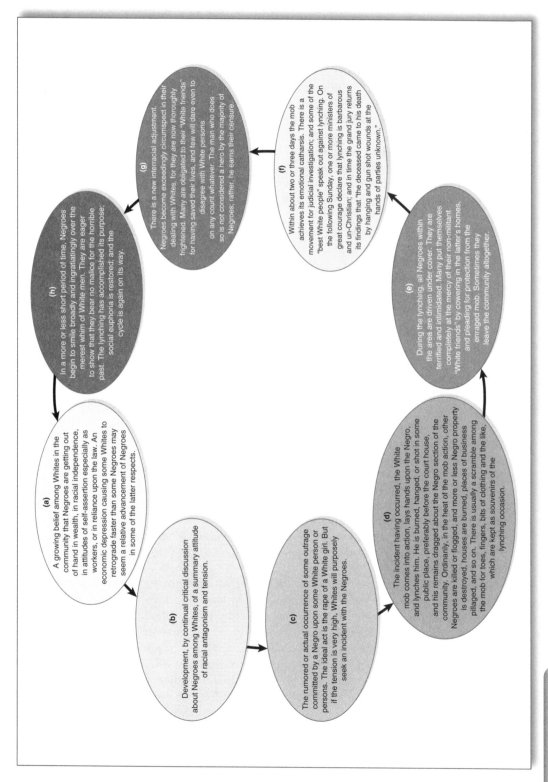

Source: The Journal of Negro education by HOWARD UNIVERSITY. Copyright 1945 Reproduced with permission of JOURNAL OF NEGRO EDUCATION in the format Textbook via Copyright Clearance Center.

Figure 1.3

Oliver Cox's Lynching Cycle

Ten years after the turn of the 20th century, African Americans were primarily Southern. Meier and Rudwick (1970) observed that "approximately three out of four lived in rural areas and nine out of ten lived in the South" (p. 213). The "Great Migration," however, changed the landscape of the North and South. By the 1950s, "Negroes were mainly an urban population, almost three fourths of them being city-dwellers" (Meier & Rudwick, 1970, p. 213). During this era, African Americans crowded into Northern cities in search of job opportunities; what they found, however, were overcrowded urban areas with assorted European immigrants either seeking similar opportunities or already established in the low-skill, low-wage jobs that African Americans had hoped to obtain. African American women were able to secure employment in domestic service, where, unfortunately, White men often sexually assaulted them. Writing of the dilemma this posed, scholar activist Angela Davis (1981) noted,

> From Reconstruction to the present, Black women household workers have considered sexual abuse perpetrated by the "man of the house" as one of their major occupational hazards. Time after time they have been victims of extortion on the job, compelled to choose between sexual submission and absolute poverty for themselves and their families. (p. 91)

African American men who did find work were also relegated to menial jobs and, from 1890 to 1930, were often used as strikebreakers (Massey & Denton, 1993). Their role as strikebreakers often led to racial violence in the North, which repeatedly culminated in race riots. From 1900 to 1919, there was a steady stream of race riots throughout the North. The riots continued into the 1920s, with Whites resisting integration "by any means necessary." As Massey and Denton (1993) documented,

> A wave of bombings followed the expansion of Black residential areas in the cities throughout the north. In Chicago, fifty-eight homes were bombed between 1917 and 1921, one every twenty days; and one Black real estate agent, Jesse Binga, had his home and office bombed seven times in one year. (p. 35)

Devastating riots followed in Tulsa, Oklahoma, in 1921 (Hirsch, 2002) and Rosewood, Florida, in 1923 (D'Orso, 1996; Russell, 1998). Because of the continuing racial tensions related to labor competition and integration attempts, race riots persisted well into the 1960s (Grimshaw, 1969).

In the 1930s, the "Scottsboro Boys" drew international attention to the plight of African Americans. The case involved several African American boys who were traveling in a freight train with several White boys and two White girls. After a fight ensued, the White boys were ejected from the train. At the next stop in Scottsboro, Alabama, the girls got off the train and claimed they had been gang-raped by the nine African American boys. Playing on the worst fears of Southern White men, the girls' accusations resulted in a mob being quickly formed in anticipation of the lynching of the boys (Carter, 1969). With the protection of law enforcement, however, the boys made it to trial. Following several trials, the boys were found guilty and received the death penalty. Although it was later revealed that the claims were a hoax, the boys spent the better part of their youth and early adulthood incarcerated for crimes they didn't commit.

During the 1930s and 1940s, there was continued interest in the subject of crime among African Americans. In the last edition of his landmark text, *Principles of Criminology* (1947), pioneering criminologist Edwin Sutherland devoted a chapter to "crime in relation to race and nativity." He first noted that, much like today, African Americans were "arrested, convicted, and committed to prisons approximately three times as frequently as White persons" (Sutherland, 1947, p. 121). Sutherland also cautioned that some of these statistics "probably reflect a bias against all of the minority races but especially against the Negro" (p. 121).

By the early 1950s, African Americans and other ethnic groups were still struggling to survive in an increasingly segregated and hostile America. Some turned to crime, whereas others turned to the United Nations for assistance. In 1951, African Americans petitioned the United Nations and charged the U.S. government with genocide against African Americans (Patterson, 1951/1970). Although the United Nations did not respond to the petition, African Americans had made the commitment to try to change their position within American society. This movement was given a further push by the 1955 kidnapping and slaying of Emmett Till in Mississippi.

The shocking and brutal killing of the 14-year-old boy for "disrespecting" a White woman spurred a movement that picked up steam with the Montgomery boycott, which started on December 5, 1955. The civil rights movement showed the national and international communities the depth of racial hatred and interracial strife in America. The demonstrations that defined the movement were seen by millions on TV, and the brutality of the police toward nonviolent demonstrators spoke to the oppressive role the police played in the African American and other minority communities.

By the 1960s, according to figures from Tuskegee Institute (Zangrando, 1980), lynchings were rare events; however, Whites had successfully used the practice to discourage any serious level of integration. Therefore, although Thurgood Marshall and his colleagues were successful in the landmark *Brown v. Board of Education* (1954) case, minority communities did not substantially change for decades. Because of "the White strategy of ghetto containment and tactical retreat before an advancing color line" (Massey & Denton, 1993, p. 45), substantial underclass communities were in existence by the 1970s. This bred a level of poverty and despair that fostered the continuation of the African American criminal classes and organized crime. The riots of the 1960s were a response to the long-standing troublesome conditions in some of these cities (National Advisory Commission on Civil Disorders, 1968).

When African Americans (especially those that comprised a growing middle class) were finally able to take advantage of the opportunities forged by the civil rights movement and desegregation, many of them left inner-city areas for the suburbs (an event known as "Black flight"). As a result, the level of stability they brought to these communities disappeared after the exodus. Those communities are now composed of what Wilson (1987) describes as "the truly disadvantaged." They are heavily dependent on the underground economy for survival (see Venkatesh, 2006, 2008), which has likely contributed to the overrepresentation of African Americans throughout the U.S. criminal justice system.

In the mid part of the first decade of the 2000s, the plight of the **truly disadvantaged** was brought to the forefront of American consciousness with the 2005 Hurricane Katrina fiasco, in which the government—at all levels—failed to provide an adequate response to the needs of poor and mostly Black New Orleans residents (Dyson,

2006; Potter, 2007). Moreover, in the absence of government response, citizens who took matters into their own hands have been portrayed as criminals (Russell-Brown, 2006). In the second decade of the 21st century, a spate of high-profile fatal shootings involved unarmed Black males. In 2012, the first shooting to receive considerable national exposure involved Trayvon Martin, a 17-year-old boy from Florida, who was killed by George Zimmerman, a community watch person (Gabbidon & Jordan, 2013). Zimmerman killed Martin after confronting him, even though he had been directed to do otherwise by the local police department. Additionally, in 2014 and 2015, the questionable deaths of Michael Brown in Ferguson, Missouri; Eric Garner in New York City; and Freddie Gray in Baltimore at the hands of police officers spurred nationwide protests and a movement that emphasizes that "Black Lives Matter" (see Chapter 4 for additional discussion of these police killings).

Even with the ongoing struggles encountered by African Americans and other Black ethnic groups, and the historical fixation on their criminality, they have contributed to every aspect of American life, from the tilling of the soil in the South and factory work in the North to produce the wealth that made America what it is, to the innumerable scientific, musical, and artistic contributions that are now considered staples of American culture.

White Ethnics

During the early 1600s, while the slave trade in South America and the West Indies was commonplace, the British colonized parts of what would later become the American colonies. This led to many of the same kinds of conflicts with Native Americans that the Spanish had quelled with unimaginable brutality. Although the British saw the colonies as somewhere they could send criminals and other undesirables, they also saw the opportunity for monetary gain, so they encouraged immigration to the colonies. Some came freely, whereas others used indentures to get themselves to the New World. Indentured servant agreements allowed immigrants to work for a period of time to pay for their travel expenses to the colonies. Once their indentures were completed, immigrants were free to pursue whatever opportunities they desired. In addition to British immigrants, Germans and Italians were among the first to immigrate to America. Many began to arrive in the early 1600s, settling first in New Amsterdam (New York) and later in Pennsylvania (Sowell, 1981).

Given this rich history of European immigration to the United States, we briefly review the history of several **White ethnic** groups. Although our review does not cover every White ethnic group that immigrated to America, we provide discussions of several of the major groups. We begin with an overview of the experience of German Americans. This is followed by a review of the experiences of Italian Americans, Irish Americans, Jewish Americans, and Arab Americans. As you will see, many of these groups have similar stories regarding their reason for making the long journey to America. In addition, many have had nearly identical experiences upon their arrival in America.

German Americans

Faust (1927) places the first German in America at the time of Leif Eriksson's pioneering journey that landed him in North America 500 years prior to Columbus's arrival.

Among Eriksson's crew was a German named Tyrker, who "is credited with discovering grapes in North America and therefore also naming the new land Vineland" (Rippley, 1976, p. 22). Not until the 1500s was there a settlement of Germans in America. Located in Port Royal, South Carolina, the settlement was composed of Huguenots (French Protestants) and Alsatian and Hessian Protestants (both of German origin). The settlement, however, was destroyed by the Spaniards, and thus only lasted four years, from 1562 to 1566. The next wave of German immigrants arrived with the first settlers in Jamestown in 1607. Often referred to as the "Dutch," which is likely "a linguistic slip that occurred because the word 'Dutch' so closely resembles a German's designation for himself, *Deutsch*" (Rippley, 1976, p. 24), they were often mistreated during the early colonial period. Consequently, they sympathized with the plight of Native Americans and "chose to remain with the Indians, preferring their friendship to that of the 'gentlemen' of Jamestown" (Faust, 1927, p. 8).

In the late 1600s, 13 German families arrived in Philadelphia and represented the beginning of mass German immigration to the United States (Coppa & Curran, 1976). Many of these immigrants came at the urging of William Penn, who told them of the religious freedoms in his colony of Pennsylvania (Sowell, 1981). Others came as a result of the disarray in their homeland. Of this, Coppa and Curran (1976) wrote, "The havoc wrought by the Thirty Years' War (1618–1648) devastated Germany for many decades: commerce declined; industry was crippled; and intellectual life sustained a deep if not mortal blow" (p. 45). The German population also increased because of the use of indentures to get them to America. Hence, those who wanted to immigrate to America signed contracts that paid their way. As one might imagine, this was shady business. Sowell (1981) writes that:

> the indentured servants were preyed upon by the dishonest. Some ship captains provided inadequate food or sold them into longer periods of bondage than actually required to work off the cost off their transportation. Germans who could not understand English were particularly vulnerable. (p. 49)

As a consequence of all these events, by the time of the Revolutionary War, there were about 225,000 German Americans in the colonies (Rippley, 1976, p. 29).

Immigration from Germany in the 1800s began slowly, but because of continuing issues in the homeland, Germans continued to hear from other groups of the promise of America. As such, around the 1830s, the number of German immigrants rose again and continued to increase throughout the 19th century. By the 1900 census, there were more than 2.6 million Germans in America (Faust, 1927). These formidable numbers made them a significant force in American culture and politics. They were outstanding farmers and glassmakers and have been credited with setting up the first paper mill. Culturally, they incorporated coleslaw, sauerkraut, hotdogs, and hamburgers into American life. Well-known Germans such as Albert Einstein, Babe Ruth, Lou Gehrig, and Presidents Hoover and Eisenhower, among others, helped shape sports, science, and political life in America.

Given their large numbers in the American colonies following the Revolutionary War, Germans, unlike some other ethnic groups, were accepted early in the development of the country. Consequently, throughout the 1800s and 1900s, there were few bumps along the path toward full **assimilation**. An exception to this was during World War I, when America went to war with Germany. The anti-German sentiment was strong, but as Sowell (1981) notes, the animus was not restricted to Germans in Germany:

> Anti-German feeling among Americans was not confined to Germany, but extended quickly to the whole German culture and to German Americans, many of whom were sympathetic to their former homeland. German books were removed from the shelves of American libraries, German-language courses were canceled from the public schools, readers and advertisers boycotted German-American newspapers. (p. 65)

Anti-German sentiment returned with World War II; however, it never approached the level of World War I. Also, it was Japanese Americans who caught the ire of patriotic Americans. After World War II, German Americans further assimilated by intermarriage and their increasing advancement within key institutions in American society. Today, Germans are no longer a distinct Census category. In fact, looking back at their history, they have long been considered a significant segment of the White American population.

Italian Americans

Centuries after Christopher Columbus "discovered" the New World other Italians would take advantage of his discovery by immigrating to the American colonies. Although few in number, Italians were among the earliest immigrants to arrive in colonial America. The small numbers were not simply because of the disinterest in immigrating to America. Some jurisdictions, such as Maryland, only allowed the settlement of immigrants from Britain (Iorizzo & Mondello, 2006). But as a result of labor shortages, these laws started to disappear in the colonies. By 1648, Maryland had also changed its practice and passed legislation that "encouraged French, Dutch and Italians to come to its shores" (Iorizzo & Mondello, 2006, p. 26). To further encourage immigration to the colonies, in 1649 the Toleration Act was passed, which ensured religious freedom for Catholics. From the 1600s through the mid-1800s, immigration from Italy was steady but, mirroring the trend of other White ethnic groups, really picked up in the late 1800s. Those Italians who immigrated were trying to escape the turmoil in their homeland or simply looking for better economic opportunities. Among them were not only poor people, but various artists and political dissidents who were middle class and others who were revolutionaries. Settling mostly in northern cities, they contributed to the diversity of cities such as Boston, New York, and Philadelphia (Iorizzo & Mondello, 2006).

By 1920, more than 4 million Italians had arrived in the United States. To some, this was not necessarily a welcome development. Leading up to this period, during the late 1800s and early 1900s, heavy anti-Italian sentiment had resulted in numerous killings and hangings (Marger, 1997). Therefore, to stem Italian immigration to the United States, the Immigration Act of 1924 placed a stringent quota on the number of Italians who could immigrate to the country. In 1929, that number "was only 5,802, compared with 65,721 for British Immigrants" (Feagin & Booher Feagin, 2012, p. 98). Similar to the experience of other ethnic immigrant groups, their religion, Catholicism, also became a point of contention, along with stinging stereotypes, which, as noted in the experience of other ethnic groups, have often been created to demonize new immigrants. Italians were perceived by many to be "dangerous" and "inferior" to other European immigrants. The perception was enhanced by the image of the Italian Mafia (also referred to as the "Black Hand"; Marger, 1997).

The belief that Italians were heavily involved in organized crime likely originated from the fact that many of the immigrants came from Sicily, where the mafia was a social institution. However, in America, Italian organized crime became an obsession. The terms *organized crime* and *mafia* became synonymous with Italians. They were considered a lawless race. One congressional report described them as morally deficient, excitable, superstitious, and vengeful (Iorizzo & Mondello, 2006). These negative and racist characterizations were clearly unfair considering that the Irish, German, Jewish, and Polish immigrants had preceded them in organized criminal activity (Iorizzo & Mondello, 2006). In fact, as Sowell (1981) has aptly stated, "Organized crime was an existing American institution, and the Italian Americans had to literally fight their way into it" (p. 125). Despite the prevailing criminal stereotype, in the early part of the 20th century, Italians had "*lower* [emphasis added] crime rates than other Americans" (Sowell, 1981, p. 125). Although Italians eventually assimilated into American society and are presently subsumed under the White racial category, some of the early stereotypes remain.

Irish Americans

According to Meagher (2005), "The first Irishman came to America in 1584 as part of Sir Walter Raleigh's ill-fated expedition to the Outer Banks of North Carolina" (p. 1). Later, the Irish came in great numbers to America, looking for opportunities to escape extreme poverty in Ireland. Meagher has observed that 60% of those who came in the 17th century did so by way of indentures. Others were given the option of leaving Ireland instead of serving a prison sentence for a criminal conviction. Those who came in the mid-1800s as a result of the potato famine in Ireland, which killed (through starvation and disease) an estimated 1 million people, contributed to the exponential increase of Irish Americans. For example, during the 100-year period from 1820 to 1920, about 5 million Irish arrived in America (Meagher, 2005). They settled in areas throughout the country; however, many landed in northern states such as New York, Massachusetts, Pennsylvania, and Illinois. In addition, by the early 1860s, one-third of the Irish population could be found in the Western and Midwestern parts of the United States. Wherever the Irish settled, because of the prevailing nativist views and their predominantly Catholic backgrounds (some were Protestant), they often were ostracized and relegated to the worst areas of cities.

Historians have generally agreed that few immigrant groups have encountered the harsh treatment the Irish received in 19th-century America. Many of the Irish immigrants did bring alcoholism and fighting habits to American shores. As a result, they often caught the attention of police officials, who called police vans "paddy wagons" because so many Irish were occupants. In some cities, such as New York, the areas where the Irish dominated were some of the toughest.

The highly acclaimed 2002 movie *Gangs of New York* depicts the immigration of the Irish to New York during a period when there was a strong sense of resentment and hate directed toward immigrants. Largely based on actual events, the movie shows how ethnic antagonism between the native population (English) and newest immigrant group (Irish) resulted in brutal gang wars. The Irish are portrayed as a criminogenic ethnic group who bring their bad habits to an already overcrowded and notorious district of New York. The movie culminates with the "Draft Riots," which were provoked by ethnic tensions and Whites who objected to being drafted into the Union army to fight for the liberation of African American slaves, while they themselves were struggling to survive. Prior to the September 11, 2001, terrorist attack on the World Trade Center buildings, the Draft Riot was considered the single event to have caused the largest loss of life in New York City history (more than 1,000 deaths).

Not until the second- and third-generation families did the Irish truly start to become a part of the American social fabric. In fact, during the early and mid-20th century, they became major contributors to the arts and were prominently featured in major motion pictures. Nevertheless, they were still faced with challenges. In particular, restrictive immigration quotas in the 1920s also hit them hard, and there were still barriers in place that restricted them from reaching their full potential occupationally. For example, Irish women, unlike other White ethnic females, had to take jobs as domestic servants to make ends meet. As noted previously with the experience of Black female domestics, these were dangerous jobs that often resulted in sexual harassment, rape, or, out of desperation, a descent into prostitution (Meagher, 2005). Nevertheless, large numbers of the Irish headed to college, and research shows that in the 1920s and 1940s, they were as successful as the native-born European immigrants. By 1960, "Irish occupational status exceeded national averages and was higher than every other White ethnic group except Jews" (Meagher, 2005, p. 132). In short, after initial resistance to their presence in America, the Irish had fulfilled the promise of the "American Dream." It is significant that despite the resistance to their presence in America, the Irish were able to swiftly rise out of the doldrums of their early American experience. This is likely attributable to the fact that, as time went on, the Irish became integrated into the fabric of American society and assimilated into the status of White Americans (T. W. Allen, 1994; Ignatiev, 1996).

Jewish Americans

Interestingly, the first Jews who arrived in America were of Hispanic origin. In 1654, 23 Sephardic Jews from Spain and Portugal arrived in New Amsterdam (Finkelstein, 2007). Their arrival in the New World began with controversy when the captain of the ship that brought them to America sued them because their fares had not been paid. To pay their fares, "The court ordered two of the new arrivals imprisoned and the belongings of all 23 passengers sold at auction" (Finkelstein, 2007, p. 31). Moreover, the governor of New Amsterdam, Peter Stuyvesant, wanted them to leave. In short, he viewed Jews as repugnant and originating from a "deceitful race" (Finkelstein, 2007, p. 31). Stuyvesant was so anti-Semitic that he banned Jews from building a synagogue and restricted their enlistment in the military. Thus, the first American synagogue was not built until the 1720s. Henceforth, Jews began to branch out and started to become somewhat more accepted within American society. This was fostered by the advent of American Freemasonry, in which Christians and Jews interacted. Although discrimination remained a part of the Jewish American landscape, Article VI of the U.S. Constitution, which banned religious discrimination, provided some respite for Jews who aspired to public office.

The 19th century saw a considerable increase in the Jewish presence in America. Whereas there were only 3,000 Jews in America in 1820, 40 years later there were 200,000 (Finkelstein, 2007). Tied together by religious and cultural traditions, many arrived from Russia, Poland, and other Eastern European countries, where they had long been persecuted for their religious beliefs and customs. To preserve their culture, in 1843, 12 German Jews gathered in a New York café and founded B'nai B'rith, which means "Sons of the Covenant." The mission of the organization was ambitious, but it laid the grounds for an organization that, by 1861, was "operating in every major Jewish community in America" (Sachar, 1993, p. 71). The mission of the organization was as follows:

> Uniting Israelites in the work of promoting their highest interests and those of humanity; of developing and elevating the mental and moral character of the people of our faith; of inculcating the purest principles of philanthropy, honor, and patriotism; of supporting science and art; of alleviating the wants of the victims of persecution; providing for, protecting and assisting the widow and orphan on the broadest principles of humanity. (Finkelstein, 2007, p. 64)

Recounting Jewish history, Feagin and Booher Feagin (2012) write,

> From the Egyptian and Roman persecutions in ancient times to massacres in Spain in the 1400s to brutal pogroms in Russia in the 1880s to German Nazi massacres, Jews might be regarded as the most widely oppressed racial or ethnic group in world history. (p. 115)

Seeking relief from persecution in European countries, Jews continued to arrive in America en masse. In the 40 years from 1880 to 1920, 2 million Jews arrived in America. As the persecution continued, many more arrived and eventually assimilated into the American way of life while maintaining their Jewish traditions. However, coinciding with this significant wave of immigration was an increase in anti-Semitism. Describing this turbulent period for Jews, Finkelstein (2007) writes, "Much of this was fueled by the stereotypes brought over from Europe by the large numbers of newly arrived Christian immigrants. Jews faced growing restrictions in housing, employment, and education" (p. 79).

During the first quarter of the 20th century, the mass immigration and squalid living conditions of Jews resulted in abundant numbers of Jewish youth hanging out on the streets. This produced rising juvenile delinquency rates, which became the target of a number of Jewish organizations. In a similar vein, whereas the 1920s and 1930s were periods of considerable Jewish progress, Brodkin Sacks (1997) noted that Jewish success in organized crime was also critical to their upward mobility. She specifically mentioned that "Arnold Rothstein transformed crime from a haphazard, small-scale activity into a well-organized and well-financed business operation. Consider also Detroit's Purple Gang, Murder Incorporated in New York, and a host of other big-city Jewish gangs in organized crime" (p. 399). These illicit activities were also found among other ethnic groups striving to move up the social ladder, albeit through criminality, in urban areas.

The period also saw quotas established restricting the number of Jews who could attend prestigious universities such as Harvard. Thus, although they were progressing in terms of their status in American society, there remained barriers to full assimilation. Jews, however, continued to be successful in educational pursuits and small businesses. In 1921, Albert Einstein won the Nobel Prize in Physics, and Jews were among the most successful immigrants. Because of their success in education, Finkelstein (2007) notes that "by the end of World War II . . . most Jews had established themselves firmly into the middle class, with large numbers employed in 'economically secure' jobs as civil servants: Teachers, accountants, lawyers, and medical professionals" (pp. 129–130). As a result, many moved out of the ghettos and into the suburbs, where they were largely unwelcome. In time, however, Jews assimilated and were also categorized as White Americans (Brodkin, 1999; Brodkin Sacks, 1997).

Each of the aforementioned White ethnic groups came to America seeking prosperity but was immediately thrust into dire socioeconomic conditions. In many instances, crime provided the means to rise above their condition (Bell, 1960; Light, 1977). Initially, each group was labeled criminal, but after a period of decades, most were able to rise out of their situations and assimilate into America—as White Americans (Gans, 2005). In recent years, some Whites have become concerned about their status as White Americans. This has led to a resurgence of nativist movements—largely tied to immigration concerns (Mudde, 2012). One group that is currently classified by the U.S. Census Bureau as White American that, in the last decade, has had a divergent experience from other White ethnics is Arab Americans. We provide a brief overview of their experience in the next section.

Arab Americans

Arab Americans have a long history in the United States. Before reviewing their experience, it is important that readers understand that the terms *Arab Americans* and *Muslim Americans* are not synonymous. In other words, not all Muslims are Arab. And similarly, not all Arab Americans are Muslims. Arab Americans are a cultural group in the United States, and Muslim Americans are those persons from all races and ethnic backgrounds who follow the Islamic religious tradition. Our focus here is on Arab Americans, who are people from Lebanon, Egypt, Syria, Palestine, Jordan, and a host of other Middle Eastern countries. Orfalea (2006) separates the Arab American experience into three significant waves of immigration. The first wave commenced in 1878 and continued through 1924. There are multiple reasons given for why Arabs immigrated to the United States in the late 19th century. It has been suggested that economics, political conflict, religious strife, and the pursuit of fortune contributed to Arab immigration to America. Not unlike other **White immigrants**, Arab Americans viewed the United States as having "streets of gold" (p. 51). These varying motivations resulted in approximately 200,000—mostly Christian—Arab Americans in the country during the 1920s (Feagin & Booher Feagin, 2012; Kayyali, 2006).

Just as the immigration of other ethnic groups was reduced by legislation, Arab Americans were also affected by the notorious 1924 Immigration Act that severely restricted the total immigration to the United States to fewer than 160,000 (Federal Reserve Archival System for Economic Research, n.d.). The second wave of Arab

American immigration followed World War II and spanned the years 1947 to 1966. With the relaxing of immigration policies, Arabs fled war-torn areas in the Middle East. Some came as political refugees in the 1950s and 1960s when the United States passed the Refugee Relief Act that was targeted at Palestinian refugees. In total, 6,000 Palestinians made use of this Act (Kayyali, 2006). The late 1960s saw the third wave of Arab immigration to the United States. Following the Arab defeat in the 1967 Six-Day War against Israel, Arabs became "disillusioned and pessimistic about the future of the Arab world and chose to move to the United States and other non-Arab countries" (p. 33). This resulted in more than 400,000 Arab immigrants arriving in the United States between the 1960s and the 1990s (p. 33).

On the surface, the Arab American story mirrors that of other White ethnics, as they also had to endure negative stereotypes leveled at them by other more established immigrant groups. The Arab American story was considerably altered following the events of September 11, 2001 (hereafter 9/11). While other groups quietly assimilated into whiteness, the 9/11 terrorist attacks returned Arab Americans to the status of a recognizable minority (Jamal & Naber, 2008). The racial animus that had previously targeted minority groups such as Blacks and Latinos also targeted Arab Americans (and Muslim Americans) because of the Middle Eastern backgrounds of the 9/11 terrorists. In particular, Arab Americans were perceived to be the group most likely to engage in terrorist activities; therefore, citizens and policing officials alike were supportive of **racial profiling** of people of Middle Eastern descent. This led to the harassment of Arab Americans and to the term *flying while Arab,* which refers to the additional scrutiny Arab Americans are perceived to receive when traveling by airplane (Baker, 2002; Schildkraut, 2009). Despite this recent harassment directed at them, the estimated 1.8 to 3.7 million Arab Americans remain a vital force in the United States (Brown, Guskin, & Mitchell, 2012).

Latino Americans

Prior to the 2000 census, the term *Hispanic* was used to refer to persons from Mexico, Puerto Rico, Cuba, and Central and South America. Feagin and Booher Feagin (2012) noted that the term *Latino* emerged because it "recognizes the complex Latin American origins of these groups. It is a Spanish-language word preferred by many Spanish-speaking scholars, activists, and others" (p. 209). Our review of their history focuses on the two largest ethnic groups under the Latino category: Mexicans and Puerto Ricans. The data presented earlier in Table 1.2 clearly illuminate the diversity of the American Latino population.

Mexicans

Between 1500 and 1853, the Spanish conquered and ruled Mexico. During these three centuries, the Spanish exploited the Mexican population for their labor. Many Mexicans became Americans with the annexation of Texas. Following the Mexican-American War (1846–1848) and the Treaty of Guadalupe Hidalgo (1848), Mexicans had the option to stay in the United States or return to Mexico. According to Feagin and Booher Feagin (2012), although many returned, others stayed in America.

Sowell (1981) wrote that Mexicans immigrated to America in three great waves. The first wave of Mexicans came to America by railroad—and ironically, over the years, railroads became one of the largest employers of Mexicans. Specifically, they were employed "as construction workers, as watchmen, or as laborers maintaining the tracks. Many lived in boxcars or in shacks near the railroads—primitive settlements that were the beginning of many Mexican-American communities today" (p. 249). Before World War I, other industries employing Mexicans were agriculture and mining. Mexican workers in America were paid considerably more than they were in Mexico. As a result, there was a steady flow of seasonal workers crossing the Mexican border to earn money to take back home to Mexico. Labor shortages caused by World War I resulted in formalized programs to encourage such practices. About 500,000 Mexicans came to America to work during this period (Tarver, Walker, & Wallace, 2002). Beginning in this period, Mexicans also were subject to negative stereotypes, such as being considered "dirty," "ignorant," and lacking standards of appropriate behavior (Sowell, 1981). Even so, they were tolerated because of the dire need for their labor. With the arrival of the Depression, "Fears of the unemployed created an anti-immigrant movement, and immigration laws were modified to deport the 'undesirables' and restrict the numbers of foreign-contract laborers" (Tarver et al., 2002, p. 54).

About the same time as the notorious Scottsboro cases were being tried, the federal government, under the direction of President Herbert Hoover, commissioned the first national crime commission. Commonly referred to as the "Wickersham Report," for its director, George Wickersham, the commission's report, published in 1931, covered almost every aspect of American criminal justice. The report included a review of the state of Mexicans and crime; it found that there were varying levels of crime among Mexicans in California and Texas. In general, however, the report noted that, like African Americans, Mexicans were treated with considerable prejudice by the justice system (Abbott, 1931). The report suggested that the criminality of the Mexicans was overstated. There was also brief mention of Filipinos, who were overrepresented in offenses related to gambling, and Japanese, who were "among the most law abiding of all population groups" (p. 415).

The second wave of Mexican immigrants came to the United States during World War II. Another war had resulted in another labor shortage, which produced the **Bracero Program**, which brought in thousands of agricultural workers. *Bracero* is a Spanish term that was used to describe guest workers coming from Mexico to the United States. When the Bracero Program ended in 1964, 5 million Mexican workers had been imported into the United States (Tarver et al., 2002, p. 54).

The third wave of Mexican immigration is tied to the various immigration laws from the 1970s to the present, which have sought to protect, defend, or curtail Mexican immigration to the United States. One such law, the Immigration Reform and Control Act of 1986, provided temporary residency for some illegal aliens. Furthermore, those who had come to America before 1982 were given permanent resident status. According to Tarver et al. (2002),

> This Act had an enormous impact on Mexican immigration, with 1,655,842 people entering the United States during the decade of the 1980s. Since the first decade of the twentieth century, this was the largest number of immigrants from a single country. (p. 55)

Another law aimed at Mexican illegal immigration is the Illegal Immigration Reform and Immigrant Responsibility Act of 1996. In addition to shoring up the borders in California and Texas, the Act "increased the number of investigators monitoring workplace employment of aliens, passport fraud, and alien smuggling" (Tarver et al., 2002, p. 55). In 2010, because of the continuing fears about illegal immigration (estimated to be 11 to 12 million illegal immigrants in America; Hsu, 2010), Arizona passed Immigration Bill SB 1070, known as the "Support Our Law Enforcement and Safe Neighborhoods Act." In its original form, among other things, the bill required immigrants to carry their alien registration information and provided law enforcement officials with the discretion to question persons who they believed were illegal immigrants (referred to as the "papers please" provision). After the law was passed, there were lawsuits challenging the constitutionality of its assorted provisions. These challenges were eventually decided in the U.S. Supreme Court case *Arizona v. United States* (2012). The split decision upheld the "papers please" provision of the law that "required state law enforcement agents to demand immigration papers from anyone stopped, detained, or arrested in the state whom officers reasonably suspect is in the country without authorization" (Sacks, 2012).

It is apparent from this type of legislation that some Americans believe the heavy influx of Mexicans is changing the fabric of the country. Besides concerns about job competition and the strain on social services caused by considerable illegal immigration, Americans have continued their fascination with the perceived connection between immigration and crime (Guevara Urbina, 2012; Hickman & Suttorp, 2008; Higgins, Gabbidon, & Martin, 2010; Martinez & Valenzuela, 2006; Stowell, 2007). As you should know by now, this fear-based fascination is not new—it is the American way (Martinez, 2006). Ironically, very few commentators have taken note of the views of the Hispanics on illegal immigration. Box 1.3 provides a summary of public opinion data collected in 2013 that examines the Hispanic viewpoint on undocumented immigration.

BOX 1.3

Race and Crime in the Media

How U.S. Latinos Feel About Undocumented Immigration

As the debate over immigration reform takes center stage across the country, a new national survey finds that in the last 3 years, there has been a marked increase in the number of Latinos who think the effects of undocumented immigration in their community have been largely positive.

Forty-five percent of Hispanic adults say the impact of unauthorized immigration is positive, compared to 29 percent who had the same opinion in 2010, according to the survey by the Pew Research Hispanic Trends Project.

Authors Mark Hugo Lopez and Ana Becerra state that "it is possible that in 2010, a combination of a weak economy and a hardening political environment around immigration may have led to a more downbeat assessment of illegal immigration's impact on U.S. Latinos."

"In 2010, the nation was emerging from the Great Recession and Arizona had passed its SB 1070 law that authorized local police to check the immigration status of anyone they suspected of being in the U.S. illegally," they add.

(Continued)

(Continued)

The increase in the more favorable view of unauthorized immigration is seen more among foreign-born Latinos. Over half—53 percent—say unauthorized immigration has been positive, up 19 points since 2010, when it was 34 percent.

Yet among native-born Latinos, the views are more generational—and in some groups there is much less support for undocumented immigration.

While 42 percent of second-generation Latinos say undocumented immigration has been generally positive for the U.S. Latino community, only 29 percent of third-generation Hispanics think the same, though in both groups, the numbers have increased over 10 points since 2010.

The report also found differences among Latinos by language, country of origin, and educational attainment.

Spanish-dominant Latinos were more positive about the impact of unauthorized immigrants—55 percent—whereas opinions are split among English-dominant Hispanics. Thirty-one percent see a positive effect, 30 percent see a negative effect and 33 percent say there is no impact one way or the other.

Dominicans (59 percent) and Salvadorans (57 percent) are the most likely to say the effect of undocumented immigration on U.S. Hispanics is positive, followed by about half of other Central Americans, 47 percent of Mexicans, and 47 percent of South American Latinos.

The views are more mixed among Cubans and Puerto Ricans. Thirty-eight percent of Cubans say the impact of undocumented immigration is positive, but 28 percent say it is negative, and 27 percent say there is no impact one way or the other. Among Puerto Ricans, it is split more equally—34 percent say it is positive, 29 percent negative, and 29 percent think there is no effect.

In terms of education, 52 percent of Hispanics with less than a high school diploma and almost half who are high school graduates have a favorable view of undocumented immigration.

Latinos with a bachelor's degree are more mixed in their views. Thirty-four percent say the effect of unauthorized immigration has been positive, 33 percent say it is negative, and 27 percent say it has had no effect on the U.S. Latino community.

The report comes out as Latino groups around the country plan high-profile marches and events on Saturday to bring attention to the issue of undocumented immigration and the lack of legislation out of Congress.

Source: Lilley (2013).

1. Why do Latinos' views on undocumented immigration vary by language, country of origin, and educational attainment?

Puerto Ricans

In the late 1400s, the island of Puerto Rico was colonized by the Spanish. But it was not until 1897 that Puerto Ricans gained their independence. The year after achieving independence, in 1898, the Spanish-American War resulted in the U.S. taking over the island. In the 1950s, Puerto Rico became a commonwealth of the United States, granting Puerto Ricans more independence in their governance. From 1945 to the 1970s, the high unemployment rate resulted in one in three Puerto Ricans leaving the island (Feagin & Booher Feagin, 2012). Significant numbers of Puerto Ricans headed to New York and other states, such as New Jersey and Delaware. Thus, after having only

2,000 Puerto Ricans in New York in 1900, there was significant Puerto Rican immigration to the United States, which resulted in an increase to 70,000 in 1940 and 887,000 by 1960 (Feagin & Booher Feagin, 2012). Upon their arrival, as with other immigrants who headed to the "promised land," they were faced with high levels of unemployment and poverty. In fact, these dire circumstances resulted in what has been referred to as "circular migration." That is, after the opportunities they were seeking did not materialize, Puerto Ricans would head home, but then return because of the lack of opportunities in Puerto Rico. Mirroring the experience of other racial and ethnic groups, over time, Puerto Ricans were also saddled with negative stereotypes, such as "lazy," "submissive," "violent," and "criminal." Moreover, because they cannot always "pass" as White, they have been unable to assimilate like some other ethnic groups. As a result of their varying skin tones and backgrounds, they often are categorized as either White or Black.

A Brief Note on Other Latino Americans

Cubans are also a notable segment of the Latino population. With much of their immigration coming after Fidel Castro's takeover of the government in 1959, they currently number about 2 million (Brown & Patten, 2013). With the relaxing of sanctions against Cuba and the lifting of some travel restrictions under the Obama Administration, there is the strong potential for improved relations with Cuba in the coming years. Combined, South Americans from the Dominican Republic, El Salvador, and Colombia also represent another substantial portion of the Latino population. Given these figures, it is no wonder that Latinos have become the largest minority group in the United States. They have also, however, suffered from some of the same crime-related concerns as other ethnic groups before them. Notably, however, they have not experienced the same levels of crime and violence as African Americans (Martinez, 2002; Martinez, Stowell, & Lee, 2010). This may reflect the fact that many Latinos have come to the United States specifically seeking opportunities for employment, with a willingness to take the most undesirable jobs in the labor market. For many, these jobs provide much more financial compensation than the available employment in the various Latin American countries from which a substantial portion of Latino immigrants originate. Nevertheless, some Latinos have drifted into gangs and other criminal activities as a way to survive in America. Unfortunately, their criminal activities have been exaggerated by the news media and Hollywood, which has resulted in continuing stereotypes (Martinez, Lee, & Nielsen, 2001). Notably, some recent research suggests some improvement in the news media coverage of Blacks and Latinos in Los Angeles (Dixon, 2015).

Asian Americans

Asian Americans provide another interesting case study of ethnic group acculturation in America. Like Latinos, they belong to a number of ethnic groups, such as Filipino, Korean, Japanese, and Vietnamese. Table 1.5 provides an overview of the population of the various Asian American groups. We begin our review with a brief discussion of the Chinese American experience.

Table 1.5

U.S. Population Estimates of Asian Americans, 2013

Asian American Group	Estimate	Percentage
Asian Indian	2,960,584	19.4
Chinese	3,578,774	23.4
Filipino	2,604,783	17.1
Japanese	785,003	5.0
Korean	1,438,725	9.0
Vietnamese	1,649,951	10.8
Other Asian	2,214,142	14.5
Total Asian American	15,231,962	100.0*

Source: U.S. Census Bureau, 2009–2013 5-Year American Community Survey.

Note: * Total percentage slightly off due to rounding.

Chinese Americans

According to Daniels (1988), there were Chinese in America as early as the late 1700s. Not until the California gold rush of the mid-1850s was there any significant Chinese immigration to America: Between 1849 and 1882, nearly 300,000 Chinese came to America (Daniels, 1988). The **Chinese Exclusion Act of 1882** limited immigration until the 1940s. Most of the early Chinese immigrants were male (90%) and came to work in America temporarily. However, they came in significant enough numbers to represent nearly 10% of California's population between 1860 and 1880 (Daniels, 1988). Those who did stay were subjected to considerable violence due to anti-Chinese sentiment. Chinatowns had existed since the arrival of the Chinese in America; they embraced these areas because there they were free to maintain their culture without fear of hostility—although some areas occupied exclusively by Chinese inhabitants were "shabby looking, vice-infested, and violence prone" (Sowell, 1981, p. 141).

The Chinese were quite successful as laborers as well as in independent businesses such as restaurants and laundries (Daniels, 1988; Sowell, 1981). Yet, as with other immigrant groups, the Chinese were not immune to engaging in illegal activities. Daniels (1988) wrote that prostitution and gambling flourished in the "bachelor society" created by the dearth of Asian women in America. In 1870, "More than 75% of the nearly 3,000 Chinese women workers in the United States identified themselves as prostitutes" (Perry, 2000, p. 104). Brothels and opium-smoking establishments became popular among both Asians and Whites. Regarding opium use among early Chinese immigrants, Mann (1993) suggested that 35% of the Chinese immigrants smoked opium regularly, which "led to the first national campaign against narcotics" (p. 59), and the subsequent legislation was aimed at "excluding Chinese participation in American society" (p. 59). On the participation of the Chinese in these illegal activities, Daniels (1988) noted, "Since all of these activities were both lucrative and illegal, it seems clear that police and politicians in the White community were involved in sanctioning and profiting from them" (p. 22).

Eventually, following the pattern of other immigrants, Asian organized crime emerged, and secret societies such as "tongs" were formed. Describing these organizations, Perry (2000) indicated that such societies were originally created to assist Asian men in adjusting to America. But, as Perry notes, over time, many evolved into criminal organizations or developed links with Chinese "triads." Consequently, the tongs came to dominate prostitution, along with gambling, drugs, and other vice crimes. So, in addition to providing sexual outlets, they also created other opportunities for recreation and escapist behavior. Despite the profits reaped by Whites from the legal and illicit activities of the Chinese, heavy anti-Chinese sentiment persisted in California, which led to numerous negative campaigns against the population. Pointing to the roots of this negative sentiment, Sowell (1981) wrote, "The Chinese were both non-White and non-Christian, at a time when either trait alone was a serious handicap. They looked different, dressed differently, ate differently, and followed customs wholly unfamiliar to Americans" (pp. 136–137). Once they began to receive jobs in competition with Whites, they became targets of increasing violence and, in several instances, were massacred. By and large, the Chinese were generally relegated to the most menial and "dirty" occupations, such as mining, laying railroad tracks, and agricultural work. As a result of the Chinese Exclusion Act of 1882, unlike other ethnic minorities, the Chinese population decreased from the late 1880s through the mid-1940s. Since then, their numbers have increased, and they have remained the largest segment of the Asian American population. Until the last 30 years of the 20th century, Japanese Americans represented the second-largest group among Asians in the United States. Several other Asian groups have now surpassed them in population (most notably, Filipinos). We briefly discuss the Japanese American experience below.

Japanese Americans

Before arriving on the shores of North America in the last quarter of the 19th century, a considerable contingent of Japanese workers (30,000) arrived in Hawaii. They were contract workers who came to the island to provide much-needed labor for sugar plantations and "to serve as a counterweight to the relatively large number of Chinese in the islands" (Daniels, 1988, pp. 100–101). Like the Chinese before them, the Japanese also arrived on North American shores as a result of labor needs, and the relatively small number of Japanese men who made it to America (about 2,200 by 1890) filled the continuing need for laborers on California farms (Daniels, 1988). Like the Chinese and other groups, some Japanese immigrants turned to illicit activities, such as prostitution and other petty crimes, to survive.

Over time, the number of Japanese in America began to increase, with 24,326 in 1900, 72,157 in 1910, and nearly 127,000 by 1940. Mirroring the experience of the Chinese, anti-Japanese sentiment arose in the United States, culminating with the arrival of World War II. During World War II, negative sentiment toward the Japanese reached new heights; they were hated and mistrusted by many Americans. Once the attack on Pearl Harbor occurred, in December, 1941, life for Japanese Americans would never be the same. In February, 1942, President Roosevelt issued Executive Order 9066 (Dinnerstein & Reimers, 1982). The order, which was upheld by the Supreme Court, required that all Japanese from the West Coast be rounded up and placed in camps called **relocation centers**. In all, about 110,000 were rounded up on five days' notice and were told they could take only what they could carry. The camps were nothing more than prison facilities with armed military police on patrol watching for escapes.

Following the war, the Japanese population remained low in the United States due to immigration restrictions that were not lifted until the 1960s. At that time, Japanese Americans represented 52% of the Asian American population. However, over the next 20 years, the number of Japanese who immigrated to America declined. This trend was largely a result of the increased need for labor in Japan, which stunted the immigration of the Japanese to America (Takaki, 1989). The Japanese who were already here or among those who came after stringent quotas were lifted in the 1960s would go on to become some of the most successful immigrants. Today, economic indicators related to income and unemployment levels all reveal a positive trend for Japanese Americans. Nonetheless, Japanese Americans are still targets of discrimination. Two other Asian groups whose numbers have increased over the last few decades are Filipinos and Koreans. We provide brief overviews of their American experiences in the next section.

Filipinos and Koreans

Filipinos have been in the United States since the 1700s. But, as you might expect, much of their most significant immigration to the United States occurred in the 19th and 20th centuries. Many headed to plantations in Hawaii due to labor shortages. Unfortunately, when they arrived in America, they encountered violent attacks from Whites. In California, they competed with White farm workers; besides receiving lower wages than their counterparts, they were the targets of continuing violence. In fact, in 1929 and 1930, there were brutal riots that were brought on by anti-Filipino sentiment (Feagin & Booher Feagin, 2012). During this same time, the 1924 immigration law restricted the number of Filipinos who could enter the country to 50 (Kim, 2001). Since this early period, although their population has increased precipitously, they remain the targets of violence, and in post-9/11 America, some have been targeted as potential terrorists.

Photo 1.1

Japanese American internees await processing in 1942.

Russell Lee / Corbis.

Like Filipino Americans, Korean Americans headed to Hawaii in the early part of the 20th century to fill labor shortages. Koreans also followed other Asian groups to California. In the case of Koreans, the place of choice was San Francisco. Limited by immigration restrictions, much of Korean immigration followed World War II. Not until 1965 were the stringent immigration restrictions lifted. This policy change coincided with more Koreans (mostly from South Korea) arriving in America. Looking for opportunities, Koreans headed to inner-city communities, where they set up dry cleaners and convenience stores. Unfortunately, the relations between Koreans and urban residents are tenuous at best: Koreans are resented for entering largely African American communities and "setting up shop," as some have noted. Therefore, besides feeling mistreated by clerks in Korean establishments, some African Americans have felt that these businesses should be owned by community members. This sentiment spilled over in the Los Angeles riot of 1992 (Kim, 1999). Tensions remain between the two communities, but the dialogue continues. In 2007, Korean Americans received negative attention because the perpetrator of the Virginia Tech massacre was an immigrant from South Korea. Moreover, the 2012 Oikos University shooting in Oakland, CA that killed seven people and involved Korean native One L. Goh brought additional negative attention to the Korean community.

Asian Indians

Asian Indians are the second most populous Asian group in America. They began to arrive from India and other South Asian countries in the United States in the early 1800s, but only 17,000 made it to American shores between 1820 and 1965 (Schaefer, 2011). Many of these early immigrants were employed in railroad and agricultural industries on the West Coast (Feagin & Booher Feagin, 2012). Following the easing of immigration restrictions, the number of Asian Indian immigrants began to rise. In particular, the need for skilled workers resulted in the immigration of highly educated and skilled Asian Indians. Many initially headed to northeastern states such as New York; however, after the rise of Silicon Valley, California quickly became the destination of choice for many of the more technologically savvy Asian Indians. In addition to the highly skilled and educated immigrants from India, there is also a contingent of Asian Indians who are heavily engaged in the service sector occupations including driving taxicabs, managing motels, and operating convenience stores (Schaefer, 2011). Their success in the professions has resulted in many Asian Indians moving directly to suburban areas, as opposed to urban areas where most immigrants normally begin their ascension up the rungs of American society (Feagin & Booher Feagin, 2012). Asian Indians clearly represent one of the true immigrant success stories.

In closing, the difference between Asians and ethnic groups who came to be classified as White is that, although they have attained high levels of achievement, Asians have never fully assimilated. This leaves them, as one author put it, "as perpetual outsiders" (Perry, 2000). Like African Americans, Native Americans, and some Latinos, Asian Americans have maintained a distinct racial categorization in the Census. L. A. Gould (2000) has suggested that physical characteristics unique to their race (e.g., skin color, facial characteristics, size) have barred them from full assimilation and acceptance in America.

Despite not being able to fully assimilate, Asian Americans have been labeled the *model minority* because of their success in education. Some see their success as proof that all groups can succeed if they "put their best foot forward." Others see this label as problematic (Wu, 2002), noting that all Asians are not equally successful. For example, as Perry (2000) noted, "Koreans and Vietnamese consistently lag behind Chinese, Japanese, and Asian Indians on most indicators of socioeconomic status" (p. 100). Furthermore, the continuing discrimination in employment, income, and education is masked by the model minority label. Nevertheless, over the last century, Asian Americans have been a productive force in the United States.

❖ Conclusion

Since the categorization of races in the late 1700s, societies have, unfortunately, used the social construct to divide populations. In America, the notion of race was not of considerable use until the 1660s, when color was one of the deciding factors in the creation of the slave system. It was at this time in history that the category "White" began to take on increased importance.

Along with "Whiteness" came racism, which justified the system from the point of view of the dominant population. For the next two and a half centuries, as more White ethnic immigrants came to the United States looking for opportunities, they were looked down on as well. However, at some point, each group was allowed to fully assimilate and truly "become White," and over time, the stereotypes with which they had been identified eventually dissipated (see Table 1.6). In the case of Native Americans, African Americans, Asians, and Latinos, however, this process has been more difficult because of distinct physical traits that have limited their ability to fully assimilate. Recent years have also seen an increasing intolerance of Arab Americans following 9/11.

Our review of the historical antecedents of race and crime in America has revealed that, over the past few centuries, although the level of crime in each group

Table 1.6

Early Stereotypes of Racial and Ethnic Minorities (1600s–1900s)

Native American	Irish	Jewish	African American	Mexican American	Puerto Rican	Chinese/ Japanese
childlike	temperamental	too intelligent	bad odor	lazy	emotional	devious
cruel	dangerous	crafty	lazy	backward	lazy	corrupt
thieves	quarrelsome	clumsy	criminal	lawless	criminal	dirty
wild beasts	idle		apelike	violent		crafty
exotic	apelike			shiftless		docile
powerful				improvident		dangerous

*All groups were thought to be "biologically inferior" to the native White population.

has varied over time, most racial/ethnic groups have committed the same kinds of offenses and have had similar offenses perpetrated against them by the dominant culture. Initially, Whites criminally brutalized Native Americans and African Americans. As time went on, ethnic immigrants such as the Germans, Italians, and Irish, also were subjected to harsh treatment and sometimes violence. As these "White ethnic" groups assimilated into the populace, they, in turn, became part of the oppressive White population, continuing at times to engage in racial violence against other minority groups.

In short, the history of race and crime in America is a story of exploitation, violence, and, in the case of most racial/ethnic groups, the common use of crime as a way to ascend from the lower rungs of American society. The next chapter examines official crime and **victimization data** for the various races.

Discussion Questions

1. Explain the origin of race and its implications for race and crime.

2. Does DNA evidence support the existence of distinct races?

3. What role has the law played in the experiences of the groups portrayed in the chapter? Provide some examples using specific laws.

4. How does racial/ethnic oppression intersect with the study of race and crime?

5. What role does "Whiteness" play in understanding race and crime?

Internet Exercises

1. Visit the U.S. Bureau of the Census Web site (http://www.census.gov) and provide another logical way of categorizing the various groups in American society.

2. Visit the Forensic DNA website (http://nij.gov/topics/forensics/evidence/dna/pages/welcome.aspx) and view some of the advances in DNA identification in crime solving.

3. Visit the U.S. National Archives and Records Administration (http://www.archives.gov/) website and view some of the tools people use to investigate their racial/ethnic heritage.

Internet Sites

Forensic DNA website: http://nij.gov/topics/forensics/evidence/dna/pages/welcome.aspx

U.S. Bureau of the Census: http://www.census.gov

Ellis Island: http://www.nps.gov/elis/index.htm

Pew Research Hispanic Trends Project: http://www.pewhispanic.org/

Supplemental materials for *Race and Crime* are available online at
study.sagepub.com/gabbidon4e.

Extent of Crime and Victimization

CHAPTER 2

> *The falsity of past claims of race-neutral crime statistics and color-blind justice should caution us against the ubiquitous referencing of statistics about black criminality today, especially given the relative silence about white criminality.*
>
> —Muhammad (2010, p. 277)

Race and crime have been inextricably linked throughout American history. As noted in Chapter 1, early stereotypes of some Americans implied their criminality. Over time, beliefs about the inferiority and criminality of certain groups, including African Americans, Native Americans, White immigrants, and others, fostered the eugenics movement of the early 20th century and the "law and order" campaigns that came later. Muhammad (2010) provides a historical account of how the statistical link between race and crime occurred during the time when crime data first became available. Since then, although not created to do so, crime data often are used to support (erroneous) beliefs about minorities and crime. Between 1850 and the early 1900s, census data about convicted persons were the primary source of criminal statistics. At that time, distinctions were made between foreign and native-born convicts. Most foreign convicts were immigrants from European countries and were classified based on their place of origin (France, Germany, etc.). Despite opposition, in 1930, the U.S. Congress mandated that the Federal Bureau of Investigation (FBI) collect and report crime data. By the 1960s, the increase in crime recorded in the FBI's Uniform Crime Reports (UCR)—especially in urban areas—was used to justify the implementation of more punitive crime control policies. "The link between race and crime is as enduring and influential in the twenty-first century as it has been in the past" (Muhammad, 2010, p. 1).

Sullivan and McGloin (2014) identify several kinds of official criminal justice system data, including police contacts, arrests, court involvement, conviction, and incarceration. Today, the FBI continues to collect crime and arrest data from law enforcement agencies, and the **Bureau of Justice Statistics (BJS)** provides information on nonfatal victimizations. During the past several years, the BJS has enhanced dynamic online analyses of arrests, crime trends, victimizations, and other topics with data analysis tools. Other federal agencies facilitate online analyses of crime-related topics as well (see Table 2.1).

The use of **crime statistics** in empirical research and efforts to determine their reliability and validity are ongoing (see, e.g., O'Brien, Shichor, & Decker, 1980; Skogan, 1981; Steffensmeier, Feldmeyer, Harris, & Ulmer, 2011). Arrest and victimization data play an important role in research about race and crime. While informative, some of the research that relies on crime statistics leads to misperceptions about race and crime. The media also contributes to these misperceptions by its unbalanced focus on violent crime. As a result, many Americans continue to believe that Blacks are the perpetrators of more violent crimes than is actually the case. This is due, at least in part, to their overrepresentation in violent crime arrests and victimizations. For example, in 2013, African Americans made up about 13% of the population in the United States and an estimated 28% of all persons arrested, 52.2% of persons arrested for murder, 56.4% of persons arrested for robbery, and 33.9% of persons arrested for aggravated assault (FBI, 2014a). Some of these arrest patterns have persisted throughout the 20th and into the 21st century. It's easy to lose sight of the facts:

- The majority of Americans, regardless of their race/ethnicity, are neither arrested nor victimized.
- The majority of Americans and persons arrested are White.
- Of persons who are arrested, regardless of their racial categories, fewer are arrested for violent crimes such as murder, rape, robbery, and aggravated assault than for property offenses, most notably larceny/theft.
- Native Americans and persons of two or more races have higher violent **victimization rates** than either Whites, African Americans (Blacks), or Hispanics (Truman & Langton, 2014).
- Less than half of violent victimizations (46%) are reported to the police (Truman & Langton, 2014).

Despite the fact that most Americans are not involved in crime, over time, both crime and the administration of justice have become racialized (Covington, 1995; Keith, 1996). Covington (1995) used the concept of racialized crime to describe the process of generalizing the traits, motives, or experiences of individual Black criminals to the whole race or communities of noncriminal Blacks. The concept also can be applied to other minorities. For example, consider media portrayals of illegal immigrants, most notably Latinos, and perceptions about their involvement in gangs and violent crime. Is there a relationship between immigration, crime, and victimization? As discussed in Chapter 1, immigrants and their involvement in crime have been a concern since the 1800s, often resulting in restrictive immigration quotas. Today a considerable amount of attention is focused on crimes committed by and victimizations of undocumented/illegal immigrants. Some will be surprised to learn that most illegal immigrants are arrested for immigration violations and not for their involvement in violent crime (U.S. Government Accountability Office, 2011). Although crime statistics were not initially designed to label certain groups of people as criminals, this is exactly what has occurred.

Table 2.1

Sources of Crime and Victimization Statistics

Source	Sponsor	Inception	Methodology	Scope	Race Included	Ethnicity Included	Data Analysis Tool
Behavioral Risk Factor Surveillance System (BRFSS)	CDC	1984	Annual survey	Health and behavior risks	Yes	Yes	Yes
Campus Safety and Security	DOE, OPE	2010	Crimes reported	Person and property crimes	No	No	Yes
Civil Rights Data Collection	DOE	1968	Biennial survey	School and student characteristics	Yes	Yes	Yes
Crime in the United States (UCRs)	FBI	1930	Crimes reported to the police	• Crimes reported • Crimes cleared • Persons Arrested • Law enforcement personnel	Yes	Yes	Yes—Arrest Data Analysis Tool
Human Trafficking	FBI	2013	Crimes reported to the police	• Offense data • Arrest data	Yes	Yes	No
Human Trafficking Reporting System	BJS	2005	State and local task force reports	• Victims • Suspects	Yes	Yes	No
Indicators of School Crime and Safety	BJS and DOE: National Center for Education Statistics (NCES), Institute of Education Sciences (IES)	1997	Annual survey	• Teachers • Principals • Students	Yes	Yes	No

Source	Sponsor	Inception	Methodology	Scope	Race Included	Ethnicity Included	Data Analysis Tool
National Crime Victimization Survey (NCVS)	BJS	1972	Interviews	• Victims • Offenders • Offenses	Yes	Yes	Yes
Sourcebook of Criminal Justice Statistics	BJS	1973	Compendium of justice statistics 1973–2013	• Criminal justice data • Public attitudes	Yes	Yes	No
Statistical Briefing Book	Office of Juvenile Justice and Delinquency Prevention	1999	Compendium of juvenile data	• Juvenile crime victims • Offenders	Yes	Yes	Yes
Supplemental Homicide Reports	FBI	1980	Homicides reported to the FBI	Characteristics of homicide incidents	Yes	Yes	Yes—Criminal Justice Archive (ICPSR)
Yearbook of Immigration Statistics	DHS	2004	Annual statistics	Criminal aliens	No	No	No

In this chapter, we present a brief overview of the history of crime and victimization statistics, limitations of crime and victimization data, and analyses of arrest and victimization data. Although there are numerous sources of data on topics relevant to the study of race and crime, here, we focus on the UCR *Crime in the United States,* compiled by the FBI, and *Criminal Victimization,* the NCVS annual publication funded by the DOJ (BJS) and compiled by the U.S. Bureau of the Census. Race and crime data is presented in subsequent chapters as well. The goals of this chapter are to familiarize students with (1) arrest and victimization trends in the United States, (2) what arrest and victimization trends do and do not tell us about race and crime, (3) lynching and **hate crime** incidents, and (4) the policy implications of historical and contemporary race, crime, and victimization trends. At the outset, we acknowledge that race, class, and gender are difficult to assess with currently available crime and victimization data. First, an overview of the history of collecting crime and victimization data in the United States is presented.

❖ History of Crime and Victimization Statistics in the United States

The history of crime statistics in the United States dates back to the 19th century. L. N. Robinson (1911) was one of the first to analyze crime statistics and noted,

> The purpose of criminal statistics is two-fold: (1) that one may judge of the nature and extent of criminality in a given geographical area, and (2) that one may determine the transformation, if any, which is occurring in these two phases. The results, when known, may give direction to many movements of one kind or another, but the purpose of the statistics is to furnish these two sets of data. Their application is another question. (pp. 27–28)

Some states started collecting crime and justice data in the early 19th century. Several state legislatures mandated the collection of statistics on crime and criminals in two categories: judicial and prison statistics. Judicial statistics included information on persons appearing before the courts and their offenses. New York (1829) and Pennsylvania (1847) required clerks of the courts to submit transcripts or statements of convictions and/or criminal business. In 1832, Massachusetts mandated that the attorney general report his work and the work of the district attorneys to the legislature. In Maine (1839), county attorneys were required to report the number of persons prosecuted and their offenses to the attorney general, who also was required to submit a report to the governor. Twenty-five states legislated the collection of judicial criminal statistics between 1829 and 1905 (L. N. Robinson, 1911). State prison statistics were collected in two ways: Sheriff and prison officials sent information to either the secretary of state or a state board of charities and corrections. Massachusetts required reports as early as 1834; most other states mandated prison statistics later in the 1800s or early in the 20th century. Robinson described these statistics as less comprehensive than judicial statistics.

At the federal level, the collection of crime statistics was the responsibility of the U.S. Bureau of the Census during the 1800s. Beginning in 1850, the sixth census of the population required U.S. Marshals to collect population statistics for free inhabitants of jails and penitentiaries. In addition to counting inmates, data were collected on the sex, age, nativity, and color (of the native born) of convicted persons and prisoners (L. N. Robinson, 1911). For the native born, the categories of Native, White, and Colored were included. Knepper and Potter (1998) attributed distinctions between foreign-born and native-born criminals to immigration in the last two decades of the 1800s. A shift from nativity to biological conceptions of race in crime statistics paralleled developments in eugenics and criminal anthropology (Knepper, 1996; Knepper & Potter, 1998).

According to L. N. Robinson (1911), federal crime statistics really began with the 1880 census, when prisoner, judicial, and police statistics were collected and published for the first time. Noted penologist Frederick H. Wines was given the responsibility of revising the crime statistics for the 1880 census. Since 1880, there have been several changes in the collection of census crime statistics, but, for the most part, they continue to be prison criminal statistics.

In 1870, Congress passed a law requiring the attorney general to report statistics on crime annually, including crimes under federal and state laws. A year later, in 1871, the organizing conference that created the National Police Association (now known as the International Association of Chiefs of Police) called for "crime statistics for police use" (Maltz, 1977, p. 33). The 1880 and 1890 censuses collected police statistics, although they were not reported; it would be several more decades before police crime statistics became available.

❖ The Uniform Crime Reporting Program

The history of the FBI's **Uniform Crime Reporting program** began in 1927, when a subcommittee of the International Association of Chiefs of Police (IACP) was charged with the task of studying uniform crime reporting. In 1930, the FBI began collecting data from police departments. At the time, there was considerable debate about what data should be collected, the responsible federal agency, and the reliability of the data (Maltz, 1977). Wolfgang (1963) noted that Warner (1929, 1931) was opposed to the federal government collecting statistics on crimes known to the police. Warner (1931), in a report on crime statistics for the National Commission on Law Observance and Enforcement (the Wickersham Commission), recommended that police crime statistics not be collected by the federal government. He believed that the UCRs would do more harm than good because they were both inaccurate and incomplete. By publishing crime statistics, the federal government would give credence to the UCRs, which, in turn, would influence public opinion and legislation.

Despite support for the U.S. Bureau of the Census to collect crime data, in 1930, the FBI was mandated by Congress to compile crime data collected by the police. Reports were issued monthly (1930–1931), quarterly (1932–1941), semi-annually with annual accumulations (1942–1957), and annually beginning in 1958. UCR contributors compile information on crimes reported, cleared, persons arrested, and law enforcement personnel, and they forward it to either a state UCR program or directly to the FBI. Seven offenses comprised what was known as the crime index—murder/nonnegligent manslaughter, forcible rape, robbery, aggravated assault, burglary, larceny/theft, and motor vehicle theft—until 1979, when arson was added. The UCR

Photo 2.1

At its headquarters, 69 Fifth Avenue, New York City, the NAACP flew a flag to report lynchings until, in 1938, the threat of losing its lease forced the association to discontinue the practice.

Library of Congress, Prints and Photographs Division, reproduction number LC-USZ62-33793.

program's Supplementary Homicide Report (SHR) provides information about murder victims, offenders, and incidents. Throughout its history several changes have occurred in the UCR program. In 1957, a Consultant Committee on Uniform Crime Reporting made 22 recommendations for changes, although only two were implemented, including changes in statistical presentation and revisions in classification of the crime index (Wolfgang, 1963). In 1980, the UCR renamed arrest race categories to include American Indian or Alaskan Native and Asian or Pacific Islander. During the 1980s, efforts began to modernize the UCR program, which culminated in implementation of the **National Incident-Based Reporting System (NIBRS)** in 1988, created to enhance the quantity, quality, and timeliness of crime statistical data collected by the law enforcement community and to improve the methodology used for compiling, analyzing, auditing, and publishing the collected crime data (Rantala & Edwards, 2000). The NIBRS has several advantages over the UCR program, although not all states participate in it. In 2013, only 15 of the 33 states that were certified submitted all their crime data to NIBRS (FBI, 2014c). NIBRS does include information on several crimes excluded from the UCR, including human trafficking and white collar crime. In 2004, upon the recommendation of the Advisory Policy Board, the FBI discontinued use of the UCR Crime Index and replaced it with two categories, violent crime total and property crime total (FBI, 2010a).

When President George H. W. Bush signed the Hate Crime Statistics Act into law in April, 1990, the FBI developed the National Hate Crime Data Collection Program (NHCDCP) and began reporting hate crime statistics in 1992 (Nolan, Akiyama, & Berhanu, 2002). Hate/bias crime statistics include information on victims, offenders, and incidents for eight crimes, as well as simple assault, intimidation, and destruction/damage/vandalism. The Matthew Shepard and James Byrd Jr. Hate Crime Prevention Act, enacted in 2009, amended the 1990 legislation to include gender, gender identity bias, and crimes committed by and directed against juveniles under the age of 18. The number of police agencies participating in the NHCDCP has continued to increase since 1991. In 2013, 15,016 agencies participated in the program (FBI, 2014b).

One of the most important recent changes in the UCR program is the reporting of Hispanic/Latino arrests in a separate category, which began in 2013. This means that persons arrested who are Hispanic/Latino are no longer included in the White category. Another significant change is the revised definition of rape, which removed the word "forcible" and now includes all victims (regardless of gender; FBI, 2012). According to then–Attorney General Holder, "This new, more inclusive definition of rape will provide us with a more accurate understanding of the scope and volume of these crimes" (FBI, 2012b). Efforts to improve the UCR program are ongoing.

❖ Victimization Surveys

Letting citizens self-report their victimizations is another way to study the extent of crime, especially crime that is not reported to the police. One of the earliest victimization surveys was conducted in the 1960s by the National Opinion Research Center for the President's Commission on Law Enforcement and the Administration of Justice. In 1972, the Law Enforcement Assistance Administration implemented the NCVS, originally known as the National Crime Survey. Since its inception, the U.S. Bureau of the Census has administered the NCVS for the BJS. Criminal victimization reports have been issued annually since 1973 and are now prepared by BJS statisticians. Today, the NCVS is the primary source of information on victims of nonfatal violent and property crimes in the United States. The early surveys included about 100,000 persons and 50,000 households in 26 cities that collected information about victims and offenders from a representative sample of households. At the time, interviews of persons 12 years old and over identified attempted and completed crimes that "are of major concern to the general public and law enforcement authorities" (BJS, 1992, p. iii).

The NCVS also has undergone changes since its inception. In 1992, the name was changed after a redesign of the survey was implemented (Kindermann, Lynch, & Cantor, 1997). The Crime Survey Redesign Consortium recommended numerous changes in the crime survey to improve its accuracy (B. M. Taylor, 1989). The redesign specifically focused on improving the collection of data by expanding the capability of the survey to prompt recall by respondents. Enhanced screening questions are believed to have improved recall of respondents about domestic violence, rape, and sexual attacks, which has led to higher estimates of some victimization rates (Kindermann et al., 1997). The Crime Victims with Disabilities Awareness Act of 1998 mandated the inclusion of victims with disabilities in the NCVS (Harrell & Rand, 2010) and in 2000, questions were added to identify victims of hate crimes (Harlow, 2005). In 2005, the Human Trafficking Reporting System (HTRS) began collecting state and local agency human trafficking incident data (Banks & Kyckelhahn, 2011). In 2008, BJS requested that a panel of experts recommend guidelines for conducting the NCVS, in light of funding constraints and their impact on its value as a social indicator (Groves & Cork, 2008). Do changes in the NCVS survey design limit its ability to determine victimization experiences of Americans? This and other limitations of the UCR and NCVS are discussed next.

❖ Limitations of Arrest and Victimization Data

Ever since their inception, the limitations of crime statistics have been acknowledged. One problem is the amount of time between data collection and publication. For example, UCR and NCVS data collected in one year usually isn't available until well into the next year. Another criticism is that crime statistics are unreliable because they cannot tell us how much crime takes place, how many persons were arrested, or how many crime victims there actually are. At most, arrest statistics are no more than "descriptions of the persons who, for a veritably endless array of reasons (many of which are beyond our knowledge) are subjected to arrest" (Geis, 1972, p. 65). As previously noted, there was opposition to the collection of police crime statistics early in the 20th century due, in part, to their limitations. Table 2.2 provides a summary of the limitations of UCR arrest and NCVS victimization data. Despite many improvements, each program still has problems, including definitions of racial categories; variations in reporting and recording; and the utilization of estimates for population, crimes, arrests, and victimizations. These limitations are briefly described next (for a comprehensive overview of these limitations, see Mosher, Miethe, & Hart, 2011).

Table 2.2

Limitations of Arrest and Victimization Data

Limitation	UCR Arrest (Police) Data	NCVS Victimization Data
Counting only the most serious crime	X	
Definition of ethnic categories	X	X
Definition of racial categories	X	X
Estimates of arrests	X	
Estimates of crime offenses	X	
Estimates of the population	X	X
Estimates of victimizations		X
Offenses included		X
Possible manipulation of data for political gain	X	
Recording of information by interviewers		X
Recording of information by police	X	
Reporting by citizens	X	X
Underreporting by citizens	X	X

Definitions of Racial Categories

Knepper (1996) noted that there is no scientific definition of race, that social categories of race are both simplistic and wrong, and that official racial categories are the result of legal definitions that date back to slavery. He stated, "Race is a political concept. . . . [It] represents a powerful means of reinforcing an ideology of distinct races that began during the colonial period and was cemented during Jim Crow" (p. 86). Knepper argued that contemporary race-coded statistics descended from an ancestry of scientific racism. He questioned how analyses using official statistics can provide objective findings if race cannot be objectively defined. Racial categories in the 2000 and 2010 censuses were guided by Directive No. 15, issued by the Office of Federal Statistical Policy and Standards in 1977. The 2000 and 2010 censuses expanded racial categories to reflect the diversity of multiracial Americans. Despite improvements in racial categories in the census and other federal statistical compilations, they are still problematic.

Racial data first appeared in the UCR in 1933 and included three categories: Whites, Blacks, and Others. In 1934, the UCR included a Mexican category that was dropped in 1941. Initially, age, sex, and race of persons arrested were compiled from fingerprint cards submitted by police departments to the FBI. Since 1953, race has been taken from the reported arrest information. Arrests for Whites (foreign and native born), Negroes, Indians, Chinese, Japanese, Mexicans, and others were reported separately. In 1970, Chinese and Japanese were in the Asian American category (LaFree, 1995). Today, there are five racial categories: White, Black, American Indian and Alaskan Native, Asian, and Native Hawaiian or other Pacific Islander. The Native Hawaiian or other Pacific Islander category first appeared in 2013. According to Tapia and Harris (2012), "The most problematic logistical issue facing scholars of Latinos and crime today is the structure of official data collection mechanisms" (p. 96). A Hispanic ethnic category was available between 1980 and 1985, although it did not distinguish between Hispanic/Latino groups (Puerto Rican, Mexican, Cuban, etc.). Since then (and before), Hispanics/Latinos have been included in the White category. The NIBRS program collected Hispanic/Latino arrest data before 2013 when the UCR included an ethnicity category in Table 43. Counting American Indians is also problematic because they are located in a variety of jurisdictions under numerous police agencies (Greenfield & Smith, 1999). The NCVS has included racial categories since its inception in 1973. Initially, victimizations for Blacks, Whites, and Others were reported. The "Other" category was used for Asian Pacific Islanders, American Indians, Aleut and Eskimos. Hispanics were omitted until 1977.

Despite efforts to develop and improve racial/ethnic categories, they are fatally flawed for two reasons. First, they are unable to capture intraracial and intraethnic heterogeneity. As Georges-Abeyie (1989) correctly noted, there is no Black ethnic monolith. All Blacks are not the same; they have different cultural and ethnic backgrounds representing numerous countries and different social classes. Other racial/ethnic categories also suffer from this limitation. Asian Americans, Latinos/Latinas, Native Americans, and Whites have varying backgrounds, experiences, and cultures that cannot be captured by counting them as if they were all the same. This is true for the "two or more races" category that arguably will not fit into any of the other racial and ethnic categories. Second, how racial categories and ethnicity are determined is questionable and often inaccurate. In both the UCR and NCVS, discretionary determinations about race and ethnicity for both arrestees and victims occur. In the past, race was initially determined by the interviewer's observation, and respondents were asked about the racial/ethnic identity of the offender.

Variations in Reporting and Recording

Wolfgang (1963) noted the problems associated with efforts to obtain uniform reporting when police agencies participate and report voluntarily to the UCR program. Throughout the history of the UCR, some agencies have submitted incomplete reports or no reports. For several reasons, citizens do not report and police do not record all crimes. Likewise, and perhaps more germane, some police selectively enforce the law, which might contribute to variations by race. Variations in crime categories, counting only the most serious crimes, and nonreporting to the police by victims are also problematic. For example, Native American arrests are lower than expected in comparison to victimizations reported to the NCVS (Greenfield & Smith, 1999). Recording and reporting discrepancies by interviewers affect the NCVS as well. Recent changes implemented in both programs impact reporting and recording as well. For example, when agencies transition from the traditional definition of rape (against women) to the new one, there may be errors.

Utilization of Population, Crime, Arrest, and Victimization Estimates

Estimations are an important part of the methodology and findings reported in both the UCR and NCVS. The UCR uses population estimates to calculate crime and **arrest rates**. According to Mosher et al. (2011), these estimates are misleading because the census only counts the population every 10 years. Another problem is that not all persons are counted by the census. The undercounting of minorities by the census is well known (Nasser & Overberg, 2012). Some citizens don't receive the census forms, some who have received the forms don't respond, and citizens choose not to participate for a variety of reasons. Noncitizens don't want to be included. If the population estimates are inaccurate, so are the crime and arrest rates. The NCVS uses a sample of the population to estimate crime victimization experiences and rates. Their estimation procedures are reported in the methodology section. Although efforts are made to minimize differences between the sample population and the total population, there are limitations related to recall and estimates of multiple victimizations by respondents (BJS, 1992). Estimation inaccuracies are particularly relevant to understanding racial victimizations. First, it is unclear how representative the samples are because they are based on census data. Second, survey estimates are based on sampling units that may not adequately capture all racial groups in the population. Third, for Asians and American Indians, the sample size is so small that it affects the reliability of the estimate (Rennison, 2001b).

The limitations of arrest and victimization statistics, although important, do not outweigh their value and utility for examining historical and contemporary patterns and trends by race/ethnic categories. What patterns and trends have remained the same over time? What patterns and trends have changed? Why? To answer these questions, we present analyses of arrests, victimizations, homicide, lynching, and single-bias hate crime incidents.

❖ Arrest Trends

The UCR provide crime data for eight offenses (formerly known as Part I offenses), four violent crimes against the person—murder/nonnegligent manslaughter (herein used interchangeably with homicide), forcible rape, robbery, and aggravated assault—and four property crimes—burglary, larceny/theft, motor vehicle theft, and arson. UCR crime data is presented in tables that include numbers and rates for crimes reported. The rates (per 100,000 population) facilitate temporal and jurisdictional comparisons. In 2013, the FBI estimates that 1,163,146 violent crimes and 8,632,512 property crimes occurred in the United States. The 2013 violent crime rate (367.9) was much lower than the property crime rate (2,730.7), and crimes reported decreased 4.4% compared to 2012 (FBI, 2014d). Information on persons arrested for violent crimes, property crimes, and other crimes are included in the Persons Arrested Section of the UCR in numbers and percentages.

In the early years (1933–1941), both White and Black arrests increased steadily, declined for Whites between 1942 and 1944, and declined for Blacks between 1942 and 1943. There was fluctuation in arrests of Mexicans, Indians, Chinese, Japanese, and "Other" races during this period. The downward trend in total arrests and arrests for Blacks ended in 1944 and for Whites in 1945. Arrests continued to increase between 1945 and 1953; by 1953, there were more than 1 million arrests of Whites, and by 1960, more than 1 million arrests of Blacks. By 1970, the number of total arrests had surpassed 6 million; by 1978, the number was 9 million, and in 1992 arrests peaked at almost 12 million. Snyder (2011) provides a comprehensive analysis of arrest rates by gender, age, and race from 1980 to 2009 for several violent and property crimes, weapons and drug violations. "Over the 30-year period the black arrest rate for murder averaged 7 times the white rate" (p. 3). The Black arrest rate fluctuated during the period and fell sharply between 1991 and 2009, while the White rate gradually declined. "The American Indian/Alaskan Native (AI/AN) rate averaged twice the white arrest rate, while the Asian/Pacific Islander (API) rate averaged half the white rate" (p. 3).

Historically, Whites are more likely than persons in other racial categories to be arrested for rape, aggravated assault, and all property crimes. Blacks are overrepresented in arrests for violent and property crimes, especially homicide and robbery. Even though they don't outnumber Whites arrested, their arrests are disproportionate to their representation in the population. Since 2009, arrests for violent crimes have continued to decrease. In 2013 there were an estimated 9,014,635 persons arrested—a 4.1% decrease from the previous year—91,467 persons for violent crimes and 1,254,696 for property crimes; the remainder were arrested for what were formerly known as Part II offenses (FBI, 2014a). Table 2.3 presents arrests by racial categories for violent crimes between 2009 and 2013. During that period total arrests declined, although there is variation within racial categories. Most notably, arrests for aggravated assault, rape, and robbery decreased for Blacks and Whites. Although reported arrests for American Indians (AI) and Asian Pacific Islanders (A/PI) are much lower, there was more fluctuation for rape (AI), aggravated assault (A/PI), and robbery (A/PI).

Compared to earlier decades, the number of arrests have trended downward in all racial categories. Whether or not reported decreases are accurate or can be interpreted to mean Americans, especially Blacks, are less likely to be involved in violent crime is debatable. Some believe that decreases in Blacks' violent crime arrests might be related to their improved economic and social integration (Tonry & Melewski, 2008; LaFree, Baumer, & O'Brien, 2010). Other possible explanations are

Table 2.3

Reported Violent Crime Arrests by Race, 2009–2013

Year	Offense	Total Arrests by Race						Percentage Distribution					
		Total Arrests	Black	American Indian or Alaskan Native	Asian or Pacific Islander	Native Hawaiian or Other Pacific Islanders	White	Total Percentage Distribution	Black	American Indian or Alaskan Native	Asian or Pacific Islander	Native Hawaiian or Other	White
2009	Murder	9,739	4,801	100	97		4,741	100.0	49.3	1.0	1.0		48.7
	Rape	16,362	5,319	169	230		10,644	100.0	32.5	1.0	1.4		65.1
	Robbery	100,496	55,742	726	989		43,039	100.0	55.5	0.7	1.0		42.8
	Aggravated Assault	330,368	111,904	4,613	3,929		209,922	100.0	33.9	1.4	1.2		63.5
2010	Murder	8,641	4,209	91	80		4,261	100.0	48.7	1.1	0.9		49.3
	Rape	15,503	4,925	214	186		10,178	100.0	31.8	1.4	1.2		65.7
	Robbery	87,587	48,154	617	910		37,906	100.0	55.0	0.7	1.0		43.3
	Aggravated Assault	317,435	106,382	4,854	3,924		202,275	100.0	33.5	1.5	1.2		63.7
2011	Murder	8,341	4,149	105	87		4,000	100.0	49.7	1.3	1.0		48.0
	Rape	14,611	4,811	170	126		9,504	100.0	32.9	1.2	0.9		65.0
	Robbery	82,436	45,827	619	547		35,443	100.0	55.6	0.8	0.7		43.0
	Aggravated Assault	305,220	102,597	4,540	3,102		194,981	100.0	33.6	1.5	1.0		63.9

Year	Offense	Total Arrests by Race						Percentage Distribution					
		Total Arrests	Black	American Indian or Alaskan Native	Asian or Pacific Islander	Native Hawaiian or Other Pacific Islanders	White	Total Percentage Distribution	Black	American Indian or Alaskan Native	Asian or Pacific Islander	Native Hawaiian or Other	White
2012	Murder	8,506	4,203	102	100		4,101	100.0	49.4	1.2	1.2		48.2
	Rape	13,886	4,512	183	164		9,027	100.0	32.5	1.3	1.2		65.0
	Robbery	80,135	44,002	601	771		34,761	100.0	54.9	0.7	1.0		43.4
	Aggravated Assault	299,943	102,371	4,312	4,755		188,505	100.0	34.1	1.4	1.6	0.1	62.8
2013	Murder	8,383	4,379	98	101	6	3,799	100.0	52.2	1.2	1.2	0.1	45.3
	Rape	13,515	4,229	160	173	7	8,946	100.0	31.3	1.2	1.3	0.1	66.2
	Robbery	78,538	44,271	579	649	94	32,945	100.0	56.4	0.7	0.8	0.1	41.9
	Aggravated Assault	291,031	98,748	4,356	4,423	412	183,092	100.0	33.9	1.5	1.5	0.1	62.9

Source: FBI.

the deglamorization of violence, grassroots efforts to "stop the violence," and changing policing priorities (e.g., immigration, homeland security, terrorism). Steffensmeier,
Feldmeyer et al. (2011) posit that crime statistics that measure Black involvement in
violent crime are confounded with how Hispanics are undercounted. The "Hispanic
effect" refers to "growth in the Hispanic population and the ways it might affect the
measurement of racial disparities in violent crimes reported in national databases"
(p. 210). In their analysis they used adjustment procedures to estimate and remove
the Hispanic effect to create "clean" UCR arrest counts. They found little overall
change in the race-violence relationship from 1980–2008. The research challenges
conventional beliefs about decreased arrests for Blacks involved in violent crime,
social integration, and the arrest-incarceration gap. While intriguing, there are
limitations to their research as well. The adjustment procedures might not be accurate because they are based on the Hispanic/Latino populations in California and
New York, which are not representative of other states. Additionally, just because
these two states include Hispanic/Latino arrests doesn't mean that they are accurate.
Although not generalizable, these findings highlight the importance of disaggregating
Hispanics/Latinos from Whites in UCR arrest data. The 2013 FBI arrest data estimates
that 700,913 Hispanic or Latino persons were arrested. In the violent crime categories,
most Hispanic/Latinos (18 and over) were arrested for aggravated assault (40,073),
followed by robbery (6,651), rape (1,751), and murder (963). Since it is estimated
that Hispanic/Latinos represent 17% of the population (see Chapter 1), they were
disproportionally arrested for violent crimes (23.3%), as well as for motor vehicle theft
(see Appendix A.2). There is no way to determine the number of Hispanics/Latinos
still included in the White category because not all agencies report ethnicity data.

The continued focus on violent arrests and victimizations minimizes the importance of other arrest trends. Again, most Americans are not arrested for serious
violent crimes; the data actually reveal that more Americans are arrested for other
types of offenses including larceny/theft, drug abuse violations, driving under the
influence, drunkenness, disorderly conduct, liquor law violations, and other assaults.
Between 2006 and 2010, most Whites were arrested for driving under the influence,
most Blacks were arrested for drug abuse violations, most American Indian/Alaskan
Natives were arrested for other assaults, and most Asian or Pacific Islanders for
driving under the influence. Whites outnumbered Blacks arrested for drug abuse
violations, and American Indian/Alaskan Natives outnumber Asian/Pacific Islanders
arrested for driving under the influence (Gabbidon & Taylor Greene, 2013). In 2013,
most Whites (815,181), Blacks (365,785), and Native Hawaiians (858) were arrested for
drug abuse violations; AIAN for other assaults (14,041); and Asians for driving under
the influence (16,831) (FBI, 2014).

❖ Victimization Trends

Since its inception, the NCVS has collected information on persons age 12 and older
who report they were victims of either nonfatal violent or property crimes in the United
States. Unlike the UCR, since 1977 the NCVS has included separate categories for
"Hispanic/Latino" and, more recently, "Two or More Races." In the past, the BJS periodically published reports on victimization trends and analyses for specific racial groups

(see, e.g., Bastian, 1990; Greenfield & Smith, 1999; Harrell, 2007, 2009; S. W. Perry, 2004; Rennison, 2001b, 2002; Whitaker, 1990). Today victimization trends by race can be examined using the National Crime Victimization Survey Analysis Tool (NCVSAT). The NCVS also provides information on victims of domestic violence/intimate partner violence, hate crimes, human trafficking, rape, and sexual assault, as well as victimization of persons with disabilities (Banks & Kyckelhahn, 2011; Catalano, 2013; Harlow, 2005; Harrell & Rand, 2010; Langton & Planty, 2011; Sinozich & Langton, 2014).

According to Catalano (2013), the number of rapes/sexual assaults, robberies, and other assaults (both aggravated and simple) has declined since 1994, with some fluctuation (p. 1). For both females (44.6%) and males (43.3%), physical attacks including hitting, slapping, and knocking down were most common. For females (36.1%), grabbing, tripping, holding, pushing, or jumping were also common. Victimization statistical data is also available for rape and sexual assault for college-age females who are students and nonstudents (Sinozich & Langton, 2014). In both groups, the offenders are known about 80% of the time, incidents occur in a home, and very few seek or receive victim services (see Box 2.1).

BOX 2.1

Domestic Violence and Interpersonal Violence Victimization

Emily's Story

I was 19, a student in my second year at college, when I met the man of my dreams in one of my classes. He was tall, blonde, blue-eyed, and all-American—with a smooth demeanor and a knack for saying all the right things. He treated me like a princess. Gifts, surprise visits to my dorm room and classes, frequent phone calls to see where I was and how I was doing. He told me he loved me within the first month of our relationship, and he wanted to be near me all the time. . . . Then, two weeks after our first anniversary, I found him in bed with an ex-girlfriend. I immediately broke up with him. It was only then that I began to truly see his controlling nature. I started to see him everywhere I went. He showed up to my classes and sat two rows behind me. I caught glimpses of him walking a couple paces behind me on campus. Pretty soon, he started calling my cell phone constantly, leaving up to twenty voice messages a day begging me to reconsider our relationship. . . . I returned home one evening after going to a meeting on campus, and he was on my doorstep. He was drunk, and he was angry. As his anger escalated, he began to shove me around and pin me by my neck against my front door, smashing empty beer bottles against the corner of the building and holding the shattered glass up to my face. He had simply snapped. I escaped to a friend's house an hour later with a broken rib, a sprained wrist, a black eye, and bruises from head to toe. . . . I used my cell phone to call the police. A week later, he would break bail and leave the country. I would never see him again. The experience did change me—sometimes for the worse, but (I hope) mostly for the better. I had to struggle with fear, anger, depression, insomnia, and even nausea. I had to mend the breach of trust that my parents felt when they found out about my situation after the fact. I've had to fight to break down my defensive walls, so that I could be less guarded in my romantic relationships and less cautious in my friendships. It has not been easy.

Source: National Domestic Violence Hotline (2015).

(Continued)

(Continued)

Do you know anyone who is a victim of domestic/interpersonal violence? These offenses often occur regardless of one's race, ethnicity, age, or class. The majority of victims are females and many are young. According to *Nonfatal Domestic Violence, 2003–2012,* rates of domestic violence are highest for persons between 18–24 years of age. For several decades female scholars have been instrumental in bringing attention to this issue. Domestic violence victimization (DVV) refers to both fatal and nonfatal incidents that take place in families, between intimate partners, or with other friends/acquaintances. They include but are not limited to murder, physical assaults, rape, sexual assaults, verbal abuse, and battering. Information on fatal DVV is available in the FBI *Supplemental Homicide Reports* and the NIBRS. Nonfatal DVV is collected in the NCVS. However, for various reasons, many domestic violence victimizations are not reported to either the police or NCVS interviewers. These victims are often afraid to come forward because they may have been threatened not to do so by the offender, they are embarrassed, or they don't think reporting will make any difference.

When the Bureau of Justice Statistics published a report titled *Homicide Trends in the United States, 1980–2008,* they reported that more than half of White homicide victims were killed by offenders in either an intimate or family relationship. This was also the case for Blacks, although not as often (Cooper & Smith, 2011). Rates of DVV vary by race; persons of two or more races had the highest nonfatal DVV (22.5 per 1,000) between 2003–2012. Whites (1.2 per 1,000) had higher rates by immediate family members than Blacks (0.7) and Hispanics (0.6; Truman & Morgan, 2014).

Several policy initiatives have been enacted to address violence between immediate family members, other relatives, intimate partners, and acquaintances.

1. Do you think domestic violence/intimate partner violence is a problem in your community?

2. Do you think enough is being done by state and local justice officials to prevent intimate partner violence?

Violent victimization rates (VVRs) fluctuate over time. Between 1986 and 1990, the VVR steadily increased to 31.7 per 1,000 persons. During this period, Whites had higher victimization rates for simple assault, whereas Blacks had higher victimization rates for aggravated assault and robbery. Black females had a pattern of higher victimization rates for rape than did White females. Victimization levels and rates for larceny/theft with contact were higher for Blacks than Whites, and larceny/thefts without contact victimization were higher for Whites than Blacks. This pattern occurred regardless of gender. Rates of burglary incidents and motor vehicle thefts were much higher for Blacks and others than for Whites (Bastian, 1992). In 1993, the VVR was 69.3; in 2001 it was 29.7; in 2005 it was 28.6; and in 2009 the VVR was at the lowest rate ever, 16.9 per 1,000 population age 12 or older (Harrell, 2007). Estimates of Hispanic victimizations between 1992 and 2000 fell from 63 to 28 per 1,000. Similar to violent victimization in other racial categories, simple assaults were common, and Hispanic males were victimized most often (Rennison, 2002). The Hispanic VVR fluctuated more between 1993 and 2000; the highest rate was reported in 1994 (61.6) and the lowest rate in 2002 (23.6). An examination of violent victimizations in the 2000s shows that a decline that began in 1994 continued until 2002 (Rennison & Rand, 2003). In 2001, Americans experienced approximately 24.2 million victimizations, 18.3 million property victimizations, and 5.7 million violent victimizations. Average annual violent victimizations between 2001 and 2005 indicate that Blacks have higher VVRs for rape/sexual assault and robbery, although American Indian/Alaska Natives have the highest VVR (56.8; Catalano, 2006). The victimization patterns in 2009 are similar to previous years: higher VVR for males (18.4), Blacks (26.8), and youth aged 12 to 15 (36.8) (Gabbidon & Taylor Greene, 2013). Table 2.4 presents the most recent NCVS information on VVRs for 2004, 2012, and 2013. According to the table, VVRs decreased from 27.8 in 2004 to 23.2 in 2013. There is variation within racial categories; while White VVRs decreased, other racial categories had more fluctuation, especially the AINA and Two or More Races categories.

Table 2.4

Violent Victimization, by Victim Demographic Characteristics, 2004, 2012, and 2013

Victim Demographic Characteristic	Violent Crime[a]			Serious Violent Crime[b]		
	2004	2012	2013	2004	2012	2013
Total	27.8	26.1	23.2[‡]	9.5	8.0	7.3
Sex						
Male	30.2	29.1	23.7[†]	10.6	9.4	7.7
Female	25.5	23.3	22.7	8.4	6.6	7.0
Race/Hispanic origin						
White[c]	28.5	25.2	22.2	9.0	6.8	6.8
Black/African American[c]	30.2	34.2	25.1[†]	16.3	11.3	9.5
Hispanic/Latino	20.1	24.5	24.8	6.5	9.3	7.5
American Indian/Alaska Native[c]	165.6	46.9	56.3	46.1[!]	26.2[!]	39.0[!]
Asian/Native Hawaiian/other Pacific Islander[c]	11.3	16.4	7.0[†]	3.9	9.1	1.6[††]
Two or more races[c]	77.6	42.8	90.3[†]	11.6[!]	9.5[!]	26.8[†]
Age						
12–17	49.7	48.4	52.1	13.7	9.9	10.8
18–24	55.4	41.0	33.8	19.9	14.7	10.7
25–34	31.2	34.2	29.6	10.9	10.9	10.2
35–49	28.0	29.1	20.3[†]	9.9	9.5	7.1
50–64	15.4	15.0	18.7	5.7	4.6	6.9
65 or older	25	5.7	5.4	0.8	1.6	1.1

(Continued)

(Continued)

Victim Demographic Characteristic	Violent Crime[a]			Serious Violent Crime[b]		
	2004	2012	2013	2004	2012	2013
Marital status						
Never married	46.2	40.7	36.3	16.5	11.9	9.6
Married	13.8	13.5	10.7[‡]	4.5	3.9	3.2
Widowed	9.3	8.3	8.6	1.8[!]	2.6	5.2
Divorced	36.7	37.0	34.4	11.8	10.9	16.0
Separated	110.7	83.1	73.2	38.9	39.5	33.3

Note: Victimization rates are per 1,000 persons age 12 or older. See appendix table 10 for standard errors.

[†] Significant change from 2012 to 2013 at the 95% confidence level.

[‡] Significant change from 2012 to 2013 at the 90% confidence level.

[!] Interpret with caution. Estimate based on 10 or fewer sample cases, or the coefficient of variation is greater than 50%.

a. Includes rape or sexual assault, robbery, aggravated assault, and simple assault.

b. Includes rape or sexual assault, robbery, and aggravated assault.

c. Excludes persons of Hispanic or Latino origin.

Source: NCVS.

Victims of human trafficking are not part of the NCVS, although data collection recently began. Both race and crime in human trafficking are understudied, even though the majority of victims and suspects are minorities (see Box 2.2). This is due, at least in part, to the fact that human trafficking was not a priority for the federal government until passage of The Trafficking Victims Protection Act in 2000 (Ensor, 2010). While efforts in the U.S. to prevent and control trafficking have improved as a result of police training and state and local task forces, the need for better data collection and reporting continues (Farrell, McDevitt, & Fahy 2010; Stolz, 2010). Homicide victims are also excluded from the NCVS. Homicide arrests and victimizations are reported in the FBI UCR and Supplemental Homicide Reports.

BOX 2.2

Race and Human Trafficking

The Trafficking Victims Protection Act (TVPA) of 2000 defines human trafficking as "the recruitment, harboring, transportation, provision, or obtaining of a person for one of three purposes" (Banks & Kyckelhahn, 2011, p. 2). These purposes include persons trafficked for labor or other services and for adult and juvenile coercive commercial sex acts. Human trafficking is an issue of international and national importance. According to the U.S. Department of State, (2014, p. 397), "The United States is a source, transit and destination country for men, women, and children, both U.S. citizens and foreign nationals." The 2005 reauthorization of the TVPA mandated that the Human Trafficking Reporting System (HTRS) collect and report state and local level data every two years. In 2013, the FBI began collecting data on crimes reported and persons arrested for human trafficking crimes, although they are not yet included in its publications.

The recent inception of the HTRS and its limitations make it difficult to describe and understand patterns and trends. Like other crimes, these incidents are underreported. According to the HTRS, in 389 confirmed incidents, most of the persons trafficked for labor were adults (25 and older) while most sex trafficking victims were 17 or younger (Banks & Kyckelhahn, 2011). One surprising finding is that of 527 victims and suspects identified between 2008–2010, most were Black, Latino, and U.S. citizens. Among 488 confirmed suspects, most sex trafficking suspects were Black and labor trafficking suspects were Latino. Fewer than 30 Asian victims and suspects were confirmed in the report.

1. Do you think racial and ethnic disparities reported by the HTRS reflect the reality of trafficking in the U.S.? Explain.

2. Why doesn't the overrepresentation of Blacks and Latinos as victims and traffickers receive as much media attention as other types of criminal offenders?

Homicide Victimizations

The violent crime of murder/nonnegligent manslaughter, often referred to as homicide, is of concern to most Americans. If you watch the nightly news, you might conclude that homicide offenses occur quite often; in fact, compared to other offenses, they are rare. Homicide is one of the more accurately measured offenses (Schwartz, 2010). Historically, homicide research focused on Blacks and Whites. Arrest trend analyses indicate that with only a few exceptions (1950 and 1951, 1979–1981, 1984–1986, 2003–2005, and 2010), the number of Blacks arrested for homicide has outnumbered Whites. Between 1952 and 1962, homicide arrests for both Blacks and Whites tripled. Between 1963 and 1972, Black arrests for murder steadily increased and tripled from 2,948 to 8,347, while arrests for Whites doubled. Between 1976 and 1994, homicide arrests continued to fluctuate, both increasing and decreasing until 1994. Between 1994 and 2000, homicide arrests steadily decreased (Gabbidon & Taylor Greene, 2013). LaFree, Baumer, and O'Brien (2010), in a study of 80 large cities, analyzed Black and White homicide arrest trends between 1960 and 2000 to determine whether or not the Black/White gap in arrests was decreasing. They found that while the gap appeared to decrease between 1960 and the mid-1980s, it stalled and then reversed through the mid-1990s. Today, regardless of race, arrests for murder are much lower than during several earlier decades. In 2013, in the traditional racial categories there were 8,383 reported arrests for murder, considerably fewer than the number of arrests in these categories reported in the late 1960s through the late 1990s. In the ethnicity category, Hispanics/Latinos were disproportionately arrested for murder.

Arrest trends for murder/nonnegligent manslaughter also can be analyzed by type of jurisdiction where the arrest occurred. As Schwartz (2010) states, "Homicide is rare, but it is more common in some groups, places, or time periods than in others . . . Homicide offenders and victims tend to be concentrated more heavily in communities characterized by economic and social disadvantages." (p. 294)

Between 2009 and 2013, Blacks arrested for murder outnumbered Whites arrested in cities. In metropolitan and nonmetropolitan counties and suburban areas, the number of Whites arrested for murder outnumbered Blacks (see Table 2.5).

Hate Crime Trends

Lynching was one of the earliest types of hate crimes. Due to prevailing attitudes about race and crime in the 19th and the 20th centuries, lynching was not always viewed as a crime, and lynchers were not always viewed as criminals. There is no mention of lynching in the early historical analyses of crime statistics (see, e.g., Maltz, 1977; L. N. Robinson, 1911; Wolfgang, 1963), and it remains unclear how lynchings were reported and recorded in crime data. The *Chicago Tribune* collected and reported data on lynchings as early as 1882 (Perloff, 2000). During the early 20th century, Tuskegee Institute and the National Association for the Advancement of Colored People (NAACP) also collected lynching data. These compilations only included Whites and Negroes (the classification at the time), even though Latinos, Native Americans, and Asian Americans also were victimized (Gonzales-Day, 2006). Mexicans were targeted in Arizona, California, New Mexico, and Texas and, like Blacks, were often lynched for "acting 'uppity,' taking away jobs, making advances toward a white woman, . . . with one exception, Mexicans were lynched for acting 'too Mexican'—speaking Spanish too loudly or reminding Anglos too defiantly of their Mexicanness" (Delgado, 2009, p. 299). Delgado also noted that even though there is very little information on Latino lynching, the rate of lynching for Blacks and Latinos was similar during and immediately after Reconstruction. Carrigan and Webb (2003) found that more than 400 Latinos/Mexicans were lynched between 1848 and 1890.

The earliest available data for Whites and Negroes show that lynchings of Negroes appeared to be most frequent between 1884 and 1901 (Raper, 1933; Zangrando, 1980). Between 1889 and 1932, there were 3,745 lynchings reported; 2,954 were Negroes and 791 were Whites (Raper, 1933). In 2015, the Equal Justice Initiative (EJI) released *Lynching in America: Confronting the Legacy of Racial Terror,* which states,

> Lynching profoundly impacted race relations in American and shaped the geographic, political, social, and economic conditions of African Americans in ways that are still evident today . . . Lynching reinforced a legacy of racial inequality that has never been adequately addressed in America. (EJI, 2015b, p. 3)

Focusing specifically on lynchings in Southern states between 1877–1950, they identified 3,959 lynchings, including 700 that were previously unknown. EJI found that many that might have been victims of what the EJI refers to as "terror lynchings" were often forced to migrate from the South. In spite of several attempts, such as the 1922 Dyer Anti-Lynching Bill, federal legislation was never enacted.

Today, the terms *hate crime* and *bias crime* refer to offenses committed against individuals because of their race, religion, ethnicity, sexual orientation, or disability. Hate/bias crime information is available in the FBI Hate Crime Statistics and NIBRS programs as well as in the NCVS. The FBI Hate Crime Statistics include information on characteristics of incidents, offenses, victims, and known offenders. The NCVS

Table 2.5

Reported Arrests for Murder by Race, 2009–2013, in Cities, Metropolitan Counties, Non-metropolitan Counties, and Suburban Areas

	Total	Black	White	American Indian or Alaskan Native	Asian or Pacific Islander	Percentage Black	Percentage White	Percentage American Indian or Alaskan Native	Percentage Asian or Pacific Islander
2009									
City	7,149	3,896	3,112	65	76	54.5	43.5	0.9	1.1
Metropolitan county	1,840	694	1,121	8	17	37.7	60.9	0.4	0.9
Nonmetropolitan county	750	211	508	27	4	28.1	67.7	3.6	0.5
Suburban areas	2,903	1,184	1,683	12	24	40.8	58.0	0.4	0.8
2010									
City	6,350	3,406	2,832	46	66	53.6	44.6	0.7	1.0
Metropolitan county	1,655	636	997	11	11	38.4	60.2	0.7	0.7
Nonmetropolitan county	636	167	432	34	3	26.3	67.9	5.3	0.5
Suburban areas	2,675	1,075	1,560	18	22	40.2	58.3	0.7	0.8
2011									
City	6,072	3,329	2,601	69	73	54.8	42.8	1.1	1.2
Metropolitan county	1,565	639	908	6	12	40.8	58.0	0.4	0.8
Nonmetropolitan county	704	190	491	30	2	25.7	69.7	4.3	0.3
Suburban areas	2,599	1,113	1,442	26	38	42.8	55.5	0.7	1.0

(Continued)

(Continued)

	Total	Black	White	American Indian or Alaskan Native	Asian or Pacific Islander	Percentage Black	Percentage White	Percentage American Indian or Alaskan Native	Percentage Asian or Pacific Islander
2012									
City	6,302	3,439	2,723	65	75	54.6	43.2	1.0	1.2
Metropolitan county	1,564	629	902	9	24	25.4	72.4	0.8	1.4
Nonmetropolitan county	640	135	476	28	1	21.1	74.4	4.4	0.2
Suburban areas	2,659	1,143	1,458	17	41	43.0	54.8	0.6	1.5
2013									
City	6,154	3,568	2,455	76	50	58.0	39.9	1.2	0.8
Metropolitan county	1,607	647	929	20	10	40.3	57.8	1.2	0.6
Nonmetropolitan county	622	164	415	5	38	26.4	66.7	0.8	6.1
Suburban areas	2,580	1,164	1,363	35	17	45.1	52.8	1.4	0.7

collects information on victims' perceptions of incidents based on the offenders use of hate language and symbols. Hate crime is more likely to involve crimes against the person (intimidation, simple assault, and aggravated assault) than crimes against property (B. Perry, 2002; FBI, 2014b). Most hate crimes motivated by race occur at the victim's residence. Hate crime also is more likely to be interracial; the race of most known offenders is White (FBI, 2011g; see Box 2.3). The Civil Rights Division of the DOJ "enforces federal **statutes** prohibiting discrimination on the basis of race, color, sex, disability, religion, familial status and national origin" (U.S. DOJ, 2011f). As previously mentioned, the Matthew Shepard and James Byrd Jr. Hate Crimes Prevention Act, enacted in October 2009, broadened the scope of the original 1990 hate crime legislation. The first person convicted for a violation of the 2009 Act was Sean Popejoy, a 19-year-old White male and resident of Green Forest, Arkansas. Thomas E. Perez, Assistant Attorney General for the DOJ Civil Rights Division, stated, "It is unacceptable that violent acts of hate committed because of someone's race continue to occur in 2011, and the department will continue to use every available tool to identify and prosecute hate crime whenever and wherever they occur" (U.S. DOJ, 2011a).

BOX 2.3

Race and Crime in the Media

FBI Investigating Hate Site Linked to Accused Charleston Shooter

The FBI is investigating a website that emerged Saturday and was registered under the name of Dylann Roof, the 21-year-old white man accused of killing nine people at a Bible study group last Wednesday evening at a historic Black church in Charleston, South Carolina.

Roof was arrested Thursday in North Carolina and later transported back to South Carolina. On Friday, just before Roof was charged with nine counts of murder and one count of weapon possession, Governor Nikki Haley told the *TODAY* show the act was a "hate crime" deserving of the death penalty. Among the victims was the church's pastor, Reverend Clementa Pinckney, who also served as a state senator.

The website includes a racist manifesto and what appear to be pictures of Roof. The website's URL, "LastRhodesian.com," refers to the majority-Black, White-run nation that existed in what is now Zimbabwe. Roof wore the Rhodesian flag on his coat in a photo released by authorities after the shooting.

The site includes a lengthy, racist screed that begins, "I was not raised in a racist home or environment" before detailing his disdain for and hatred of Black people, Hispanics and Jews. The Associated Press, citing anonymous law enforcement sources, reported Saturday that the FBI was reviewing the website, which the New York *Times* reports online records show was registered under Roof's name in February. The manifesto's writer mentions the case of Trayvon Martin—the Black teen who was shot dead by George Zimmerman, a neighborhood watch volunteer, in 2012—as "the event that truly awakened me."

The case led the manifesto's writer to start researching Black-on-White crime, which the writer said was being ignored by the media. In the final section, the writer states: "I chose Charleston because it is most historic city in my state, and at one time had the highest ratio of Blacks to Whites in the country. [...] someone has to have the bravery to take it to the real world, and I guess that has to be me."

Source: D'Addario (2015).

(Continued)

(Continued)

The June 18, 2015, killings at the Emmanuel African Methodist Church in Charleston shocked the conscience of many Americans. Though the perpetrator's method was unique, attacks against Black churches are not. These places of worship have been set on fire, Molotov cocktails have been thrown into them, hate speech has been painted on them, vandals have broken into them, and cross burnings have been reported (Patterson, Andrews, & Barber, 2015; "Violent History," 2015). According to the 2013 UCR hate crime statistics, although killings are not reported as often as other offenses, White males are the majority of hate crime offenders (FBI, 2014c).

1. If the killings in the Charleston, SC, church are hate crimes, how should they be classified by the Hate Crime Statistics Program ?

2. How pervasive do you think racial/ethnic hatred is among young males between the ages of 18 and 25 in the United States?

Hate crimes are "severely underreported" (Gerstenfeld, 2010, p. 263) and there are differences in how hate crimes are recorded by police agencies (Gerstenfeld, 2010, 2011). That hate crimes continue to be racially motivated against Blacks is supported by the NCVS: Victims perceive race to be the primary offender motivation (Harlow, 2005; Langton & Planty, 2011; Sandholtz, Langton, & Planty, 2013). Of the 5,928 hate crimes reported in 2013, the majority were bias incidents based on race (2,871) and anti-Black (1,856); of those based on ethnicity (655), most were anti-Hispanic or Latino (331; see Table 2.6). The total number of single-bias incidents fluctuated between 2009 and 2013, as did incidents occurring within racial categories.

❖ Conclusion

The purpose of this chapter was to examine crime and victimization statistics, their limitations, and how they contribute to our understanding of race and crime. For more than 80 years, the UCR has been the primary source of crime statistics, and for more than 30 years, the NCVS has provided victimization data. Researchers rely on these two data sets to analyze patterns and trends by race, especially for Blacks and Whites. At best, we can conclude that Americans are arrested for a variety of offenses, including violent crimes, property crimes, alcohol-related offenses, and drug abuse violations. Fewer persons are arrested for violent personal crimes, although they tend to receive the most attention in the study of crime. Decades of comparisons made between Blacks and Whites as arrestees and victims have resulted in several misperceptions. Support for this idea can be easily found by asking students enrolled in criminal justice courses a few questions about persons arrested before presenting the material. Invariably, they believe that more Blacks than Whites are arrested, especially for drug offenses and rape. Even though many still believe that Blacks are arrested more often than Whites, they are not. Blacks do continue to be involved in crime at a level that is disproportionate to their representation in the population. With only a few exceptions over time, Blacks continue to be arrested for murder more often than any other race,

Table 2.6

Hate/Bias Crime Incidents Reported by Race and Ethnicity, 2009–2013

	2009	2010	2011	2012	2013
Total single-bias incidents	6,604	6,624	6,216	5,790	5,922
Single-bias race	6,598	3,135	2,917	2,797	2,871
Anti-Black	2,284	2,201	2,076	1,805	1,856
Anti-White	545	575	504	657	653
Anti-American Indian or Alaskan Native	65	44	61	101	129
Anti-Asian	126	150	138	121	135
Anti-Native Hawaiian or other Pacific-Islander					3
Anti-multiple races	179	165	138	113	95
Ethnicity	984	847	720	667	655
Anti-Hispanic	483	534	405	384	331
Anti-other ethnicity/national origin	294	313	315	283	324

Source: Hate Crime Statistics, FBI, UCR Incidents and Offenses, 2009–2013

although reported murders and arrests have decreased (compared with earlier decades), and Black homicide victimizations are at their lowest levels. Martinez, Stowell, and Lee (2010) noted that lethal violence research doesn't contribute to our understanding of nonlethal violence and property crime, especially among immigrants.

Despite what they do tell us, what these two sources of crime statistics do not tell us is just as important. The limitations of these data sets have persisted since their inception and efforts to improve them are ongoing. Even though the racial and ethnic categories, use of estimates, and variations in reporting and recording are problematic, arrest and victimization data help us understand changes over time. Now that Hispanics/Latinos are the largest minority group, and a separate category for their arrests has been added, we will be better informed about Black, White, and Hispanic/Latino arrest patterns in the future. Arrest patterns for other racial and ethnic categories also are important and should not be overlooked simply because of their smaller proportion of the population. The BJS Data Analysis Tools will be useful in increasing our understanding of race, ethnicity, arrests, crime, and victimization. The legislatively mandated collection of data continues to include racial and ethnic groups that should receive more attention in the race and crime discourse. One example of this is the category of "two or more races" that receives limited attention in the research in spite of their overrepresentation as crime victims. Most important, crime statistics tell us either nothing (UCR) or little (NCVS) about class and crime. The extent of race and crime as reported in arrest and victimization data is useful, although not definitive.

Finally, why are lynchings and other types of racial violence excluded from the race and crime discourse? Although hate/bias crimes have occurred for several hundred years, the collection of hate crime statistics is rather recent. With the expansion of the focus of hate crime legislation, it remains to be seen whether or not "new" victims of hate crimes will vary by race and ethnicity. Even though White violence such as lynching may not be a crime problem today, assaults and intimidation against individuals based on their race and/or ethnicity still occur. The EJI (2015b) contends that "the history of lynching continues to contaminate the integrity and fairness of the justice system" (p. 3). Most important, the policy implications of the disproportionality by race that has persisted for decades, if not centuries, should receive more attention. It is unclear why patterns and trends in arrests and victimizations have not received more attention from federal, state, and local elected officials. Miller (2013) states,

> By recognizing the enormous variation in exposure to violence across different segments of society, we can see much more clearly how political agendas can be driven into more punitive directions not so much by mass democratic politics, but by the insufficient political voice and representation of those most affected by violence and those who support their interests. (p. 306)

Discussion Questions

1. What is the importance of arrest and victimization data in the study of race and crime?

2. How do you think the arrests of Hispanics/Latinas/Latinos will compare to other racial categories when the category is reported in arrest data?

3. Do you think racial categories should be excluded from arrest and victimization statistics?

4. Why do you think some minorities are disproportionately arrested and victimized?

5. Why is there less publicity about anti-Black hate crimes than about Black arrests and victimizations?

Internet Exercises

1. Use The Campus Safety and Security Data Analysis Cutting Tool (http://ope.ed.gov/security/) to examine and summarize reported crime at your institution and at least one other institution in your region.

2. Use the UCR Table-Building Tool (http://www.ucrdatatool.gov/) to construct a table. Analyze one violent crime and one property crime in a city and state of your choice.

3. Use the NCVS Victimization Data Analysis Tool (http://www.bjs.gov/index.cfm?ty=nvat) to construct and analyze a table that includes race or ethnicity (or both) and violent victimizations.

Internet Sites

American Bar Association Commission on Domestic and Sexual Violence: http://www .americanbar.org/groups/domestic_violence.html

Bureau of Justice Statistics Data Analysis Tools: http://www.bjs.gov/index.cfm?ty=daa

Department of Education, The Campus Safety and Security Data Analysis Cutting Tool: http://ope.ed.gov/security/

Federal Bureau of Investigation Crime Statistics: http://www.fbi.gov/stats-services/ crimestats

The Office of Victims of Crime: http://www.ovc.gov/

Supplemental materials for *Race and Crime* are available online at
study.sagepub.com/gabbidon4e.

Theoretical Perspectives on Race and Crime

A wide variety of sociological, psychological, and biological theories have been proposed to explain the underlying causes of crime and its social, spatial, and temporal distribution. All of these theories are based on the assumptions that crime is accurately measured. But when variation in crime patterns and characteristics is partially attributable to unreliability in the measurement of crime, it is impossible to empirically validate the accuracy of competing criminological theories.

—Mosher, Miethe, and Hart (2011, p. 205)

C onsidering the historical and contemporary crime and victimization data and statistics presented in Chapter 2, the logical next question is this: What explains the crime patterns of each race? Based on this question, we have formulated two goals for this chapter. First, we want to provide readers with a rudimentary overview of **theory**. Second, we want to provide readers with a summary of the numerous theories that have relevance for explaining race and crime (see Box 3.1). In addition to this, where available, we also discuss the results of tests of the theories reviewed. Last, we also document some of the shortcomings of each theory.

Decades ago, criminology textbooks devoted a chapter to race and crime (Gabbidon & Taylor Greene, 2001). Today most texts cover the topic, but only in a cursory way. In general, because of the additional focus on race and crime, scholars have written more specialized books, such as this one, to more comprehensively cover the subject. But even in these cases, many authors devote little time to reviewing specific theories related to race and crime (Walker, Spohn, & DeLone, 2012). In her 1993 tome on race and crime, *Unequal Justice: A Question of Color,* Mann provided one of the most comprehensive reviews of theories that have been applied to race and crime. More recent texts have been solely devoted to assessing how well theories explain disparities tied to race and crime and have updated and expanded Mann's coverage (Gabbidon, 2015). We attempt to provide an overview of the vast number of major and lesser-known theories that have been applied to understanding racial patterns in crime

BOX 3.1

Public Views on the Causes of Crime: Are There Racial Differences?

You've likely heard the saying, "Everyone has an opinion on crime." Well it is true! Criminologists study this topic for a living and have produced countless theories, some of which are highlighted throughout this chapter. In recent years, though, Gabbidon and Boisvert (2012) put the question of crime causation to a diverse sample of Philadelphia area residents. Their study examined whether resident views on crime fell under some of the well-known paradigms within the discipline of criminology, such as biological theories, sociological theories, social control theories, critical theory, and so on. With nearly an even split between Blacks and Whites, the authors were able to compare whether the views of Whites and Blacks were similar or different. Table 3.1 provides a summary of the significant findings out of the 37 questions that were asked (for the full set of questions, see Gabbidon & Boisvert, 2012, p. 54). The table shows that Blacks showed significantly greater support than Whites for only three crime causation items that were tied to classic/general strain theory and critical theory.

1. What do you think accounts for the differences by race noted in Table 3.1?

Table 3.1

Public Opinion on Crime Causation by Race[a]

Criminological Theory/Item	Whites/Mean(SD)	Blacks/Mean(SD)	t-test
Genetics	3.25 (2.03)	2.75 (2.01)	2.24*
Psychological theory	15.36 (3.49)	14.24 (4.34)	2.57*
Drugs/alcohol problems	5.63 (1.52)	4.88 (1.84)	4.03***
Social disorganization theory	18.46 (4.75)	16.75 (5.17)	3.10**
No sense of belonging	4.81 (1.74)	4.32 (2.03)	2.39*
Immigrants	3.62 (1.83)	2.95 (1.90)	3.24***
Stressful events	3.85 (1.75)	4.32 (1.93)	–2.34*
Subcultural theory	13.02 (4.37)	11.23 (4.73)	3.61***
Different values/morals	3.93 (1.89)	3.34 (2.08)	2.72**
Acceptable in neighborhoods	4.76 (1.99)	3.58 (2.16)	5.19***
Social learning theory	19.36 (4.65)	18.89 (5.49)	2.96**
Imitating family/friends/others	4.86 (1.54)	4.27 (1.99)	2.53**
Learned	5.10 (1.57)	4.58 (2.11)	2.53**
Family/friends/others approve	5.38 (1.50)	4.88 (2.06)	2.49*

(Continued)

(Continued)

Criminological Theory/Item	Whites/Mean(SD)	Blacks/Mean(SD)	t-test
Social control/general theory	20.18 (4.98)	18.38 (5.94)	2.96**
Can't control impulses	4.59 (1.80)	4.04 (2.01)	2.63**
Called "criminal" enough times	4.19 (1.84)	3.77 (2.01)	2.02*
Some have lots/others have nothing	4.38 (2.01)	4.82 (2.03)	−1.97*
Poverty	4.73 (1.94)	5.17 (2.00)	−2.03*

Source: Gabbidon and Boisvert (2012).

Notes: a. To reduce the length of the paper, only the significant findings are presented. The full results are available from the authors.

*p < 0.05; **p < 0.01; ***p < 0.001.

and victimization. Before we begin, however, we review the fundamentals of theory, noting what theory is, distinguishing the various types of theories, and discussing the usefulness of having theory.

❖ What Is Theory?

According to Bohm and Vogel (2010), "A theory is an explanation" (p. 1). Some theory can be found in practically everything we do. When it comes to explaining crime, just about everyone has an opinion. All of these insights, however, might not qualify as *scientific* theory. Curran and Renzetti (2001) noted that a scientific theory is "a set of interconnected statements or propositions that explain how two or more events or factors are related to one another" (p. 2). Furthermore, scientific theories are usually logically sound and empirically testable (Curran & Renzetti, 2001).

Theories can be further categorized as macro theories, micro theories, or bridging theories (Williams & McShane, 2010). Macro theories focus on the social structure and are generally not concerned with individual behavior; conversely, micro theories look to explain crime by looking at groups, but in small numbers, or at the individual level (Williams & McShane, 2010). Bridging theories "tell us both *how social structure comes about and how people become criminals*" (Williams & McShane, 2010, p. 8). Many of the theories reviewed in this chapter fit some of these criteria, whereas others do not, but in our view, they nonetheless provide useful insights into race and crime. Thus, we discuss some nontraditional approaches that have not been folded into the mainstream of scientific criminological theory. It is important to note here that this chapter does not review every criminological theory. Our aim was to simply examine some of those that have been applied to the issue of race and crime. Others, such as rational choice theory, might also have some relevance, but they were left out because there is limited scholarship that makes the connection between the perspective and racial disparities in crime and justice.

Theories are valuable for a number of reasons. Curran and Renzetti (2001) provided an important summary of the usefulness of theory:

> Theories help bring order to our lives because they expand our knowledge of the world around us and suggest systematic solutions to problems we repeatedly confront. Without the generalizable knowledge provided by theories, we would have to solve the same problems over and over again, largely through trial and error. Theory, therefore, rather than being just a set of abstract ideas, is quite practical. It is *usable knowledge.* (p. 2)

There are several paradigms within criminological theory that are reviewed here. We review biological approaches that look to physical features and/or genetic inheritance to explain crime; other theories that have their foundations in the American social structure, social processes, or one's culture; and theories that have psychological foundations. Theorists have also sought to integrate some of these approaches (Agnew, 2004; Messner, Krohn, & Liska, 1989). As one might expect, many of these theories have been applied to explain race and crime. We begin with a review of biological explanations of crime.

❖ Biology, Race, and Crime

Early Developments in Biological Explanations

The linking of biology and crime has its roots in Europe. Reid (1957) wrote that "[in] the year 1843 a Spanish physician Soler was [the] first to [mention] the concept of the born criminal" (p. 772). It was also in Europe that phrenology, the study of the external shape of the head, was first popularized (Vold, Bernard, & Snipes, 1998). Darwin's *On the Origin of Species* (1859) and *Descent of Man* (1871) were also influential in this era. Once the ideas became accepted, **Cesare Lombroso**, a doctor in the Italian Army in the 19th century and the so-called father of criminology, began studying army personnel from the southern portions of Italy where, in addition to being considered inferior beings, the citizens were thought to be "lazy, incapable, criminal, and barbaric" (Vold et al., 1998, pp. 42–43).

In Lombroso's first major work, *Criminal Man* (1876/1911), he made clear the importance of race in explaining crime. He mentioned that some tribes in parts of India and Italy had high **crime rates** due to "ethnical causes" (p. 140). He added, "The frequency of homicide in Calabria, Sicily, and Sardinia is fundamentally due to African and Oriental elements" (p. 140). When Lombroso took on the task of explaining criminality among women, he again saw race as being an important contributor to crime. In his view, "Negro" women and "Red Indian" women were manly looking, which contributed to their criminality. His works were widely hailed and were translated into English, by which time the notion of biological determinism had already taken hold on American shores.

As in Lombroso's work, in the United States, racial and ethnic groups were the focus of ideas that inferior "stocks" were polluting society. The most virulent attacks were reserved for African Americans. Books such as Charles Carroll's (1900) *The Negro a Beast* spoke to the notion that African Americans were not human; they were more akin to apes. Relying heavily on biblical interpretations, Carroll sought to show why the White race was superior to the African American race. Around the same time, there was the thought that because of their genetic inferiority, African Americans would eventually die off (Hoffman, 1896). Although these notions were vigorously challenged here and abroad, such ideas dominated the late 19th- and early 20th-century literature and gave rise to the racist eugenics movement. However, as noted in Chapter 1, with increased immigration to the United States, these ideas were also applied to the unwelcome new arrivals (see Hooton, 1939a, 1939b). There were, however, continuing critics of this early work (Bonger, 1943; Merton & Ashley-Montagu, 1940).

Recent Developments in Biological Explanations

Crime and Human Nature

Because of the persistent criticism of the biological perspective, support for the ideology lay dormant until 1985, when Wilson and Herrnstein resurrected it with their publication of *Crime and Human Nature*. In their chapter on race and crime, Wilson and Herrnstein pointed to constitutional factors that may contribute to the overrepresentation of Blacks in crime; such constitutional factors "merely make a person somewhat more likely to display certain behavior; it does not make it inevitable" (p. 468). Wilson and Herrnstein next suggested that Black males tend to be more mesomorphic (muscular) than White males; in addition, because they have higher scores on the Minnesota Multiphasic Personality Inventory (MMPI) than Whites, they are "less normal." Another constitutional factor mentioned by the authors is low **IQ**. This connection is discussed further in the next section of the chapter.

As with their predecessors, Wilson and Herrnstein (1985) have had their critics. Most notably, there were concerns about the clarity of concepts and other measurement issues. Another concern related to their exclusive use of the theory to explain crime in the streets, not "crimes in the suites" (Lilly, Cullen, & Ball, 2001, pp. 212–213). This obviously speaks to race and crime because it is clear that these conservative thinkers have more interest in explaining crimes associated with racial minorities than those overwhelmingly committed by middle- and upper-class Whites.

Intelligence, Race, and Crime

With the development and acceptance of intelligence tests, another linkage was developed: intelligence and crime (S. Gould, 1996). Much of the early literature suggested that criminals were of low intelligence or "feebleminded." This line of thinking was based on Richard Dugdale's 19th-century Jukes study, which chronicled the genealogy of a family that had experienced generations of immorality and criminality.

Building on the Jukes study, in the early 1900s, Henry H. Goddard studied the lineage of a family in New Jersey. Goddard found that one side of the family produced primarily descendants of superior intelligence, whereas the other side of the family produced offspring that were considered immoral, criminal, and alcoholics. Goddard's study was later found to be faulty because he had his assistant, Elizabeth S. Kite, conduct the research, and she failed to use an IQ test to determine feeblemindedness. Instead, she made her assessments based on physical appearance (Knepper, 2001). In addition, it was found that Goddard had altered some of the pictures in his books to make study participants look diabolical. The notion of a link between intelligence and crime had existed prior to the aforementioned studies, but the development of the IQ test gave proponents of the idea a tool with which to test their beliefs.

Because of a critical review of numerous studies on IQ and crime by Edwin Sutherland, as well as Simon Tulchin's (1939) classic *Intelligence and Crime*, intelligence-based theories disappeared from the criminological literature until the 1970s. At this time, two prominent criminologists, Hirschi and Hindelang (1977), conducted a review of the literature on intelligence and crime. On the issue of race, they wrote, "There can be no doubt that IQ is related to delinquency within race categories" (p. 575). From their research, they concluded that students with low intelligence had difficulty in school and, as a result, were more likely to engage in delinquency—ergo, given that Blacks have traditionally scored lower on IQ tests, they are likely to commit more crimes.

The debate lingered until Herrnstein and Murray (1994) published their controversial work, *The Bell Curve*. The book picked up where the debate left off. They suggested that low IQ contributed to a host of factors, including crime, poverty, illegitimacy, unemployment, welfare dependency, and others. How? Well, the authors present a few ways in which this connection materializes. First, they state that low IQ results in school failure, which tends to lead to crime. Second, they argue that low IQ leads to people being drawn to danger and having "an insensitivity to pain or social ostracism, and a host of derangements of various sorts" (p. 240). Combined, these factors, in their minds, were precursors for a criminal career. Finally, the authors suggest that those with low IQs would have a hard time following ethical principles. According to their theory,

> [People with low IQ might] find it harder to understand why robbing someone is wrong, find it harder to appreciate values of civil and cooperative social life, and are accordingly less inhibited from acting in ways that are hurtful to other people and to the community at large. (pp. 240–241)

Implicit in their thinking is that, because Blacks tend to have lower IQs, they are likely at greater risk for engaging in criminality.

Following the publication of *The Bell Curve*, the American Psychological Association convened a committee of scholars to assess the state of knowledge on IQ. The committee found that IQ does predict school performance and that there are unexplained racial differences in IQ. There were concerns expressed by the committee that IQ doesn't cover all dimensions of intelligence, such as creativity, wisdom, practical sense, and so on (Neisser et al., 1996). Critics of IQ tests continue to assert that if a lack of intelligence is associated with crime, then what explains the fact that persons with high IQs commit white-collar and political crime (M. Lanier & Henry, 1998)?

Long after the dust settled from the IQ debate inspired by *The Bell Curve*, biosocial criminology, with some of its lineage connected to the IQ and crime debate, emerged as a growing paradigm in the field (Barnes & Boutwell, 2015). There are a few incarnations of the perspective. One incarnation is the r/K selection theory, which is based largely on evolutionary foundations. And recently, John Wright has integrated evolutionary and biosocial foundations to offer a perspective to explain offending among Blacks in particular. We review both theories below.

Contemporary Biosocial Criminology and Race

r/K Selection Theory

One of the more controversial criminological theories related to race in general and crime in particular is the r/K selection theory. Created by Harvard biologist E. O. Wilson to explain population growth and the decline in plants and animals, the theory has been adapted to humans by Rushton (1999), the late professor of psychology at Western Ontario University. This gene-based evolutionary theory links many of the differences among the races, including crime patterns, to migrations out of Africa.

Rushton (1999) agreed with the hypothesis that all humans came out of Africa. It was his contention, however, that there was a split of the population before humans left Africa and that this split is responsible for the current position of Blacks, Whites, and Asians. As he saw it, those who stayed in Africa (now referred to as Black people) were subjected to unpredictable droughts and deadly diseases, which caused them to die young. Those who migrated to Eurasia (now referred to as Whites and Asians) had to deal with other concerns, such as "gathering and storing food, providing shelter, making clothes, and raising children during the long winters" (p. 85). These tasks were more mentally demanding and, according to Rushton, required greater intelligence. Moreover, "They called for larger brains and slower growth rates. They permitted lower levels of sex hormones, resulting in less sexual potency and aggression and more family stability and longevity" (p. 85).

At the heart of the r/K selection theory are reproduction, climate, and intelligence. R-selected organisms are those that evolved to survive in less crowded, but unstable, environments. K-selected organisms have the ability to compete successfully for limited resources in a stable environment. Because Africans were faced with early death, they often had to bear more children to maintain their population, which left them unable to provide significant care for their offspring. Conversely, those falling under the K-strategy, Whites and Asians (Rushton acknowledged only three races: Negroid, Caucasoid, and Mongoloid), reproduced less and generally spent more time caring for their offspring.

Rushton's theory relates to race and crime in that aggression, impulsive behavior, low self-control, low intelligence, and lack of rule following are all associated with criminals and, according to Rushton, those who fall under the r-strategy, namely, Black people. To support his approach, Rushton conducted cross-national studies that looked at race and crime (see Rushton, 1995; Rushton & Templer, 2012; Rushton & Whitney, 2002). Other scholars have also adopted some of Rushton's ideas in the areas of crime (Ellis, 1997; Ellis & Walsh, 1997, 2000; Walsh, 2004; Walsh & Ellis, 2003; J. Wright, 2009) and skin color and intelligence (Lynn, 2002).

As with all theories, there have been several notable criticisms of the r/K selection theory. First, Rushton generally ignored sociological factors. Most of his cross-national comparisons point strictly to numbers, without taking into account variables such as socioeconomic status, discrimination, and other important sociological variables. Second, in the 21st century, there are few "pure" races, especially in the United States, where, as noted in Chapter 1, White sexual aggression against Black females during the slave era produced countless mixed-race offspring. Therefore, the rigorous adherence to the Black-White-Asian split is problematic. Finally, if Rushton's theory were true, what would explain White aggression as early colonizers and their current involvement in wars and violence across the globe? In contrast to Rushton's theory, Bradley (1978) argued that, as a result of migration to colder regions, since the beginning of humanity, Whites have been the global aggressors.

John Wright's Biosocial Thesis on Race and Offending

In recent years, the connection between biology and behavior has emerged as a more accepted area of study in criminology (Cullen, 2009). Contemporary adherents to this theory point to the influence of biological and social factors in criminal behavior (Walsh & Beaver, 2009; Wright & Boisvert, 2009). In particular, the researchers have called for the consideration of neuroscience and genetics in criminological research. Among the assertions by biosocial theorists is that race does matter in biosocial criminology (Walsh, 2004). For example, John Wright (2009), drawing on evolutionary and biological considerations, argues that there is an "inconvenient truth" pertaining to the existence of race and the evolutionary basis of race-based patterns of behavior. While acknowledging the potential role of past societal injustices in America, he points to the persistent pattern of high crime in Black communities in America and abroad as further evidence that something biological is likely a contributing factor.

Moving away from structural and racism-based explanations, Wright (2009) offers two reasons for race and problem behavior that "are highly couched in an evolutionary understanding of race differences and, as such, overlap with one another" (p. 147). He turns first to executive functions, which are "a range of brain-based activities housed in the frontal, prefrontal, and orbital frontal cortex. These abilities are highly heritable and provide humans with their unique abilities to plan, organize their lives, and control their emotions" (p. 147). Self-control and IQ are two key components of executive functions. Wright's argument here rests on the belief that those with low self-control will have difficulties throughout the life course, and this will be reflected in problems in education and employment. Although he believes these problems can befall all racial groups, he does add the caveat that "due to the distribution of low IQ and low self-control found in black populations, it is more often reflected in the lives of blacks" (p. 148). Wright next proffers that

> collective social behavior is an evolved ability and set the stage for the beginning of complex societies we see today . . . it entails individuals making a choice to sacrifice or risk something they value personally for the overall good. (p. 149)

Wright (2009) believes that in neighborhoods where most residents exhibit collective social behavior and enforce basic social norms, crime will be minimized. In his view, this is simply not the case in Black neighborhoods. Specifically, Wright closes his perspective with the following:

In many black neighborhoods, but especially in inner cities and ghettos, there are too few individuals with the ability to act collectively and there are too many who violate basic social norms and laws. And the undeniable fact is that individual differences in IQ and other executive functions, which tend to cluster within neighborhoods by race, is intimately tied to the lack of collective social behavior, to the lack of social control . . . and to the violation of rudimentary norms of appropriate conduct. (p. 150)

Wright's (2009) theory doesn't explain within-race class differences. That is, if his theory is correct, then wouldn't all Black neighborhoods—not just "many"—exhibit the same levels of social norm and law violation? In other words, if all Blacks of all classes suffer from "deficits in executive functions," then it stands to reason that the same problems should be found among all groups in that population. If that is not the case, then the role of class is being underemphasized in favor of race. Furthermore, the lack of collective social behavior could be a product of cultural inclinations that are a product of past inaction on the part of criminal justice officials. As such, the observed unwillingness of Blacks to follow "rudimentary norms of appropriate conduct" might be simply an artifact of the longstanding "no snitch" cultural norm that is pervasive in many of the inner-city communities that appear to be the targets of Wright's theory. Also, since Blacks reside in the most depressed areas of inner cities, it stands to reason that they might turn to violating norms of appropriate conduct to survive.

In large part, biosocial criminologists have relied on data from The National Longitudinal Study of Adolescent Health (Add Health) to test ideas related to their suppositions. Though this stream of scholarship is fairly new, some findings have begun to emerge that partially support biosocial assertions regarding the intersection of race, gender, behavior, and alleles (Vaske, Beaver, Wright, Boisvert, & Schnupp, 2009; Vaske, Makarios, Boisvert, Beaver, & Wright, 2009). Notably, none of these findings support any of the evolutionary aspects of Rushton's (1999) or Wright's (2009) work.

In summary, many of the current biologically oriented theories either directly or indirectly point to some race and crime linkage. Nevertheless, for more than a century, opponents of such approaches have countered with alternative sociological perspectives, some of which are reviewed in the next section.

❖ Sociological Explanations

Early Sociological Explanations

Sociological explanations for crime in general have existed for nearly two centuries. Beginning with the early work of the cartographic school, led by Adolphe Quetelet, who some have said produced the first scientific work on crime (see Quetelet, 1833/1984), this approach looked to sociological factors to explain criminality (age, social class, poverty, education level, etc.). Quetelet was likely among the first to aver some relationship between race and crime when he divided French citizens into distinct races and offered explanations why each group was engaged in crime (Mosher et al., 2011). Several decades after the publication of Quetelet's work, as noted earlier, biological notions related to crime were being espoused in America.

Numerous American scholars, however, challenged the biological approach using sociological analyses of crime problems. With the development of the first sociology department at the University of Chicago in 1892, and other such programs at universities across the United States, scholars saw this new discipline and a sociological approach as a means to solve some of the pressing issues particularly plaguing overcrowded northern cities.

In the late 1890s, Philadelphia was one of those cities looking for answers to its concerns regarding the burgeoning African American population. At the time, city officials sought out **W. E. B. Du Bois** to conduct a study of Philadelphia's notorious Seventh Ward. Du Bois (1899/1996) conducted a comprehensive review of the ward, outlining the conditions in the area and also pointing to several possible explanations for crime among African Americans. One of his explanations was as follows:

> Crime is a phenomenon of organized social life, and is the open rebellion of an individual against his social environment. Naturally then, if men are suddenly transported from one environment to another; the result is lack of harmony with the new conditions; lack of harmony with the new physical surroundings leading to disease and death or modification of physique; lack of harmony with social surroundings leading to crime. (p. 235)

He felt that the mass migration from the South to the North produced problems of adjustment for African Americans, who were previously familiar only with Southern life.

Du Bois's ideas were in line with the concept of **social disorganization**. Like Quetelet earlier, to explain criminality in the Seventh Ward, Du Bois pointed to issues related to age, unemployment, and poverty. Du Bois, however, added the sociological variable of discrimination, noting that Blacks were arrested for less cause than Whites, served longer sentences for similar crimes, and were subject to employment discrimination (Gabbidon, 2007; Taylor Greene & Gabbidon, 2000). Other early studies would echo similar sentiments on crime in the African American community (Grimke, 1915; K. Miller, 1908/1969; R. Wright, 1912/1969). Recently, Unnever and Gabbidon (2011) have offered an expansion of Du Bois's ideas and argued for the consideration of **racial discrimination** as a potential contributor to African American offending. Their theory is reviewed at the end of the chapter.

Social Disorganization

Northern cities, such as Chicago, were also experiencing the same social problems that Du Bois found in Philadelphia as a result of population booms caused by the mass immigration by racial and ethnic groups outlined in Chapter 1. With unparalleled philanthropic support from numerous foundations (Blumer, 1984), by the 1920s, the University of Chicago had put together a formidable cadre of scholars to investigate the social ills plaguing the city. Together, these scholars combined their ideas to formulate what is now known as the "Chicago School."

The leaders of the school were Robert Park and Ernest Burgess. They viewed the city as an environment that functioned much like other ecological environments: It was formed based on the principles of invasion, dominance, and succession. In short, one group moves in, battles the previous group until they dominate the area, after which, to continue the cycle, it is likely that another group will invade the area and pursue dominance. This ecological approach was believed to explain the conflict that occurred in emerging cities across the United States. Moreover, it was Burgess (1925) who had earlier conducted a study that produced the notion that towns and cities "expand radially from its central business district—on the map" (p. 50). From this, he and Park produced their now famous map of Chicago. The map divided the city into several concentric circles or "zones," as described by Park and Burgess. Of the numerous zones, Zone 2 is of most significance to the theory. This area was referred to as "the capital zone in transition" or "the slums," which, according to the theory, is where most of the crime should take place. As predicted by the theory, the farther one moves away from this zone, the more crime decreases (Shaw & McKay, 1942/1969).

In the tradition of Quetelet's earlier work, two researchers, Clifford Shaw and Henry D. McKay, who worked at the University of Chicago's Institute for Juvenile Research but were not faculty members, tested the theory by examining juvenile delinquency. To do so, they made use of 20 different types of maps. Each of the maps charted out different characteristics of Chicago's residents and delinquent youth. For example, there were maps that outlined neighborhood characteristics such as population fluctuations, percentage of families on welfare, monthly rents, percentage of foreign-born and Negro residents, and distribution of male delinquents (Shaw & McKay, 1942/1969). Their results were striking. As postulated by the theory, over several decades and with several changes in ethnic groups, Zone 2 had the most delinquency. Describing this dramatic finding, Shaw and McKay (1942/1969) wrote,

> the proportions of Germans, Irish, English-Scotch, and Scandinavians in the foreign-born population in 8 inner-city areas underwent, between 1884 and 1930, a decided decline (90.1 to 12.2 per cent); while the proportion of Italians, Poles, and Slavs increased . . . the 8 areas maintained, throughout these decades, approximately the same rates of delinquents relative to other areas. (pp. 150–151)

In the end, the scholars concluded that the crime in these areas was caused by social disorganization. Social disorganization refers to areas characterized by the following conditions: (a) fluctuating populations, (b) significant numbers of families on welfare, (c) families renting, (d) several ethnic groups in one area, (e) high truancy rates, (f) high infant mortality rates, (g) high levels of unemployment, (h) large numbers of condemned buildings, and (i) a higher percentage of foreign-born and Negro heads of families (Sampson & Groves, 1989; Shaw & McKay, 1942/1969).

During the late 1930s and early 1940s, a 1923 graduate of the "Chicago School," Norman Hayner, utilized social disorganization theory while investigating crime in diverse communities populated by Whites, Asian Americans, African Americans, and Native Americans (Hayner, 1933, 1938, 1942). These studies by Hayner all revealed that the more Asians and Native Americans were exposed to American culture, the more their rates of crime and delinquency started to mirror that of Whites.

Contemporary Social Disorganization Theory

Since these early articles, scholars have continued to explore the viability of social disorganization to explain crime, particularly in urban areas. Sampson (1987) found a connection between Black male joblessness and economic deprivation and violent crime. This connection was an indirect one mediated by family disruption (i.e., female-headed households). Another important article by Sampson and Groves (1989) expanded the theory and found considerable support for it. Building on this prior research and the important research of William Julius Wilson (1987), Sampson and Wilson (1995) posited a theory targeted at explaining race and crime with structural and cultural constructs:

> [Our] basic thesis is that macro social patterns of residential inequality give rise to the social isolation and ecological concentration of the truly disadvantaged, which in turn leads to structural barriers and cultural adaptations that undermine social organization and hence the control of crime. This thesis is grounded in what is actually an old idea in criminology that has been overlooked in the race and crime debate—the importance of communities. (p. 38)

The theory, which is referred to as the "racial invariance thesis," draws heavily on two of W. Wilson's (1987) concepts from *The Truly Disadvantaged*. The first, concentration effects, speaks to the fact that Whites and Blacks live in considerably different areas. In his research, Wilson found that many African Americans live in areas where there are significant concentrations of poverty. Once neighborhoods reach this point, working-class and middle-class African Americans abandon them.

This removes important **social buffers** (role models) who show neighborhood youths that there are successful people who go to work, day in and day out. When all the "social buffers" have abandoned a community, Wilson (1987) suggested that the remaining individuals are in a state of *social isolation*, which he defined as "the lack of contact or of sustained interaction with individuals and institutions that represent mainstream society" (p. 60). The notion of social isolation adds the cultural component to the theory. By not being exposed to mainstream individuals and institutions, socially isolated people tend to develop their own norms within these isolated areas. In a series of publications, Lauren Krivo and Ruth Peterson of Ohio State University have tested some of the ideas of Wilson (1987) and Sampson and Wilson (1995) and have found considerable support for them (see Krivo & Peterson, 1996, 2000; Peterson & Krivo, 1993, 2005, 2010). Returning to the perspective, Sampson and Bean (2006) have called for a revision of the theory to account for concentrated immigration and culture, both of which have profound implications for communities.

Scholars have also applied social disorganization theory to diverse groups such as Native Americans and found partial or full support for the theory (Bachman, 1991; Lanier & Huff-Corzine, 2006). Besides Native Americans, Martinez (2003) and Lee and Martinez (2002) have found support for aspects of the perspective in Latino communities. Velez (2006) argues that there is a lower level of social disorganization in Latino communities. This speaks to the so-called "Latino Paradox" that finds that even though Latinos are exposed to the same social disadvantages as other groups, they tend not to exhibit the extreme adverse effects (e.g., extreme levels of crime). Velez outlines four characteristics for this difference. First, she notes that there are lower levels of concentrated disadvantage in such communities. This includes things such as male joblessness and female-headed households. Moreover, in contrast to conventional wisdom, she argues that the presence of immigrants "provide protective mechanisms against crime" (p. 92). This supposition contradicts the longstanding immigration and crime perception held by the public (Higgins, Gabbidon, & Martin, 2010). And recent research has supported the notion that immigration does not increase crime but has actually contributed to a reduction of some crimes in Latino communities (Feldmeyer, 2009; Ferraro, 2015; MacDonald, Hipp, & Gill, 2013; Stowell, Messner, McGeever, & Raffalovich, 2009; Velez, 2009). Third, she indicates that Latino communities have better relations with economic officials, the police, and local politicians, all of whom are key "players" in all communities. Finally, she argues that Latinos tend to benefit from living in communities that are close to advantaged Whites. She provides data from Chicago that support her assertions (Velez, 2006).

Mass Incarceration and Social Disorganization

In the late 1990s, Dina Rose and Todd Clear (1998) articulated an expansion of social disorganization theory. Contrary to the punitive approach being heralded at the time, Rose and Clear posited that mass incarceration actually exacerbated social disorganization in the most depressed communities. According to their thesis, this happens for three reasons. First, it impacts the socioeconomic nature of the community. Second, because mass incarceration results in people leaving for prison and then being released from prison, it increases the mobility in certain communities. Finally, mass incarceration increases the heterogeneity of communities. This occurs because offenders who spend time in correctional institutions learn new antisocial behaviors that they bring back to their communities (for a complete articulation of the perspective, see Clear, 2007; see also Western, 2006; Western & Wildeman, 2009). Using data from Florida, they found support for their theory (Clear, Rose, & Ryder, 2001; Clear, Rose, Waring, & Scully, 2003). More recent research has also noted that mass incarceration inflicts collateral damage on the mental health of those residing in neighborhoods with high levels of incarceration (Hatzenbuehler, Keyes, Hamilton, Uddin, & Galea, 2015).

❖ Collective Efficacy

In the 1990s, Sampson, Raudenbush, and Earls (1997) sought to determine why urban communities differ in their levels of crime. From their research, they concluded that crime was related to the amount of **collective efficacy** found in a particular community. They defined collective efficacy as "social cohesion among neighbors combined with their willingness to intervene on behalf of the common good" (p. 918). In short, in the communities where residents do not retreat behind their locked doors and actively look out for one another, there is a diminished likelihood that they will have many of the ills found in other urban areas. Since their work, other scholars have found some support for collective efficacy among African Americans (Sampson, 2012; Simons, Gordon Simons, Burt, Brody, & Cutrona, 2005). Other research has suggested that the impact of collective efficacy is not as significant in communities as more official strategies such as **community policing** (Xu, Fiedler, & Flaming, 2005).

Both social disorganization and collective efficacy theories generally speak to high-crime urban areas. Because not all African Americans live in high-crime urban areas, some have wondered whether those in middle-class areas also encounter higher crime rates than those in similarly situated White areas. To investigate this question, Pattillo (1998) conducted participant observation and 28 in-depth interviews in one such area of Chicago. She found that "middle class Black areas tend to be nestled between areas that are less economically stable and have higher crime rates" (p. 751). In addition, many of the Black residents who make it to middle-class areas are "unstable" middle-class residents and struggle to maintain their status. In some instances, they cross over the line into crime to do so. Therefore, Pattillo also found that such residents were "given a degree of latitude to operate in the neighborhood" (p. 770). Based on the premise of social organization, which, along with being goal oriented, "stresses the importance of kin and neighborly ties for the social control of crime and disorder," Pattillo showed how these communities maintain order while allowing "the integration of licit and illicit networks both working toward common goals, with variant strategies" (p. 770). Recent research by Hassett-Walker (2009, 2010) has also investigated crime among the Black middle class and found that structural factors were not as significant a contributor to middle-class delinquency as peer influence.

There is both support for and persistent criticisms of social disorganization theory in the research literature. The most often-cited weakness of the social disorganization perspective is the so-called ecological fallacy. This refers to the fact that the perspective is usually tested at the aggregate level, but researchers still use the data to make assertions about individuals. The theory also does not explain how certain groups, such as Asians and Jewish communities, maintained low levels of crime and delinquency, although they lived in areas that might be categorized as socially disorganized (Lanier & Henry, 1998). Moreover, although there were high levels of delinquency in the study areas, the theory does not explain why, in general, most juveniles in these areas do not become delinquent.

❖ Culture Conflict Theory

Originally formulated by criminologist Thorsten Sellin in the late 1930s, culture conflict theory, according to Williams and McShane (2010), is heavily based on the work of Chicago School graduates Louis Wirth and Edwin Sutherland (who collaborated with Sellin). A central idea of the theory relates to the rules or norms within a culture. Sellin (1938) suggested that, over a period of time, certain behavior becomes accepted within a culture, so that "the violation of [it] arouses a group reaction. These rules or norms may be called *conduct norms*" (p. 28).

Sellin's (1938) theory states that all societies have conduct norms, which vary from one culture to the next and could result in violations in one society not being a violation of conduct norms in another. Within each society, those in power can control the definitions of conduct norms and hence determine what behaviors become crimes. This leads to the potential for culture conflict. In general, Sellin pointed to three ways that conflicts between various cultural codes arise: (a) when the codes clash on the border of contiguous cultural areas; (b) when, as may be the case with legal norms, the law of one cultural group is extended to cover the territory of another; or (c) when members of one cultural group migrate to another.

Summarizing these ideas, Sellin (1938) formulated two types of culture conflicts. Regarding the first type, called *primary conflicts*, he noted,

> [If] the immigrant's conduct norms are different from those of the American community and if these differences are not due to his economic status, but to his *cultural origin*, then we speak of a conflict of norms drawn from different cultural systems or areas. Such conflicts may be regarded as *primary* culture conflicts. (p. 104)

Sellin (1938) described *secondary conflicts* as "conflicts of norms which grow out of the process of social differentiation which characterize the evolution of our own culture" (p. 105). As an example of the applicability of his perspective, Sellin used Native Americans as an illustrative population:

> We need only to recall the effect on the American Indian of the culture conflict induced by our policy of acculturation by guile and force. In this instance, it was not merely contact with the White man's culture, his religion, his business methods, and his liquor, which weakened tribal mores. In addition, the Indian became subject to the White man's law and this brought conflicts as well, as has always been the case when legal norms have been imposed upon a group previously ignorant of them. (p. 64)

Although the theory clearly has relevance for Native Americans and the various ethnic immigrants who were arriving in America during the early part of the 20th century, in recent decades, it has received limited attention (Lee, 1995). Criminologists have generally neglected culture conflict theory; they have, however, borrowed some ideas from the theory and formulated related theories, such as **strain theory**, subcultural theory, and conflict theory. We look at these theories in the following sections.

❖ Strain/Anomie Theory

In the same year as the publication of Sellin's work on culture conflict, another important theory was presented. The 1938 publication of Robert K. Merton's "Social Structure and Anomie" produced what is likely one of the most cited theories in criminology: strain or anomie theory. The theory was influenced by the classic work of Emile Durkheim, who first made use of the word *anomie* in a criminological sense. According to Akers (2000), "Durkheim (1951[1897]) used the term anomie to refer to a state of normlessness or lack of social regulation in modern society as one condition that promotes higher rates of suicide" (p. 143). Merton's (1938) work showed that in every society, there are "culturally defined goals, purposes, and interest" (p. 672). He also suggested that there are generally "acceptable modes of achieving these goals" (p. 673). Turning to American society, Merton recognized that "the extreme emphasis upon the accumulation of wealth as a symbol of success in our own society mitigates against the completely effective control of the institutionally regulated modes of acquiring a fortune" (p. 675). In short, in pursuit of the "American Dream," some people turn to alternative means to secure this cultural goal. When applying the theory to race and crime, Merton recognized the special case of African Americans:

> Certain elements of the Negro population have assimilated the dominant caste's values of pecuniary success and advancement, but they also recognize that social ascent is at present restricted to their own caste almost exclusively. The pressures upon the Negro which would otherwise derive from the structural inconsistencies we have noticed are hence not identical to those upon lower class Whites. (p. 680)

Merton (1938) understood that the strain experienced by African Americans was unlike any other in American society. Basically, no matter how much they sought to achieve the "American dream," they could never "legitimately" reach the status of Whites, so they maintained lower aspirations and were resigned to achieving a lower level of success and advancement. Such a situation likely contributed to a strain that resulted in some African Americans turning to crime. Some well-known tests of the theory have shown mixed results (Cernkovich, Giordano, & Rudolph, 2000; Epps, 1967). Notably, in the early 2000s, McCluskey (2002) applied strain theory to Latinos and found that the theory was a weak predictor of delinquency. As a result, she argued for a culturally specific model that supports the notion that criminological research pertaining to Latinos needs to consider the unique nuances of their experience.

Limitations of Strain/Anomie Theory

Most of the criticisms of strain theory have been leveled at Merton's original formulation of the theory. Bohm (2001), for example, noted that anomie theories have a middle-class bias; they presume that lower class individuals commit crimes in an effort to reach middle-class status. As was seen by some of the research reviewed, this is not always the case. Another persistent criticism is that the theories do not explain white-collar and government crimes. Given that people at this level have already achieved middle-class status, why, then, do they engage in crime? Even in its various incarnations, the theory is generally silent on this issue.

Bohm (2001) also suggested that the theory suffers from overprediction. As he put it, "If strain is caused by the inability to achieve the American dream and is as widespread as Merton implies, then there ought to be much more crime than occurs" (p. 80). Because of the shortcomings of strain/anomie theory, Agnew (1992, 2006) developed a revised version of the theory.

❖ General Strain Theory

Robert Agnew, first in a pioneering *Criminology* article in 1992 and later in a book-length exposition (Agnew, 2006), renewed interest in strain theory by adding that the removal (or loss) of positive or introduction of negative stimuli into an environment can cause a strain that, as with blocked opportunities, can result in criminal behavior.

As for the removal of positively valued stimuli, Agnew (1992) specifically pointed to the following: "loss of a boyfriend/girlfriend, the death of or serious illness of a friend, moving to a new school district, the divorce/separation of one's parents, suspension from school, and the presence of a variety of adverse conditions at work" (p. 57). Turning to the presentation of negative stimuli, Agnew pointed to the following: child abuse and neglect, criminal victimization, physical punishment, negative relations with parents, negative relations with peers, adverse or negative school experience, stressful life events, verbal threats and insults, physical pain, unpleasant odors, disgusting scenes, noise, heat, air pollution, personal space violations, and high density.

Building on these ideas, Jang and Johnson (2003) used the National Survey of Black Americans (composed of a sample of 2,107 African American adults) to test whether Agnew's theory holds true for African Americans. In addition to testing core tenets of Agnew's work, they sought to determine whether African American religiosity, an area in which research has consistently shown more commitment by African Americans than by other ethnic groups, has any impact on helping them cope when strain occurs. In contrast to the earlier research of Cernkovich et al. (2000), these authors found support for Agnew's modified version of strain theory, noting the following regarding the role of religiosity:

> We find that individuals who are religiously committed are less likely than those who are not to engage in deviant coping in reaction to personal problems because their religiosity buffers the effects of negative emotions on deviance as well as directly and indirectly (via outerdirected emotions) affects their coping strategies. (Jang & Johnson, 2003, p. 98)

Studies have continued to find support for the theory (Eitle & Turner, 2003; Rocque, 2008; Simons, Chen, Stewart, & Brody, 2003). In the Simons et al. (2003) research study, the authors found that experiencing discrimination was a significant predictor of delinquency. Eitle and Turner's (2003) work revealed that disparities in crime commission were largely attributable to African Americans' increased exposure to stressors. Jang and Johnson (2005) found additional support for their earlier research on the benefit of religiosity when coping with strain (see also Jang & Lyons, 2006). In addition, some research has also shown that there are ethnic-specific strains that influence delinquency among Hispanics (Perez, Jennings, & Giver, 2008).

Kaufman, Rebellon, Thaxton, and Agnew (2008) have devoted an article to clarifying how **general strain theory** can explain racial differences in criminal offending. In particular, they posit that "A GST explanation of racial differences in offending . . . implies that African-Americans experience disproportionate strain in the social environment and/or have fewer resources for coping with strain in conventional ways" (p. 424). Kaufman and his colleagues point to economic strains, family strains, community strains, and a host of other strains that Blacks are more likely to encounter (e.g., discrimination in all aspects of life). Their work has provided additional clarity for how general strain theory applies to African Americans. Despite these clarifications, at least one empirical study has found only mixed support for the theory as applied to race and offending (Piquero & Sealock, 2010). We now turn our attention to subcultural theory.

❖ Subcultural Theory

In the 1950s, several theories were formulated that considered criminality to be tied to the development of subcultures among White middle-class youth. In *Delinquent Boys*, Albert Cohen (1955) argued that gang delinquency was associated with juveniles being unable to achieve status among their peers. When they were unable to meet established White middle-class standards, they established their own values, which generally involved activities and behaviors that were in conflict with middle-class values.

While examining a diverse, lower class area in Boston, Walter Miller (1958) also formulated a subcultural theory. Referred to as the "focal concerns" theory, Miller's thesis was based on three years of field research. His focal concerns were considered values to which lower class residents adhered. These included trouble, toughness, smartness, excitement, fate, and autonomy. *Trouble* referred to youth engaging in risk-taking activities. *Toughness* represented the notion that one was fearless and could "handle oneself" in a physical encounter. *Smartness* referred to street smarts, which are valued in lower class communities. *Excitement* is the pursuit of thrill seeking. *Fate* is the belief among lower class youth that their lives are controlled by things over which they have no control. *Autonomy* was the final focal concern and represents the resentment that lower class youth have regarding the control others have over their lives (Miller, 1958).

Two years after Miller's work, Cloward and Ohlin's (1960) *Delinquency and Opportunity* pointed to opportunity structure as the key to understanding gang activities. They suggested that when there are limited opportunities, youth join gangs with one of three orientations. Those who cannot find legitimate opportunities join criminal gangs whose aim is to make money through a variety of illegitimate avenues. If, however, there remain few illegitimate opportunities, the youth might join a "conflict" gang. Such gangs primarily engage in violent activities, doing whatever is necessary to maintain their status in the streets. Youth who end up in "retreatist" gangs are what Cloward and Ohlin refer to as "double failures." Because such youth did not make it in either legitimate or illegitimate opportunities, they retreat to drug usage.

The same year Miller published his theory, noted criminologist M. Wolfgang (1958) published *Patterns in Criminal Homicide*. This was significant because, as an outgrowth of this pioneering work, less than a decade later he, along with Franco Ferracuti, formulated the subculture of violence theory, which has been used to explain homicide, particularly in the African American community. We review this theory next.

The Subculture of Violence Theory

As reflected in Chapter 2, African Americans and Latinos are overrepresented in the violent crime categories. In the case of African Americans, this is nothing new. In the late 1950s, while studying homicides in Philadelphia, Wolfgang (1958) found high homicide rates among African Americans in Philadelphia. In addition, Wolfgang found interesting results related to sex differences, victim-offender relationships, weapons involved, and motives for the homicides. From this research and that of his colleague Franco Ferracuti, who had also conducted homicide research in Italy, Wolfgang and Ferracuti (1967) formulated the subculture of violence theory. Their theory, which draws from several other criminological theories, consists of seven propositions.

These propositions speak to a range of factors that encapsulate the subculture of violence. Some of these factors include the fact that those invested in the subculture of violence are not violent all the time. Although the subculture is found in all age segments of society, it is found most in those in the late-adolescence to middle-age categories. Because those vested in the subculture do not see violence as "illicit conduct," they have no feelings of guilt about their actions (Wolfgang & Ferracuti, 1967).

Several authors have either critiqued or tested the theory as it relates to race and the commission of violent crimes. Hawkins (1983) provided one of the earliest and most comprehensive critiques of the theory. In doing so, he also provided an alternative perspective. We begin with a summary of his critique; then we turn to a brief overview of his alternative theory. Hawkins pointed to the following five major weaknesses of the theory:

1. There is an extreme emphasis on mentalistic value orientations of individuals— orientations that in the aggregate are said to produce a subculture.

2. The theory lacks empirical grounding and, indeed, is put in question by some empirical findings.

3. Much of the theory has tended to underemphasize a variety of structural, situational, and institutional variables that affect interpersonal violence. For Blacks, these variables range from historical patterns developed during slavery to the immediate social context of an individual homicidal offense to the operation of the criminal justice system, past and present.

4. Subcultural theory underemphasizes the effects of the law on patterns of criminal homicide.

5. There are other plausible ways apart from the inculcation of values by which the economic, political, and social disadvantages of American Blacks may produce high rates of homicide. (pp. 414–415)

Hawkins's (1983) alternative theory provided three propositions that were meant to address the holes in the subculture of violence theory. Proposition 1 states, "American Criminal Law: Black life is cheap but White life is valuable" (p. 415). Here, Hawkins believes that, based on history, Black lives have taken on less value than White lives; as a result, African Americans can kill other African Americans without fear of being punished. In line with this argument, Hawkins expanded the work of G. Johnson (1941) and presented a hierarchy of homicide seriousness, interpolated between the least and most serious types of homicides (see Figures 3.1 and 3.2). Hawkins's (1983) second proposition states the following: "Past and present racial and social class differences in the administration of justice affect Black criminal violence" (p. 422). This proposition speaks to the lack of attention paid to prehomicide behaviors in the Black communities. Hawkins believes that, because various prehomicidal assaults in the African American community do not receive the attention they deserve, homicides that could be prevented are not. Such inattention is also a product of the poor relationship between African Americans and police agencies (Brunson, 2007; Jones-Brown, 2007; Rios, 2011; Stewart, 2007).

Rating	Offense
Most Serious	Negro versus White, White versus White
Least Serious	Negro versus Negro, White versus Negro

Figure 3.1

Johnson's Hierarchy of Homicide Seriousness

Source: Hawkins (1983, pp. 420–421).

Rating	Offense
Most Serious	Black kills White, in authority
	Black kills White, stranger
	White kills White, in authority
	Black kills White, friend, acquaintance
	Black kills White, intimate, family
	White kills White, friend, acquaintance
	White kills White, intimate, family
	Black kills Black, stranger
	Black kills Black, friend, acquaintance
	Black kills Black, intimate, family
	White kills Black, stranger
	White kills Black, friend, acquaintance
Least Serious	White kills Black, intimate, family

Figure 3.2

Hawkins's Hierarchy of Homicide Seriousness

Source: Hawkins (1983, pp. 420–421).

As a product of poor relations with the police, in some instances, response times are slower, and at some point, African Americans lose faith in the police and refuse to call on them for assistance in certain instances. Relatedly, once a homicide is committed and the police are called in, their lack of serious attention provides no deterrent effect to the community. The final proposition—that "economic deprivation creates a climate of powerlessness in which individual acts of violence are likely to take place" (p. 429)—speaks to the association between socioeconomic disadvantage and violence, a connection generally lacking in the subculture of violence theory, but that was incorporated into Sampson's (1985) test of Wolfgang and Ferracuti's (1967) version of the theory. Sampson tested the theory, looking at disaggregated homicide rates for 55 of the largest American cities. According to Sampson (1985), if the theory were correct, he would find that "Black offending rates should be related positively to percent of Black violent crimes, independent of other structural characteristics, particularly poverty and inequality" (p. 52). Using a variety of sophisticated methods, no support was found for the theory.

During the 1990s, the theory also was tested to determine its applicability to Black women. Mann (1990a) examined homicide data from six major cities and found Black women comprised 77% of female murderers. However, after taking all factors into consideration, she concluded, "These women are not part of a 'subculture of violence' but of a 'subculture of hopelessness.' Their fierce independence, their tendency to batter or to kill when battered and their almost insurmountable economic obstacles represent a constant struggle" (Mann, 1990a, p. 198). When Ray and Smith (1991) took up the subject the following year, they noted that if there is a "subculture of violence" among African American females, there must also be one among White females who had identical offending patterns, primarily committing homicides against males of the same race with whom they have a close relationship.

During the mid-1990s, Harer and Steffensmeier (1996) did find support for the subculture of violence theory. Their research made use of prison misconduct data and examined the theory as applied to institutional violence. They found that Blacks were twice as likely to be found guilty of violent misconduct as were Whites, even after controlling for standard variables. Even so, they pointed out that the differences also could be attributable to racial discrimination in the disciplinary process, something their research did not take into consideration.

Cao, Adams, and Jensen (2000) tested the theory using General Social Survey (GSS) data from 1983 to 1991 (excluding 1985). Focusing on all core elements of the theory, the authors found that, in contrast to the theory, "Whites are found to be significantly more vocal than Blacks in expressing their support for the use of violence in defensive situations, with the effects of other factors held constant" (p. 54). Finally, the authors concluded with this:

> Based on our data and analyses, there is enough evidence to conclude that Blacks in the general U.S. population are no more likely than Whites to embrace values favorable to violence. Our findings thus repudiate the idea that the causes of Black crime are rooted in unique aspects of Black culture. (p. 58)

They suggested that, given the limited support for the theory, for scholars to continue to promote it as an explanation for racial differences in violence implies that all African Americans are violent, something that is "unfair and potentially racist in nature" (Cao et al., 2000, p. 58). More recent results have been mixed, with some scholarship finding little support for the perspective (Chilton, 2004; Pridemore & Freilich, 2006), and other research finding qualified support for the theory (Doucet, D'Antonio-Del Rio, & Chauvin, 2014; Staff & Kreager, 2008).

Other criticisms also have been leveled at the theory. Covington (2003) noted that supporters of the theory "fail to explain how [the] Black subculture of violence came to be more combative than the White subculture of violence" (p. 258). Psychologists also have argued that Wolfgang and Ferracuti (1967) "ignore the psychological underpinnings of [the] subculture" (Poussaint; cited in Covington, 2003, p. 259).

The Code of the Streets

One of the more recent subcultural theories that has some connections to several of the approaches previously reviewed is the **code of the streets** (Anderson, 1994, 1999). Based on his research in Philadelphia, Elijah Anderson, an urban ethnographer, published a highly acclaimed article, "The Code of the Streets," which focused on interpersonal violence in an impoverished Philadelphia neighborhood and how residents in the area adopted the "code of the streets" to survive. Anderson (1994) believes that "at the heart of the code is the issue of respect—loosely defined as being treated 'right,' or granted deference one deserves" (p. 82). In such an environment, something that has little meaning to one person might be interpreted as "dissing" by someone else and result in a confrontation that could lead to violence. Being able to defend oneself is also an important part of the code. Within such depressed neighborhoods, Anderson suggested, there are "decent" and "street" families. Decent families "tend to accept mainstream values more fully and attempt to instill them in their children" (pp. 82–83). Such families are also strict and teach their children to respect authority and act in a moral way. In addition, they are not seriously tied to the code.

In contrast, Anderson (1994) described "street families," who loosely supervise their children and, in many cases, are unable to cope with them (see Box 3.2). Unlike the decent families, "they believe in the code and judge themselves and others according to its values" (Anderson, 1994, p. 83). Consequently, their lives "are marked by disorganization" (p. 83). In such families, children learn early on that they must fend for themselves. This produces a cycle in which they also become vested in the code and take to the streets to prove their "manhood," which involves securing pretty women, being able to defend themselves, and being able to support themselves "by any means necessary."

BOX 3.2

Race and Crime in the Media

Is crime in the Black community cultural or is it the product of racial bias?

In a 2014 *Washington Times* article titled "Family Secret: What the Left Won't Tell You About Black Crime," author Jason Riley presents a conservative argument that moves away from blaming the criminal justice system for the overrepresentation of Blacks in the justice system. In particular, he points to the continuing high rates of Black violence in Southern and Northern cities as evidence of the limited role of discrimination in producing violence in the Black community. Furthermore, he writes that "Black crime and incarceration rates spiked in the 1970s and 1980s in cities such as Baltimore, Cleveland, Detroit, Chicago, Philadelphia, Los Angeles, and Washington under Black mayors and Black police chiefs. Some of the most violent cities in the United States today are run by Blacks." Riley blames the current state of crime in the Black community on cultural factors. In particular, he writes,

> Black people are not shooting each other at these alarming rates in Chicago and other urban areas because of our drug laws or a criminal justice system that has it in for them. The problem is primarily cultural—self-destructive behaviors and attitudes are all too common among the Black underclass. The problem is Black criminal behavior, which is one manifestation of a Black pathology that ultimately stems from the breakdown of the Black family. Liberals want to talk about what others should do for Blacks instead of what Blacks should do for themselves. But if we don't acknowledge the cultural barriers to black progress, how can we address them? How can you even begin to fix something that almost no one wants to talk about honestly?

More about Jason Riley: http://jasonrileyonline.com/

1. Do you support Riley's perspective? Why or why not?

Source: Riley (2014).

Research conducted within the last two decades has provided some support for Anderson's ideas focusing on Blacks (Baumer, Horney, Felson, & Lauritsen, 2003; Brezina, Agnew, Cullen, & Wright, 2004; Chilton, 2004; Stewart, Simons, & Conger, 2002; Stewart & Simons, 2006), Hispanics (Lopez, Roosa, Tein, & Dinh, 2004), and, more recently, young Black women (Brunson & Stewart, 2006; N. Jones, 2010). Other studies have also noted the role of rap music in the perpetuation of the code of the streets (Kubrin, 2005). In contrast to these positive findings, Stewart, Schreck, and Simons (2006) found limited support for the perspective. In line with the theory, they postulated that adhering to the code of the streets would reduce one's likelihood of being victimized. However, their research revealed the opposite: Adherents to the code of the streets reported *higher* levels of victimization (see also McGee, 1999; McGee, Barber, Joseph, Dudley, & Howell, 2005; Stewart, Schreck, & Brunson, 2008).

Besides the need for nationwide replications of the theory, there have been other concerns expressed about the viability of Anderson's ideas. Commenting on one of the life histories presented in Anderson's work, J. Miller (2001) wrote that, based on the way Anderson described the person's prison experience, it could be that the prison, not the streets, is the more powerful contributor to the development of the code of the streets. Elaborating on this point, he wrote,

> I do not feel that Professor Anderson gives enough weight to the influences of prison on the code of the streets. It is no accident that most of the known violent gangs in California developed in the institutions of the California Youth Authority or the California prisons. Leadership is confirmed by a stint in prison. The walk, the "pose," the language, the argot, the dress, the focus of one's eyes, and the studied indifference all bespeak prison. (p. 157)

Wacquant (2002) provided a more expansive critique of Anderson's work, pointing to the "loose and over-expansive definition of the code of the streets" (p. 1491). Another point of concern is that "there is considerable confusion as to the origins and vectors of the code of the streets" (p. 1491). Wacquant further observed,

> Because he starts from an overly monolithic vision of the ghetto and conflates folk with analytic concepts, Anderson cannot relate the *moral distinctions* he discovers in it to the internal *social stratification*. He thus boxes himself into a culturalist position with deeply disturbing political implications insofar as they render ghetto residents responsible for their own plight through their deviant values or role ineptness. (p. 1500)

Anderson took exception to Wacquant's (2002) critique and produced a rejoinder that suggested that Wacquant had misread his work and distorted its findings. Outside commentators on the debate have noted that both scholars had valid arguments (Wilson & Chaddha, 2009).

In general, a common shortcoming of subcultural theories is that they ignore criminality in the middle and upper classes (Hagan, 2002). In addition, as noted in the critiques of Hawkins (1983) and Cao and his colleagues (2000), tests of the theory (specifically the popular subculture of violence theory) have found minimal support. Another persistent criticism of subcultural theories is that, in most instances, they speak only to male criminality (Lilly et al., 2001). Rocque, Posick, and Felix (2015) have also recently proposed that subcultural theories have the potential to be strengthened by integrating biological factors. In particular, they believe that the structural pressures and concentrated violence that are found in some communities can create prolonged stress on the brain and contribute to violence and aggression.

One of the most popular theories used to explain racial differences in offending is conflict theory. Our discussion of the theory is presented next.

❖ Conflict Theory

Conflict theory likely represents the most popular theoretical framework used to explain race and crime. The theory, which has seeds in many of the ones previously discussed, has some of its origins in Germany. Specifically, the works of German scholars Karl Marx, George Simmel, and Max Weber have been credited with providing the impetus for the theory. According to Lilly, Cullen, and Ball (2011), "Theories that focus attention on struggles between individuals and/or groups in terms of power differentials fall into the general category of *conflict theory*" (p. 166). In short, when applying conflict theory to race and crime, one would look to whether the enforcement of laws and the distribution of punishment are done in a discriminatory manner. Although social class and gender also would be important to investigate, the way in which the White power structure administers justice would be of central concern to conflict theorists.

Conflict Theory, Race, and Crime

An early observer of race and crime, W. E. B. Du Bois studied under Weber and produced one of the earliest works to incorporate a conflict analysis (Gabbidon, 1999, 2007; Taylor Greene & Gabbidon, 2000). In 1901, he published an article on the convict-lease system (for more discussion on this system, see Chapter 8), which spoke to the conflict perspective. Du Bois (1901/2002) traced the history of the system whereby immediately after the passage of the Thirteenth Amendment, states leased convicts out to private landowners who no longer had the free labor of African American slaves.

Du Bois (1901/2002) wrote about how states strategically enacted various laws (referred to as the "Black codes") to snare Blacks into the criminal justice system so they could be returned to the labor force, which helped maintain the power and privileged status of Southern White landowners. In the article, Du Bois also rebutted the biological theorists of his day by declaring,

> Above all, we must remember that crime is not normal; that the appearance of crime among Southern Negroes is a symptom of wrong social conditions— of a stress of life greater than a large part of the community can bear. The Negro is not naturally criminal; he is usually patient and law-abiding. If slavery,

the convict-lease system, the traffic in criminal labor, the lack of juvenile reformatories, together with the unfortunate discrimination and prejudice in other walks of life, have led to that sort of social protest and revolt we call crime, then we must look for remedy in the sane reform of these wrong social conditions, and not in intimidation, savagery, or legalized slavery of men. (p. 88)

By this time, as reviewed earlier, Du Bois had already made significant statements on crime, pointing to discrimination, segregation, lynching, and the attitudes of the courts as explanations for African American criminality (Gabbidon, 2001; Taylor Greene & Gabbidon, 2000). Other prominent scholars would find considerable support for Du Bois's ideas (Myrdal, 1944; Sellin, 1928, 1935; Work, 1900, 1913). In each case, the authors wrote of the discrimination and economic conditions that were contributing to African American involvement in the criminal justice system—matters that directly speak to conflict theory.

It would be some time, however, before the formal articulation of conflict theory (also referred to as "critical criminology") and a little longer before it incorporated race as a central component. The development of conflict theory over the last 40 years is often credited to the writings of Chambliss (1964, 1969), Turk (1969), and Quinney (1970). Much of these writings were class-based analyses that suggested that capitalism, class structure, and the manipulation of laws were significant contributors to crime, and, as such, changing the structure of society would go a long way toward eliminating crime.

In addition to these scholars, in his classic work *Crime and Privilege*, Krisberg (1975), while articulating a critical perspective (referred to then as "New Criminology"), clearly added the dimension of race to the theory by integrating the history of criminal justice practices used to control oppressed groups and also highlighting the prison writings of George Jackson, Angela Davis, and other high-profile African American prisoners of the early 1970s. Notably, building on the work of Blauner (1972), Krisberg (1975) devoted a whole section of the work to race privilege, which in recent years has been translated into the notion of "White privilege" (see McIntosh, 2002). This notion of White privilege within criminal justice translates into more focus on "crimes in the streets," as opposed to "crimes in the suites." This focus criminalizes the actions of other races and poor Whites while minimizing or looking past the crimes of Whites in power. Over the years, in several editions of his classic text *The Rich Get Richer, and the Poor Get Prison* (2004), Reiman has spoken of this in terms of white-collar crimes, environmental crimes, and other corporate crimes that kill thousands of people, who are primarily poor and American minorities, but rarely result in anyone being severely punished.

Hawkins (1987) further expanded the conflict model by examining it in terms of race, crime, and punishment. He emphasized the need to consider race discrimination in conflict theory. According to Hawkins, other considerations usually lacking in conflict theory included victim characteristics, region, and accounting for race-appropriate behaviors. Whereas the first two characteristics are self-explanatory, for the latter, Hawkins noted that anomalies found in some studies do not take into account behaviors that are generally committed by one race and that, when committed by another race, result in a punishment that seems out of line. Finally, Hawkins also suggested that too often conflict theorists do not consider the power threat approach of Blalock (1967). The approach, which some have called a "power threat version of conflict theory" (Ellis & Walsh, 2000, pp. 384–385), argues that once a majority population sees a minority group encroaching on spheres traditionally reserved for majority group members, they respond in a number of ways, including imposing additional social control (Hawkins, 1987). This usually comes in the form of increased investments in police forces. According to past and recent scholarship, there is support for the "power threat" thesis (see D'Alessio, Eitle, & Stolzenberg, 2005; Jackson, 1989; R. King, 2007; Sharp, 2006). Recent scholarship has also found support that Hispanics represent a new minority threat (Eitle & Taylor, 2008; Stewart, Martinez, Baumer, & Gertz, 2015).

Around the same time of Hawkins's important research, Wilbanks (1987), a professor of criminal justice at Florida International University, published his controversial work, *The Myth of a Racist Criminal Justice System*. In contrast to conflict theorists, who argue that discrimination is a significant reason why minorities are overrepresented in the criminal justice system, Wilbanks argued that, although he believed there was some discrimination in the criminal justice system (using the analogy of having a few bad apples in a barrel), contrary to what was being espoused in much of the race and crime literature,

> I do not believe that *the system* is characterized by racial prejudice or discrimination against Blacks; that is, prejudice and discrimination are not "systematic." Individual cases appear to reflect racial prejudice and discrimination by the offender, the victim, the police, the prosecutor, the judge, or prison or parole officials. But conceding individual cases of bias is far different from conceding pervasive racial discrimination. (pp. 5–6)

Wilbanks' perspective became known as the "no discrimination thesis" (NDT). Wilbanks's (1987) book and its perspective initiated a series of debates between Wilbanks and Coramae Richey Mann. In contrast to Wilbanks's position, Mann (1990b) felt,

> The racism in the criminal justice system has become institutionalized in the same way that it has in other organizational segments of the nation such as education, politics, religion, and the economic structure; and the barrel *is* rotten. (p. 16)

Mann's perspective became known as the "discrimination thesis" (DT). Although the debates became heated, the two had brought to the fore an issue that lay below the surface among criminologists for many years. In 1993, Mann responded with her contemporary classic *Unequal Justice: A Question of Color*. Although the debate cooled after the publication of her book, the level of discrimination in the criminal justice system continued to be a central focus of race and crime researchers (Walker, Spohn, & DeLone, 2007; see Box 3.3). Moreover, although Wilbanks never produced the second edition he planned to write (Wilbanks, 1987, p. x), other scholars have continued in his tradition (see, e.g., Beaver et al., 2013; DeLisi, 2011; DeLisi & Regoli, 1999; DiLulio, 1996a; MacDonald, 2003, 2008).

BOX 3.3

Walker, Spohn, and DeLone's (1996) Discrimination-Disparity Continuum

Building on the "no discrimination thesis" (NDT) and "discrimination thesis" (DT) articulated by Wilbanks and Mann, Samuel Walker, Cassia Spohn, and Miriam DeLone created the "discrimination-disparity continuum," which was presented in the first edition of their book, *The Color of Justice* (1996). The continuum provides a useful framework for the NDT/DT debate. As they see it, discrimination in the criminal justice and juvenile justice systems can fall somewhere along their continuum (see Figure 3.3). At the one end of the continuum is systematic discrimination, whereby discrimination takes place "at all stages of the criminal justice system, at all times, and at all places" (Walker, Spohn, & DeLone, 2007, p. 19). At the other end of the continuum, there is pure justice, which suggests that there is no discrimination in the criminal justice system and the overrepresentation of minorities in the criminal justice system is likely a product of offending patterns. In between these poles, you have institutionalized discrimination, contextual discrimination, and individual acts of discrimination. Walker et al. (2007) defined institutional discrimination as "racial and ethnic disparities in outcomes that are the result of the application of racially neutral factors, such as prior criminal record, employment, and demeanor" (p. 19).

Figure 3.3 Discrimination-Disparity Continuum

Systematic Discrimination	Institutionalized Discrimination	Contextual Discrimination	Individual Acts of Discrimination	Pure Justice

Source: From WALKER/SPOHN/DELONE. *The Color of Justice*, 3E. © 2003 South-Western, a part of Cengage Learning, Inc. Reproduced by permission. www.cengage.com/permissions.

Contextual discrimination is discrimination that occurs only in certain contexts. The examples presented by the authors include discrimination found in "certain regions, particular crimes, or special victim-offender relationships" (Walker et al., 2007, p. 19). Individual acts of discrimination occur when there are simply individuals within the criminal justice and juvenile justice systems—not whole agencies—engaged in discrimination.

After presenting their continuum, the authors surveyed the current race and crime literature and concluded that although the criminal justice and juvenile justice systems were once characterized by systematic discrimination, that is no longer the case. Their most recent review of the literature suggests that the two justice systems are now characterized by contextual discrimination (see Walker et al., 2007, p. 420).

1. Pick a topic related to race and crime (e.g., the death penalty, racial profiling) and find three refereed journal articles on the subject. After reviewing the articles, see whether, as a whole, you also find that contextual discrimination pervades your selected area of race and crime.

Along with Hawkins's (1987) concern about the oversimplification of the theory, a few other shortcomings of conflict theory have been noted. Bohm (2001) noted that the perspective does not take into account individual differences. That is, not all people who are oppressed or discriminated against will respond the same way. Finally, some have suggested that, in some of its forms, the theory is not testable. A perspective related to conflict theory that has been applied to race and crime is the colonial model.

❖ The Colonial Model

The **colonial model** has its foundations in the work of psychiatrist and activist Frantz Fanon (Tatum, 1994). Although Fanon used the model to examine the relations between Blacks and Whites in colonial settings, Blauner (1969) and Staples (1975), leaning heavily on intellectuals of the Black power movement, such as Stokely Carmichael and Charles Hamilton, were among the first to substantively apply the theory to crime. Applying the perspective to the conditions of African Americans, Blauner (1969) provided the following definition of colonialism:

> Colonialism traditionally refers to the establishment of domination over a geographically external political unit, most of them inhabited by people of a different race and culture, where this domination is political and economic, and the colony exists subordinated and dependent on the mother country. Typically the colonizers exploit the land, the raw materials, the labor, and other resources of the colonized nation; in addition a formal recognition is given to the difference in power, autonomy, and political status, and various agencies are set up to maintain this subordination. (p. 395)

Blauner (1972) also generally applied the model to Native Americans. In the work *Gringo Justice*, Mirande (1987) reviewed the historical treatment of Mexican Americans by the criminal justice system and formulated a theory of "gringo justice," integrating the colonial model and conflict theory. Although African Americans were not colonized in the sense that Native Americans or Mexican Americans were, according to Tatum (1994), internal colonialism, which is "when foreign control of a state or territory is eliminated and the control and exploitation of subordinate groups passes to the dominant group within the newly created society" (p. 41), produces many of the same characteristics of the more traditional **colonization** process. Such characteristics include "a caste system based in racism, cultural imposition, cultural disintegration and recreation and members of the colonized being governed by representatives of the dominant power" (p. 41). Such characteristics within a society leave the colonized with feelings of alienation, which results in either crime and delinquency or the desire to assimilate or protest.

All articulations of the theory note the important role that agents of the criminal justice system (or "internal military agents," as they are called by Staples, 1975) play in maintaining order in a colonial society. In the words of Blauner (1969),

> The police are the most crucial institution maintaining the colonized status of Black Americans. . . . Police are key agents in the power equation as well as the drama of dehumanization. In the final analysis they do the dirty work for the larger system by restricting the striking back of Black rebels to skirmishes inside the ghetto, thus deflecting energies and attacks from the communities and institutions of the larger power structure. (pp. 404–405)

R. Austin (1983) was one of the first to empirically test the theory. Using violence rates before and after the decolonization of the Caribbean island of St. Vincent, he sought to determine whether crime rates declined following the removal of British colonial rule. Although he did find that crime rates declined after the end of colonial rule, this did not hold true when he examined data related to murder and manslaughter. Here, Austin noted that the increasing availability of guns might have played a role in this finding.

Tatum (2000) provided one of the more comprehensive tests of the theory. In her test of the theory, she formulated several propositions related to the model, including the connections among race, class, and oppression; how race and class are associated with the availability of social support; and issues related to alienation. Relying on survey data from African American, Mexican American, and White juniors and seniors at two high schools in a major southwestern urban area, she found limited support for the model.

The colonial model has applicability for racial groups who have been subjected to colonization (most notably, Native Americans, African Americans, and Mexican Americans). There have been mixed results when the theory has been tested, and there need to be more direct tests of it. Tatum (1994) also noted several additional concerns with the theory. First, as reflected in other structural models, she noted that two people can be exposed to the same oppression yet respond differently; in such instances, the model does not account for the different adaptations. Second, as with conflict theory, the model is difficult to test. Another weakness of the model is that it does not adequately address class issues (Tatum, 1994).

Criminologist Agozino (2003) also has considered colonialism in his ground-breaking work *Counter-Colonial Criminology: A Critique of Imperialist Reason*. In the work, he argued that "criminology is concentrated in former colonizing countries, and virtually absent in the former colonized countries, because criminology is a social science that served colonialism more directly than many other social sciences" (p. 1). More specifically, Agozino focused on

> how imperialism used criminological knowledge and how it can be seen as a criminological project—imprisonment with or without walls, a widening of the net of incarceration, and how the close kinship between the two fields of knowledge and power, criminology and imperialism, served both. (p. 6)

He also highlighted that the discipline of criminology originated "at the height of European colonialism" (p. 6). As a product of these origins, he noted that "criminology is dominated by scholars in former colonial centres of authority," which has led to what he considers "theoretical underdevelopment through the concealment of the bloody legacy of colonialist criminology" (p. 6). Although on the surface his ideas might seem controversial, it is clear that Agozino's work provides a critical new direction for race and crime theorists.

In general, however, the impact of colonialism on countries around the globe has been considerably neglected by criminologists. Notably, scholars have begun to revisit the role of colonialism in crime and justice (see Bosworth & Flavin, 2007; Gabbidon, 2009; Hawkins, 2011; Saleh-Hanna, 2008).

❖ Integrated and Nontraditional Theories on Race and Crime

Integrated theories of crime and nontraditional theories of race and crime receive less attention in crime and justice textbooks. Integrated theories incorporate more than one theory to explain criminal behavior. Nontraditional theories tend to have nontraditional ideas behind them. They also tend to be controversial. The integrated and nontraditional theories discussed here include structural-cultural theory; the abortion, race, and crime thesis; critical race theory; and Unnever and Gabbidon's (2011) recent theory of African American offending.

Structural-Cultural Theory

In the 1980s, Oliver (1984) proposed that to explain Black male criminality one needs to use an integrated theory combining structural conditions of African Americans and their cultural adaptations to such conditions. In one of his early articles, he explored Black males and their "tough guy image" or, as he called it, the "Black compulsive masculinity alternative." Oliver believes that because of racial oppression, Black males exhibit masculine behavior that places an overemphasis on "toughness, sexual conquest, manipulation, and thrill-seeking" (p. 199).

Oliver (1984) has argued that Black males act this way for two reasons. First, "lower-class Black males who adopt the compulsive masculinity alternative do so in order to mitigate low self-esteem and negative feelings which emerge as a consequence of their inability to enact the traditional masculine role" (p. 199). The second reason relates to the notion that males who adopt the masculine approach pass it on to other males. In later publications, Oliver (1989a, 1989b) applied his theory to sexual conquest and the adaptation of an Afrocentric perspective to ameliorate social problems in the African American community, and he also has examined violence among African Americans in barroom settings (Oliver, 1994). More recently, he has continued to refine his perspective (see Oliver, 2003, 2006).

One limitation of Oliver's perspective relates to the central role of low self-esteem. There has been some debate as to whether low self-esteem is really the central problem contributing to social problems among African Americans generally and African American males in particular (see Ross, 1992). Covington (2003) also has argued that Oliver's approach labels activities "race specific" that Whites also engage in. For example, many of the functions that bars serve for African Americans serve the same functions for Whites. Finally, Covington noted that in one of his studies, Oliver's "sample of African-American participants in violent transactions report that many of their fights seem to have been precipitated for non-race-specific reasons that apply equally well to violent Whites" (p. 266).

Abortion, Race, and Crime

In a highly controversial paper, Donohue and Levitt (2001) proposed that more than 50% of the crime drop in the 1990s could be attributed to the 1973 *Roe v. Wade* Supreme

Court decision that legalized abortion. They pointed to three important factors that support this thesis. First, they noted that the decline in crime coincided with the landmark decision and the period when those who would have been born would have reached their peak years of criminal activity (ages 18–24). Second, they suggested that the states that legalized abortion three years before the *Roe v. Wade* decision experienced earlier crime drops than the remaining states. Finally, they pointed to the fact that states that have the highest abortion rates also have had the largest declines in crime.

At the core of the theory are two premises. First, abortion reduces the pool of individuals who would later engage in crime. Second, the theory relates to race and crime in that, according to this view, abortion is not random. According to their thesis, those likely to have abortions include unwed women, teenagers, and Blacks. As such, because of a host of challenges often faced by such parents, they would be less than ideal parents and would place their children "at risk" for criminal activity. Donohue and Levitt's thesis, which has been widely disseminated in the scholarly community as well as in Levitt and Dubner's (2005) best-selling book *Freakonomics*, has garnered significant attention.

Among scholars, there has been vigorous debate about the veracity of their thesis, with some scholars supporting the thesis (Barro, 1999), and other researchers (some of whom conducted re-analyses of Donohue and Levitt's data) having found little to no support for the thesis (Chamlin, Myer, Sanders, & Cochran, 2008; Foote & Goetz, 2006; Hay & Evans, 2006; Joyce, 2004a, 2004b; Lott & Whitley, 2007). More recently, scholars have tried to apply the abortion and crime thesis to England and Wales and found no support (Kahane, Paton, & Simmons, 2008). Some noted scholars, such as Al Blumstein, have suggested that, although creative, the thesis does not give enough "attention to other factors, such as the decline in crack cocaine street dealing, the booming economy, and the efforts of police to keep guns away from juveniles" ("Renowned Criminologist Eschews Alarmist Theories," 1999, p. B5). Overall, although Donohue and Levitt (2004, 2006) have vigorously defended their perspective, there has not been a major shift toward using their thesis to explain the significant crime dip of the 1990s.

Critical Race Theory

In addition to theories based on biological, sociological, or other traditional perspectives, critical race theory (CRT), which emanated from the critical legal studies movement during the 1970s (K. Russell, 1999) and closely aligns with radical criminology (Delgado & Stefancic, 2001, p. 113), represents another perspective that has proved useful for contextualizing race and crime. Founded by Derrick Bell, Richard Delgado, and other legal scholars, in recent years it also has become more widely known in social science circles. The perspective has two goals. The first is to understand how the law is used to maintain White supremacy and continue to oppress people of color. The second is countering or stopping the use of the law to maintain White supremacy (K. Russell, 1999). It is here that critical race theorists have expressed concern about laws (e.g., "three strikes and you're out") and practices (e.g., racial profiling, **wrongful convictions**) that directly impact racial and ethnic minorities.

In addition to the aforementioned goals, there are several tenets of the perspective. First, racism is ever present in American society and is, thus, a daily occurrence.

The second tenet is referred to as "interest convergence," or the notion that Whites benefit (materially and in other ways) from racism, so they "have little incentive to eradicate it" (Delgado & Stefancic, 2001, p. 7). Third, critical race theorists believe race to be socially constructed, manufactured classifications. Here, critical race theorists are particularly concerned about the racialization of groups. Specifically, they express concern about "the ways the dominant society racializes different minority groups at different times, in response to shifting needs such as the labor market" (p. 8). Critical race theorists also believe that, because of their distinct histories and experiences, racial and ethnic minorities have a "unique voice of color" perspective to offer society.

There have been a few persistent criticisms of the theory. First, because much of the work is based on storytelling and personal narratives, which move away from "objective" or "value-free" analyses, some critics have concluded that the perspective is unscientific. Also, according to K. Russell (1999), some have argued that "CRT amounts to academic whining about women and minorities" (p. 183). Even with these criticisms, the perspective has become a standard legal theory, especially among women and minority legal scholars. In addition, criminologists have also started to use the theory as the foundation for studies in the discipline (Glover, 2009; Longazel, Parker, & Sun, 2011; Ross, 2010).

Theory of African American Offending

In 2011, Unnever and Gabbidon published their book *A Theory of African American Offending: Race, Racism, and Crime*. In the book, the authors argue that African Americans have had a unique experience in America that requires a specific theory to explain their overrepresentation in the justice system. Admittedly, there has been considerable interest in identifying the origins of overrepresentation in the justice system, but there has been less scholarship devoted to how racial discrimination contributes to the racial disparities in crime commission. Moreover, researchers have also neglected the nuances of African American offending, such as differences by ethnic group, gender, color, and so on. Unnever and Gabbidon believe any theory devoted to explaining African American offending needs to account for these within-group distinctions. Even so, they do not totally discount the value of general theories—they simply believe that such theories can be complementary to an overall race-centered perspective.

Unnever and Gabbidon (2011) assert that many African Americans share a similar worldview that has been informed by America's past and current history of racial injustice. Taking into account the frequency and intensity of this racial injustice, they believed that some African American offending is tied to these experiences. In particular, they "posit that the belief that the criminal justice system is racist heightens the tendency for African Americans to perceive criminal justice injustices and to react to them with shame, anger, hostility, and defiance" (p. 173). The authors continue:

> We hypothesize that these emotive responses substantially undermine the potential of the law to restrain offending behavior. That is, it is difficult for African Americans to believe that they should obey the law when they see it as a racist means to disrespect, harass, humiliate, bully, and unfairly imprison them. (p. 173)

Central to their theory is also the belief that exposure to racial discrimination is tied to offending. This connection has been supported in recent research (Burt, Simons, & Gibbons, 2012).

Unnever and Gabbidon (2011) believe that encountering racial discrimination has the potential to increase African American offending in two ways. First, they believe that experiencing racial discrimination will hinder African Americans from bonding with White-dominated social institutions such as schools. As predicted by social control theory, weak bonds to schools can result in increased offending. Unnever and Gabbidon also argue that negative stereotypes represent another form of racial discrimination that potentially increases the likelihood that African Americans will offend. The authors identify three pathways by which pejorative stereotypes can increase the likelihood of African American offending. First, drawing on the secondary deviance concept of labeling theory, the authors argue that, at times, African Americans will internalize the negative depictions that are often portrayed throughout American society and imitate them. Second, the authors believe that pejorative stereotypes negatively impact African Americans in the same way as racial discrimination. As such, the authors posit,

> Pejorative stereotypes of African Americans—particularly when there is chronic exposure—are debilitating. That is, they deplete ego resources as African Americans are continually confronted with negative stereotypes that "put them down." We assert that the negative emotions that arise can oscillate between depression-humiliation and anger-defiance. (p. 179)

Finally, the authors believe that encountering negative stereotypes increases the likelihood of African American offending because it also diminishes bonds with White-dominated social institutions.

Considering that their theory relies heavily on encountering racial discrimination and negative racial stereotypes, there is the potential to overpredict offending among African Americans because nearly every African American will be subjected to one or both of these. To address this concern, the authors devoted attention to the following question: Why do so many African Americans encounter racial discrimination but *do not* offend? They provide two concrete answers to the question. First, they argue that a key aspect of offending is tied to the degree of exposure to experiences with racial injustices. More specifically, the authors "argue that the degree of exposure to racial injustices should be measured across multiple dimensions, including . . . age of onset (i.e., At what age did the individual first encounter racial injustice?), who committed the racial injustice (e.g., Was it a person in authority, such as a school teacher or a police officer?), the frequency of exposure (i.e., How often was the individual exposed? Was it daily, weekly, or monthly?), and the duration of the exposure (i.e., Did it persist across the person's life course?). We further posit that scholars should assess the degree to which the individual is embedded in networks that both sensitize and reinforce perceptions of racial injustices" (p. 183).

Another factor that Unnever and Gabbidon (2011) believe distinguishes African Americans who are more likely to offend from those who don't resort to offending is racial socialization practices. Racial socialization refers to "specific verbal and non-verbal messages transmitted to younger generations for the development of values, attitudes, behaviors, and beliefs regarding the meaning and significance of race and racial stratification, intergroup and intragroup interactions, and personal and group identity" (Lesane-Brown, 2006, p. 400). Unnever and Gabbidon (2011) believe that through this process—which two-thirds of African American families practice—"parents proactively attempt to prepare their children for encounters with criminal justice injustices, racial discrimination, and the invidious consequences of being depreciatively stereotyped" (p. 183). The authors discuss several types of racial socialization practices, but they generally suggest that neglecting to racially socialize African American children "puts them at greater risk for experiencing the deleterious consequences of racial injustices that are related to offending (e.g., anger-hostility-defiance-depression and weak social bonds)" (p. 184). Unnever and Gabbidon believe that in the absence of parents racially socializing their children, children will construct their racial identity from peers and street culture. The authors also believe that African Americans whose parents "overly emphasize the mistrust of whites and encourage their children to become overly defiant in the presence of racism are likely to develop stigma sensitivity and stigma consciousness…researchers have found that these heightened states of sensitivities may cause African Americans to have less self-control, a factor that is unequivocally related to offending" (p. 185). A schematic presentation of the entire theory is presented in Figure 3.4.

Unnever and Gabbidon (2011) also provide insights into the nuances of differences in African American offending tied to within-group characteristics such as gender, place, and ethnicity. The authors posit that "gender differences in offending are related to gender disparities in the *degree* to which African American males and females encounter criminal justice injustices, racial discrimination, and racial injustices" (p. 192). Since African American males are more likely to encounter these despicable practices, they are more susceptible than African American females to the deleterious consequences of them—including offending. The authors also suggest that the differences in racial socialization practices between African American males and females account for differences in offending. Specifically, "African American parents are more likely to socialize their daughters with a greater sense of pride than their sons. The research shows that a strong positive racial identity decreases the likelihood of offending and enhances academic commitment and performance" (p. 193). Positive racial socialization that occurs in churches—attended by African American females more than African American males— is another reason for lower offending among African American females.

Unnever and Gabbidon readily recognized—as demonstrated in more than a century of community studies beginning with Du Bois's *The Philadelphia Negro* (1899)— the role of place or the disadvantaged places that African Americans live and its influence on offending. The authors devote considerable attention to the contribution of segregation and neighborhood disadvantage to African American offending. Finally, the authors also mention the difference in offending across the ethnic spectrum of Black Americans. Unnever and Gabbidon believe that a central part of the difference in offending among the various Black ethnic groups is tied to their level of acceptance of the worldview of native Black Americans. In particular, the authors believe that "…less offending should occur among first generation foreign-born blacks who have immigrated to the United States" (p. 202). Moreover, once the immigrants embrace the worldview held by native born Black Americans, they hypothesize that "second generation blacks will approach the same level of offending as native-born African Americans, everything else being equal" (p. 203).

Figure 3.4

Theory of African American Offending

Source: Unnever & Gabbidon (2011).

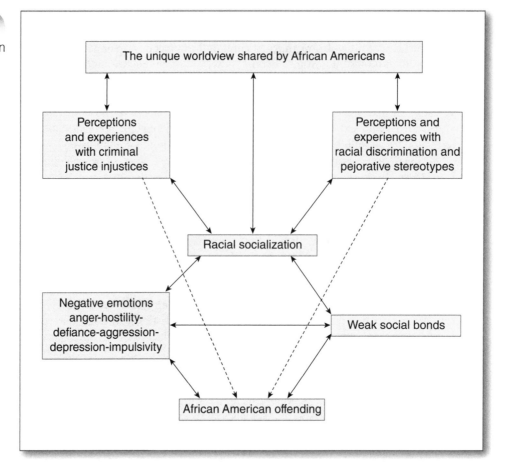

On the whole, the response to Unnever and Gabbidon's theory has been generally positive (Arnold, 2014; Bonnet, 2012; Hawkins, 2014; Lee, 2012; Shedd, 2015; Polizzi, 2013). Moreover, the limited tests of the theory have found support for its basic tenets (Unnever, 2014), as well as its nuances tied to the differing worldviews of native-born Black Americans and foreign-born Blacks (Unnever & Gabbidon, 2015). Amid the praise, criticisms also surfaced. Some authors challenged the assertion that African Americans have a uniquely oppressive experience in America given that Native Americans were also brutally treated (Kindle, 2012). Scholars have expressed concern that the schematic presentation of the theory does not include mention of gender and community factors as being central, as well as the lack of discussion about lifespan development among African American males (Kindle, 2012).

In closing, it is likely that in years to come there will not only be additional tests/articulations of Unnever and Gabbidon's theory (see Unnever, 2015), there will be the continuing realization that general theories alone are not the answer to understanding the complexities of crime as they relate to African Americans or other racial/ethnic groups.

❖ Conclusion

Just as there is little consensus among criminologists about the causes of crime (Cooper, Walsh, & Ellis, 2010; Ellis & Walsh, 1999), there is even more debate about which theory best explains racial patterns in crime and victimization. However, one thing is apparent from the coverage in this chapter—numerous theories have been applied to the question of race and crime (see Table 3.2). In the beginning, scholars turned to the biology of African Americans, Native Americans, and Asian Americans to answer this question; however, over the years, this has changed. The decline in popularity of the biological approach gave rise to the sociological approach. Beginning with scholars such as Du Bois, the sociological approach continues to be a mainstay of those interested in studying race and crime. Subcultural approaches seem to have also maintained their place in the race and crime literature. Conflict theory now represents one of the more popular theoretical frameworks when studying race and crime. In addition, scholars are beginning to re-examine the role of colonization in race, crime, and justice.

There are clearly limits to the utility of these various theories. Even with the increasing scholarship on race, crime, and gender (Gabbidon, 2015), there remains a dearth of knowledge as to minority female offending. It is also noteworthy that much

Table 3.2

Theoretical Contexts of Race and Crime

Theory	Context
Biological	White superiority, genetic inferiority, low IQ, physical characteristics, evolutionary factors
Biosocial	Interaction of biological and environmental factors
Sociological	Social conditions, social structure, heterogeneity, mobility, mass migration, impact of mass incarceration on communities
Culture conflict	Cultural differences, violation of social norms within a community
Subcultural	Street culture, code of honor rooted in violence
Conflict	Racial discrimination in criminal justice
Colonial/counter-colonial	Role of imperialism, criminology's role in imperialism
Structural-cultural	Social structure, culture, and Black masculinity
Legalized abortion	Unborn "at-risk" children
Critical race theory	Law maintains White supremacy
Theory of African American Offending	Unique worldview, race discrimination, perceptions of criminal injustice, racial stereotypes, racial socialization

of the existing theoretical research on race and crime is centered on African Americans (and males in particular). While it is obvious that the research on Latinos and crime is on the rise, scholars need to test the existing theories to determine their relevancy for other racial/ethnic groups. In fact, with Unnever and Gabbidon arguing for race/ethnic-centered perspectives, this approach might be the norm in decades to come.

Finally, with the return of the biological-sociological debate in the form of biosocial criminology, the discipline has come full circle. Moreover, with the discoveries tied to the Human Genome Project, scholars have become even more interested in the influence of genetics on human behavior and also in explaining racial disparities in offending. When one reviews the various theories, it seems safe to say that, although the research methodologies have become more sophisticated, many of the same ideas presented about race and crime 100 years ago remain popular today. Chapter 4 looks at the police and their historical and contemporary roles in handling race and crime.

Discussion Questions

1. Why are theoretical perspectives so critical for race and crime researchers?

2. Do you believe biosocial perspectives can help explain racial differences in crime trends?

3. Which sociological theory best explains racial differences in crime trends?

4. What is colonialism? How does it explain the disproportionate involvement of racial and ethnic minorities in certain criminal offenses?

5. Do you believe race/ethnic-specific theories are necessary? Why or why not?

Internet Exercises

1. View the index offenses presented at http://www.fbi.gov/ucr/ucr.htm and discuss which of the theories presented in this chapter can provide an explanation for homicide trends by race.

2. Spend 30 minutes at the Eugenics Archives (http://www.eugenicsarchive.org/eugenics/) examining some of the history and materials related to the Eugenics Movement.

Internet Sites

Eugenics Archive: http://www.eugenicsarchive.org/eugenics/

W. E. B. Du Bois: http://www.pbs.org/wnet/jimcrow/stories_people_dubois.html

Supplemental materials for *Race and Crime* are available online at
study.sagepub.com/gabbidon4e.

CHAPTER 4

Policing

Those of us in law enforcement must redouble our efforts to resist bias and prejudice. We must better understand the people we serve and protect—by trying to know, deep in our gut, what it feels like to be a law-abiding young black man walking on the street and encountering law enforcement . . . . We must work—in the words of New York City Police Commissioner Bill Bratton—to really see each other . . . . But the "seeing" needs to flow in both directions. Citizens also need to really see the men and women of law enforcement . . . . They need to give them the space and respect to do their work, well and properly.

—Comey (2015)

Police are on the front line of the criminal justice system. This means that a citizen's introduction to the administration of justice often begins with contact with a police officer. Most Americans have positive attitudes toward the police, although minorities have always been less likely to view the police as favorably as Whites do. During the 1960s, when the National Opinion Research Center conducted a national survey for the President's Commission on Law Enforcement and the Administration of Justice (1967), they found that 67% of the general public responded that their police did an "excellent" or "good" job, and 77% responded that police did a "pretty good" to "very good" job of protecting people in their neighborhoods. Non-Whites (primarily Blacks) gave a rating of "very good" half as often as Whites and a "not so good" rating twice as often. Blacks were also more likely to view the police as discourteous. In 1979, according to the National Crime Survey, while 54% of White victims of crime evaluated their local police as "good," only 25% of Blacks and 19.2% of Hispanic victims did (Carter, 1983).

This pattern of differences in levels of confidence by race and ethnicity continues today. For example, between 2002–2011, the majority of Whites continued to have the most confidence in the police. The confidence of Blacks increased in 2011 to

43%, although it was still much lower than in 2005 when it was at its highest level in the decade (Gabbidon & Taylor Greene, 2013). More recently, Blacks and Hispanics continue to have less confidence than Whites in the police (see Figure 4.1).

While there are many factors that have contributed to this reduction in confidence in the police, aggressive tactics, "shadow immigration enforcement" (see Sweeney, 2014), homeland security/terrorism reduction initiatives, recurring incidents of use of deadly force/brutality, and racial profiling continue to frame confidence in the police. In their book *Police in a Multicultural Society,* Barlow and Barlow (2000, p. 53) state, "Police have historically enforced laws that are today widely regarded

Figure 4.1

Good Cop, Bad Cop

Source: "Latino confidence in local police lower than among whites," Pew Research Center, Washington, DC (August 2014) http://www.pewresearch.org/fact-tank/2014/08/28/latino-confidence-in-local-police-lower-than-among-whites/

Note: Survey conducted Aug. 20–24, 2014. Voluntary responses of "None" and "Don't know/Refused" not shown. Blacks and Whites include only non-Hispanics. Hispanics are of any race.

Source: Pew Research Center/USA Today (http://www.pewresearch.org/fact-tank/2014/08/28/latino-confidence-in-local-police-lower-than-among-whites).

Good Cop, Bad Cop
How much confidence do you have in police officers in your community ...

... to do a good job of enforcing the law?

	JUST SOME/VERY LITTLE	A GREAT DEAL/FAIR AMOUNT
Hispanic	37%	63%
Black	47	52
White	16	83

... to not use excessive force on suspects?

Hispanic	54	45
Black	59	36
White	24	74

... to treat Hispanics and Whites equally?

Hispanic	51	46
Black	55	41
White	25	72

... to treat Blacks and Whites equally?

Hispanic	48	47
Black	62	36
White	27	72

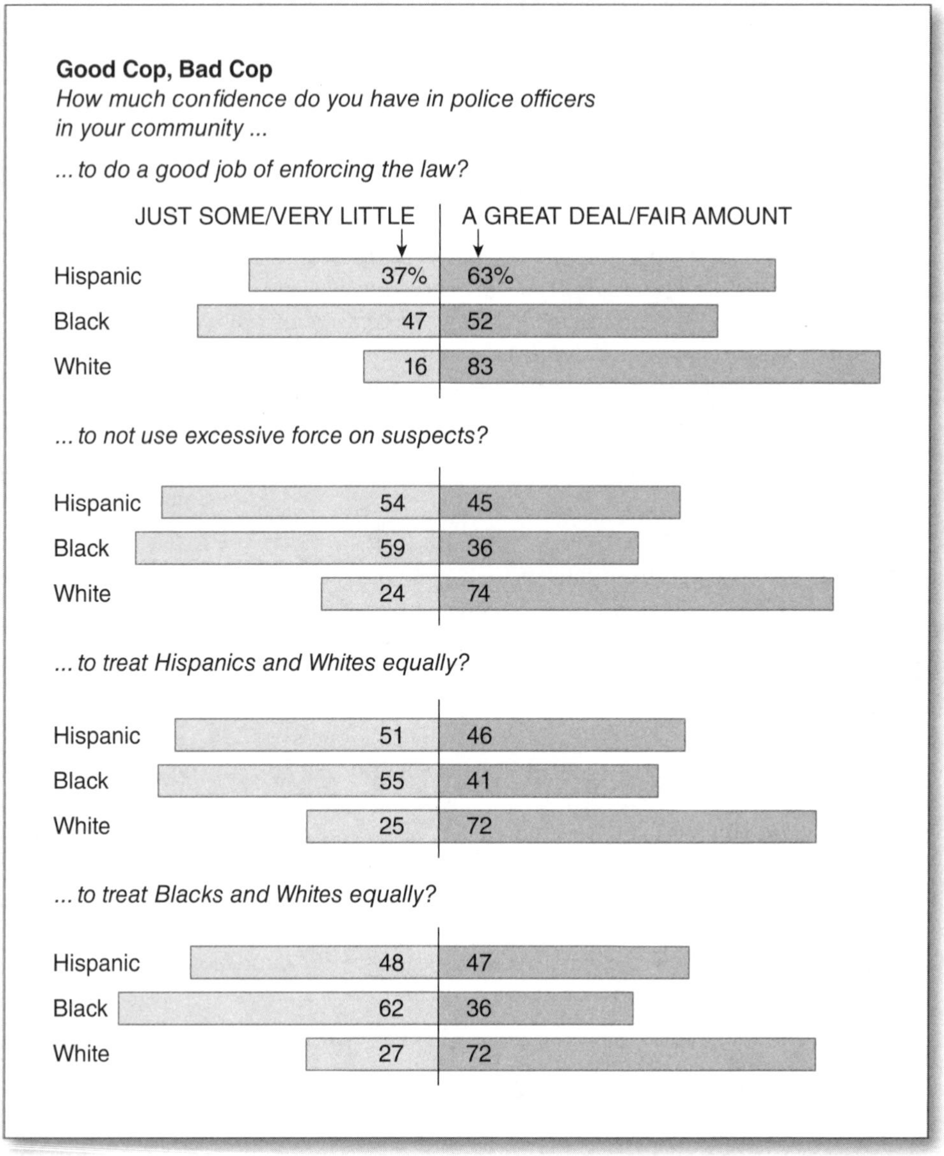

as violations of the human rights of racial and ethnic minorities." Russell-Brown (2004) noted, "the historically oppressive relationship between police and African-Americans is lost in contemporary discussions" (p. 66). That is why FBI Director Comey's remarks on February 12, 2014 (Abraham Lincoln's birthday), at Georgetown University in Washington, DC, are so important. Not only did he acknowledge the history of poor relations between police and communities of color, he also emphasized that everyone has a vested interest in addressing it. Today police agencies are more diversified, professional, and technologically advanced than at any other time in our history. There are more minority, female, and educated officers. Many departments have a website, utilize computer mapping, and have access to numerous databases and information systems that increase their capabilities to "serve and protect." Agencies can now issue crime alerts and use Reverse 911 calls to inform residents of emergencies.

Sherman (2002) described a criminal justice paradox characterized by improvements in fairness and effectiveness but not in public trust and confidence. He identified three domains that affect public trust: the conduct and practices of the criminal justice system, the changing values and expectations of the culture the system serves, and the images of the system presented in electronic media. Too many deadly police confrontations with Black males during the past two years confirm that these domains of trust are still applicable (see Box 4.1).

BOX 4.1

Police Deadly Confrontations

The killings of men of color by police officers has garnered media attention and incited peaceful demonstrations, civil disturbances, policy initiatives, task forces, research, and a search for how to resolve this dilemma. Even though the February 2012 killing of Treyvon Martin in Sanford, Florida, by George Zimmerman was not a deadly police officer confrontation, it garnered public attention and galvanized Americans. At that time, it was unclear what role, if any, the Sanford Police Department had played in the incident. Kimani Gray, 16 years old, was killed in Brooklyn, New York, in March 2013 after allegedly pointing a gun at plainclothes police officers. In July 2014, the killing of Eric Garner in Staten Island, New York, by a police officer using an illegal choke hold was the first of several incidents that year. Garner was stopped, questioned about selling untaxed cigarettes, and asked to move on. Garner's death was recorded on video, and he can be heard several times telling police officers that he cannot breathe. After the officer involved was not charged, protesters around the country chanted, "I can't breathe" as they marched. Michael Brown, an unarmed Black teenager, was shot six times following an altercation with Officer Darren Wilson in Ferguson, Missouri, on August 9, 2014. Brown was allegedly shot while his hands were raised in submission. Tamir Rice, a 12-year-old child, was shot and killed by two Cleveland, Ohio, police officers in November 2014 after he allegedly pointed a toy gun at the officers who responded to a call that he was pointing his toy gun aimlessly in a park. The cops who confronted Rice shot him several times within seconds after exiting their patrol car and didn't give him a chance to drop his toy gun. In April 2015, within days of each other, there were two deaths of Black males, Walter Scott in North Charleston, SC, shot in the back while fleeing after a

(Continued)

(Continued)

traffic stop, and Freddie Gray, killed while in police custody in Baltimore, MD. The death of Freddie Gray in Baltimore, MD, led to peaceful marches, civil unrest, police officer injuries, and considerable property damage in various locations.

The public outcry has forced policy makers, citizens, and law enforcement officials to re-examine the historic conflict between people of color and law enforcement agencies. Policing in America has an institutional history that includes more punitive social control of Blacks and other minorities. Since the 1700s, slave catchers served as a bastion of White supremacy to protect the profits of White slaveholders and remind slaves of their inferior position in American society. In the North, Blacks also dealt with oppressive and dehumanizing police tactics, although the North was seen as a place of refuge during the great migration. Fast forward to the contemporary era, and many Blacks still believe that the police treat Blacks and other minorities differently than Whites. Also, Whites are often more likely to see police officers as individuals who seek to serve and protect without bias or prejudice. For example, a recent national survey conducted by the Pew Research Center found that Blacks are twice as likely as Whites to believe that the killing of Michael Brown raises important questions about race that need to be discussed (Pew Research Center, 2014b). The survey also found that the public is divided over whether the police went too far in responding to the Mike Brown shooting protests in Ferguson: 65% of African Americans and 33% of Whites polled believed that the police went too far (Pew Research Center, 2014b).

Black and White Americans experience policing differently. Crime control policies designed to maintain order and circumvent more serious crimes, such as "stop and frisk" and "broken windows policing," often place people of color under more scrutiny. For example, in Ferguson, Missouri, in 2013, Blacks were 3.5 times as likely as Whites to be stopped by police (Office of the Missouri Attorney General, 2014). The majority of Black drivers (57%) who were stopped in Ferguson were stopped for a license or equipment problem, while the majority of White drivers were stopped for moving violations (Office of the Missouri Attorney General, 2014). Although Blacks are more likely to have vehicle code violations than Whites, these differences do not account for the disproportionate rate of stops of Black drivers for non-moving violations (Office of the Missouri Attorney General, 2014). The disparities mentioned above provide context to the outrage that many Ferguson residents and citizens throughout the world feel about the killing of Michael Brown.

A similar problem was reported in New York City. Unfortunately, many New Yorkers of color have been subjected to aggressive police tactics for minor offenses. The killing of Eric Garner by a New York City police officer serves as an example of the threat that order-maintenance policing poses to minorities living in inner cities. Between 2003 and 2013, 82% of New Yorkers who were arrested or received a summons were Black and Hispanic (Chauhan, Fera, Welsh, Balazon, & Misshula, 2014). Yet, order-maintenance policies such as broken windows policing and stop and frisk have only had a modest impact on the serious crime rate (Jones-Brown, Stoudt, Johnston, & Moran, 2013) .

Since the killing of two police officers in New York City in 2015, many police officers nationwide have argued that policing is increasingly dangerous and that many police organizations are working in neighborhoods that are essentially battlefields. Thus, throughout the country the turn to military tactics to police urban areas is an accepted ideology in many law enforcement agencies. According to data from the National Law Enforcement Officers Memorial Fund (2015), which maintains the largest database of police officer line-of-duty deaths, 2013 had 107 law enforcement deaths, compared to 117 in 2014. Even though law enforcement firearms-related fatalities increased from 38 in 2013 to 48 in 2014, firearms-related fatalities for these two years are the lowest for the decade.

1. What do you think is the primary cause of increased police killings of minority males?

2. What is the best approach for reducing the number of minorities killed by the police?

The "terrorist era of policing" (Forst, 2003) that began after the 9/11 terrorist attacks has resulted in less community involvement, increased federalism, loss of civil liberties, greater reliance on private security, militarization, and a propensity toward errors of justice. The 2001 USA PATRIOT Act (and its subsequent reauthorizations) was enacted to counter terrorism, although it is viewed by some as infringing on the rights of citizens. Today there is increased concern about privacy and due process for all Americans, as well as closer scrutiny of "new" minority groups, including Middle Easterners and Muslims, and those who are identified as belonging to groups perceived as threatening (although they may not be), such as Sikhs. Has the shift in focus to terrorism, terrorists, and homeland security improved or exacerbated the strained relationship between police and minority groups?

The goals of this chapter are to provide an overview of policing in America, present the history of race and policing minority groups in America, and examine several contemporary issues in race and policing including police deviance, police bias and racial profiling, militarization, immigration law enforcement, and community policing.

Our focus is primarily on policing in municipal (local) police agencies, for three reasons. First, many historical accounts of police usually focus on cities like Boston (MA), New York City (NY), Philadelphia (PA), Chicago (IL), and Charleston (SC). Second, most sworn officers are employed at the local level in cities and counties. Third, race and policing continues to be a critical issue in the nation's urban areas. We forgo an extensive overview of policing that can be found in most introductory law enforcement and criminal justice textbooks. The overview does describe the major **components of the policing industry** in America and recent minority employment trends. The historical information on the experiences of Native Americans, African Americans, Asian Americans, Latinos, and immigrant Whites presented in Chapter 1 continues in this chapter, with an emphasis on policing from the colonial era to the present. By examining the past, we are able to better understand the complexities of race and policing that define the relationship Director Comey refers to in the chapter's opening quotation.

❖ Overview of Policing in America

Police are the most visible symbol of governmental authority in our country. There are more than 18,000 federal, local, and state agencies, which vary in size and are bureaucratic and quasi-military in structure. In addition, there are Native American (tribal) police agencies, special police agencies with limited jurisdiction (e.g., transit police), and private police. The roles and functions of police agencies are specified in federal and state statutes and local ordinances. In municipal agencies, the police role consists primarily of maintaining the social order, preventing and controlling crime, and enforcing the law. Police have a considerable amount of discretion (decisional latitude) and are authorized to use force in the performance of their duties. After 9/11, the increased emphasis on homeland security changed the role of local law enforcement to include "greater surveillance capabilities, enhanced punishments for crimes related to terrorism, and . . . improving relationships and communication between federal and local law enforcement" (Oliver, 2007, in Oliver, 2009, p. 254). Today, as in the past, federal, state, and local police agencies continue to work together to address problems, including gangs, human trafficking, illegal immigration, narcotics law enforcement, and cybercrime.

Diversity in law enforcement agencies has improved in the past 50 years as a result of several factors, including legislation, litigation, and recruitment efforts. Diversity varies from one jurisdiction to another, and the progress made in many larger agencies differs from more limited progress in some smaller agencies and locales. "A wide range of barriers may undermine diversity at every stage of the recruiting, hiring, and selection process" (U.S. DOJ & EEOC, 2015, p. 3). The majority of police officers are White males, even in many locales where minorities are a large percentage of the population (Ashkenas & Park, 2014; Badger, Keating, & Elliott, 2014). Between 1990 and 2000, minority representation in large city police agencies increased from 29.8% in 1990 to 38.1%, Hispanic representation increased from 9.2% to 14.1% (the largest increase), followed by Blacks (18.4% to 20.1%; Reaves & Hickman, 2002b). At that time, minority officers outnumbered White officers in some agencies, although the ratio of minority police officers to minority group members in large cities had increased only slightly, from .59 in 1990 to .63 in 2000. This means that there were 63 minority officers for every 100 minority citizens. The ratio for Blacks increased to .74, for Latinos to .56, and for other minorities to .37 (Reaves & Hickman, 2002b). Although many officers are employed in large cities, 63% of local police departments only employ between 2 and 24 sworn officers (Reaves & Hickman, 2002a).

The Bureau of Justice Statistics has not provided information on minority and female representation in local police agencies since 2007. At that time, there were an estimated 12,575 local police agencies that employed 463,000 full-time sworn personnel (Reaves, 2010, p. 6). Table 4.1 shows the race and ethnicity of sworn and nonsworn employees in state and local government protective services reported by the U.S. Census. Between 2006 and 2010, there were more than 2,766,630 sworn male and female police, 64.6% were White, 18.7% were Black, and 12% were Latino (U.S. Census, 2013). The Bureau of Labor Statistics (BLS, 2014) indicates that of the 680,000 police and sheriffs, 1.8% were Asian, 15.6% were Black, 13.2% were Latino, and 12.4% were women. Sometimes relying on percentages masks the actual representation of minorities in policing. Minority representation in smaller police departments as well as in state and federal agencies is still relatively low.

At the federal level, the U.S. Attorney General is the chief law enforcement officer in the country and the U.S. Department of Justice (DOJ) is the lead agency for enforcing the law, preventing and controlling crime, and ensuring fair and impartial administration of justice (U.S. DOJ, 2015). DOJ works closely with other federal, state, and local law enforcement agencies; the U.S. Congress; and law enforcement interest groups. In 2002, the Homeland Security Act created the **Department of Homeland Security** (DHS) in order to provide a more integrated approach to security in the United States. The legislation transferred all or part of 22 federal agencies to the DHS, making it the largest employer of federal law enforcement officers, and created the Transportation Security Administration (Reaves & Bauer, 2003). Prior to the creation of the DHS, the Department of Justice (DOJ) and Department of Transportation (DOT) were the largest employers of federal officers with arrest and firearm authority. In 2008, there were approximately 120,000 federal full-time police personnel authorized to arrest and carry firearms (Reaves, 2012). Most federal law enforcement officers are employed by the DHS, U.S. Customs and Border Protection (CBP), the FBI, and U.S. Immigration and Customs Enforcement (ICE; see Table 4.2). Most federal officers are White males, and about one-third belong to a racial or ethnic minority group (Reaves, 2012; see Figure 4.2). Throughout the history of American policing, efforts to make it a more diverse profession often were met with resistance by both police officers and citizens.

❖ Historical Overview of Race and Policing

Historical accounts of the police often exclude the horrendous treatment of minorities by the police, and instead focus on the need for social control of these "threatening" groups. Facts about policing minorities and some White immigrants in earlier centuries are often omitted from criminal justice and law enforcement textbooks. It is impossible to separate the history of policing minority groups from the general history of the experiences of minorities in the United States, which were presented in Chapter 1. Similar to their treatment by most segments of our society, Native Americans, African Americans, Asian Americans, Latino/Hispanic Americans, and some White immigrants were treated differently (from the so-called law-abiding native Whites) by the police. Here, we provide (a) a brief summary of the history of policing in America, beginning with the colonial period to the present; and (b) a discussion of the historical treatment of racial/ethnic groups by the police. It is important to remember that historical research on some groups is still limited and that policing practices varied considerably from one time to another and from one locale to another.

According to Walker and Katz (2002), "American policing is a product of its English heritage" (p. 24). During the colonial era, there were no formal police departments. Like their British counterparts, the colonists initially made policing the responsibility of every citizen and later utilized the sheriff, constable, and watch system (Uchida, 1997). During this time, there were regional differences in policing. For example, in some places, like Boston and New Amsterdam, NY, night watches were established, whereas in the South, slave patrols were more common. Over time, social disorder and crime increased so much, especially in Northern cities, that the early forms of policing proved ineffective and were gradually replaced with more formal police agencies patterned after the British model (Fogelson, 1977; Lane, 1967; Monkkonen, 1981; Richardson, 1970). Unlike the British police, American police agencies were decentralized, locally controlled, and influenced by politics. "The history of American police during the nineteenth century is the history of separate forces in separate cities" (Emsley, 1983, p. 101). For example, White immigrants dominated police forces in some Northern cities, and slave patrollers in the South were usually poorer Whites. Slave patrols relied on a more military style of policing. The first African American police were "free men of color" who served in police organizations in New Orleans between 1805 and 1830. For the most part, they were responsible for slaves (W. Dulaney, 1996). D. Johnson (1981) mentioned that social tensions among immigrants, Blacks, and native Whites often resulted in conflicts and crime. Examples of these conflicts include verbal and physical abuse of abolitionists, race riots, labor strikes, and draft riots (Barlow & Barlow, 2000). Outside the urban areas, especially on the frontier, policing was characterized as

Table 4.1

Race and Ethnicity of Sworn and Nonsworn Employees in State and Local Government Protective Services by Sex and Race/Ethnicity, 2006–2010

| Subject | Total, Race and Ethnicity | Hispanic or Latino | | Not Hispanic or Latino, One Race | | | | |
		White Alone Hispanic or Latino	All Other Hispanic or Latino	White Alone	Black or African American Alone	AIAN Alone	Asian Alone	NHPI Alone
Protective service: sworn								
Total, both sexes								
Number	2,970,135	220,540	137,010	1,885,850	578,930	27,285	61,325	8,580
Percentage	100.0	7.4	4.6	63.5	19.5	0.9	2.1	0.3
Male								
Number	2,378,150	178,580	108,285	1,583,425	389,255	20,515	51,790	6,660
Percentage	80.1	6.0	3.6	53.3	13.1	0.7	1.7	0.2
Female								
Number	591,980	41,960	28,725	302,425	189,670	6,770	9,540	1,920
Percentage	19.9	1.4	1.0	10.2	6.4	0.2	0.3	0.1
Protective service: nonsworn								
Total, both sexes								
Number	287,175	18,735	12,370	204,990	36,085	1,935	5,765	610
Percentage	100.0	6.5	4.3	71.4	12.6	0.7	2.0	0.2
Male								
Number	136,140	9,635	5,595	98,100	14,985	1,025	3,265	155
Percentage	47.4	3.4	1.9	34.2	5.2	0.4	1.1	0.1
Female								
Number	151,035	9,100	6,770	106,890	21,095	905	2,505	450
Percentage	52.6	3.2	2.4	37.2	7.3	0.3	0.9	0.2

Source: U.S. Department of Commerce.

Notes: The EEO Tabulation is sponsored by four Federal agencies.

a. AIAN refers to American Indian and Alaska Native.

b. NHPI refers to Native Hawaiian and Other Pacific Islander.

c. X means that the estimate is not applicable or not available.

| | Not Hispanic or Latino, Two or More Races | | | | | | |
White and Black	White and AIAN	White and Asian	Black and AIAN	NHPI[b] and White (Hawaii only)	NHPI and Asian (Hawaii only)	NHPI and Asian and White (Hawaii only)	Balance of not Hispanic or Latino
7,240	13,360	8,390	3,635	X[c]	X	X	17,980
0.2	0.4	0.3	0.1	X	X	X	0.6
5,825	10,510	6,705	2,725	X	X	X	13,875
0.2	0.4	0.2	0.1	X	X	X	0.5
1,415	2,850	1,690	910	X	X	X	4,105
0.0	0.1	0.1	0.0	X	X	X	0.1
1,260	1,820	1,330	280	X	X	X	2,000
0.4	0.6	0.5	0.1	X	X	X	0.7
635	785	630	20	X	X	X	1,305
0.2	0.3	0.2	0.0	X	X	X	0.5
630	1,035	700	260	X	X	X	695
0.2	0.4	0.2	0.1	X	X	X	0.2

Table 4.2

Female and Minority Federal Officers in Agencies Employing 500 or More Full-Time Officers, September 2008

			Percent of Full-Time Federal Officers					
					Racial/Ethnic Minority			
Agency	Number of Officers	Female	Total Minority	American Indian/ Alaska Natives[a]	Black/ African American[a]	Asian/ Pacific Islander[a]	Hispanic/ Latino Origin	Two or More Races[a]
U.S. Customs and Border Protection	37,482	12.1%	45.3%	0.4%	3.5%	3.3%	38.0%	–%
Federal Bureau of Prisons	16,993	13.6	40.0%	1.4	24.1	1.6	12.9	0.0
Federal Bureau of Investigation	12,925	18.8	18.1%	0.4	5.4	3.9	8.1	0.2
U.S. Immigration and Customs Enforcement	12,679	15.7	37.1%	0.7	8.3	3.8	24.3	–
U.S. Secret Service[b]	5,226	10.5	19.7%	0.6	11.2	2.7	5.2	–
Administrative Office of the U.S. Courts	4,767	46.2	33.8%	0.6	14.3	1.8	16.5	0.7
Drug Enforcement Administration	4,388	9.6	19.6%	0.4	7.1	2.6	9.3	0.0
U.S. Marshals Service[b]	3,359	10.2	19.4%	0.7	7.4	2.2	9.6	0.1
Veterans Health Administration	3,175	7.8	37.2%	1.7	23.5	2.6	9.4	0.0
Internal Revenue Service	2,655	31.5	25.5%	0.1	11.0	5.7	8.5	0.2
Bureau of Alcohol, Tobacco, Firearms and Explosives	2,562	13.0	18.9%	1.1	8.5	2.1	5.8	1.6

Agency	Number of Officers	Female	Total Minority	Racial/Ethnic Minority				
				American Indian/ Alaska Natives[a]	Black/ African American[a]	Asian/ Pacific Islander[a]	Hispanic/ Latino Origin	Two or More Races[a]
U.S. Postal Inspection Service	2,324	22.2	36.5%	0.3	20.4	5.1	10.8	0.0
U.S. Capitol Police	1,637	18.5	37.1%	0.3	29.7	2.1	4.9	0.0
National Park Service—Rangers	1,416	18.6	12.7%	3.0	2.1	2.2	4.8	0.6
Bureau of Diplomatic Security	1,049	10.8	19.2%	0.7	8.1	4.0	6.4	0.0
Pentagon Force Protection Agency	725	12.4	51.2%	0.8	43.0	1.5	4.3	1.5
U.S. Forest Service	648	15.9	17.3%	4.8	4.2	1.5	6.8	0.0
U.S. Fish and Wildlife Service	603	8.8	15.8%	3.6	1.8	2.3	7.1	0.8
U.S. Park Police	547	13.2	21.8%	0.2	11.9	3.3	5.9	0.5

Percent of Full-Time Federal Officers

Source: Bureau of Justice Statistics, Census of Federal Law Enforcement Officers, 1996 and 2008.

Note: Includes personnel with arrest and firearm authority in U.S. territories. Detail may not sum to total due to rounding. See table 5 for sex and race data for personnel in offices of inspectors general.

a. Excludes persons of Hispanic/Latino origin.

b. Percentages are from 2004 because agency did not provide data for 2008.

–Less than 0.05%.

Figure 4.2

Percentage
of Female
and Minority
Federal Officers
With Arrest
and Firearm
Authority, 1996
and 2008

Source: Bureau of
Justice Statistics,
Census of Federal Law
Enforcement Officers,
1996 and 2008.

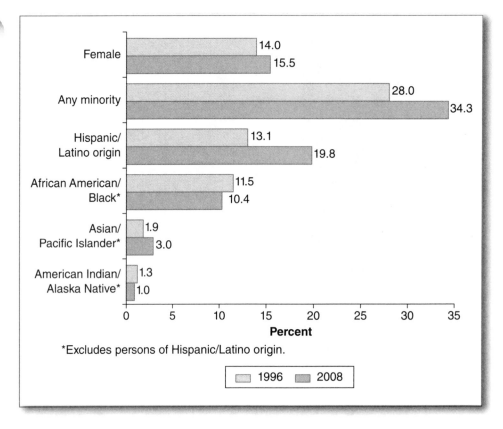

*Excludes persons of Hispanic/Latino origin.

vigilante in nature. Although paid police forces that emerged in the 1800s were viewed as better than the night-and-day watches of the colonial era, social disorder and crime continued to be challenges. This led to the formation of private police, such as the Pinkerton Agency, and the reorganization of public police.

Many law enforcement and criminal justice textbooks allude to two important reform efforts. The first, during the late 1800s, attempted to reduce political control of the police. The next occurred during the early 20th century and focused on developing more professional police forces (McCamey, Scaramella, & Cox, 2003; Thurman, Zhao, & Giacomazzi, 2001; Walker & Katz, 2002). These reforms are important because some police were abusing their powers and resorting to unsavory practices such as corruption and the "third degree" (discussed later). Although the reform movement in the beginning of the 20th century was significant, much-needed personnel, policy, and training reforms did not occur until much later. During the 1960s, police were closely scrutinized following a great deal of civil unrest and several U.S. Supreme Court decisions, including *Mapp v. Ohio* (1961), *Escobedo v. Illinois* (1964), and *Miranda v. Arizona* (1966). Between 1970 and the present, policing has changed dramatically due to the convergence of several previously mentioned factors, including the hiring of minorities and women, technological developments, community policing, and the research revolution.

Kelling and Moore (1988) identified three eras in the history of policing often cited in many law enforcement textbooks: the political (1840s to early 1900s), reform (1930s to 1960s), and community problem-solving eras (1970s to present). Williams and Murphy (1990) viewed Kelling and Moore's analysis as incomplete:

> The fact that the legal order not only countenanced but sustained slavery, segregation, and discrimination for most of our nation's history—and the fact that the police were bound to uphold that order—set a pattern for police behavior and attitudes toward minority communities that has persisted until the present day. . . . The existence of this pattern . . . meant that, while important changes were occurring in policing during our Nation's history, members of minority groups benefited less than others from these changes. (p. 2)

The following sections describe how the police (and other governmental officials) interacted with minority groups to uphold the legal and social order throughout American history.

Policing Native Americans

In the foreword to F. Cohen's (1971) classic book *Handbook of Federal Indian Law*, Robert L. Bennett and Frederick M. Hart described the complexities of understanding Indian law due to the numerous treaties, statutes, judicial decisions, and administrative rulings that emerged during the 1800s and 1900s. F. Cohen noted further that "Indian country" must be viewed temporally because federal and tribal law had changed over time. For example, although the Act of May 19, 1796 set the boundary between Indian country and the United States, by 1799, the boundary was changed to give federal courts jurisdiction over U.S. citizens who committed crimes against Indians. The Act of March 3, 1817 further extended federal law to prevent "White desperados" from escaping federal and state law (F. Cohen, 1971, p. 6). Indian country and/or territory was defined as "country within which Indian laws and customs and federal laws relating to Indians are generally applicable" (p. 5).

Following the Civil War, the United States minimized the political autonomy of tribal leaders and encouraged government representatives to deal with individual Indians and families (Tyler, 1973). As early as 1878, Congress established the U.S. Indian Police, which by 1881 was composed of 40 agencies, 162 officers, and 653 privates (Tyler, 1973). By the 1880s, the West was becoming rapidly developed and settled by Whites, which precipitated the demand for the acquisition of Indian land and resources. According to Tyler, there were chiefs of Indian police on the reservations who often mediated between White man's law and Indian custom. At the same time, the decimation of tribal leadership often resulted in the breakdown of social control. In 1887, the General Allotment or Dawes Act permitted tribal lands to be allotted to individual Indians, making them landowners and farmers.

Although not applicable to all tribes initially, over time, the Dawes Act was extended to the Five Civilized Tribes in Indian Territory (Cherokees, Choctaws, Creeks, Chickasaws, and Seminoles) by the Curtis Act of 1898. By the turn of the century, the allotments were primarily an opportunity for the U.S. government and White settlers to secure both land and natural resources. Interestingly, the FBI's first major homicide investigation involved Native Americans. During the 1800s, oil was discovered on the land of the Osage Indian tribe of Oklahoma. Beginning in the late 1800s, the reservations began yielding barrels of oil. By the early 1900s, the tribe was extremely wealthy considering that "in 1923 alone, the Osage Tribe received $27 million. In two decades, the Osage would receive more money from oil than all the old west gold rushes combined had yielded" (Hogan, 1998, p. 28). Eventually, this made them the target of elaborate schemes to defraud them of their wealth. After asking for assistance from the government, during the 1920s, the FBI infiltrated the tribe and uncovered a major scheme that involved intermarriage and murder. In the end, the FBI solved the case but had local officials make the arrests "since Special Agents of the FBI did not have the power of arrest (or the authority to carry firearms) at the time" (Hogan, 1998, p. 194).

On August 15, 1953, **Public Law 280** transferred federal responsibility for criminal and civil jurisdiction, including law enforcement duties, to six states (Alaska, California, Minnesota, Nebraska, Oregon, and Wisconsin) and made it optional for several other states to assert jurisdiction (Luna-Firebaugh, 2003; Tyler, 1973). Although P.L. 280 did not terminate tribal jurisdiction, it was the belief that states and sheriffs were now responsible for law enforcement. When it was widely recognized that states were not providing adequate policing services, some tribal governments sought to reestablish and strengthen tribal police services. In 1974, almost a century after the federal government first established police in Indian country, police protection on reservations was described as follows:

> On reservations where State laws apply, police activities are administered in the same manner as elsewhere. On reservations where State laws do not apply, tribal laws or Department of the Interior regulations are administered by personnel employed by the Bureau of Indian Affairs, or by personnel employed by the tribe, or by a combination of both. (Bureau of Indian Affairs, 1974, p. 27)

In February, 1973, a group of young Indians seized the village of Wounded Knee, South Dakota, to protest conditions on the Pine Ridge reservation. Federal agents were called in to end the takeover, which lasted 71 days. Afterward, relations between the FBI and the American Indian Movement, a more radical American Indian rights group, continued to be tense. By 1976, the Bureau of Indian Affairs and/or tribes maintained law enforcement services on 126 reservations assigned to 61 Indian agencies. These agencies were responsible for around 200,000 square miles, 416,000 Indians, and numerous other non-Indians (Bureau of Indian Affairs, 1976). In the 1990s, more than 56 million acres of land were owned and policed by tribal nations in the United States. "Indian country" includes reservations in 34 states, most of which are located west of the Mississippi River (Wakeling et al., 2001). The workload of officers in Indian police departments has increased as a result of several factors, including more reliance on the police (instead of traditional methods) and more crime and emergencies (Wakeling et al., 2001). Tribal police have responsibility for large land areas and often share criminal jurisdiction with federal and state agencies, "depending upon the particular offense, the offender, the victim and the offense location" (M. Hickman, 2003, p. 4). There are several administrative arrangements for policing Native Americans that include cross-deputization agreements with neighboring tribes, neighboring nontribal authorities, and federal law enforcement agencies

(Perry, 2005). According to the Census of State and Local Law Enforcement Agencies, 2004, there were 154 tribal police agencies with 2,490 sworn personnel (Reaves, 2007). In 2008 there were 178 law enforcement agencies, 157 general purpose police departments, and 21 agencies with special jurisdiction concerned with the enforcement of natural resources laws (Reaves, 2011). As previously mentioned, tribes have assumed responsibility and control of policing on many reservations. The typical department is small, and therefore there is considerably less police protection than in other urban and rural agencies.

The Navajo and Seminole police departments are the largest tribal agencies, but most tribal agencies have fewer than 50 full-time sworn personnel. The Relocation Program of the Bureau of Indian Affairs transplanted Native Americans to cities in the early 1950s. By 1973, more than 100,000 Native Americans had relocated to urban areas, where they were faced with social, economic, and psychological challenges (Fixico, 2000). Historical research does not focus on either police-Indian relations in urban areas or crime among Indians who relocated, although considerable attention is devoted to the problem of alcohol-related crimes both on and off the reservation. More recent research has also been devoted to the nature of policing in Indian Country (Perry, 2009).

Policing African Americans

African Americans have posed a unique problem for America since they arrived as slaves in the 16th century and were labeled "inferior." By the early 18th century, most of the early colonies regulated the movement and activities of free and enslaved Negroes by enacting special codes to totally control them. During the antebellum period, slaves were unprotected from crimes by slave owners, including murder, rape, assault, and battery (Kennedy, 1997). According to Dulaney (1996), by the mid-1700s, "patterrollers," or slave patrols, the first distinctively American police system, existed in every Southern colony. Slave patrols carried out numerous duties, including checking passes of slaves leaving plantations, routinely searching slave quarters for stolen property, and administering whippings (Websdale, 2001). Relatedly, slave revolts were of increasing concern and, along with slavery, mandated a brutal policing mechanism to both protect Whites and dehumanize Blacks (T. Jones, 1977).

During the 1800s, in the North and South, both before and after Emancipation, free Blacks were treated like slaves. Their movements were regulated: They were prohibited from entering several states and had to be employed to remain in states; in Virginia, an emancipated slave had to leave the state within 12 months or forfeit his freedom (Taylor Greene & Gabbidon, 2000). Kennedy (1997) describes the unwillingness of Southern Whites to recognize Blacks' rights to protection and the failure of local authorities to restrain or punish violence against them.

African Americans were excluded from policing in most cities until the mid-1800s. Black police did serve in Washington, DC, as early as 1861 (Kuykendall & Burns, 1980). The first wave of Black police officers in the United States appeared during Reconstruction. Several cities in the North and South employed Blacks, including Chicago; Philadelphia; Columbia and Charleston, South Carolina; and several cities in Mississippi and Texas. However, by the 1890s, most Blacks had been eliminated from police agencies in the South (Dulaney, 1996).

As discussed in Chapter 2, lynching was a serious problem after the Civil War. Less well known is that some police/sheriffs and other justice officials participated in lynchings or silently supported attacks against African Americans by White mobs (Russell-Brown, 2004). In his book *An American Dilemma: The Negro Problem and Modern Democracy,* Gunnar Myrdal (1944) states,

> The average Southern policeman is a promoted poor White with a legal sanction to use a weapon. His social heritage has taught him to despise the Negroes, and he has had little education which could have changed him. . . . The result is that probably no group of Whites in America have a lower opinion of the Negro people and are more fixed in their views than Southern policemen. (pp. 540–541)

The underprotection of Blacks by police was a problem in both the North and South during the Race Riots in the 19th and early 20th centuries. Race riots were clashes between Black and White citizens, in which the police were often accused of indifference, brutality, and leaving the scene. With few exceptions, police did not protect Blacks from these attacks on their persons and property, and sometimes they even participated in these events. Police officers played a pivotal role in race riots in East St. Louis (1917), Chicago (1919), Tulsa (1921), Detroit (1943), and Washington, DC (1919). In the 20th century, efforts were made to protect Blacks in some instances, and federal troops were sometimes called in to assist in restoring order (Grimshaw, 1969).

There were approximately 50 Black policemen by 1940. At the time, three-fourths of the Black population lived in the South. Alabama, Georgia, Louisiana, Mississippi, and South Carolina, the states with the largest Black populations, had no Black policemen (Rudwick, 1960). Police officers were also on the front lines of the Civil Rights Movement, often as adversaries protecting the social order at that time. Substantial gains were made by Blacks in law enforcement after the 1960s, although it would take numerous court battles to integrate police departments, and the problems of underprotection and police violence persisted into this century. Since the 1970s, there has been an increase in the number of Black police officers and police administrators. Black police organizations and police leaders have been instrumental in calling attention to police use of deadly force, brutality, and racial profiling, issues of concern to Black Americans (as well as other minorities). It is important to note that employment gains by Blacks in law enforcement have caused some citizens to complain that their treatment by Black officers often is just as problematic as the historical treatment by White officers.

Policing Asian Americans

As discussed in Chapter 1, many Chinese immigrated to the United States as laborers. In 1876, there were 151,000 Chinese in the United States, and 116,000 were in the state of California. Like others, many Chinese immigrated to California in search of gold, although they were also known to serve as cooks, laundrymen, and servants (Norton, 2004). Early laborers were indentured servants who financed their passage by agreeing to work for merchant creditors (Courtwright, 2001). Around 1880, El Paso, Texas, became a point of entry for Chinese laborers from Mexico after the United States made entry for Chinese workers illegal. Often referred to as "coolies," the Chinese were involved in laying tracks for the Southern Pacific Railroad or remained in El Paso after completing railroad tracks that originated in the West (Dickey, 2004; Institute of Texan Cultures, 1998).

The fact that many Chinese immigrants were illegal did not seem to matter as much as their opium smoking and **opium dens**. Opium smoking was common among Chinese immigrants and confined to them between 1850 and 1870. Soon after, opium and opium dens gained popularity with the underworld of gamblers, prostitutes, and other criminals (Courtwright, 2001). In 1883, several dens were operating in El Paso and were frequented by members of both the lower and upper classes. Many believe that the opium dens were eventually targeted by the police and other governmental officials because of concerns that Whites were mixing with Chinese, viewed by some as "polluting" (Institute of Texan Cultures, 1998). In the 1870s and 1880s, federal, municipal, and state governments passed laws that penalized opium smoking. According to Courtwright (2001), "Dens patronized by Whites were the most likely to be raided" (p. 77). By 1909, federal legislation banned the importation of opium for smoking by stipulating that it could be imported only for medicinal purposes.

After the anti-opium smoking legislation, imports decreased and coincided with a decrease in the size of the Chinese population that was also related to more restrictive immigration policies. During most of the 20th century, Asian Americans were more likely to remain in cultural enclaves and less likely to be involved in crime in their communities. Thus, although Asian gangs in California and other jurisdictions are still involved in drug distribution (heroin, ice), prostitution, and other illegal activities, the fact that most Asian Americans are insulated from police attention is due, at least in part, to their cultural values, ethnic isolation, and language barriers. More recent Southeast Asian immigrants and some second-generation Asian Americans target other Asian immigrants, Asian Americans, and businesses (http://www.asian-nation.org/gangs.shtml). These individuals, often belonging to gangs, are more likely to come to the attention of police today.

Policing Latinos

Research on the experiences of Mexican Americans in the Southwest and Los Angeles is more readily available than studies of the historical experiences with the police of other Latino groups such as Colombians, Dominicans, El Salvadorans, Guatemalans, Hondurans, and Puerto Ricans. Trujillo (1974/1995) described how American capitalists who colonized the Southwest during the 1850s and 1860s created a cheap labor force and perpetuated an atmosphere of violence against Chicano immigrants. He maintained that repression of Chicanos by the police, military, and vigilantes led to the formation of protective guerilla units and bandits that are misrepresented in American history. According to Chabrán and Chabrán (1996), Latino migrant workers in the Southwest received the harshest treatment. Because many of them were illegal immigrants, they were minimally protected by the American legal system. Similar to the experiences with the police of other minorities, Latinos also were subjected to acts of brutality that included lynchings and other murders. As early as 1823, the Texas Rangers engaged in questionable practices ranging from threats to torture, flogging, castration, and lawless executions (Duran, 2012). According to Duran, "The high number of lynchings and killings of Mexicans by Anglo mobs continued without punishment from 1848–1916" (p. 44). The number of brutal incidents in California and Texas prompted the Mexican ambassador to formally protest the mistreatment of Mexicans in 1912 (Kanellos, 1977).

In the 1931 Wickersham Commission Report on Crime and the Foreign Born, three chapters specifically address the Mexican American immigrant. The focus is primarily on arrests, although there is some information on discriminatory treatment by the police. For example, P. Taylor (1931) found several individuals who noted how the police in Chicago and Gary, Indiana, were more likely to arrest Mexican Americans than Poles for drunkenness.

By the 1940s in Los Angeles, where many Mexican Americans resided and Chicano youth were viewed as a social threat, police-Chicano relations had deteriorated to what Escobar (1999) described as extreme hostility and suspicion toward each other. On June 3, 1943, several White sailors stated that they were attacked by a group of Mexicans, which marked the beginning of what is referred to as the "**zoot suit riots**" or "sailor riots." The sailors retaliated by going to East Los Angeles and attacking Mexican Americans, especially those wearing zoot suits. The riots continued until June 7, when the Navy finally put an end to the wanton attacks by declaring Los Angeles off limits to military personnel. The police and sheriff arrested several sailors, although none were charged with crimes. In contrast, hundreds of Chicano youth were arrested without cause (Suavecito Apparel Co., 2004).

During the latter part of the 20th century and early 21st century, Latinos, like African Americans, continued to have strained relations with the police due, at least in part, to controversial immigration policing tactics (see Immigration and Policing, below). Recent legislation and activism by stakeholders has heightened awareness of the ongoing scrutiny of "Browns" by federal, state, and local police. Perceptions and misperceptions about the problems of illegal immigration, human trafficking, and drug smuggling, especially in the country's southwest region and other locales, have strained relationships between Latinos and police at all levels. The representation of Latinos in local police agencies increased from 4.5% in 1987 to 10.3% in 2007 (Reaves, 2010) and is estimated to be 11.9% today (see Table 4.1). Very little is known about the role of these officers, especially in places where Latinos are the majority of the population, and it is not known whether police-Latino relations are better in those communities.

Policing White Immigrants

Throughout American history, the majority of immigrants have been of European descent. During the 1800s, immigration increased considerably as waves of Germans, Irish, and the "new immigrants" (Italians, Poles, Greeks, Portuguese, Jews, and others) arrived in the United States. These new immigrants were viewed less favorably than those who had arrived prior to 1850. This was due, at least in part, to beliefs that "incoming migrants from eastern and central Europe brought many negative social characteristics often attributable to their race," a term used rather carelessly to refer to nationality and/or culture (Graham, 2004, p. 25). By the late 1800s, immigration was seen by Progressive Era reformers as a threat to democracy, social order, and American identity (Graham, 2004). Poverty, illiteracy, unemployment, and underemployment in the ethnic ghettos meant that various types of criminal enterprises were common, including gambling, prostitution, theft, and con men (Fogelson, 1977).

The police experiences of White immigrants were drastically different from those of Native Americans, African Americans, Asian Americans, and Latinos. First, it was easier for foreign-born Whites to gradually blend into American society. Second, many White immigrants were able to secure jobs as police officers. Third, White immigrants often were assisted by the police in their transition to life in a new country. As early as the 1850s, the Boston police provided firewood and other necessities to Irish immigrants. Decades later, one function of the Boston police department was to distribute free soup in station houses, especially during the winter (Lane, 1967). Police also assisted parents looking for lost children (Monkkonen, 1981) and accommodated overnight lodgers (Lane, 1967; Monkkonen, 1981).

By the turn of the 20th century, tension between upper- and middle-class native-born and foreign-born Whites often resulted in more aggressive policing that emphasized law enforcement more than service. In some cities, policing of White immigrants depended on whether the police were controlled by political machines friendly to either immigrants or Progressive Era reformers seeking to restrict the immorality of immigrants (Brown & Warner, 1992). Ironically, because policemen were recruited from the lower and lower middle classes, they "had little or no inclination to impose the morality of the upper middle and upper classes on the ethnic ghettos" (Fogelson, 1977, p. 38). Later in the 20th century, serial killers, including Theodore Bundy, David Berkowitz, and John Wayne Gacy; White supremacists Randy Weaver and the Ruby Ridge incident; and domestic terrorists Timothy McVeigh and Terry Nichols, who bombed the Alfred P. Murrah Federal Building in Oklahoma City, were key factors in the development of criminal profiles and revisions to training and policy especially at the federal level.

Photo 4.1

A group of Hispanic men stand chained together on their way to court in June, 1943.

Corbis.

It is easy to lose sight of the fact that, throughout history, most persons who have been arrested (i.e., have had contact with the police) have been White. Historically, interactions between the police and Whites were less controversial than encounters between police and minority groups. Compared with early periods in American history, policing minorities has gradually improved as a result of the civil rights movement, federal legislation, affirmative action policies, human rights advocates, community policing, minority political empowerment, minority ascendancy in police organizations, policing research, and increased media attention focusing on police behaviors. Despite improved **police-community relations**, there are several contemporary issues regarding race and policing that continue to negatively impact citizen confidence in the police, which are discussed next.

❖ Contemporary Issues in Race and Policing

As noted at the beginning of the chapter, the majority of Americans view the police favorably even though there is variation in citizen satisfaction with the police. Minorities continue to be overrepresented as victims of racial profiling, stop and frisk, use of force, and less-than-lethal conducted-energy devices (CEDs, i.e., **Tasers**). Here, we present several contemporary issues in race and policing, including police deviance, police bias and racial profiling, militarization, immigration and policing, and community policing.

Police Deviance

Police deviance is a broad term used to refer to "police officer activities that are inconsistent with the officer's official authority, organizational authority, values, and standards of ethical conduct" (Barker & Carter, 1991, p. 4). Use of excessive force (including both police homicides and police brutality), corruption, perjury, having sex, sleeping and drinking while on duty, discrimination, and failure to enforce the law are examples of police deviance (Barker & Carter, 1991). Police deviance has been known to exist since the 1800s (see, e.g., Fogelson, 1977; Richardson, 1970; Sherman, 1974). When President Herbert Hoover established the Wickersham Commission to investigate the shortcomings of the administration of justice, the third degree, a mostly secret and illegal practice, was a common form of police deviance. The Report on Lawlessness in Law Enforcement stated,

> After reviewing the evidence obtainable the authors of the report reach the conclusion that the third degree—that is, the use of physical brutality, or other forms of cruelty, to obtain involuntary confessions or admissions—is widespread. (National Commission on Law Observance and Enforcement, 1931b, p. 4)

Deviant police practices continued to receive considerable attention throughout the 20th century. During the civil unrest of the 1960s, following several questionable police homicides during the 1970s and 1980s, and after the Rodney King beating in 1991, police abuse of their authority precipitated research and legislative changes. Another egregious incident of police deviance occurred in 1999 in Tulia, Texas, when

46 people (the majority of whom were Black) were arrested by Officer Tom Coleman and charged with being cocaine dealers. Many of them went to prison and later were pardoned by Governor Rick Perry after an appellate judge accused Coleman of lying, falsifying evidence, and racism (Drug Policy Alliance, 2008). A similar incident occurred in Hearne, Texas, in 2000 when 27 were arrested (Frontline, 2004).

In 2001, more than a dozen police departments, including Cincinnati (OH), New York City (NY), Detroit (MI), New Orleans (LA), and Tulsa (OK), were under investigation by the DOJ Office of Civil Rights (OCR), to determine whether they engaged in patterns and/or practices of two types of police deviance, discrimination and brutality (Roane, 2001). In 2010, the OCR was investigating 17 police departments across the country. Since 2010, the OCR also has investigated several agencies including the Albuquerque (NM), Cleveland (OH), Puerto Rico, Portland (OR), Seattle (WA), and Ferguson (MO) police departments.

Another explanation of how discrimination manifests itself in police behavior is referred to as "reasonable racism." Kennedy (1997) explained,

> Most courts . . . have authorized police to use race in making decisions to question, stop, or detain persons so long as doing so is reasonably related to efficient law enforcement and not deployed for purposes of racial harassment. (p. 141)

More troubling is the fact that "reasonable" racial discrimination continues to be viewed as "a practical aspect of good law enforcement" (p. 141). He went on to state,

> Reasonableness, then, is not a definite, arithmetic objective quality that is independent of aims and values. It is a concept that is considerably more subtle, complex, malleable, and mysterious than the simplistic model of human decision making relied upon by those who accept at face value the "reasonableness" and "rationality" of conduct that not only expresses controversial moral and political judgments but that also expresses deep seated, perhaps unconscious, affections, fears, and aversions. (pp. 144–145)

Police discrimination is not as blatant and overt today as it was in the past. Yet, the recent increases in deadly police confrontations require one to consider whether or not discrimination is a factor.

Police Use of Deadly Force

What happened in Ferguson (MO) after an officer killed Michael Brown, an unarmed Black male, in August 2014, and the protests that followed, are perfect examples of the importance of the domains identified by Sherman (2002): conduct and practices of the criminal justice system, changing values and expectations of the culture, and images of the system presented in electronic media. While Black males are the most likely victims of recent deadly police confrontations, other minorities have also been killed, including two illegal immigrants, Antonio Zambrano-Montes, killed in Pasco, WA, on February 15, 2015, and Ruben Garcia Villapando, killed in Grapevine, TX, on February 20, 2015, and an unarmed 19-year-old, Hector Morejon, shot and killed in Long Beach, CA, on April 23, 2014. Most viewers were stunned to see

Ferguson, MO, Police Department (FMPD) officers in tanks and military gear. Both the killing and apparent militarization of the FMPD kept Ferguson, MO, in the news for months. The Ferguson grand jury's decision not to indict the officer involved in the killing of Michael Brown rekindled concerns. When the DOJ OCR released the results of their investigation, Attorney General Holder held a press conference and summarized the findings and recommendations (see Box 4.2).

BOX 4.2

Race and Crime in the Media

Justice Department Announces Findings of
Two Civil Rights Investigations in Ferguson, Missouri

Department of Justice

Office of Public Affairs

FOR IMMEDIATE RELEASE Wednesday, March 4, 2015

The Justice Department announced the findings of its two civil rights investigations related to Ferguson, Missouri, today. The Justice Department found that the Ferguson Police Department (FPD) engaged in a pattern or practice of conduct that violates the First, Fourth, and Fourteenth Amendments of the Constitution. The Justice Department also announced that the evidence examined in its independent, federal investigation into the fatal shooting of Michael Brown does not support federal civil rights charges against Ferguson Police Officer Darren Wilson.

"As detailed in our report, this investigation found a community that was deeply polarized, and where deep distrust and hostility often characterized interactions between police and area residents," said Attorney General Eric Holder. "Our investigation showed that Ferguson police officers routinely violate the Fourth Amendment in stopping people without reasonable suspicion, arresting them without probable cause, and using unreasonable force against them. Now that our investigation has reached its conclusion, it is time for Ferguson's leaders to take immediate, wholesale and structural corrective action. The report we have issued and the steps we have taken are only the beginning of a necessarily resource-intensive and inclusive process to promote reconciliation, to reduce and eliminate bias, and to bridge gaps and build understanding."

"While the findings in Ferguson are very serious and the list of needed changes is long, the record of the Civil Rights Division's work with police departments across the country shows that if the Ferguson Police Department truly commits to community policing, it can restore the trust it has lost," said Acting Assistant Attorney General Vanita Gupta of the Civil Rights Division. "We look forward to working with City Officials and the many communities that make up Ferguson to develop and institute reforms that will focus the Ferguson Police Department on public safety and constitutional policing instead of revenue. Real community policing is possible and ensures that all people are equal before the law, and that law enforcement is seen as a part of, rather than distant from, the communities they serve."

. . . . The investigation focused on the FPD's use of force, including deadly force; stops, searches and arrests; discriminatory policing; and treatment of detainees inside Ferguson's city jail by Ferguson police officers. In the course of its pattern or practice investigation, the Civil Rights Division reviewed more than 35,000 pages of police records; interviewed and met with city, police and court officials, including the FPD's chief and numerous other officers; conducted hundreds of in-person and telephone interviews, as well as participated in meetings with community members and groups; observed Ferguson Municipal Court sessions, and analyzed FPD's data on stops, searches and arrests. It found that the combination of Ferguson's focus on generating revenue over public safety, along with racial bias, has a profound effect on the FPD's police and court practices, resulting in conduct that routinely violates the Constitution and federal law. The department also found that these patterns created a lack of trust between the FPD and significant portions of Ferguson's residents, especially African Americans.

The department found that the FPD has a pattern or practice of:

- Conducting stops without reasonable suspicion and arrests without probable cause in violation of the Fourth Amendment;
- Interfering with the right to free expression in violation of the First Amendment; and
- Using unreasonable force in violation of the Fourth Amendment.

The department found that Ferguson Municipal Court has a pattern or practice of:

- Focusing on revenue over public safety, leading to court practices that violate the 14th Amendment's due process and equal protection requirements.
- Court practices exacerbating the harm of Ferguson's unconstitutional police practices and imposing particular hardship upon Ferguson's most vulnerable residents, especially upon those living in or near poverty. Minor offenses can generate crippling debts, result in jail time because of an inability to pay and result in the loss of a driver's license, employment, or housing.

The department found a pattern or practice of racial bias in both the FPD and municipal court:

- The harms of Ferguson's police and court practices are borne disproportionately by African Americans and that this disproportionate impact is avoidable.
- Ferguson's harmful court and police practices are due, at least in part, to intentional discrimination, as demonstrated by direct evidence of racial bias and stereotyping about African Americans by certain Ferguson police and municipal court officials.

The findings are laid out in a 100-page report that discusses the evidence and what remedies should be implemented to end the pattern or practice. The findings include two sets of recommendations, 26 in total, that the Justice Department believes are necessary to correct the unconstitutional FPD and Ferguson Municipal Court practices. The recommendations include changing policing and court practices so that they are based on public safety instead of revenue; improving training and oversight; changing practices to reduce bias; and ending an overreliance on arrest warrants as a means of collecting fines.

1. Do you think the practices identified in Ferguson, MO, by the DOJ OCR are occurring elsewhere in the United States? Explain.

2. What strategies would you recommend to a police department to improve its relationship with its residents?

Source: U.S. Department of Justice.

Goldkamp (1982) identified two perspectives that help us to understand why minorities are overrepresented as victims of police use of force. Belief Perspective I points to differential law enforcement and the possible effects of prejudice and discrimination. Belief Perspective II posits that minorities are involved in crimes that increase their likelihood of victimization by the police. The OCR findings in the investigation of the Ferguson (MO) police department (as well as other agencies) lends some support for Belief Perspective I. The National Organization of Black Law Enforcement Executives (NOBLE) offers some support for Belief Perspective I as well. They believe that justice is a system of people influenced by biases and stereotypes that are often incorporated into police decision making and actions. Over a decade ago they noted that the use of excessive force, brutality, and shootings of unarmed minority suspects and undercover officers are "symptoms and manifestations of biased-based policing" (NOBLE, 2001, p. 4)

The U.S. Supreme Court in *Tennessee v. Garner* (1985) ruled that shooting fleeing felons was unconstitutional. Ironically, the police officer and victim in that case were both Black. Before the Court ruled in the Garner decision, researchers and practitioners were questioning the disproportionate number of minorities shot and killed by the police (see, e.g., Fyfe, 1981, 1982; Sherman, 1980; Takagi, 1974). In 1989, the U.S. Supreme Court addressed the issue of reasonable force by police officers in *Graham v. Connor* and concluded that the perspective of a reasonable officer, as well as the facts and circumstances, must be considered (Novak, 2009; Terrill, 2009). More recently, the impact of an officer's perceptual distortions during police shootings and how such distortions might relate to "reasonableness" has garnered attention in the research (Engel & Smith, 2009; Klinger & Brunson, 2009). Goldkamp's Belief Perspective II has some support as well. The disproportionate involvement of minorities (especially Blacks) in arrests for violent crimes, as discussed in Chapter 2, leads to more contact with the police. The Death in Custody Reporting Act of 2000 mandates that all states collect and report data on arrest-related deaths. The first reported findings provide some support for Belief Perspective II; between 2003 and 2005, 2,002 deaths were reported. Of these, 1,095 arrest-related homicides were by police officers, and 75% involved arrests for a violent crime. In 80% of the homicides, a weapon was used by the arrestee. Relatedly, 16 of the 24 CED-related deaths were of persons arrested for violent crimes (Mumola, 2007). More recently, in 2009, police homicides accounted for 497 of 729 deaths in custody. Although Whites (340) comprised the majority, Blacks (218) and Hispanics (130) together accounted for more than half of decedents (Burch, 2011). An examination of police officers feloniously killed in the line of duty might be considered to be support for Belief Perspective II as well. In 2006, 48 officers were killed; 12 died during arrest situations, 10 were ambushed, 8 were responding to disturbance calls, and 8 were killed during traffic pursuits or stops (FBI, 2006c). Since 2009, the number of officers killed during felonious incidents has fluctuated between 48 and 72. More recently, 51 officers were killed in 2014, a noticeable increase from 2013 when the fewest (35) were killed (Wagner, 2015).

Opponents of Goldkamp's Perspective II argue that many victims of police use of excessive force are not engaged in violent criminal acts when they are beaten or killed by police. Before Rodney King refused to stop his car, was he involved in a violent crime? In New York City, several controversial incidents of police use of deadly force were not preceded by a violent crime, including those involving Abner Louima (savagely sodomized and beaten in 1997), Amadou Diallo (a Guinean immigrant shot and killed by New York City police in 1999), Sean Bell (killed by police after leaving a Queens strip club in 2007) and Eric Garner (killed by an officer's choke hold in 2014). Russell-Brown (2004) has succinctly noted,

> There is no evidence that the level of police assaults against Blacks increases and decreases on the basis of the rate of Black offending. Further, according to this reasoning, the majority of Blacks are required to pay the debt incurred by the small percentage of the group who are offenders. (p. 60)

In 2008, an estimated 776,000 people—about 1.9% of the 40 million U.S. residents who had contact with police that year—reported police use of force or threat of force. Although there were fewer such incidents than in 2002 and 2005, in 2008, males, Blacks, and younger persons were more likely to have had contact with police that resulted in the use of force (Eith & Durose, 2011, p. 11). Many conclude that police bias is a contributing factor to the overrepresentation of minorities in police-citizen encounters.

Police Bias

Lately, **implicit bias** or hidden bias has received considerable attention in an effort to understand what role it plays in criminal justice and how it can be both prevented and controlled (Gove, 2015). Implicit bias is "shaped by both history and cultural influences" (p. 45). *Biased-based policing* is a term used to describe how some officers' decisions are based upon stereotypes and negative attitudes about certain people—in this case, racial and ethnic minorities. Police bias is not new and has existed since the 19th century. During what Kelling and Moore (1988) refer to as the Political Era, the police were responsible to certain ethnic groups with political power in their neighborhoods. These groups excluded Blacks (Williams & Murphy, 1990) and other minorities.

As presented in Chapter 2, Blacks have been overrepresented in arrest statistics since their inception, and differential enforcement by the police, though controversial, has a long history in our country. There is evidence that "Some parts of the apparent excessive criminality of the Negro people find its explanation in police discrimination" (Reuter, 1927, in Muhammad, 2010, p. 245). In the past, not only did the police have the authority to arrest, coerce confessions, and recommend charges, they "frequently aided and abetted mob attacks against blacks" (Ovington, 1911, in Muhammad, 2010, p. 233), especially during the Jim Crow era of racial violence. As previously stated, the problem of police bias was included in the Wickersham Commission's Report Volume 11 on the "third degree." Various forms of police maltreatment and killings also were included in the reports of organizations following race riots in the early 20th century (see, e.g., reports of The Chicago Commission on Race Relations, The National Association for the Advancement of Colored People, National Urban League; see Muhammad, 2010) and civil unrest later in the 20th century (Kennedy, 1997; National Advisory Commission on Civil Disorders [The Kerner Commission]; the President's Commission on Law Enforcement and the Administration of Justice). During the 1960s, the FBI's Counter Intelligence Program (COINTELPRO) was an example of how police bias can manifest in police tactics and operations. Many White, Black, and Latino individuals and organizations labeled "agitators" were targeted, including Dr. Martin Luther King Jr. and his associates, members of the Black Panther Party, American Indians, and Vietnam War protesters.

In spite of numerous efforts to improve police-community relations, and progress since the Rodney King incident decades ago, police bias and discrimination are still with us today. The continued overrepresentation of racial and ethnic minorities in police-citizen encounters has led to renewed efforts to reduce and control police bias. On December 18, 2014, President Barack Obama signed Executive Order 13684 that established the President's Task Force on 21st Century Policing. The task force will identify **best practices** and make recommendations to the president on building public trust and improving collaboration between local police and the communities they serve (U.S. DOJ, 2014).

Unfortunately, a few incidents where police bias is apparent can do extensive damage to confidence in and perceptions of police. In spite of a long history in American policing, strategies to prevent and reduce bias since the 1940s have had mixed results. These efforts include screening during recruitment, in-service training, early warning systems that monitor complaints about officers' behaviors, videotaping, and most recently the use of body cameras. Recommendations for reducing police bias include developing a comprehensive program that promotes impartial policing and clear policies that specify criteria that must be met before officers "interdict or detain based on race or ethnicity" (Gove, 2015, p. 6). Another recommendation is to minimize "the influence of unconscious racial stereotypes on police behavior by changing officers' beat assignment and units (Smith & Alpert, 2007, pp. 1279–1280). Last, police and citizens should get to know each other better. As FBI Director Comey pointed out, both have an obligation to better understand each other. Perhaps the most problematic and best example of bias policing is racial profiling.

Racial Profiling

Racial profiling refers to "any action that results in the heightened racial scrutiny of minorities—justified or not" (Russell-Brown, 2004, pp. 98–99). This definition recognizes that racial discrimination (i.e., profiling) is experienced by consumers (Gabbidon & Higgins, 2007), travelers (Gabbidon, Penn, Jordan, & Higgins, 2009), those crossing borders (Higgins, Gabbidon, & Martin, 2010), as well as those subject to searches by police and other governmental officials (Gau, 2013; Gau & Brunson, 2012; Higgins, Jennings, Jordan, & Gabbidon, 2011; Rojek, Rosenfeld & Decker, 2012). According to Batton & Kadleck (2004), "The roots of racial profiling run deep" (p. 32). Arguably, racial profiling has always existed in American policing and therefore is best understood in both cultural and historical contexts. During the 1990s, "**driving while Black/brown**" (DWB) was the most visible form of racial profiling. At that time, profiling on the highways and in the streets was much more dangerous because it was based on beliefs about those who might commit crimes (predictive), rather than those who have committed them (descriptive); it was less formal (based on empirical support) and more informal (i.e., based on empirical support and personal experiences; Harris, 2002).

In one well-known incident that occurred early in the morning of May 8, 1992, members of the Wilkins family were driving home to Washington, DC, from a funeral of a family member in Chicago, when they were stopped by a Maryland state police officer. Unfortunately for them, they fit the profile of drug traffickers. When the family refused to consent to a search, they were "sniffed by a dog for contraband" (Ogletree, 2012, p. 105). Robert Wilkins, a passenger, the driver's cousin, and a Harvard Law School graduate, decided to take legal action that culminated in *Wilkins v. Maryland State Police* (1993). The case was instrumental in highlighting the overrepresentation of African Americans in stops by Maryland state police. Harris (2002) credited lawyers in the New Jersey case of *State v. Soto* (1996) with demonstrating that, at least in New Jersey, criminal profiling had become racial profiling.

In 1996, in the case of *Whren v. United States,* the U.S. Supreme Court granted police officers the power to stop persons suspected of drug crimes under the pretext of probable cause for a traffic violation. Whren and Brown, two Black males, argued that the police officers were racist, and that if they had been White, the traffic stop would not have occurred. Cooper (2001/2002) pointed out that the more troubling aspect of the *Whren* decision was the Court's ruling that a police officer's state of mind is irrelevant if probable cause for his or her action exists. For many observers, by ignoring the importance of an officer's racial prejudices, *Whren* opened the door to racial profiling during traffic stops (Russell, 2002). Since *Whren,* the Supreme Court has granted police even greater powers over drivers and passengers (American Civil Liberties Union, 1999). Today, racial profiling of minorities during traffic stops— initially referred to as driving while Black—includes driving while Asian, driving while Latino, or driving while any other minority category that is perceived to pose a threat.

Another type of racial profiling, referred to as either "stop, question, and frisk" or "stop and frisk," occurs when police stop pedestrians as they go to and from work or school and ride the subway (Jones-Brown, Stoudt, Johnston, & Moran, 2013). Commonly referred to as "walking while Black," these stops occur daily and are viewed as necessary by police and intrusive and unwarranted by citizens (p. 1). **Street stops** don't occur as often as traffic stops, but when they do, fewer pedestrians (71%) report that police behave properly compared to drivers (88%) involved in traffic stops (Langton & Durose, 2013). The 1968 U.S. Supreme Court decision in *Terry v. Ohio* granted police officers the right to stop and detain a person when there is reasonable suspicion that a crime is either in progress or about to occur. Data on police pedestrian stops (PPS) is not readily available, although some large cities—including New York City, Philadelphia (PA), and Los Angeles (CA)—that do collect data have reported increases in pedestrian stops (Jones-Brown et al., p. 4). In New York City, the number of reported PPS increased from 160,851 in 2003 to 685,724 in 2011 and decreased to 532,911 in 2012 (p. 3). The majority of persons stopped were Blacks and Hispanics, who were stopped nine times more often than Whites (p. 24). Since the 1990s, a coalition of individuals and organizations have challenged the city's stop-and-frisk practices, culminating in several class action lawsuits, most notably *Floyd et al. v. City of New York* (2008), which did not go to trial until 2013. In January 2014, the City of New York and Center for Constitutional Rights (CCR) finally reached an agreement that includes a reform process and monitors (CCR, 2014).

Interest in racial profiling has produced countless articles, books, and reports on the topic (Archbold, Dahle, Fangman, Wentz, & Wood, 2013; Batton & Kadleck, 2004; Cochran & Warren, 2012; Lange, Johnson, & Voas, 2005; Langton & Durose, 2013; Meehan & Ponder, 2002; Ogletree, 2012; Rice & White, 2010; Weitzer & Tuch, 2006;

Withrow, 2006) and other forms of profiling have been studied, including "walking and shopping while Black" (Gabbidon, 2003; Gabbidon, Craig, Okafo, Marzette, & Peterson, 2008; Gabbidon & Higgins, 2007; Higgins & Gabbidon, 2008; Jordan, Gabbidon, & Higgins, 2009; Russell, 2002) and **profiling in airports** (Gabbidon, Higgins, & Nelson, 2011; Gabbidon, Penn, Jordan & Higgins, 2009). Public opinion polls about racial profiling indicate that most Americans believe it exists (Higgins, Gabbidon, & Vito, 2010; McMahon, Garner, Davis, & Kraus, 2002). Fredrickson and Siljander (2002) argued that racial profiling does not exist because race is just one of several factors considered in the process of police profiling. Rather, they posited that criminal profiling may sometimes be racially biased and discriminatory. It remains unclear whether DWB traffic stops are driven by honest efforts to control drug trafficking, are the result of biased and racist beliefs about minority involvement in the drug trade, or are a more sinister and less recognized opportunity for police to seize drug assets.

Ogletree (2012) provides an interesting thesis about racial profiling in his account of the arrest of Professor Henry Louis Gates at his home in Cambridge, Massachusetts, in July, 2009. Gates's arrest set off a firestorm of controversy that culminated in President Obama inviting both Dr. Gates and Sergeant Crowley, the arresting officer, to join him for a beer at the White House. Ogletree notes that when it comes to Black males, the police seem to presume guilt instead of innocence. What was most surprising to Ogletree was the number of upper and middle class Black males who wrote to him describing their experiences with the police, challenging the notion that racial profiling only occurred in certain areas and was limited to Blacks in the lower class.

For several decades, researchers have been unable to agree on the extent of racial profiling. Most previous studies have both theoretical and methodological limitations, including conceptual/definitional issues, as well as measurement and analytical challenges (Batton & Kadleck, 2004). In spite of this, racial profiling/traffic stop research provides overwhelming support for the overrepresentation of Blacks and Latinos in traffic stops (Durose, Smith, & Langan, 2007; Eith & Durose, 2011; Engel & Calnon, 2004; Gau, 2013; Gau & Brunson, 2012; Harris, 2002; Racial Profiling Data Collection Resource Center, 2003; Warren, Tomaskovic-Devey, Smith, Zingraff, & Mason, 2006). The 2015 U.S. DOJ OCR report on its investigation of the FMPD (see Box 4.2) concluded, "Ferguson police officers routinely violate the Fourth Amendment in stopping people without reasonable suspicion, arresting them without probable cause, and using unreasonable force against them."

Every three years, BJS conducts the Police Public Contact Survey, and its data is often used in racial profiling research. Since 2002, in both BJS reports and research using the data, the overrepresentation of minorities, especially Black males, in traffic and street stops has been well documented (Eith & Durose, 2011; Gau & Brunson, 2012; Pickerill, Mosher, & Pratt, 2009; Rosenfeld, Rojek, & Decker, 2012; Tillyer, Klahm, & Engel, 2012). According to Eith & Durose (2011), between 2002 and 2008 face-to-face contact with police decreased, and the majority of contacts continued to occur during traffic stops. During that time, Black drivers were about three times as likely as White drivers, and about two times as likely as Hispanic drivers, to be searched during a traffic stop (p. 1). According to the 2011 PPCS, traffic stops continue to occur more often than street stops, and more than 80% of drivers involved in traffic stops believed the police acted properly regardless of race and ethnicity. All racial/ethnic groups perceived that the traffic stop was legitimate (Langton & Durose, 2013; see Table 4.3).

Table 4.3

Involuntary Contact With Police Among Persons Age 16 or Older, by Demographic and Type of Contact

Demographic Characteristics	Street Stops[a]			Traffic Stops[b]		
	Percentage of All Persons	Percentage of Stopped Persons		Percentage of All Drivers[d]	Percentage of Stopped Drivers	
		Total	Police Behaved Properly[c]		Total	Police Behaved Properly
Total	0.6	100	70.7	10.2	100	88.2
Sex						
Male	0.8	67.5	69.8	11.9	58.8	86.9
Female	0.4	32.5	72.7	8.4	41.2	89.9
Race/Hispanic origin						
White[e]	0.6	65.2	77.6	9.8	69.3	89.4
Black/African American	0.6	12.4	37.7	12.8	12.6	82.7
Hispanic/Latino	0.7	15.3	62.9	10.4	12.2	86.5
American Indian/Alaska Native	0.5[f]	0.6	100	15.0	0.6	74.2
Asian/Native Hawaiian/other Pacific Islander	0.4	3.6	85.0	9.4	4.0	89.5
Two or more races	1.8	3.1	76.6	13.4	1.3	94.8

(Continued)

(Continued)

Demographic Characteristics	Street Stops[a]			Traffic Stops[b]		
		Percentage of Stopped Persons			Percentage of Stopped Drivers	
	Percentage of All Persons	Total	Police Behaved Properly[c]	Percentage of All Drivers[d]	Total	Police Behaved Properly
Age						
16–17	1.5	8.5	67.4	9.0	1.8	92.3
18–24	1.6	31.7	72.1	17.8	19.5	85.1
25–34	0.9	27.1	64.4	12.7	22.4	88.1
35–44	0.4	10.6	81.6	11.3	19.8	87.9
45–54	0.4	10.9	79.7	9.4	17.9	88.7
55–64	0.2	5.5	62.2	7.1	11.4	89.7
65 or older	0.2	5.7	68.8	4.8	7.2	92.3

Source: Bureau of Justice Statistics, *National Crime Victimization Survey, Police–Public Contact Survey, 2011.*

Notes:

[I]Interpret with caution. Estimate based on 10 or fewer sample cases or the coefficient of variation is greater than 50.

a. Includes persons stopped by police during the past 12 months for whom the most recent contact involved being stopped by police on the street or in public but not in a moving motor vehicle.

b. Includes persons stopped by police during the past 12 months for whom recent contact was as a driver in a traffic stop.

c. Includes persons stopped by police during the past 12 months for whom recent contact was as a driver in a traffic stop.

d. Denominator includes approximately 2 of respondents who did not report whether police behaved properly.

e. Excludes persons of Hispanic or Latino origin.

During the last decade, research interest in **consent searches** following traffic stops has increased (see, e.g., Engel & Calnon, 2004; Higgins, Jennings, Jordan, & Gabbidon, 2011; Housholder, 2005; Pickerill, Mosher, & Pratt, 2009; Rojek, Rosenfeld, & Decker, 2004; Schafer, Carter, Katz-Bannister, & Wells, 2006; Tillyer & Klahm, 2011; Paoline & Terrill, 2005), due at least in part to the use of this type of search in the war on drugs (Gau & Brunson, 2012) and the high search rates of African American males (Pickerill, Mosher, & Pratt, 2009; Rojek, Rosenfeld, & Decker, 2012; Tillyer, Klahm, & Engel, 2012). Gau and Brunson (2012) analyzed the 2008 PPS data in an effort to determine perceptions of the legitimacy of consent searches. Their findings found significant support for negative perceptions among White drivers, but only marginal support among Black drivers that they attribute to drivers' expectations, leading them to conclude that "racial profiling is a complex, nuanced phenomenon and that race is more symbolic than predictive of stopped drivers' attitudes toward police" (p. 250). Interestingly, Gau and Brunson found no support among Hispanics for negative perceptions of police following a traffic stop. However, they note the limitations of small Black and Hispanic sample sizes. Are traffic stops and consent searches used as a pretext for curtailing illegal immigration, especially among Hispanics? Increased attention has been placed on this immigration and policing issue, discussed next.

Immigration and Policing

America has always been a country of immigrants, and the role of law enforcement in controlling illegal immigration is not new. What is new is the increased concern about homeland security since 9/11 and the disparate impact it has had on Mexicans and other Latinos in immigration enforcement actions. Latinos have always been subjected to brutality and dehumanizing processes at border crossings and either under-policed or over-policed in their barrios (Duran, 2012). Their presence in, and migration to, the United States has existed for centuries. For the most part, the current focus on illegal immigration is ahistorical and omits the importance of Mexican and other Latinas/Latinos to the U.S. economy. According to Posadas and Medina (2012), since the 1870s, "American employers have long courted Mexican immigrants" (p. 81). As early as 1910, they were subjected to oppressive conditions, and abuses often occurred when they attempted to enter the United States to work. For decades they made their way across the country and into the U.S. labor pool in both agricultural and industrial jobs. Since the 1950s, changes in federal migrant worker policies and increased anti-immigrant sentiments have resulted in selective immigration enforcement. Today, Mexicans and other Latinos appear to have transitioned from migrant workers to criminal illegal immigrants, due at least in part to what Posadas and Medina describe as a "lockdown through legislation" (p. 86).

Immigration enforcement is the responsibility of the federal government. Three agencies within the DHS are responsible for the enforcement of immigration laws: the U.S. Customs and Border Protection (CBP), the U.S. Immigration and Customs Enforcement Services (ICE), and the U.S. Citizenship and Immigration Services (UDCIS; Blumberg & Niederhoffer, 1970). In 2009, the DHS ICE implemented *Secure Communities: A Comprehensive Plan to Identify and Remove Criminal Aliens* (S-Comm). It initially was envisioned as an effort to improve public safety that included technological advances and cooperation with local and state law enforcement agencies (LEAs). It was a multi-faceted and multi-agency effort that required stakeholders in federal agencies as well as tribal LEAs to work with ICE and other LEAs to apprehend and remove criminal aliens. At the time, more than 100 localities entered into Memorandums of Agreement with ICE to participate in S-Comm through Section 287(g) of the Immigration and Nationality Act (Gabbidon & Taylor Greene, 2013). Even before S-Comm was implemented, some states enacted legislation requiring state and local law enforcement officers to act as federal immigration agents (Kirk, Papachristos, Fagan, & Tyler, 2012; "Minnesota Advocates for Human Rights," 2008). In some locales, status checks became routine, not only during traffic stops but also at work sites, in shopping areas, and elsewhere. In 2010, Arizona enacted SB 1070, a controversial immigration law that requires police to enforce federal laws and to check immigration status upon "reasonable suspicion" that someone is an illegal immigrant. SB 1070 was copied by other states as well.

Activists, scholars, police administrators, and officers have taken varying positions on the role of state and local officials in immigration law enforcement and S-Comm. In May, 2011, Illinois Governor Pat Quinn withdrew from the program after discovering that many deportees had never been convicted of any crime (La Mala, 2011). In July, 2011, the National Latino Peace Officers Association sent a letter to S-Comm task force members expressing concern about how the program has eroded police-community relations (Holub, 2011). At issue is whether an aggressive strategy of verifying residency during traffic stops results in racial profiling of immigrants (S. Williams, 2007; Sweeney, 2014; Young, 2007). Sweeney (2014) uses the term *shadow immigration enforcement* to refer to

> the distorted exercise of regular policing powers by a state or local officer who has no immigration enforcement authority for the purpose of increasing immigration enforcement . . . [that] involves the disproportionate targeting of vulnerable "foreign-seeming" populations for hyper-enforcement. (p. 228)

The DOJ OCR has investigated and found racial profiling against Latinos in Maricopa County, AZ; East Haven, CT; and Alamance County, NC (U.S. DOJ, 2011b, 2011c, 2011d). On March 26, 2012, by a vote of 5–3 (Justice Kagan recused), the U.S. Supreme Court ruled in *Arizona v. United States* that some provisions of SB 1070 did interfere with the power of the federal government to enforce immigration laws, including being in the state without legal papers, seeking employment in the state, and arresting persons without a warrant (ACLU, 2012). However, the Court let stand the most controversial provision that allowed Arizona police to hold anyone involved in a crime who is believed to be illegally in the country (ACLU, 2012). After years of controversy and its negative impact on both citizens and efforts to enforce immigration laws, DHS Secretary Jeh Charles Johnson discontinued S-Comm in November, 2014.

The number of DHS deportations has steadily increased since 2003 (Pew Research Center, 2014c). In 2013, DHS apprehended approximately 662,000 aliens and removed approximately 438,000. The countries of origin for most of the persons removed were Mexico (64.1%), Guatemala (11.1%), Honduras (9.7%), and El Salvador (7.7%). Most apprehensions occur on the Texas, Arizona, and California borders, and the majority of aliens are returned to Mexico (49.4%), Canada (13.4%), the Philippines (12.1%), and China (6.6%). According to USCIS (Simanski, 2014), most aliens who were removed had a prior criminal record and were removed for immigration violations (31.3%), drug offenses (15.4%), and criminal traffic offenses (15%). Even though the number of criminal alien deportations decreased between 2012 and 2013, the deportations of

Table 4.4

Aliens Removed by Criminal Status and Country of Nationality: Fiscal Years 2011 to 2013

Country of Nationality	2013 Total	2013 Criminal[*]	2013 Non-Criminal	2012 Total	2012 Criminal[*]	2012 Non-Criminal	2011 Total	2011 Criminal[*]	2011 Non-Criminal
Total	438,421	198,394	240,027	418,397	200,143	218,254	387,134	188,964	198,170
Mexico	314,904	146,298	168,606	303,745	151,444	152,301	288,078	145,133	142,945
Guatemala	46,866	15,365	31,501	38,900	13,494	25,406	30,343	11,718	18,625
Honduras	36,526	16,609	19,917	31,740	13,815	17,925	22,027	10,825	11,202
El Salvador	20,862	9,440	11,422	18,993	8,674	10,319	17,381	8,507	8,874
Dominican Republic	2,278	1,805	473	2,868	2,182	686	2,893	2,142	751
Ecuador	1,491	580	911	1,763	706	1,057	1,716	704	1,012
Colombia	1,421	956	465	1,591	1,055	536	1,899	1,048	851
Brazil	1,411	366	1,045	2,397	424	1,973	3,350	550	2,800
Nicaragua	1,337	691	646	1,400	731	669	1,502	696	806
Jamaica	1,101	993	108	1,319	1,150	169	1,474	1,225	249
All other countries, including unknown	10,224	5,291	4,933	13,681	6,468	7,213	16,471	6,416	10,055

Source: U.S. Department of Homeland Security, ENFORCE Alien Removal Module (EARM), January 2014. Enforcement Integrated Database (EID), November 2013.

Note: Excludes criminals removed by Customs and Border Protection (CBP). CBP EID does not identify whether aliens removed were criminals.

[*] Refers to persons removed who have a prior criminal conviction.

noncriminals (i.e., those removed for immigration violations) has increased since 2011 (see Table 4.4).

Public opinion about immigration is fairly consistent regardless of race. Most Americans (41%) believe that immigration levels should decrease, including (non-Hispanic) Whites (37%), Blacks (29%), and Hispanics (30%), and that border security should be tightened (83%): Whites (85%), Blacks (84%) and Hispanics (74%). Forty-three percent believe that controlling the U.S. borders to halt illegal immigrants is very important, and 37% believe we should have new laws dealing with immigration: Whites (39%), Blacks (34%), and Hispanics (32%; Gallup, 2014).

We know less about whether or not Americans believe racial profiling of Latinos exists during immigration enforcement efforts. We do know that, "While strict immigration laws are often touted politically as ways to ensure public safety, the enactment and enforcement of harsh immigration laws may actually undercut public safety by creating a cynicism of the law in immigrant communities" (Kirk et al., 2012, p. 81). Very little is known about how the militarization of the police along the southern borders impacts public safety. This issue is discussed next.

Militarization of the Police

Students are taught that police departments have both bureaucratic and quasi-military characteristics that include a centralized and hierarchical command structure, ranks, rules and regulations, and use of military terminology. Historically, police departments were distinguishable from military forces. More than 40 years ago, Blumberg and Niederhoffer (1970) described the growing militarization of urban police departments as "the most ominous development that has occurred as a concomitant of police professionalism" (p. 13). At the time, they attributed this development to the growth of police agencies that "take on the characteristics of an army rather than a police force" (p. 13). When the FMPD used military equipment to disperse and control protesters following the grand jury's decision not to indict the officer involved in the killing of Michael Brown, it was obvious that the distinction between police and the military had become less clear. Most Americans were either surprised and/or appalled that the FMPD officers looked like they were on a battlefield, not on the streets of a small American city with a population of about 21,000.

Since the 1990s, military equipment has been available to federal and state agencies through the Department of Defense's 1033 Program. Initially the equipment was designated for drug enforcement, primarily at the border (Cox & Cook, 2014). Since 1997, equipment has been available to local agencies as well. The DOJ also supported the militarization of the police through the Edward Byrne Memorial Justice Assistance Grant (JAG) program. Kraska (2007) argued that the distinctions between the military and the police have become blurred and that each has taken on characteristics of the other (i.e., the police and crime control have become militarized, and the military has become more involved in police matters, especially internal security). Kraska explains the concepts of militarism and militarization as follows,

> Militarism . . . is an ideology focused on the best means to solve problems . . . a set of beliefs, values, and assumptions that stress the use of force and threat

of violence as the most appropriate and efficacious means to solve problems. Police militarization . . . is simply the process whereby civilian police increasingly draw from, and pattern themselves around, the tenets of militarism and the military model. (p. 3)

He also refers to the rise of a crime control enterprise (i.e., a military and criminal justice complex similar to the military-industrial complex).

The movement of some police agencies from having quasi-military characteristics to using military tactics in crime control is problematic. As the ACLU (2014, p. 2) states, "Neighborhoods are not war zones and police officers should not be treating us like wartime enemies." Special Weapons and Tactics (SWAT) teams and Paramilitary Police Units (PPU) are at the center of militarized policing. Along with both come overly aggressive tactics and a paramilitary culture. According to the ACLU, "Not all communities are equally impacted by this phenomenon; the disproportionate impact of the War on Drugs in communities of color has been well documented" (p. 16).

The ACLU study of **police militarization** expressed concern about how the program has eroded police-community relations. In the aftermath of criticisms related to the Ferguson and Baltimore police departments, President Obama limited the sale of military equipment to local law enforcement agencies. Immigration law enforcement and the militarization of police agencies appear to have eroded both confidence in the police and progress made in building better police-community relations through community policing initiatives, discussed next.

Community Policing

Community policing (COP) has been utilized for more than two decades in numerous jurisdictions in the United States and abroad. It is a proactive approach that provides opportunities for citizens and police to work together to solve problems of crime and disorder. When it emerged in the 1980s, it was viewed as an alternative to traditional policing strategies. At the time, it was the latest of several efforts to improve police and community relationships that began long ago, and in the 1960s-1980s included the establishment of police-community relations (PCR) units, team policing, foot patrol, and other innovations. In the early 1990s, COP had begun to spread across the country before President Clinton included it in his election campaign. At the time, although many agencies had adopted varying forms of COP, others were not convinced of its utility. When the 1994 Crime Control Act made federal funds available for hiring COP officers, it became a major impetus for the adoption of COP by agencies willing to accept federal money to do so.

Many Black police administrators, including Lee P. Brown, Hubert Williams, Rueben Greenberg, and other members of NOBLE, were early proponents of COP. In the 1980s, Brown and Williams were among the first in a cadre of progressive chiefs of police to successfully implement foot patrol programs in an effort to reduce the fear of crime in Houston, Texas, and Newark, New Jersey, respectively. COP was attractive to many progressive police administrators because it could be tailored to fit the needs of a particular neighborhood or jurisdiction. Other administrators and police officers resisted COP because it required a completely different police role; crime control was replaced with addressing not only crime, but also problems of disorder.

Today, most COP programs have a problem-solving component that originated in problem-oriented policing (POP). POP, as conceived by Goldstein (1979), differs from (early) COP programs in that it is a reactive approach that initially did not require citizen input. POP uses a process known as scanning, analysis, response, and assessment (SARA) to identify and respond to problems (Dempsey, 1999). Oliver (2000) described three generations of COP: innovation (1979–1986), diffusion (1987–1994), and institutionalization (1995-present). Whether or not COP has been institutionalized is debatable, depending on what "institutionalized" means. Does it mean that more agencies have mission statements that reflect a COP philosophy and approach than in the 1980s when it first emerged? Does it mean that agencies have a department-wide COP philosophy; continue to train officers; and have identifiable COP strategies, officers, and daily face-to-face interaction with citizens? In 2000, Oliver and other COP proponents could not foresee the impact that 9/11 would have on the institutionalization of COP after federal funding priorities shifted to homeland security. The Office of COP Services in the DOJ was instrumental in federal COP initiatives. Like other DOJ agencies, COP's budget has been reduced since 2002.

COP research includes descriptive studies of implementation, organizational issues, evaluative studies, and analyses of citizen and officer perceptions of COP, as well as its progress and obstacles. COP has had varied responses in different places, and the verdict is still out as to whether or not it improves police-community relations. Some municipal agencies have excelled at adopting a philosophy of COP that is emphasized in their organizations' mission statements and values, although they have had more limited success in gaining support from minority groups. Kusow, Wilson, and Martin (1997) noted that citizen satisfaction with the police, as well as community trust and confidence, are prerequisites to successful COP programs. COP initiatives in some minority and immigrant communities have improved relationships between police and citizens. During the past decade, COP research has decreased substantially.

Even though relationships built with citizens by utilizing COP strategies can be helpful in detecting threats to the homeland, citizens are more reluctant to cooperate with police when they don't trust them. Do you think the FMPD utilized community policing strategies?

❖ Conclusion

Race and policing is an important topic in the study of crime. This chapter provided a brief overview of policing and traced the history of policing racial and ethnic groups. Several contemporary issues, including police deviance, police bias and racial profiling, immigration and policing, police militarization, and community policing were examined. The quality of policing has improved dramatically during the past 200 years. Countless individuals and organizations have labored to ensure that citizens are provided with police who understand their role to protect and serve. New recruits receive more training and are better educated than ever before. Today, many officers who successfully complete the police academy are more likely to be representative of minorities in their communities. The changing face of police officers did not occur overnight and was initially resisted by the police establishment.

Today, there is still a need for affirmative action at all levels of government, there are still patterns and practices of violations of civil rights by police, and there is racial conflict within some police departments and communities. Despite progress, citizen confidence in the police, especially among minorities, hasn't improved very much. And police deviance and misconduct are ongoing problems. These are indicators of the need to continue to identify best practices to prevent and control deviance, bias, and selective enforcement. Recent efforts to curtail illegal immigration have led to more allegations of racial profiling during traffic stops. The data collected on racial profiling attest to differential treatment of minorities (Blacks and Hispanics). The increase in deadly police confrontations continues to have disparate impacts. The formal elimination of the DHS Secure Communities is important, although whether or not it continues to be used (less formally) is unclear.

Discussion Questions

1. What needs to be done in order to increase confidence in the police among minorities?

2. Why do you think minorities are often involved in brutality and use of force incidents?

3. Do you think police militarization contributes to more effective law and order?

4. Do you think the DOJ findings on the police in Ferguson, MO, might be found elsewhere as well?

5. How can community policing and policing for homeland security coexist?

Internet Exercises

1. Visit the Harvard University Project Implicit website (https://implicit.harvard.edu/implicit/research/) and take one of the Implicit Bias Tests. The site requires that you register.

2. Review the annual report *Immigration Enforcement Actions: 2013* prepared by the Office of Immigration Statistics (http://www.dhs.gov/publication/immigration-enforcement-actions-2013). Do you think the data support the belief of some that legal and illegal Latino (especially Mexican) immigrants are targeted? Explain.

Internet Sites

Bureau of Justice Statistics Special Report: Police Behavior During Traffic and Street Stops, 2011: http://www.bjs.gov/content/pub/pdf/pbtss11.pdf

Department of Homeland Security: http://www.dhs.gov/index.shtm

DOJ National Initiative for Building Community Trust and Justice: http://trustandjustice.org/

Supplemental materials for *Race and Crime* are available online at
study.sagepub.com/gabbidon4e.

CHAPTER 5

Courts

*My experience in the criminal court is that the colored defendant, even in
bailable cases, is unable to give bail. He has to stay in jail, and therefore his
case is very quickly disposed of by the prosecutor. Defendants locked up are
usually tried first. The colored man is more apt to be out of work than the
White man, and that is a possible reason for the large number of arrests of
Negroes. His sphere is very limited, and if there is any let up in the industry
that is involved in that sphere, he is a victim. I have often wondered if you
could change the skin of a thousand White men in the city of Chicago and
handicap them the way the colored man is handicapped today, how many
of those White men in ten years' time would be law-abiding citizens.*

—Judge Kickham Scanlan
(cited in Chicago Commission on
Race Relations, 1922, p. 356)

A s one of the key components of the criminal justice process, the courts
represent an entity in which nationally billions of dollars are spent each year.
Moreover, according to the Bureau of Justice Statistics' most recent data, annually, more than one million adults are convicted of felonies (Rosenmerkel,
Durose, & Farole, 2009), most of which are handled in state courts. Furthermore, 38%
of those convicted in state courts are Black (Rosenmerkel et al., 2009). Given these
statistics, prior to and following Judge Scanlan's telling comments, the question of
the courts and their treatment of persons of color piqued scholarly interest. It is also
important to note here the central role that class and social status play in the justice
received in the courts.

Considering the significance of the courts in the race and crime discourse, our
objectives for this chapter are threefold. First, we provide an overview of how the
American courts operate. This is followed by a brief historical overview of race and
the American courts. Last, we examine some contemporary issues related to race
and the courts. Our primary focus here is on the various aspects of the court process

and whether discrimination (on the basis of race or gender) remains a problem. In addition, we examine drug courts, which, over the past decade, have served as a way to handle the overflow of drug cases. Because racial minorities are frequently diverted to drug courts, after reviewing drug courts' structure and philosophy, we examine some recent evaluations.

❖ Overview of American Courts: Actors and Processes

Like so many other facets of American life, the American court system owes much to the English justice system (Chapin, 1983). In general, as American society gained its independence, the courts became more complex with the development of the federal court system and the Supreme Court (Shelden, 2001). Today, because of these early changes, the U.S. court system is referred to as a "**dual-court system**." There are both state and federal courts, each with trial courts at the lowest level and appellate courts at the top of the hierarchy. The federal court system starts with U.S. magistrate courts, "who hear minor offenses and conduct preliminary hearings" (Shelden & Brown, 2003, p. 196). U.S. District Courts are trial courts that hear both civil and criminal cases. Positioned above the U.S. District Courts is the U.S. Court of Appeals, which is the final step before reaching the U.S. Supreme Court. The Supreme Court represents the highest court in the land and has the final say on matters that make it to that level. The American court system (both state and federal) involves several actors and processes. Over time, some of these actors and processes have come under scrutiny for a variety of reasons, including race- and class-related concerns (Reiman, 2007). As for actors, the court is generally composed of three main figures: the judge, the prosecutor, and the defense attorney. Although the system is theoretically based on the ancient system of "trial by combat," in practice, it has been suggested that these main figures are part of the "courtroom workgroup" who actually work together to resolve matters brought before the court (Neubauer & Fradella, 2014).

Photo 5.1

The U.S. Supreme Court Justices, 2010. Back row (left to right): Sonia Sotomayor, Stephen G. Breyer, Samuel A. Alito, and Elena Kagan. Front row (left to right): Clarence Thomas, Antonin Scalia, Chief Justice John G. Roberts, Anthony Kennedy, and Ruth Bader Ginsburg.

Roberts Court (2010)—The Oyez Project.

There are several processes involved when one is navigating through the court system. First, there is a pretrial process, where the decision is made whether to move forward with a particular case. If the case is moved forward, the question of pretrial detention and **bail** is decided next. Other processes in the court system include the preliminary hearing, grand jury proceedings, and the arraignment, at which time a defendant first enters his or her plea. Although **plea bargaining** determines the outcome in most cases, if the case happens to go to trial, there are other processes that move the case along. Once the decision to go to trial is made, unless the case is going to be decided solely by a judge (referred to as a "bench trial"), the next process would be jury selection. Following the completion of jury selection, the trial begins. If the defendant is found guilty, the sentencing phase begins (this phase is discussed in detail in Chapter 6).

A Note on the Philosophy, Operation, and Structure of Native American Courts

Because of the unique history and worldview of Native Americans, much of the previous dialogue on American courts does not apply to Native American courts. Consequently, we provide a brief overview of the extent, philosophy, operation, and structure of their court system. Recent figures reveal that there are more than 200 courts in Native American jurisdictions. These courts have "approximately 200 judges, 153 prosecutors and 20 peacemakers. Nearly half of all tribes rely on state courts for judicial services due to a lack of resources and shortage of personnel" (J. Smith, 2009, p. 574). J. Smith (2009) noted that there are three fundamental differences between Native American courts and American courts. First, Native American courts have limited jurisdiction:

> Tribal courts only have jurisdiction when (a) both the offender and victim are Native Americans, (b) the crime occurs on the reservation, and (c) the punishment does not result in longer than a year imprisonment or exceed $5,000 in fines. (p. 574)

Second, because Native American tribes are considered sovereign nations, they are not bound by the Constitution. Finally, the American and Tribal Courts operate under two distinct philosophies. The philosophy of tribal courts certainly follows a different paradigm than Anglo-American justice systems (see Table 5.1). Tarver et al. (2002) noted that the indigenous justice paradigm follows an approach that includes spirituality and oral customs, which are not welcome in non-Native American courts.

As was mentioned in Chapter 4, after the enactment of Public Law 280 in 1953, the jurisdiction for criminal and civil cases on tribal lands in several states was turned over to local and state governments (Tarver et al., 2002). Other jurisdictions were also impacted by this new law, which "gave to state and local police the enforcement authority in Indian communities, and cases would be adjudicated in state courts" (p. 88). The complexity of jurisdictional issues on tribal land is illuminated in Table 5.2.

Table 5.1

Comparison of American and Indigenous (Native) Justice Paradigms

American Justice Paradigm	Indigenous (Native) Justice Paradigm
Vertical power structure	Circular structure of empowerment
Communication is rehearsed	Communication is fluid
Written statutory law derived from rules and procedures	Oral customary law learned as a way of life
Separation of church and state	The spiritual realm is invoked in ceremonies and with prayer
Time-oriented process	No time limits on the process

Source: TARVER, MARSHA; WALKER, STEVE; WALLACE, HARVEY, MULTICULTURAL ISSUES IN THE CRIMINAL JUSTICE SYSTEM, 1st, Copyright©2002. Printed and Electronically reproduced by permission of Pearson Education, Inc., Upper Saddle River, New Jersey.

Table 5.2

Indian Country Jurisdiction in Criminal Cases

Suspect	Victim	Jurisdiction
Indian	Indian	Misdemeanor: Tribal jurisdiction Felony: Federal jurisdiction No state jurisdiction No federal jurisdiction for misdemeanors
Indian	Non-Indian	Misdemeanor: Tribal jurisdiction Felony: Federal jurisdiction No state jurisdiction
Non-Indian	Indian	Misdemeanor: Federal jurisdiction Felony: Federal jurisdiction Normally not state jurisdiction (the U.S. Attorney may elect to defer prosecution to the state) No tribal jurisdiction
Non-Indian	Non-Indian	Misdemeanor: State jurisdiction Felony: State jurisdiction Normally U.S. Attorney will decline prosecution No tribal jurisdiction
Indian	Victimless	Misdemeanor: Tribal jurisdiction Felony: Federal jurisdiction
Non-Indian	Victimless	Misdemeanor: Usually state jurisdiction Felony: Usually state jurisdiction Normally U.S. Attorney will decline prosecution

Source: TARVER, MARSHA; WALKER, STEVE; WALLACE, HARVEY, MULTICULTURAL ISSUES IN THE CRIMINAL JUSTICE SYSTEM, 1st. Copyright,©2002. Printed and Electronically reproduced by permission of Pearson Education, Inc., Upper Saddle River, New Jersey.

Although almost no research examines whether there are American Indians who are discriminated against in their own court system, it remains important to provide an overview of how their courts operate. To do this, we focus on the courts of the Navajo, the second largest American Indian tribe (U.S. Census Bureau, 1995). Tso (1996) noted that over the years, Navajo courts have been structured like Anglo courts. There are several judicial districts; as is seen in Table 5.2, the jurisdiction is based on the parties involved (i.e., Indian or non-Indian). In general, however, district courts are courts of general civil jurisdiction and of limited criminal jurisdiction. Civil jurisdiction extends to all persons residing within the Navajo Nation or who cause an act to occur within the nation. The limitations of criminal jurisdiction are determined by the nature of the offense, the penalty to be imposed, where the crime occurred, and the status and residency of the individual charged with an offense (Tso, 1996).

There are also children's courts within each district. These courts hear "all matters concerning children except for custody, child support and visitation disputes arising from divorce proceedings, and probate matters" (Tso, 1996, p. 172). The Navajo also have a Supreme Court and Peacemaker Courts. The Navajo Nation Supreme Court "hears appeals from final lower court decisions and from certain final administrative orders" (Tso, 1996, p. 173). Peacemaker Courts rely on mediation to resolve some lesser matters.

Any prospective judicial candidates are screened by the Judiciary Committee of the Navajo Tribal Council. Using the Navajo Tribal Code as its basis for selection, the committee selects those who are most qualified. In Navajo courts, where the Navajo Tribal Code prevails, people can represent themselves; however, only members of the Navajo Bar Association can represent others in the courts. These include actual lawyers who have attended law school and those who have followed nontraditional pathways (i.e., passing a certified Navajo Bar Training Course or having served as a legal apprentice). More than a decade ago, the Navajo Nation Council revamped the Navajo Nation Criminal Code to reflect more indigenous practices.

The irony of the Navajo justice system is that, with the emerging acceptance of the philosophy of restorative justice, American courts are trying to operate more like Native American courts. This is especially true of juvenile justice systems in some states (such as Pennsylvania), where the guiding philosophy is now restorative justice. We now turn to a historical overview of race and the courts.

❖ Historical Overview of Race and the Courts in America

Native Americans

It is widely accepted that America had its beginnings long before Europeans began arriving in colonial America, and the record shows that the Native Americans who were here had already created their own norms and ways of handling deviants. As Friedman (1993) noted, once Europeans began to come en masse, there was a "clash of legal cultures" (p. 20). In many instances, this clash resulted in the conqueror Europeans imparting their system onto Native Americans and African Americans, who also began to arrive en masse after the slave trade began. Due to the smallness of 142 communities in colonial America, these early court procedures were more informal, which, as noted before, owed much to the English system. In fact, the courts were also places where community members looked for social drama (Friedman, 1993).

Early on, both Native Americans and African Americans had similarly low status in American society. As such, other than being a means of social control, the courts were generally not concerned about their lives. In Massachusetts, for example, the courts treated Native Americans with indifference (Higginbotham, 1978). For example, according to Higginbotham (1978), "The general court of the colony enforced the English right to take the Indians' 'unimproved' land in 1633" (p. 69). This action was followed by the courts treating Native Americans more harshly (Higginbotham, 1978). During this period, it was not unusual for the Massachusetts courts to use the punishment of either enslavement or banishment for Native Americans (Higginbotham, 1978). On occasion, however, magistrates were concerned about uprisings that could occur if Native Americans felt they were being mistreated by the courts. Because of this concern, on occasion, "The magistrates involved other Indians, either as viewers of the trial and punishment or ideally as witnesses of the accused" (Chapin, 1983, p. 117).

As noted by J. Smith (2009), formal court systems in Native American communities have been around since the 1880s. At that time, the Court of Indian Offenses was established by the Department of the Interior and the Bureau of Indian Affairs. These courts were created to handle minor offenses (J. Smith, 2009). In the 1930s, tribal courts were enacted in concert with the Indian Reorganization Act. Such courts were established with the intention of having Native Americans "enact their own laws and establish their own court system to reflect those laws" (J. Smith, 2009, p. 574). Notably, more than 50% of tribes have such courts today. Box 5.1 discusses some recent concerns about whether Tribal courts are equipped to handle domestic violence cases involving tribal and non-tribal members.

BOX 5.1

Race and Crime in the Media

Are Tribal Courts Developed Enough for VAWA? Pascua Yaqui Proves It

The *American Bar Association Journal* summed up the situation this way in a recent article on Reclaiming Sovereignty: "Indian tribes are retaking jurisdiction over domestic violence on their own land."

And as part of that effort, the Pascua Yaqui Tribe of Southern Arizona, one of three pilot project tribes chosen by the Justice Department, recently held the first Violence Against Women Act Trial Advocacy training at their Casino Del Sol Conference Center in Tucson.

Attendees came from tribes across the country like Aleisha Pemberton, a domestic and sexual assault prosecutor from the Red Lake Minnesota Band of Chippewa, who said, "Our system is developed, but with domestic violence involving both tribal and non-tribal members being a growing problem, we're hoping to better our program with this current knowledge."

(Continued)

(Continued)

Frank Demolli is Chief Judge of the Santa Clara Pueblo in Espanola, New Mexico, where tribal council for its nearly 900 tribal members is discussing the issue. "The pueblo would like to implement VAWA, but where do we get the money?" he asks, admitting that the eight pueblos under his purview were staunch opponents of the Indian Civil Rights Act in the 1960s and fought against some of the standards imposed in the current legislation, particularly federal government oversight of tribal court decisions and having non-Indians on a jury pool.

According to a *Washington Post* story, "Some members of Congress fought hard to derail the legislation, arguing that non-Indian men would be unfairly convicted without due process by sovereign nations whose unsophisticated tribal courts were not equal to the American criminal justice system."

That's a bum rap according to the Pascua Yaqui tribe's Attorney General Alfred Urbina. "Historically, people argued that tribal courts couldn't treat people fairly – but that's not a true snapshot of what tribal courts are now. Today, tribal tribunals are as sophisticated as any municipal court in Arizona in terms of how they operate. There are a lot of tribes already doing a great job administering justice in different ways consistent with their community values."

Urbina and Pascua Yaqui Chairman Peter Yucupicio were part of a contingent that went to Washington last year to present the tribe's $21 million state-of-the-art courthouse and point to the fact that there are over 300 other tribal courts on sovereign land throughout the U.S.

Development of the Yaqui legal complex was necessary to serve the 5,000 tribal members who lived with, worked with, and often dated or married non-Natives. More than 500 non-tribal members live in the 2-square-mile reservation that employs 800 non-Indian casino and resort employees. Conditions were ripe for trouble. The poverty rate hovered in the 40-45 percent range. Unemployment was at 25 percent. Over 40 percent of the populace was single moms with children. Substance issues were problematic in struggles involving alcohol and drug abuse, gangs, and domestic violence.

During the year-long pilot project, "We recorded 20 DV cases, nearly half involving injuries, with 16 defendants representing Hispanic, Afro-American, Asian, and Caucasian cultures," according to the tribe's Chief Prosecutor Oscar "OJ" Flores. "Fourteen female victims were involved along with 18 children (from infant to 11 years old) present during the incidents. These cases represented 25 percent of all the domestic violence cases on the reservation during the trial period."

"About half the cases during the trial were dismissed early on because charges didn't ultimately qualify," adds tribal Public Defender Melissa Acosta. "The one case that did go before a jury was a weak one, a same sex couple where their specific relationship could not be established in court. This is an on-going learning experience, and as each case is different, it presents a new challenge. We're learning as we go."

Melvin Stoof (Rosebud Sioux), a 40-year veteran of the legal profession, sat in on all the cases during the Pascua Yaqui trial period. "We've seen a lot of substantial changes in the past decade, more collaborative efforts, and more cases being prosecuted. This pilot project will certainly be a model for much of Indian country and what's happening here will hopefully spread like wildfire as other tribes get on board to keep their women and children safe and make batterers more accountable. This is the ground floor and I'm proud to be a part of it."

Source: Allen (2015).

Whether the courts were a place where justice prevailed for Native Americans is subject to debate. In Chapter 6, we look a bit more closely at early sentencing patterns, shedding some light on this topic. For now, we turn our attention to a brief historical overview of African Americans and the courts.

African Americans

Much of the early race-related legislation, which guided the courts, was directed at Blacks (Higginbotham, 1978). However, some legislation did target White ethnic group members. An example of such early legislation was Act VI, which was passed by the Virginia legislature in the 1600s and "required Irish servants arriving in the colony without indentures to serve longer terms than their English counterparts" (Higginbotham, 1978, p. 33). As one reviews the early literature, it becomes apparent that legislation contributed to the inequities observed in the courts. Given these connections, it is also apparent that politics played a key role in how the courts ruled. Therefore, even after the Revolutionary War and the subsequent ratification of the Constitution, Southern states still had a vested interest in controlling African American slave labor. Legal scholar Randall Kennedy (1997) wrote,

> In terms of substantive criminal law and in terms of punishment, slaves were . . . prohibited from testifying or contradicting Whites in court. Moreover, in some jurisdictions, such as Virginia, South Carolina, and Louisiana, slaves were tried before special tribunals—slave courts—designed to render quick, rough justice. (p. 77)

For those who did not go before slave courts, "plantation justice" prevailed solely under the discretion of the master or overseer (Friedman, 1993). To refer to plantation justice as being brutal is an understatement. Even minor events resulted in serious punishments. Friedman (1993) provided an example of how one slave, Eugene, was disciplined:

> William Byrd of Westover, Virginia, recorded the following in a dry, matter-of-fact tone in his diary: On November 30, 1709, Eugene, a house hand, "was whipped for pissing in bed." On December 3, Eugene repeated this offense, "for which I made him drink a pint of piss." On December 16, "Eugene was whipped for doing nothing yesterday." Three years later, on December 18, 1712, "found Eugene asleep instead of being at work, for which I beat him severely." (p. 53)

Byrd's actions were sanctioned by slave codes, which, several decades earlier, had made it a minor offense for a master to kill a slave in colonial Virginia (Higginbotham, 1978).

With the abolition of slavery in Northern states and the arrival of emancipation in 1863, it was anticipated that justice would prevail more often for African Americans. At least in the South, such conventional wisdom did not prevail. As is further discussed in Chapter 6, the courts became a cog in the operation of the convict-lease system, which, as was noted in Chapter 1, allowed states to lease out convicts to Southern landowners.

Using familiar tactics, legislators enacted laws to snare African Americans. The courts were eager participants and ensured that an ample labor supply flowed to Southern landowners (Sellin, 1976). When these "legal" measures failed to produce the desired outcome, Southerners resorted to trickery and violence (Friedman, 1993). Such actions led many African Americans to lose faith in both the political and justice systems (Du Bois, 1901/2002).

Well into the 20th century, little changed regarding the treatment of African Americans and the courts. Higginbotham (1996) provided a classic review of how courts were bastions of racism. By the very nature of the segregated practices that prevailed in courtrooms, one could presume that the courts were places where White supremacy prevailed and African Americans received little justice. Providing reviews of cases where there were segregated courtroom seating, cafeterias, and restrooms, Higginbotham noted how such discriminating practices reminiscent of "Apartheid" stood in the way of African Americans receiving equal standing in court. Of equal concern was the practice of referring to African Americans by their first names while addressing Whites by their last names and using their appropriate titles (e.g., Mr. or Mrs.). Again, such forms of disrespect produced an air of inequality, which translated into African Americans being at a disadvantage in courts.

During the 1960s and 1970s, there were national inquiries into civil disorders (riots) and also the state of racism in the criminal justice system. One such inquiry looking at the courts was prepared by the National Minority Advisory Council on Criminal Justice (1979), which was created in 1976. The report, "Racism in the Criminal Courts," surveyed the literature to determine the prevalence of racism in the courts. Drawing on the literature and public hearings in 13 cities, the report noted particular concerns with the paucity of minority judges at both the federal and state levels. Many of the other concerns expressed with the courts remain with us today (see section below on "Contemporary Issues in Race and the Courts"). For example, the council expressed concerns about unfairness in the bail process, the potentially discriminatory use of **peremptory challenges** in jury selection, the quality of public defense, and prosecutorial misconduct in the plea-bargaining process.

Latinos

The early literature on Latinos and the courts is quite sparse, and much of that early literature discussed Mexicans and immigration concerns. Another central focus of the literature is Mexicans' experience with the criminal justice system in the Western and Midwestern United States. The 1931 Wickersham Commission report, *Crime and the Foreign Born,* noted a common problem when dealing with persons, such as Mexicans, who did not speak English:

> With the best intentions in the world, an investigating officer, a prosecutor, or a court will have the greatest difficulty in getting at the exact truth and all the facts in the case when the accused is a non-English-speaking immigrant. (National Commission on Law Observance and Enforcement, 1931a, p. 173)

The report also noted that in California, Mexican defendants were abused by bail bondsmen, loan sharks, and "shyster lawyers" (p. 175). The report also mentioned that Los Angeles had an excellent **public defender system** in the 1920s, which "very frequently appear[ed] on behalf of the foreign born, especially the penniless Mexican" (p. 175).

Paul Warnshuis (1931), as part of the Wickersham Commission report, conducted a study of how Mexicans were faring with criminal justice agencies in Illinois. Besides the notion that Mexicans were often arrested on flimsy charges, an overriding theme in the report is that Mexicans were at a serious disadvantage in the court process because of language concerns. In many instances, interpreters, although needed, were not used, which resulted in the swift conviction of Mexicans. In some instances, judges simply ruled on the evidence and, if convinced of the defendants' guilt, proceeded without hearing testimony (Warnshuis, 1931). As one can imagine, the courts were a place where, for Mexicans, justice was not always received.

During the 1940s, the "Sleepy Lagoon Case" became the high-profile case that brought the issue of Latinos and the courts to the fore. The case revolved around the murder of Jose Diaz. Following the murder, 22 Mexicans were arrested, whereas another 17 were convicted (the convictions were overturned two years later). According to most reports, the trial was unfair. The media played a large role in this by creating a moral panic. Friedman (1993) wrote that the media spewed headlines calling for concern about the "zoot-suit gangsters" and "pachuco killers." One representative from law enforcement stated the following to the grand jury:

> Mexicans [have] a "biological" tendency to violence. They were the descendants of "tribes of Indians" who were given over to "human sacrifice," in which bodies were "opened by stone knives and their hearts torn out while still beating." Mexicans had "total disregard for human life"; the Mexican, in a fight, will always use a knife; he feels "a desire . . . to kill." (Friedman, 1993, p. 382)

Outrageous statements such as these colored the way in which society viewed Mexicans. A year after the Sleepy Lagoon case, the city of Los Angeles exploded with the "zoot suit riots." The riots ignited after rumors spread that a Mexican had killed a serviceman, and the city broke out into four days of rioting. During this time, "servicemen and off-duty policemen chased, beat, and stripped 'zoot-suiters'" (Friedman, 1993, p. 382). As for the courts, little is ever mentioned of them punishing those who attacked the Mexicans.

In later years, the National Minority Advisory Council on Criminal Justice (1979) would also express concern about the treatment of Hispanics in the courts. As in the case of African Americans, they expressed concern about the treatment of Hispanics throughout the court system. Particularly disturbing to the council was the lack of Hispanics in significant judiciary roles. The report also noted that nearly 50 years after the Wickersham report, language remained a problem, commenting,

> Non-English speaking minorities have special problems of access to courts, to legal counsel and representation because of language and the failure of the courts and priorities of resources to have trained, impartial translators at every stage of courts and trial-related proceedings. (p. 63)

Asian Americans

As was mentioned in Chapter 1, when Asians began arriving in the United States, they were primarily located on the West Coast. Similar to other new immigrants, Asian Americans were despised by the general public. Friedman (1993) described some of the more gruesome early incidents:

In 1871, a mob in Los Angeles killed nineteen Chinese. In the 1880s, riots in Rock Springs, Wyoming, left twenty-eight Chinese dead; Whites in Tacoma, Washington, put the torch to the Chinatown in that city; and there were outrages in Oregon, Colorado, and Nevada. (p. 98)

Eventually, as in the case of other minorities, legislation in concert with the courts was used to deal with Asian Americans. But in the case of Asian Americans, the aim of such actions was to remove them from the country. Friedman (1993) put it best, writing, "The goal of anti-Chinese policy was not suppression but expulsion. . . . The keystone of Asian policy was immigration law, exclusion, and deportation" (p. 100).

Although our focus now turns to contemporary issues in race and the courts, the unfortunate reality is that many of the same issues from our historical overview are still with us. One would have anticipated that problems related to racial bias in the courts would have been resolved, but, from the literature we review next, we can see that this is not always the case.

❖ Contemporary Issues in Race and the Courts

Many of the contemporary issues pertaining to race and the courts are related to whether there is either race or gender discrimination in the various court processes (Spohn, 2014). Drug courts have also emerged as an institution that has provided some hope in stemming the tide of drug addiction and its residual effects. Given the heavy presence of racial minorities circulating through drug courts, we examine the structure, philosophy, and effectiveness of these specialized courts. We begin with a review of the literature that examines whether race or gender has been found to have an influence on each respective court process. Our first review examines the role of race and gender during the bail and pretrial processes.

Bail and the Pretrial Process

Although bail is not guaranteed by the Constitution, the **Eighth Amendment** does state that when given, it should not be "excessive." Since the creation of this amendment, various **pretrial release** options have been used. During the early 1950s and 1960s, the Vera Institute of New York conducted studies on bail practices in Philadelphia and New York. The early study in Philadelphia found that "18% of persons jailed pending trial because they could not afford bail were acquitted, whereas 48% of persons released on bail were acquitted" (Anderson & Newman, 1998, p. 215). In the 1960s, the Vera Institute created the Manhattan Bail Project, which was meant to see whether those released on their own recognizance (ROR) absconded any more often than those released on monetary bail. The project convincingly showed that "the rate of return for ROR releases was consistently equal to or better than the rate for those on monetary bail" (Anderson & Newman, 1998, p. 215). It is noteworthy that many of the defendants in the pioneering Manhattan Bail Project were minorities, the majority of whom did return for trial (Mann, 1993). Even with these findings, during the Reagan presidency, the Bail Reform Act of 1984 provided judges more discretion as to who can be given pretrial release. In general, judges can hold defendants in jail if they consider them either a risk for flight or if they pose a danger to the community. Because of risk concerns, the courts consider a variety of factors when making the decision to grant pretrial release on bail. In fact, some states, such as New York, have bail statutes that require judges to consider risk factors such as the nature of the offense, prior record, patterns in prior court appearances, employment status, community ties, and the weight of the evidence against a defendant.

There are generally three broad categories of pretrial release: nonfinancial release, financial release, and emergency release (Cohen & Reaves, 2007; see Table 5.3). Nonfinancial release means the accused is released without having to provide any monetary collateral. This typically comes in the form of ROR or citation releases, which are

Table 5.3

Types of Pretrial Release Used in State Courts

Type of Release	Defendant	Financial Liability for Failure to Appear	Liable Party
Financial			
Surety bond	Pays fee (usually 10% of bail amount), plus collateral if required, to commercial bail agent.	Full bail amount	Bail agent
Deposit bond	Posts deposit (usually 10% of bail amount) with court, which is usually refunded at successful completion of case.	Full bail amount	Defendant
Full cash bond	Posts full bail amount with court.	Full bail amount	Defendant
Property bond	Posts property title as collateral with court.	Full bail amount	Defendant
Nonfinancial			
Release on recognizance (ROR)	Signs written agreement to appear in court (includes citation releases by law enforcement).	None	N/A
Conditional (supervised) release	Agrees to comply with specific conditions such as regular reporting or drug use monitoring.	None	N/A
Unsecured bond	Has a bail amount set, but no payment is required to secure release.	Full bail amount	Defendant
Emergency release	Released as part of a court order to relieve jail crowding.	None	N/A

Source: BJS.

typically administered by law enforcement. Other such releases include conditional releases that involve having to either contact or report to some official to ensure compliance with the conditions of release (e.g., drug treatment). Under this type of release, a third party can also be entrusted to ensure the return of the accused. The final release is referred to as an "emergency release" and occurs when, due to jail crowding, the defendant is given pretrial release under generally non-stringent release conditions.

Reaves (2013) provides 2009 figures on pretrial releases of felony defendants in state courts. His report notes that in the 75 largest United States counties, 62% of felony defendants were released prior to a final decision. Of those released prior to trial, 38% were on financial release and the remainder were on nonfinancial release (24%). Defendants who were not released prior to the final disposition were most often held on bail (34%). In terms of offenses, defendants charged with more serious offenses were less likely to receive pretrial release. Table 5.4 highlights the most recent

Table 5.4

Type of Pretrial Release or Detention for State Court Felony Defendants in the 75 Largest Counties, 1990–2004

Detention-Release Outcome	State Court Felony Defendants in the 75 Largest Counties	
	Number	Percentage
Total	424,252	100
Released before case disposition	264,604	62
Financial conditions	125,650	30
Surety bond	86,107	20
Deposit bond	23,168	6
Full cash bond	12,348	3
Property bond	4,027	1
Nonfinancial conditions	136,153	32
Personal recognizance	85,330	20
Conditional release	32,882	8
Unsecured bond	17,941	4
Emergency release	2,801	1
Detained until case disposition	159,647	38
Held on bail	132,572	32
Denied bail	27,075	6

Source: BJS (2007).

Note: Counts based on weighted data representing 8 months (the month of May from each even-numbered year). Detail may not add to total because of rounding.

data on the type and number of pretrial releases from the 75 largest counties from the period of 1990 to 2004. Surety bond and ROR represent the most frequent types of pretrial releases.

Turning to the race and gender of those encountering the pretrial process, Cohen and Reaves (2007) found that females (74%) were more likely than males (60%) to be granted pretrial release. Also, as shown in Table 5.5, Whites (68%) were more likely

---

Table 5.5

State Court Felony Defendants in the 75 Largest Counties Released Prior to Case Disposition, 1990–2004

Variable	Percentage Released	Predicted Probability of Release (percentage)
Most serious arrest charge		
Murder	19	11**
Rape	53	44**
Robbery	44	36**
Assault	64	59*
Burglary	49	49**
Motor vehicle theft	49	50**
Larceny/theft	68	66
Forgery	72	67
Fraud	82	76**
Drug sales (reference)	63	63
Other drug (non-sales)	68	70*
Weapons	67	65
Driving-related	73	76**
Age at arrest		
Under 21 (reference)	68	64
21–29	62	63
30–39	59	60**
40 or older	62	60**

(Continued)

(Continued)

Variable	Percentage Released	Predicted Probability of Release (percentage)
Gender		
Male (reference)	60	60
Female	74	69**
Race/Hispanic origin		
White non-Hispanic (reference)	68	66
Black non-Hispanic	62	64
Other non-Hispanic	65	63*
Hispanic, any race	55	51**
Criminal justice status at arrest		
No active status (reference)	70	67
Released on pending case	61	63
On probation	43	49**
On parole	26	37**
Prior arrest and court appearance		
No prior arrests (reference)	79	65
Prior arrest record without FTA	59	62*
Prior arrest record with FTA	50	58*
Most serious prior conviction		
No prior convictions (reference)	77	70
Misdemeanor	63	64**
Felony	46	51**

Source: BJS (2007).

Note: Logistic regression (predicted probability) results exclude the year 1990 because of missing data. Asterisks indicate category differed from the reference category at one of the following significance levels: * ≤ .05; ** ≤ .01. Not all variables in the model are shown.

to be released than Blacks (62%) and Hispanics (55%). Of particular significance to the pretrial process is pretrial misconduct, or whether the defendant fails to appear, is rearrested, or is a fugitive after a year. Table 5.6 highlights the nuances of pretrial misconduct. It shows that males have higher rates of misconduct than females and Blacks and Hispanics have higher misconduct rates than Whites.

Table 5.6

State Court Felony Defendants in the 75 Largest Counties Charged With Pretrial Misconduct, 1990–2004

Variable	Number of Defendants	Percentage of Released Defendants Charged With Pretrial Misconduct			
		Any Type	Rearrest	Failure to Appear	Fugitive
Type of pretrial release					
Release on recognizance	80,865	34	17	26	8
Surety bond	78,023	29	16	18	3
Conditional release	31,162	32	15	22	6
Deposit bond	20,993	30	14	22	7
Unsecured bond	17,001	36	14	30	10
Full cash bond	11,190	30	15	20	7
Property bond	3,649	27	17	14	4
Emergency release	2,656	52	17	45	10
Most serious arrest charge					
Murder	741	19	12	9	1
Rape	3,481	18	9	10	2
Robbery	12,947	35	21	21	6
Assault	32,931	23	12	14	4
Burglary	18,377	37	19	25	6
Larceny/theft	26,667	33	16	25	7
Motor vehicle theft	6,415	39	20	29	7
Forgery	8,374	33	15	24	7
Fraud	9,094	21	8	15	5
Drug trafficking	47,182	39	21	27	8
Other drug	50,547	37	18	29	8
Weapons	8,574	27	13	17	5
Driving-related	8,148	28	14	18	5
Age at arrest					
20 or younger	55,505	33	20	21	5
21–29	90,768	34	17	24	7

(Continued)

(Continued)

Variable	Number of Defendants	Percentage of Released Defendants Charged With Pretrial Misconduct			
		Any Type	Rearrest	Failure to Appear	Fugitive
30–39	71,049	33	16	24	7
40 or older	44,701	28	13	20	6
Gender					
Male	211,396	34	18	23	6
Female	52,291	28	12	21	6
Race/Hispanic origin					
Black, non-Hispanic	96,348	36	19	25	7
White, non-Hispanic	64,571	28	14	19	4
Hispanic, any race	49,544	34	17	25	8
Other, non-Hispanic	5,165	23	13	14	3
Criminal justice status at arrest					
On parole	6,012	47	25	32	7
On probation	25,765	44	26	30	6
Released pending prior case	25,955	48	30	30	7
No active status	167,227	27	12	19	6
Prior arrests and FTA history					
Prior arrest record with FTA	59,468	49	27	35	8
Prior arrest record, no FTA	75,806	30	17	18	5
No prior arrests	85,366	23	8	18	7
Most serious prior conviction					
Felony	75,187	43	25	28	6
Misdemeanor	44,989	34	19	23	5
No prior convictions	129,975	27	12	19	7

Source: BJS (2007).

The most recent data on pretrial release (2008–2010) actually examines this phase of the criminal justice process at the federal level. This data shows wide racial/ethnic disparities in terms of who receives pretrial release and for what offenses. Table 5.7 shows pretrial release patterns in the federal system by assorted demographic characteristics.

Although these county and federal figures provide a preliminary overview of the workings of the pretrial process across the country, scholars have investigated the complexities of the influence of a host of factors (including race and gender) on pretrial. In the next section, we review some of the recent studies in this area.

Table 5.7

Defendants Released Pretrial for Cases Disposed in Federal District Courts, by Demographic Characteristics, Citizenship Status, and Most Serious Offense Charged, FY 2008–2010

Demographic Characteristic and Citizenship Status	All Offenses		Percent Released, by Most Serious Offense Charged					
	Total	Percent Released[a]	Violent	Property	Drug	Public-Order	Weapons	Immigration
All defendants	283,358	36%	30%	71%	38%	65%	32%	12%
Sex								
Male	243,863	31%	26%	66%	34%	63%	30%	11%
Female	39,121	65	62	80	62	80	71	34
Age								
17 or younger	339	50%	67%	74%	28%	^	^	28%
18–19	6,513	37	43	57	43	66%	36%	17
20–29	97,829	31	32	62	37	62	27	11
30–39	95,175	31	23	65	35	59	30	11
40 or older	83,118	47	31	80	42	71	44	15
Race/ethnicity								
White[b]	60,427	65%	30%	82%	60%	73%	46%	41%
Black/African American[b]	54,346	43	22	76	36	57	27	34

(Continued)

(Continued)

Demographic Characteristic and Citizenship Status	All Offenses		Percent Released, by Most Serious Offense Charged					
	Total	Percent Released[a]	Violent	Property	Drug	Public-Order	Weapons	Immigration
Hispanic/Latino	155,036	20%	23%	48%	26%	49%	24%	11%
American Indian/Alaska Native[b]	4,049	54	42	78	62	58	35	53
Asian/Pacific Islander[b]	5,569	66	42	78	59	76	41	52
Citizenship status								
U.S. citizen	148,348	55%	31%	82%	47%	69%	34%	59%
Legal alien	15,100	43	35	71	30	60	39	46
Illegal alien	116,321	10	5	28	5	21	5	8

Source: Administrative Office of the U.S. Courts, Office of Probation and Pretrial Services Automated Case Tracking System, 2008–2010.

Note: Detail may not sum to total due to missing information for demographic characteristics and citizenship status. Race/ethnicity excludes defendants classified as other race. Information on race and ethnicity was available for 99.0% of defendants, sex was available for 99.9%, age was available for 99.9%, and citizenship status was available for 98.7%.

^ Too few cases to provide a reliable rate.

a. Includes defendants who were never detained and those who were also detained for part of the pretrial period.

b. Excludes persons of Hispanic or Latino origin.

❖ Scholarship on Race/Ethnicity, Bail, and Pretrial Release

At best, the scholarship on the discriminatory nature of bail and the pretrial process is mixed (Spohn, 2014). Since the early 2000s, scholars have continued to investigate the influence of race/ethnicity and gender in the bail and pretrial process. Researchers who examine this question seek to determine whether legal or extra-legal factors play a role in the outcomes of the decisions related to bail, pretrial release, and sentencing (discussed in Chapter 6). Legal factors are factors that are specifically related to the criminal justice system, such as seriousness of offense, prior convictions, and type of attorney (public or private). Examples of extra-legal factors, or those elements of a case that are unrelated or extraneous to the criminal justice system, include race/ethnicity, age, gender, employment status, marital status, and educational level.

The research produced during the 2000s sought to correct some of the problems present in earlier research, such as the lumping of Hispanics in with Whites that is believed to mask the punitiveness toward Hispanics and contribute to the nonsignificant findings between Blacks and Whites in pretrial research. In addition, earlier studies did not "distinguish and analyze separately pretrial release decisions as compared to pretrial release outcomes. . . . The decisions are the preventative [sic] detention decision, the financial/nonfinancial release decision, the bail amount decision, and the ability to pay decision" (Demuth & Steffensmeier, 2004, p. 224). These decisions clearly impact the prospects for release. But by researching the two stages separately, one can determine whether groups are being differentially impacted during the decision or outcome part of the pretrial process. With these caveats in mind, Demuth and Steffensmeier examined four years of data concerning felons charged in state courts in the 75 most populous counties. Their results showed that females received more favorable pretrial decisions (e.g., nonfinancial release, lower bail amounts) than males, and Black and Hispanic defendants received less favorable treatment than White defendants. In particular, "Black and Hispanic defendants were more likely to receive pretrial decisions that discouraged pretrial release (e.g., financial release options, higher bail amounts) than White defendants, and they were less likely to gain pretrial release than White defendants" (pp. 237–238). Although White females had the most favorable decisions (no pretrial detention), White males also received particularly favorable decisions that the authors felt was a product of their

> greater ability to make bail. Relative to similarly situated gender and race-ethnic subgroups, white defendants of both sexes apparently have greater financial capital or resources either in terms of their personal bankroll/resources, their access to family or social networks willing to pay, or their greater access to bail bondsmen for purposes of making bail. (p. 238)

The last decade has seen a limited stream of scholarship on bail and pretrial release. This research includes a handful of studies that examine race/ethnicity, bail, and the pretrial process. Some of these studies continue to support the findings of Demuth and Steffensmeier (2004), but emphasize that Hispanics receive the least favorable pretrial decisions.

Turner and Johnson (2005), for example, found that, among a sample of more than 800 felony defendants in Nebraska, "Hispanic defendants charged with bailable offenses were found to receive higher bail amounts than other similarly situated African American and White defendants" (p. 49). Schlesinger (2005), using a national sample of 36,709 felony defendants, found that "both Blacks and Latinos receive less beneficial pretrial release decisions and outcomes than Whites" (pp. 185–186).

Recent studies have also found that extra-legal factors matter in the bail and pretrial process. Freiburger and Hilinski (2010) studied the role of race, gender, and age on the pretrial process. Focusing on one urban county in Michigan, they found support for the findings of Demuth and Steffensmeier (2004). More specifically, they found that

> A strong race effect was found prior to entering the economic variables into the model, with Black defendants less likely to be released pretrial than Whites. Once these variables were included, however, race was no longer significant. . . . Therefore, it appears that Black defendants are more likely to be detained because they do not have the financial means necessary to secure release. (Freiburger & Hilinski, 2010, p. 330)

The authors point to the fact that inequalities in the larger society might be contributing to the disadvantages Blacks face in the pretrial release process. Other findings were that Black females (of all age groups) were least likely to be detained and that legal factors were less relevant for females than males. For the latter finding, the authors surmise that judges believe males who commit a serious offense pose a greater risk to society than similarly situated females (p. 330). A study by Wooldredge (2012) considered the role of race in the pretrial process in a large trial court in Ohio. The findings revealed that young Black males (18–29) were less likely to receive ROR than all other defendants. This finding also held true for African Americans eligible for bond. In particular, Wooldredge found that "African American males were also assigned significantly higher bond amounts relative to white males, although the additional age breakdown created a wider gap in the average bond amounts" (p. 63). Findings related to race have also been supported in the preliminary work of Liu, Johnson, & Vidmar (2014), whose small study of Halifax, North Carolina found that the type of bond differed by race and that Blacks stayed in jail longer than Whites (303 days vs. 125 days) when both groups were unable to post bond.

Taken together, the past and more recent research suggests that there are a variety of nuances related to understanding whether extra-legal factors such as race and gender influence the bail and pretrial process. Even so, the most recent scholarship makes clear that—at some level—race/ethnicity, gender, class, and age are all factors that must be considered in an effort to determine whether this early stage of the criminal justice system is characterized by bias.

Legal Counsel

As a result of the blatant racism in the previously discussed Scottsboro case, since 1932, the U.S. Supreme Court has mandated that indigent defendants in capital cases have the right to adequate counsel (see *Powell v. Alabama,* 1932). Three decades later, in *Gideon v. Wainwright* (1963), the Court ruled that all felony defendants have a right to counsel, a ruling that was expanded in 1972 when the Court mandated that counsel be provided for defendants in misdemeanor cases if there was the possibility of incarceration (see *Argersinger v. Hamlin,* 1972). To meet these Supreme Court mandates, states created several legal defense systems. Many states have adopted a public defender system in which, as with a district attorney, the local or state government hires a full-time attorney to provide legal counsel for indigent defendants. In other cases, defendants are assigned counsel from a list of private attorneys who are selected on a case-by-case basis by a judge. Another option is the use of contract attorneys. These people are also private attorneys who are contracted to provide legal representation to indigent defendants (DeFrances & Litras, 2000). In the following section, we review some recent national governmental studies that examine the operation of these systems.

Defense Counsel

Most indigent offenders (82%) are represented by public defenders (DeFrances & Litras, 2000). A 2007 survey of public defender offices found nearly 1,000 such offices in 49 states. These offices handled more than 5.5 million cases and had more than 15,000 attorneys (4,000 at the state level and 11,000 at the county level) and nearly 10,000 full-time staff members (investigators, paralegals, and administrative staff). The total expense for indigent defense services in 2012 was $2.3 billion (Herberman & Kyckelhahn, 2014). Table 5.8 lists the criteria used to determine eligibility for public defense services, by system (state or county).

The public defense systems clearly show signs of strain, with the average state public defense system receiving "82 felony (non-capital) cases, 217 misdemeanor cases, and two appeals cases per full-time equivalent litigating attorney" (Langton & Farole, 2009, p. 2; see also Farole & Langton, 2010). County public defense systems have

Table 5.8

State and County Public Defense Systems' Most Commonly Used Criteria for Determining Indigence

State Criteria for Indigence	County Criteria for Indigence
• Income level	• Income level
• Defendant's receipt of public assistance	• Sworn defendant's application
• Sworn defendant's application	• Judge's discretion
• Defendant's debt level	• Defendant's residence in a public institution
	• Defendant's debt level

Source: BJS (2009).

somewhat lighter loads, with 100 felony (non-capital) cases and 146 misdemeanor cases per attorney at any given time. Langton and Farole (2010) also note that nearly 70% of the 22 states that have statewide public defense systems did not have the requisite number of attorneys to meet caseload guidelines.

Considering the investment in public defense systems, one wonders how defendants fare with the use of public defenders. Several studies have examined whether defendants represented by public defenders receive more or less favorable outcomes than similarly situated defendants who are represented by assigned counsel or private attorneys. On the whole, the literature has found that type of representation is not significant (Hanson & Ostrom, 1998; Hartley, Ventura Miller, & Spohn, 2010; Spohn & Holleran, 2000; Williams, 2002). The most recent comprehensive analysis of legal representation using data from the 75 most populous counties in the United States during 2004 and 2006 also found no significant differences in the outcome of cases handled by public defenders and private attorneys. Cohen (2011) did, however, find that defendants represented through assigned counsel programs received less favorable outcomes (conviction, imprisonment, and sentence length).

Despite Cohen's (2011) recent findings, there has been some evidence to support the notion that public defender offices might be at a disadvantage in carrying out their duties. A study of Pennsylvania's public defense systems provided a snapshot of the functioning of the system. The survey revealed some troubling findings. First, only the Philadelphia office provided any formalized training to their new public defenders. Even with this training, the public defenders were then thrust into positions where they were overworked and underpaid (Pennsylvania Supreme Court, 2003). They generally also had fewer resources than the district attorney's office. These findings were repeated when comparing them with the data from the other Pennsylvania jurisdictions. Most troubling was that "most court-appointed lawyers and many public defenders do not make use of investigators, and therefore do not conduct independent investigations of cases" (p. 185). Because of the paucity of resources, one jurisdiction pointed out "that a case that might require a psychologist or forensic expert might exhaust the whole budget" (p. 185). A study published shortly after the release of the Pennsylvania study provides a glimpse of the potential result of inferior public defense systems. Hoffman, Rubin, and Shepherd (2005) found that defendants represented by public defenders in Denver received more severe sentences than those represented by private attorneys.

In July 2011, the Justice Policy Institute released the report *System Overload: The Costs of Under-Resourcing Public Defense*. The report provided a variety of stunning figures regarding the sparse resources devoted to public defense. In 2008, for example, there were nearly $104 billion spent on policing, $74.1 billion spent on corrections, and $5.3 billion spent on public defense. Even more revealing was the data presented in the report from Tennessee that provided a comparison of the annual spending on public defense and prosecution. In 2005, Tennessee spent between $130 to $139 million on prosecution and a paltry $56.4 million on public defense (K. Taylor, 2011, p. 9).

In support of the previously reviewed Pennsylvania Supreme Court's findings nearly a decade earlier, K. Taylor (2011) outlined the sparse resources being devoted to the public defense office across the county. In the report, the situation in Cumberland County, New Jersey, is provided as an example. In that jurisdiction, it was revealed that

> public defenders . . . handle about 90 percent of all criminal cases, but there are twice as many lawyers and more than seven times as many investigators working on criminal cases in the prosecutor's office than the public defender's office. (p. 9)

The report also outlines five primary ways in which poor public defense can increase incarceration: unnecessary pretrial detention, increased pressure to plead guilty, wrongful convictions and other errors, excessive and inappropriate sentences that fail to take into account the unique circumstances of the case, and increased barriers to successful reentry into the community. Each of these points speaks to the wide-ranging impact that poor public defense can have on whether defendants end up in prison, for how long, and whether they can make it once they are released. The report concludes with the suggestion that public defense systems should adopt the American Bar Association's (ABA) minimum standards for public defense (see Box 5.2).

BOX 5.2

Ten Principles of a Public Defense Delivery System

1. The public defense function, including the selection, funding, and payment of defense counsel, is independent.

2. Where the caseload is sufficiently high, the public defense delivery system consists of both a defender office and the active participation of the private bar.

3. Clients are screened for eligibility, and defense counsel is assigned and notified of appointment, as soon as feasible after clients' arrest, detention, or request for counsel.

4. Defense counsel is provided sufficient time and a confidential space within which to meet with the client.

5. Defense counsel's workload is controlled to permit the rendering of quality representation.

6. Defense counsel's ability, training, and experience match the complexity of the case.

7. The same attorney continuously represents the client until completion of the case.

8. There is parity between defense counsel and the prosecution with respect to resources, and defense counsel is included as an equal partner in the justice system.

9. Defense counsel is provided with and required to attend continuing legal education.

10. Defense counsel is supervised and systematically reviewed for quality and efficiency according to nationally and locally adopted standards.

Source: American Bar Association.

The Justice Policy Institute also provided additional recommendations. First, public defense systems should integrate a holistic and community-based approach to public defense. In short, they should also consider the root causes of justice system involvement as a way to prevent future encounters with the justice system. Second, better data should be collected and there should be more evaluations of the impact of public defense systems on society and the criminal justice system. Third, the Institute recommended that both the public defenders and the community be involved in the policymaking process. Finally, the Institute called on the collaboration of policy makers, researchers, and advocates to seek out additional voices from those who have used public defense services to help better understand the nuances of how the system operates (K. Taylor, 2011, p. 34).

Even though the empirical literature suggests that defendants (of all racial/ethnic backgrounds) have minimal disadvantage when represented by public defenders, there is still a heavy reliance on plea bargaining. We provide a brief overview of the plea-bargaining process and the potential influence of race.

Plea Bargaining

Before actually proceeding to the trial phase, in any given year, an estimated 96% of convictions are reconciled through a guilty plea in the plea-bargaining process (Reaves, 2001). Early in American history, however, plea bargaining was frowned on by justice system officials and, as a result, comprised a small percentage of how cases were resolved. Only since the 20th century have courts accepted it as an important part of the criminal justice process (Shelden & Brown, 2003). Predictably, a process involving no real oversight and such broad discretion has come under scrutiny because of concerns related to race and class.

An example of how racial bias can influence the plea-bargaining process can be seen in a comprehensive study of California criminal cases conducted by the *San Jose Mercury News* in 1991. Using a computer analysis of nearly 700,000 criminal cases from 1981 to 1990, the study found,

> At virtually every stage of pretrial plea bargaining Whites were more successful than minorities. All else being equal, Whites did better than African-Americans and Hispanics at getting charges dropped, getting cases dismissed, avoiding harsher punishment, avoiding extra charges, and having their records wiped clean. (Donzinger, 1996, p. 112)

In addition, the study found that, although one-third of Whites who started out with felony charges had their charges reduced to misdemeanors, African Americans and Hispanics received this benefit only 25% of the time (Donzinger, 1996). Seeking to explain some of these results, one California judge stated that there was no conspiracy among judges to produce such outcomes. When put to a public defender, he explained the disparities this way:

> If a White person can put together a halfway plausible excuse, people will bend over backward to accommodate that person. It's a feeling, "You've got

a nice person screwing up," as opposed to the feeling that "this minority person is on track and eventually they're going to end up in state prison." It's an unfortunate racial stereotype that pervades the system. It's an unconscious thing. (p. 113)

More recent scholarship has continued to study whether extra-legal factors such as race, class, or gender matter in the plea-bargaining process. O'Neill Shermer and Johnson (2010) studied the role of plea bargaining in U.S. Federal District Courts. The authors found that males were less likely than females to receive charge reductions through the plea-bargaining process. Other findings of note include the following: Young minority youth were not less likely than other similarly situated offenders to receive charge reductions, and "older white males, young white females and young and old Hispanic females are significantly more likely to receive charge reductions, but these effects are driven by gender rather than by race/ethnicity" (p. 413). The authors also noted that offense matters in the plea-bargaining process, with property offenders being twice as likely to receive a charge reduction as violent offenders. The researchers also note that immigration offenses were among the offenses least likely to receive charge reductions. Further, offenders who accepted responsibility for their offense also received a significant charge reduction. Finally, the authors found that "male offenders were especially unlikely to be given charge reductions for drug and violent crimes and black and Hispanic offenders were disadvantaged in charging decisions for weapons offenses" (p. 421). Hence, while some extra-legal factors did appear to matter, O'Neill Shermer and Johnson conclude that "despite public concern, widespread prejudices do not seem to dominate prosecutorial decision-making at the federal level" (p. 424).

Another recent plea-bargaining study examined the prosecutorial decision making involving misdemeanor marijuana arrests in New York City during 2010–2011 (Kutateladze, Andiloro, & Johnson, 2014). In particular, relying on a diverse sample of Whites, African Americans, Hispanics, and Asians, the researchers sought to determine whether the offenders' race/ethnicity impacted on pleas for a lesser charge or for a noncustodial sentence. The authors did find differences by race/ethnicity but observed that "much of the observed racial and ethnic disparity was explained away by legal considerations, evidentiary factors, prosecutor and defense characteristics, and socioeconomic proxies" (p. 22). Also of note, though, was that other racial disparities remained even after controlling for all relevant factors. As an example, the authors found that "black defendants, and to a lesser extent Latino defendants, were substantially more likely to receive charge bargains that involved pleas to the current charge as opposed to reduced charges" (p. 22). The research also found that Asians in the study received the most favorable plea bargains, as compared to Whites and the other minority groups in the study. On the whole, the authors pointed to prior arrest history as the most important factor in their analyses.

In the rare event that a case is not resolved during the plea-bargaining process, the next stage of the process requires preparation for a jury trial. Jury selection begins this phase of the process.

Jury Selection

Once the decision has been made to prosecute an offender, the case will either be decided by a jury or solely by a judge in a bench trial (where a judge alone is responsible for the determination of guilt or innocence). In the event of a jury trial, the jury selection process begins with a *venire,* or the selection of a jury pool. This provides the court with a list of persons from which to select the jury members. The Constitution requires that citizens be tried before a jury of their peers. Those in the legal profession generally agree that this should translate into juries being representative of the community in which the defendant resides. In the jury selection process, however, race and gender concerns have continued to pervade the process. The Scottsboro case discussed in Chapter 1 was an example of how racial bias in jury selection resulted in all-White juries trying African Americans because of long-standing discrimination in the courts. Although times have changed, in some jurisdictions, when minorities are underrepresented on juries in their own communities, questions have been raised and radical action has been taken, with some judges delaying trials until juries have acceptable diversity (Mandak, 2003). But in other instances, the courts have refused to intervene. Results from a study commissioned by the Pennsylvania Supreme Court (2003) on racial and gender bias have provided some examples of how issues related to race and gender influence the makeup of jury pools.

To investigate ethnic and gender bias in jury selection in Pennsylvania, researchers sent surveys to every county in the state to assess the various practices. More than 80% of the 67 counties returned the surveys (Pennsylvania Supreme Court, 2003). Once the surveys were tabulated, it was revealed that there were a variety of barriers to minorities and women participating in jury service. For minorities, these barriers included receiving fewer summonses for jury duty, transportation issues, child-care issues, and employer issues. Minorities, more so than others, have transportation difficulties that result in them being unable to serve on juries. Often, they are also impeded from serving on juries because they are unable to secure appropriate childcare. In some instances, employers of hourly wage employees are unsupportive of jury service. The second part of the study, which looked in depth at four of Pennsylvania's largest counties (Allegheny, Lehigh, Montgomery, and Philadelphia), found that "African Americans were under-represented in juror yield in all four counties; Latinos were under-represented in juror yield in three of the counties; and Asian Americans were under-represented in juror yield in Philadelphia County" (p. 70).

In addition to surveys, the committee charged with completing the study also heard public testimony. When they queried one Pittsburgh attorney on the state of affairs concerning the racial composition of juries, he responded,

> In all of the cases in which I have tried on behalf of African American plaintiffs in the past five years, a grand total of one African American was involved in the deliberations that determined the outcome of the case. Indeed, in most of the cases, the only African American in the courtroom was my client. (Pennsylvania Supreme Court, 2003, p. 74)

Turning to the underrepresentation of women on juries, the report revealed some of the interconnections between race and gender. Women were generally the ones responsible for childcare; therefore, they were often unable to serve on juries. The committee also noted that women had difficulty reaching the courthouse, a concern shared by non-Whites. In certain situations, women, like men, were unable to serve on juries due to economic hardships. A final gender-related concern was "[the finding of] evidence that the interpersonal dynamics within the jury room can operate to the detriment of female jurors" (Pennsylvania Supreme Court, 2003, p. 106). More specifically, "Women in Pennsylvania were less likely than men to be chosen as presiding jurors" (p. 106).

Once the jury pool is formed, the opportunity for race and gender bias does not end there. There have been concerns with the subsequent **voir dire** process, during which jurors are screened for their fitness to serve on a particular case.

Voir Dire

Considering the difficulty in locating non-White jurors, it would seem that once the final juror selection process begins, non-White jurors would not be the targets for removal. To the surprise of some, this is not the case. Both the defense and prosecution often use their peremptory challenges to remove jurors based, in large part, on their race. In general, peremptory challenges can be used to remove jurors without cause. This was challenged in the 1965 case of *Swain v. Alabama*. In the case, Robert Swain, a Black teenager, was convicted of raping a White teenager (Cole, 1999). During the case, the prosecution "struck all six prospective Black jurors," and after investigation, it was revealed "that no Black had ever served on a trial jury in Talladega County, Alabama," despite the fact that Blacks made up 25% of the county population (p. 119). Based on this information, the conviction was challenged, and the Supreme Court decided to hear the case. However, the Supreme Court found no problem with striking the prospective Black jurors, indicating among other things that, "in the quest for an impartial and qualified jury, Negro and White, Protestants and Catholic, are alike subject to being challenged without cause" (p. 119). But according to the 1986 Supreme Court decision in **Batson v. Kentucky**, race or gender must not be the deciding factor. It is notable that, six years later, in *Hernandez v. New York* (1991), the Supreme Court ruled

> that a criminal defendant's Fourteenth Amendment rights to equal protection were not violated when a prosecutor exercised a peremptory challenge excluding potential Latino/a jurors who understood Spanish on the basis that they might not accept the court interpreter's version as the final arbiter in the case. The defendant had argued that the elimination of potential Latino/a jurors violated his right to a trial by his peers in violation of his constitutional rights. (cited in Morin, 2005, p. 78)

In the eyes of the Supreme Court, the prosecutor's reason for the removal of Latino/a jurors was "race neutral" (Morin, 2005, p. 78).

Prior to the *Batson* decision, studies of jurisdictions in Texas and Georgia found that peremptory challenges were used to strike 90% of Black jurors (Cole, 1999). In fact, in large cities such as Philadelphia, district attorneys were given clear instructions to strike non-White jurors. A now infamous training tape by one Philadelphia assistant district attorney declared,

> Young Black women are very bad. There's an antagonism. I guess maybe they're downtrodden in two respects. They are women and they're Black . . . so they somehow want to take it out on somebody, and you don't want it to be you. (p. 118)

Scholars have also noted that, in certain instances, defense attorneys follow similar practices (Cole, 1999).

Since the *Batson* decision, prosecutors have turned to deception to strike non-White jurors. According to Cole (1999), prosecutors are masking their race-based actions by using neutral explanations to remove jurors. In some instances, for example,

> Courts have accepted explanations that the juror was too old, too young, was employed as a teacher or unemployed, or practiced a certain religion. They have accepted unverifiable explanations based on demeanor: the juror did not make eye contact or made too much eye contact, appeared inattentive or headstrong, nervous or too casual, grimaced or smiled. And they have accepted explanations that might often be correlated to race: the juror lacked education, was single or poor, lived or worked in the same neighborhood as the defendant or a witness, or had previously been involved with the criminal justice system. (pp. 120–121)

Gabbidon, Kowal, Jordan, Roberts, and Vincenzi (2008) confirmed these findings after reviewing five years' worth of litigation in which plaintiffs sued because they felt allegedly race-neutral peremptory challenges were race-based. Based on an analysis of 283 cases from the U.S. Court of Appeals, the researchers found that Blacks were the ones most likely to be removed from juries. The explanations used to justify their removal include questionable body language, questionable mannerisms, medical issues, child-care issues, limited life experiences, and unemployment. The courts accepted these explanations, considering that 79% of the appellants lost their cases (Gabbidon et al., 2008). For those who actually won their appeal, there was an extremely high burden of proof. However, at the heart of winning was being able to show some inconsistency on the part of the attorney who made the removals. As an example, Gabbidon et al. noted that in one instance, the prosecutor struck a juror "because he was concerned that she did not seem to understand or respond appropriately to certain *dire* questions" (p. 64). But after further review, "the courts ruled against the prosecutor because they found that the prosecutor declined to strike white jurors whose answers were far more inappropriate or unresponsive" (p. 64).

Sommers and Norton (2007) conducted an experiment using 90 undergraduate college students, 81 advanced law students (second and third year), and 28 practicing attorneys to determine several things, including (a) to what extent does race affect jury selection judgments, and (b) if decision makers fail to report the influence of race on jury selection judgments, how do they justify their decisions? On the first point, the authors found that "across three samples, this investigation provides clear empirical evidence that a prospective juror's race can influence peremptory challenge use and that self-report justifications are unlikely to be useful for identifying this influence" (p. 269). Furthermore, the researchers reported that when justifying their reason for removing Black jurors, the respondents used a race-neutral explanation. Thus, as Sommers and Norton (2007) aptly note, "The practical implications of these findings are clear: even when attorneys consider race during jury selection, there is little reason to believe that judicial questioning will produce information useful for identifying the bias" (p. 269).

Considering the frequent removal of racial and ethnic minorities from jury pools, one wonders how jurors perceive the jury selection process. McGuffee, Garland, and Eigenberg (2007) explored this question based on a survey sent to Tennessee residents summoned for jury service. In general, most of the 138 respondents felt that most jury verdicts are correct (92%) and "that juries try hard to do the right thing" (p. 456). Fewer respondents reported that they felt the system was fair (83%). As for questions related to race and the jury system, the authors found that

> About half the respondents (52%) agreed that it is important for African-Americans to have African-Americans on the jury in order to get a fair trial. Similarly one-half of the respondents (49%) reported that if you are African American you want other African-Americans on the jury to get a fair trial. (p. 457)

Other findings showed that the respondents were less likely to feel that having Whites on the jury was critical for Whites to receive a fair trial. Also, a little more than 25% of the respondents felt that African Americans were "more likely to be dismissed from jury duty than are whites. Furthermore, about one-fifth (18%) of the respondents believed that whites are more apt to convict than minorities." In terms of fairness in decision making, "only 7% of the respondents believe that whites are fairer than minorities in jury decisions" (McGuffee et al., 2007, p. 457). It is also important to note that most of the respondents (57%) felt that race had nothing to do with jury selection or jury verdicts (68%).

Even with these generally positive sentiments from admittedly a limited sample of jurors, prosecutors and defense attorneys still resort to peremptory challenges to remove racial and ethnic minorities from jury pools. Recently the Equal Justice Initiative (2010) published a monograph, *Illegal Racial Discrimination in Jury Selection: A Continuing Legacy* (see Stevenson, 2010). The report confirms the findings from the empirical research regarding the exclusion of racial minorities from juries. In fact, the Supreme Court of Mississippi is quoted in the report as saying "racially motivated jury selection is still prevalent twenty years after *Batson* was handed down" (p. 24). In response to the disappointing findings, the Initiative proposed 14 recommendations to help remedy the problem (see Box 5.3). Concerns regarding **jury nullification** likely lie at the heart of the practice. We review jury nullification and the fears surrounding it in the next section.

BOX 5.3

Equal Justice Initiative: Recommendations to Reduce Bias in the Jury Selection Process

1. Dedicated and thorough enforcement of anti-discrimination laws designed to prevent racially biased jury selection must be undertaken by courts, judges, and lawyers involved in criminal and civil trials, especially in serious criminal cases and capital cases.

2. The rule banning racially discriminatory use of peremptory strikes announced in *Batson v. Kentucky* should be applied retroactively to death row prisoners and others with lengthy sentences whose convictions or death sentences are the product of illegal, racially biased jury selection but whose claims have not been reviewed because they were tried before 1986.

3. To protect the credibility and integrity of criminal trials, claims of illegal racial discrimination in the selection of juries should be reviewed by courts on the merits and exempted from procedural bars or technical defaults that shield and insulate from remedy racially biased conduct.

4. Prosecutors who are found to have engaged in racially biased jury selection should be held accountable and should be disqualified from participation in the retrial of any person wrongly convicted as a result of discriminatory jury selection. Prosecutors who repeatedly exclude people of color from jury service should be subject to fines, penalties, suspension, and other consequences to deter this practice.

5. The Justice Department and federal prosecutors should enforce 18 U.S.C. §243, which prohibits racial discrimination in jury selection, by pursuing actions against district attorney's offices with a history of racially biased selection practices.

6. States should provide remedies to people called for jury service who are illegally excluded on the basis of race, particularly jurors who are wrongly denigrated by state officials. States should implement strategies to disincentivize discriminatory conduct by state prosecutors and judges, who should enforce rather than violate anti-discrimination laws.

7. Community groups, civil and human rights organizations, and concerned citizens should attend court proceedings and monitor the conduct of local officials with regard to jury selection practices in an effort to eliminate racially biased jury selection.

8. Community groups, civil and human rights organizations, and concerned citizens should question their local district attorneys about policies and practices relating to jury selection in criminal trials, secure officials' commitment to enforcing anti-discrimination laws, and request regular reporting by prosecutors on the use of peremptory strikes.

9. States should strengthen policies and procedures to ensure that racial minorities, women, and other cognizable groups are fully represented in the jury pools from which jurors are selected. States and local administrators should supplement source lists for jury pools or utilize computer models that weight groups appropriately. Full representation of all cognizable groups throughout the United States easily can be achieved in the next five years.

10. Reviewing courts should abandon absolute disparity as a measure of underrepresentation of minority groups and utilize more accurate measures, such as comparative disparity, to prevent the insulation from remedy of unfair underrepresentation.

11. State and local justice systems should provide support and assistance to ensure that low-income residents, sole caregivers for children or other dependents, and others who are frequently excluded from jury service because of their economic, employment, or family status have an opportunity to serve.

12. Court administrators, state and national bar organizations, and other state policy makers should require reports on the representativeness of juries in serious felony and capital cases to ensure compliance with state and federal laws barring racial discrimination in jury selection.

13. The criminal defense bar should receive greater support, training, and assistance in ensuring that state officials do not exclude people of color from serving on juries on the basis of race, given the unique and critically important role defense attorneys play in protecting against racially biased jury selection.

14. Greater racial diversity must be achieved within the judiciary, district attorney's offices, the defense bar, and law enforcement to promote and strengthen the commitment to ensuring that all citizens have equal opportunities for jury service.

Source: © 2014 Equal Justice Initiative, http://www.eij.org

Jury Nullification

Given the numerous measures being taken in some jurisdictions to diversify jury pools, one would think that keeping non-Whites on the jury would be a high priority. On the contrary, as discussed in the previous section on peremptory challenges, prosecutors and defense attorneys alike often eliminate jurors based on race if they believe it will help them secure a victory. The underlying premise is surely a lack of trust, particularly of non-White jurors. Why else would someone not want non-Whites on juries? The concern relates to the practice of jury nullification. According to Walker et al. (2007),

> Jury nullification . . . occurs when a juror believes that the evidence presented at trial establishes the defendant's guilt, but nonetheless votes to acquit. The juror's decision may be motivated either by a belief that the law under which the defendant is being prosecuted is unfair or by an application of the law to a particular defendant. (p. 223)

In the past two decades, there has been increasing debate on this practice. In 1995, Paul Butler, a professor of law at George Washington University, published a seminal and controversial article on the utility of African Americans engaging in jury nullification. Since Professor Butler published his controversial article, he has continued to refine his perspective (Butler, 2009). During the beginning of his tenure as a federal prosecutor, Butler (1995) wrote that "we would lose many of our cases, despite having persuaded a jury beyond a reasonable doubt that the defendant was guilty. We would lose because some Black jurors would refuse to convict Black defendants who they knew were guilty" (p. 678). After considering the concept, Butler used two case studies to show how the practice can send a message to society regarding injustices. The first case study reviewed the case of *United States v. Barry* (1991). After a long and expensive federal investigation, Marion Barry, the former mayor of Washington, DC, was observed on videotape in a sting operation smoking crack cocaine. Two prominent and controversial African American leaders, Reverend George Stallings and Minister Louis Farrakhan, were provided with passes by Barry to attend the trial. However, in both cases, they were denied access because the presiding judge felt they might influence juror sentiment. The American Civil Liberties Union (ACLU) took up the cases and argued that they both had a right to attend the trial. In the end, the trial court conceded and let the two attend the trial; however, they were given "special rules" that had to be followed (Butler, 1995). Although Barry was clearly guilty, at the end of the trial, he was found guilty of only 1 of 14 charges.

The second case study involved John T. Harvey III, a prominent Washington, DC, attorney. During a trial in the early 1990s, Harvey's attire became the subject of controversy while he was representing a client. Along with a traditional suit, Harvey wore a stole made of *Kente* cloth, which has roots in African culture. During the pre-trial process, a judge warned him about wearing the cloth. Apparently, the judge felt that wearing the cloth would "send a hidden message to jurors" (Butler, 1995, p. 685). Given his convictions on the matter, the judge offered Harvey three options: "He could refrain from wearing the *Kente* cloth; he could withdraw from the case; or he could agree to try the case before the judge, without a jury" (p. 685). After considerable wrangling, Harvey was allowed to wear the *Kente* cloth. The judge even suggested that Harvey be charged for the time devoted to the *Kente* cloth issue. Eventually, "Harvey's client is tried before an all-Black jury and is acquitted" (p. 686).

On the whole, Butler (1995) advocated the use of jury nullification to fight against unfair practices, which are outlined in his two case studies, as well as unjust laws, such as the controversial crack cocaine laws, which annually send a disproportionate number of people of color to jail and prison. In Butler's (1995) words

> The Black community is better off when some nonviolent lawbreakers remain in the community rather than go to prison. The decision as to what kind of conduct by African-Americans ought to be punished is better made by African-Americans themselves, based on the costs and benefits to their community, than by the traditional criminal justice process, which is controlled by White lawmakers and White law enforcers. Legally, the doctrine of jury nullification gives the power to make this decision to [African-American jurors who sit in judgment of] African-American defendants. (p. 679)

Although acknowledging some merits of Butler's arguments, Krauss and Schulman (1997) see the general concern of Black juror nullification as being based on anecdotal evidence. In their analysis, the discussion comes down to the following equation: "Black defendant + Black jurors + non-conviction = miscarriage of justice" (p. 60). As they see it, those who believe in this equation ignore the fact that, in some of these cases, "Black jurors are being condemned for doing exactly what jurors are supposed to do: demanding that the prosecution prove its case beyond a reasonable doubt" (p. 60). Furthermore, they view the continuing outrage over jury nullification as a response to an article published in the *Wall Street Journal* shortly after the conclusion of the O. J. Simpson trial in 1995. The article provided figures showing that nationwide there was an overall acquittal rate of 17%, whereas in jurisdictions such as the Bronx, New York, and Washington, DC, the acquittal rates were 47.6% and 28.7%, respectively. The authors countered these figures, showing that the acquittal rate nationally was closer to 28% (p. 62). Subsequently, contrary to the notion of jury nullification, the authors noted that the Bronx rate was likely a result of "(1) jurors doing their jobs well, [and] (2) prosecutors who are not doing their jobs well" (p. 63).

Krauss and Schulman (1997) also noted that there is the belief that only White jurors can be color-blind. They responded that it is impossible to have a color-blind jury because race is the first thing that people see in others. Another important point discussed by the authors relates to police testimony. Although in many instances the testimony of police officers is believed without challenge, the authors pointed out that, because of their historically negative experiences with police officers, persons of color give equal weight to police testimony and that of other witnesses, even when they differ (pp. 70–71).

❖ Drug Courts

Drug courts are a fairly recent initiative. Dade County, Florida is credited with starting the first one in 1989 (Goldkamp & Weiland, 1993). Since then, partly as a result of Title V of the Violent Crime Control and Law Enforcement Act of 1994, which awarded federal monies to drug court programs (U.S. General Accounting Office [GAO], 1997), the number of drug courts increased to more than 2,800 in 2013 (National Institute of Justice, 2015). Table 5.9 shows the assorted types of drug courts in the United States. These courts surfaced when drug-related cases began to overwhelm traditional courts, which was largely due to the wide-scale use of mandatory minimum drug sentences (Fox & Huddleston, 2003). This sentencing approach had a disparate impact on minorities (see Chapter 6), and consequently many of those persons diverted to drug courts are minorities (Fielding, Tye, Ogawa, Imam, & Long, 2002). Before we discuss the effectiveness of drug courts, we review the structure and philosophy of the courts.

Structure and Philosophy of Drug Courts

Court Structure

Drug courts (also referred to as "drug treatment courts") attempt to provide "a bridge between criminal justice and health services" (Wenzel, Longshore, Turner, & Ridgely, 2001, p. 241). This bridge results in a combination of court oversight and therapeutic services and the use of "an intense regimen of drug treatment, case management, drug testing, and supervision, while reporting to regularly scheduled status hearings before a judge" (Fox & Huddleston, 2003, p. 13). The judge, the prosecutor, defense

Table 5.9

Number and Type of Drug Courts (as of June 30, 2013)

Type of Drug Court	Number
Adult drug courts	1,485
Juvenile drug courts	447
Adult drug/DWI	422
Family	311
DWI	229
Veterans	145
Tribal	119
Co-occurring	39
Reentry	31
Federal drug	25
Campus	5
Federal veterans	4

Source: U.S. Department of Justice, Office of Justice Programs, National Institute of Justice (2015).

attorney, treatment provider, law enforcement officer, probation officer, case manager, and program coordinator are part of the "drug court team" (p. 13).

Based on a report commissioned by the U.S. Department of Justice and the National Association of Drug Court Professionals, there are 10 key components of drug courts (Fox & Huddleston, 2003). To receive federal funding, drug courts must adhere to the following components. First, they must use a multidisciplinary process to address the needs of persons who are diverted to the court. Second, the courts are also seen as nonadversarial. Going against the traditional philosophy of courts, all parties work together to ensure that the participant has the best chance of success. Early identification is the third component of drug courts. Here, the courts try to get to prospective participants as early in the criminal justice process as possible. The fourth component of the court is to offer a "continuum of treatment and rehabilitation services" (p. 16). This acknowledges the diverse needs of those who come under the purview of the court. Regular alcohol and drug testing is another key component. Such random testing, which should be observed by a program official, is essential to ensure participants have not had relapses.

The sixth key component of the court is to have regular meetings to discuss the progress of participants. Philosophically, these meetings should not take on a punitive tone (Fox & Huddleston, 2003). In line with the sixth component, the seventh requires that there should be ongoing interaction with the judge. Evaluation is the eighth essential component of a drug court. Using goals and objectives as a starting point, each court should periodically measure its effectiveness. The ninth component requires that team members seek out additional education or training to stay abreast of current drug court practices. The final key component of drug courts is developing community partnerships. Drug courts are encouraged to make links to "enhance program effectiveness and general local support" (p. 17).

Court Philosophy

In short, the underlying philosophy of the court is that persons with drug addictions need treatment rather than prison sentences. That is, because some of the problems that result from drug abuse are related to criminal justice, drug courts seek to address the addiction problem through treatment services in the hopes of producing the following positive outcomes: a reduction in drug use, less criminal activity, lower recidivism, better health, better social and family functioning, better educational/vocational status, and residential stability (Fischer, 2003; Wenzel et al., 2001). Taking into consideration the unique approach and philosophy of drug courts, the next section looks at how effective they have been.

Effectiveness of Drug Courts

After more than 20 years in existence, drug courts have been the focus of a considerable number of evaluations. In 1997, the GAO reviewed 20 studies that evaluated the effectiveness of drug courts. The GAO noted the serious shortcomings in many of the evaluations that had been done up to that point. In general, the report found mixed results. Some programs recorded relapse rates from 7% to 80%, with some programs reporting recidivism rates ranging from 0% to 58%. In addition, completion rates were mixed, ranging from 1% to 70%, with an average of 43%. A review of studies conducted for drug courts in California, Florida, and Delaware found that Hispanics and African Americans were less likely to complete the programs. In Nevada, however, researchers reported "no difference in the termination rates between ethnic groups and between male and female participants" (p. 77).

Los Angeles County started its first drug court in 1994. By June, 2001, there were "11 pre-plea drug court programs . . . operating in 11 of Los Angeles County's 24 judicial districts" (Fielding et al., 2002, p. 218). Like others around the country, the court "provide[s] a treatment alternative to prosecution for non-violent felony drug offenders" (p. 218). To measure the effectiveness of the drug court, the researchers used a quasi-experimental design with three sample groups. The first group included those who participated in the drug court program. The second group participated in another diversion program, whereas the third group was composed of felony defendants who went to trial. The study aimed to investigate the program completion and recidivism rates of the groups. Most of the persons in the three groups were male and minorities, with an average age in the low 30s. When Fielding et al. (2002) examined recidivism among the three groups, they found that

Drug court participants were less likely to be re-arrested than drug diversion participants or felony defendants. However, results differ by risk strata. Low risk study participants' re-arrest rates did not differ significantly from those of the diversion sample. However, for those classified at medium or high risk, the re-arrest rate for drug court participants was significantly below those of the diversion and/or felony defendant groups. (pp. 221–222)

Moreover, the time to rearrest was longer for those who participated in drug courts than those who were in the other groups. This held true for time to new drug arrests. On the whole, drug court graduates fared better than those in the other groups. A final area of interest to the researchers was cost. The cost for drug court ranged from nearly $4,000 to nearly $9,000. Yet the alternatives to drug courts—prison ($16,500) and residential treatment centers ($13,000)—were considerably more expensive.

Other studies have also found the courts to be effective in reducing recidivism (Gottfredson, Najaka, & Kearley, 2003; Johnson Listwan, Sundt, Holsinger, & Latessa, 2003; Mitchell, Wilson, Eggers, & MacKenzie, 2012), improving the participants' job prospects and self-image (Creswell & Deschenes, 2001), and reducing costs (Carey, Finigan, Crumpton, & Waller, 2006). Additional research has found that drug court participants in a nonmetropolitan area were also more successful that nonparticipants (Galloway & Drapella, 2006). Howard (2014) also recently investigated the role of individual-level and neighborhood-level variables on graduation from drug courts. He found that neighborhood-level factors, such as level of social disadvantage and crime rates, reduced the significance of race but not of other individual-level predictors of drug court graduation, such as education and employment.

Still other research has examined the effectiveness of family treatment drug courts (FTDCs), which are designed to get drug-addicted parents the treatment they need "to be reunited with their children" (Green, Furrer, Worcel, Burrus, & Finighan, 2007, p. 44). In such instances, the courts often work in conjunction with the child welfare system. Green et al. conducted an assessment of FTDCs at multiple sites using a quasi-experimental approach. The research revealed that

Participants in FTDCs entered treatment more quickly, stayed in treatment longer, and were more likely to successfully complete treatment, even when controlling for a host of risk factors. Moreover, FTDC participants were more likely to be reunited with their children, and children were placed in permanent living situations more quickly compared to those in the comparison groups. (p. 56)

Although some of the earlier research on drug courts found mixed results (J. Anderson, 2001; Bavon, 2001; Cooper, 2003; Fischer, 2003; Harrell, 2003; Johnson Listwan et al., 2003), recent studies on drug courts have yielded positive results (Marlowe, 2011; Rossman, Roman, Zweig, Rempel, & Lindquist, 2011). That is, in most studies, drug court participants are faring better than those in comparison groups. Even when the outcomes are quite similar, the cost of the drug court is far lower than the alternative. In addition, offenders who are supervised through drug courts are able to improve family relationships and continue to make a living. As a result, in the

2011 National Drug Control Strategy, drug courts are lauded as "a proven method for addressing substance-abusing offenders" (p. 45). Despite the praise surrounding drug courts, the funding for such courts peaked in FY 2010 at $45 million and was at a low of $35 million in FY 2013. Table 5.10 shows the overall gains for treatment-oriented courts and initiatives.

Table 5.10

Historical Federal Funding for Drug Courts, Substance Abuse, and Mental Health Initiatives

	Drug Courts	MIOTCRA*	Mental Health Jail Diversion	Substance Abuse Treatment Courts
FY 2009	$40 million	$10 million	$6.7 million	$37.6 million
FY 2010	$45 million	$12 million	$6.7 million	$67.6 million
FY 2011	$37 million	$12 million	$7.0 million	$44 million
FY 2012	$35 million	$9 million	$7.0 million	$43 million
FY 2013	$35 million	$9 million	$6.7 million	$67.3 million

Source: National Center for State Courts (2015).

Note: *Mentally Ill Offender Treatment and Crime Reduction Act

❖ Conclusion

This chapter examined race and the American court system. From the earliest period of American history, race/ethnicity and class have played a role in the operation of American courts. More recent research has shown race effects during every aspect of the court process. However, unlike in the past when the discrimination was blatant, some of the bias is now masked, such as in the jury selection process and the use of peremptory challenges to remove racial/ethnic groups from jury pools. It is clear from the research in this area that both defense and prosecutors do not trust racial/ethnic minorities to make reasoned decisions when serving on juries. This mistrust leads to actions that deny minority defendants the opportunity to have minorities (their peers) serve on their juries.

Finally, drug courts were discussed as a way to reduce the prison population, while also giving drug-addicted offenders the treatment they need. We reviewed their structure, philosophy, and promise for dealing with some of the addiction problems. Although the results of early evaluative studies were mixed, more recently the initiative has shown considerable promise for diverting racial minorities and other drug-addicted offenders out of regular courts. Closely tied to the courts is the sentencing process. Chapter 6 looks at how racial minorities fare in the sentencing phase of the court process.

Discussion Questions

1. Discuss the most significant demographic factors in pretrial release.

2. Do you believe Native American courts and their unique philosophy are equipped to handle all types of offenses? Explain why or why not.

3. Discuss why the discrimination thesis (DT) and the no-discrimination thesis (NDT) are critical considerations in the American court process.

4. Are you for or against peremptory challenges? Explain your position.

5. Make an argument to either decrease or increase funding for drug courts.

Internet Exercises

1. Visit http://www.jurybox.org and read the statements from significant American figures concerning jury nullification. Do any of their thoughts sway your feelings on jury nullification? Take a look at the other links and see whether you agree with the suggestions for improving the jury system.

2. Visit the Equal Justice Initiative Website (http://www.eji.org/eji/) and read their report, "Illegal Racial Discrimination in Jury Selection: A Continuing Legacy."

Internet Sites

National Center for State Courts: http://www.ncsc.org

U.S. Supreme Court: http://www.supremecourt.gov

National Drug Court Institute: http://www.ndci.org

Supplemental materials for *Race and Crime* are available online at
study.sagepub.com/gabbidon4e.

CHAPTER 6

Sentencing

The social responsibility for crime is so widely recognized that when the criminal is arrested, the first desire of decent modern society is to reform him, and not to avenge itself on him. Penal servitude is being recognized only as it protects society and improves the criminal, and not because it makes him suffer as his victim suffered.

—Du Bois (1920, p. 173)

Sentencing represents the stage of the criminal justice process when, following conviction, a defendant is given a sanction for committing his or her offense. Sanctions that are regularly used because they are not in violation of the Eighth Amendment's cruel and unusual punishment clause include fines (which cannot be excessive); being placed on **probation**, given an intermediate sanction (something in between probation and incarceration), and/or incarceration; and the death penalty. Such a process has considerable potential for discrimination and errors. It is important to consider, however, that, like the laws that set the criminal justice process in motion, state and federal legislatures are primarily responsible for determining the appropriate sentence for each offense. Although the legislature has a significant role to play in the creation of sentences, in many instances, judges also have considerable discretion in the sentencing process. Therefore, a variety of legislative enactments (e.g., sentencing guidelines) have been created to "equalize" or reduce the disparities in the sentencing process, yet sentences still can be influenced appreciably by judicial discretion. Because of this, over the years, the actions of the judiciary have been scrutinized more closely by citizens and social scientists alike.

In this chapter, we examine the following three areas related to sentencing: (a) sentencing philosophies, (b) historical overview of race and sentencing, and (c) contemporary issues in race and sentencing. The first section reviews the various sentencing philosophies (also called justifications) that influence the direction of sentencing policies. Such philosophies generally shift based on political leanings, which are also discussed. Our historical overview provides some early examples of patterns in race and sentencing. Finally, the last segment of the chapter explores contemporary race and sentencing issues.

❖ Sentencing Philosophies

Punishment is meted out in the sentencing phase of the criminal justice process. According to van den Haag (1975), "'punishment' is a depravation, or suffering, imposed by law" (p. 8). Drawing on the works of English philosopher H. L. A. Hart, Cassia Spohn (2009), a leading scholar in the area of sentencing, wrote that there are five necessary elements of punishment: It must (a) involve pain or other consequences normally considered unpleasant, (b) be enacted for an offense against legal rules, (c) be imposed on an actual or supposed offender for his offense, (d) be intentionally administered by human beings other than the offender, and (e) be imposed and administered by an authority constituted by a legal system against which the offense was committed.

Spohn (2009) added that some scholars feel that, in addition to the five elements outlined by Hart, there must also be an appropriate justification for the punishment. These justifications amount to what are generally referred to as "philosophies of punishment" or "sentencing philosophies." Generally speaking, there are four different sentencing philosophies: (a) justice/retribution, (b) incapacitation, (c) deterrence, and (d) treatment/rehabilitation. According to van den Haag (1975), "Justice [or retribution] is done by distributing punishments to offenders according to what is deserved by their offenses as specified by law" (p. 25). Incapacitation suggests that as long as offenders are detained, society is protected from them. Deterrence operates under the premise that the public will be affected by seeing others punished (van den Haag, 1975). There are two forms of deterrence: specific and general. Specific deterrence operates under the notion that when you punish someone, he or she will be deterred from further criminal activity. General deterrence suggests that when you punish someone, the larger society is deterred from committing crimes (van den Haag, 1975). Making the offender better is the overriding aim of the treatment or **rehabilitation** philosophy. In some instances, each of these might be present in a sentence; however, one will typically predominate (Anderson & Newman, 1998). Predictably, each of these philosophies is tied to politics. We discuss this connection next.

Sentencing and Politics

Sentencing philosophies are germane to any discussion of punishment because such considerations tend to drive the nature of what happens at the "back end" of the system (i.e., corrections). Thus, depending on the prevailing philosophy, sentences could be longer and harsher, or, conversely, sentences could be lighter and more treatment oriented. Each of these two possibilities has consequences for society as a whole. For example, when sentences are longer, jails and prisons often reach or exceed their capacity; government officials justify such expensive policies by pointing to cases in which people who were released early went out and committed new crimes. However, when sentences are lighter and more treatment oriented, government officials argue that a shorter sentence under the rehabilitation approach is cheaper and more effective. Therefore, more often than not, politics at the local, state, and federal levels dictate the prevailing philosophy (Beckett & Sasson, 2000; Hagan, 2010; Scheingold, 1984).

A good example of this is the formulation of the crime control and due process models of criminal justice decision making constructed by Herbert Packer (1968) in the late 1960s, which 20 years later was refined by Samuel Walker (1989). In both formulations, there are those who adhere to a more conservative approach when handling crime control, and, on the other side, there are those who adhere to a more liberal approach. In short, those who adhere to the conservative approach take a hard line stance on crime and are generally supportive of sentencing philosophies that are both punitive and deterrent in orientation. Adherents to the liberal philosophy lean more toward the rehabilitation/treatment approach. They tend to believe that people can be "cured" or, at the least, made better through a variety of treatments. Therefore, they generally recommend shorter jail or prison sentences combined with appropriate treatment. Such thinking reigned during the 1960s, when some literature actually pointed to the counterproductiveness of punishment (see, e.g., Menninger, 1966). However, during the punitive decades of the 1980s and 1990s, some liberals, particularly those in inner cities, were influenced by the conservatism that swept the country. This era witnessed some people calling for "personal responsibility" and more punitive sanctions for those engaging in urban violence.

The liberal and conservative approaches have predominated for the last 40 years. As is widely acknowledged, the rehabilitation approach was dealt a near fatal blow in the 1970s by the increasing crime rate and the controversial Martinson (1974) report, which reviewed numerous treatment-oriented approaches and suggested that few were having their desired outcome. In the end, Martinson's study was interpreted as saying when it comes to rehabilitation, "nothing works." Such a dismal forecast set in motion a movement toward the conservative philosophy, which most would agree remains the predominant approach.

❖ Historical Overview of Race and Sentencing

Punishment in Colonial America

A good place to begin a historical overview of race and sentencing is colonial America. This era provides us with a sense of the punishments that were rendered in the early years of the colony. Moreover, a review of court records and other documents also provides us with some indication as to racial/ethnic disparities in sentencing.

As has been previously noted, much of the law in colonial America was based on English practices. The remainder of the laws that were created originated from the colonists or the Bible (Chapin, 1983). The colonists took biblical influence one-step further by having some cases actually handled by religious congregations. In general, it is thought that summary proceedings administered by judges were the primary way many cases were handled. For those who desired a trial by jury, Chapin wrote, "A defendant could have a jury in almost any kind of case if he asked and paid for it" (p. 41). It is obvious from this practice that class bias was present from the earliest colonial times and was also present when administering punishments.

Wilson Chinn, a freed slave from Louisiana, poses with equipment used to punish slaves. Such images were used to set Northern resolve against slaveholders during the American Civil War.

Kimball / Corbis.

One of the first things the colonists did when they began to construct their justice system was to do away with the excessive use of the death penalty, which prevailed in England. Many of the more brutal sentences were reserved for servants and "lesser men." One such servant was Richard Barnes, whose offense, aggravated contempt, resulted in him having "his arms broken and his tongue bored through and [he] was forced to crawl through a guard of forty men who kicked him" (Chapin, 1983, p. 50). Certainly, the colonists did execute people and were fond of corporal punishment and other public displays. Some people were whipped in public (see Photo 6.1), but class lines again prevailed because those who were considered "gentlemen" could substitute some other satisfaction (likely money) to fulfill their sentences. According to Chapin, however, "The most common punishment was a fine payable in money or tobacco" (p. 51). As they are today, the punishments were incremental. For example, "A convicted burglar or robber in Connecticut and Massachusetts was branded on the forehead with the letter 'B' for a first offense, branded and whipped for a second, and executed as incorrigible for a third conviction" (p. 49). This example also suggests that, although the moniker might be new, three-strikes laws are not.

Early Colonial Cases

The colonists were clearly sensitive to economic issues, which, along with their xenophobia, translated into unfairness in the justice system. One way to examine this unfairness is to review early cases and their sentencing patterns. To get a glimpse of the justice that prevailed for African Americans in early America, some scholars have turned to Helen Tunnicliff Catterall's (1926/1968) four-volume work, *Judicial Cases Concerning American Slavery and the Negro,* which provides brief summaries of early relevant cases (see also Higginbotham, 1978; Russell, 1998). Four cases decided in colonial Virginia that have received considerable attention by legal scholars seeking to see how race impacted on sentences in early America are *Re Davis, Re Sweat, Re Negro John Punch,* and *Re Negro Emmanuel.* The summary from the 1630 trial of *Re Davis* reads,

Hugh Davis to be soundly whipt before an assembly of negroes and others for abusing himself to the dishonor of God and shame of Christianity by defiling his body in lying with a negro, which fault he is to acknowledge next Sabbath day. (Catterall, 1926/1968, p. 77)

Here, one could interpret the transcript as saying that Davis was White and he had violated the law by sleeping with a Black woman. His obvious sentence was penance on the next Sabbath day. But the mere suggestion that he defiled his body by sleeping with the woman suggests notions of superiority and inferiority. As noted earlier by Higginbotham (1978), religion also played a key role in maintaining African Americans and other undesirables in their "place." A decade later, *Re Sweat* (1640) also spoke to the criminal liaisons between White men and Black females, but in this case, where a child resulted, the penalties were distinctly different. The case summary reads,

> Whereas Robert Sweat hath begotten with child a negro woman servant belonging unto Lieutenant Sheppard, the court hath therefore ordered that the said negro woman shall be whipt at the whipping post and the said Sweat shall tomorrow in the forenoon do public penance for his offense at James city church in the time of divine service according to the laws of England in that case provided. (Catterall, 1926/1968, p. 78)

Here, Sweat was given part of the punishment as Davis in the prior case; however, the whipping was reserved for the Black woman. Although the punishments were obviously disparate, the sentence was likely even more stinging for the Black woman considering that, given the time period, it is likely that the relationship was not consensual. Thus, there is the possibility that a convicted rapist did penance while the victim was whipped for being raped. Such contradictions or inequities were also present in other trials. In *Re Negro Punch,* the case record stated the following:

> Whereas Hugh Gwyn hath . . . Brought back from Maryland three servants formerly run away . . . the court doth therefore order that the said three servants shall receive the punishment of whipping and to have thirty stripes apiece one called Victor, a Dutchman, and other a Scotchman called James Gregory, shall first serve out their times with their master according to their Indentures, and one whole year apiece after the time of their service is Expired . . . and after that service . . . to serve the colony for three whole years apiece, and that the third being a negro named John Punch shall serve his said master or his assigns for the time of his natural Life here or elsewhere. (Catterall, 1926/1968, p. 78)

In this case, the punishments rendered suggest that the two White servants received less punishment than the Black servant. The two Whites received extended indentures and service to the colony, with the Dutchman also receiving a whipping. Yet the Black servant received *lifetime* servitude. Another case that shows the early disparities in sentencing is *Re Negro Emmanuel*. In *Re Negro Emmanuel,* a plot to run away was foiled. Again, the summary of the case is illuminating:

> Complaint . . . by Capt. Wm. Pierce, Esqr. That six of his servants and a negro of Mr. Reginolds has plotted to run away unto the Dutch plantation . . . and did assay to put the same in Execution. They "had . . . taken the skiff of . . . Pierce . . . and corn, powder and shot and guns . . . which said persons sailed down . . . to Elizabeth river where they were taken . . . order that . . . Emmanuel the Negro to receive thirty [lashes] and to be burnt in the

cheek with the letter R, and to work in shakle one year or more as his master shall see cause. (Catterall, 1926/1968, p. 77)

Except for Emmanuel, each of the conspirators received additional service to the colony, with one White conspirator also being branded and whipped. Although Emmanuel received no additional service, which some have suggested was an indication that he was already in lifetime servitude (Higginbotham, 1978), he was whipped, branded with "R" (presumably so everyone would know he had previously run away), and made to wear shackles for a year.

Scores of related cases existed in the colonial era. Based on an analysis of these cases, Catterall (1926/1968) noted that a hierarchy of social precedence developed (see Figure 6.1). According to her analysis, at the top of the hierarchy were White indentured servants, whereas at the bottom of the hierarchy were Black slaves. Based on the case studies presented, one can confidently assume that justice in the courts was distributed in line with this hierarchy.

Figure 6.1

Catterall's
Hierarchy
of Social
Precedence

Source: H. Catterall (1926/1968) Judicial cases concerning American Slavery and the Negro (Vol 1). New York: Negro University Press.

1. White indentured servants
2. White servants without indentures
3. Christian Black servants
4. Indian servants
5. Mulatto servants (Black or Indian)
6. Indian slaves
7. Black slaves

To further investigate these early disparities in case outcomes, we turn to one of the more diverse colonies, New York. From the late 1600s through the 1700s, New York was the gateway for an influx of racial and ethnic groups. Therefore, looking at data from this colony provides a more expansive picture than the cases presented by Catterall.

Crime and Justice in Colonial New York

Greenberg (1976) provided data on more than 5,000 cases that were prosecuted in New York from 1691 to 1776. Of these cases, nearly 75% involved persons of English background, most of whom were males. As seen in Table 6.1, the remaining persons were of a variety of racial and ethnic backgrounds. What stands out most in the figures is that both the Dutch and slaves had sizeable populations but were under-represented in the criminal cases.

In the case of the Dutch, Greenberg (1976) surmised that, given that in some estimates they were nearly 50% of the population of the colony, they were likely

Table 6.1

Ethnic Distribution of Criminal Cases in Colonial New York, 1691–1776

Ethnic Group	Number Accused	Percentage of All Accusations
English	3,889	73.4
Dutch	693	13.1
Jewish	44	0.8
Other Whites	252	4.8
Slaves	353	6.7
Free Blacks	35	0.7
Indians	31	0.6
Total	5,297	100

Source: Reprinted from *Crime and Law Enforcement in the Colony of New York,* 1691–1776, by Douglas Greenberg. Copyright 1976 by Cornell University. Used by permission of the publisher, Cornell University Press.

misidentified and undercounted in the case figures. The discrepancy related to slaves was explained differently. Because they were constantly under the threat of being brutally punished, they were less likely to engage in criminal activity. Furthermore, as noted previously, virtually every aspect of slave life was controlled, which naturally resulted in fewer offenses. Greenberg (1976) also pointed out,

> [Another] factor that accounts for the apparently small volume of slave crime is that prosecutions for what was probably the most common and, from the master's point of view, the most costly of slave crimes—running away—appear very infrequently in the records, since slave runaways were seldom captured. (p. 45)

Before looking at the case outcomes, it is important to review the distribution of crimes by ethnic group (see Table 6.2). The review resulted in no unusual patterns except that the English and Blacks predominated in thefts. Explaining the large number of Blacks involved in theft, Greenberg (1976) wrote,

> Prosecutions for theft were almost twice as frequent among Blacks as in the defendant population at large. This figure is a function both of the "real" position of Blacks in the eighteenth century and prevailing ideas *about* Blacks. On the one hand, slaves stole because they were deprived, and on the other, they were deprived because people believed them inherently sinful. (p. 61)

Conviction patterns also speak to how ethnic and racial groups were treated in this early period. Here, as noted in Table 6.3, although slaves represented 6.7% of

Table 6.2

Ethnic Distribution of Major Categories of Crime in New York, 1691–1776

Crime	English	Dutch	Jews	Whites	Blacks	Indians	N
Crimes of violence*	871	156	27	65	18	3	1,140
Thefts	585	30	4	19	86	3	727
Contempt of authority	221	79	1	10	1	0	312
Crimes by public officials	137	47	0	15	0	0	199
Disorderly houses	163	17	0	10	3	0	193
Violations of public order	795	135	6	48	7	6	997
Crimes against masters**	3	0	0	0	217	8	228

Source: Reprinted from *Crime and Law Enforcement in the Colony of New York, 1691–1776,* by Douglas Greenberg. Copyright 1976 by Cornell University. Used by permission of the publisher, Cornell University Press.

* Against persons, not resulting in death.

** By servants or slaves.

Table 6.3

Patterns of Judgment for Ethnic Groups in New York, 1691–1776

Ethnic Group	Number Accused	Percentage of All Accusations	Number Convicted	Percentage Convicted of Those Accused	Percentage of All Convictions	Number Acquitted	Percentage Acquitted of Those Accused	Percentage of All Acquittals
English	3,889	73.4	1,809	46.5	71.3	542	13.9	68.0
Dutch	693	13.1	329	47.5	13.0	118	17.0	14.0
Jews	44	0.8	14	31.8	0.6	16	36.4	2.0
Other Whites	252	4.8	115	45.6	4.5	48	19.0	6.0
Slaves	353	6.7	242	68.6	9.5	59	16.7	7.4
Free Blacks	35	0.7	13	37.0	0.5	6	17.1	0.8
Indians	31	0.6	16	51.6	0.6	8	25.8	1.0

Source: Reprinted from *Crime and Law Enforcement in the Colony of New York, 1691–1776,* by Douglas Greenberg. Copyright 1976 by Cornell University. Used by permission of the publisher, Cornell University Press.

the accusations, they represented nearly 10% of all convictions (Greenberg, 1976). Tables 6.3 and 6.4 illustrates that slaves had higher conviction rates than other ethnic or racial groups, with an overall conviction rate of 68.6%. American Indians had the next highest conviction rate (51.6%). Given their status within colonial America, for obvious reasons, slaves would not have been expected to receive the same consideration as other racial or ethnic groups. Their higher conviction rates speak to their low status in American society.

Closely related to conviction trends are sentencing dispositions. Although Greenberg's (1976) analysis does not provide sentences by ethnic or racial group, he does note that the nature of punishments changed in the mid-1750s. In particular, he observed that whereas before 1750, most thefts resulted in whippings and few executions, after 1750, the number of whippings for theft dropped, whereas the use of branding and the number of executions increased dramatically. Although Greenberg did not make the connection, this change in sentencing practices could have been a response to the increasing number of racial or ethnic minorities who were engaging in theft to survive. Although the first two sections of our historical overview presented information on early cases from two distinct colonies, we now review some early national figures on race and sentencing.

Early National Sentencing Statistics

Following the Revolutionary War, in terms of treatment, little changed for racial or ethnic minorities. Although it was a major development when the new government

Table 6.4

Conviction Patterns for Slaves in Colonial America, 1691–1776

Crimes by Slaves	Number of Accusations	Number of Convictions	Percentage Convicted of Those Accused	Percentage of All Convictions Against Slaves
Thefts	69	38	55.1	15.7
Crimes against masters	214	149	69.6	61.6
Crimes against morality (all Sabbath breach)	32	32	100.0	13.2
Crimes of violence not resulting in death	16	13	81.3	5.4
Total (these crimes)	331	232	71.0	95.9
Total (all cases involving slaves)	353	242	68.6	100.0

Source: Reprinted from *Crime and Law Enforcement in the Colony of New York, 1691–1776*, by Douglas Greenberg. Copyright 1976 by Cornell University. Used by permission of the publisher, Cornell University Press.

created federal courts, including the Supreme Court, criminal justice remained a place where race and class bias persisted (Shelden, 2001). The development of these courts only provided new mechanisms to reinforce the race and class bias in state judiciaries (Shelden, 2001). Accurate sentencing trends from the 18th and 19th centuries are difficult to ascertain because there were no national statistics until the 1880 census (Cahalan & Parsons, 1986, p. 31). Taken from penitentiaries, the data in that first report revealed that: "99% [of the offenders] were reported to be under sentence at the time of the survey . . . and 88% had sentences listed over 1 year" (Cahalan & Parsons, 1986, p. 31). In jails, "about 55% of the inmates were under sentence and of these only 8% had sentences of 1 year or longer" (p. 31).

The 1890 census provided even more detailed information of the characteristics of offenders, noting the ethnicity of those who were sentenced. At that time, the most severe average sentence was for crimes against the person, at 7.8 years (Cahalan & Parsons, 1986; see Table 6.5). Table 6.6 shows the average sentences by race, nativity, and gender. The figures show that Chinese received the longest average sentences (6.58 years), followed by Indians (5.64 years). When looking for the female group with the longest average sentence, Negroes were highest (2.8 years), with persons of Chinese origin closely behind (2.54 years; Cahalan & Parsons, 1986). Although the data do not speak to offense trends by specific racial group, they do show that, from the earliest records available, disparities by race were present.

Table 6.5

Average Sentence in Years, by Gender and Offense, 1890

Offense Against	Male	Female
Government	2.76	1.75
Society	.79	.67
Person	7.8	6.99
Property	3.9	2.29
On high seas	2.75[a]	
Other	4.67	.8

Source: BJS (1986).

a. Not separately enumerated.

How far have we come in race and sentencing? Before answering this question, we examine how politics and the "get tough" philosophy have impacted sentencing over the last 30 years. The last section of the chapter takes a deeper look at contemporary issues related to race and sentencing.

Table 6.6

Average Sentence in Years, by Gender and Nativity and Race, 1890

Color, Nativity, Race	Male	Female
White	3.66	1.12
Native	3.79	1.51
Parents native	4.25	1.76
One parent foreign	3.66	1.08
Parents foreign	3.10	1.08
Unknown	2.47	1.28
Colored	5.04	2.79
Negroes	5.01	2.80
Chinese	6.58	2.54
Indians	5.64	.2

Source: BJS (1986).

The 1980s to 2000s: The Changing Nature of Sentencing Practices

Coinciding with the 1980 election of President Ronald Reagan was the largest number of homicides in U.S. history. That year, according to the FBI's Uniform Crime Reports, there were 23,040 homicides. Pointing to this unprecedented level of violent crime, to reduce these figures, President Reagan championed a conservative and more punitive approach (Hagan, 2010). Following the lead of the federal government, most states moved away from sentencing policies that were generally more indeterminate in nature, which had allowed for minimum and maximum sentences and gave justice officials the discretion to release offenders when they were thought to be rehabilitated. Observers from all sides felt such a sentencing approach was unfair and in too many instances resulted in bias against poor people and racial minorities. Nevertheless, over time, the public also bought into the punitive approach.

During the mid-1990s, a national opinion survey on crime and justice of more than 1,000 randomly selected U.S. citizens revealed that when asked whether the government should focus on rehabilitation or punishing and putting away violent offenders, nearly 60% responded "punish," whereas only 27% said "rehabilitate" (Gerber & Engelhardt-Greer, 1996). There were, however, significant differences by race. Nearly half of the Black respondents (46%) indicated that rehabilitation should be the focus, with Hispanics (38%) also being more receptive to rehabilitation than Whites (23%) (Gerber & Engelhardt-Greer, 1996).

In line with national sentiment, states created "get tough" approaches such as determinate sentencing, sentencing guidelines that included mandatory minimum statutes, three-strikes-and-you're-out legislation, and truth-in-sentencing laws (Spohn, 2009). In addition to being more punitive, proponents of these approaches suggested that such policies also reduced judicial discretion, which some felt contributed to leniency in some instances and racial disparities in other instances. One of the first alternative sentencing approaches enacted by states was determinate sentencing.

In contrast to indeterminate sentencing, this approach required states to create "a presumptive range of confinement for various categories of offenses. The judge imposed a fixed number of years from within this range, and the offender would serve this term minus time off for good behavior" (Spohn, 2009, p. 231). In the few states that did enact this form of sentencing, the results were mixed; therefore, most states lost interest in the approach (Spohn, 2009).

One of the most popular sentencing approaches adapted during the 1970s was presumptive sentencing guidelines. Such guidelines based sentencing decisions on the various aspects of the crime and the offender history. According to Spohn (2009), there are several common aspects of this approach. First, there is generally some sentencing commission or committee that makes the recommendations for the guidelines. Second, the guidelines take into consideration "the severity of the offense and the seriousness of the offender's prior criminal record" (Spohn, 2009, p. 234). Finally, although this approach allows for some judicial discretion, judges who deviate from the specified sentence must justify their decision An often-cited example of this approach is the Minnesota Sentencing Guidelines (see Figure 6.2).

Following the lead of states, the federal government created its own guidelines. Once the Federal Sentencing Guidelines were enacted in 1984, federal parole was eliminated (Hickey, 1998). Moreover, during this process, in 1987, the U.S. Sentencing Commission was created. Spohn (2009) noted that the commission was created "to develop and implement presumptive sentencing guidelines designed to achieve 'honesty,' 'uniformity,' and 'proportionality' in sentencing" (p. 239).

Mandatory minimum sentences were created in the 1970s and 1980s in response to concerns about drug dealing and violent crimes involving guns. Such sentences stated a minimum penalty for a particular offense, and in some instances there were mandatory penalties for using a gun in the commission of a crime. Generally, the proscribed minimums were fairly harsh and provided little, if any, room for judicial discretion in sentencing. Prosecutors generally have the leeway to charge the offender with an offense that carries a particular sentence. As a result, under such an approach, prosecutors determine the nature of one's sentence (Spohn, 2009).

Popularized in the 1990s by the states of Washington and California, three-strikes-and-you're-out legislation caught on, as evidenced by the fact that "as of 2004, 23 states and the federal government had adopted some variation of the three-strikes-you're-out laws" (Spohn, 2009, p. 264). Although from state to state there were different versions of the legislation, the common theme was, like a batter in a baseball game, when an offender committed his or her third "strike" (felony offense), he or she was "out" (sentenced to 25 years to life or some other draconian sentence).

Presumptive Sentence Lengths in Months

Italicized numbers within the grid denote the range within which a judge may sentence without the sentence being deemed a departure. Offenders with non-imprisonment felony sentences are subject to jail time according to law.

Severity Level of Conviction Offense (Common offenses listed in italics)		Criminal History Score						
		0	1	2	3	4	5	6 or more
Murder, 2nd Degree (intentional murder; drive-by-shootings)	XI	306 261-367	326 278-391	346 295-415	366 312-439	386 329-463	406 346-480[2]	426 363-480[2]
Murder, 3rd Degree Murder, 2nd Degree (unintentional murder)	X	150 128-180	165 141-198	180 153-216	195 166-234	210 179-252	225 192-270	240 204-288
Assault, 1st Degree Controlled Substance Crime, 1st Degree	IX	86 74-103	98 84-117	110 94-132	122 104-146	134 114-160	146 125-175	158 135-189
Aggravated Robbery, 1st Degree Controlled Substance Crime, 2nd Degree	VIII	48 41-57	58 50-69	68 58-81	78 67-93	88 75-105	98 84-117	108 92-129
Felony DWI	VII	36	42	48	54 46-64	60 51-72	66 57-79	72 62-86
Assault, 2nd Degree Felon in Possession of a Firearm	VI	21	27	33	39 34-46	45 39-54	51 44-61	57 49-68
Residential Burglary Simple Robbery	V	18	23	28	33 29-39	38 33-45	43 37-51	48 41-57
Nonresidential Burglary	IV	12[1]	15	18	21	24 21-28	27 23-32	30 26-36
Theft Crimes (Over $2,500)	III	12[1]	13	15	17	19 17-22	21 18-25	23 20-27
Theft Crimes ($2,500 or less) Check Forgery ($200-$2,500)	II	12[1]	12[1]	13	15	17	19	21 18-25
Sale of Simulated Controlled Substance	I	12[1]	12[1]	12[1]	13	15	17	19 17-22

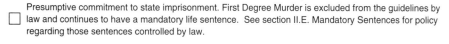

Presumptive commitment to state imprisonment. First Degree Murder is excluded from the guidelines by law and continues to have a mandatory life sentence. See section II.E. Mandatory Sentences for policy regarding those sentences controlled by law.

Presumptive stayed sentence; at the discretion of the judge, up to a year in jail and/or other non-jail sanctions can be imposed as conditions of probation. However, certain offenses in this section of the grid always carry a presumptive commitment to state prison. See sections II.C. Presumptive Sentence and II.E. Mandatory Sentences.

Figure 6.2

The Minnesota Sentencing Guidelines Grid

Source: Minnesota Sentencing Guidelines Commission.

1. One year and 1 day.

2. M.S. § 244.09 requires the Sentencing Guidelines to provide a range of 15% downward and 20% upward from the presumptive sentence. However, because the statutory maximum sentence for these offenses is no more than 40 years, the range is capped at that number.

Another sentencing innovation was the Truth in Sentencing Act of 1997. Clearly falling under the incapacitation philosophy, the Act "awarded funds to states that kept their offenders—particularly those serving time for violent offenses—in prison for at least 85% of their sentences" (Blumstein, 2002, p. 461). It was anticipated that such a policy would have serious implications for preventing serious crimes and also for the size of correctional populations. It is notable that although crime did decrease during the 1990s, whether this sentencing strategy produced the reductions has been subject to debate (Blumstein & Wallman, 2005). Each of the aforementioned sentencing approaches, in varying magnitudes, contributed to an increasing number of persons being incarcerated (see Chapter 8). In fact, many of those who bore the brunt of such policies were poor persons and racial minorities. Another set of legislative enactments from the 1980s through the 2000s, which influenced the nature of sentencing, targeted the "**War on Drugs**."

The "War on Drugs"

Declaring a "War on Drugs" in the late 1980s was also a major contributor to the increase in punitive sentencing policies during the last 20 years. Beginning with Ronald Reagan and taking shape under George H. W. Bush, the White House Office of National Drug Control Policy, which was officially established under the Anti-Drug Abuse Act of 1988 and extended under the Violent Crime Control and Law Enforcement Act of 1994, was created to "establish policies, priorities, and objectives for the Nation's drug control program" (Office of National Drug Control Policy, n.d.). In line with its purpose, "The goals of the program are to reduce illicit drug use, manufacturing, and trafficking, drug-related crime and violence, and drug-related health consequences" (Office of National Drug Control Policy, n.d.). In some ways, the role of the director (also referred to as the "drug czar") is symbolic in that that person is the face of drug control for each president. Although the director drafts and promotes the annual *National Drug Control Strategy* report (United States, 2014), he or she does not actually carry out the activities proposed to meet its goals. Nevertheless, because the director is a component of the Executive Office of the President, he or she does "[advise] the President regarding changes in the organization, management, budgeting, and personnel of Federal Agencies that could affect the Nation's anti-drug efforts; and regarding Federal agency compliance with their obligations under the Strategy" (Office of National Drug Control Policy, n.d.).

With such an influential role, the director can push either punitive or treatment-oriented drug-control strategies. However, given that the position is an appointed one, it is likely that the director will simply follow the party line on most issues. Again, as in the sentencing strategies discussed in the previous section, the party line on such issues in the 1980s and early 1990s was punitive in orientation. Even with the election of President Bill Clinton (a Democrat) and the appointment of Lee P. Brown as director, who championed rehabilitative and education-oriented initiatives, such punitive approaches had become so institutionalized that during Clinton's administration one of the most punitive crime bills in history was enacted. During the first two decades of the 21st century, the collateral consequences of the punitive ideology had actually brought the system back to rehabilitation. Why? Because states finally realized that they could not afford to maintain the correctional building programs of the 1980s and 1990s. In more recent times, states have increasingly looked for ways to divert or release nonviolent drug offenders—an option that was not on the table during the height of the "War on Drugs." Moreover, the positive reception for the legalization of marijuana sales and use in states across the country provides further evidence of the loosening of the punitive ideology surrounding drugs (Harvard Public Opinion Project, 2014).

❖ Contemporary Issues in Race and Sentencing

We begin our discussion of contemporary issues with a review of current sentencing patterns at the state and federal levels. Following this initial discussion, we examine race and sentencing scholarship, as well as the role of judges in **sentencing disparities**.

Felony Convictions in State Courts

In 2006, more than 1.1 million adults were convicted of a felony in state courts; nearly 70% of them were sentenced to either jail (28%) or prison (41%), with the remainder being sentenced to probation (Rosenmerkel et al., 2009). In 2006, the average sentence was 4 years and 11 months. For those who committed murder and nonnegligent manslaughter, the average was 20 years. In line with the arrest statistics presented in Chapter 2, most persons convicted for felony offenses were Whites; however, Blacks were overrepresented in nearly every category (see Table 6.7). In 2006, for example, Blacks, who make up 12% of the population, represented 38% of those persons convicted of a felony in state courts and 39% of convicted felons who committed a violent crime. Other races (American Indians, Alaska Natives, Asian and Pacific Islanders) represented 2% of all felony convictions and the same percentage of convictions for violent crime (Rosenmerkel et al., 2009). Table 6.8 provides a glimpse of the different sentences being received by Blacks and Whites for certain offenses.

Convictions in Federal Courts

In addition to state-level data, there are also data on offenders convicted in federal court. In FY 2013, the **United States Sentencing Commission** (2014) reported 80,035 offenders at the federal level. First, we discuss the nature of the offenses. The majority of the cases (82.3%) involved the following four offenses: drugs, immigration, firearms, or fraud. Immigration (31.2%) and drug trafficking offenses (31.2%) were the most frequent federal offenses. Turning to trends related to race/ethnicity, we see that Blacks—and especially Hispanics—are overrepresented as offenders in the federal system. In fact, more than half the offenders (51.5%) were Hispanic, with Whites (23.8%) and Blacks (20.6%) rounding out the majority of the federal offender population. Also, nearly 45% of all federal offenders were noncitizens. Hispanics represented slightly more than half of the offenders charged with federal immigration offenses (51.6%) and nearly half of the federal drug offenders (47.9%).

Table 6.7

Gender and Race of Persons Convicted of Felonies in State Courts, by Offense, 2006

Most Serious Conviction Offense	Percentage of Convicted Felons					
		Gender		Race		
	Total	Male	Female	White	Black	Other[a]
All offenses	100	83	17	60	38	2
Violent offenses	100	89	11	58	39	3
Murder/nonnegligent manslaughter	100	90	10	46	51	3
Sexual assault	100	97	3	74	24	3
Rape	100	96	4	70	28	2
Other sexual assault[b]	100	97	3	77	21	2
Robbery	100	91	9	42	57	1
Aggravated assault	100	86	14	59	39	3
Other violent[c]	100	88	12	69	28	3
Property offenses	100	75	25	65	33	3
Burglary	100	90	10	66	32	2
Larceny	100	75	25	64	34	2
Motor vehicle theft	100	86	14	70	26	5
Fraud/forgery[d]	100	59	41	66	32	2
Drug offenses	100	82	18	55	44	1
Possession	100	80	20	62	36	2
Trafficking	100	83	17	50	49	1
Weapon offenses	100	95	5	43	55	2
Other specified offenses[e]	100	87	13	67	30	3

Source: BJS (2009).

Note: Data on gender were reported for 86% of convicted felons and data on race for 74%. Detail may not sum to total because of rounding. Racial categories include persons of Latino or Hispanic origin.

a. Includes American Indians, Alaska Natives, Asians, Native Hawaiians, and other Pacific Islanders.

b. Includes offenses such as statutory rape and incest with a minor.

c. Includes offenses such as negligent manslaughter and kidnapping.

d. Includes embezzlement.

e. Consists of nonviolent offenses such as vandalism and receiving stolen property.

Table 6.8

Type of Felony Sentences Imposed in State Courts, by Offense and Race of Felons, 2006

Most Serious Conviction Offense	Total	Percentage of Felons Sentenced					
		Incarceration			Nonincarceration		
		Total	Prison	Jail	Total	Probation	Other
White							
All offenses	100	66	37	29	34	29	4
Violent offenses	100	74	52	23	26	22	3
Murder/ nonnegligent manslaughter	100	93	92	2	7	4	3
Sexual assault[a]	100	81	64	16	19	16	4
Robbery	100	83	70	14	17	15	2
Aggravated assault	100	69	40	29	31	27	3
Other violent[b]	100	68	40	28	32	27	4
Property offenses	100	65	36	29	35	30	5
Burglary	100	71	46	25	29	25	4
Larceny	100	66	32	34	34	30	4
Fraud/forgery[c]	100	59	31	27	41	35	6
Drug offenses	100	61	31	30	39	34	5
Possession	100	63	28	35	37	33	4
Trafficking	100	59	33	26	41	35	6
Weapon offenses	100	73	45	28	27	23	4
Other specified offenses[d]	100	69	34	35	31	27	4
Black							
All offenses	100	72	45	27	28	25	4
Violent offenses	100	78	58	20	22	19	3
Murder/ nonnegligent manslaughter	100	95	93	2	5	3	2

(Continued)

(Continued)

Most Serious Conviction Offense	Percentage of Felons Sentenced						
		Incarceration			Nonincarceration		
	Total	Total	Prison	Jail	Total	Probation	Other
Sexual assault[a]	100	80	65	15	20	16	4
Robbery	100	86	71	14	14	12	2
Aggravated assault	100	72	46	26	28	23	4
Other violent[b]	100	68	37	31	32	28	4
Property offenses	100	69	41	28	31	27	4
Burglary	100	78	57	20	22	20	3
Larceny	100	69	36	33	31	28	3
Fraud/forgery[c]	100	60	30	30	40	35	5
Drug offenses	100	70	43	27	30	25	4
Possession	100	71	38	33	29	24	5
Trafficking	100	70	46	25	30	26	4
Weapon offenses	100	73	45	28	27	25	2
Other specified offenses[d]	100	70	38	31	30	27	3

Source: BJS (2009).

Note: For persons receiving a combination of sentences, the sentence designation came from the most severe penalty imposed—prison being the most severe, followed by jail, probation, and then other sentences, such as a fine, community service, or treatment. *Prison* includes death sentences. In this table, *probation* is defined as straight probation. Details may not sum to total because of rounding. Racial categories include persons of Latino or Hispanic origin.

a. Includes rape.

b. Includes offenses such as negligent manslaughter and kidnapping.

c. Includes embezzlement.

d. Consists of nonviolent offenses such as vandalism and receiving stolen property.

Given the large numbers of Blacks and Hispanics convicted of felony offenses in either state or federal courts, the next question is whether there are racial disparities in sentencing. In recent years, there has been an explosion of literature investigating this question. We review a sampling of these studies next.

Scholarship on Race and Sentencing

There have been countless studies on race and sentencing, beginning in the early 20th century. Since then, scholars have relied on a variety of methodologies to determine the nature and scope of racial discrimination in the sentencing process. To provide context for the first 50 years of these studies, Marjorie Zatz (1987) organized the research into four waves. Her important work is outlined in the next section. Our discussion of her work is followed by reviews of recent summaries on the topic.

Zatz's Four Waves of Race and Sentencing Research

Separating sentencing research into four waves, Zatz (1987) provided a summary of the diverse research on race and sentencing. During Wave I (1930s to mid-1960s), the literature "showed clear and consistent bias against non-Whites in sentencing" (p. 71). Most of the early research suggested that Blacks and foreigners received biased sentences in the courts. A noted concern of this early research was its lack of methodological sophistication. On this point, Zatz wrote, "These studies were flawed by a number of serious methodological problems. The most damning flaw was the lack of controls for legally relevant factors, especially prior record" (p. 72).

Wave II (late 1960s to 1970s) followed on the heels of the successful civil rights movement. During this period, studies began to emerge that indicated that discrimination in sentencing had subsided. Moreover, more sophisticated studies began to suggest "that minorities were overrepresented in the criminal justice system and prisons because of their greater proportional involvement in crime, and not because of any bias in the system" (Zatz, 1987, p. 73). Studies were also beginning to show that race might have a "cumulative effect" by indirectly impacting minority offenders through other variables. In addition, "extralegal attributes of the offender could *interact* with other factors to influence decision making" (p. 73).

In Wave III (studies conducted in the 1970s and 1980s), the Wave II studies that suggested discrimination had subsided were reanalyzed and produced different results. Previously unaccounted for in earlier studies, Zatz (1987) noted that, "depending on the degree of victimization and the relative social harm perceived, minority members were treated more harshly in some situations and Whites in others" (p. 74). In addition, Zatz pointed to selection bias and specification error as two other common problems with earlier research. Here, she was concerned that some people were dropped out of study samples too early in the process, which can invalidate the results of studies. With specification error, in some instances, researchers were not considering interaction effects. Such effects highlight when

> race/ethnicity can operate *indirectly* through its effect on other factors. It can interact with other variables to affect sentencing. That is, the impact of other variables (e.g., prior record, type of offense) could differ, depending on the defendant's race/ethnicity. (p. 75)

Another important type of indirect effect is referred to as "cumulative disadvantage." Here, race/ethnicity has a small effect on the initial stages of the process; however, "as the person moves through the system, these add up to substantial, and often statistically significant, disparities in processing and outcomes for different social groups" (Zatz, 1987, p. 76).

At the time of the publication of her article, Zatz (1987) indicated that Wave IV (data from the late 1970s to 1980s, conducted in the 1980s) was underway and substantive issues were emerging. Determinate sentencing was beginning to garner significant attention. Researchers were beginning to investigate the outcomes produced by this sentencing strategy.

Race and Sentencing Research Post-Zatz

In the years following the publication of Zatz's (1987) article, a multitude of scholars have provided extended summaries of the existing race and sentencing research. Some of these have found that region, prior record, crime seriousness, percentage Black in the population, and employment status all play a role in sentencing decisions (Chiricos & Crawford, 1995), while others have found that only one variable—severity of the offense—was tied to sentence length (Pratt, 1998). When Cassia Spohn (2000) conducted a major synthesis of the existing research on race and sentencing for the National Institute of Justice, she concluded that

> Considered together . . . race and ethnicity do play an important role in contemporary sentencing decisions. Black and Hispanic offenders sentenced in State and Federal courts face significantly greater odds of incarceration than similarly situated White offenders. In some jurisdictions, they also may receive longer sentences or differential benefits from guideline departures than their White counterparts. (p. 458)

More specifically, the studies reviewed by Spohn (2000) showed that "Racial minorities are sentenced more harshly than Whites if they (1) are young and male, (2) are unemployed, (3) are male and unemployed, (4) are young, male, and unemployed, (5) have lower incomes, and (6) have less education" (p. 462).

Spohn (2000) also found that, in several studies, when looking at the interaction between the offenders' race and process-related factors, "Racial minorities are sentenced more harshly than Whites if they (1) are detained in jail prior to trial, (2) are represented by a public defender rather than a private attorney, (3) are convicted at trial rather than by plea, and (4) have more serious prior criminal records" (p. 462). Other studies looking at the interaction between offender race and victim race revealed that "racial minorities who victimize Whites are sentenced more harshly than other race of offender/race of victim combinations" (p. 463). Finally, Spohn's review found studies that showed interaction effects between offender race and type of crime: "Racial minorities are sentenced more harshly than Whites if they are (1) convicted of less serious crimes, or (2) convicted of drug offenses or more serious drug offenses" (p. 463).

Following Spohn's (2000) comprehensive review, researchers continued to examine the question of race and sentencing (Engen, Gainey, Crutchfield, & Weis, 2003; B. Johnson, 2003; Steffensmeier & Britt, 2001; Steffensmeier & Demuth, 2000, 2001; Ulmer & Johnson, 2004), and, unfortunately, they continued to find that race and ethnicity mattered in the sentencing process. For example, an increasing finding in studies of both state (Steffensmeier & Demuth, 2001) and federal (Steffensmeier & Demuth, 2000) courts is that Hispanics are receiving the harshest sentences. In addition, studies are beginning to look at more contextual factors, noting that African Americans and Hispanics tend to be sentenced more harshly in areas where they are the majority populations (Ulmer & Johnson, 2004).

In the mid-2000s, a meta-analysis by Mitchell (2005) again sought to determine whether race matters in a large selection of empirical studies. Mitchell (2005) found that "even after taking into account offense seriousness and prior criminal history, African-Americans were punished more harshly than whites" (p. 456). He did note, however, that

> the observed differences between whites and African-Americans generally were small, suggesting that discrimination in the sentencing stage is not the primary cause of overrepresentation of African-Americans in U.S. correctional facilities. The size of unwarranted sentencing disparities grows considerably, however, when contrasts examined drug offenses, imprisonment decisions, discretionary sentencing decisions, and recently collected Federal data. (p. 462)

Although some of the more recent research has continued to find that Blacks and Hispanics are more likely to be prosecuted (Crow & Johnson, 2008) and treated more harshly (Brennan & Spohn, 2008; Spohn & Brennan, 2011) than Whites, other recent research (examining federal sentencing data) has found that Blacks had longer sentences than Whites, but Hispanic sentences were not significantly longer than those received by Whites (Feldmeyer & Ulmer, 2011). Feldmeyer and Ulmer also found that "district percentages of Blacks and Hispanics make no difference in terms of the average district sentence lengths of *all* defendants" (p. 254).

Two underexplored aspects of the race and sentencing research has been the experience of Asians and Native Americans in courts. Johnson and Betsinger (2009) made a notable contribution to the area by studying whether Asian Americans were sentenced any differently than other racial ethnic minorities in federal courts. In other words, they studied whether the positive "model minority" stereotype influences sentencing outcomes. Using data from the U.S. Sentencing Commission, the authors found that punishments were race graded, in that "Black and Hispanic offenders typically receive more severe outcomes than their similarly situated white counterparts, whereas Asian offenders do not" (p. 1076). In particular, young Asian offenders did not receive as severe sentences as young Black and Hispanic males—especially in terms of incarceration decisions. The researchers also found that citizenship status worked against Blacks and Hispanics, as compared to Asians. Taken together, the research supported the "model minority" thesis in that Asians were treated more leniently than not only Blacks and Hispanics, but Whites as well. Additional sentencing research using county-level data has also found Asians receiving more advantageous outcomes (Kutateladze, Andiloro, Johnson, & Spohn, 2014). Another underexplored aspect of race and sentencing is tied to Native Americans. Very little is known about their sentencing experiences. Franklin's (2013) pioneering study of the sentencing outcomes of cases involving Native Americans in U.S. Federal Courts (from 2006–2008) found that young Native American males received the most punitive treatment compared to other racial/ethnic minorities and Whites. Franklin's important work makes a strong argument for scholars to invest in the study of Native American sentencing.

Eric Baumer (2013) conducted the most recent synthesis and critique of the race and sentencing scholarship. Notably, Baumer's analysis also included the opinions of 25 sentencing scholars who answered a few questions tied to sentencing research. Baumer's work begins by recognizing the "meta-goals" of the existing research has tended to include the following: "(1) detecting racial disparities; (2) detecting racial discrimination; (3) assessing how or why race influences legal decision makers and/or legal decisions; and (4) evaluating whether a given policy intervention has modified observed racial disparities or discriminatory outcomes" (p. 234). Baumer concludes that the existing body of research is not particularly useful in weighing in on any of these issues. Baumer believes that the existing scholarship is too simplistic to capture the multiple influences on sentencing outcomes. Figure 6.3 is Baumer's heuristic model of racial influence on sentencing outcomes. It provides a clear picture of the multitude of factors that have the potential to influence sentencing outcomes. Unfortunately, according to Baumer and the sentencing scholars he interviewed, very few research studies are able to capture the complexity of the issue and, thus, are unable to definitively move beyond simply identifying racial disparities.

Figure 6.3

Baumer's Heuristic Model of Racial Influences on Sentencing Outcomes

Source: Baumer (2013, p. 239).

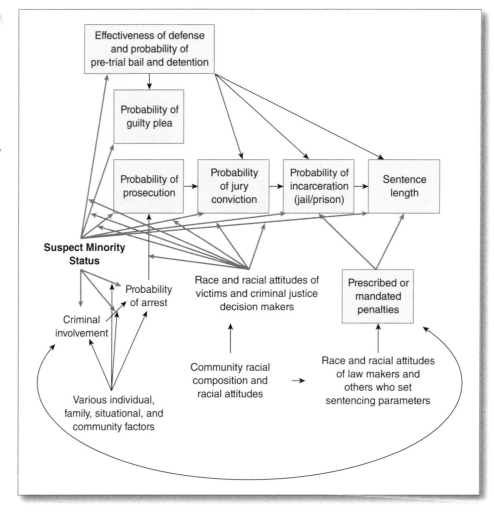

Race and Misdemeanor Sentencing

Although much of the research reviewed earlier focused on felony defendants, studies have examined race and misdemeanor sentencing. Munoz and McMorris (2002) reviewed more than 8,000 misdemeanor cases in Nebraska to determine whether racial/ethnic bias was present. Their analysis found that, in line with studies focusing on felony sentencing,

> Non-Whites in comparison to Whites were charged with more serious misdemeanors and more total number of offenses. Latinos experienced unfavorable outcomes in comparison to Whites, but not to the extent Native Americans did. In addition to having the highest average total number of offenses, Native Americans were most likely to find themselves charged with alcohol/drug, property, and assault-related offenses. (p. 254)

Mirroring felony studies, legal variables such as prior record and seriousness of the offense were the best predictors of sentence severity. Extralegal factors such as race and gender were also contributors to the observed disparities (see also Munoz, McMorris, & DeLisi, 2005; Munoz & Freng, 2008).

Leiber and Blowers (2003) tested whether, in the case of misdemeanor offenses, African Americans were punished more severely than Whites. With a sample of more than 1,700 defendants, they examined the influence of extralegal variables (race, age) and legal variables (crime type, weapons use, property loss, and prior arrest). The findings of Leiber and Blowers revealed that "race does not have a direct effect on the conviction and incarceration decisions" (p. 477). They contextualized their findings by noting that the race effect was indirect. That is, in their study, the race effect was masked through the procedural variables of case status and continuance. On this finding they wrote,

> The prioritizing of a case and not having a continuance increase the chances of being convicted and incarcerated. Because African Americans are more likely to have their case classified as a priority and not have a continuance, they have a greater probability than Whites to be convicted and incarcerated. (p. 477)

Brennan (2006) examined a sample of female misdemeanants from New York City courts to determine whether there were any racial/ethnic disparities in sentencing. By restricting her sample to females, she was able to take a more critical look at outcomes among females. Her study of nearly 700 Black, Hispanic, and White females revealed that race/ethnicity did not directly affect sentencing outcomes. The study did, however, find that

> class discrimination resulted in indirect racial discrimination. Both Black and Hispanic women were less likely to be high school graduates than White women. They were also less likely to be employed. Ultimately, both limited educational attainment and unemployment indirectly increased the chances that Black and Hispanic women would serve jail terms. (p. 89)

Golub, Johnson, and Dunlap (2007) examined whether misdemeanor marijuana arrests during the height of the "quality of life" policing initiative in New York City discriminated against Blacks and Hispanics. In particular, the authors investigated "marijuana in public view" arrests in New York City from 1980 to 2003. Their analysis found that Blacks and Hispanics were overrepresented in the marijuana in public view arrests. The disparities persisted as the authors analyzed several additional aspects of the data. Specifically, Blacks and Hispanics were more likely than Whites to be detained, and they were also two times more likely to be convicted of marijuana in public view offenses than Whites (p. 149). Golub et al. concluded that Blacks and Hispanics were punished more severely than Whites.

Each of these studies reviewed in this section provides evidence (either direct or indirect) that racial disparities in sentencing are not limited to felony cases. The "War on Drugs" has also been suggested as a substantial contributor to racial disparities in criminal justice. This is discussed next.

Sentencing Disparities and the "War on Drugs"

As noted earlier in the chapter, the "War on Drugs" rang in a new era of punitive sanctions. Unfortunately, as has been noted by several researchers, minorities have been impacted most by the war (Donzinger, 1996; J. Miller, 1996; Mitchell, 2009; Tonry, 1995). On the federal level alone, Tonry (1995) noted that, in 1980, drug offenders represented 22% of the admissions to institutions, but by 1989, this had risen to 39%, and by 1990, this had risen to 42%. Strikingly, by 1992, 58% of federal inmates were drug offenders (Tonry, 1995). At the state level, Shelden and Brown (2003) noted that, "between 1980 and 1992, sentences on drug charges increased by more than 1,000%" (p. 252). They continued by noting that when taking race into consideration, "The number of African Americans sentenced to prison on drug charges increased by over 90%, almost three times greater than White offenders" (p. 252). Shelden and Brown also pointed to figures that show that, during the 10-year period of 1985 to 1995, "the number of African American inmates sentenced for drug offenses increased by 700%" (p. 252). Reflecting on the striking figures related to race and the War on Drugs, Tonry (2011) recently had the following to say:

> So there it is. When all the relevant data are pulled together, it is clear that black people bear most of the brunt of the War on Drugs. It is also clear that racial disparities among people imprisoned for drug offenses arise primarily from racial profiling by police, deliberate police policies to focus drug law enforcement on inner-city drug markets, and deliberate legislative decisions to attach the longest prison sentences to drug offenses for which blacks are disproportionately arrested. I have purposely not used the word racism to this point, but it is difficult not to wonder. (p. 75)

During the mid-1980s to mid-1990s, crack cocaine became a significant concern for the government, which led to the formulation of differential mandatory minimum penalties. At the time, someone with 500 grams of powder cocaine would receive a mandatory minimum sentence of 5 years, whereas someone with 5 grams of crack cocaine would receive the same 5-year mandatory minimum penalty. For those caught with 50 grams of crack cocaine, the mandatory minimum penalty was 10 years, whereas those caught with 5,000 grams of powder cocaine also received a 10-year mandatory minimum sentence. Unfortunately, although minorities are overrepresented in the use of crack cocaine, the majority of those who use crack cocaine are White, yet most of those serving time under these federal policies are African Americans and Hispanics (Russell-Brown, 2004).

Tracing the origin of this much-maligned 100-to-1 crack cocaine-to-powder cocaine sentencing differential, Russell (1998) suggested that the sudden death of University of Maryland basketball star Len Bias contributed to this "moral panic" or unsupported fear about crack cocaine (Brownstein, 1996; Jenkins, 1994). Because Bias's death was initially linked to crack cocaine, a cheaper form of cocaine, many public officials felt that this was a sign that crack would devastate the Black community.

It is important to note that, in the ensuing legislative debates, according to Kennedy (1997), Black legislators such as Charles Rangel and Major Owens argued vociferously for their legislative colleagues to move quickly in drafting legislation to head off a potential epidemic in the African American community. Although Kennedy noted that the legislators didn't call for the differential penalties that ensued, "Eleven of the twenty-one Blacks who were then members of the House of Representatives voted in favor of the law which created the 100–1 crack-powder differential" (p. 370).

Many observers would agree the early efforts to stave off an impending epidemic were noble, but others have argued that because of these actions, an "incarceration epidemic" ensued (Mauer, 1999; Radosh, 2008; Tonry, 1995). Moreover, once it became clear that the sentencing differential was leading to massive incarceration disparities, in 1995 and 1997, the government had two opportunities to rectify the situation. But according to Russell (1998), Congress overwhelmingly voted against taking such action, although it was recommended by the U.S. Sentencing Commission. To the surprise of many in the African American community, President Clinton did not follow the recommendations of the Commission. In response to this inaction, prisoners at several federal correctional facilities rioted (Russell, 1998). Congress returned to the matter in 2002, when the Senate held hearings on the federal cocaine policy (see U.S. Senate, 2002). The U.S. Sentencing Commission did provide Congress with an important report on the topic in 2002 and again in 2007. Both reports made similar recommendations.

In particular, the 2002 Commission report provided three recommendations. First, they recommended "increas[ing] the five-year mandatory minimum threshold quantity for crack cocaine offenses to at least 25 grams and the ten-year threshold quantity to at least 250 grams (and repeal the mandatory minimum for simple possession of crack cocaine)" (U.S. Sentencing Commission, 2002, p. viii). Second, rather than having a blanket mandatory minimum sentence, they recommended providing sentencing enhancements based on the nature of the offense. Such enhancements would take into consideration whether a weapon was used, bodily injury occurred, the person was a repeat offender, and so on. Finally, the Commission recommended maintaining the current powder cocaine thresholds, but also incorporating the said sentencing enhancements.

In 2007, the Commission returned to similar themes from the 2002 report, noting the continuing "universal criticism from representatives of the Judiciary, criminal justice practitioners, academics, and community interest groups" (p. 2). In addition, the report noted that the major conclusions from the 2002 report remained valid. During 2007, however, the Commission had the benefit of two Supreme Court cases that provided additional impetus to change the disparity. The cases of *Blakely v. Washington* (2004) and *United States v. Booker* (2005) both involved issues related to sentencing. In the *Blakely* case, the Court ruled that judges could not enhance penalties based on facts outside of those noted by the jury and the offender. In doing so, they violated one's Sixth Amendment rights to a jury trial. In the *Booker* case, the Court affirmed this decision. Thus, when mandatory sentences are in place and they go against a jury's findings, the judge can view such mandatory penalties as being advisory. Consequently, the draconian mandatory crack cocaine sentences can be seen as advisory, and, with these decisions, judicial discretion was permissible. In December 2007, the Supreme Court ruled in the case of *Kimbrough v. United States* that mandatory crack penalties were advisory in nature and judges could take into account the crack and powder cocaine disparities when sentencing. Given all these significant cases and the longstanding efforts of numerous entities, the Commission's recommended changes were partially adopted and made "sentences for crack offenses between two and five times longer than sentences for equal amounts of powder" (*Kimbrough v. United States,* 2007). Not until August, 2010, however, was there a significant legislative change in the crack cocaine and powder cocaine sentencing disparity. At that time, President Barack Obama signed the Fair Sentencing Act of 2010, which included the provision that the sentencing disparity between the two forms of cocaine be reduced from 100 to 1 to 18 to 1.

Since the passage of the Fair Sentencing Act, Hispanics (47.9%) and Blacks (26.5%) still represent the largest share of the drug offenders at the federal level (U.S. Sentencing Commission, 2014). Moreover, Blacks still represent the majority of crack offenders at the federal level (82.7%), and Hispanics represent the largest share of the methamphetamine cases (55.7%; U.S. Sentencing Commission, 2014). In 2015, Congressman Robert C. "Bobby" Scott introduced several bills that sought to address past and present sentencing disparities. The first bill, The Fair Sentencing Clarification Act of 2015, provides offenders convicted prior to the 2010 Fair Sentencing Act to

Photo 6.2

U.S. President Barack Obama (C) signs the Fair Sentencing Act in the Oval Office of the White House, August 3, 2010. Also in the picture (L-R) Attorney General Eric Holder, Democratic Senator Patrick Leahy of Vermont, Democratic Representative Bobby Scott of Virginia, Democratic Senator Dick Durbin of Illinois, Republican Senator Jeff Sessions of Alabama, Republican Senator Orrin Hatch of Utah, and Democratic Representative Sheila Jackson-Lee of Texas.

Pool/Pool/Getty Images.

retroactively have their sentence reduced. This Act would affect 8,829 offenders who could petition for a sentence reduction. In addition, Congressman Scott introduced the Fairness in Cocaine Sentencing Act, which would equalize the penalties for crack and powder cocaine offenses. It is noteworthy that, along with these promising bills, the federal government has also increasingly moved away from pursuing the prosecution of drug cases (see Box 6.1).

BOX 6.1

Race and Crime in the Media

Attorney General Eric Holder Sees Success in Fewer Drug Prosecutions

Washington (CNN)—Federal prosecutors are bringing fewer prosecutions for illegal drugs and less often seeking mandatory minimum sentences, changes that Attorney General Eric Holder is hailing a major success of his tenure.

At the same time, the crimes being prosecuted carried higher minimum sentences on average because less-serious cases aren't being pursued by federal prosecutors, according to Attorney General Eric Holder, citing data from the U.S. Sentencing Commission.

In a speech Thursday at the National Press Club, Holder pointed to the new data as showing the fruits of his Smart on Crime initiative, an effort focused on reducing federal sentences for non-violent drug crimes. Holder plans to leave office in the coming weeks, pending the Senate approval of U.S. Attorney Loretta Lynch.

Holder views the sentencing changes as a civil rights issue, because he and others argue that tough drug sentencing laws have a disproportionate impact on black and other minority defendants. The tough sentencing laws has also led to high incarceration rates and high prison costs, an issue drawing attention from both liberal and conservative political leaders.

"For years prior to this administration, federal prosecutors were not only encouraged — but required — to always seek the most severe prison sentence possible for all drug cases, no matter the relative risk they posed to public safety. I have made a break from that philosophy," Holder said. "While old habits are hard to break, these numbers show that a dramatic shift is underway in the mindset of prosecutors handling nonviolent drug offenses. I believe we have taken steps to institutionalize this fairer, more practical approach such that it will endure for years to come."

A similar effort to soften mandatory sentences for non-violent drug crimes has gained bipartisan support in Congress, joining liberals like Sens. Dick Durbin and Patrick Leahy with libertarian-leaning conservatives such as Sens. Mike Lee and Ted Cruz. But those changes face an uphill climb with other law-and-order conservatives who hold leadership posts in the new Republican majority.

Sen. Charles Grassley, chairman of the Senate Judiciary Committee, recently took to the Senate floor to dispute what he says are myths about mandatory minimum sentences. He says the existing laws have been key to encouraging criminals to provide information to help prosecutors target bigger criminals.

"We are not sending huge numbers of nonviolent drug offenders to federal prison under lengthy mandatory minimum sentences," Grassley said. He criticized the bipartisan Senate proposal to change sentencing laws as possibly reducing sentences for terrorists who used drug trafficking to finance terror.

Holder, in his speech, cites the new data showing that prosecutors are pursuing mandatory minimums in just over 51% of drug cases in fiscal year 2014, down from nearly 64% of such cases in fiscal 2013.

(Continued)

(Continued)

The changes come amid reductions in prison populations and generally low crime rates, Holder said. "This newly unveiled data shows we can confront over-incarceration at the same time that we continue to promote public safety," Holder says in prepared remarks. "Already, in fiscal Year 2014, we saw the first reduction in the federal prison population in 32 years. Meanwhile, since President Obama took office, we've presided over a continued decline in the overall crime rate. This marks the first time that any Administration has achieved side-by-side reductions in both crime and incarceration in more than forty years."

Source: Perez (2015).

Throughout the last 30 years, some citizens (particularly racial and ethnic minorities) have often questioned the neutrality of judges when racial disparities are revealed. As such, a consistent theme in policy considerations related to the judiciary is the assumption that if there were more minority judges, the courts would be run more equitably. Drawing on the scholarly literature, we investigate this supposition next.

Minority Judges

More than 150 years ago, Robert Morris became the first African American to be appointed as a judge (Washington, 1994). Less than 20 years later, during the Reconstruction period, another milestone was reached when Jonathan Jasper Wright was elected to the Supreme Court of South Carolina in 1872 (Washington, 1994). Since these early breakthroughs, few minorities have served as judges. Although this could be a product of the fact that in 2010 Blacks and Hispanics combined represented less than 8% of American lawyers (U.S. Bureau of Labor Statistics, 2010), proactive measures have resulted in some increases in minority judicial appointments.

Looking at federal judicial appointments during the last 40 years, one does notice a considerable improvement in diversity—but only during the tenure of four presidents (Carter, Clinton, the second Bush, and Obama) were there substantial gains (Maguire, 2011b; see Table 6.9). During the Carter era, approximately 14% of the appointments were African American, and approximately 6% were Hispanic (Alliance for Justice, 2014). During this span, significant gains were also made for women. In particular, during the Obama administration nearly 42% of the appointments were female—compared to 8.8% during the Reagan era. The racial/ethnic diversity of the federal judiciary also peaked during the Obama presidency with 17.4% African American, 10.9% Hispanic, and 7.2% Asian appointees being confirmed (Alliance for Justice, 2014).

Two things stand out from these data. First, Asian Americans and Native Americans are minimally represented in the appointment figures. The absence of qualified Native American judges could be a product of many of them serving in such positions on reservations. In the case of Asian Americans, although their population figures are low, by now there are surely an ample number of potential nominees. It is promising

Table 6.9

Federal Judicial Appointments by Gender and Ethnicity, From President Carter to President Obama

President (Term)	Total	Male	Female	White	African American	Hispanic	Asian Pacific	Native American	Native Hawaiian or Other Pacific Islander	Openly GLBT	People With Disabilities
Obama confirmed	265	154 (58.1%)	111 (41.9%)	172 (64.9%)	46 (17.4%)	29 (10.9%)	19 (7.2%)	1 (0.4%)	1 (0.4%)	8	1
Obama pending	26	12 (46.2%)	14 (53.8%)	16 (61.5%)	8 (30.8%)	2 (7.7%)	0	0	0	2	0
Obama withdrawn/not renominated	14	9	5	7	5	0	1	1	0	2	0
Obama total	305	175	130	195	59	31	20	2	1	12	1
Bush II (2001–2008) confirmed	327	256 (78.2%)	71 (21.8%)	269 (82.2%)	24 (7.3%)	30 (9.1%)	4 (1.2%)	0	0	0	2
Clinton (1993–2000) confirmed	378	267 (70.6%)	111 (29.4%)	285 (75.3%)	62 (16.4%)	25 (6.6%)	5 (1.3%)	1 (0.2%)	0	1	3
Bush I (1989–1992) confirmed	193	157 (81.3%)	36 (18.7%)	172 (89.1%)	13 (6.7%)	8 (4.1%)	0	0	0	0	1
Reagan (1981–1988) confirmed	383	351 (91.6%)	32 (8.8%)	360 (93.9%)	7 (1.8%)	14 (3.6%)	2 (0.5%)	0	0	0	1
Carter (1977–1980) confirmed	262	221 (84.3%)	41 (15.7%)	205 (78.2%)	37 (14.1%)	16 (6.1%)	3 (1.1%)	1 (0.3%)	0	0	1

Source: Alliance for Justice (www.afj.org).

that 7.2% of President Obama's appointments were Asian American. Nevertheless, are there differences between minority judges' decisions and those of White judges? We explore this question next.

Do Minority Judges Make a Difference?

Most people are familiar with the instant classic *Black Robes, White Justice* by New York State Judge Bruce Wright (1987). Judge Wright's poignant criticism of the justice system served as a much-needed case study of how, in his experience, race operated in the courts. Since the publication of his work, several observers have investigated the impact of minority judges, such as Wright, to see whether they are bringing balance to the bench. In essence, because many minority judges have experienced racism along the way, some observers believe they will be more sensitive to the plight of minorities who come before them. Other observers believe that because of the nature of the judicial role, minority or female judges are more apt to conform to the norm so they can fit in (Spohn, 2009).

Reviewing the literature on the subject, Spohn (2009) noted that there were few differences between the sentences dispensed by Black, Hispanic, and White justices. In fact, in some instances, both Black and White judges sentenced Black defendants more harshly than White defendants. Spohn suggested that minority judges could be more sensitive to the justice given to Black *victims,* as opposed to being sensitive to the plight of Black offenders. Yet others contend that at times Black judges hand down longer sentences because they sit on the bench in high-crime areas (see Muhlhausen, 2004). Worse yet, minority judges might accept the notion that minorities are more dangerous than Whites. One thing is clear from Spohn's (2009) review: The current body of macrolevel studies does not provide definitive answers to this question.

Since Spohn's summary of the issue, Kastellec (2013) has conducted a study that considered the topic of minority influence on the judiciary. Specifically, Kastellec examined whether the addition of a minority judge on the judicial panels at the U.S. Court of Appeals influenced the outcomes of 182 affirmative action cases heard by the courts between 1971 and 2008. During this period, the affirmative action cases consisted of 152 cases that had no Black judges, 28 cases that had one Black judge, and one case that had two Black judges. After observing that support for affirmative action was nearly 90% among Black judges, Kastellec's research found that "nonblack judges who sit [on an appellate review panel] with a black colleague uphold affirmative action plans about 80% of the time" (p. 179).

Even with the interesting results from Kastellec's (2013) study, could it be that society expects too much from minority judges? In line with this question, the late Judge A. Leon Higginbotham noted,

> No Black judge should work solely on racial matters. I think that would be a profoundly inappropriate abstention, and I would further argue that there is no special role that a Black jurist should play. (cited in Washington, 1994, p. 4)

Reviewing the decision of Supreme Court Justice Clarence Thomas in the case of *Hudson v. McMillian* (1992), in which two prison guards assaulted a Black prisoner while he was shackled at the hands and feet, Higginbotham added,

A Black judge, like all judges, has to decide matters on the basis of the record. But you would hope that a Black judge could never be as blind to the consequences of sanctioning violence and racism against Blacks by state officials as Clarence Thomas was in the *Hudson* case. (cited in Washington, 1994, p. 5)

So, barring exceptional cases, according to one of the leading African American jurists of the 20th century, we should not expect anything different from minority judges; irrespective of race, the facts should dictate case outcomes.

Although this debate will likely rage on in scholarly and other circles ad infinitum, the larger issue likely relates to opportunity. Whether a minority or female judge rules in accordance with Whites is, in some ways, beside the point. The more central issue is that qualified minority and female attorneys should be afforded equal opportunities to serve in these important roles. Although it could be that in modern times race discrimination continues to be a factor in not appointing more minority attorneys, such a trend could also be tied to politics. That is, which political party is in office might be an equally strong explanation as to why some minorities are selected for the judiciary and others are not.

❖ Conclusion

This chapter reviewed race-related issues in the sentencing phase of the criminal justice process. After a historical review of early cases that illustrated sentencing patterns, it was shown that race and class disparities have always existed in the American justice system. Following a review of the American sentencing process and its various philosophies, we noted that during the 1990s more punitive philosophies prevailed. As such, numerous "get tough" approaches were devised to deal with offenders. Most notably, mandatory minimum, three-strikes-and-you're-out, and truth-in-sentencing policies swelled prison populations with minorities and poor persons. The "War on Drugs" also contributed to the sway toward punitive policies with the passage of the 1986 and 1988 Anti-Drug Abuse Acts, which also contributed to the infamous disparities between penalties for crack cocaine and powder cocaine and further pronounced the racial disparities in sentencing outcomes. It was promising to note that the Fair Sentencing Act of 2010 was a big step in the right direction toward equality in sentencing. The increasing legalization of marijuana at the state level is also likely to reduce the emphasis on punitive sentencing for drugs.

Next, we reviewed the extant scholarship on race and sentencing. This review showed the numerous characteristics that predict whether minorities will be sentenced more harshly than Whites. Some of these characteristics include being young, male, poor, and unemployed; being detained prior to trial; and victimizing Whites. In contrast to the harsh treatment of Blacks and Hispanics during sentencing, some recent research has shown that Asians receive leniency in the sentencing process. Turning to the judiciary, we also examined the discretion wielded by judges and investigated the conventional wisdom that by having more minority judges, the scales of justice would be more balanced. The existing literature on the topic is mixed, with some literature showing some minority influence and others showing no change in outcomes due to increasing judicial diversity. We concluded that the most important concern is that qualified minority judges should be afforded equal opportunities to serve in the judiciary.

Discussion Questions

1. Discuss the sentencing disparities found in colonial America.

2. What do you see as being the most effective sentencing strategy with the least potential for racial/ethnic bias?

3. Explain the impact of the "War on Drugs" on racial and ethnic minorities.

4. Discuss the difference between the research found in Zatz's (1987) four waves of sentencing research and the post-Zatz sentencing research.

5. Explain the trends regarding racial/ethnic minorities and judicial appointments.

Internet Exercises

1. Go to https://www.whitehouse.gov/ondcp/national-drug-control-strategy and examine how much of the most recent *National Drug Control Strategy Report* focuses on drug treatment or law enforcement.

2. Listen to the following podcast by scholar John McWhorter and see whether you agree with his suggestion to end the War on Drugs: http://www.cato.org/multimedia/daily-podcast/race-relations-war-drugs

3. Visit the Families Against Mandatory Minimums (FAMM) website (http://www.famm.org/) and read some of the profiles on injustice.

Internet Sites

The Sentencing Project: http://www.sentencingproject.org

U.S. Sentencing Commission: http://www.ussc.gov

National Drug Control Strategy: https://www.whitehouse.gov/ondcp

Supplemental materials for *Race and Crime* are available online at
study.sagepub.com/gabbidon4e.

The Death Penalty

The history of American Indian executions is clearly nestled within a sociopolitical context of genocidal colonialism calculated to dispossess American Indians of their Indianism by removing them from their sacred tribal territories, disrupting their traditional cultures, and continuing their marginalized status in the U.S. society today.

—David V. Baker (2007, pp. 316–317)

Over the years, there has been considerable debate about the merits of the death penalty as a form of punishment. Although some debates have centered on whether it is cruel and unusual punishment, a considerable portion of the debate has centered on who receives the death penalty. Racial minorities remain overrepresented among those who are sentenced to death and those who, in the end, are executed. This chapter begins with a review of several significant Supreme Court decisions, followed by a historical overview of race and the death penalty. The chapter also reviews the following related areas: current death penalty statistics, recent scholarship on race and the death penalty, public opinion and the death penalty, the Capital Jury Project, wrongful convictions, the death penalty moratorium movement, and judicial overrides in death penalty sentencing.

❖ Significant Death Penalty Cases

The Peach State and the Foundational Death Penalty Cases

The continued use of the death penalty in America can be credited to a series of Supreme Court cases in the 1970s involving the state of Georgia that reaffirmed its constitutionality. The cases also provided guidance for the application of the death penalty. The first of these was the 1972 decision in *Furman v. Georgia*. The case centered on a 25-year-old Black man (William Henry Furman) with an IQ of 65 who was charged with killing a 30-year-old White man (Bohm, 2007). Furman's lawyers argued that because of the lack of instructions given to jury members about deciding which cases warrant the death penalty and which ones do not, the way the death penalty was being administered violated Furman's Fourteenth Amendment right to due process and was also a violation of the Eighth Amendment, which protects citizens against cruel and unusual punishment. In a decision in which the nine justices each wrote a separate opinion, the majority agreed that the death penalty was being administered in an arbitrary and capricious manner. That is, there was little uniformity across states as to who should receive the death penalty and under what circumstances. Those in the majority also pointed out that the death penalty had been applied in a discriminatory manner. Concurring with the majority decision, Justice Douglas wrote,

> It is cruel and unusual punishment to apply the death penalty selectively to minorities whose numbers are few, who are outcasts of society, and who are unpopular, but whom society is willing to see suffer though it would not countenance general application of the same penalty across the boards. (*Furman v. Georgia,* 1972, p. 1)

Given some of these considerations, in the end, Furman's sentence was commuted to life in prison (he was paroled in 1985). As Baker (2003) noted,

> The aftermath of *Furman* saw the Court vacate 120 cases immediately before it and some 645 other cases involving death row inmates. The decision rendered defective the death penalty statutes of thirty-nine states, the District of Columbia, and the federal government. (p. 180)

The *Furman* decision, however, would stand only four years. In the 1976 case of **Gregg v. Georgia**, the Court indicated that states that used **guided discretion** statutes removed concerns regarding previous procedures that were considered to be arbitrary and capricious. According to Bohm (1999), such statutes

> set standards for juries and judges when deciding whether to impose the death penalty. The guided discretion statutes struck a reasonable balance between giving the jury some discretion and allowing it to consider the defendant's background and character and circumstances of the crime. (p. 25)

The year following the *Gregg* decision, the Court provided states with further guidance on the application of the death penalty. Specifically, in **Coker v. Georgia** (1977), the Court ruled that sentencing rapists to death was cruel and unusual punishment. Considering that between 1930 and the 1970s, 405 Black men were executed in the South for the crime of rape, whereas only 48 Whites were executed for the same offense during this period (Holden-Smith, 1996), it is perplexing that the Court skirted around the racial dynamics of the historical use of executions for rapists. With about 90% of such death sentences being given to Blacks (who presumably had raped White women), it appears that this punishment was historically reserved for Blacks.

In June of the same year as the *Coker* decision, the court also ruled in *Eberheart v. Georgia* (1977) that kidnappings not resulting in death cannot be punished with the death penalty. A decade later, the 1987 decision in **McCleskey v. Kemp** represents another important Supreme Court case, which challenged the constitutionality of the death penalty based on racial discrimination in its application.

McCleskey v. Kemp

Warren McCleskey, a Black man, was convicted of the 1978 shooting of a White police officer during an armed robbery. Once caught, tried, and convicted following Georgia's death penalty statute, the jury found beyond a reasonable doubt that the murder had occurred with one of their statutorily defined aggravating circumstances. In this case, however, there were two aggravating circumstances. First, McCleskey had committed the murder during an armed robbery, and second, the victim was a police officer. In the course of his appeals, McCleskey claimed that Georgia's death penalty process was being administered in a racially discriminatory manner, which violated his Eighth and Fourteenth Amendment rights. As evidence of this discrimination, McCleskey's defense showed that

> even after taking account of numerous nonracial variables, defendants charged with killing Whites were 4.3 times more likely to receive a death sentence in Georgia as defendants charged with killing Blacks, and that Black defendants were 1.1 times as likely to receive a death sentence as other defendants. (*McCleskey v. Kemp,* 1987, p. 1)

After working its way through the courts, the case finally made its way to the Supreme Court in 1986. In an opinion written by Justice Powell and joined by four other justices (Rehnquist, White, O'Connor, and Scalia), the majority held

> the statistical evidence was insufficient to support an inference that any of the decision makers in the accused's case acted with discriminatory purpose in violation of the equal protection clause of the Fourteenth Amendment, since (a) the accused offered no evidence of racial bias specific to his own case, and (b) the statistical evidence alone was not clear enough to prove discrimination in any one case; (2) the study was insufficient to prove that the state violated the equal protection clause by adopting the capital punishment statute and allowing it to remain in force despite its allegedly discriminatory application; and (3) the study was insufficient to prove that the state's capital punishment system was arbitrary and capricious in application and that therefore the accused's death sentence was excessive in violation of the Eighth Amendment. (*McCleskey v. Kemp,* 1987, pp. 1–2)

Conversely, the dissenting justices in the case (Brennan, Marshall, Stevens, and Blackmun) provided a host of contrasting points. First, as noted in previous cases, justices Brennan and Marshall reiterated that the death penalty was cruel and unusual and therefore violated the Eighth and the Fourteenth Amendments. Furthermore, in their eyes, the statistical evidence was valid and showed that there was "an intolerable risk that racial prejudice influenced his particular sentence" (*McCleskey v. Kemp*, 1987, p. 2). In his dissenting opinion, Justice Blackmun, who was joined by justices Marshall and Stevens, suggested that the statistical data showed

> (1) The accused was a member of a group that was singled out for different treatment, (2) the difference in treatment was substantial in degree, and (3) Georgia's process for seeking the death penalty was susceptible to abuse in the form of racial discrimination. (*McCleskey v. Kemp*, 1987, p. 2)

The study that was debated by the majority has come to be known as the "Baldus study" (see Baldus, Woodworth, & Pulaski, 1990). Leading up to the *McCleskey* case, Baldus et al. had conducted two important death penalty studies: the procedural reform study and the charging and sentencing study. The first study was designed to

> compare how Georgia sentenced defendants convicted of murder at trial, before and after the statutory reforms prompted by *Furman v. Georgia,* and to assess the extent to which those reforms affected the levels of arbitrariness and discrimination observed in its sentencing decisions. (p. 42)

For the second study, Baldus and his colleagues (1990) were hired by the NAACP Legal Defense Fund to conduct the study "with the expectation that the results might be used to challenge the constitutionality of Georgia's death sentencing system as it has been applied since *Gregg v. Georgia* (1976)" (p. 44). In the end, the second study was the one considered but rejected in the *McCleskey* decision. Using a sophisticated methodological design, which controlled for hundreds of variables, the Baldus study remains the standard when examining race and the death penalty. Probably the most discussed and important finding from the study was the strong race-of-the-victim effect, which showed that Black offenders in Georgia who victimized Whites were considerably more likely to receive death sentences than White persons who victimized Blacks. In fact, looking at this dynamic nationally over a 370-year period (1608–1978), only 30 Whites in the United States have been executed for killing African Americans (Radelet, 1989).

It has been suggested that had the Supreme Court ruled in McCleskey's favor, it would have opened "a Pandora's box of litigation" (Kennedy, 1997, p. 333). In short, ruling in McCleskey's favor would have, as Justice Powell stated, "throw[n] into serious question the principles that underlie our entire criminal justice system" (cited in Kennedy, 1997, p. 333). Moreover, he noted that such a decision would produce similar claims "from other members of other groups alleging bias" (p. 333). Nonetheless, the fact remains that those who support the death penalty outnumber those who oppose it. Even so, given the historical and contemporary racial disparities in who receives the death penalty, in 1988, Congressman John Conyers introduced the Racial Justice Act, which prohibits executions if there is a pattern of racial discrimination in death sentences at the state and federal levels. Such laws have been tried in some states. North Carolina, for example, passed a Racial Justice Act in 2009, but the legislation was repealed in 2013 (See Box 7.1).

BOX 7.1

Race and Crime in the Media

North Carolina Repeals Law Allowing Racial Bias Claim in Death Penalty Challenges

A law that allowed death-row inmates to challenge their sentences based on racial bias claims was repealed by the North Carolina legislature on Wednesday, paving the way for executions to resume in a state that has 152 people on death row.

The law, the only one of its kind in the country, allowed inmates to use state and county statistics and other material to claim that race played a role in their sentencing. Since the law took effect in 2009, nearly everyone facing execution—not all of them Black—has used it in hopes of reducing sentences to life in prison.

In the weeks before the State House of Representatives took up the Racial Justice Act, most lawmakers acknowledged it was headed for repeal. Still, the legislative debate stretched over two days and was noteworthy for both its emotion and its ideology.

Those who voted to rescind it recited the names of people whose killers were on death row and said the law had clogged the courts and denied justice to victims.

It was also called a deeply flawed piece of legislation.

"It tries to put a carte blanche solution on the problem," said Representative Tim Moore, a Republican. "A White supremacist who murdered an African-American could argue he was a victim of racism if Blacks were on the jury."

Defenders of the act spoke of innocent Black men on death row who had been exonerated and shared deeply personal experiences with racism. They spoke against the death penalty and pointed to the state's history of tension between Blacks and Whites.

"It's incredibly sad," said Representative Rick Glazier, a Democrat who has long been a supporter of the act. "If you can't face up to your history and make sure it's not repeated, it lends itself to being repeated."

After one more perfunctory pass through the State Senate, which already passed a version of the measure, the bill repealing the act will head to Gov. Pat McCrory, a Republican elected last year who has said he will sign it.

A section of the law rescinding the act will now prevent doctors, nurses, and other health care professionals from being punished by regulatory boards if they assist in executions. The state medical board in 2007 said it would penalize medical professionals who participated, a policy the State Supreme Court later said was beyond the board's authority.

The floor debate over the Racial Justice Act began a day after 151 people were arrested in Raleigh as opposition grows to a newly conservative government in a state that has long been considered centrist.

Preserving the act, which was passed when there was a Democrat in the governor's office and the legislature was not as heavily controlled by Republicans, was among dozens of issues brought up by protesters who have been gathering every Monday since April.

Monday's protest, organized by the N.A.A.C.P., drew more than a thousand people. Since the protests began, about 300 people have been arrested on trespassing charges and other charges related to acts of civil disobedience.

Conservatives have been chipping away at the Racial Justice Act since its inception four years ago. In 2012, the legislature severely limited how statistics could be used and put a stronger burden of proof on the inmate making the appeal.

Backers had hoped that the law would have stood long enough to be tested in the state's highest court.

(Continued)

(Continued)

Judges in two counties have used the act. One, a Cumberland County judge who reduced sentences in four cases, cited a Michigan State University legal study of cases between 1990 and 2010 that found that state prosecutors had removed Black people from murder-trial juries at more than twice the rate of others.

Although the State Supreme Court had agreed to review cases from earlier decisions, their fate remains unclear.

"I think there's going to be intense years of litigation over this," Mr. Glazier said.

Source: Severson (2013).

After reviewing these significant cases, one is left to wonder whether or not race has always mattered in the application of the death penalty. We examine this question in the next section.

❖ Historical Overview of Race and the Death Penalty

As with other sentences, the death penalty followed colonists from their homeland, where English law provided for so many offenses resulting in death that it was referred to as the "**bloody code**." In a pioneering article on the death penalty as it relates to Native Americans, Baker (2007) notes that besides the well-known early genocidal actions of Europeans, since their arrival there have been at least 450 formal executions of Native Americans. The 1639 execution of Nepauduct was the first execution of a Native American. Moreover, during the 17th century, there were 157 executions of Native Americans (Baker, 2007).

Besides the execution of Native Americans, Banner (2002) has documented that the colony had numerous death penalty statutes that were solely applied to Blacks. There were a variety of such statutes, beginning in New York in 1712. However, it is in the South where many of these statutes prevailed. Because of the greater number of slaves in the South, there was considerable concern that they might rebel; therefore, as a means of deterrence, there were wide-ranging capital statutes. For example, "In 1740 South Carolina imposed the death penalty on slaves and free Blacks for burning or destroying any grain, commodities, or manufactured goods; on slaves for enticing other slaves to run away; and on slaves maiming or bruising Whites" (Banner, 2002, pp. 8–9). Other statutes made it punishable by death for slaves to administer medicine (to guard against poisoning); "strike Whites twice, or once if a bruise resulted"; or burn a house (Banner, 2002, p. 9; see Box 7.2). It is noteworthy that Black female slaves were not spared the death penalty, unlike White women, who rarely received the death penalty. Baker (2008) found that the first recorded execution of a Black woman was in 1681 when Maria, a slave, was executed for arson and murder. After this initial execution, 58 more slave women were executed before 1790, with another 126 being executed prior to the Civil War (Baker, 2008).

BOX 7.2

Slave-Era Capital Crimes and Slave Owner Compensation in Virginia, 1774–1864

One little-known fact from the slave era relates to slave owners being compensated for capitally sentenced slaves. Thus, whenever slaves committed an executable offense, the state had a set fee that was given to slave owners. Why? Phillips (1915) asserted that "to promote the suppression of crime, various colonies and states provided by law that the owners of slaves capitally sentenced should be compensated by the public at appraised valuations" (p. 336). Using Virginia as his study site, Phillips noted that the first such vouchers were distributed in the 1770s. Besides serving as a window into crimes committed by slaves, the practice also showed how critical the loss of a slave was for Southern landowners. In terms of the records, though incomplete, they provide a look at 1,117 out of 1,418 capital crimes committed by slaves from the 1700s to the 1860s. An analysis of the crimes reveals that murder represented the largest share of the offenses (347). Of these, Phillips extracted a bit more context from the state records:

Murder of the master, 56; of overseer, 7; of the White man, 98; of mistress, 11; of other White woman, 13; of master's child, 2; of other White child, 7; of free Negro man, 7; of slave man, 59; of slave woman, 14; of slave child, 12 (all of which were murders by slave women of their own children); of persons not described, 60. Of the murderers 307 were men and 39 were women. (p. 337)

The remaining convictions are summarized in Table 7.1. While Phillips noted that most of the crimes were typical of the era, he did note a few unusual punishments. In one case, after one slave killed

Table 7.1

The Capital Crimes of Slaves in Virginia, 1774–1864

Crime	Number of Offenses
Murder	346
Rape/attempted rape	105[a]
Poisoning	55[b] (40 men and 15 women)
Administering medicine to Whites	2[c]
Assault/attempted murder	111[d]
Insurrection/conspiracy	91
Arson	90
Burglary	257
Highway robbery	15
Horse theft	20
Other theft	24
Forgery	2

Source: Phillips (1915), pp. 336–340.

Notes:

a. According to records, all of these appear to have been of White women.

b. These were mostly targeted at Whites.

c. One of these persons was pardoned and transported away from the colony.

d. Only two of these crimes involved Black victims.

(Continued)

(Continued)

another, the offending slave "had his head cut off and stuck on a pole at the forks of the road" (p. 338). In another instance, a slave stole a silver spoon from his owner's kitchen and was put to death.

Source: Phillips (1915).

As shown in Figure 7.1, the compensation for the lives of the capitally sentenced slaves fluctuated from the 1700s to the 1800s. The rates fluctuated from a low of less than $300 in the 1700s to a high of $4,000 in 1864. Although a host of economic factors likely accounted for these fluctuations, the reality is that the state continuously provided some compensation to slave owners for their losses attributable to slaves sentenced to death.

In general, a few critical things stand out from the Virginia data. First, the state was so wedded to the economics of the slave system that it felt a need to compensate slave owners for the loss of their "property." Second, the data reveal the wide range of offenses for which slaves were executed. It is likely that executing slaves for so many offenses was used as a tool to control the slave population. Third, it is plausible that many of the property crimes were committed by slaves in response to the deprivation inherent in the slave system, and personal crimes may have been a way for slaves to fight back against the brutal system of slavery.

1. Do you think reparations should be paid to the descendants of slaves? Explain your opinion.

Figure 7.1 Compensation for Capitally Sentenced Slaves, 1700s–1860s

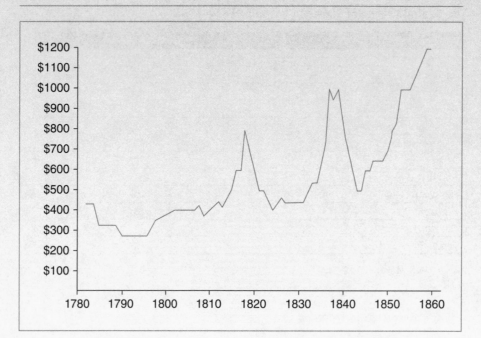

Source: Phillips (1915, pp. 336–340).

The obvious undercurrent with early death penalty statutes was that landowners were intent on controlling the slave population by fear and state-sanctioned brutality. Banner (2002) noted that colonial officials "streamlined" the process by cutting out juries and using local justices of the peace to ensure the "justice" was rapid. As one can imagine, although a host of capital offenses also applied to Whites, the processes that prevailed in the slave era resulted in disparities. Looking at one state, North Carolina, the record shows that "at least one hundred slaves were executed in the quarter-century between 1748 and 1772, well more than the number of Whites executed during the colony's entire history, spanning a century" (p. 9).

Predictably, such disparities persisted well into the 19th century. Not until 1880, however, were there national statistics on capital punishment (Cahalan & Parsons, 1986). In that first report, there were 80 people listed as "present under the sentence of death" (p. 9).

These early reports provided information on the number of state-sanctioned executions, as well as those that were considered illegal (lynchings). Tables 7.2 and 7.3 highlight two important trends. First, Table 7.2 reveals that, from 1890 to 1984, 5,726 persons were executed, of which 54% (2,915) were non-Whites (Cahalan & Parsons, 1986). Furthermore, Table 7.3 shows that of the 4,736 illegal lynchings that occurred between the 1880s and the 1960s, nearly 73% (3,442) were of Blacks (Cahalan & Parsons, 1986). Given this early history, scholars have continued to research race and the death penalty. Our review of the death penalty continues with a review of current statistics at both the state and federal levels.

❖ Current Statistics on the Death Penalty

State Death Penalty Statistics

Using the year following the *Gregg* decision as a reference point, from 1977 to 2013, there were 1,359 inmates executed (Snell, 2014). The racial/ethnic breakdown of these figures reveal that approximately 57% of those executed since 1977 were White and about 34% have been Black. Strikingly, the following five states accounted for nearly two-thirds of the executions since 1977: Texas (508), Virginia (110), Oklahoma (108), Florida (81), and Missouri (70; Snell, 2014). There were 2,979 persons under a death sentence at the end of 2013. Of the persons under sentence of death, 98% were male, more than 90% had a high school diploma/GED or less, and more than half had never been married (54.8%; Snell, 2014). Of those under sentence of death, 41.9% were Blacks and 55.8% were Whites. Hispanics accounted for 14.4% of those prisoners under death sentence, whereas all other races accounted for 2.3%. There were 56 females under sentence of death in 2013. More than two-thirds (38) of them were White, 25% (14) were Black, and the remaining women were categorized as "Other races" (Snell, 2014). In 2013, 39 persons were executed. Of these, 23 were White, 13 were Black, and 3 were Hispanic. On average, these persons had been serving a death sentence for nearly 16 years.

Snell (2014) also provides additional information on inmates under a death sentence. In particular, he reviews their criminal histories. Most of the offenders sentenced to death had prior convictions, but fewer than 10% had a prior conviction for homicide. This held true across race/ethnicity. Also, approximately 60% of the offenders had no

Table 7.2

Executions per Decade Under Civil Authority and Illegal Lynchings, 1890–1984

	1890s[a]	1900s	1910s	1920s	1930s	1940s	1950s	1960s	1970s	1980–1984	Total
Total under state authority	155	289	636	1,038	1,523	1,177	684	192	3	29	5,726
Race											
Number non-White	70	157	286	481	745	706	361	99	1	9	2,915
Percentage non-White	55	62	47	49	52	63	56	52	33	31	54
Race unknown	(27)	(37)	(26)	(51)	(79)	(55)	(32)	(1)	(0)	(0)	(308)
Offense											
Murder	155	281	570	961	1,383	980	564	152	3	29	5,078
Rape	0	5	40	69	112	172	91	28	0	0	518
Other	0	3	26	8	28	23	19	8	0	0	115
Offense unknown	(0)	(0)	(0)	(0)	(0)	(2)	(9)	(4)	(0)	(0)	(15)
Total under local authority	1,060	901	406	131	147	110	35	0	0	0	2,790
Total under civil authority (state and local)	1,215	1,190	1,042	1,169	1,670	1,287	719	192	3	29	8,516
Illegal lynchings	1,540	895	621	315	130	33	8	1	—[b]	—[b]	3,543
Total per decade (legal and illegal)	2,755	1,995	1,663	1,484	1,800	1,292	721	192	3	29	12,059

Source: BJS (1986).

Notes:

a. The earliest recorded execution under state authority was in 1864. Between 1864 and 1890, 57 persons were reported executed under state authority.

b. No lynchings were reported after 1962.

Table 7.3

Illegal Lynchings by Race and Offense by Decade, 1880–1962

	1880s[a]	1890s	1900s	1910s	1920s	1930s	1940s	1950s	1960s[b]	Total
Total	1,203	1,540	895	621	315	130	33	8	1	4,736
Race										
Number Blacks	534	1,111	791	568	281	119	31	6	1	3,442
Percentage Blacks	44	72	89	91	89	92	94	75	100	
Offense reportedly causing lynchings										
Homicide	537	606	372	278	100	39	5	0	0	1,937
Felonious assault	4	37	56	51	40	14	2	1	0	205
Rape	259	317	154	88	70	22	0	1	0	911
Attempted rape	9	75	99	56	22	21	6	0	0	288
Robbery and theft	58	87	33	38	6	6	4	0	0	232
Insults to White persons	4	10	11	31	17	8	2	1	0	85
All other causes	331	408	160	79	60	20	14	5	1	1,078

Source: BJS (1986).

Notes:

a. Statistics for 1880s are for 1882 through 1889.

b. Statistics for 1960s are for 1960, 1961, and 1962; no lynchings recorded after 1962.

charge pending at the time of the offense. Nonetheless, slightly more than 25% of them were on probation or **parole** when they committed the offense that resulted in a death sentence. A recent survey of states found that the death penalty remains an option in 34 states. Despite this, very few executions are actually carried out.

Federal Death Penalty Statistics

Largely as a result of the increasing number of death penalty statutes passed during times of heightened concern regarding drug-related activity, throughout the 1980s and 1990s there was increased attention on the federal death penalty. In March, 1994, the House Judiciary Subcommittee on Civil and Constitutional Rights produced a report looking at racial disparities in federal death penalty prosecutions over a six-year period (1988–1994). Out of concern that the federal death penalty provisions in the 1988 Anti–Drug Abuse Act were contributing to this, the committee examined the existing prosecution data. What they found was troubling. When looking at data on those who had been prosecuted under the so-called drug kingpin law, "Twenty-nine [78%] of the defendants have been Black and 4 have been Hispanic. All ten of the defendants approved by Attorney General Janet Reno for capital prosecution have been Black" (Subcommittee on Civil and Constitutional Rights, 1994, p. 3). The report also noted that, although Whites had traditionally been the ones executed under federal law (85% between 1930 and 1972), the new drug kingpin laws were causing a dramatic change in this trend—so dramatic, in fact, that the report called for remedial action (p. 4).

In January, 1995, a policy was adopted whereby a death penalty "protocol" was instituted. This policy resulted in a process in which "United States Attorneys are required to submit for review all cases in which a defendant is charged with a capital-eligible offense, regardless of whether the United States Attorney actually desires to seek the death penalty in that case" (U.S. Department of Justice, 2000, p. 2). During this process, some of the cases are withdrawn, whereas others are dismissed (some or all charges). Five years after the passage of this protocol, the Department of Justice conducted an analysis of the federal death penalty system (U.S. Department of Justice, 2000). The report began by showing that overall the use of the death penalty at the federal level pales in comparison to its use at the state level. It also showed that, between 1930 and 1999, the federal government executed 33 defendants, and up until the report was written, no one had been executed since 1963 (Timothy McVeigh and two other federal inmates have been executed since 2001). At the end of 2014, there were 63 persons with pending federal death sentences. Of these, 28 were Black, 26 were White, 7 were Latino, 1 was Native American, and 1 was Asian (Death Penalty Information Center, 2015).

❖ Scholarship on Race and the Death Penalty

For decades, scholars have considered a variety of issues related to the death penalty, including whether race matters when death sentences are administered (Garfinkel, 1949). Because of the expansive nature of the literature, our emphasis here is on a brief overview of select areas of death penalty research.

More than four decades ago, Wolfgang and Riedel (1973) concluded that, after controlling for numerous factors, racial discrimination was likely the reason that Blacks received the death penalty more often than Whites. Since this pioneering research, numerous studies have been done that focus on racial disparities in the administration of the death penalty. With the development of more sophisticated methodological approaches, researchers have confirmed that discrimination permeates the initial charging and sentencing phases of capital cases (Bowers & Pierce, 1980; Paternoster, 1983). Yet, as noted earlier in the chapter, it was the Baldus study that most potently brought to the fore the issue of the race-of-victim effects (Baldus et al., 1990; see also U.S. GAO, 1990).

During the 2000s, researchers have continued to study and find race-of-victim effects and other race/ethnicity-related aspects of the death penalty (for a cogent review of post 1990s research, see Baldus & Woodworth, 2003). Stauffer, Smith, Cochran, Fogel, and Bjerregaard (2006) investigated whether the race-of-victim effect applies to situations involving not only White female victims, but females in general. Their research built on the work of M. Williams and Holcomb (2004), who found that the death penalty was more likely in cases involving White female victims. Based on data from more than 950 North Carolina capital cases, Stauffer et al. (2006) did not find any significant differences between cases involving Black and White female victims. Hence, they argued that there was a general "gender [effect] versus a racial effect in sentencing outcomes" (p. 110). Explaining this result, the authors wrote: "We may likely find that female victim cases are disproportionately selected for capital prosecution in North Carolina because they fit the profile (such as it is) of a murder that evokes a particularly severe criminal justice reaction" (p. 110). The authors also note other aggravating factors, such as females are generally perceived as being vulnerable, and their murders often involve other acts that might provoke an additional level of outrage (e.g., rape).

Not all the recent literature has supported the race-of-victim effect. In fact, Berk, Li, and Hickman (2005) disputed some of the earlier findings of Paternoster and Brame's (2003) research examining racial disparities in the application of the death penalty in Maryland that revealed significant race-of-victim effects. In their re-analysis of the Paternoster and Brame data using a new analytical approach, the race-of-victim effect was less pronounced; Berk and his colleagues concluded that there was no definitive support for the findings from the Maryland data. Paternoster and Brame (2008) responded to the re-analysis with another paper, which included new analyses that affirmed their earlier findings. This stalemate suggests that, in this and other instances, the selected analysis procedure might have an influence on the results reported. Berk and his colleagues have certainly opened up questions on the nature of the analyses used in most studies that examine race and the death penalty. Interestingly, other recent studies on race and the death penalty in Tennessee (Scheb, Lyons, & Wagers, 2008) and Texas (Petrie & Coverdill, 2010) have found that race of the victim was not significant in death sentences for racial minorities even when controlling for the standard legal and extralegal factors. Despite these findings, which as with all state-level studies are limited in their generalizability, the bulk of the studies on race and the death penalty continue to find Blacks receiving the death sentence more often when they kill Whites (for a cogent recent summary, see Kavanaugh-Earl, Cochran, Smith, Fogel, & Bjerregaard, 2008; Phillips, 2012; Pierce & Radelet, 2011).

Hispanics and the Death Penalty

Although much of the existing death penalty research has centered on Black and White experiences, little research has solely examined how Hispanics fare regarding capital cases (Urbina, 2011). To fill this gap in the literature, C. Lee (2007) analyzed death penalty data from San Joaquin County, California. More specifically, using data from 128 death penalty cases from 1977 through 1986, she sought to determine whether Hispanics were treated more like Blacks or Whites in death penalty cases. Lee's diverse sample included defendants with the following racial characteristics: 34% White, 33% Hispanic, 25% African American, and 7% Asian American. The results from her analysis were rather telling. First, cases involving White victims "netted the most death-eligible charges" (p. 21). Next, the study showed that "A death-eligible charge was never levied against Asian American defendants" (p. 21). Turning to race-of-victim effects, C. Lee noted the following: "In a case where the victim was Hispanic or African American, the defendant was less likely to be charged with a capital homicide than if the victim was White or Asian" (p. 21). Furthermore, as found in the study by Stauffer and her colleagues, there was a strong gender effect. Here, it was revealed that "Defendants in male victim cases were *forty-three times* [emphasis added] less likely to face a death-eligible charge than those accused of killing a woman" (p. 22). To explain this effect, C. Lee turned to similar explanations postulated by Stauffer et al. (2006; e.g., vulnerability, additional offenses involved). Lee's results point to a clear need to move beyond the Black/White emphasis in death penalty research.

We turn our attention to the substitution thesis, which has, over the years, emerged as a way of contextualizing the racial disparities in the use of the death penalty in the United States.

Substitution Thesis/Zimring Analysis

One important area of research related to race and the death penalty has been the notion that, following the reduction in illegal lynchings, states "substituted" state-sanctioned executions for lynchings (Ogletree & Sarat, 2006; Tolnay & Beck, 1995; Vandiver, 2006). Referred to as the "substitution thesis," scholars have found support for this supposition (see J. Clarke, 1998; Tolnay & Beck, 1995; Vandiver, 2006). Zimring (2003) has also made a strong case for this perspective. In his death penalty research, Zimring has noted that, of all the industrialized nations, America remains one of the few that use the death penalty. He noted that, within the last 50 years, European nations such as Italy (1944), West Germany (1949), Austria (1950), Britain (1969), Portugal (1976), Spain (1978), and France (1981) have all abolished the death penalty (Zimring, 2003). Given this trend, he wonders why America has not abolished the death penalty. To answer the question, he turned to an analysis of executions by region, noting similarities between the current patterns in the use of the death penalty and historical lynching trends.

These data show that, from 1889 to 1918, lynchings were predominantly carried out in the South (88%). When one looks at the executions during the same period, again, the South predominated, producing 56% of the executions. During this early period, the North accounted for nearly 23%. Turning to the modern era of the death penalty (1977–2000), Zimring noted the similarities to the lynching patterns of earlier times (see Figure 7.2).

During the current period, 81% of the executions were in the South, with the Midwest (10%) and the West (8%) carrying out nearly all of the remaining executions. After considering these striking similarities, Zimring (2003) surmised that the South has a "culture of punishment." Of this culture, he wrote,

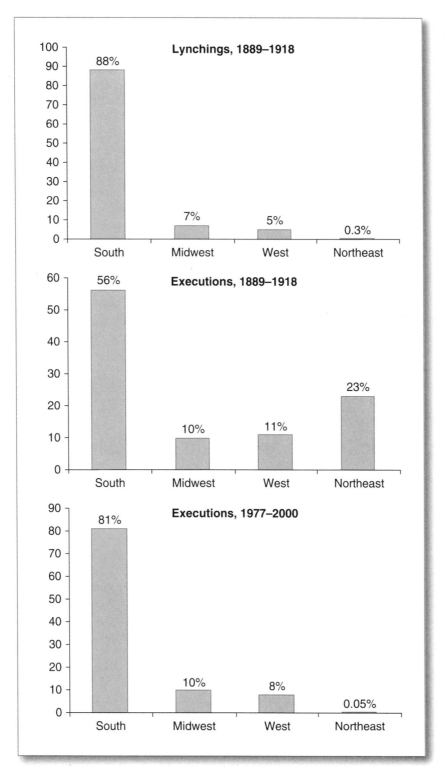

Figure 7.2

Regional
Percentage
Distributions of
Lynchings and
Executions

Source: Death Penalty
Information Center. 2002.
Available at http://www
.deathpenaltyinfo.org.

The Southern inclination towards high levels of punishment cannot be separated from the vigilante tradition itself. Rather than two separate traditions, the values and practices associated with extensive uses of the plantation prison, high levels of corporal and capital punishment, and those associated with lynchings and vigilante nostalgia overlap extensively with each other and with racial repression. Racism, vigilantism, and high levels of punishment were concurrent conditions in the South when high levels of punishment came to characterize the region. (p. 116)

On the racial dynamics of this culture, he opined,

It is likely that the long tradition of viewing punishments as a community rather than state institutions and the coercive White supremacist context in which such punishments took place were defining elements of the Southern propensity to punish. . . . The larger willingness to punish was a function of the particular targets and the particular context of punishment. (pp. 116–117)

Zimring's (2003) arguments are provocative and provide an important analysis that shows the parallels between illegal lynchings and state-sanctioned executions, which some have considered modern-day lynchings (J. Jackson & Jackson, 1996). Because of analyses such as Zimring's, there continues to be considerable debate about the application of the death penalty.

Over the years, public opinion researchers have measured public sentiment on the use of the death penalty. Next, we review some recent public opinion poll data on the death penalty.

❖ Public Opinion and the Death Penalty

According to Bohm (2007), public opinion on the death penalty is important for the following five reasons. First, strong public support for the death penalty is the likely reason that it is still used as a punishment in the United States. Consequently, politicians will continue to support the death penalty as long as support from the public remains high. Second, because the public wants the death penalty, Bohm believes that prosecutors are willing to appease them by seeking the death penalty in cases in which other penalties might be more suitable. Third, feeling the pressure from public sentiment, judges, like prosecutors, might feel undue pressure to impose death sentences (Bohm, 2007). Fourth, governors are also swayed by public opinion in their decisions to commute sentences. If public support for the death penalty is strong, few governors are willing to risk political disfavor by going against such sentiment. Finally, because state supreme courts and the U.S. Supreme Court consider public sentiment in their decisions regarding whether the death penalty is cruel and unusual punishment, the results of public opinion polls take on an added measure of significance.

Beginning in 1936, the Gallup poll began an annual tradition of asking Americans their opinions related to the death penalty. That early poll showed that 61% of those polled were in favor of the death penalty (Bohm, 1991). Since then, such polls have been annually conducted by several American polling organizations. Over time, support for the death penalty has ranged from a low of 42% in 1966 to a high of

80% during the early 1990s (Bohm, 1991). Over the 50-year period between 1936 and 1986, public support for the death penalty has averaged about 59% (Bohm, 1991). Recent polls continue to indicate considerable support for the death penalty, with overall support at 63% among adults in 2014 (Swift, 2014). According to 2014 Gallup data presented in Table 7.4, the number one reason (35%) that Americans support the death penalty is that they believe in the ancient concept of "an eye for an eye" (Swift, 2014). Table 7.5 shows that the number one reason people oppose the death penalty is that they believe it is "wrong to take a life."

Table 7.4

Reasons to Support the Death Penalty

Why do you favor the death penalty for persons convicted of murder? (Open-ended; Based on sample of those who favor the death penalty in murder convictions)

	1991 %	2001 %	2003 %	2014 %
An eye for an eye/They took a life/Fits the crime	50	48	37	35
Save taxpayers money/Cost associated with prison	13	20	11	14
They deserve it	–	6	13	14
They will repeat crime/Keep them from repeating it	19	6	7	7
Deterrent for potential crimes/Set an example	13	10	11	6
Depends on the type of crime they commit	–	6	4	5
Fair punishment	–	1	3	4
Serve justice	3	1	4	4
If there's no doubt the person committed the crime	–	2	3	3
Support/believe in death penalty	–	6	2	3
Don't believe they can be rehabilitated	–	2	2	3
Biblical reasons	–	3	5	3
Life sentences don't always mean life in prison	–	2	1	2
Relieves prison overcrowding	–	2	1	2
Would help/benefit families of victims	–	1	2	1
Other	11	3	4	1
No opinion	2	1	2	4

Table 7.5

Reasons to Oppose the Death Penalty

Why do you oppose the death penalty for persons convicted of murder? (Open-ended; Based on sample of those who oppose the death penalty in murder convictions)

	2001 %	2003 %	2014 %
Wrong to take a life	41	46	40
Persons may be wrongly convicted	11	25	17
Punishment should be left to God/religious belief	17	13	17
Need to pay/suffer longer/think about their crime	–	5	9
Depends on the circumstances	–	4	9
Unfair application of death penalty	6	4	5
Does not deter people from committing murder	7	4	4
Costs more to keep prisoners on death row	–	–	2
Possibility of rehabilitation	6	5	2
Other	16	3	1
No opinion	6	4	3

Even with the continuing high level of support for the death penalty, the differences in levels of support for the death penalty have been attributed to a variety of characteristics, including race, political party affiliation, region, education level, occupation, religion, and gender (Longmire, 1996). Such differences have remained constant over time. Racial differences in support for the death penalty have also been consistent.

Race and Support for the Death Penalty

During the 1970s, there was a consistent trend in support for the death penalty; however, Black support was considerably less than White support (Longmire, 1996). This trend has continued into the 21st century. In a 2013 public opinion poll, White support for capital punishment was at 63% compared to 40% for Hispanics and 36% for Blacks (Pew Research Center, 2014b).

So what accounts for the racial differences in support for the death penalty? Barkan and Cohn (1994) explored the notion that racial prejudice might play a role. Using 1990

GSS data, they examined questions that might speak to prejudice, such as whether Whites strongly favor or strongly oppose "living in a neighborhood where half your neighbors were Black" and "having a close relative or family member marry a Black person" (p. 203). Based on questions on the survey, they constructed a racial stereotyping scale out of questions that were meant to measure "the degree to which they thought Blacks were lazy, unintelligent, desirous of living off welfare, unpatriotic, violent, and poor" (p. 203). Barkan and Cohn's results showed that "many White people are both prejudiced against Blacks and are more likely to support the death penalty" (p. 206).

Bobo and Johnson's (2004) study on attitudes toward the death penalty found that more than 80% of Whites and slightly more than 50% of Black respondents favored the death penalty. Such support was not mediated when the researchers introduced respondents to concerns regarding bias in the administration of criminal justice. There was, however, an effect when respondents were told that if someone murdered a White person he was more likely to receive the death penalty than if he murdered a Black person. This caveat significantly reduced Black support for the death penalty, whereas White support was not significantly impacted. When Bobo and Johnson posed a hypothetical question involving executing innocent people on death row, there were only slight changes in the views of Whites and Blacks toward support for the death penalty.

Analyzing 14 years' worth of GSS data, spanning from the 1970s to 2002, related to attitudes toward the death penalty, Unnever and Cullen (2007) also reported that African Americans were significantly more likely than Whites to oppose the death penalty. Their research also found that "respondents with more years of education, who resided in the central city, and often attended church were significantly less likely to support the death penalty, and males and Americans who feared being victimized were significantly more likely to support the death penalty" (pp. 140–141). Income was also a significant variable in determining support for the death penalty. Here, respondents with higher incomes were more likely to support the death penalty. In general, this study, like other recent ones, found considerable support for the "racial divide" in public opinion on the death penalty (see also Cochran & Chamlin, 2006).

Scholars have found that White racism accounts for a percentage of the racial divide in support for the death penalty (Unnever & Cullen, 2007). Hurwitz and Peffley (2010) also found that White racism was a factor in White support for the death penalty. They conducted an experiment that asked a sample of respondents for their views about the death penalty, and to measure the influence of certain factors on the level of support for the punishment, they informed the respondents that "some" people believe that it is administered in a discriminatory fashion. This caveat caused "African Americans . . . to become even more oppositional to the penalty, while, shockingly, a nontrivial number of Whites became *more* supportive once informed that the punishment is administered disproportionately to Blacks" (p. 473). Another consideration related to the death penalty public opinion research is called the **Marshall hypotheses**.

The Marshall Hypotheses

Drawing on the statements of the late Supreme Court Justice Thurgood Marshall in *Furman v. Georgia*, researchers have presented hypotheses derived from his suggestions that (a) "American citizens know almost nothing about capital punishment," and (b) "[people] fully informed as to the purposes of the penalty and its liabilities, would find the penalty shocking, unjust, and unacceptable." Marshall qualified his second supposition by noting that this would not be the case if someone adhered to the retributive sentencing philosophy.

On the whole, scholars have found support for Marshall's first hypothesis—that the public is uninformed about the death penalty (Bohm, Clark, & Aveni, 1991; Lambert & Clarke, 2001). However, Lambert and Clarke (2001) noted that "of the five studies that directly attempt to test Marshall's second hypothesis, three found small decreases in support for the death penalty after subjects were presented with information concerning capital punishment" (p. 218). Guided by this past research, Lambert and Clarke conducted a study to determine whether reading an essay would influence college students' views on the death penalty.

To do so, Lambert and Clarke (2001) created three different essays. The first essay spoke to the major reasons for punishing criminals. The second essay presented empirical research on "the deterrence effect of the death penalty" (p. 222). The third essay discussed the "possibility and frequency of sentencing the innocent to death" (p. 222). Making use of a self-administered survey design, more than 700 students were randomly given surveys with one of these essays in it. The first section of the survey asked questions regarding the students' initial knowledge and attitudes toward the death penalty (serving as a pretest); the authors wanted to see whether their views changed depending on their exposure to one of the essays. Thus, following their review of the essay, students were again queried about their views on the death penalty. Although their research did show support for Marshall's second hypothesis, that an informed citizen would not support the death penalty, Lambert and Clarke wrote, "The type of information is critical. Although those who read the deterrence essay stated that their view of the death penalty had changed, only the innocence essay group had a statistically significant reduction in support for capital punishment" (p. 227). Although those who had read the essays on convicting innocent people showed statistically significant changes in their views, the authors did note that the change was slight. A decade later re-analysis of their data continued to support the Marshall hypotheses (Lambert, Camp, Clarke, & Jiang, 2011).

Cochran and Chamlin (2005) used a pretest/posttest design to determine whether students' views on the death penalty would be influenced by exposure to materials presented in a course on the death penalty. The authors did find mixed support for the supposition "that death penalty attitudes and beliefs were inversely associated with student's level of knowledge" (p. 582). The researchers also found that exposure to knowledge about the death penalty decreased the level of support for capital punishment and increased students' support for life without parole as an alternative to capital punishment (see also Cochran, Sanders, & Chamlin, 2006).

A. Mitchell (2006) also examined whether Marshall's suppositions could be supported using a pretest/posttest approach with a seminar course as the experimental stimulus. An interesting finding from his research was that the views of White and Hispanic students were minimally impacted by the seminar. In contrast, following exposure to the materials in the seminar, Blacks' opposition to the death penalty significantly increased (A. Mitchell, 2006). A. Mitchell attributed this finding to the legacy of Blacks being disproportionately sentenced to the death penalty. When comparing the experimental group to a control group that did not take the seminar, the study did find that the seminar increased the participants' knowledge of the death penalty.

In recent tests of the Marshall hypotheses, researchers continue to find minimal or no change in attitudes toward the death penalty of experimental subjects who were exposed to additional information on the death penalty (Cox, 2013; Lee, Bohm, & Pazzani, 2014). LaChappelle (2014) has recently expanded the Marshall hypothesis research literature by illustrating that educating the public about international context (i.e., the fact that most countries do not utilize capital punishment) can reduce support for the death penalty among Americans.

Because of the importance of the Capital Jury Project, wrongful convictions, the death penalty moratorium movement, and judicial overrides in death penalty sentencing, we conclude the chapter with brief discussions of these topics.

❖ Contemporary Issues in Race and the Death Penalty

Capital Jury Project

Funded by the National Science Foundation in 1991, the Capital Jury Project (CJP) was originally founded to investigate the following research objectives:

(1) to systematically describe jurors' exercise of capital sentencing discretion; (2) to assess the extent of arbitrariness in jurors' exercise of capital discretion; and (3) to evaluate the efficacy of the principal forms of capital statutes in controlling arbitrariness in capital sentencing. (University at Albany, School of Criminal Justice, 2011)

In addition, the CJP has secured additional funds to investigate "the role played by jurors' race in making the life or death sentencing decision" (University at Albany, School of Criminal Justice, 2011). To date, nearly 1,200 jurors from 353 capital trials in 14 states have been interviewed. Drawn from a combination of structured and unstructured questions, the interviews conducted for the project typically lasted from three to four hours.

The project has already yielded some general findings and also some related to race and capital juror decision making (Bowers, Sandys, & Steiner, 1998; Bowers, Steiner, & Sandys, 2001; Fleury-Steiner & Argothy, 2004). As an example, Fleury-Steiner and Argothy (2004) considered what happens in Latino capital cases. Making use of 35 juror narratives from 14 cases involving Latino capital defendants from Texas and California, the authors illuminated the racialized perceptions that jurors had of Latinos. Such racialized views manifested themselves in narratives that included the concepts of "colorblindness," "ethnic threat," and "ethnic deceit" (p. 74). With the concept of colorblindness, it is commonly thought that there is a general denial that racism exists in American society. As such, in capital cases involving Latinos, it impacts "the ways jurors evaluate witnesses, deliberate with other jurors, and justify their decisions to impose the death penalty" (p. 75). The concept of ethnic threat centers on the notion that Latinos are prone to violence and, as a result, the "belief in 'dangerous hombres' may *itself* play a role in capital sentencing jurors' decision to impose the death penalty" (p. 77). The notion of ethnic deceit relates to the belief that Latinos will do anything to enter the United States. As such, they simply cannot be trusted. Thus, Fleury-Steiner and Argothy believe that "racial deceit may be activated at various points in the trial process, including when a Latino defendant who happens not to speak English testifies" (p. 79).

Summarizing some of the major findings from the CJP, Fleury-Steiner (2009) writes that jurors were found to "have their minds made up on punishment before the sentencing phase of the trial had begun" (p. 91). Thus, jurors are neglecting the Supreme Court mandate to consider aggravating and mitigating factors in the capital sentencing process. Jurors also "[do] not believe that a life sentence actually means that the defendant will remain in prison the rest of his or her life" (p. 92). In short, because they cling to the belief that the offender might eventually be released, rather than risk the offender being released and harming someone else, they sentence the person to death. As for race, the results revealed that the possibility of being convicted was higher when there were fewer non-Whites on the jury. Even more disturbing was the finding that, in cases involving Black offenders and White victims, "a strong majority of White jurors as compared to Black jurors are more likely to be predisposed to the death sentence even before the sentencing trial begins" (p. 92). Finally, jurors were less likely to consider mitigating circumstances in cases involving Black offenders and White victims. In an earlier study, Brewer (2004) also weighed in on this general finding and provided additional context. Using a subset of the CJP data, he found that "only when Black jurors are faced with killing an out-group member, White victim, that they become significantly more receptive to mitigation than their White colleagues on the jury" (p. 542).

Taken together, the CJP has provided findings that align with the thoughts of some notable jurists (see Higginbotham, 1996) as well as yield new insights into capital jurors and their decision-making process. Whereas in the past researchers conducted simulations involving nonjurors to study jury decision making, the CJP has provided key insights into how *actual* jurors weigh in on capital cases. Such insights might hold the key to changing misperceptions that too often influence jury decision making. An obvious reason that this project is so critical relates to the potential for misguided verdicts and sentencing practices, which, in their worst manifestation, can result in wrongful convictions. We review various aspects of wrongful convictions in the next section.

❖ Wrongful Convictions

Concerns regarding innocent people being convicted are not new. Early on, both American (Borchard, 1932) and British (Brandon & Davies, 1973) scholars investigated this issue. Generally, however, most American citizens understand that, given the nature of our justice system, at times the guilty will go free and at other times innocent people will be sent to jail or prison. Therefore, when it comes to criminal justice, we generally adhere to a utilitarian philosophy. That is, because the system works for most citizens, we can tolerate it when a small number of citizens are wrongfully convicted. Essentially, this is the price we are willing to pay to maintain our adversarial "trial by combat" justice system. Although such a philosophy might be acceptable if the stakes were low, that is not the case with the American justice system. Considering that the United States still maintains the death penalty, to some, adhering to such a system leaves us open to executing innocent people. In fact, pioneering research in this area suggests that the United States has already executed hundreds of innocent people (Radelet, Bedau, & Putnam, 1992).

Numerous authors have elucidated the major contributors to wrongful convictions (Bedau, 2009; Castelle & Loftus, 2002; Christianson, 2004; S. Cohen, 2003; Gould & Leo, 2010; Harmon, 2001, 2004; Huff, 2004; Huff, Rattner, & Sagarin, 1996; Leo, 2002; Martin, 2002; Smith & Hattery, 2011; Zalman, 2011; Zimmerman, 2002). Of these, the most consistent contributors are (a) eyewitness error, (b) police misconduct, (c) prosecutorial misconduct, (d) plea bargaining, (e) community pressure for conviction, (f) inadequacy of counsel, (g) false confessions, (h) mistaken identity, (i) fabrication of evidence, (j) having a criminal record, (k) misinformation from criminal informants, and (l) race. Most of these contributors are self-explanatory; therefore, given the focus of this book, we concentrate on the role of race in wrongful conviction cases.

Bedau and Radelet (1987) were among the first to discuss race as a factor in wrongful conviction cases: Of the 350 capital cases they reviewed, 40% involved instances in which Blacks were wrongly accused. Huff et al. (1996) have also noted that historically there have been disproportionate numbers of Blacks and Hispanics among those wrongly convicted. He and his coauthors alluded to the fact that many of the early instances of wrongful convictions involving minorities were likely a result of being tried by racist prosecutors, who also had all-White, prejudiced juries on their sides.

According to Parker, Dewees, and Radelet (2002), the 40% figure generally holds true across studies. One exception to this is the research done by Barry Scheck and Peter Neufeld, in which their **Innocence Project** (housed at Cardozo Law School at Yeshiva University in New York) has found that, of those exonerated by the use of DNA, 57% have been Black (Parker et al., 2002). Parker et al. also surmised that, based on past criminal justice practices, "Among those wrongly convicted of felonies, Black defendants are significantly less likely than White defendants to be vindicated" (p. 118).

Another contribution of the Parker et al. (2002) paper is that it attempts to link theoretical explanation to the disproportionate representation of minorities among the wrongly convicted. Among their individual explanations, they pointed to racism, stereotyping, and Blacks being easy targets for a variety of reasons, including their lack of access to resources. As for structural explanations, Parker et al. relied on the conflict-oriented (see Chapter 3) power threat hypothesis; according to this perspective, "Because Blacks are perceived as a threat to Whites, they face higher conviction rates, even wrongfully as Whites respond to this perceived threat" (p. 125). The authors also noted that urban disadvantage might play a role in minorities being overrepresented in instances of wrongful convictions. As they opined,

> The racial patterns in cases of wrongful conviction, particularly the finding that Blacks are more likely to be erroneously convicted, are crystallized under these conditions. That is, these conditions—residential segregation, concentrated poverty, joblessness, and other forms of concentrated disadvantage—reinforce racial disparities in the treatment of minorities in the criminal justice system, including racial bias in convictions of the innocent. (p. 126)

In a recent book that builds on past scholarship on race and wrongful convictions, Free and Ruesink (2012) analyzed more than 300 cases (from 1970 to 2008) in which African American males have been wrongfully convicted. Their research showed that the three states with the highest number of wrongful convictions of African Americans were Texas, Illinois, and Ohio. More than half the cases involved instances in which the African Americans were wrongly convicted of murder or attempted murder. Other significant offenses that were represented among the cases included rape, sexual assault, drug offenses, and robbery. The authors also found that in more than 90% of the rape and sexual assault cases there were witness errors that often involved cross-race identification issues. Other factors in the wrongful conviction included forensic errors, police and prosecutorial misconduct, and questionable informants (Free & Ruesink, 2012). This important work will hopefully lead to additional empirical research on race and wrongful convictions. In particular, we note the dearth of information on race, sex, and wrongful convictions.

Addressing Wrongful Convictions in the 21st Century

It is notable that C. Ronald Huff devoted his 2001 American Society of Criminology presidential address to the topic of wrongful conviction and public policy (Huff, 2002). Although he repeated many of the previously discussed facts and figures, his address laid out several important policy considerations aimed at reducing the number of persons wrongfully convicted. First, Huff recommended that those wrongly convicted should be adequately compensated and also provided the appropriate social services to deal with the trauma and reintegration. Second, he suggested replacing the death penalty with sentences of 20 years, 30 years, or life imprisonment without parole. Third, he advocated granting prisoners access to DNA tests. In line with this policy suggestion, the Innocence Protection Act of 2003, if enacted, would require DNA tests when federal inmates claim they are innocent. Fourth, Huff suggested ensuring that qualified expert witnesses be used to minimize misidentification, which is a major contributor to wrongful convictions. Fifth, legal counsel should be present when any identification procedure is used. Sixth, police interrogations of suspects should be taped. Seventh, criminal justice officials who engage in unethical, unprofessional, or illegal activity should be removed and prosecuted. Finally, Huff recommended that individual states and the federal government establish innocence commissions to handle these situations.

There can be no doubt that instituting Huff's proposed policies would go a long way toward reducing the number of wrongful convictions in general. In recent years, states have responded to public concern about wrongful convictions. Norris (2011) recently assessed the compensation statutes for the wrongly convicted across the United States. Using the Innocence Project's compensation provision as the model standard, he compared how well states' policies stacked up. The Innocence Project recommends $50,000 minimum for each year spent in prison plus $25,000 for time spent on parole or probation. The model policy also recommends other types of compensation such as mental and physical services, child support payments, and so on. None of the 27 states that have such statutes included all the provisions recommended in the model policy. Notably, only four states matched the $50,000 annual compensation recommendation. After scoring the states on the comprehensiveness of their statutes, Texas emerged as a leader. In particular, Texas provides $80,000 per year compensation and also provides vocational training and tuition and fees at a state university or college (p. 16). Medical and support services are also available for one year, and the Texas statute was also the only one to pay child support for exonerees.

Another recent development in the fight to reduce wrongful convictions is the development of Conviction Integrity Units (CIUs) housed in District Attorney offices (Center for Prosecutorial Integrity, 2014). These units are tasked with investigating wrongful conviction claims. Under the direction of Craig Watkins in Dallas, the first CIU was created in 2007. In 2014, there were 16 such units across the United States.

It is apparent that some states have taken heed of the concerns surrounding wrongful convictions and, in response, have enacted moratoriums on the death penalty. We briefly review this movement next.

Death Penalty Moratorium Movement

Because of the increasing recognition that errors were being made in capital cases, states have begun to consider moratoriums on executions. Governor George Ryan of Illinois (a past nominee for the Nobel Peace Prize) was the first governor to take such drastic action. When asked why he felt a need to enact such a policy, he noted,

> We have now freed more people than we have put to death under our system—13 people have been exonerated and 12 have been put to death. . . . There is a flaw in the system, without question, and it needs to be studied. ("Illinois Suspends Death Penalty," 2000)

Like Illinois, other states such as Nebraska and Pennsylvania have considered such action ("Illinois Suspends Death Penalty," 2000; "Pennsylvania Panel Advises Death Penalty Moratorium," 2003), but it has not passed muster with the legislatures of these states. In 2002, former Maryland governor Parris Glendening issued a moratorium, only to have his successor, governor Robert Ehrlich, lift it shortly after he was sworn in the next year. Citizens in some states have formed groups that are aimed at pressuring state governments to enact moratoriums in order to study the fairness of the death penalty. Although the movement is clearly picking up momentum, few other states that currently use the death penalty have gone as far as Illinois did without turning back. A 2003 poll sheds some light on why more states have not followed Illinois's lead. A January, 2003 ABC/*Washington Post* national poll of 1,133 citizens found that when asked, "Would you support or oppose it if the governor in your state changed the sentence of every death row inmate to life in prison instead?" only 39% supported such a policy, whereas the majority (58%) did not (ABC/*Washington Post* Poll, 2003). Such figures indicate that death penalty opponents have considerable work to do in order to increase the number of moratoriums nationwide. It is notable, however, that as a result of the efforts of the New Jerseyans for a Death Penalty Moratorium, in December, 2007, the New Jersey legislature approved legislation to abolish the death penalty in the state (Hester & Feeney, 2007). In 2015 there were 18 states that had abolished the death penalty. In the last two years, two states, Washington (2014) and Pennsylvania (2015), have also issued moratoriums on executions (see Table 7.6).

Table 7.6

States With and Without the Death Penalty

States With the Death Penalty (32)		
Alabama	Louisiana	Pennsylvania (moratorium 2015)
Arizona	Mississippi	South Carolina
Arkansas	Missouri	South Dakota
California	Montana	Tennessee
Colorado	Nebraska	Texas
Delaware	Nevada	Utah
Florida	New Hampshire	Virginia
Georgia	North Carolina	Washington (moratorium 2014)
Idaho	Ohio	Wyoming
Indiana	Oklahoma	
Kansas	Oregon	**ALSO**
Kentucky		U.S. Government
		U.S. Military

States Without the Death Penalty (18) (year abolished in parentheses)		
Alaska (1957)	Michigan (1846)	West Virginia (1965)
Connecticut** (2012)	Minnesota (1911)	Wisconsin (1853)
Hawaii (1957)	New Jersey (2007)	
Illinois (2011)	New Mexico* (2009)	**ALSO**
Iowa (1965)	New York (2007)#	Dist. of Columbia (1981)
Maine (1887)	North Dakota (1973)	
Maryland (2013)	Rhode Island (1984)^	
Massachusetts (1984)	Vermont (1964)	

Source: Death Penalty Information Center (2015).

Notes:

* In March 2009, New Mexico voted to abolish the death penalty. However, the repeal was not retroactive, leaving two people on the state's death row.

** In April 2012, Connecticut voted to abolish the death penalty. However, the repeal was not retroactive, leaving 11 people on the state's death row.

^ In 1979, the Supreme Court of Rhode Island held that a statute making a death sentence mandatory for someone who killed a fellow prisoner was unconstitutional. The legislature removed the statute in 1984.

In 2004, the New York Court of Appeals held that a portion of the state's death penalty law was unconstitutional. In 2007, they ruled that their prior holding applied to the last remaining person on the state's death row. The legislature has voted down attempts to restore the statute.

Judicial Overrides in Death Penalty Sentencing

One of the more recent "hot button" contemporary death penalty issues is the use of judicial override in capital cases, particularly in Alabama. A report by the Equal

Justice Initiative has brought this issue front and center in Alabama. Alabama is one of the few states that allow judges to override the sentence recommended by the jury in death penalty cases. The override can involve the changing of a life without parole sentence to a death sentence or, alternatively, it can reduce a death sentence to life without parole. Currently, only three states allow judicial overrides (Alabama, Florida, and Delaware). Yet only in Alabama is the practice regularly used. The Equal Justice Initiative found that in Delaware, the judicial override has been largely used by judges to override death sentences and impose life sentences. In Florida, the practice hasn't been used in more than a decade.

In contrast to Delaware and Florida, judicial overrides in Alabama are a common practice in death penalty cases. Judges in Alabama consistently override jury verdicts in death penalty cases. In fact, "more than 20% of the people currently sentenced to death in Alabama were condemned by a judge after the jury voted for life" (Stevenson, 2011, p. 8). To date, 92% of the overrides have involved the changing of life sentences to death sentences. It is believed that because judges in Alabama are elected they take tough stances by overriding jury sentencing decisions that might appear lenient. The Equal Justice Initiative (2011) has gone further by outlining the following potential reasons for the heavy use of overrides in Alabama:

> The data suggests that override in Alabama is heavily influenced by arbitrary factors such as the timing of judicial elections, the politics of the county where the accused is prosecuted, and the outsized enthusiasm of certain judges for overriding jury life verdicts. (p. 8)

While there has been at least one legal challenge to the practice, the courts have found that it is not unconstitutional for Alabama judges to use overrides.

The racial dynamics of the judicial overrides have also been noted. As with other death penalty research, race appears to play a role in the judicial overrides in Alabama. In particular, it has been found that "African Americans in Alabama constitute 26% of the total population, but more than half of the overrides in Alabama have imposed the death penalty on African Americans" (Stevenson, 2011, p. 18). In addition, the Alabama data reveal that "While just 6% of all the murders in Alabama involve black defendants and white victims, in 31% of Alabama override cases, the trial judge condemned a person of color to a death sentence for killing someone white" (p. 18). It is apparent from the existing data that the practice of judicial overrides, even with the requirement that judges explain their decisions, has the potential to produce racial disparities.

To stem the concerns related to judicial overrides, in 2007 the Alabama legislature considered a bill that would disallow their use; the bill failed. Others have suggested that electing judges is part of the problem and should be eliminated because decision making might be tied to concerns about re-election (Serwer, 2011). In general, judicial overrides in death penalty cases is a problem that is only now receiving national attention, but it clearly has been a concern in Alabama for some time. With the U.S. Supreme Court potentially hearing cases tied to judicial overrides (see Box 7.3), the national spotlight on the issues will certainly cause Alabama to reconsider its policy and, more generally, cause the nation to think about the way in which judges are selected.

BOX 7.3

Race and Crime in the Media

U.S. Justices May Review Capital Cases in Which Judges Overrode Juries

WASHINGTON—In 2009, an Alabama jury convicted Christie Scott of murdering her 6-year-old son by setting a fire in her home. It then voted to spare her life.

Judge Terry L. Dempsey of the Circuit Court in Russellville rejected that verdict and sentenced Ms. Scott to death. "This jury was probably emotionally and mentally worn out," he said, adding that jurors might have been swayed by testimony from the victim's family seeking leniency.

A year later, on the other side of the state, a jury unanimously recommended that Courtney Lockhart, a veteran of the Iraq war, be spared the death penalty for murdering Lauren Burk, a college student.

Judge Jacob A. Walker III of the Circuit Court in Opelika overrode the jury's verdict and sentenced Mr. Lockhart to death—but for the opposite reason. Judge Walker said Ms. Burk's family had asked for the death penalty, which "weighs in favor of judicial override."

The Supreme Court will soon consider whether to hear one or both of the cases—*Scott v. Alabama*, No. 14-8189, and *Lockhart v. Alabama*, No. 14-8194—and to take a new look at the unusual power Alabama gives to its judges.

The court has lately been interested in other aspects of capital sentencing, agreeing on Monday to consider a challenge to Florida's system in *Hurst v. Florida*, No. 14-7505.

Alabama is one of three states with laws on the books allowing judges to reject juries' sentencing recommendations in capital cases. In the past decade, it has been alone in sending defendants to death row after juries determined that the just sentence was life in prison.

Alabama law allows judges to override jury recommendations in either direction: from life to death or from death to life. But Alabama judges mostly choose death.

Since the Supreme Court reinstated the death penalty in 1976, judges in Alabama have overridden recommendations of life 101 times and of death just 10 times.

Twenty years ago, the Supreme Court upheld Alabama's capital-sentencing system. But at least two justices seem ready to reconsider that ruling.

In a 2013 dissent, Justice Sonia Sotomayor, joined by Justice Stephen G. Breyer, said it was time for the court to re-examine a system that let "a single trial judge's view to displace that of a jury representing a cross-section of the community."

Alabama jurors are not notably squeamish about the death penalty, and those opposed to it are automatically excluded from service. In Mr. Lockhart's case, the prosecution excluded 10 potential jurors based on doubts about their commitment to capital punishment.

Delaware and Florida also allow overrides. But no one has been sentenced to death in Florida as a result of a judicial override since 1999, and no one is on death row in Delaware as a consequence of an override.

In Alabama, by contrast, more than 20 percent of the inmates on death row are there because of judicial overrides.

Mr. Lockhart's case is already on the Supreme Court's radar. Justice Sotomayor's dissent, in a case involving a different condemned inmate, included an unusual footnote about Mr. Lockhart. She seemed to want to describe an extreme case.

Justice Sotomayor wrote that the jury's 12-to-0 vote in favor of sparing Mr. Lockhart's life had been "influenced by mitigating circumstances relating to severe psychological problems Lockhart suffered as a result of his combat in Iraq."

"Lockhart spent 16 months in Iraq; 64 of the soldiers in his brigade never made it home, including Lockhart's best friend," she added. "The soldiers who survived all exhibited signs of post-traumatic stress disorder and other psychological conditions. Twelve of them have been arrested for murder or attempted murder."

"The trial judge nonetheless imposed the death penalty," Justice Sotomayor concluded.

Mr. Lockhart is one of five inmates on Alabama's death row in spite of life verdicts from unanimous juries, according to the Equal Justice Initiative, which represents Mr. Lockhart and Ms. Scott. (The vote in favor of life in Ms. Scott's case was 7 to 5.)

Justice Sotomayor said she had a theory about Alabama judges' "distinctive proclivity" for overrides in favor of death.

"The only answer that is supported by empirical evidence," she wrote, "is one that, in my view, casts a cloud of illegitimacy over the criminal justice system: Alabama judges, who are elected in partisan proceedings, appear to have succumbed to electoral pressures." She cited a study showing that overrides were more common in election years.

Judges in Delaware, by contrast, are appointed. They generally use their authority to reject death sentences.

But even appointed judges are more prone to sentence defendants to death than juries are. A study in the current *Journal of Empirical Legal Studies* that looked at three decades of data from Delaware, which has experimented with several systems, found that "the shift to judge sentencing significantly increased the number of death sentences."

Three veterans' organizations and the Constitution Project, a legal research and advocacy group, filed a brief supporting Mr. Lockhart. It said Alabama's judicial overrides interfered with the jury's role in violation of the Sixth Amendment.

But the more promising line of attack may be under the Eighth Amendment, which bans cruel and unusual punishment.

In a 1988 dissent, long before Alabama found itself alone in using overrides, Justice Thurgood Marshall said that allowing judges to overrule juries could not be reconciled with that amendment.

"The death penalty's cruel and unusual nature is made all the more arbitrary and freakish," he wrote, "when it is imposed by a judge in the face of a jury determination that the appropriate penalty is life imprisonment."

1. Do you believe judges should be able to override jury sentencing decisions in capital cases? Why or why not?

Source: U.S. Justices May Review Capital Cases in Which Judges Override Juries, Dave Martin, Associated Press, © Academy of Criminal Justice Sciences, reprinted by permission of Taylor & Francis Ltd, www.tandfonline.com on behalf of Academy of Criminal Justice Sciences.

❖ Conclusion

This chapter reviewed several aspects of race and the death penalty. Our historical overview showed that the death penalty has been applied in a discriminatory fashion since colonial times. Sadly, recent state and federal death penalty figures do not show much promise for resolving this issue in the immediate future. After reviewing several significant Supreme Court cases on the death penalty, we reviewed public opinion on the subject. Although support has remained strong, it has varied based on characteristics such as race, class, area of residence, education level, political party affiliation, and religion.

We concluded the chapter by focusing on the Capital Jury Project, wrongful convictions, the death penalty moratorium movement, and judicial overrides in death penalty cases. These areas are clearly intertwined in the search for justice. Moreover, this literature has shown that the criminal justice system is not infallible. In fact, several hundred people have been wrongly convicted of capital offenses in the United States, and some of these persons have actually been executed. Scholars have suggested a variety of reasons for these errors, all of which should be the focus of policy makers to ensure that the justice system works. Because of the furor over wrongful convictions involving death sentences, several states have either abolished the death penalty or issued temporary moratoriums on its use.

In Chapter 8, we turn our attention to corrections and the race-related issues that plague the so-called back end of the criminal justice system.

Discussion Questions

1. What was the nature of capital punishment during the colonial era?

2. Describe the significance of *Gregg v. Georgia* and *McCleskey v. Kemp*.

3. Discuss two reason why people support and oppose the death penalty.

4. Explain the significance of the Conviction Integrity Units.

5. What are five of the most significant contributors to wrongful convictions?

Internet Exercises

1. Go to the Death Penalty Information Center (http://www.deathpenaltyinfo.org), and select the link for the list of exonerees from death row since 1973. Using the data provided, summarize the overall racial trends and also the average time between conviction and exoneration.

2. Visit the website for the National Coalition to Abolish the Death Penalty (http://www.ncadp.org/) and see whether the arguments presented concerning the abolishment of the death penalty are convincing.

3. After reading the report on Conviction Integrity Units at http://www.prosecutorinteg rity.org/wp-content/uploads/2014/12/Conviction-Integrity-Units.pdf, take a position as to whether every prosecutorial office in the United States should have a CIU.

Internet Sites

Capital Jury Project: http://www.albany.edu/scj/13189.php

Death Penalty Information Center: http://www.deathpenaltyinfo.org

The Innocence Project: http://www.innocenceproject.org

National Coalition to Abolish the Death Penalty: http://www.ncadp.org

Supplemental materials for *Race and Crime* are available online at
study.sagepub.com/gabbidon4e.

CHAPTER 8

Corrections

In many prisons, one feels as if there is an invisible sign on the front door that reads: Only Blacks and Hispanics Need Apply.

—National Trust for the Development of
African American Men (cited in Petersilia, 2003, p. 26)

Once offenders are convicted and sentenced, the courts generally turn them over to correctional officials. Correctional departments typically oversee inmates sentenced to probation, jail, and prison. Another key component of the criminal justice system, **corrections** represents one of the most costly expenditures of the system. Billions of dollars are spent each year to carry out this difficult function. To reduce such expenditures, over the last several decades, more nontraditional approaches, such as community-based initiatives, have expanded the umbrella of corrections (see Clear & Dammer, 2003). Even with the adoption of more innovative initiatives, prison overcrowding has continued to plague correctional systems throughout the United States. In fact, there has been an increasing concern in society about the expense of corrections. Multiple reports in recent years have lamented about the robust state-level funding for corrections and comparatively sparse expenditures on educational systems (NAACP, 2011; The Pew Center on the States, 2008). This concern is further illustrated in Box 8.1 and Figure 8.1, which illustrate state-level expenditures on corrections and education.

Along with financial concerns, the correctional system has also remained an arena in which race-related concerns have persisted. Considering that in 2013, 59% of sentenced male prisoners in state and federal facilities in the United States were Black and Hispanic (Carson, 2014), questions have arisen about social justice. In line with Goldkamp's (1982) belief perspectives presented in Chapter 4, one question of critical concern is whether disparities in corrections are based on discrimination or whether they exist because minorities commit more serious offenses and should expect to be overrepresented in prison populations (DeLisi & Regoli, 1999; MacDonald, 2008; Mann, 1993; Wilbanks, 1987). As noted next, this chapter aims to explore this and other related questions.

BOX 8.1

Race and Crime in the Media

States Are Prioritizing Prisons Over Education, Budgets Show

If state budget trends reflect the country's policy priorities, then the United States currently values prisoners over children, a new report suggests.

A report released this week by the Center on Budget and Policy Priorities shows that the growth of state spending on prisons in recent years has far outpaced the growth of spending on education. After adjusting for inflation, state general fund spending on prison-related expenses increased over 140 percent between 1986 and 2013. During the same period, state spending on K–12 education increased only 69 percent, while higher education saw an increase of less than six percent.

Figure 8.1 State Corrections Spending Has Grown Much Faster Than Education Spending

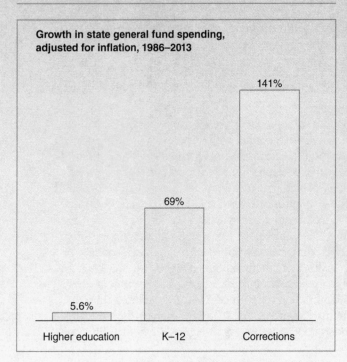

Growth in state general fund spending, adjusted for inflation, 1986–2013

Source: CBPP analysis data from National Association of State Budget Officers.

State spending on corrections has exploded in recent years, as incarceration rates have more than tripled in a majority of states in the past few decades. The report says that the likelihood that an offender will be incarcerated has gone up across the board for all major crimes. At the same time, increases in education spending have not kept pace. In fact, since 2008, spending on education has actually declined in a majority of states in the wake of the Great Recession.

According to the brief, rates of violent crime and property crime have actually fallen over the years, even while incarceration rates have risen. Therefore, it appears that states' more aggressive incarceration policies are behind the higher prison rates.

Michael Mitchell, a co-author of the report and a policy analyst with the Center on Budget and Policy Priorities, suggested that education spending could actually help lower incarceration rates. "When you look at prisoners, people who get sent to prison and their educational levels, [the levels are] typically much lower than individuals who are not sent to prison," he told The Huffington Post. "Being a high school dropout dramatically increases your likelihood of being sent to prison."

"Spending so many dollars locking up so many people, those are dollars that inevitably cannot be used to provide pre-K slots . . . or financial aid for those who want to go to college," Mitchell added.

The report suggests that states' spending practices are ultimately harming their economies, while not making the states especially safer. The authors ultimately conclude that if "states were still spending the same amount on corrections as they did in the mid-1980s, adjusted for inflation, they would have about $28 billion more available each year for education and other productive investments."

"The types of investments to help people out of poverty and break that school-to-prison pipeline are investments in early education, helping youth stay in school and getting them onto college campuses," said Mitchell.

Source: Klein (2014).

1. Provide three policy suggestions to help resolve this problem.

The purpose of this chapter is to provide an overview of corrections and the race-related issues that are connected to its operation. Our coverage of corrections begins with a brief overview of the structure, function, and public opinion pertaining to corrections in America. A brief historical overview of race and American corrections is presented next. We then review the current state of corrections in America. The chapter concludes by focusing on several contemporary issues in corrections. Specifically, our focus here is reviewing explanations for disparities in correctional populations, **prisoner re-entry** into the community, and felon disenfranchisement.

❖ Overview of American Corrections

Often referred to as the "back end" of the criminal justice system, corrections is generally the place where the system ends. Although there is the perception that *corrections* is synonymous with incarceration, approximately 70% of those persons in the corrections phase of the criminal justice system are actually being supervised in the community (Glaze & Kaeble, 2014). Clear and Cole (2000) suggested that "the central purpose of corrections is to carry out the criminal sentence" (p. 7). Furthermore, describing the scope of American corrections, they wrote that "corrections . . . encompasses . . . the variety of programs, services, facilities, and organizations responsible for managing people accused or convicted of criminal offenses" (p. 8). Within this description, they are distinguishing between the various correctional options. We discuss these options in turn.

American corrections include a continuum of sanctions that range from being incarcerated in a jail or prison facility to being sentenced to a fine or restitution (Clear & Cole, 2000). Depending on the nature of their offenses, those who are incarcerated are placed in minimum-, medium-, or maximum-security prisons. Nationwide, there are also approximately 57 "supermax" prisons in 40 states that hold approximately 25,000 prisoners (Amnesty International, 2014; Mears & Watson, 2006). According to Clear and Cole (2003), "These institutions are designed to hold the most disruptive, violent, and incorrigible prisoners" (p. 252). Persons who are awaiting trial and are unable to secure bail are held in jails. In addition, persons who are sentenced to a year or less are typically housed in jails. Because of overcrowding, however, some jurisdictions have turned to housing more serious offenders in jails (Allen, Simonsen,

& Latessa, 2004). Other sanctions falling under the corrections umbrella include fines, community service, drug and alcohol treatment, probation, home confinement, and **intensive probation** supervision. Each of these sanctions provides nonincarcerative options for offenders. Such options are also attractive to corrections officials because they are considerably cheaper than incarcerating offenders.

All of these various correctional options have also resulted in considerable employment opportunities. For example, in 1983, there were 146,000 correctional workers (U.S. Census Bureau, 2003); however, more than 30 years later, in 2014, there were approximately 400,000 correctional officers. Blacks (20.6%) and Hispanics (16%) were beneficiaries of this growth. Females also took advantage of this growth, representing 28.6% of those employed as bailiffs, correctional officers, and jailers (U.S. Bureau of Labor Statistics, 2014).

As with sentencing philosophies, public opinion and politics play important roles in the way the correctional system operates. Given the importance of public opinion research, we briefly review some recent public opinion research on corrections.

Public Opinion on Corrections

Because of the various "get tough" laws that were legislated in the 1980s and 1990s, jails and prisons have become considerably overcrowded (Alexander, 2010). This overcrowding coincided with the decline in support for rehabilitation that began in the 1970s (Flanagan, 1996). Since then, the support for punitive policies has increased dramatically. Even with the support for this punitive approach being strong nationally, especially from the 1980s into the 2000s, there remain considerable differences in opinion by race and gender. In particular, there have been consistent cleavages in public opinion on the topic with a gradient in views by race/ethnicity with Whites being most punitive, Hispanics being less punitive than Whites, and Blacks being the least punitive (Ghandnoosh, 2014).

A 2009 national poll by Rasmussen Reports found increasing support for rehabilitation. When asked "To fight crime, what is more important—funding programs for the rehabilitation of criminals, hiring more police or building more prisons?" respondents from across the nation placed rehabilitation (34%) just below hiring more police (42%). Building more prisons was only endorsed by 12% of the respondents (Rasmussen Reports, 2009). It is important to note that the increased interest in rehabilitation or alternative programs might be tied to fiscal concerns because of budget shortfalls across the country in the last part of the first decade of the 21st century. In California, for example, when former Governor Arnold Schwarzenegger proposed the release of 22,000 nonviolent offenders to ease state spending on prison and correction, there was sizeable support within a state that had previously championed the three-strikes-and-you're-out policies. More specifically, a statewide poll found that nearly half the population was in favor of the governor's proposal. As expected, the support varied by political affiliation, with Democratic support at 55%, whereas Republican support was nearly 20 points lower at 37% (Public Policy Institute of California, 2008).

More recent national public opinion research on the criminal justice system has found that the country remains split on whether the focus of the system should be punitive (54%) or rehabilitative (46%) in orientation (Mizell, 2014). Moreover, Americans are similarly split on whether alternatives to incarceration (i.e., offering probation, treatment, counseling, and payment of damages instead of prison time) for nonviolent offenders should be increased (48%), kept the same (43%), or cut back (9%; Mizell, 2014, p. 18).

On the whole, racial minorities have been the ones disproportionately affected by what some have called America's "imprisonment binge" (Alexander, 2010; J. Austin & Irwin, 2001; Baadsager, Sims, Baer, & Chambliss, 2000; Clear, 2007; Tonry, 2011; Western, 2006). This was borne out by one national poll of African Americans that revealed that 19% of African Americans had an immediate family member incarcerated in either a prison or juvenile detention facility (National Urban League Poll, 2001).

Unnever (2008) examined public opinion as to why African Americans were disproportionately imprisoned. In general, African Americans and Whites had differing views. African Americans, more so than Whites, felt that police bias (71% vs. 37%) and unfair courts (67% vs. 28%) were big reasons why African Americans were disproportionately incarcerated. Another big difference in opinion was with denial of jobs. African Americans were much more likely than Whites to see this as a big reason (59% vs. 37%). Both African Americans and Whites felt that poverty was a big reason (67% vs. 63%) for the disproportionate incarceration of African Americans. Unnever (2008) noted that a big reason for the "racial divide" in opinions has to do with personal experience:

> The more African Americans report that they have encountered racial discrimination the more likely they are to attribute the disproportionately high rates of imprisonment among black males to structural disadvantages such as bad schools and a lack of job opportunities and to racial discrimination within the criminal justice system. (Unnever, 2008, pp. 531–532)

Nelson, Gabbidon, and Boisvert (2015) recently published the results of a study that built on Unnever's work. In particular, the scholars sought to determine public views on the causes of the disproportionate representation of Blacks and Hispanics throughout the entire criminal justice system. Notably, their research found that Philadelphia-area residents felt that similar factors to those found in Unnever's research, including economics and education, played a significant role in racial/ethnic disparities in the U.S. criminal justice system.

Has race always mattered in corrections? The next section looks into this question by providing a historical overview of race and corrections.

❖ Historical Overview of Race and Corrections

Because of the uneven nature of the historical scholarship and statistics on groups other than African Americans, chronicling the history of race and corrections is a considerable challenge. However, even with these limitations, we attempt to provide some insight into how race has historically intersected with American corrections. We begin our discussion with a brief overview of the history of race and corrections.

Early History of Race and Corrections

American corrections had its origins in the European workhouses, which were places where vagrants and other minor offenders were sent (Langbein, 1976). According to Shelden (2001), the first such institution to house offenders opened in Amsterdam in 1596. Referred to as the *Rasphaus,* the purpose of this facility was to "discipline the inmates into accepting a regimen analogous to an 'ideal factory,' in which the norms required for capitalist accumulation were ingrained in the code of discipline" (Shank, 1978; cited in Shelden, 2001). Shelden proposed that these facilities were more appropriately called "poorhouses," which were essentially modeled to support the need for industrial workers. As a result, "When released from these workhouses, the inmates would theoretically willingly adapt to the regimentation of the factory and other forms of labor under the new capitalist system" (Shelden, 2001, p. 155).

Over time, England developed three types of facilities: (a) jail, (b) house of corrections, and (c) workhouse (Collins, 1997). By the founding of colonial America in the early 17th century, some of these facilities made their way to America. Similar to today, in colonial times, jail and prisons were expensive to build and maintain (Chapin, 1983). As a result, most offenders were rarely sentenced to prison, with fines, corporal punishments (e.g., whippings), and banishment serving as the most common punishments (Chapin, 1983; Shelden, 2001). Chapin (1983) noted that "jails were used most commonly to hold persons accused of serious crimes before trial and to detain convicted persons until they could pay fines or make restitution" (p. 52).

Because of economic considerations, it was rare to find slaves, Native Americans, or indentured servants incarcerated. On this subject, Collins (1997) wrote,

> Jailing of slaves was not profitable for the slave owners, so very few slaves were ever incarcerated for an extended period of time. Instead, prior to the Civil War, Black slaves would be imprisoned in plantation-built jails and punished for crimes committed (for example, running away, stealing, assaulting an overseer, or disobeying an order) by the slave master who had unlimited power, including deadly force. (p. 6)

To legitimize their actions, slave masters created "Negro courts," which meted out punishments (Sellin, 1976).

In 1790, legislation was passed to create an institution in which solitary confinement and hard labor were required (Clear & Cole, 2000). In response to the legislation, the Quakers restructured the **Walnut Street Jail** (which began to receive prisoners in 1776) to fit the required specifications. At that moment, the Walnut Street Jail became America's first prison (Shelden, 2001). Reviewing the early prison records (1795–1826), McIntyre (1992) noted that the free African American population in Philadelphia ranged from 4.6% in 1790 to 9.4% in 1810. When she looked at prisoner statistics in the Walnut Street Jail, McIntyre found,

> Throughout the period from 1795 to 1826 in Philadelphia City and County, Blacks comprised 35% with "Mulattoes" equaling an additional 9%. This 44% reflected an inmate population for African Americans more than 13 times greater than the state's and nearly 5 times greater than the city's total African American population. (pp. 170–171)

Race and Corrections in the 1800s

As one might expect, soon the Walnut Street facility became overcrowded. To alleviate this overcrowding, as happens today, the legislature approved the construction of two prisons: Western Penitentiary (1826) and Eastern Penitentiary (1829). As a prelude of things to come, Clear and Cole (2000) noted that Prisoner Number 1, who arrived at the Eastern Penitentiary (near Philadelphia) on October 25, 1829, was "Charles Williams, an 18-year-old African American from Delaware County, Pennsylvania . . . serving a two-year sentence for larceny" (p. 35). Inmate records from 1829 to 1841 show that a steady stream of African Americans followed Williams into Eastern Penitentiary. An inspector's report of the records revealed that there were 1,353 prisoners from 1829 to 1841, "with a breakdown of 846 White inmates (823 males and 23 females) and 508 Black inmates (456 males and 52 females). The Black men represented 37.5% of all males, and the Black women equaled 66% of the females" (McIntyre, 1992, p. 171).

Other states had similar trends in relation to the racial composition of early correctional facilities. For example, from 1812 to 1832, the Maryland state prison in Baltimore "held 45% African American males and 68% African American females for a 51% overall Black inmate population" (McIntyre, 1992, p. 172). Over a 10-month period, from 1832 to 1833, records show that in Richmond, Virginia, on average 28% of the inmates were African American. Although African American men represented 22% of this number, African American women represented 100% of the female inmates (McIntyre, 1992).

Strikingly, according to these statistics, White women did not commit any crimes requiring incarceration during this period. A more likely explanation is that "the chivalry factor" was in effect for White women, but not Black women. That is, Southerners might have done all they could to protect White women from entering prisons, but such a consideration was not given to Black women.

So how did early observers of the system explain these disparities? When Beaumont and Tocqueville (1833/1964) visited the United States in the early 1800s to examine the feasibility of applying the American penitentiary system to France, they provided some early commentary on these disparities. Examining the trends in crime across the country, Beaumont and Tocqueville wrote, "In order to establish well-founded points of comparison between the various states, it would be necessary to deduct from the population of each the foreigners, and to compare only the crimes committed by the settled population" (p. 93). Even after doing this, Beaumont and Tocqueville (1833/1964) noted that Maryland had a high crime rate, which was, as they put it,

> explained by a cause peculiar to the southern states—the colored race. In general it has been observed, that in those states in which there exists one Negro to thirty Whites, the prisons contain one Negro to four White persons. (p. 93)

In their view, "The states which have many Negroes must therefore produce more crimes" (p. 93). Beaumont and Tocqueville (1833/1964) speculated that crime was high not just in Southern states, but, more specifically, those states that manumitted slaves. On this point, they opined,

> We should deceive ourselves greatly were we to believe that the crimes of the Negroes are avoided by giving them liberty; experience proves, on the

contrary, that in the south the number of criminals increases with that of manumitted persons; thus, for the very reason that slavery draws nearer to its ruin, the number of freed persons will increase for a long time in the south, and with it the number of criminals. (p. 93)

Without much more said, such statements could have been interpreted as arguing for the continued enslavement of Blacks. In addition, Christianson (1998) has aptly wondered why the two men did not see slavery as being criminogenic.

The mid-1800s brought African Americans closer to their eventual emancipation. However, as noted in Chapter 1, following their emancipation in 1863 and the passage of the Thirteenth Amendment in 1865, Southern landowners were devastated. Sellin (1976) noted that, following the passage of the Thirteenth Amendment,

The penal laws of the southern states became applicable to all offenders regardless of race. This was a distressing prospect for states which had created industrial penitentiaries for offenders from the master class and now faced the rapidly growing criminality of poor, unskilled, bewildered ex-slaves cast into a freedom for which few of them were prepared. (p. 145)

Sellin added that, although Blacks were legally free, Southern landowners "did not change their opinions on the status of Blacks in a society dominated by Whites" (p. 145). Because of Whites' "reluctance to labor," they created a system to maintain an able-bodied labor force (Sellin, 1976). Taking advantage of the language in the Thirteenth Amendment, which allowed slavery and involuntary servitude as punishment for certain crimes, Southern landowners created the convict lease system, which

Reintroduce[d] a species of slavery for Negro criminals and lower-class Whites. They were to be forced to do work which would more than compensate the state for their keep. The sole aim of the convict lease system was financial profit of the lessees who exploited the labor of the prisoners to the fullest, and to the government which sold the convicts to the lessees. (Sellin, 1976, p. 146)

Southern states invested in the system because it was profitable while also keeping taxes down (Oshinsky, 1996). To make the system work, the change in the racial composition of prison populations was dramatic. Oshinsky (1996) wrote,

In Alabama and Arkansas, Texas and Virginia, Florida and Georgia, North and South Carolina, Louisiana and Mississippi, the convict populations were overwhelmingly Black. Of South Carolina's 431 state prisoners in 1880, only 25 were White; of Georgia's 1,200 state prisoners in that year, almost 1,100 were Negro. (p. 63)

Furthermore, in Georgia, "Between 1870 and 1910, the convict population grew ten times faster than the general one. Prisoners became younger and Blacker, and the length of their sentences soared" (Oshinsky, 1996, p. 63). Records from Georgia prisons in the late 1800s showed that Blacks were serving sentences twice as long as Whites, with 50% of the inmates serving sentences of more than 10 years (Oshinsky, 1996).

Myers (1998) has shown the full extent of the racial dimension of punishment in Georgia. Looking at the Georgia system from 1870 to 1940, she chronicled the ups and downs of the convict lease system, as well as the use of other punishments (e.g., chain gangs) to provide services to the state (e.g., public roads projects). She noted that the trends in punishments were often dictated by economic factors such as depressions and recessions (Myers, 1998).

During the 1800s, race also intersected with gender in corrections. For a long time, women prisoners were housed in the same facilities as men (Young & Reviere, 2006). Because of overcrowding issues and scandals such as women prisoners becoming impregnated, during this time, several states built reformatories for women (Collins, 1997; LeFlouria, 2011). Although White women were initially housed in these facilities, Black women were later housed in segregated cottages. Prison officials justified their actions with ridiculous rationales, such as "a peculiar attraction has been found to exist between 'colored' and White women in confinement which intensifies much danger, always present in an institution, of homosexual involvement" (Lekkerkerker, 1931, cited in Collins, 1997, p. 10). Some officials, such as Katherine Bemet Davis, the first female corrections commissioner of New York City, refused to segregate female prisoners. More significant segregation took place in the housing of Black women in penitentiaries, whereas White women were housed in treatment-oriented reformatories. This segregation reduced the chance that Black women would be successful on their release from prison (Collins, 1997).

Early National Prison Statistics

The earliest national statistics on corrections were recorded in 1850, when the national census on prisons took a one-day count and recorded 6,737 prisoners. By 1860, there were an additional 13,000 prisoners, with records indicating 19,086 prisoners. Dramatic increases would occur over the next several decades: 1870 (32,901), 1880 (30,659), 1890 (45,233), and 1904 (57,070; Cahalan & Parsons, 1986). Tracking the trends by race and ethnicity, Table 8.1 shows that not only did state and federal prison populations increase, but the percentage of Blacks incarcerated also increased, from 31% in 1923 to 37% in 1960 (Cahalan & Parsons, 1986).

Figures from the 1931 Wickersham Commission Report show that in 1926, native-born Whites represented 68% of those in federal and state prisons. The racial breakdown for the remainder of the inmates was 8% foreign-born White, 21% Negro, and 3% Other (Indian, Mexican, Chinese, Japanese, and all other races; National Commission on Law Observance and Enforcement, 1931a). During this same period, Black females were also considerably represented in the nation's prisons. Russell-Brown (2004) presented figures that show that, from 1926 to 1946, the percentage of Black female prisoners fluctuated from a low of 21% to a high of 40% of the female inmates.

In the decades between the Reconstruction period and 1960, although much changed in terms of overall advancements for racial minorities, much stayed the same, with Blacks continuing to be overrepresented in state and federal correctional institutions. However, the 1960s saw the civil rights movement, the increasing visibility of Black Muslims, and the Black Power movement influenced both Black prisoners and various segments of the Black community.

Table 8.1

Characteristics of Persons in State and Federal Prisons, Institutional Population Census Data, 1910–1980

Year	Number of Prisons	Inmates Present	Female	Foreign-Born	White	Black	Other Races	Spanish Origin[a]	Juvenile (under 18)
					Percentage				
1910	61	67,871	4	—[b]	—[b]	—[b]	—[b]	—[b]	—[b]
1923	64	80,935	4	12	68	31	1	—[b]	2.0
1933[b]	117	137,997	3	(5)	(74)	(23)	(3)	—[b]	(3.9)
1950[c]	158	178,065	4	3	65	34	1	—[b]	2.9
1960[d]	1,072	226,344	4	1	61	37	2	—[b]	2.3
1970[e]	633	198,831	3	—[b]	58	41	—[b]	7	2.2
1980[f]	2,560[g]	302,377	5	3	47	44	—[b]	10	—[b]

Source: BJS (1986).

Notes:

a. Persons of Spanish origin may be of any race.

b. Not available or not obtained.

c. Except for the 3% female prison population, which is calculated on the basis of inmates present (137,997), details are calculated on the basis of prisoners received from courts (62,801) according to available data.

d. 1940 is excluded because juvenile facilities were not separated from state and federal. However, only those over 14 were enumerated. Detail data in 1950 were calculated on 3½% sample with an estimated base of 181,080 for total prison population; the complete count is 178,065.

e. Data based on 25% sample.

f. Data based on 20% sample.

g. Counted each budget unit as individual facility.

Black Muslims, the Black Panther Party, Political Prisoners, and the Prisoners' Rights Movement

Although each of the above movements can be credited with bringing to the fore issues related to police brutality, they each played a role in the evolution of corrections during the 1960s and 1970s as well. Prior to this period, Black inmates essentially accepted their status without any resistance (Reasons, Conley, & Debro, 2002). Reasons et al. (2002) noted that, although Blacks were exposed to inhumane conditions, they did not protest because "(1) the courts had a hands-off policy with respect to penal conditions and issues, and (2) the institutions were located primarily in rural areas and thus functioned in relative isolation, and the guards were all White" (p. 271). Discussing the importance of the mass migration from the South to northern and western states among African Americans, Reasons et al. wrote, "This demographic shift made racial segregation more difficult and expensive to maintain in all institutions, including penal institutions" (p. 271). Another contributor to change was the fact that leaders from the civil rights movement (e.g., Martin Luther King, Jr., Ralph Abernathy, and Medgar Evers), Black Panther movement (e.g., Stokely Carmichael, H. Rap Brown, Huey Newton, and Angela Davis), and Black Muslim movement (most notably, Malcolm X) were all incarcerated at some point and spoke out about their experiences (Reasons et al., 2002). It was, however, the Black Muslim and Black Panther movements that had the greatest influence on correctional systems.

Photo 8.1

Two chain gang prisoners in Georgia (1937).

Bettmann/Corbis.

According to Conley and Debro (2002), the Black Muslim (also known as the "Nation of Islam") movement in California prisons can be traced to San Quentin in the late 1950s. On the one hand, the movement was popular among Black inmates because, along with preaching racial pride, instituting strict discipline, and pushing for economic self-sufficiency, the group preached that Whites were evil and the cause of the current plight of African Americans (Reasons et al., 2002). On the other hand, correctional officials saw the movement as both a threat and "management problem," so they took steps to suppress the movement using a variety of strategies, including dispersing the members. Even with these strategies, the Black Muslims continued to challenge correctional policies in court.

Beginning with the 1962 case of *Fulwood v. Clemmer,* courts began to recognize the Black Muslim religion. Furthermore, this decision sparked the prisoners' rights movement, which resulted in thousands of lawsuits being filed by inmates. Some of these lawsuits resulted in substantive changes in the way correctional institutions were run. For example, in *Battle v. Anderson* (1974), following an earlier loss in the courts to maintain the right to read literature that was considered inflammatory, the courts reinforced inmates' First Amendment rights and provided that "prison officials had the burden of proving to the court that the publications *Elijah Muhammad Speaks* and *The Message to the Black Man in America* present[ed] a threat to security, discipline, and order within the institution" (Palmer, 2010, p. 86). A related case, *Northern v. Nelson* (1970), ruled that Black Muslims should have access to religious literature. Other cases challenged the request of Black Muslims to be served a pork-free diet (*Young v. Robinson,* 1981), the right to correspond with their religious leaders (*Desmond v. Blackwell,* 1964), and the right to free access to ministers (*Jones v. Willingham,* 1965). The efforts of Black Muslims to challenge correctional officials represent a monumental contribution to prisoners' rights.

One could argue that the early concerns expressed by correctional officials were somewhat exaggerated, but it also is likely that some of the disturbances caused by Black Muslims were instigated by prison officials (Conley & Debro, 2002). In recent years, the group has continued to be involved in correctional settings through the Nation of Islam Prison Reform Ministry, which has received several awards (Gabbidon, 2004).

During the 1960s and 1970s, the Black Panther Party also impacted corrections through its nationwide efforts to steer Black youth away from the criminal justice system. But it was the party's influence on several high-profile inmates that highlighted the abuses in correctional facilities. Inmates such as George Jackson typified the inmates who adhered to the "Black power" philosophy of the Black Panther Party. These inmates were often considered **political prisoners** or individuals who, based on their political, social, or environmental beliefs, are brought within the jurisdiction of the criminal justice system, with most of them eventually being incarcerated. Historically, the term *railroaded* was used to describe the swift and unfair manner in which political prisoners are handled. According to Aptheker (1971), some inmates become political prisoners while they are incarcerated. In particular, she writes that, "as soon as they give expression to their political views they become victims of politically inspired actions against them by the prison administration and the parole boards" (p. 47). Because of George Jackson's activism in prison, he represents one of the most notable political prisoners in American correctional history. Jackson's story began when he was 18 years old and

[He] was accused of stealing $70 from a gas station in Los Angeles. Though there was evidence of his innocence, his court-appointed lawyer maintained that because Jackson had a record (two previous instances of petty crime), he should plead guilty in exchange for a light sentence in the county jail. He did, and received an indeterminate sentence of one to life. Jackson spent the next ten years in Soledad Prison, seven and a half of them in solitary confinement. (G. Jackson, 1970, p. ix)

Jackson's case became a cause célèbre and was brought to even more prominence with his critically acclaimed work *Soledad Brother: The Prison Letters of George*

Jackson. The year after his book was published, Jackson was shot, on August 21, 1971, allegedly trying to escape. Jackson's influence was so wide, even among prisoners in other states, that the next day at Attica prison in New York,

> Inmates . . . graphically demonstrated their reaction to the shooting of Jackson. Instead of the usual banter and conversation of inmates coming out of their cells to line up for the march to breakfast, officers on many companies were greeted by somber inmates who moved silently out of their cells and lined up in rows of twos with a Black man at the head of each row; many of them wore Black armbands. (New York State Special Commission on Attica, 1972, pp. 139–140)

A few weeks later, Attica erupted in a riot that lasted four days, with 43 people killed and 80 wounded. Most of the dead (39 people) and all of the wounded were the result of the state police operation to take back the institution. Referring to that infamous assault, the preface to the report investigating the riot noted, "With the exception of the Indian massacres in the late 19th century, the State Police assault which ended the four-day prison uprising was the bloodiest one-day encounter between Americans since the Civil War" (New York State Special Commission on Attica, 1972, p. xi). In 2000, more than 25 years after the riot, former inmates and families of those inmates killed received a settlement of $12 million. However, the families of the employees of Attica never received any compensation. In an effort to remedy this, former New York Governor George Pataki appointed a task force to look into the claims of former correctional employees (Public Report of the Forgotten Victims of Attica, 2003).

The Attica riot rang in an era in which more scholars began to examine correctional institutions. What they found were highly segregated institutions with increasing Black and Hispanic populations (L. Carroll, 1974; Davidson, 1974). Each of these populations was struggling for control, which increased the level of violence within institutions. Coupled with the inhumane treatment and emerging overcrowding, the prisons throughout the country were susceptible to "rage riots," which, unlike the political riots of the late 1960s and early 1970s, were "very spontaneous and expressive, as most of the violence was directed at fellow inmates, rather than prison officials or the 'system' itself. Often they were the result of racial conflicts, especially between rival gangs" (Shelden & Brown, 2003, p. 304).

Prison Gangs

Prevalence and Racial/Ethnic Backgrounds of Prison Gangs

One of the earliest prison gangs was the "Gypsy Jokers" in Washington State prisons, where gangs have been present since the 1950s (Fleisher & Decker, 2001). Some researchers have estimated that the population of prison gang members ranges from 15,000 (Trulson, Marquart, & Kawuncha, 2006) to somewhere between 50,000 and 100,000 (Fleisher & Decker, 2001), while other researchers have estimated that 13% of the jail population, 12% to 17% of the prison population, and 9% of the federal prison population are gang members (Pyrooz, Decker, & Fleisher, 2011). Over time, the gangs have formed along racial/ethnic lines, which, with the burgeoning prison population, has perpetuated conflict within institutions. Some of the more infamous gangs include the Mexican Mafia (*La Eme*), the Black Guerilla Family, the Aryan Brotherhood, *Nuestra Familia* ("our family"), and the Texas Syndicate (Fleisher & Decker, 2001). The Mexican Mafia was the first prison gang with nationwide ties, whereas the Black Guerilla Family had its origins in the larger Black Panther movement and was politically oriented, having Marxist-Leninist leanings (Fleisher & Decker, 2001). The Aryan Brotherhood, a White supremacist gang, was started in 1967 "by inmates who wanted to oppose the racial threat of Black and Hispanic and/or counter the organization and activities of Black and Hispanic gangs" (Fleisher & Decker, 2001, p. 4). *Nuestra Familia* is a Hispanic prison gang that formed to provide protection against the Mexican Mafia. The Texas Syndicate is primarily composed of Mexicans/Hispanics.

Race and Prison Gang Activity

Other well-known street gangs such as the Crips and the Bloods have also been found in correctional institutions around the country. Table 8.2 provides a comparison of the characteristics of prison gangs and street gangs. Each of the various racial/ethnic gangs and the new ones that continue to emerge has caused its share of problems within correctional institutions. Some have argued that a considerable amount of the violence and drugs in prisons are attributable to prison gangs (G. M. Camp & Camp, 1985; Fleisher & Decker, 2001; Gaes, Wallace, Gilman, Klein-Saffran, & Suppa, 2002; Huebner, 2003; Varano, Huebner, & Bynum, 2011).

Griffin and Hepburn (2006) examined the notion that prison gangs have an impact on violence in prisons. In their study of a diverse sample of more than 2,000 Arizona inmates, they found support for this belief, reporting that: "Inmates with no gang affiliation were significantly less likely than those with either street gang affiliation or prison gang affiliation to have been guilty of violent misconduct in the first 3 years of confinement" (p. 434). The authors also found that

> assault misconduct was significantly more likely to occur among younger inmates and among White inmates. Compared to White inmates, African American inmates, Mexican American inmates, and inmates who were Mexican Nationals were significantly less likely to be guilty of a major misconduct for assault. Native American inmates, in contrast, were no more or less likely than White inmates to commit assault. (p. 436)

Sorenson, Cunningham, Vigen, and Woods (2011) studied serious assaults on prison staff in Texas during 14 months in 2007 and 2008 and found that nearly half the assaults were of White correctional officers (48.2%), followed by assaults on Hispanic (36.5%), and Black officers (14.1%). The attacks were largely on male correctional officers (76.7%). The researchers found that although Blacks represented slightly less than 40% of the inmates, they were involved in nearly 70% of the assaults. Black and White inmates were heavily involved in interracial assaults, while Hispanics were as likely to victimize other Hispanics as they were those outside their group. In their models, the authors found that "Black inmates and gang members were each three times more likely to be among the assaulters as the controls" (Sorenson et al., 2011, p. 148).

Given the security issues raised by the presence of prison gangs, correctional officials have had to use intelligence and other strategies to control institutions (Carlson, 2001; Scott, 2001). One strategy that had been used previously in California

Table 8.2

A Comparison of Prison and Street Gangs

Variable	Prison Gang	Street Gang
Race	Single race or ethnicity	Mostly single race or ethnicity
Age	Concentrated in mid-20s, with members into 30s-40s	Average age in upper teens
Organizational structure*	Hierarchical	Situational/hierarchical
Sources of violence	Symbolic and instrumental; core activity	Symbolic; core activity
Offending style**	Entrepreneurial	Cafeteria style
Visibility of behavior	Covert	Overt
Drug trafficking	Major activity; organized, collective	Varies; mostly individualistic
Loyalty to gang	Absolute	Weak bonds
Key to membership	Unqualified fidelity, abide by gang rules; willingness to engage in violence	Real or perceived fidelity; hanging out; abide by street rules
Key psychological attribute***	Oppositional, intimidation, control, manipulation	Oppositional, intimidation, camaraderie

Source: Original author/s, the journal title, volume, issue, page numbers and the copyright designation "© Emerald Group Publishing Limited all rights reserved."

Notes:

* *Situational* refers to structural flexibility from loose to more rigid.

** *Entrepreneurial activity* refers to specific types of profit-generating activity. *Cafeteria-style activity* refers to a range of profit-generating and nonprofit activities.

*** *Oppositional* refers to attitudes toward correctional supervision in the case of prison gangs. For street gangs, it reflects a generalized opposition to authority.

was to segregate offenders by race. However, in the Supreme Court case *Johnson v. California* (2005), it was ruled that such practices were unconstitutional. Prisons use other measures such as segregating gangs into separate units, using prison informants, isolating gang leaders, locking down institutions, prosecuting gang members who engage in crime, interfering with gang communications, and scrutinizing gang offenses (Pyrooz et al., 2011). Unfortunately, there has been limited research evaluating these measures. Winterdyk and Ruddell (2010) took up this challenge by sending surveys to 37 correctional systems (incarcerating 1.19 million inmates) representing public and private correctional facilities across the United States to determine the effectiveness of some prison gang suppression measures. Table 8.3 provides a summary of the

Table 8.3

Effectiveness of STG Management Strategies

Programs or Responses	Percentage			
	Very Effective	Somewhat Effective	Not Effective	Not Applicable
Segregation/isolation	75	18.8	0	6.3
Specialized housing units	50	18.8	0	31.3
Restrictions on privileges				
Visits	64.7	17.6	5.9	11.8
Program participation	29.4	58.8	5.9	5.9
Commissary/canteen	31.3	25.0	6.3	37.5
Participation in employment	31.3	18.8	12.5	37.5
Access to community	25	12.5	12.5	50.0
Access to communication	42.9	21.4	0	35.7
Loss of good-time credits	31.3	18.8	0	50.0
Delay parole eligibility	37.5	12.5	0	50.0
Control release destination	26.7	13.3	0	60.0
Increase of security rating/ classification	41.2	23.5	0	35.3
Gang-free prisons	6.7	20.0	0	73.3

Source: Winterdyk & Ruddell (2010).

effectiveness of the various gang management strategies (also referred to as security threat group strategies, or STG) being used in prisons across the country. As seen in the table, segregation/isolation, specialized housing units, and restrictions on privileges are perceived to be the most effective strategies. This important study hopefully represents the first of many that will assess the measures being used to suppress violent and disruptive prison gangs. The next section reviews the current state of corrections.

❖ Contemporary State of Corrections

In 2013, there were more than 2.2 million people incarcerated in the United States (Glaze & Kaeble, 2014). The incarceration rate in 2013 was 478 persons per 100,000 persons in the U.S. population (Carson, 2014). Table 8.4 shows the incarceration rate from 2003 to 2013. It shows a small but steady reduction. The figures for persons under **community**

Imprisonment Rate of Sentenced State and Federal Prisoners per 100,000 U.S. Residents, by Sex, Race, Hispanic Origin, and Age, December 31, 2013

Age	Total[c]	Male					Female				
		Total Male[a]	White[b]	Black[b]	Hispanic	Other[a,b]	Total Female[a]	White[b]	Black[b]	Hispanic	Other[a,b]
Total[c]	478	904	466	2,805	1,134	963	65	51	113	66	90
18–19	181	340	115	1,092	412	344	14	7	33	17	24
20–24	755	1,382	601	3,956	1,617	1,472	95	73	154	100	131
25–29	1,607	1,937	954	5,730	2,289	2,082	168	140	260	173	232
30–34	1,187	2,183	1,104	6,746	2,529	2,257	180	156	277	169	235
35–39	1,071	1,994	1,009	6,278	2,321	1,951	151	133	240	133	178
40–44	917	1,713	938	5,244	2,007	1,730	131	113	224	107	144
45–49	782	1,464	827	4,486	1,700	1,495	112	90	202	99	135
50–54	567	1,082	615	3,382	1,382	1,171	70	54	128	72	94
55–59	348	679	389	2,132	1,016	750	36	26	72	44	52
60–64	208	415	252	1,269	714	497	19	14	34	25	27
65 or older	70	153	108	406	301	206	5	4	7	8	8
Total number of sentenced prisoners	1,516,879	1,412,745	454,100	526,000	314,600	118,100	104,134	51,500	23,100	17,600	11,900

Sources: Bureau of Justice Statistics, National Prisoner Statistics Program, 2013; Federal Justice Statistics Program, 2013; National Corrections Reporting Program, 2012; Survey of Inmates in State and Federal Correctional Facilities, 2004; and U.S. Census Bureau, resident population estimates for January 1, 2014.

Note: Counts based on prisoners with sentences of more than a year under the jurisdiction of state or federal correctional officials. Imprisonment rate is the number of prisoners under state or federal jurisdiction with a sentence of more than a year per 100,000 U.S. residents of corresponding sex, age, and race or Hispanic origin. Resident population estimates are from the U.S. Census Bureau for January 1 of the following year. Nevada did not submit 2013 data to NPS, and Alaska did not submit sex-specific counts or sentence length data in 2013.

a. Includes American Indians, Alaska Natives, Asians, Native Hawaiians, Pacific Islander, persons of two or more races, or additional racial categories in the reporting information systems.

b. Excludes persons of Hispanic or Latino origin.

c. Includes persons age 17 or younger.

supervision also show modest declines since 2005. In 2013, there were 4,751,400 adults under community supervision, including probation and parole (Glaze & Kaeble, 2014).

Reviewing the trends by race/ethnicity and gender, in 2013, Black males had the highest incarceration rates at 2,805 inmates per 100,000 Black male U.S. residents. This incarceration rate amounted to "Almost 3% of black male U.S. residents of all ages being imprisoned on December 31, 2013" (Carson, 2014, p. 8). Hispanics/Latino males followed Blacks with an incarceration rate of 1,134 per 100,000 (1% of Hispanic/Latino males), and Whites had the lowest rate at 466 per 100,000 (0.5% of White males; p. 8). While there has been some reduction in prison populations, Black men still comprised the largest share of inmates in state or federal prisons (526,000 prisoners). Whites were second (454,100 prisoners), followed by Hispanic males (314,600; Carson, 2014). One particularly disturbing racial disparity revealed by an analysis of the imprisonment data was that Black males in the age group 18 to 19 were "more than 9 times more likely to be imprisoned than white males" (p. 8).

Turning to the state of incarcerated women, the data also show that Black females had the highest incarceration rates at 113 per 100,000, followed by Hispanic females at 66 per 100,000, and White females at 51 per 100,000. Notably, there was a similar racial disparity in the 18- to 19-year-old imprisonment data for females; in particular, Black females in this age group were five times more likely than White females to be imprisoned. In actual numbers, in 2013, there were more White women incarcerated (51,500) in state and federal prisons than Black women (23,100) and Hispanic women (17,600; Carson, 2014, p. 9).

❖ Jails

Table 8.5 shows the significant increases in jail populations from 2000 to 2013. During this period, the number of Whites in jails increased from 260,500 in 2000 to 344,900 in 2013, whereas the number of Blacks increased from 256,300 to 261,500. Over the same period, the number of Hispanics held in jails increased from 94,100 in 2000 to 107,900 in 2013 (Minton & Golinelli, 2014). In 2013, the racial composition of jails was as follows: 47% White, 36% Black, and 15% Hispanic (Minton & Golinelli, 2014).

There are also separate jail facilities in Indian country (see Table 8.6). According to Minton (2014), in 2013, there were 2,287 inmates in 79 jails located in Indian country. Of the inmates incarcerated in these facilities, 32% were being held for violent offenses (domestic violence, assault, and rape or sexual assault), 17% for public intoxication, 8% for DWI/DUI, and 4% for drug law violations. Overall, the trend in many Indian country jails was a decrease in admissions and short stays averaging about 5.9 days (Minton, 2014).

Probation and Parole

In 2013, there were 4,751,400 men and women being supervised on probation or parole. Racial and ethnic data from 2013 for those on probation reveals that Whites comprised 54% of those on probation, with Blacks representing 30%, Hispanics 14%, and Asians and American Indians each representing 1% (Herberman & Bonczar, 2014). Of those on parole in 2013, Whites represented 43%, Blacks 38%, Hispanics 17%, 1% Asians, and 1% American Indian/Alaskan Native (Herberman & Bonczar, 2014). At the federal level, Table 8.7 shows that there were 131,732 offenders under supervision, either on probation, parole,

Table 8.5

Number of Inmates in Local Jails, by Characteristics, Midyear 2000 and 2005–2013

Characteristic	2000	2005	2006	2007	2008	2009	2010	2011[a]	2012[a]	2013[a]
Total[b]	621,149	747,529	765,819	780,174	785,533	767,434	748,728	735,601	744,524	731,208
Sex										
Male	550,162	652,958	666,819	679,654	685,862	673,728	656,360	642,300	645,900	628,900
Female	70,987	94,571	99,000	100,520	99,670	93,706	92,368	93,300	98,600	102,400
Adult	613,534	740,770	759,717	773,341	777,829	760,216	741,168	729,700	739,100	726,600
Male	543,120	646,807	661,164	673,346	678,657	667,039	649,284	636,900	640,900	624,700
Female	70,414	93,963	98,552	99,995	99,712	93,176	91,884	92,800	98,100	101,900
Juvenile[c]	7,615	6,759	6,102	6,833	7,703	7,218	7,560	5,900	5,400	4,600
Held as adult[d]	6,126	5,750	4,835	5,649	6,410	5,846	5,647	4,600	4,600	3,500
Held as juvenile	1,489	1,009	1,268	1,184	1,294	1,373	1,912	1,400	900	1,100
Race/Hispanic origin[e]										
White[f]	260,500	331,000	336,500	338,200	333,300	326,400	331,600	329,400	341,100	344,900
Black/African American	256,300	290,500	295,900	301,700	308,000	300,500	283,200	276,400	274,600	261,500
Hispanic/Latino	94,100	111,900	119,200	125,500	128,500	124,000	118,100	113,900	112,700	107,900
American Indian/Alaska Native[f,g]	5,500	7,600	8,400	8,600	9,000	9,400	9,900	9,400	9,300	10,200
Asian/Native Hawaiian/Other Pacific Islander	4,700	5,400	5,100	5,300	5,500	5,400	5,100	5,300	5,400	5,100
Two or more races	. . .	1,000	700	800	1,300	1,800	800	1,200	1,500	1,6000

Sources: Bureau of Justice Statistics, *Annual Survey of Jails,* 2000 and midyear 2006–2013, and the *Census of Jail Inmates.*

Note: Detail may not sum to total due to rounding.

. . . Not collected.

a. Data for 2011–2013 are adjusted for nonresponse and rounded to the nearest 100.

b. Midyear count is the number of inmates held on the last weekday in June.

c. Persons age 17 or younger at midyear.

d. Includes juveniles who were tried or awaiting trial as adults.

e. Data adjusted for nonresponse and rounded to the nearest 100.

f. Excludes persons of Hispanic or Latino origin.

g. Previous reports combined American Indians and Alaska Natives and Asians, Native Hawaiians, and other Pacific Islanders into an Other race category.

Table 8.6

Inmates Confined in Indian Country Jails, by Demographic Characteristic, Conviction Status, and Offense, Midyear 2000 and 2010–2013

Characteristic	Number of Inmates[a]					Percentage of Inmates				
	2000	2010	2011	2012	2013	2000	2010	2011	2012	2013
Total	1,775	2,119	2,239	2,364	2,287	100	100	100	100	100
Sex										
Male	1,421	1,639	1,743	1,831	1,699	80	77	78	78	76
Female	354	480	496	526	551	20	23	22	22	24
Age group										
Adults	1,498	1,866	2,002	2,109	2,060	84	88	89	89	92
Male	1,214	1,479	1,583	1,660	1,581	68	70	71	70	70
Female	284	387	419	449	479	16	18	19	19	21
Juveniles	277	253	237	248	190	16	12	11	11	8
Male	207	160	160	171	118	12	8	7	7	5
Female	70	93	77	77	72	4	4	3	3	3
Conviction status										
Convicted	1,072	1,240	1,247	1,279	1,243	61	59	57	56	56
Unconvicted	689	879	928	993	964	39	41	43	44	44

Characteristic	Number of Inmates[a]					Percentage of Inmates				
	2000	2010	2011	2012	2013	2000	2010	2011	2012	2013
Type of offense										
Violent offense	. . .	651	646	692	697	. . .	31	30	32	32
Domestic violence	. . .	276	262	314	332	. . .	13	12	15	15
Aggravated or simple assault	. . .	226	254	188	216	. . .	11	12	9	10
Rape or sexual assault	. . .	39	36	36	44	. . .	2	2	2	2
Other violence	. . .	110	94	154	105	. . .	5	4	7	5
Burglary	. . .	. . .	. . .	. . .	36	. . .	. . .	. . .	. . .	2
Larceny-theft[b]	. . .	. . .	. . .	. . .	30	. . .	. . .	. . .	. . .	1
Public intoxication[c]	. . .	. . .	. . .	. . .	368	. . .	. . .	. . .	. . .	17
DWI/DUI[d]	274	218	231	219	178	17	10	11	10	8
Drug offense	133	95	116	115	93	8	5	5	5	4
Other offense[e]	. . .	1,144	1,175	1,108	780	. . .	54	54	52	36
Not reported	. . .	11	71	230	105	/	/	/	/	/

Source: Bureau of Justice Statistics, *Annual Survey of Jails in Indian Country,* 2000 and 2010–2013.

Notes: Detail may not sum to total due to incomplete data. Totals based on facilities who reported characteristic data.

. . . Not collected.

/ Not reported.

a. The number of inmates held on the last weekday in June.

b. Excludes motor vehicle theft.

c. Includes drunk and disorderly.

d. Includes driving while intoxicated and driving while under the influence of drugs or alcohol.

e. In 2013, BJS started collecting data on burglary, larceny-theft, and public intoxication. As a result, other unspecified offenses in prior years are not comparable to 2013.

Table 8.7

Characteristics of Offenders Under Federal Supervision, September 30, 2012

Offender Characteristic	Total Offenders Under Supervision		Probation		Supervised Release		Parole	
	Number	Percentage	Number	Percentage	Number	Percentage	Number	Percentage
All offenders*	131,732	100	22,307	100	107,802	100	1,623	100
Sex								
Male	106,875	81.3	13,893	63.2	91,396	84.8	1,586	97.7
Female	24,526	18.7	8,093	36.8	16,396	15.2	37	2.3
Race								
White	74,302	56.8	14,488	66.6	59,242	55.2	572	35.7
Black/African American	49,203	37.6	5,586	25.7	42,622	39.7	995	62.0
American Indian/Alaska Native	3,207	2.5	721	3.3	2,459	2.3	27	1.7
Asian/Native Hawaiian/Other Pacific Islander	3,479	2.7	796	3.7	2,676	2.5	7	0.4
Two or more races	530	0.4	170	0.8	357	0.3	3	0.2
Hispanic/Latino origin								
Hispanic/Latino	28,920	22.3	4,392	20.4	24,393	22.9	135	8.5
Non-Hispanic/Latino	100,733	77.7	17,137	79.6	82,151	77.1	1,445	91.5
Age								
18 or younger	301	0.2	249	1.1	52	–	0	. . .
19–20	1,586	1.2	749	3.4	836	0.8	1	0.1
21–30	31,851	24.2	5,804	26.4	25,925	24.0	122	7.5
31–40	45,168	34.4	5,510	25.1	39,290	36.4	368	22.7
41 or older	52,464	39.9	9,639	43.9	41,694	38.7	1,131	69.7

Source: Bureau of Justice Statistics, based on data from the Administrative Office of the U.S. Courts, Federal Probation and Supervision Information System (FPSIS), 2012.

Note:

* Total includes offenders whose offense characteristic could not be determined.

— Less than 0.05%.

. . . No cases of this type occurred in the data.

or supervised release. The table shows that most of the federal offenders under supervision are either White (56.8%), Black (37.6%), or Hispanic/Latino (22.3%; Motivans, 2015).

Taken together, the statistics presented in this section have led some to speculate about the causes of the considerable growth of American corrections. In Box 8.2, two leading figures in the **mass incarceration** dialogue tackle some of the most persistent myths pertaining to incarceration. As the figures presented in this chapter reveal, Blacks and Hispanics are overrepresented in nearly all areas of corrections. Whether this is a product of discrimination has been an ongoing question during the last two decades (Mann, 1993; MacDonald, 2003, 2008; Morgan & Smith, 2008; Walker et al., 2012; Wilbanks, 1987). Along with this question, race-related topics surface when considering correctional systems in America. In the next section, we begin with a review of the most salient scholarship that has been used to explain the disparities reviewed here. Furthermore, we look at several other contemporary issues related to race and corrections: prisoner reentry and felony disenfranchisement.

BOX 8.2

Five Myths About Incarceration

No country on Earth imprisons more people per capita than the United States. But for America, mass incarceration has proved a losing proposition. The Supreme Court recently found California's overcrowded prisons unconstitutional, and state legislators want to cut the vast amounts of public money spent on prison warehousing.

Why are so many Americans in prison, and which ones can be safely released? Let's address some common misunderstandings about our incarceration problem.

1. Crime has fallen because incarceration has risen.

U.S. crime rates are the lowest in 40 years, but it's not clear how much of this drop is a result of locking up more people.

In Canada, for example, violent crime declined in the 1990s almost as much as it did in the United States. Yet, Canada's prison population dropped during this time, and its per capita incarceration rate is about one-seventh that of the United States. Moreover, while U.S. incarceration rates have steadily risen for four decades, our crime rate has fluctuated—rising through the 1970s, falling and then rising in the 1980s, and falling since 1993.

Harvard University sociologist Bruce Western believes that increased incarceration accounts for only about 10 percent of the drop in crime rates; William Spelman, a professor of public affairs at the University of Texas, puts the figure at about 25 percent. Even if the higher figure is accurate, three-quarters of the crime decline had nothing to do with imprisonment. Other causes include changes in drug markets, policing strategies, and community initiatives to reshape behavior.

2. The prison population is rising because more people are being sentenced to prison.

In the 1980s and early 1990s, the number of people sent to prison grew mainly because of the war on drugs. The number of drug offenders sentenced to state prisons increased by more than 300 percent from 1985 to 1995.

(Continued)

(Continued)

Since then, however, longer prison terms more than new prison sentences have fueled the prison population expansion. These are a result of mandatory sentencing measures such as "three strikes" laws and limits on parole release. Today, 140,000 prisoners, or one of 11 inmates, are incarcerated for life, many with no chance of parole.

Longer stays in prison offer diminishing returns for public safety. As prisoners age, the likelihood that they will commit crimes drops, but the cost of their imprisonment rises, primarily because of increased medical care. Harsher sentences also offer little deterrence: When people consider committing crimes, they may think about whether they will be caught, but probably not about how harshly they will be punished. In 1999, the Institute of Criminology at Cambridge University reviewed studies of deterrence and sentencing and found no basis "for inferring that increasing the severity of sentences generally is capable of enhancing deterrent effects."

3. Helping prisoners rejoin society will substantially reduce the prison population.

Ninety-five percent of American prisoners will return home someday. While reentry programs can aid reintegration into the community, they do little to reduce our reliance on incarceration. Prison appears to make inmates as likely to commit crime as not; about half of released inmates return to prison within three years. Congress appropriated only $83 million for reentry in fiscal year 2011, or less than $120 per released prisoner. Even with additional state funds, one is not likely to overcome a lifetime of low educational attainment, substance abuse and/or mental health disabilities with this meager commitment.

Investing in prevention and treatment instead of imprisonment is more likely to shrink the prison population. The Washington State Institute for Public Policy, for example, found that home-based supervision of juvenile offenders produced $28 in taxpayer benefits for every dollar invested.

4. There's a link between race and crime.

Yes, African Americans and Latinos disproportionately commit certain crimes. But in a 1996 study of crime rates in Columbus, Ohio, criminologists from Ohio State University concluded that socioeconomic disadvantages "explain the overwhelming portion of the difference in crime."

Nowhere are racial disparities in criminal justice more evident than in drug law enforcement. In 2003, black men were nearly 12 times more likely to be sent to prison for a drug offense than White men. Yet, national household surveys show that Whites and African Americans use and sell drugs at roughly the same rates. African Americans, who are 12 percent of the population and about 14 percent of drug users, make up 34 percent of those arrested for drug offenses and 45 percent of those serving time for such offenses in state prisons. Why?

In large measure, because police find drugs where they look for them. Inner-city, open-air drug markets are easier to bust than those that operate out of suburban basements, and numerous studies show that minorities are stopped by police more often than Whites. For example, a Center for Constitutional Rights study found that 87 percent of the 575,000 people stopped by the police in New York City in 2009 were African American or Latino.

5. Racial disparities in incarceration reflect police and judges' racial prejudice.

Shocking instances of racism still come to light in the justice system. But racist cops and courts are not the primary reason for racial disparities in incarceration.

Consider increased penalties for drug offenses in school zones. Though not racially motivated, these laws disproportionately affect minorities, who more often live in densely populated urban areas with many nearby schools. In New Jersey, for example, 96 percent of people incarcerated under such laws in 2005 were African American or Latino. Judges didn't necessarily want to sentence these defendants to more prison time than those convicted outside school zones, but under the law, they had to.

Where we spend money also contributes to the problem. The Violent Crime Control and Law Enforcement Act of 1994 appropriated $9.7 billion for prisons and $13.6 billion for law enforcement, but only $6.1 billion for crime prevention. Politicians eager to be seen as tough on crime too often find ways to fund new prison cells, even though they know that minorities will predominantly fill them. This isn't the fault of racist individuals. It's the fault of a system that fails to take the promise of equality seriously.

The United States imprisons a larger proportion of its population than Russia or Belarus. Our incarceration rate is eight times that of France. These tragic statistics force us to ask: Would the American public accept these rates if incarceration were distributed more equally across race and class?

Source: Mauer and Cole (2011).

1. Do you believe that there would be less acceptance of the current rates of incarceration if they "were distributed more equally across race and class"?

❖ Contemporary Issues in Race and Corrections

Explaining Racial Disparities in Corrections

Blumstein's Pioneering Work

During the early 1980s, scholars began to examine in earnest the racial disparities in corrections (see, e.g., Christianson, 1981; Petersilia, 1983). It is, however, the work of Blumstein (1982) that is most used as the benchmark study for explaining racial disproportionality in prisons. In Blumstein's state-level study, he investigated the role of discrimination in Black overrepresentation in prisons. Taking into account arrest patterns of Blacks and Whites, Blumstein found "that 80% of the actual racial disproportionality in incarceration rates is accounted for by differential involvement in arrest" (pp. 1267–1268). Although he noted that this explains the majority of the racial differences in incarceration, Blumstein also noted that if the unexplained 20% (which at the time translated to 10,500 prisoners) of overrepresentation of Blacks in prison "were attributable to discrimination, that would be a distressing level of discrimination" (p. 1268). It is important to note that, although Blumstein's work has become one of the benchmark studies in this area, his analysis is based on arrest statistics, which, as noted in Chapter 2, have serious limitations.

Pointing to other possible explanations for the disproportionality, Blumstein (1982) suggested that although Blacks are more involved in the most serious types of offenses, they may also be involved in the more serious "versions *within* each of the offense types (e.g., *stranger-stranger* homicides, in the *armed* robberies, etc.)" (p. 1268). Furthermore, he pointed to the possibility that Black offenders might accumulate longer criminal records. Noting the complexity of various extraneous factors that could impact on the accuracy of studies like his, Blumstein pointed to research that showed that, in some instances, "Discrimination in the criminal justice system might work in the opposite direction, resulting in Black offenders receiving more favorable treatment than White offenders" (p. 1269). More specifically, using rape cases as an example, he wrote,

> Because less certain and less severe punishment results when the victim is Black, and because the victims of Black offenders more often are Black, this could result in Black defendants being treated less severely than White defendants. Thus, this act of discrimination against Black *victims* could result in discrimination in favor of Black *offenders.* (p. 1269)

Blumstein also suggested that regional issues, educational issues, and socioeconomic factors could all play roles in explaining the unexplained 20%. He noted, however,

> Even after taking into account all factors that are at least arguably legitimate and that could explain the racial disproportionality in prison, it would certainly not be surprising to find a residual effect that is explainable only as racial discrimination. (Blumstein, 1982, p. 1270)

Following the publication of Blumstein's work, other scholars sought to test some of his findings. Focusing on arrest and prison admissions data for three years in North Carolina, Hawkins (1986) found that from 1978 to 1979, 30% of the prison disproportionality was explained by arrest patterns.

For the subsequent two years, Hawkins (1986) noted that the figures increased to 40% and 42%. In line with Blumstein's earlier supposition for certain crimes, Hawkins's research showed that Blacks received more favorable sentences than Whites. Specifically, Hawkins found that "fewer Blacks than White assault offenders received prison sentences. Fewer Blacks than Whites also received prison terms for larceny and armed robbery" (p. 260). These findings were in line with Hawkins's earlier work noting that, in certain contexts, Black life was devalued and resulted in justice officials minimizing Black-on-Black offenses, which manifested itself in less serious punishments for such offenses (Hawkins, 1983).

Using state-level arrest and prison data for 39 states (with a 1% or greater Black population), Hawkins and Hardy (1989) found some variation across states. For example, their study revealed,

> In nine states the level of arrest explains only 40% or less of Black-White imprisonment rate differences. On the other hand, for six other states the level of arrests explains more than 80%. Thus, even allowing for some discrepancy due to differences in data sources, Blumstein's figure of 80% would not seem to be a good approximation for all states. (Hawkins & Hardy, 1989, p. 79)

Racial Disparities in Corrections Scholarship

The 1990s found more researchers concentrating on racial disparities in corrections. At the beginning of the decade, two nonprofit organizations, the Sentencing Project and the National Center on Institutions and Alternatives (NCIA), released reports that highlighted the control rates for African Americans. Russell-Brown (2004) noted that such rates "refer to the percentage of a population that is under the jurisdiction of the criminal justice system—on probation, parole, in jail, or in prison. It provides a snapshot of a group's overall involvement in the justice system" (pp. 123–124).

In 1990, the Sentencing Project released a report that showed that "almost one in four African American males in the age group of 20–29 was under some form of criminal justice supervision" (Mauer, 1990). In April 1992, J. G. Miller (1992a) of the NCIA reported,

> On an average day in 1991, 21,800 (42%) of Washington, D.C.'s 53,375 African American males ages 18 through 35 were either in jail or prison, on probation or parole, out on bond awaiting disposition of criminal charges or being sought on an arrest warrant. (p. 1)

Five months later, J. G. Miller (1992b) returned to the subject, reporting that "of the 60,715 African American males age 18–35 in Baltimore, 56% were under criminal justice supervision on any given day in 1991" (p. 1). Updating their report in 1995, the Sentencing Project found things had worsened since 1990, reporting that "nearly one in three (32.2%) of African American males in the age group 20–29—827,440—is under criminal justice supervision on any given day—in prison, or jail, on probation or parole" (Mauer & Huling, 1995). An update of the NCIA's reports also noted that things had worsened in Washington, DC (Lotke, 1998).

During the release of these important reports, Blumstein (1993) also returned to the task of seeking to explain some of these disparities. Blumstein noted that the situation had marginally worsened, with 24% of the disproportionality of Blacks in prison not being explained by offending patterns. More specifically, he wrote,

> The bulk of the disproportionality is a consequence of the differential involvement in the most serious kinds of crime like homicide and robbery, where the ratio of arrests is between five and ten to one. For these crimes, the race ratio in prison is still very close to that at arrest. (Blumstein, 1993, p. 6)

However, there was a disparity related to less serious offenses (i.e., drug offenses). To explain these disparities, Blumstein (1993) surmised that, because of the increased level of discretion in less serious offenses, factors such as discrimination could be contributing to the disparity.

The early 1990s also saw concerns being expressed about the increasing expenditures on prisons and the decreasing spending on education (Chambliss, 1991). Sometime during the decade, prisons became "hot commodities"; unlike in prior years, communities, especially in rural areas hit hard by economic downturns, saw them as desirable for their overall economic impact (Lotke, 1996). Some states, like Florida, created brochures to promote the economic impact of prisons for prospective communities. Residents were told that a 1,100-person rated capacity prison could produce $25 million annually in revenue and create 350 jobs (Lotke, 1996). Downtrodden rural communities bit on the carrot, which is reflected by the fact that 5% of the increase in rural populations between 1980 and 1990 was attributed to prisons (Lotke, 1996).

Huling (2002) noted that, prior to 1990, 36% of prisons were built in nonmetropolitan areas. Furthermore, according to her figures, "Between 1990 and 1999, 245 prisons were built in rural and small town communities—with a prison opening somewhere in rural America every fifteen days" (p. 198). Noting that the economic impact is often overstated, she pointed to the "hidden" costs, such as increasing cost for local court and police services and the fact that some industries might be discouraged from investing in an area where a prison was located. Another unanticipated consequence of placing prisons in rural areas is the prevalence of racism in many rural communities. Such racism is a problem for guards and inmates. Huling (2002) provided an illustration of such problems:

> In at least six states, guards have appeared in mock Klan attire in recent years. Guards have also been accused of race-based threats, beatings and shootings in ten states. Lawsuits have been filed in at least thirteen states by Black guards alleging racist harassment or violence from White colleagues. (pp. 208–209)

In Washington State, a rural institution (Clallam Bay Correctional Center) had only 4 Black officers out of 326 correctional officers. The Black officers eventually filed a lawsuit (which was settled out of court for $250,000), claiming,

> Black officers were denied promotions, subject to threats and racial epithets like "coon," and the minority prisoners were harassed and set up for beatings. Some White guards had taken to calling Martin Luther King, Jr., Day "Happy Nigger Day" and a handful of guards openly bragged about associations with hate groups such as the Ku Klux Klan. (Huling, 2002, p. 209)

The late 1990s and early 2000s saw scholars seeking to explain disparities in corrections with radical critiques that referred to the "**prison-industrial complex**." Writers such as Parenti (1999) and Dyer (2000) have argued that government and citizens were profiting from the mass incarceration of principally African Americans and Hispanics. Private prison companies such as Corrections Corporation of America and the GEO Group, Inc. were in some cases found unknowingly in the retirement portfolios of many Americans (Dyer, 2000). As such, society was "investing" in prisons, which obviously relied on an ample supply of prisoners to keep the prison boom going (Dyer, 2000; Hallett, 2006; Price, 2006). Other writers of the period stressed the rebirth of the convict lease system in the form of the modern-day use of cheap prison labor by private companies partnering with state corrections departments (Davis, 1997, 2000, 2003). Scholars of this genre believe that because of the continuing need for bodies to keep the prison-industrial complex going, disparities in corrections will likely persist. Today, there remains a continuing reliance on privatization. In fact, **private prisons** housed 7% of the incarcerated adults in state and federal prisons in 2007 (Sigler, 2010). In addition, 35 states (and Washington, DC) have private prisons. The federal government has 11.5% of their inmates housed in private prisons, while "at the end of 2007, Immigration and Customs Enforcement housed about 38% of its detainees in privately managed facilities" (Sigler, 2010, p. 150).

In response to the growing prison-industrial complex that has become a global problem (see Sudbury, 2005), the critical resistance movement was forged after a national conference in 1998 (see http://www.criticalresistance.org). The aim of the movement is to dismantle the prison-industrial complex "by challenging the belief that policing, surveillance, imprisonment, and similar forms of control make . . . communities [of color] safe." To date, the movement has sued the California Department of Corrections to prevent it from building a new maximum-security prison. In addition, several regional chapters have been formed, and the organization has focused on educating communities about the prison-industrial complex. In September, 2008, the organization held its 10th anniversary conference in Oakland, California.

In the 2000s, scholars have continued to examine disparities (Crutchfield, 2004; Fernandez & Bowman, 2004; Mauer, 2004, 2006; Sorenson, Hope, & Stemen, 2003; Western, 2006), but there has been more of an emphasis on the consequences of mass incarceration on communities in general and minority communities in particular (see Alexander, 2010; Clear, 2007; Loury, 2008; Wacquant, 2000, 2001, 2011; Wildeman & Wakefield, 2014). Disparities in prisons create what some call "**collateral consequences**" or by-products of the decision to incarcerate so many minority offenders. Two additional concerns related to corrections are prisoner reentry and felony disenfranchisement. We discuss prisoner reentry concerns first.

Prisoner Reentry Concerns

Reentry is a critical concern because one recent report placed the **recidivism** rate (as measured by three-year return to prison rate) across the United States at approximately 40% (The Pew Center on the States, 2011). More recently, a Bureau of Justice Statistics report that relied on data from 30 states found that 67.8% of the 404,638 state prisoners released in 2005 had recidivated by 2008; after five years, that figure rose to 76.6% (Durose, Cooper, & Snyder, 2014). Thus, because of the mass incarceration that took place in the 1980s and 1990s, America has more offenders being released and likely to be recidivists than ever before (Durose et al., 2014; Glaze & Bonczar, 2010; Petersilia, 2003; Travis, 2005). Table 8.8 shows the recidivism trends by offense and race and ethnicity.

Moreover, because sentences were extended and 16 states eliminated parole (Hughes, James Wilson, & Beck, 2001), more prisoners than ever before have spent and continue to spend extended periods of time incarcerated. Herberman and Bonczar (2014) indicated that, at the end of 2013, there were 853,200 persons on parole (see Table 8.8). In addition to those on parole, thousands of persons "max out," or complete their entire sentences and leave prison without any supervision. Considering that a large share of those persons sentenced to jails and prisons are minorities, it is only logical that the majority of those coming home will also be minorities. Unfortunately, in 2013, 14% of those persons exiting parole were either returned to incarceration, absconded, or failed to meet the conditions of supervision (Herberman & Bonczar, 2014, p. 8). Such figures speak to the need to explore prisoner reentry issues.

Petersilia (2003) defined *prisoner reentry* as "all activities and programming conducted to prepare ex-convicts to return safely to the community and to live as law-abiding citizens" (p. 3). According to Petersilia (2002), the key factors that contribute to failure on both probation and parole (which has been eliminated at the federal level and in some states) include the following:

Table 8.8

Recidivism of Prisoners Released in 30 States in 2005, by Race or Hispanic Origin, Most Serious Commitment Offense, and Time From Release to First Arrest

Race/Hispanic Origin and Most Serious Commitment Offense	Cumulative Percent of Released Prisoners Arrested Within—							
	6 Months	1 Year	2 Years	3 Years	4 Years	5 Years
All released prisoners	28.2%	43.4%	59.5%	67.8%	73.0%	76.6%
White[a]	25.6%	39.7%	55.5%	63.9%	69.3%	73.1%
Violent	21.9	33.6	48.2	55.6	61.1	65.1
Property	31.2	47.6	63.9	71.9	76.9	80.0
Drug	23.6	37.7	53.4	62.4	68.2	72.6
Public order[b]	21.5	33.9	50.1	60.2	65.6	69.5
Black/African American[a]	29.1%	45.8%	63.2%	71.7%	77.2%	80.8%
Violent	26.1	41.5	58.1	66.4	72.6	76.9
Property	33.9	51.3	68.5	76.5	81.8	84.5
Drug	28.5	45.5	63.7	72.6	77.9	81.5
Public order[b]	27.3	44.4	61.4	69.9	75.3	79.1
Hispanic/Latino	32.3%	46.3%	60.7%	68.1%	72.2%	75.3%
Violent	28.1	40.9	54.9	62.7	67.5	71.3
Property	39.8	55.7	71.1	77.6	80.2	83.0
Drug	29.0	42.2	57.0	65.0	69.8	72.5
Public order[b]	34.9	50.4	61.7	68.4	72.2	75.9
Other[a,c]	25.7%	42.7%	58.3%	67.3%	72.1%	75.0%
Violent	19.9	34.7	51.9	58.9	62.0	66.6
Property	36.5	55.4	69.3	78.3	81.6	83.7
Drug	19.4	39.5	57.0	67.3	76.5	78.1
Public order[b]	23.0	37.3	51.1	62.4	68.4	71.2

Source: BJS (2014).

Note: Prisoners were tracked for 5 years following release. Inmates could have been in prison for more than one offense; the most serious one is reported in this table. Data on the prisoner's race or Hispanic origin were known for nearly 100% of cases. See appendix table 16 for standard errors.

a. Excludes persons of Hispanic or Latino origin.

b. Includes 0.8% of cases in which the prisoner's most serious offense was unspecified.

c. Includes persons identified as American Indian or Alaska Native; Asian, Native Hawaiian, or other Pacific Islander; and persons of other races.

Conviction crime (property offenders have higher rates), prior criminal record (the more convictions the higher the recidivism), employment (unemployment is associated with higher recidivism), age (younger offenders have higher rates), family composition (persons living with spouse or children have lower rates) and drug use (heroin addicts have the highest recidivism rates). (p. 491)

Because minorities are more likely to fit some of these characteristics, they are at even higher risk for reentry problems (Pager, 2007a, 2007b). Employment and maintaining family ties are especially big concerns for minorities (Bushway, Stoll, & Weiman, 2007; Visher, 2007; Western & Wildeman, 2009; Wildeman & Wakefield, 2014). To address these issues, in 2003, the federal government passed the Serious and Violent Offender Reentry Initiative (Lattimore, 2007). This Act, which allocated $100 million for grants, focuses on "employment-based programming for inmates" (p. 88). Moreover, the Marriage and Incarceration Act was enacted to address "family programming for adult male inmates" (p. 88). Even with these initiatives, because of the bias against ex-cons, some have turned to creative measures to get their foot in the door of employers. In his highly acclaimed work *When Work Disappears,* W. J. Wilson (1996) noted the stereotypical views of employers in the Chicago region. When he asked employers about their perceptions of inner-city workers (especially young Black males), many of the 197 participating firms referred to them as "uneducated," "uncooperative," and "dishonest" (p. 111). Such perceptions have obvious implications for ex-cons. Building on the work of Wilson, Pager (2007b) sought to determine the impact of race and criminal histories on employment in entry-level jobs. Her experimental study of Milwaukee-area businesses found that Whites with criminal records had a better chance at employment than Blacks without criminal records. Such findings can only continue the cycle of recidivism among Blacks. In recent years, however, some cities and states have loosened some of the requirements tied to ex-cons and employment applications (see Box 8.3).

BOX 8.3

A Criminal Record May No Longer Be a Stumbling Block to Employment in Some Places

When Dwyane Jordan got busted four years ago on felony drug-peddling charges, he was thankful to get probation and addiction treatment rather than prison time.

What he didn't bargain for was the haunting effect that being branded a felon would have on his ability to lawfully earn a living—a burden he shares with roughly 70 million U.S. adults who have criminal records. "It reminds me of 'The Scarlet Letter,'" said Jordan, 43, of Washington, DC.

Jordan's criminal past comes up nearly every time he applies for a job, because most employment applications ask him to check a box if he has been convicted of a felony. He has been tempted to

(Continued)

(Continued)

lie about his conviction, because he believes marking the box has prompted multiple employers to reject him in the past year. But if the employer runs a background check and learns the truth, he'd be disqualified anyway.

A criminal record is such a stumbling block to employment that many states, cities and counties are passing laws to remove the question from applications for government jobs. Increasingly, some are forcing private employers to ban the question, too.

So far this year, Delaware and Nebraska have passed legislation to "ban the box" from application forms for most state, city, and county jobs. In the past five years, California, Colorado, Connecticut, Illinois, Maryland, Massachusetts, New Mexico, Minnesota, and Rhode Island and the District of Columbia have banned the box for most state jobs. Hawaii was the first state to ban the box in 1998.

Georgia Gov. Nathan Deal, a Republican, plans to ban the box from applications for most state jobs by executive order as soon as next month, according to spokeswoman Sasha Dlugolenski. Legislation is pending in New Jersey. And more than 60 cities and counties—from Indianapolis to Kansas City, Missouri, to Alameda County, California—have adopted similar laws for government employment. Rochester, New York, did so this week.

Four states—Hawaii, Massachusetts, Minnesota, and Rhode Island—have extended the ban to include private employers. San Francisco did it in February. And the Baltimore City Council last month voted to impose the rule on businesses with 10 or more employees.

Some of the nation's biggest employers, such as Wal-Mart and Target, also have banned the box.

Tommy Wells, a member of the DC City Council, wants Washington, DC, to extend the city's 2010 law banning the box on city employment applications to private businesses.

"The biggest challenge they [people returning from prison] face is getting housing and employment," Wells said. "[Banning the box] is one thing we can do to help."

Not Forced to Hire Felons

Ban-the-box laws don't prevent employers from rejecting applicants because of their criminal pasts. However, they typically prohibit asking the question or running a criminal background check until the first or second interview or until an offer is made. The goal is to prevent employers from blackballing people based solely on their criminal background.

Postponing the question gives a prospective employee an opportunity to explain the circumstances of the crime, to point out how long it has been since it was committed, and to present evidence of rehabilitation.

"You're not required to hire anyone," said Michelle Rodriguez, a lawyer with the National Employment Law Project (NELP), one of several non-profit groups which have been pushing ban-the-box legislation. "This is about letting people get their foot in the door, and not being automatically disqualified."

States and localities typically exempt jobs in law enforcement, child or nursing care, schools or other areas in which other laws require background checks for safety or security reasons. The same is true for jobs in the private sector that require background checks for licensing, such as drivers or day care workers.

Some laws say employers cannot ask about misdemeanors, arrests without convictions, or convictions that are expunged or annulled. They don't allow the checks without the applicant's permission. Some say applicants cannot be disqualified if their convictions don't relate to the type of work they'd be doing.

Numbers Help Drive the Push

Several factors have converged to drive the growing movement to ban the box. Chief among them is the huge number of people who have criminal records.

NELP's estimate that 70 million U.S. adults have arrest or conviction records is based on federal Bureau of Justice statistics compiled from federal, state, and local law-enforcement and courts. And that's a conservative figure, Rodriguez said. Tougher sentencing laws, especially for drug offenses, have swelled that total.

In Washington, DC, about 8,000 people are released from prison every year, according to Wells of the DC council. In DC, which has a large African-American population, Black men comprise a disproportionate share of that total. The same holds true around the country: A 2010 study by the Pew Charitable Trusts (which funds *Stateline)* found that one in 87 working-age White men was incarcerated, while the numbers for African-Americans and Hispanics were one in 12 and one in 36, respectively.

Similarly disproportionate figures prompted the U.S. Equal Employment Opportunity Commission in 2012 to update guidelines for hiring people with criminal records. The guidelines stop short of ban-the-box laws, but they warn employers they could violate federal civil rights laws if they reject an African-American applicant based on his criminal record but hire a White one with a comparable record.

Similar to many of the state laws, the guidelines urge employers to consider the seriousness of an applicant's crime, the time that's passed since conviction, and the nature of the job.

Do Old Criminal Records Matter?

Kiminori Nakamura, assistant professor of criminology and criminal justice at the University of Maryland, said most people who return to prison do so within three to five years. The longer they're out, he said, the less likely they are to return.

Nakamura co-authored a 2009 study that found people with a criminal record are at no greater criminal risk after they've been out seven to 10 years than those with no record. "Very old criminal records are not very useful in predicting risk," he said.

Evolv, a data firm that analyzes workforces, has found that people convicted of a crime—about 13 percent of its database of hourly workers—were slightly more productive than those with no records when it studied workers handling customer support phone calls.

Massachusetts has had a ban-the-box law for business since 2010. The state's Commission Against Discrimination says businesses have generally complied and that it's received only a "handful" of filings from applicants who said they'd been improperly asked about their criminal history. Those businesses brought their hiring policies into compliance, the commission said, and the state hasn't had to initiate any complaints.

Bill Vernon, who heads the Massachusetts chapter of the National Federation of Independent Business (NFIB), said he hasn't heard of any small businesses being in trouble over the state law. But, he said, small businesses also are more likely to hire ex-offenders when they return to the community because they know them.

But businesses, especially small ones, remain wary of the laws.

"A blanket ban-the-box policy doesn't make good business sense for small business," said Elizabeth Milito of the national office of the NFIB, which represents about 350,000 small and independent businesses nationwide.

Most businesses aren't the size of Wal-Mart or Target, she said, or state or city government. Some don't have human resources departments. And she said businesses that have to adhere to federal or state laws on background checks—such as transportation or security firms—shouldn't have to put off asking people about their criminal history.

To ask small employers to wait until they're ready to offer somebody a job before asking about a criminal record is "kind of wasting the business owners' time," she said.

Wells said he has heard similar complaints from many Washington businesses. But he's determined to press ahead. "We did it for city government and it seemed to work," he said.

(Continued)

(Continued)

Dwyane Jordan knows banning the box won't guarantee him a job. During his struggles last year to find work, he got an offer from a company that didn't ask about his criminal history on the application. But that offer was rescinded after he gave permission for a background check and the results came in.

Jordan now has a job as a server at a restaurant. He knows it's a "high risk" job for a recovering addict because he's around alcohol. But he's been clean almost three years. He's no longer living in shelters. Because tips have been good, he's paid his rent three months in advance. And he's talking about going back to school to build on his already four years of college.

But he also knows it may take him another decade to work his way up the economic ladder. If he has a consistent job history during that period, he hopes, the "scarlet letter" on his record will no longer matter.

Source: Stinson (2014).

As for maintaining family ties, concerns about Black inmates and their families are not new (Swan, 1977). However, given the overrepresentation of Blacks and Hispanics among those who are incarcerated and eventually come home, it is important to note the consequences of fractured families. Studies have shown that "imprisonment and parole affects family stability and childhood development" (Petersilia, 2002, p. 494). Incarcerated and paroled inmates have increased chances of separation and divorce, which in the long run can impact their children. Petersilia (2002) wrote, "Children of incarcerated and released parents often suffer confusion, sadness, and social stigma; and these feelings often result in school-related difficulties, low self-esteem, aggressive behavior, and general emotional dysfunction" (p. 494). More disturbingly, "Children of incarcerated parents are five times more likely to serve time in prison than are children whose parents are not incarcerated" (p. 494). Employment also intersects with family concerns in that, among other things, being unemployed raises the risk that there will be violence in the home of a recently released offender (Petersilia, 2002). Recent scholarship has continued to confirm some of these problems associated with families coping with the incarceration of a loved one (see Braman, 2002; Richie, 2002).

With a change in tone at the state and federal levels regarding crime and criminals, there has been considerable effort to address the reentry problem (Travis, 2007; Visher, 2007). One way to combat reentry concerns is through the development of **reentry courts**. Jeremy Travis developed this concept in 1999. The idea moves the role of reentry to the judicial branch of government. Based largely on the concept of drug courts, reentry courts require that a parolee and the parole officer work with the courts to formulate a reentry plan. Each month parolees are required to provide evidence of their progress. Travis (2005) argues that the court can be effective:

The judges are able to marshal community resources, and wield both "carrots" and "sticks" in their efforts to promote successful reintegration. The carrots are services, positive reinforcement, family and community support, and a forum for the acknowledgment of success. The sticks are enhanced levels of supervision (such as curfews, more intensive drug treatment, or more frequent drug testing), and ultimately short periods of incarceration, typically measured in days rather than months. (p. 59)

The reentry court model is still new, with pilot sites in Delaware, Florida, Iowa, Kentucky, New York, Ohio, and West Virginia (E. Miller, 2007). These courts, drawing on Travis's model, are based on four core components: a reentry transition plan, a range of supportive services, regular appearances for oversight of the plan, and accountability to victims or communities (E. Miller, 2007). To date, E. Miller (2007) has identified three major challenges faced by reentry courts: health, employment, and housing. As for health, E. Miller notes that inmates are typically troubled by numerous ailments, and, in fact, some observers have noted that Black males live longer in prison than they do outside institutions because of the easier access to health care (Martin, Harris, & Jack, 2015; Pittman, 2011). This represents yet another challenge reentry courts need to consider. As for employment, it goes without saying that this represents an essential key to the successful reentry of formerly incarcerated people. Programs such as the Center for Employment Opportunities (CEO) in New York could serve as models for other communities struggling with this issue. The nonprofit organization "provides immediate, paid employment for people coming home with criminal records, followed by placement in a permanent job and job retention services" (Tarlow & Nelson, 2007, p. 138). Their program includes a few days of job-readiness instruction, after which there are two months of paid transitional work, followed by permanent employment largely in the private sector. A recent movement across the nation tied to reentry concern is the Ban the Box movement that seeks to prevent employers from asking felons on job applications about their criminal history. This has been a stumbling block for many ex-felons seeking employment. In June 2015, New York City Mayor Bill de Blasio signed into law the Fair Chance Act (also referred to as "banning the box"). The new law requires that "employers will only be allowed to run background checks and ask questions about an applicant's criminal background after they have made a conditional job offer. In addition, the employers will be required to obtain a written copy of the request and provide supporting documentation to the applicants" (Pazmino, 2015). Because of various legislative mandates, securing housing can be quite a challenge during the reentry process. As such, it might actually require changes to current policies to open more options for ex-inmates (E. Miller, 2007; see Box 8.4).

BOX 8.4

Race and Crime in the Media

Finding a Home After Prison Tough for Released Felons

SIOUX FALLS, S.D.—Stacie Schroder's search for a home began the day she regained her freedom.

Finding an apartment can be a complicated, time-consuming process for anyone. Schroder didn't expect her search to be easy, but she also wasn't prepared for the months of dead ends, denials and desperation that would come to define her housing search.

Schroder spent almost four years in prison after a 2007 arrest on drug-related charges. After prison, she learned that finding a place to live for an ex-convict is one of the biggest barriers to getting back on your feet.

(Continued)

(Continued)

"Trying to find a landlord that takes felons is hard," Schroder said.

Under the law, landlords are free to discriminate against people with criminal records. A popular police-sponsored rental housing program in Sioux Falls and other cities encourages property managers to reject renters with recent criminal histories.

While criminal background checks by landlords might deter crime on their properties and reassure tenants, they pose a major barrier for people who have made mistakes, served their time, and are trying to get a fresh start on life. People coming out of prison often depend on a lucky break from a relative or Good Samaritan, or else face turning to the same people whose influence steered them to crime in the first place.

"It's a vicious circle. They see no light, no hope and they fall into the same circle, again," said Paul Flogstad, Sioux Falls' fair housing ombudsman.

The limited housing options for people with felony records raises questions about the community's ability to rehabilitate criminals and get them off a path that leads back to an overcrowded corrections system.

"It's just nearly impossible in this town with a felony to get housing," said Melanie Bliss of the Sioux Empire Homeless Coalition. "Being a felon or sex offender are serious barriers for people for the rest of their lives."

Calvin Dunham knows he caught a lucky break.

Dunham was serving a three-year prison sentence for selling prescription pills when he met his future boss and landlord at Bible study in the Minnehaha County prison.

Three days after his release from prison, Dunham had an interview for a job fixing up properties. He got the job. His new boss then offered him a place to rent after Dunham's five-month stay at a halfway home.

"I'm just highly blessed," Dunham said. "Society owes us nothing but maybe a chance. I think everyone deserves a second chance if they are changing."

Tenants Feel Safe

Property managers, though, have real incentives for not giving people such as Dunham a second chance.

More than 200 property managers in Sioux Falls, including some of the city's largest housing companies, now participate in the city's crime-free housing program, which offers marketing materials and police consultations to participants who agree to certain practices. They include:

- Performing background checks on all applicants.
- Denying rental to anyone on the sex-offender registry or anyone with an assault or drug conviction in the past five years.
- Installing security features such as deadbolts, peep holes that provide 180-degree views, lift and slide protection on windows and patio doors, and adequate lighting in hallways and parking lots.

"It's a proven program; it's a good program," said Flogstad, the city's fair housing ombudsman.

It's a marketing tool for landlords, and for tenants it brings a peace of mind that their neighbor isn't a sex offender or drug dealer.

But it also makes it difficult for people such as Dunham to find a home after prison, Flogstad said. Discrimination still would exist, even if the crime-free program didn't.

Sioux Falls police officer Jim Larson, who oversees the crime-free housing program in the city, said people with criminal records are not a protected class when it comes to housing discrimination, so landlords can freely refuse to rent to any ex-convict.

"A landlord, a managing company, or an owner has the right to refuse anyone for any reason except for reasons like sexual orientation, creed and color, as long as they're consistent with it," Larson said.

Sioux Falls adopted the Crime-Free Multi-Housing Program in March 1997. The program is based on a national program that originated in Mesa, Ariz., in 1991. Since then, it's spread to about 2,000 cities in 48 states, five Canadian provinces, England, Nigeria, and Puerto Rico.

Lloyd Cos., one the largest apartment companies in Sioux Falls, is a member of the crime-free housing program. Nicholas Blau, regional manager, said one of the first questions prospective renters ask is whether they are members of the crime-free program.

Blau said the companies follow the minimum requirements of the crime-free housing program but also impose further restrictions against those with felonies on their criminal records.

"The general rule we use is any felony record of criminal action which would adversely affect the health, safety, and welfare of residents is grounds for denial," Blau said.

Help for Ex-Convicts

Instead of Craigslist or the classifieds, people with criminal records often need to look to people such as Jeff Haverhals.

He is director of Kingdom Boundaries Prison Aftercare, the ministry that connected Dunham to his future boss and landlord as he was transitioning from prison.

Haverhals spent years interacting with convicts behind prison walls through a mentorship program. It gave him an intimate view of the struggles convicts face once they leave prison. For the past four years, he has worked with ex-convicts to reintegrate into society.

"A lot of guys don't have a lot of hope. They are scared. They don't have anybody to help them. They feel stuck," he said. "When people get stressed, they go back to doing what they were doing that got them in trouble in the first place."

At the moment, he is working with six people to help them find a place to live, get a job, and get back on their feet. He admits sometimes it doesn't work out the way he hopes—leaving him feeling like a failure. But that comes with dealing with human nature and sin, he said.

"What hurts the most is when we help and help and help and they want to go back to that life and end up back in jail," Haverhals said.

Another program that helps ex-convicts transition into housing after prison is the Glory House, one of the few programs of its kind.

Executive Director Dave Johnson said their work helps not only those in need of a second chance but also the community.

"The reality is that for people coming out of the correction system, 96 percent of them are going to come out in the community and they will be our neighbors," Johnson said. "I'd rather have them know the basics on how they live so they don't struggle."

Schroder stayed at the Glory House in Sioux Falls after her release from prison in 2011. She said they worked hard to find her a place to live, but it was tough to find anyone who would look past the felonies on her record, a reminder of her old self.

"People change," said Schroder, who is now an engineering supervisor at a manufacturing plant. "People have the ability to be better, productive members of society. God forgives us, so why can't everyone else."

After more than half a year of searching, Schroder finally found a sympathetic landlord in Tea, S.D., who, after hearing her story, was willing to lease an apartment to her.

"A lot of people don't give you that chance," Schroder said. "A lot of people think that because you're felons you're a bad person. That's not the case. People make mistakes."

Source: Walker (2015).

1. Draft a policy that you believe will address the difficulties ex-convicts have in securing decent housing.

Faith-based reentry programs also have flourished and worked in conjunction with reentry courts (Herz & Walsh, 2004). As with other faith-based initiatives, faith-based reentry programs are eligible for federal funds. In general, faith-based initiatives range from "faith-saturated" to those that have no apparent faith component (Mears, 2002). Whatever role such programs fall under, they "cannot expend funds for inherently religious activities such as worship, religious instruction or proselytization" (p. 30). It is also critical to note that, to date, little substantive research has examined the effectiveness of these programs. Consequently, there is little evidence that faith-based reentry programs are more effective than other reentry programs (Mears, 2002).

Although many reentry issues concern all inmates, as noted earlier, minorities are particularly hard hit with such concerns. Until these issues are addressed in a serious way, the cycle of recidivism will continue to pervade minority communities. A promising development occurred when former President George W. Bush announced in his 2004 State of the Union address that he was planning to implement a $300 million mentoring program to help ex-felons entering the job market (Kroeger, 2004). As part of this commitment, the Second Chances Act that was passed in 2008 has numerous provisions for reentry, including monies for jurisdictions to start reentry courts. Given the magnitude of the reentry problem, however, this was only a start.

In January 2011, the first Federal Interagency Reentry Council was held with former Attorney General Eric Holder. The Council's threefold mission is "to make communities safer by reducing recidivism and victimization; to assist those returning from prison and jail in becoming productive, taxpaying citizens; and to save taxpayer dollars by lowering the direct and collateral cost of incarceration" (The Council of State Governments Justice Center, 2015). Although the initiative is relatively new, it appears to address many of the key issues related to reentry. In 2014, the Department of Justice funded an evaluation of several reentry courts, and the findings were largely favorable (Lindquist et al., 2014).

Another collateral consequence of being convicted of a felony is the loss of the right to vote. In recent years, felon disenfranchisement has become a major focus of scholars and community activists. In the next section, we review the history, current state, and implications of this practice.

Felon Disenfranchisement

Being able to vote is a fundamental right in a democracy. Nevertheless, beginning in ancient times, taking away a criminal offender's right to vote "was thought to offer both retribution and a deterrent to future offending" (Behrens, Uggen, & Manza, 2003, p. 562). Although such laws may seem "race neutral," recent research has challenged these notions (Behrens et al., 2003; Fellner & Mauer, 1998; Manza & Uggen, 2006; Preuhs, 2001; Shapiro, 1997; Uggen & Manza, 2002; Uggen, Manza, & Behrens, 2003). The United States' adoption of the practice dates to the colonial era. Initially, only a few offenses resulted in disenfranchisement. But according to Behrens et al. (2003), "Many states enacted felon disenfranchisement provisions in the aftermath of the Civil War. Such laws diluted the voting strength of newly enfranchised racial minority groups, particularly in the Deep South but in the North as well" (p. 563). Since these early times, the prevalence of such laws has grown. For example, "Whereas 35% of states had a broad felon disenfranchisement law in 1850, fully 96% had such a law by 2002, when only Maine and Vermont had yet to restrict felon voting rights" (p. 564).

Behrens et al. (2003) sought to determine whether the composition of prison populations is associated with the enactment of state felony disenfranchisement laws from 1850 to 2002. Their results showed,

> The racial composition of state prisons is firmly associated with the adoption of state felon disenfranchisement laws. States with greater non-White prison populations have been more likely to ban convicted felons from voting than states with proportionately fewer non-Whites in the criminal justice system. (p. 596)

Such findings suggest an effort to minimize the impact of the votes of felons.

A study by Uggen and Manza (2002) investigated the potential impact of felony disenfranchisement on past elections. Noting that the disenfranchised population represents 2.3% of the electorate, Uggen and Manza controlled for turnout and voter choice, which estimates the level at which felons would have participated in the election process and their party preferences. Their estimates revealed that, "On average . . . about 35% of disenfranchised felons would have turned out to vote in presidential elections, and that about 24% would have participated in Senate elections during nonpresidential election years" (p. 786). Estimates for political party preference showed,

> Democratic candidates would have received about 7 of every 10 votes cast by the felons and ex-felons in 14 of the last 15 U.S. Senate election years. By removing those Democratic preferences from the pool of eligible voters, felon disenfranchisement has provided a small but very clear advantage to Republican candidates in every presidential and senatorial election from 1972 to 2000. (pp. 786–787)

When Uggen and Manza (2002) examined the impact of these figures on senatorial elections from 1978 to 2000, they found "7 outcomes that may have been reversed if not for the disenfranchisement of felons and ex-felons" (p. 789). Although seven outcomes might not seem substantial, they noted that this could have resulted in the Democrats controlling the Senate during the 1990s, which could have impacted on the nature of the punishment policies during the decade. Finally, when examining the 2000 presidential election, Uggen and Manza found that, without the restrictions on felons and ex-offenders, Al Gore would have won the popular election by 1 million votes, as opposed to 500,000, and, more important, "If disenfranchised felons in Florida had been permitted to vote, Democrat Gore would certainly have carried the state, and the election" (p. 792).

Given the implications of felony disenfranchisement, one wonders how the public feels about the practice. Manza, Brooks, and Uggen (2004) investigated this question in a national poll. More specifically, they were interested in finding out whether the public supported the enfranchisement of offenders and whether this support was contingent on "the level of supervision or the specific nature of the crime" (Manza et al., 2004). Their poll showed that the majority of the public was willing to enfranchise probationers (68%); however, with a slight change in the phrasing of the question, which included the word *prison,* the support slipped to 60%. The aversion to supporting enfranchisement for those imprisoned was also seen with a direct question on the matter, which showed only 31% of the respondents supporting such a policy. Eighty percent of the public supported enfranchising ex-felons. But when the ex-felon category was disaggregated by offense, in some cases, the support was lower, with 63% supporting enfranchisement for white-collar offenders and 66% supporting enfranchisement for violent offenders (Manza et al., 2004). The lowest level of support was found for enfranchising sex offenders (52%).

There have been considerable changes in felony disenfranchisement laws across the nation because of the hard work of scholars and activists. Their efforts led to considerable public exposure and debate on the topic. This led to legislatures across the country revisiting their felon disenfranchisement laws. According to Porter (2010), since 1997, 23 states have revised their policies. In Porter's assessment of the changes, she highlights the following:

- Nine states either repealed or amended lifetime disenfranchisement laws.
- Two states expanded voting rights to persons under community supervision (probation and parole).
- Eight states eased the restoration process for persons seeking to have their right to vote restored after completing their sentence.
- Three states improved data and information sharing. (Porter, 2010, p. 1)

Because of these changes, Porter (2010) estimates that 800,000 persons "have regained their right to vote" (p. 2). Despite these promising developments, there remain more than five million people who have lost the right to vote as a result of a felony conviction—a large number of whom are racial/ethnic minorities (Porter, 2010). Given this reality, it is likely that scholars and activists will continue to apply pressure to those who can continue to change the landscape regarding felon disenfranchisement laws. In fact, emerging articles from well-known advocates are making strong arguments for allowing inmates to vote while incarcerated (Mauer, 2011).

❖ Conclusion

This chapter began by examining the structure of American corrections. The review showed that the correctional system in America includes both community-based and incarceration options. Furthermore, a historical overview of race and corrections showed that race, class, and gender have always had a place in American corrections. Currently, Black and Hispanic prisoners represent a large share of the incarcerated population in the United States. Furthermore, with hundreds of thousands of prisoners annually returning to their communities in the United States, prisoner reentry has become a major concern in recent years. One innovative approach that has been used to handle this issue is reentry courts, which are based on the drug courts model. Although new, it is hoped that these courts will help stem the tide of recidivism among recently released inmates. Another promising development is that prison populations are declining. Fiscal crises in many states have resulted in reduced inmate populations. In fact, The Sentencing Project released a report in 2011 that found that 24 states had reduced their prison populations during 2009 (Porter, 2011). In addition, several states are either closing or considering the closure of correctional facilities. These closures will reduce the number of prison beds across the nation by nearly 14,000 (Porter, 2011).

Our review of the extent and implications of felony disenfranchisement in the United States showed that Blacks and Hispanics have been disproportionately impacted by such laws. In fact, although public support is generally in favor of enfranchising most ex-cons, only two states have no restrictions on voting rights related to felony convictions. The exemplary efforts of scholars and activists have produced progressive policy changes across the nation regarding felon disenfranchisement.

Although much of our discussion in the first seven chapters has pertained to the adult criminal justice system, in Chapter 9, we turn our attention to the juvenile justice system. Operating under a separate philosophy, the juvenile justice system has also had to deal with the overrepresentation of racial minorities. Chapter 9 reviews some of the issues related to this phenomenon.

Discussion Questions

1. Discuss two historical trends related to race and corrections.
2. What is the significance of Blumstein's work related to explaining disparities in corrections?
3. Do you support Ban-the-Box legislation?
4. Name three positive benefits of reentry courts.
5. Discuss two myths about U.S. prisons.

Internet Exercises

1. Look at the data provided on the publications page of the Federal **Bureau of Prisons** website (http://www.bop.gov/resources/publications.jsp). Examine the statistical trends by race and note whether any patterns have developed during the years provided. What do you believe explains the trend(s) revealed?
2. Visit the Pew Center on the States website and review the report *One in 100: Behind Bars in America 2008* (http://www.pewtrusts.org/en/research-and-analysis/reports/0001/01/01/one-in-100). Using this report and more current statistics, compare the incarceration and education spending in your state in 2008 and now.

Internet Sites

National Institute of Corrections: http://nicic.gov

National Reentry Resource Center: http://csgjusticecenter.org/nrrc

U.S. Department of Justice Reentry Initiative: http://ojp.gov/fbnp/reentry.htm

Supplemental materials for *Race and Crime* are available online at
study.sagepub.com/gabbidon4e.

Juvenile Justice

CHAPTER 9

Existing research on the history of American juvenile justice tends to generalize from the experiences of white American and European immigrant groups. It pays limited attention to how status distinctions besides age, and particularly race and ethnicity, have contributed to variation in the notion of childhood and experiences of juvenile social control.

—Geoff K. Ward (2012, p. 34)

The quotation above appears in *The Black Child Savers,* which presents a revisionist history of race and juvenile justice from the Jim Crow era to the post–Civil Rights era of the late 20th century. Most textbooks on juvenile delinquency and juvenile justice provide only a cursory discussion of race (Taylor Greene, Gabbidon, & Ebersole, 2001) and focus primarily on statistics, police arrest decisions, gangs, and, more recently, **disproportionate minority contact (DMC).** The history of discrimination and segregation in juvenile facilities since their inception in the 1800s is often omitted, as is the important role played by minority communities in protecting their youth from involvement in crime.

With very few exceptions, historical research on race and juvenile justice focuses on White and Black youth (Adams & Addie, 2010; Brunson & Weitzer, 2009; Frey, 1981; Mennel, 1973; Pisciotta, 1983; Vaughn, Wallace, Davis, Fernandes, & Howard, 2008; Ward, 2001, 2012; Wines, 1903, cited in Pisciotta, 1983; Young, 1993), while contemporary research includes Blacks, Whites, and other minority groups. Research on Latinos/as (Cintron, 2005; Cuellar & Curry, 2007; Dillon, Robbins, Szapocznik, & Pantin, 2008; Flexon, Greenleaf, & Lurigio, 2010; Gallegos-Castillo & Patino, 2006; McCluskey, 2002; McCluskey, Krohn, Lizotte, & Rodriguez, 2002; McCluskey & Tovar, 2003; McGee et al., 2005; Miller, Barnes, & Hartley, 2011; Peguero & Shekarkhar, 2011; Shekarkhar & Gibson, 2011; Solis, Portillos, & Brunson, 2009; Vega & Gil, 1998), Native Americans (Mmari, Blum, & Teufel-Shone, 2010), and Asian Americans (Bui, 2009; Godinet, 2013; Guerrero et al., 2010; Le, Monifared, & Stockdale, 2005; Wolf & Hartney, 2005) is more readily available than in the past. Numerous government documents and edited volumes that focus on minority youth, delinquency, and justice are also available (see, e.g., Chavez-Garcia, 2012; Gray, 2014; Hawkins & Kempf-Leonard, 2005; Leonard, Pope, & Feyerherm, 1995; Parsons-Pollard, 2011; Penn, Taylor Greene, & Gabbidon, 2006; Rosenfeld, Edberg, Fang, & Florence, 2013; Sickmund & Puzzanchera, 2014; Tapia, 2012). In spite of a considerable amount of research, there is still a lack of consensus about why Blacks and other minority youth continue to be overrepresented in the juvenile justice system and the best way to address this challenge.

The goal of this chapter is to explore race effects in juvenile justice. It begins with a brief overview of juvenile justice in the United States, a historical overview of race and juvenile justice, examines race and the extent of juvenile crime and victimization, and discusses several contemporary issues, including DMC, the **school-to-prison pipeline**, minority female delinquency, life without parole sentences for juveniles, and delinquency prevention.

❖ Overview of Juvenile Justice

Many students are surprised to learn that the concepts of juvenile delinquency and juvenile justice are of a fairly recent origin. Prior to the 19th century, youth were the primary responsibility of their families and communities. Those who could not be controlled were punished like adults or sent to live with other families, usually as apprentices to learn a skill or trade. During the 1800s, separate facilities for youth in trouble were established. These early institutions included asylums, orphanages, houses of refuge, and reformatories.

Later in the century, in 1899, the first **juvenile court** opened in Cook County (Chicago), Illinois. Today, the phrase *juvenile justice system* is used to refer to the agencies and processes responsible for the prevention and control of juvenile delinquency. In fact, according to the National Center for Juvenile Justice (2004), there are actually 51 separate juvenile justice systems in the United States, and each "has its own history and set of laws and policies and delivers services to juvenile delinquents in its own way" (King, 2006, p. 1). Figure 9.1 presents an overview of case flow through a contemporary juvenile justice system. Like the criminal justice system, the juvenile system includes law enforcement, courts, corrections, and the use of discretion in decision making at several stages. The systems intersect because some juveniles are tried in criminal courts, detained in jails, and sentenced to adult prisons. Like adults, juveniles can be detained without bail before their trials (adjudicatory hearing), have procedural safeguards, have the right to an appeal (in some states), and can be placed on probation. In addition to these similarities, there are many differences between the two systems, including more parental involvement in the juvenile system, different terminology, and the fact that juveniles do not have a constitutional right to a jury trial (Lawrence & Hemmens, 2008; see *McKeiver v. Pennsylvania,* 1971).

The most important stages of the juvenile justice process are referrals (usually by police), **intake**, **adjudication**, and **disposition**. Juveniles may be diverted from the process at any stage by police, probation officers, and judges. For example, a juvenile referred to the court for a minor offense can be diverted from the process and/or detained by an intake/probation officer. A juvenile accused of a more serious crime, like rape, is less likely to be diverted. Rather, he could be formally petitioned to

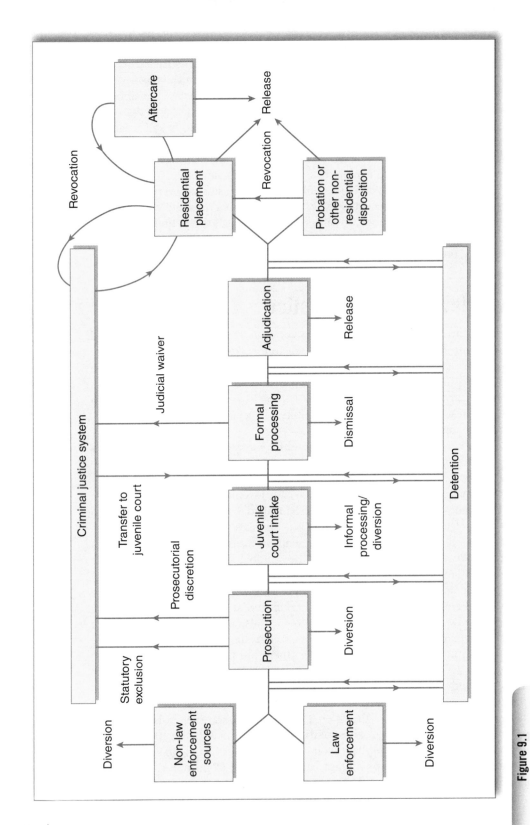

Figure 9.1

Case Processing in the Juvenile Justice System

appear in juvenile court or transferred (waived) to adult court. If the juvenile accused of rape is adjudicated as a delinquent (in juvenile court), several dispositions are available, including (intensive) probation, restitution, community service, and secure confinement. If the juvenile accused of committing a rape is waived to adult court, there also are several possible outcomes, including either plea negotiations or a trial, and if found guilty, the sentencing alternatives are similar to dispositions available in juvenile court. Unlike youth tried in juvenile court, those waived to adult court who are found guilty and sentenced to confinement will go to prison.

Another unique characteristic of the juvenile justice system is the jurisdiction of the juvenile court over delinquent youth, status offenders, and youth who are dependent, neglected, and abused. Juvenile delinquency is described by Greenwald (1993) as a "euphemism for behavioral problems of children and youth that reach beyond mere non-conformity and existed since earliest man" (p. 735). In the early 19th century, it encompassed any illegal behavior by a minor who fell under a statutory age limit and was labeled a serious social problem (Clement, 1993). In most states, juveniles include youth who are under the age of 18. Delinquent acts include both criminal and status offenses. Unlike adults, juveniles can be apprehended for offenses due solely to their status as children or adolescents. Curfew violations, underage drinking, incorrigibility, and running away are examples of status offenses. In some states, these juveniles are referred to as either "children" or "persons" in need of supervision.

The juvenile justice system today is quite different from a century ago. Initially, the goal of the early courts was to rehabilitate youth and act in their best interest. In the 1960s, a fundamental shift away from the idea of rehabilitation began to occur (Urban, St. Cyr, & Decker, 2003). Several scholars have observed a gradual transition to what is now a more accountability-driven and punitive system (Benekos & Merlo, 2008; Feld, 1999; Hinton, Sims, Adams, & West, 2007; Urban et al., 2003; Ward, 2001, 2012; Ward & Kupchik, 2009). Today, the competing goals of rehabilitation and punishment have resulted in a system that places the personal, social, and educational needs of juvenile delinquents second to the need to punish them (Urban et al., 2003). Bernard and Kurlycheck (2010) identified the cycle of juvenile justice as being driven by three ideas: Crime is exceptionally high, the present policies make the problem worse, and changing the policies will reduce juvenile crime. According to the authors, the cycle of juvenile justice continues because the social conditions that foster juvenile delinquency are never adequately addressed. How did we go from a system that focused primarily on the best interest of the child to one that emphasizes punishment? When and why did we return to policies that blur the distinction between juveniles and adults? The following section provides some answers to these questions.

❖ Historical Overview of Race and Juvenile Justice

Children and youth have always misbehaved, and there have always been varying attitudes and practices toward what has come to be known as juvenile delinquency. Clement (1993) noted that, in colonial America, Southerners were more tolerant of misbehavior than were colonists in Massachusetts, Pennsylvania, and New York. More specifically, Southerners tolerated troublesome White males, but slave owners did not tolerate misbehavior of young (or adult) slaves. In the North, as the population in cities rapidly increased due primarily to urbanization, industrialization, and immigration, there was growing concern about youth crime. During the 1700s, the problem of youth misbehavior common to all children began to be referred to as the "crimes and conditions of poor children" (Mennel, 1973, p. xxvi). It was during the 1800s that concerned citizens, referred to as "**child savers,**" coalesced to protect children and youth and work on their behalf. Early in the century, these individuals and their organizations were instrumental in establishing separate facilities for youth; later in the century, they were instrumental in the creation of the first juvenile court. From the beginning of the movement to salvage youth, Black children were excluded and treated differently. Pisciotta (1983) concluded that, "Historians have been particularly negligent in not explicating the dynamics of racism and sexism in juvenile reformatories and courts" (p. 256).

As early as 1819, a group of individuals concerned about pauperism and the plight of youth in New York City formed the Society for the Prevention of Pauperism, which later became known as the Society for the Reformation of Juvenile Delinquents. On January 1, 1825, this organization opened the New York House of Refuge; Boston and Philadelphia soon followed suit, opening **houses of refuge** prior to the 1830s. Most youth in the early houses of refuge were not committing crimes, but rather were impoverished, neglected, and homeless adolescent White males. There was a considerable amount of prejudice in these early facilities toward immigrants, especially Irish youth, as well as girls and Black delinquents. The New York and Boston houses of refuge admitted Whites and Blacks, although they were segregated. In 1849, Philadelphia opened a separate house of refuge for "colored juvenile delinquents" (Frey, 1981; Mennel, 1973). Interestingly, all Black children born in Pennsylvania after 1780 were free, even though prejudice and separation of the races were the norm well into the 20th century. Though segregated, the houses of refuge in Philadelphia sought to maintain social control over poor and delinquent youth and to instill in them a basic education, the desire to work, and a moral foundation (Frey, 1981). Early houses maintained a practice of placing youth in apprenticeships or on rural farms. Because White girls and boys were preferred, Black youth stayed in the houses for longer periods of time (Ward, 2001, 2012).

Unlike Northern states, most Southern states moved slowly to open separate facilities for youth. Young (1993) noted "that the house of refuge established in Maryland in 1840 and opened in 1855 was restricted to White children due to the slave status of Black children" (p. 557). In Kentucky, the Louisville House of Refuge, established in 1854, also was for White children only (Young, 1994). Black youth were excluded from most facilities or treated quite differently. Managers believed that placing White and Black children together would be degrading to the White children (Mennel, 1973). Before and after the Civil War, in both the North and the South, Black youth were more likely to be sent to adult jails and prisons than to juvenile facilities. In Maryland, the children of free Blacks were perceived as a threat (as were their parents) and could be either sold or bound out if their parents could not provide for them (Young, 1993).

By the 1850s, houses of refuge that had opened earlier in the century were criticized and eventually replaced with **reformatories**. Massachusetts opened its first reform school for boys in 1847 and for girls in 1856. These institutions differed from houses of refuge in several ways. First, smaller buildings that were maintained by the occupants were utilized. Second, there was a greater emphasis on education. By 1890, most states outside the South had reform schools for boys and girls (Mennel, 1973).

Like the houses of refuge, the early reformatories excluded Blacks and instead sent them to adult jails and prisons. There is little information about the treatment of Black youth in adult facilities. We know that the convict lease system in jails and prisons in the South was difficult for all prisoners (Du Bois, 1901/2002; LeFlouria, 2011; Oshinsky, 1996; Woodward, 1971; Work, 1939). As noted in earlier chapters, many Southern states used the convict lease system as both a means of generating revenue to maintain their penal institutions and for profit. Punishment was excessive, death rates were high, sexual assaults and rapes were ignored, and oversight was rare (Colvin, 1997). Black youth outnumbered other juveniles in these facilities (Ward, 2001, 2012) and were subjected to the most brutal forms of punishment. It was not until 1873 that one of the first separate reformatories for "colored boys" opened in Baltimore, MD (Ward, 2001, 2012; Young, 1993). It would take several decades for other reformatories to open for Black youth. Virginia opened its first industrial home for "wayward colored girls" in 1915 and a facility for "wayward boys" in 1920 (Young, 1994). The opening of these segregated (and often inferior) reformatories were due, in large part, to the efforts of the child savers, especially **Black child savers**.

The Child Savers

As previously mentioned, child savers were concerned with the plight of poor, vagrant, and neglected children (Siegel, 2002). These activists were middle- and upper-class females, criminal justice practitioners, and various organizations that were primarily interested in saving White children, who usually came from immigrant families struggling with the transition to life in a new country. Most of the White child savers were not concerned about Negro children, who faced challenges similar to, if not worse than, immigrant youth. Although Platt (1969) and Shelden and Osborne (1989) questioned the benevolence of the child savers and posited that they were motivated by self-interest, they do not address how child savers overlooked Negro youth and the role of Black child savers (Ward, 2001, 2012). Frederick H. Wines, a leader in the National Conference of Charities and Correction and the National Prison Association in the late 1800s and early 1900s believed that "crime and delinquency among blacks was an 'insoluble problem,'" and "because of their inherent biological, mental, and moral primitiveness . . . neither punishment or rehabilitation would work" (Wines, in Pisciotta, 1983).

Youth facilities were originally opened to separate delinquents from adults and the poor conditions found in prisons. It also was believed that youth were malleable and could be "saved" from the harmful effects of poverty and harsh living conditions. Unlike White youth, Black youth often were placed in adult facilities, evidence of what Ward (2001) referred to as "historical racial inequality" in juvenile justice. In addition, ideas of Black childhood varied between the races: Whites viewed Black childhood as developmentally limited, whereas Blacks viewed their development as critical to the future of the race (Ward, 2001).

Since the late 1800s, historically Black colleges and universities were in the vanguard of efforts to improve their race and instrumental in calling attention to Black youth. As early as 1899, at the Hampton Negro Conference, the issues of the need for clubs for girls and the dangers faced by girls migrating to the North were discussed. African American women who attended these institutions, most of them preparing to be teachers, realized that they would also need to become involved in their communities. For example, at the 1907 Hampton Conference, several women joined together to form the Virginia State Federation of Colored Women's Clubs. These women were at the forefront of the Black child savers who emerged in response to the unfair and prejudicial handling of Black youth. Like White child savers, the early Black child savers were initially women of a higher social class. However, they existed in a distinctly racially segregated community where the meaning of class was quite different. Although they held status and power in their own communities, Black child savers faced a greater challenge: a racialized justice system that was unwilling to invest in the rehabilitation of Black youth. They had to both challenge racial disparities and develop resources to finance facilities on their own (Ward, 2001).

Ward (2001, 2012) described at least three different types of Black child savers: early, reform oriented, and organizations. The early child savers were forced to work on the periphery of the justice system. The Federation of Colored Women's Clubs was at the forefront of the early Black child savers movement. These groups of women were active across the country, especially in the South, and were instrumental in creating the first reformatories for female and male Negro juveniles (Neverdon-Morton, 1989). The next group of Black child savers was more reform oriented and focused more directly on working as practitioners not only in juvenile justice, but in other agencies as well. They emerged early in the 20th century, when "African Americans were beginning to move from the periphery of juvenile justice, as community-based providers, toward its administrative center" (Ward, 2001, p. 164). These child savers were "African American participants in juvenile justice administration who aimed to affect outcomes in the legal processing of Black delinquents especially, though not exclusively" (p. 120). The National Association for the Advancement of Colored People (NAACP) provides an example of the third type of Black child savers. The organization devoted a tremendous amount of time and resources to the plight of Black youth in the justice system in the early part of the 20th century. Ward (2001) did not idealize the Black child savers in light of their incredible obstacles, although he does conclude that they probably did "improve the circumstances of Black juvenile delinquents" (p. 186). In addition, Black and White child savers coalesced in some places. Were there child savers in other minority groups? More than likely, but there are very few historical accounts currently available (see, e.g., Bush, 2010; Chavez-Garcia, 2012).

Juvenile Courts

The creation of the juvenile court was one of the most important developments in the history of juvenile justice. When the first juvenile court opened in Chicago (Cook County, IL), it was viewed as a progressive idea that recognized the special needs of children not only in juvenile facilities but in court, as well. As previously stated, the primary goal of the first juvenile courts was rehabilitation and to act in the best interest of the child. There have always been two competing views of early juvenile courts; one viewed them as a "symbol of society's concern for its young" and another as oppressive and "dedicated to controlling the indigent and powerless" (Bortner, 1984, pp. 2–3). By

the mid-1930s, most states had legislated some form of juvenile courts. Racial segregation in the juvenile courts (and reformatories) continued well into the 20th century.
Ward and Kupchik (2009) note that the U.S. Supreme Court ruling against the "separate
but equal" doctrine in the 1954 *Brown v. Board of Education* decision was one of the
earliest efforts to hold juvenile justice systems accountable to all youth.

By the 1960s, juvenile courts were criticized for lacking procedural safeguards,
insufficient training of judges and staff, and failing to control juvenile crime. During
this decade, U.S. Supreme Court rulings guaranteed juveniles in the system some
procedural safeguards in two landmark decisions (*Kent v. United States* [1966] and *In
re Gault* [1967]). There were important decisions in the 1970s as well (*In re Winship*
and [1970] *Schall v. Martin* [1984]), even though juvenile courts nationwide had begun
to shift away from an emphasis on the welfare and rehabilitation of youth to an even
more punitive "second-rate criminal court for young offenders" (Feld, 1999, p. 5).
According to Ward and Kupchik (2009),

> A two-stage and limited philosophical displacement of the rehabilitative ideal
> occurred, beginning with discourse and policy focused on system account-
> ability reforms in the 1950s, 1960s, and 1970s, followed by juvenile account-
> ability reform efforts since the 1980s that mirror the punitive tenor of broader
> juvenile justice and criminal justice policy reform. (p. 101)

Although we know quite a bit about the development of juvenile courts (and
juvenile justice), historical information about the treatment of Black and minority
youth in these courts during the early 20th century is limited. Most of the early
research consisted of case studies that examined Black delinquency in specific cities
(see Abraham, 1948; Blue, 1948, 1959; Frazier, 1939, 1949; Moses, 1933, 1936; Watts,
1941). Platt (1969, 1977, 2009) mentioned that the first juvenile court in Chicago (Cook
County) had one "colored" volunteer social worker. Frazier (1939, 1949) provided some
information on Negro youth appearing before the children's court in the District
of Columbia; Nashville, Tennessee; New York City; and other locales, although he
emphasized community and family factors and did not address race effects. In light
of segregation and treatment in the early facilities, it is doubtful that the majority of
Negro youth fared much better in juvenile courts in the early 20th century.

The Black child savers and other professionals may have played an important role in
early juvenile courts in some locales, but there were not enough of them. Although they
aimed to work in the best interest of the child, they could change neither the structural
and economic conditions nor the stereotypical attitudes of other (White) justice professionals. Among most justice practitioners, differential treatment of Black youth was
tolerated and accepted. Feld (1999) argued that, since its inception, one of the most
important functions of the juvenile court was to control ethnic and racial minorities:

> The Progressives created the juvenile court to assimilate, integrate, and control
> the children of the eastern European immigrants pouring into cities of the
> East and Midwest at the turn of the century. In postindustrial American cities
> today, juvenile courts function to maintain social control of minority youths,
> predominantly young Black males. (p. 5)

The use of waivers to remove youth from the jurisdiction of the juvenile court flourished in the late 20th century after legislative changes to transfer laws became more punitive. Judicial, legislative, and prosecutorial waivers (sometimes known as transfers and/or certifications) facilitate trying youth as adults. In some states, reverse waivers permit criminal courts to send cases back to juvenile court and utilize a juvenile disposition (Brooks & Willingham, 2009; Jordan & Myers, 2007). Between 1985 and 2007, Black youth were more likely to be waived to adult court regardless of the type of offense (person, property, drugs, public order). During the 1990s, Black youth were twice as likely as White youth to be waived for offenses against the person and more than three times as likely to be waived for drug offenses (Adams & Addie, 2010). In 2007, Black and White youth had similar likelihoods of waiver, although Black youth were still more likely to be waived for offenses against the person and drug crimes than White youth (p. 4). According to the most recent data available, Black youth were more likely than White youth to be waived for person and drug offenses, although American Indian youth had the highest percentage of waivers for person offenses (2.5%; Sickmund & Puzzanchera, 2014). DMC at this stage in the process continues to be problematic today.

In spite of efforts to deinstitutionalize youth that began with the 1974 Juvenile Justice and Delinquency Prevention Act, the 1994 Violent Crime and Safe Streets Act that allocated more funding to preventive approaches for juveniles, and recent Supreme Court decisions that abolished the death penalty and narrowed life without parole sentences for juveniles, the punishment model continues to define juvenile justice in most states. During the past two decades, the hybrid mix of rehabilitation, punishment, system accountability, and juvenile accountability has resulted in the implementation of numerous conflicting policies and programs to prevent and control juvenile delinquency. Goshe (2015) cautions that the "punitive legacy" could negatively impact progressive reforms that appear to be underway. Some of these more punitive approaches—including trying juveniles as adults, mandatory sentences, and longer sentences—were a reaction to increases in juvenile involvement in violent crime, discussed in more detail next.

❖ Race, Juvenile Crime, and Victimization

For decades, juvenile involvement in crime as perpetrators and victims has received considerable attention. Part of the concern is related to the disproportionate number of youth, especially Black and other minority youth, who are arrested and confined. Howell (2003) argued that one of the most damaging myths about juvenile crime and violence was the prediction about the emergence of a new breed of juvenile offenders, ostensibly labeled *superpredators* (DiIulio, 1995, 1996b). Implicit in the notion of the superpredator was the demonization of Black and Hispanic youth; these and other chronic offenders were projected as contributing to a youth violence epidemic in our country in the coming years (Blumstein, 1996). Although there were both increases and decreases in the number of juvenile arrests after these dire predictions, there was a "moral panic over juvenile delinquency" that resulted in more punitive measures and "a crisis of overload in the juvenile justice system" (Howell, 2003, p. 24). In fact, while the number of juveniles arrested for violent crimes is still a problem, juvenile arrests have leveled off and "the juvenile Violent Crime Index arrest rate reached a historic low in 2010" (Sickmund & Puzzanchera, 2014, p. 125).

Chapter 2 provided an overview of several sources of crime and victimization data, including the FBI Uniform Crime Reports (UCR), National Incident Based Reporting System (NIBRS), and Hate Crime Statistics, as well as the Bureau of Justice Statistics (BJS) **National Crime Victimization Survey (NCVS)**, which provide information on juveniles. In 1999, the OJJDP made its **Statistical Briefing Book (SBB)** available online (http://www.ojjdp.gov/ojstatbb/default.asp) for access to information about juvenile delinquents, victims, juvenile court statistics, and data on youth in residential confinement. The SBB data analysis tools and national data sets are very useful for analyzing race and juvenile justice. Other sources of juvenile crime and victimization data are the Monitoring the Future Study, the National Adolescent Survey, National Survey on Drug Use and Health, National Youth Gang Survey, the Pathways to Desistance Study, and the Behavior Risk Surveillance System.

Chapter 2 also addressed the strengths and limitations of available data that are relevant to understanding race, juvenile crime, and victimization. Because a separate category for Hispanic arrests was unavailable until 2013, and only aggregate arrest data is available, intersectionalities of arrests with age, race, and gender can't be examined simultaneously. Also, UCR arrest data are based on estimates, and UCR juvenile arrests estimates may vary over time (see, e.g., Snyder, 1997, 2000, 2003; Sickmund & Puzzanchera, 2014). NCVS data are also problematic. First, the NCVS excludes youth under 12 years of age. Second, NCVS data are also based on estimates. Despite these limitations, the available data do help us understand patterns and trends in juvenile participation in crime as arrestees, victims, and those who are processed in the juvenile justice system.

Juvenile arrests during the 1980s and 1990s were much more numerous than they are today. After remaining constant between 1980 and 1987, the Violent Crime Index arrest rate grew between 1987 and 1994, after which it fell to its lowest level since 1980 in 2010 (Sickmund & Puzzanchera, 2014, p. 125). Across most offenses, juvenile arrests fell proportionately more than adult arrests between 2001 and 2010 (p. 120). However, in 2010, more than one-fourth of states had a juvenile violent crime arrest rate above the national average (p. 142). According to the OJJDP SBB, juvenile arrests between 2006–2012 steadily decreased; in 2006, an estimated 2.2 million juveniles were arrested, and in 2012, an estimated 1.3 million juveniles were arrested (see Table 9.1). In 2013, the majority of juveniles arrested were either White (63%) or Black (34.4%); American Indians or Alaskan Natives and Native Hawaiians or other Pacific Islanders represented less than 3% of juvenile arrestees (see Table 9.2). In 2013, an estimated 99,018 Hispanic/Latino juveniles were arrested.

Like adults, the majority of juvenile arrestees are males, although the number of female arrestees has increased in recent years. According to the UCR, in 2006, 18.9%, and in 2009, 17% of juvenile arrestees were females (FBI, 2007a, 2010a). Although the male arrest rate had decreased since 1980, in 2010 the female rate was higher (Sickmund & Puzzanchera, 2014, p. 125). In 2013, 9% of males arrested and 11% of females arrested were juveniles (FBI, 2014a). Most juveniles arrested for violent and property crimes, regardless of age, race, ethnicity, and gender, are arrested for larceny-theft (excluding the "all other offenses" category). Blacks outnumbered Whites and others arrested for murder, robbery, prostitution and commercial vice, gambling, and

Table 9.1

Juvenile Arrest Estimates, 2006–2012

Year	Arrests	Percentage Total Arrests
2006	2,213,500	15.4
2007	2,171,200	15.3
2008	2,101,100	15
2009	1,906,600	13.9
2010	1,642,600	12.5
2011	1,470,000	11.8
2012	1,319,700	10.8

Source: OJJDP *Statistical Briefing Book Data Analysis Tool: Easy Access to FBI Arrest Statistics.*

suspicion. Black juveniles accounted for 53.3% of arrests for violent crime, whereas White juveniles accounted for 59.7 of juveniles arrested for property crime. After larceny-theft, and excluding the category of "all other offenses," more juveniles were arrested for other assaults, disorderly conduct, and drug abuse violations. Among American Indians or Alaskan Natives, more juveniles were arrested for larceny-theft and liquor law violations, whereas Asians or Pacific Islanders were more likely to be arrested for larceny-theft and other assaults (FBI, 2014a; see Table 9.2).

Youth involvement in violent crimes as both victims and offenders is of concern to families, child advocates, communities, juvenile justice practitioners, and other stakeholders. More recently, these concerns have become a national priority (see Listenbee et al., 2012). According to former Attorney General Holder's Task Force on Children Exposed to Violence, part of the Defending Childhood Initiative,

> In 1979, U.S. Surgeon General Julius B. Richmond declared violence a public health crisis of the highest priority, and yet 33 years later that crisis remains. Whether the violence occurs in children's homes, neighborhoods, schools, playgrounds or playing fields, locker rooms, places of worship, shelters, streets, or in juvenile detention centers, the exposure of children to violence is a uniquely traumatic experience that has the potential to profoundly derail the child's security, health, happiness, and ability to grow and learn—with effects lasting well into adulthood. (Listenbee et al., 2012, p. 3)

According to the National Center for Injury Prevention and Control (2010), homicide was the fourth leading cause of death for children aged 1 to 11 and second cause of death for youth aged 12 to 17. Between 2000 and 2005, there were 9,312 juvenile murder victims, many of them very young (OJJDP, 2008). In 2010, it is estimated that 1,450 youth were murdered in the U.S., many of them by parents or stepparents (see Box 9.1).

Forty nine percent of juveniles murdered were Black, and 47% were White. The Black murder rate was almost five times the White rate, and the Black-White disparity has increased since 1999 (Sickmund & Puzzanchera, 2014, p. 52). Data on juvenile victims of nonfatal crimes are reported in victimization studies discussed next.

BOX 9.1

Juveniles Murdered Between 1980 and 2010, by Offender Relationship

Offender Relationship to Victim (%)	Age of Victim					Victim Ages 0–17	
	0–17	0–5	6–11	12–14	15–17	Male	Female
Offender known	67	82	60	62	58	65	71
Total[a]	100	100	100	100	100	100	100
Parent/stepparent[b]	21	51	24	6	2	17	31
Other family member	4	5	8	6	3	4	6
Acquaintance	31	23	18	37	38	33	28
Stranger[c]	10	2	10	13	16	12	7
Offender unknown	33	18	40	38	33	35	29

Source: Sickmund and Puzzanchera (2014, p. 52).

Notes:

a. Detail may not total 100% because of rounding.

b. Female victims were far more likely than male victims to have been killed by a parent/stepparent or other family member.

c. Over the 31-year period, strangers were involved in at least 10% of the murders of juveniles. This figure is probably greater than 10% because strangers are likely to account for a disproportionate share of crimes in which the offender is unknown.

The NCVS includes reported violent victimizations (rape, sexual assault, robbery, aggravated assault, and simple assault) and property victimizations (attempted and completed theft, household burglary, and motor vehicle theft). According to Sickmund & Puzzanchera (2014), "from 1994 through 2010, youth ages 12–17 were about 2.2 times more likely to be victims of a serious violent crime . . . [and] 2.6 times more likely to be victims of a simple assault" (p. 39). Juveniles also are victims of bullying, cyberbullying, and sexual assaults.

Table 9.2

Arrests of Youth Under 18 by Race and Ethnicity, 2013

Offense Charged	Arrests Under 18						Percentage Distribution[a]		
	Race								
	Total	White	Black or African American	American Indian or Alaska Native	Asian	Native Hawaiian or Other Pacific Islander	Total	White	Black or African American
TOTAL	868,693	547,395	298,425	12,601	9,716	556	100.0	63.0	34.4
Murder and nonnegligent manslaughter	613	263	333	10	6	1	100.0	42.9	54.3
Rape[c]	2,065	1,316	709	21	18	1	100.0	63.7	34.3
Robbery	15,903	4,356	11,351	63	111	22	100.0	27.4	71.4
Aggravated assault	24,914	13,544	10,802	295	251	22	100.0	54.4	43.4
Burglary	34,610	19,948	13,913	331	385	33	100.0	57.6	40.2
Larceny-theft	150,213	90,606	54,725	2,368	2,431	83	100.0	60.3	36.4
Motor vehicle theft	9,428	5,090	4,111	135	81	11	100.0	54.0	43.6
Arson	2,928	2,157	694	43	32	2	100.0	73.7	23.7
Violent crime[d]	43,495	19,479	23,195	389	386	46	100.0	44.8	53.3
Property crime[d]	197,179	117,801	73,443	2,877	2,929	129	100.0	59.7	37.2

Source: FBI (2014a, Table 43B).

Notes:

a. Because of rounding, the percentages may not add to 100.0.

b. The ethnicity totals are representative of those agencies that provided ethnicity breakdowns. Not all agencies provide ethnicity data; therefore, the race and ethnicity totals will not be equal.

c. The rape figures in this table are an aggregate total of the data submitted using both the revised and legacy Uniform Crime Reporting definitions.

d. Violent crimes in this table are offenses of murder and nonnegligent manslaughter, rape (revised and legacy definitions), robbery, and aggravated assault. Property crimes are offenses of burglary, larceny-theft, motor vehicle theft, and arson.

* Less than one-tenth of 1%.

| | Percentage Distribution[a] | | Arrests Under 18 | | | Percent Distribution[a] | | |
| | | | | Ethnicity | | | | |
American Indian or Alaskan Native	Asian	Native Hawaiian or Other Pacific Islander	Total[b]	Hispanic or Latino	Not Hispanic or Latino	Total	Hispanic or Latino	Not Hispanic or Latino
1.5	1.1	0.1	462,583	99,018	363,565	100.0	21.4	78.6
1.6	1.0	0.2	274	89	185	100.0	32.5	67.5
1.0	0.9	*	1,775	255	1,520	100.0	14.4	85.6
0.4	0.7	0.1	8,444	1,830	6,614	100.0	21.7	78.3
1.2	1.0	0.1	13,862	3,531	10,331	100.0	25.5	74.5
1.0	1.1	0.1	19,303	5,139	14,164	100.0	26.6	73.4
1.6	1.6	0.1	77,411	14,425	62,986	100.0	18.6	81.4
1.4	0.9	0.1	4,869	1,418	3,451	100.0	29.1	70.9
1.5	1.1	0.1	1,499	295	1,204	100.0	19.7	80.3
0.9	0.9	0.1	24,355	5,705	18,650	100.0	23.4	76.6
1.5	1.5	0.1	103,082	21,277	81,805	100.0	20.6	

Some juvenile crime and victimization is the result of youth in gangs, whose members are involved in a disproportionate amount of serious and violent crime (Thornberry, 1998; Thornberry, Huizinga, & Loeber, 2004) and are more likely to be violently victimized while in a gang (Peterson, Taylor, & Esbensen, 2004). Gang-related homicides are more likely to occur in large cities and suburban counties (Egley & Howell, 2011). Youth gang activity fluctuates and varies from time to time and place to place. In 2010, there were an estimated 29,400 gangs, with about 756,000 members in jurisdictions around the country (Sickmund & Puzzanchera, 2014, p. 69). In 2012, there were an estimated 30,700 gangs with 850,000 gang members (National Youth Gang Center, 2015). Contemporary gangs include mixed racial/ethnic members, more adults than younger members, and females. Gangs continue to be composed primarily of Hispanic/Latino youth (46%), Blacks (35%), and fewer White (11%) and other youth (7%) (National Youth Gang Center, 2015). Some street gangs are involved in illegal drug sales and distribution. We can't say for sure how many youth who participate in street gangs either use or sell drugs, but drug use and sales appear to increase after joining a gang (Egley & Howell, 2011).

Juvenile drug behavior is often correlated with delinquency, although the nature of the relationship is unclear. Racial differences in drug arrest rates for Whites and Blacks changed dramatically between 1980 and 1991, increasing for Blacks and decreasing for Whites. While drug arrests increased for all youth in the 1990s, the Black rate was almost six times the White rate. More recently, between 1980 and 2010, the juvenile drug arrest rate for Whites and Blacks peaked in the 1990s, remaining constant for Whites and falling about 52% for Blacks by 2010. For males and females, the arrest rates in 2010 were above the 1980 rates (Sickmund & Puzzanchera, 2014, p. 137).

Most youthful offenders are involved with drugs or alcohol at an early age, and their involvement "increases the likelihood of chronic contact with the juvenile justice system" (Belenko, Sprott, & Petersen, 2004, p. 4). Drug and alcohol use are more common among juvenile offenders than among nonoffender students (Belenko et al., 2004).

❖ Youth in the Juvenile Justice System

Similar to patterns in FBI arrest data, most delinquency cases referred to juvenile court involve males, and most youth are referred for property offenses. In 2013, there were an estimated 1,058,500 delinquency cases in United States courts with juvenile jurisdiction. In 2013, property offenses (366,600) comprised the majority of delinquency cases. Offenses against the person (homicide, robbery, rape, and aggravated assault) accounted for 278,300 delinquency cases. Overall, with only a few exceptions, delinquency case rates have decreased since 1994 and steadily decreased since 2008, reaching a historic low in 2013. In 2013, it is estimated that 3,980 of petitioned delinquency cases were waived to adult court (OJJDP, 2015). The decline in cases waived is thought to be the result of (1) declines in juvenile involvement in violent crimes and (2) expansion of nonjudicial transfer laws (Hockenberry & Puzzanchera, 2014).

Decreases in the number of crimes committed, persons referred to juvenile courts, and juveniles waived to adult courts are important. Data limitations aside, it appears that reform efforts, including both punishment and rehabilitative approaches, work. At the same time, the overrepresentation of minorities, especially African American youth, in the juvenile justice system is an ongoing problem. Even though their referrals to juvenile court have decreased, since 2005 they continue to represent an estimated 33% of delinquency cases in juvenile court (Sickmund & Puzzanchera, 2014). What accounts for these racial disparities?

Disproportionate Minority Contact (DMC)

DMC is a term used to refer to the overrepresentation of minority youth in the juvenile justice system. As noted earlier, the concept of DMC was expanded to include disproportionate contact. This means that in addition to the disproportionate number of minority youth in confinement, DMC exists at many of the other contact/decision points and/or stages in the juvenile justice system (e.g., referral, diversion, arrest, petition, detention). According to Pope and Feyerherm (1990),

> There is evidence to suggest that processing decisions in many state and local juvenile justice systems may not be racially neutral. Race effects may occur at various decision points, they may be direct or indirect, and they may accumulate as youths are processed through the system. (p. 331)

Critical decision points where disproportionality is high include arrest, confinement, and waivers to adult court (Jones & Greene, 2014). Since we know that White and other minority youth (especially Blacks) are treated differently, the challenge "is to explain how these differences come about" (Bishop, 2005, p. 24).

The U.S. Congress formally addressed DMC in 1988 by amending the Juvenile Justice and Delinquency Prevention (JJDP) Act of 1974. For the first time, any state receiving federal funding through formula grants was required to determine whether DMC existed and, if necessary, address the problem. In 1991, OJJDP began to assist states in addressing DMC issues (Devine, Coolbaugh, & Jenkins, 1998), and in 1992 Congress made DMC a core requirement of the JJDP Act, which mandated compliance as a condition of funding. The DMC Index was created to help determine the extent of minority overrepresentation. A decade later, the JJDP Act of 2002 mandated that states failing to address DMC could forfeit 20% of their federal funding (OJJDP, 2004). According to Leiber (2002), OJJDP has adopted a judicious approach to DMC that appears to follow the "spirit" of the mandate and attempts to make inroads—"to get something done" rather than accomplishing "nothing at all" (p. 16). Unfortunately, there still are several challenges to reducing DMC that include the lack of resources, inadequate information systems, the need for the identification and development of effective intervention strategies, and the need to transition from planning (state) to implementation (local). Leiber and Rodriguez (2011) examined whether or not the DMC mandate had been a success or failure and concluded that both have occurred. They acknowledge that while the mandate has heightened awareness of the importance of promoting equity in juvenile justice, reductions in DMC have been minimal: "Efforts, however, have to be made to strengthen the 'bite' of OJJDP to entice and encourage states and localities to comply" (p. 117).

Even though there has been a considerable amount of research yielding varying results (see Leiber & Rodriguez, 2011; Davis & Sorenson, 2013), one consistent finding is that racial and ethnic youth continue to be treated differently (Bishop, 2005). In the earlier studies, some found no race effects, whereas others found direct and/or indirect race effects during intake (Leiber & Mack, 2003), detention (Wordes, Bynum, & Corley, 1994), probation (Bridges & Steen, 1998), confinement (Bridges, Conley, Engen, & Price-Spratlen, 1995), and in the child welfare system (Lau et al., 2003). In a follow-up study to the Pope and Feyerherm (1990) review of the research literature discussed at the beginning of this chapter, Pope, Lovell, and Hsia (2002) reviewed DMC studies published between 1989 and 2001 and concluded, "The majority of studies continue to provide evidence of race effects, direct or indirect, at certain stages of juvenile justice processing and in certain jurisdictions" (p. 6). Relatedly, Ward (2001) noted,

> Despite these efforts among researchers and policy makers, nearly a decade later the DMC problem is only more entrenched, and its significance amplified in the wake of a retributive turn in the philosophy and organization of juvenile justice administration. (p. 2)

More recent research has sought to identify effective strategies for reducing DMC (Cabaniss, Frabutt, Kendrick, & Arbuckle, 2007; Hsia, Bridges, & McHale, 2004; Short & Sharp, 2005) and examine DMC in the contexts of race and gender (Carr, Hudson, Hanks, & Hunt, 2008; Guevara, Herz, & Spohn, 2006; Leiber & Mack, 2003) at multiple stages instead of just one (Guevara et al., 2006), and inclusive of Blacks, Latinos/as, and American Indians (Rodriguez, 2007). The limited impact of DMC research on policy in this area extends, in part, from conceptual and empirical problems (Leiber & Rodriguez, 2011). In 2001, Ward identified the several DMC research problems that still exist today, including the conceptualization and measurement of race and how it operates at individual, cultural, and structural levels as well as within juvenile justice administration.

Why does DMC continue to challenge juvenile justice practitioners and other stakeholders? There are several plausible explanations. First, juvenile justice has always been a racialized system (Ward, 2001, 2012). Feld (1999) cited race and the macrostructural transformation of cities as two societal factors important for understanding juvenile justice policies and practices. More specifically, Feld was referring to the racial segregation in urban areas and the deindustrialization of cities that has occurred during the last few decades. Feld agreed with Sampson and Wilson's (1995) structural/cultural approach, which takes into consideration a community's structural disorganization, cultural isolation, and the concentration effects of poverty that foster criminal involvement (see Chapter 3). Another explanation is that within a racialized system, police and other justice practitioners hold stereotypical views of minority youth that often result in differential treatment (Ward, 2001, 2012). Even if discrimination and more punitive policies account for some of the overrepresentation of minorities, their involvement in serious crime in some communities is also a factor.

The overrepresentation of juveniles in arrests indicates that crime might be viewed as acceptable by some youth. Explanations for acceptance of and involvement in delinquency include alienation, reactions to discrimination, and "the street" factor. According to the colonial model (see Chapter 3), some youth turn to crime in response to their alienation (Tatum, 1994). Others are reacting to their perceptions of inequality, oppression, and discrimination (S. Johnson, 1996; Vega & Gil, 1998; Unnever & Gabbidon, 2011). Some believe that crime and delinquency are acceptable because of the lack of access to legitimate means of economic gain that many attribute to racism. Relatedly, the "street factor" often requires involvement in crime to prove one's toughness; violence is viewed favorably, often as a way of gaining status (E. Anderson, 1999), and it is therefore more likely to be tolerated and perpetuated. Unnever and Gabbidon (2011) as well as others posit that how parents socialize their youth to respond to racial discrimination can play a role in preventing youths' involvement in crime.

Some effective strategies for reducing DMC have emerged in the past decade, including data review and decision-point mapping, cultural competency training, increasing community-based detention alternatives, reducing decision-making subjectivity, reducing barriers to family involvement, and developing state leadership to legislate system-level changes (Cabaniss et al., 2007). The annual reports of the Federal Advisory Committee on Juvenile Justice (FACJJ) provide a report card on national compliance with core protections of the JJDP act. The 2013 report made the following recommendations:

- Training for school-based officers and educators to address the school-to-prison pipeline and its impact on DMC in the juvenile justice system,
- Require that grant applicants indicate how they are addressing juvenile DMC in their communities,
- That OJJDP study and research disparities within multiple youth-serving systems and their impact on juvenile DMC,
- That OJJDP support an initiative to fund and create a campaign that educates families and communities about DMC.

Have these and previous recommendations of the FACJJ made a difference to DMC efforts at the federal, state, and local levels?

The Future of DMC

Those committed to reducing DMC in this century can learn from the experiences of child savers centuries ago. Progress will require coalitions of individuals, organizations, stakeholders, and others who are willing to work together to identify best practices and develop model action plans for the coming decades. OJJDP requires states to follow a DMC Reduction Model if they accept formula grants. Many states now have DMC reduction plans in place that need continuous monitoring, evaluation, and revisions during the coming years. This will require more oversight and resources than is currently available at the federal and state levels. James Bell of the W. Haywood Burns Institute would like to see OJJDP focus more on understanding DMC at the local level, for example in cities and counties (Chu, 2014). A cadre of DMC change agents are needed in almost every state, especially those where DMC is entrenched and has seen little progress in the past 30 years. These change agents will need to continue to hold government officials accountable.

There will always be methodological issues related to the measurement of DMC. One issue that has been identified and is being addressed is the need for state information systems to accurately report and record the demographic characteristics of juveniles in contact with each stage of the juvenile process. Standards for collection and reporting information, similar to collecting and reporting arrest and victimization data, should be implemented. The DMC Relative Rate Index (RRI), designed to "quantify the nature of the decisions at each decision point for each racial group and then compare these decisions" (Snyder & Sickmund, 2008, p. 190), is now the standard for understanding disparities. It is useful because it allows for a more comprehensive understanding of DMC that focuses on multistages instead of one stage (Guevara et al., 2006). The RRI is only useful if state data collected is accurate and complete. Another issue is the complexity of defining one's racial/ethnic status. While the categories have been expanded in some data collections, most omit information on mixed-race youth, culture, class, and country of origin (Kempf-Leonard, 2007). An emerging issue in using the RRI to understand disparities is whether or not it should be based on the White population when and where they are not the majority (Jones & Greene, 2014).

As Pope and Feyerherm (1990) noted 25 years ago, the DMC problem and race effects will not end until structural and economic factors that contribute to youth involvement in delinquency are recognized and addressed. It also is important to prevent delinquency and address the challenge of making the attitudes of youth less favorable about delinquency. Similar to the problem of DMC, the overrepresentation of Blacks and Latinos in **school punishment** continues to challenge practitioners, scholars, elected officials, and other stakeholders in the United States. Is there a school-to-prison pipeline? This issue is discussed next.

The School-to-Prison Pipeline (SPP)

Since the 1990s, as a result of concerns about increases in violent crime and the number of school shooting incidents, punitive approaches to school crime, such as zero-tolerance policies and placing police officers in schools, have been implemented. By the early 2000s, concerns about the "school-to-prison pipeline" (SPP) emerged as disparities for youth of color in both school punishment and juvenile justice received more attention (see Kim, Losen, & Hewitt, 2010). The term *SPP* is used to refer to the relationship between school punishment, such as in- and out-of-school suspension and expulsion, and an increase in the likelihood of confinement in either a juvenile institution, adult prison, or both. The Children's Defense Fund (2013) uses the term *Cradle to Prison Pipeline* to emphasize that for Black and Latino boys, the pipeline begins at birth, and they have a greater lifetime risk of going to prison than Whites, due, at least in part, to both poverty and race.

Although published research on the SPP in criminology/criminal justice is limited (see Hall & Karanxha, 2012; Kupchik, 2009; Payne & Welch, 2010; Welch & Payne, 2012), there has been a considerable amount of research on school discipline in the field of education (see Houchins, Shippen, & Murphy, 2012), and disparities have been reported in many city-specific analyses (Kirwan Institute, 2014). Studies also find that schools with higher proportions of Black students use exclusionary school punishments more often (Kupchik, 2009; Payne & Welch, 2010; Welch & Payne, 2012). Other factors, including school climate, administrators' and teachers' racial biases, misperceptions about Black youth and crime, and fear of crime and victimization, influence school punishment (Welch & Payne, 2012). Teachers' racial/implicit bias has been found to be a contributing factor in racial disproportionality in school discipline and may explain why Black and White students receive different punishments for the same offenses (Kirwan Institute, 2014; Payne & Welch, 2010; Skiba, Michael, Nardo, & Peterson, 2002). Many believe that school punishment is the beginning of the SPP and that it has long-term negative effects on the life course of youth. For example, students who are punished often fall behind in class assignments, and those who believe they were wrongfully punished can develop negative feelings toward school that impact their future school performance. As adults, they might be less likely to engage in civic activities, including voting (Kupchik & Catlaw, 2014).

If confinement in a juvenile or adult facility is the last component of the SPP, then understanding whether or not school punishment is related to DMC is important. As discussed in the previous section, DMC is still problematic for minority youth at almost all stages and decision points in juvenile justice (arrest, detention, referral to juvenile court, petition, confinement, waiver, etc.). Although research that examines the relationship between school punishment and DMC is limited, there have been several studies in the state of Texas (Fowler, Lightsey, Monger, & Aseltine, 2010a, 2010b; Hall & Karanxha, 2012; Wilson, Johnson, & Greene, 2015) as a result of the efforts of child and youth advocacy organizations, including Texas Appleseed, the Children's Defense Fund-Texas, the Texas Southern University Thurgood Marshall School of Law Earl Carl Institute, and others. DMC and the SPP in Texas is presented next.

DMC and SPP in Texas

Heretofore in most states, including Texas, research on DMC in juvenile justice has received more attention than school punishment and its role in the SPP. This is due, at least in part, to federal mandates that require states to address DMC. In Texas, the Office of the Governor's Criminal Justice Division is responsible for administering OJJDP funding allocated to the state for addressing DMC. In the early 1990s, the state was found to be out of compliance with OJJDP DMC mandates (Menon, 1997). Since then, the state has continued to address DMC by working closely with the Texas A&M Public Policy Research Institute (PPRI). The PPRI has issued several reports on DMC (Carmichael, Booth, & Patnaik, 2010; Carmichael, Whitten, & Voloudakis, 2005; Menon, 1997). In Texas, the overrepresentation of minority youth at several of the juvenile justice stages, especially for African Americans, was acknowledged (Office of the Governor, Criminal Justice Division, 2014). There have been other studies of DMC in Texas (Coalition for Juvenile Justice, 2011; Davis & Sorensen, 2010, 2013; Jones & Greene, 2014; Piquero, 2008; Tracy, 2005) and ongoing efforts to address it.

In 2013, there were an estimated 35 million youth in Texas, 21.5 million Whites (81.3%), 3.3 million African Americans (12.8%), and 10 million Hispanics (38.4%). In several counties, including Bexar, El Paso, Dallas, and Harris, Blacks and Hispanics comprise the majority of the youth population (Puzzanchera, Sladky, & Kang, 2014). According to the OJJDP SBB (2015), in 2011, of the 4,671 youth in confinement in Texas, Blacks (1,506) and Hispanics (2,253) outnumbered Whites (879). Is the overrepresentation of minorities in confinement related to school punishment? In an early DMC study, Carmichael, Whitten, and Voloudakis (2005) utilized data from the Texas Education Agency and Juvenile Probation Commission (now defunct) to examine racial disparities. They found that race/ethnicity (including overt racism and systematic bias) has a small effect on justice involvement:

> Initial contact with the juvenile system predominantly occurs because youth have a discipline history at school, are male, are not excelling academically, are economically disadvantaged, or have an emotional or learning disability. (p. 58)

While all of these factors are important, even students who get good grades, attend school regularly, and have a strong attachment to school can be punished. School discipline/punishment is best understood in the context of other school factors, including demographic characteristics of students and teachers, socioeconomic status of students, and school location (see Box 9.2).

BOX 9.2

School-to-Prison Pipeline in Texas

A paradigm shift has occurred in Texas where students' misdeeds are being punished criminally, which often results in criminal records, punitive fines, and court costs for children aged 10–16. Texas Appleseed (2012) analyzed Class C ticketing for low-level student behavior and found that in many cases, ticketed behavior is often so minor that it does not warrant misdemeanor ticketing. Below are four case studies that highlight some of the issues associated with Class C ticketing, police interrogation, and searches by school police officers.

Case Study 1 (p. 146)

In Texas, zero-tolerance policies can create interesting situations for students that often subject them to unnecessary interrogations by police officers. As the police presence increases in schools, ticketing also increases.

A law enforcement officer questioned two female students about a claim of criminal mischief. The officer came on campus and questioned the two girls without the permission of school personnel and without notifying the students of their right to counsel and/or an advocate. The officer requested that school personnel escort the students from class and bring them into a room on campus for interrogation. During questioning no school officials were present. The officer claimed that both students were involved with the alleged crime, arguing that one student was driving the vehicle involved while the other student was a participant. However, the vehicle in question was in an auto body shop and both girls were in the presence of adults when the alleged crime occurred.

Case Study 2 (p. 81)

Special needs students are a population of students in Texas who are often unnecessarily subjected to Class C ticketing. Class C tickets are not processed in the juvenile court. Juveniles who are convicted of a Class C misdemeanor are not awarded the opportunity to defend themselves with legal representation. Because there is no intake process in municipal and justice court, there is no requirement for prosecutorial review. Therefore, prosecutors do not have an opportunity to exercise prosecutorial review and dismiss a case prior to trial. Also, juveniles aren't provided with defense counsel during Class C misdemeanor cases, which often results in young people pleading guilty even when they have a valid defense to a charge.

An attorney who represents special education students in school discipline cases shared one client's story with Texas Appleseed:

In Houston, a 16-year-old youth with Asperger's syndrome, who was a good student who never had any behavioral issues at school, was harassed and bullied because of his poor social skills. Although the youth's mother notified the school about her son's bully, the school failed to take any serious action and failed to inform the mother of her son's rights to move to another classroom or school. Unfortunately, the youth was later attacked by the bully, which resulted in the youth hitting the bully in self-defense. The youth with Asperger's syndrome received a brutal beating that required a trip to the emergency room for stitches. Although the youth with Asperger's syndrome was a victim in the attack, at the principal's request the school police issued citations to both youth involved in the confrontation. Fortunately, a disability rights nonprofit accepted the youth's case and notified his family of his right to self-defense under Texas criminal law and his right to switch schools to prevent future bullying and abuse. A sad reality is that most youth in similar situations agree to pleas offered by the court without legal representation, although they may have not committed a crime under Texas criminal law.

Case Study 3 (p. 98)

In Texas, Hispanic and Black students are overrepresented in Class C ticketing. The following case study describes a parent's concern with the overrepresentation of minorities in court.

A parent's 12-year-old son received a misdemeanor ticket for throwing food in the cafeteria during lunch. The ticket issued to the student was for "disturbing the educational environment." The parent and the child had to appear in court eight times and have pending dates for the following school year, which is interfering with the child's education. Because the child is biracial (Black), his mother is annoyed because the school the child attends is predominately White, yet the majority of kids that are in court from his school are minorities.

Case Study 4 (p. 101)

Gang membership is a Class C offense that is only found in the Texas Education Code. School officials often use student dress or other behavior as an indicator of gang membership, which often results in minority students receiving unnecessary Class C tickets. The following case study highlights an example of a student being profiled for alleged gang membership.

While on foot patrol at a Texas middle school, an officer was looking for signs of gang affiliation because of a fight that broke out between two gangs the previous week. Familiar with criminal street gang subcultures, the officer observed two students, Juan and Geraldo, dressed in royal blue shirts and denim jean pants. The officer observed a handshake between the two boys and identified it as a gang-related handshake. As a result, both students were detained and escorted to the police office. Geraldo received a three-day suspension, and Juan and Geraldo were both ticketed for gang membership although they were not documented by the county juvenile detention facility as having prior gang involvement.

The Office of the Governor, Criminal Justice Division's (2014) biennial report states, "The primary source of referrals into Texas' juvenile justice system are public schools" (p. 7). Of the male students with discretionary (school) disciplinary violations, 83% were Black, 74% were Hispanic, and 59% were White; of the female students, 70% were Black, 58% Hispanic, and 37% were White. More Black males (26%) and females

(14%) had contact with the juvenile justice system than male and female Hispanics (22%, 13%) and Whites (14%, 8%).

There are no federal mandates for addressing school punishment, although there have been several recommendations (see FACJJ, 2013). To date, there only have been four studies of school punishment in Texas (Advancement Project, 2010; Fowler, Lightsey, Monger & Aseltine, 2010a; Fowler, Lightsey, Monger, & Aseltine, 2010b). Fowler, Lightsey, Monger, and Aseltine (2010b) conducted a study of SPP in Texas for Texas Appleseed, focusing on Class C misdemeanor ticketing of students, arrest, and use of force in schools. In Texas school districts, administrators and teachers rely heavily on Class C misdemeanor ticketing for students' nonviolent and lower-level misbehaving (Fowler et al., 2010b). As a result of legislative changes in the 1990s, instead of juvenile courts handling Class C misdemeanor cases, they are handled by Municipal and Justice of the Peace courts that require parents' presence, fines, court costs, and payment of other fees.

When the U.S. Department of Education Office of Civil Rights made the 2011–2012 Civil Rights Data Collection (CRDC) available, it provided an opportunity for researchers to examine information on numerous school characteristics, including school punishment, in every state. The CRDC data gives stakeholders an opportunity to examine school characteristics for all schools for the first time since 2000 (U.S. DOE, 2013). The data reveal racial disparities in school punishment (and other factors) in public schools. Two recent studies used the CRDC data to examine school punishment in Texas (Greene, Johnson, & Alexander, 2014; Wilson, Johnson, & Greene, 2015).

Even though disparities do exist in school punishment and at various juvenile justice stages, how can we determine a causal relationship? Fowler et al. (2010b) examined school ticketing data, arrest data, and surveys/focus groups with confined and nonconfined youth. They found that confined youth had more disciplinary encounters. However, their findings are limited due to low response rates from schools and nonrepresentative samples. Analyses of the relationship between school punishment and DMC in Texas (and elsewhere) have several challenges. One challenge is the fact that school punishment varies from one Independent School District (ISD) to another within the same county. Another is that DMC data is not available at the ISD or neighborhood level. Lastly, data at all Texas juvenile justice decision points may not be available in the OJJDP DMC database. Greene et al. (2014) examined school punishment in ISDs in four Texas counties—Harris, Dallas, Travis, and Bexar—using the DOC OCR School Discipline data. These counties were selected because in three of them the majority of the youth population are minorities (Latino & Black). Blacks and Latinos had much higher rates of in-school and out-of-school suspensions than Whites, and Black disparities were greater than those of Latinos. Wilson et al. (2015) examined school punishment in 20 Texas ISDs, including 10 counties with majority minority populations and 10 counties with majority White populations, and also found an overrepresentation of Blacks in both types of counties. However, the relationship between school punishment and DMC was not analyzed due to limitations of the DMC data. The Texas Office of the Governor's (2014) information on school punishment and contact with the juvenile justice system indicates that at least for some minorities, there is a SPP in the state. A more definitive answer about the SPP in Texas requires more research and access to reliable data.

Minority Female Delinquency

One surprising finding of the school punishment data is the overrepresentation of girls in school punishment:

> From 2011 to 2012, black girls in public elementary and secondary schools nationwide were suspended at a rate of 12 percent, compared with a rate of just 2 percent for white girls, and more than girls of any other race or ethnicity. (Vega, 2014)

Girls' delinquency is not a new phenomenon, although it receives much more attention today. For years, researchers have considered whether females are treated differently in the juvenile justice system (see Chesney-Lind & Shelden, 2004). This is due, at least in part, to an increase in female arrests and court referrals for serious crimes. It is important to keep in mind that violent crimes are a small portion of youth arrests, that they have declined in recent years, and that more males than females are arrested for these offenses. For example, in 2006, 40 females and 724 males under age 18 were arrested for murder (FBI, 2006a). In 2013, 73 females and 541 males were arrested for murder (FBI, 2014a). Even though the number of females arrested for murder has increased, it is much lower than the number of males arrested; so is the estimated number of females under 18 arrested in 2013 for robbery (1,529) and aggravated assault (6,486).

During the 1980s and early 1990s, arrests for two offenses, aggravated assaults and other assaults, increased more for both males and females than other violent crimes (Chesney-Lind & Shelden, 2004). According to Chesney-Lind and Shelden, patterns of female juvenile arrests have not changed much during the past 25 years:

> Females have typically been arrested for the following offenses: running away, larceny-theft, liquor law violations, curfew violations, disorderly conduct, other assaults, and the catch all category "all other offenses." (p. 18)

According to the FBI, comparing 2004 and 2013 reveals that female juvenile arrests have decreased in the past 10 years. Arrests for aggravated assaults decreased by 40% and robbery by 17%.

The percentage of females referred to juvenile court for delinquency cases shows a similar trend: Referrals increased from 19% in 1989 to 24% in 1998. Those referred for offenses against the person increased to 28% by 1998 (Puzzanchera, Stahl, Finnegan, Tierney, & Snyder, 2003a). Female person offense cases continued to increase between 1994 and 2004. In 2004, females accounted for 30% of person offense cases, 17% of property, 20% of drug violation, and 18% of public order offenses in juvenile courts (Stahl, 2008a). In 2010, they accounted for 31% of person offenses, 29% of property offenses, 18% of drug violations, and 28% of public order offenses (Sickmund & Puzzanchera, 2014). According to the most recent data available, minority females comprise the majority (61%) of youth in confinement for a violent offense (Sickmund & Puzzanchera, 2014).

In 2001, the American Bar Association and the National Bar Association issued a historic report on girls and juvenile justice. The report notes that the number of girls in the system has increased, and the system is not prepared to meet their special needs. Interestingly, although the extent of female delinquency is less than male delinquency, patterns of behavior and risk factors for both groups are quite similar. For example, poverty, family problems, academic failure, dropping out of school, and substance abuse are risk factors for both sexes (Belknap & Holsinger, 2006, 2013; Chesney-Lind & Shelden, 2004; Deschenes & Esbensen, 1999; Hawkins, et al. 2000; Howell, 2003). Unlike males, female delinquents experience more physical and sexual abuse, pregnancy, and adolescent motherhood; have lower self-esteem; and have different family and school relationship issues. For example, Davis (2007, 2013) examined how family conflict and struggles for parental control with daughters might result in assaults, calling the police for assistance, and involvement in the juvenile justice system. While this is not unique to females, the family conflict issue is believed to be more harmful for them. Brown, Chesney-Lind, and Stein (2007, 2013) note that in school settings, intersectionalities of class, gender, race, and sexual identity often are overlooked in bullying programs.

Are minority female youth more delinquent than White females? This question is extremely difficult to answer because there is no specific data set that addresses this issue. Taylor, Biafora, Warheit, and Gil (1997) studied family factors and deviance in adolescent girls in Miami public schools. They found that 37.5% of the respondents engaged in serious delinquency, and Black respondents participated in more delinquent behaviors. They also reported that family factors influenced girls' delinquency differently in Hispanic, African American, and White non-Hispanic families. Dunlap, Golub, and Johnson (2003) found that many girls were compelled to have sex by the age of 13, which often resulted in various forms of independent sexual behavior, such as prostitution and teen pregnancy. According to Chesney-Lind and Shelden (2004), both Black and White girls are more likely to be arrested for traditional female offenses, like running away and prostitution. Girls in gangs were more likely to engage in violent behavior and to be victims of violent crime. Chesney-Lind and Shelden (2004) concluded that, although there are differences between Black and White girls' offending, they are not as pronounced as some might expect.

Interest in girls, delinquency, and violence in urban areas has increased due, at least in part, to the overrepresentation of minority females in the juvenile justice system. Miller (2008) and Jones (2010) focused specifically on African American girls in their research. Jones (2010) emphasizes that most teenage girls in these areas are neither in gangs nor delinquent. Miller (2008) examined sexual harassment, assaults, coercion, and relationship violence against these girls in their neighborhoods. She concludes that violence against these girls needs to be addressed and makes several recommendation while at the same time acknowledging that there are no easy solutions in light of structural challenges. Jones (2010) provides an analysis of how girls traverse their inner-city social world, which often requires them to "manage potential threats of interpersonal violence—at the risk of violating mainstream and local expectations regarding appropriate feminine behavior" (p. 9). She notes, "In distressed inner-city neighborhoods, adolescent girls must actively work to develop ways to manage the various forms of violence that they may encounter in their everyday lives" (p. 153). While informative, ethnographic research is not generalizable. The problem of violence against girls might be greater in inner cities, but it is a problem elsewhere as well. There continues to be a dearth of information about minority girls and violence in smaller urban areas, as well as suburban and rural areas.

Delinquent girls' experiences are believed to require different interventions than those usually found in community and institutional settings. Since 1992, increased attention has been devoted to providing **gender-specific programs** that take into consideration the experiences and risks that girls face. Bloom, Owen, Deschenes, and Rosenbaum (2002, 2013) examined national efforts and those in the state of California and made several policy and program recommendations. Do gender-specific programs work? For whom? Do they take racial and ethnic differences into account? One study (Wolf, Graziano, & Hartney, 2009) found that African American girls had lower rates of success in both a gender-specific and traditional program compared to other girls.

Race and Life Without Parole Sentences for Juveniles

Another contemporary issue is whether or not juveniles should be sentenced to either life without parole or death. Do you think juveniles who commit murder should be executed? The 5–4 Supreme Court decision in the 2005 case of *Roper v. Simmons* is indicative of the lack of consensus on this issue. The Court ruled that executing juveniles is unconstitutional because it violates the Eighth Amendment and converted all juvenile death sentences to life without parole. The first juvenile executed in the United States was 16-year-old Thomas Graunger, executed in 1642 in Plymouth, Massachusetts, for committing the crime of bestiality. In 1885, James Arcene, a Cherokee, was hanged for a robbery and murder that occurred in 1872; he claimed that he was 10 years old when the crime was committed (Hakins, 2004). Since World War II, the youngest known person to be executed in the United States was George Stinney, a 14-year-old African American boy who was executed in South Carolina in 1944 for murdering two White girls, aged 8 and 11. Since 1976, 22 men have been executed for crimes committed as juveniles. Prior to the Simmons decision, all juvenile offenders under sentence of death were males, and most committed their offenses at the age of 17. Forty-eight offenders (65%) were minorities—1 American Indian, 2 Asians, 30 Blacks, and 15 Latinos—and 25 were Whites (Streib, 2004). According to the National Coalition to Abolish the Death Penalty (2004), two of three children sent to death row were people of color, and two of three people executed for crimes they committed as children have been African American.

Before *Roper,* the Court had already decided several landmark cases related to the constitutionality of executing juveniles (*Eddings v. Oklahoma,* 1982; *Thompson v. Oklahoma,* 1988; *Stanford v. Kentucky,* 1989; *Wilkins v. Missouri,* 1989; *Atkins v. Virginia,* 2002). Although the era of executing juveniles in the United States is over, there are many juveniles serving life sentences for crimes committed when they were under the age of 18. The Equal Justice Initiative (2007) refers to this as "death in prison sentences" (p. 3). There are 2,570 juveniles sentenced to life without parole (ACLU, 2015), which according to Kubiak and Allen (2011), is the most severe sanction available. In 2010, the Supreme Court ruled in *Graham v. Florida* that it is unconstitutional to sentence juveniles who haven't committed a homicide to life without parole and concluded,

[There] is no penological justification for this sentencing practice . . . that life without parole for juvenile non-homicide offenders accomplishes none of the traditional goals of penal sanctions—retribution, deterrence, incapacitation, and rehabilitation. (National Conference of State Legislatures, 2010, p. 1)

At that time, 37 states, the District of Columbia, and the federal government allowed life without parole for juvenile nonhomicide offenses, six did not allow it, and seven allowed it for juveniles who committed homicide (National Conference of State Legislatures, 2010).

In most states, mandatory sentencing policies determine sentencing decisions. Juveniles as young as 12 can be tried as adults in many states, although 14 states do not set a minimum age (Kubiak & Allen, 2011). The Equal Justice Initiative (2007) identified 73 individuals sentenced to die in prison for crimes they committed when they were either 13 or 14 (p. 20); 49% were Black, 9.6% were Latino, 30% were White, and there was one Native American and one Asian American. "All of the children condemned to death in prison for non-homicide offenses are children of color. All but one of the children sentenced to life without parole for offenses committed at age 13 are children of color" (p. 21). In addition to the discriminatory manner in which life sentences appear to be imposed, they are contrary to international human rights law, such as the International Covenant on Civil and Political Rights and the United Nations Convention Against Torture and Other Cruel, Inhuman or Degrading Treatment or Punishment, both ratified by the United States (The Campaign for Fair Sentencing of Youth, 2009). There is limited research available on public opinion about life without parole sentences for juveniles (Greene & Evelo, 2013; Kubiak & Allen, 2011).

In 2012, the Supreme Court revisited the issue of life without parole for juveniles in the case of *Miller v. Alabama*. In this case, the Court considered whether or not a life without parole sentence for two teenagers who committed murders at the age of 14 was in violation of the Eighth Amendment (Kennedy, 2014). In *Miller,*

The court determined that although a person under the age of 18 may be sentenced to LWOP . . . they may not be sentenced until a judge or jury determines . . . that such a sentence is justified. (Kennedy, p. 560)

While the Court ruled that *mandatory* life without parole sentences were unconstitutional, it sidestepped the constitutionality of life without parole sentences. The Court did emphasize that differences between children and adults are important during sentencing. Since *Miller,* federal courts as well as the states of Florida, Nebraska, New Hampshire, Illinois, Mississippi, Iowa, Massachusetts, Texas, and Wyoming have made life without parole retroactive (Equal Justice Initiative, 2015a). The Court was scheduled to consider this issue in the case of *Toca v. Louisiana* before his release in January, 2015 (Simerman, 2015). At age 17, Mr. Toca was arrested after a 1984 robbery during which his best friend was accidentally shot and killed. He remained imprisoned in Louisiana for 30 years, maintained his innocence throughout, and has presented evidence that someone else was the shooter. After the Louisiana Supreme

Court ruled that *Miller* was not retroactive in that state, Mr. Toca petitioned the U.S. Supreme Court (Wegman, 2014). Juveniles under life without parole sentences challenge us to consider the best approaches to prevent juvenile involvement in crime, especially serious violent crime. This issue is addressed next.

Delinquency Prevention

More than 50 years ago, the OJJDP was established. According to the OJJDP website (http://www.ojjdp.gov/), its mission is to "provide national leadership, coordination, and resources to prevent and respond to juvenile delinquency and victimization." The federal government has provided billions of dollars to state and local governments to assist them in their efforts to prevent crime (Sherman, 1997). In FY 2014, the Office of Justice Programs (OJP) requested $332.5 million (14%) for juvenile justice programs. In FY 2015, there was a slight decrease for juvenile justice programs, $299.4 million (13%) of the request. The amount spent on prevention programs pales in comparison to what is spent on punishment and placement of youth in secure confinement. According to Taylor Greene and Penn (2005), the pendulum began to shift from punishment to prevention in juvenile justice due, at least in part, to the high cost of "get tough" policies that do not necessarily work.

How do we know what programs work? More than a decade ago, Sherman et al. (1997) conducted a study of factors that relate to juvenile crime and the effect of prevention programs on youth violence. The study was in response to a mandate from Congress to the attorney general to evaluate the effectiveness of crime prevention programs. Sherman (1997) concluded that, although some programs work, some do not, and others are promising; there is a need to identify what works in areas of concentrated poverty where homicides are rampant. In these communities there is heightened problems of fear, violence, and victimization. The three primary sources of information about programs that work are the OJJDP Model Programs Guide, The Blueprints Program of the Center for the Study and Prevention of Violence, and the Office of Justice Programs' CrimeSolutions.gov. Each of these sources provides descriptions of programs that are effective and promising. OJJDP's Model Programs Guide also includes programs found to be ineffective. Effective programs are listed in all three sources.

OJJDP's Model Program Guide (MPG) provides a compendium of evidence-based prevention and intervention programs. The prevention section emphasizes a shift from reactive to proactive delinquency prevention, referred to as the "public health model of crime prevention." The Center for the Study and Prevention of Violence has been identifying and evaluating violence prevention efforts since 1996. It selects "Blueprints Model Programs" based on several criteria for effectiveness, including evidence of a deterrent effect with a strong research design, sustained effect, and replication elsewhere (Center for the Study and Prevention of Violence, 2015). "Promising Programs" are required to meet only the first criteria. Currently, there are 13 Blueprints Model Programs and 43 Promising Programs. The Blueprints Model Programs include Big Brothers/Big Sisters of America and Functional Family Therapy (Blueprints Programs, 2015; Will President Obama's 'My Brother's Keeper' initiative become a Model Program in the future [see Box 9.3]).

BOX 9.3

Race and Crime in the Media

Foundations Pledge Nearly $200M to Help Boys, Young Men of Color

Eleven major foundations have pledged to spend a total of nearly $200 million for efforts to help boys and young men of color succeed, in concert with President Barack Obama's "My Brother's Keeper" initiative.

The foundations said in a 12-page executive summary to a still-unreleased report that the funds are to be spent over the next three years – what they hope will be the "first steps in what will be longstanding commitments from these and other funders."

Not all 11 foundations are helping fund all the efforts.

The biggest chunk of the funds, more than $81 million, is to go toward "comprehensive reforms needed to dramatically reduce racial and ethnic disparities in, and the overall use of, confinement for boys and young men," the executive summary said.

"Reliance on the juvenile and criminal justice systems locks too many young men and boys of color out of opportunity before they fully have a chance to start on the path to adulthood."

The executive summary provided little detail on specifically how the money is to be spent for that or other efforts.

The full report, "A Time for Action: Mobilizing Philanthropic Support for Boys and Young Men of Color," is expected to be released this fall.

In February, Obama announced the "My Brother's Keeper" initiative to help boys and young men of color.

"The My Brother's Keeper piece served as a catalyst for [the foundations' funding commitment] ... and sparked a new sense of urgency and focus for these foundations in ways that you probably wouldn't have seen happen so quickly otherwise," said Damon Hewitt, a senior adviser at the Open Society Foundations, one of the 11 philanthropic foundations.

"We're all in conversation with each other, which is the really important piece ... because I think this is so powerful," Hewitt told Youth Today.

He said the foundations had been working on some of the initiatives to help boys and young men of color for more than a year before the White House announced My Brother's Keeper.

"The beauty of what the White House has done [through My Brother's Keeper] is it helped the stars align and make some big things possible by focusing energies and commitments," Hewitt said.

A White House task force on My Brother's Keeper released a report on the initiative to Obama on May 30.

At the time, the 11 philanthropies released a joint statement saying, in part, "The report's emphasis on early childhood support, improving literacy, creating greater pathways to college and career success, and reducing unnecessary involvement with the justice system are all key factors toward improving the lives of boys and young men of color."

The statement noted the 11 foundations joined forces in February to provide a private-sector counterpart to the My Brother's Keeper initiative.

"Our commitment to fundamentally improving the life trajectory of young men of color is unwavering, and it is essential to build on this momentum to improve the policies and structures that currently impede the ability of many young men to participate fully in American society," the statement said.

The foundations' executive summary also outlined other funding:

- More than $55 million will to go toward "an unprecedented partnership to accelerate efforts to reduce suspensions, expulsions, school-based arrests and juvenile court referrals in our nation's elementary and secondary public schools and preschool settings." Among other things, this funding is designed to spur further efforts by the public and private sectors to reduce racial disparities in school discipline.

- More than $26 million is to be spent on efforts to help supplant negative portrayals of boys and young men of color with positive ones in print, broadcast, and social media. These funds are meant to "lift up positive narratives that affirm the value of all human beings, including boys and men of color, and to minimize the effect of implicit bias."
- More than $21 million is intended to "catalyze matching funds from other national and community foundations, corporations, and public/private partnerships to build on existing local efforts and infrastructure that offer promise of success … to help communities develop and/or expand strategies explicitly aimed at reducing disparities and improving life outcomes for boys and young men of color."
- A seed investment of more than $11 million is to spin off the Campaign for Black Male Achievement, now part of the Open Society Foundations, as an independent entity.

Along with the Open Society Foundations, the other philanthropies that have contributed to the funding are the Annie E. Casey Foundation, The Atlantic Philanthropies, Bloomberg Philanthropies, The California Endowment, the Ford Foundation, the John S. & James L. Knight Foundation, the Kapor Center for Social Impact, The Nathan Cummings Foundation, the Robert Wood Johnson Foundation and the W. K. Kellogg Foundation.

Source: Gately (2014).

On February 27, 2014, President Obama issued a memorandum that created the My Brother's Keeper (MBK) initiative to "improve measurably the expected educational and life outcomes . . . for boys and young men of color" (The White House, 2014). The presidential memorandum created an interagency task force to examine current federal policies and programs to determine what works, identify areas in need of improvement, and foster collaboration between state and local governments, businesses, and foundations. The initiative has several goals:

- Getting a healthy start and entering school ready to learn
- Reading at grade level by third grade
- Graduating from high school ready for college and career
- Completing postsecondary education or training
- Successfully entering the workforce
- Keeping kids on track and giving them second chances ("About My Brother's Keeper," 2014)

In September 2014, President Obama issued a challenge to cities, towns, counties, and tribes across the country to become "MBK Communities" by implementing a strategy to improve the life outcomes of all youth and young adults. At the time, almost 200 entities in 43 states and the District of Columbia accepted the MBK community challenge.

1. What is one strategy that you would recommend to improve the life outcomes of youth in MBK communities?

2. Have the elected officials in your locale accepted the MBK community challenge? Do you think they should?

Howell (2003) offered the "comprehensive strategy framework" for integrating the delinquency prevention and juvenile justice fields. The key components of this strategy are prevention, effective early intervention with at-risk children and families, and graduated sanctions for youth in the juvenile justice system. The comprehensive strategy is research based and flexible, and it has been implemented in several jurisdictions. It utilizes a developmental prevention approach that focuses on risk and protective factors in the family, school, peer group, community, and the individual. More recently, Lipsey, Howell, Kelly, Chapman, and Carver (2010), focusing primarily on intervention, point to the importance of evidence-based practices for reducing recidivism that take into consideration risk level of the juvenile, behavior change through personal development, as well as other factors. Are any of the strategies mentioned earlier effective for minority youth who are locked in communities and environments plagued by poverty and disorder? Will they counter the pressures and temptations of drugs and delinquency? Do they take into consideration the pressures placed on some youth to engage in delinquent behaviors in order to survive in their neighborhoods? Do they acknowledge the relationship between violence and victimization? These and other questions about delinquency prevention programs for minority youth remain unanswered.

Taylor Greene and Penn (2005) noted that identifying programs that work for minority youth is difficult. First, just because programs like the Blueprints Models, for example, have proved effective based on their deterrent effects, research design, sustained effects, and replication does not necessarily mean that they work for minority youth. If we could determine that more than 50% of the study samples of effective programs are minority youth, then we could believe that they are effective with these youth. Understanding the relationship between violence and victimization is also important to developing effective prevention programs for minority youth. Youth who witness violence in their homes and in their communities are more vulnerable to involvement in delinquency. For some, the behavior is viewed as acceptable, and for others, it is required in order to have what E. Anderson (1999) described as "juice" or status. McGee (2003) and McGee and Baker (2002) found that direct victimization as a measure of exposure to violence was a predictor of problem behaviors. Victimization was linked to both internalizing and externalizing behaviors. McGee (2003) suggested that violence prevention programs must take into consideration the specific needs of students exposed to danger and the importance of developing problem- and emotion-focused coping strategies. Relatedly, programs that emphasize resilience also are important.

Today, programs like the Safe Start Initiative target children exposed to violence. Klofas, Hipple, and McGarrell (2010) in *The New Criminal Justice* emphasize the importance of cooperation and collaborative problem solving across agencies (police, prosecutors, probation, etc.) in one locale. The Boston Gun Project, implemented in the 1990s to target gun crimes and gun-related death of youths, was one of the earliest efforts that included coordination and cooperation across justice agencies in one jurisdiction. Today, partnerships and collaboration among stakeholders are more prevalent. Payne and Button (2009) point to the importance of involving all stakeholders in planning and implementing youth violence prevention plans. Youth themselves are important stakeholders.

❖ Conclusion

This chapter traced the historical legacy of race in the juvenile justice system. It also presented information on the extent of juvenile crime and victimization and juveniles in the juvenile system. The issue of DMC was examined to shed light on the ongoing problem of minority youth in the system. When considered historically, it is not surprising that this problem exists, and it is likely to continue, if not worsen, unless society addresses the social conditions that foster delinquency and the racial attitudes that still taint the treatment of minority youth in the system. It was noted that Feld (1999) described social and demographic changes in the 1970s that produced macrostructural conditions that resulted in escalating youth violence in the 1980s. By the 1990s, the panic over violent juvenile crime adversely impacted urban Black males, who unfortunately were the perpetrators of the most violent of crimes: murder (Feld, 1999). The hybrid mix of rehabilitation and punishment that evolved in juvenile justice has had both positive and negative results. On the positive side, prevention has reemerged as a cost-effective approach to delinquency, and juvenile homicides and other violent crimes have decreased. However, the punitive era in juvenile justice has proved to be quite costly and not necessarily effective. More troubling is that DMC has only improved slightly, and school punishment disparities by race point to the possibility of a relationship between DMC and school punishment. Other contemporary issues were also presented in this chapter: the school-to-prison pipeline, female delinquency, juveniles and life without parole sentences, and delinquency prevention. It is easy to lose sight of the fact that most of the more than 72 million juveniles in our country are not delinquent, regardless of their race, class, and gender. Parents, teachers, other individuals, and numerous community organizations are dedicated to the development of American youth. It makes much better sense to invest in education, health, and delinquency prevention than it does to invest in correctional institutions. This will require the identification of prevention programs that work, can be replicated, and are adequately funded. There have been some steps in this direction since 2004, although we still need to identify and fund strategies that will reduce disparities in the juvenile justice system.

Discussion Questions

1. How relevant is the historical treatment of minority youth in juvenile justice to the DMC issue today?

2. Do you think programs for delinquent youth should vary by race/ethnicity?

3. What do you think are the best strategies for reducing the school-to-prison pipeline?

4. Is life without parole sentencing for juveniles "cruel and unusual"?

5. Does juvenile victimization in the home or the community lead to youth delinquency or future criminality?

Internet Exercises

1. Use the OJJDP Statistical Briefing Book *Easy Access to the State and County Juvenile Court Case Counts* (http://www.ojjdp.gov/ojstatbb/ezaco/asp/TableDisplay.asp) to examine cases in two states. Include your state of residence.

2. Visit the Campaign for Fair Sentencing of Youth website (http://fairsentencingofyouth.org/what-is-jlwop/) to examine the status of life without parole laws for juveniles in the United States and to read varying perspectives on the issue.

Internet Sites

Office of Juvenile Justice and Delinquency Prevention: http://www.ojjdp.gov

Blueprints for Healthy Youth Development: http://www.blueprintsprograms.com

U.S. Department of Education Office for Civil Rights Data Collection: http://ocrdata.ed.gov

Supplemental materials for *Race and Crime* are available online at
study.sagepub.com/gabbidon4e.

Conclusion

O ur examination of race and crime used a historical approach, providing overviews of components of the criminal justice system (police, courts, corrections, and juvenile justice) and examining numerous contemporary issues. Throughout the book, we presented and reviewed historical and contemporary research, relevant data, and both legal and sociohistorical factors that are important to understanding race and crime. In addition to the ongoing debate about the real meaning of the concepts of race and crime, our historical approach found that, unfortunately, little has changed over the past two centuries. Even so, a few things do stand out.

First, as we noted in Chapter 1, concerns regarding race/ethnicity are not new. They have existed since the founding of America. Beginning with the overstated "criminal aggression" of Native Americans, "superpredator" concerns expressed concerning African American and Latino youth in the 1990s, and more recently, the rash of high-profile killings of unarmed Black males during police encounters, history continues to show that there have always been groups that have garnered special attention and were viewed as a social threat, even though it was not always warranted. Over time, numerous White ethnic immigrants and some Latinos have been able to assimilate into "Whiteness" and escape such continued scrutiny. Although some Blacks have "passed" as Whites, they have never received as much attention. Changes in the classification of race and ethnicity in the 2000 Census of the Population shed light on citizens who classify themselves as "mixed" instead of the other traditional racial categories. How we define race has implications for the study of race and crime because it is not clear how mixed races fit into cultural notions about race. In the past, individuals known to be of mixed heritage or foreign born and those with any characteristics that differed from the (White) nativists were not viewed the same as Whites. Today, the distinctions are less clear, especially for those who appear to be White. Race and ethnicity continue to maintain either a cultural or subcultural context, often based on physical characteristics.

Second, in most instances, legislation was enacted to respond to the perceived criminality of racial groups. Early legislation such as the slave codes, Black codes, the Indian Removal Act, and Chinese Exclusion Act was direct and clearly targeted specific groups. Later, legislation that purported to be race neutral (e.g., death penalty and drug statutes) continued to differentially impact racial minorities. Even legislation designed to alleviate differential treatment of minority groups was underenforced (e.g., Anti-Lynching Bills and Civil Rights Acts). The role of the law cannot be overstated. It is clear that, since the founding of America, there have been laws that were either explicitly or implicitly designed to harm certain racial/ethnic groups. More often than not, the "beneficiaries" of such laws have been racial/ethnic minorities. This was the case with the Secure Communities program that was developed to identify and deport criminal aliens through information sharing with state and local police agencies. Concerns about Secure Communities included racial profiling of Latinos and the lack of procedural safeguards. Notably, the harms caused by this program resulted in its discontinuation in 2014. Although racial and ethnic minorities have been overrepresented in many criminal justice indices, legal and socioeconomic factors have undoubtedly contributed to this finding. We are left with no definitive evidence as to why elevated levels of crime have persisted in some minority communities. And it is unclear why, even though crime, especially violent crime, in these communities has decreased substantially, incarceration rates and DMC remain high. Our review of the seemingly endless theoretical perspectives on the subject pointed to a variety of potential explanations, but more research still needs to be done.

Our final thoughts relate to prospects for the future of both the study of race and crime and the plight of those in the criminal and juvenile justice systems. We are encouraged about the increased attention that race and crime has received in the discipline during the past two decades. At this point in our history, it is difficult to know whether this trend will continue without thoroughly examining indicators such as integration in scholarly research and textbooks and the number of minority and majority scholars in the field who are involved in such research. Despite the increased attention, there is still so much we do not know. The study of race and crime requires more attention to historical, methodological, and theoretical issues.

Historical research is necessary to better understand the present. There continue to be gaps in information about race and crime for certain groups and during certain periods. One example of this is research on lynching and other minority groups including Latinos, Native Americans, and Asian Americans. Another is what Ward (2014) refers to as victimization (violence, property destruction) involving state organized crime that remains hidden and understudied. Future historical research must include a more comprehensive analysis of the role of politics, and the ideologies of politicians and political parties, in order to better understand the political context of race and crime that goes beyond descriptive facts about legislation, case law, and key players in the administration of justice during different time periods. Researchers have examined race, crime, politics, and policy, although more information is needed to better understand how racist sentiments are connected to anticrime sentiments, often making crime a symbol for racism (see Alexander, 2010; Marion & Oliver, 2006; Tonry, 1995, 2011). Moore (2015) does just this in "a public policy process-centered theory and analysis" (p. 32) to understand why the policy process fails to "redress the longstanding racial divide in American criminal justice" (p. 33).

An analysis of legislative initiatives and crime and justice priorities during President Obama's administration is also important. For the first time in American history, Eric Holder, a Black person, served as Attorney General, and his replacement, Loretta Lynch, is the first Black female to hold this position. Does race matter? There have been some notable accomplishments during this administration, including revised hate crime legislation, the reduction of crack/powder cocaine sentencing disparities, and limiting the transfer of military equipment to local police agencies. The federal, state, and local Healthy Youth initiatives, Smart on Juvenile Justice, and My Brother's Keeper initiative could also reduce youth exposure to violence and prevent delinquency. These accomplishments and initiatives either directly or indirectly affect racial/ethnic minorities. In the future, theoretical research must recognize diversity not only within racial categories, but also between individuals. Explanations of race and crime should continue to contextualize race and ethnic disparities, as well as recognize that, although there is no general theory of race and crime, some theoretical concepts are more generalizable than others (such as class and labeling) and that a more global perspective can be instructive (Gabbidon, 2009). Theories of race and crime that are based on data collection and statistics must acknowledge the limitations of data and strive to improve them. One necessary change that has taken place since the last edition of this book is the distinction between Whites and Latinos in the FBI UCR arrest data (Steffensmeier, Feldmeyer, Harris, & Ulmer, 2011). Even so, the discussion about whether crime statistics should continue to be reported and recorded by race is essential. In light of the historical legacy of segregation and discrimination in justice agencies, it seems that recording racial categories is important, although some consistency from one source to another is required. Recent changes in the reporting of juvenile justice data by race/ethnicity make it easier to understand DMC at all stages. At the same time, the BJS has reduced the collection and dissemination of statistical data and removed race and ethnicity details in many publications. The online data analysis tools are useful for descriptive analyses but more disaggregated information is needed. As the primary source of most justice data, BJS should continue to report race and ethnicity information in their reports and publications.

Overall, we are not optimistic about the overrepresentation of racial minorities (primarily African Americans, Latinos, and, more recently, Native Americans) in the arrest, delinquency, victimization, and correctional figures. Unfortunately, more of the same also equates to more minority youth in the so-called "school-to-prison pipeline" who are taken into custody and more minorities being placed on death row, being wrongly accused, and incarcerated (and in the worst-case scenarios, executed) and as a consequence of such trends, in the coming years, more likely to be disenfranchised. Yet, there has been some progress, including the reduction of the crack/cocaine sentencing disparity, more attention being paid to wrongful convictions, the change in disenfranchisement laws in some states, the abolition of the death penalty for juveniles, recognition of the challenge of prisoner reentry, efforts to reduce DMC, efforts to reduce racial profiling at traffic stops, and recognition of the importance of prevention. A shift to evidence-based research is also promising, especially as it relates to reducing juvenile recidivism. At the same time, there are still challenges, including the profiling of Latinos/as in efforts to curb illegal immigration, continued injustice in the treatment of juveniles where racial issues might be more hidden, the school-to-prison pipeline, juveniles with life imprisonment sentences, juvenile involvement in hate crimes, and failure to seek alternatives to incarceration that will be less harmful to individuals, families, and communities. Further, drawing on our historical observations of racial and ethnic groups, we have noted that educational achievement holds a central place in changing the course of most minority involvement in crime.

More than a decade ago, we concluded with a dismal forecast for the possibility of reducing the racial/ethnic disparities found in the American justice system. Unfortunately, our prediction continues to be valid. As noted above, there have been some positive changes in the system, but the recent incidents of police bias against young Black males has resulted in several steps backward in the movement toward equal justice. If our dire forecast for the future is to change, a few things need to happen in the next decade. First, racial minorities must continue to look beyond governmental institutions to provide the impetus for change. By now it should be clear that the government offers no panacea and that such expectations are unrealistic. More recognition of the positive contributions of practitioners, advocates, and community entities should be identified and included in the study of race and crime. Second, legislators interested in tackling race and crime might want to heed the advice of Herbert Packer when seeking to determine what should be against the law. In his classic work, *The Limits of the Criminal Sanction* (1968), which is known for its delineation of the crime control and the due process models of justice, Packer also lays out the following criteria that serve as guidelines for determining what should be against the law:

1. The conduct is prominent in most people's view of socially threatening behavior and is not condoned by any significant segment of society;

2. Subjecting it to the criminal sanction is not inconsistent with the [societal] goals of punishment;

3. Suppressing it will not inhibit socially desirable conduct;

4. It may be dealt with through even-handed and nondiscriminatory enforcement;

5. Controlling [the conduct] through the criminal process will not expose that process to severe qualitative or quantitative strain; and

6. No reasonable alternatives to the criminal sanction exist for dealing with the behavior. (p. 298)

If legislators followed most of Packer's guidelines, we would be much closer to ending the centuries-old trend of criminal justice legislation unfairly impacting racial minorities.

Third, legislators need to be open to more thoughtful approaches to investigating and handling certain offenses. For example, since September 11, 2001, police agencies across the country are devoting more attention to preventing terrorism. Many American law enforcement agencies have adopted the British model for preventing terrorism that advocates increased public surveillance (Klinger & Grossman, 2002). Although most Americans are willing to give up some rights in the interest of protecting the country from terrorism, the dangers of the abuse of powers are of concern, particularly to American minorities. The focus on homeland security during the current era must not diminish the importance of police and the citizenry working together to solve problems of crime and disorder. Relatedly, manpower and financial resources that have been diverted to fighting terrorism and homeland security could have a negative impact on both street crimes and progress made in the last decade in the extent of reported crime (see Lehrer, 2007).

Finally, there must be acknowledgment of the failure of both research and policy to ameliorate the historical and socioeconomic conditions that have contributed to the nexus of race, crime, and the administration of justice. Legislators must understand that the development of a nation's youth is an important component of national security. It is more fiscally sound to invest in the welfare of children, youth, and young adults than to ignore the adverse socioeconomic, biological, and psychological conditions that often lead to criminality. The cost of incarceration that does not work (for most offenders) is much more than the cost of investing in developmental prevention. If there is any hope for reducing the disproportionate involvement in crime by minorities in this century, legislation that adequately funds prevention research and requires evidence-based programs is critical. Recent efforts, including the new criminal justice and predictive policing, should be assessed to determine how they impact youth and whether or not they contribute to long-term crime and delinquency prevention. Finally, perhaps it is time for a shift in focus from offenders and delinquents to practitioners' implicit bias, in order to better understand the racial divide in criminal and juvenile justice.

Appendix

Table A.1

Arrests by Race, 2013—Under 18

Uniform Crime Reports Table 43B

[11,951 agencies; 2013 estimated population 245,741,701]

| Offense Charged | Arrests Under 18 | | | | | | Percentage Distribution[1] | | |
| | Race | | | | | | | | |
	Total	White	Black or African American	American Indian or Alaska Native	Asian	Native Hawaiian or Other Pacific Islander	Total	White	Black or African American
TOTAL	**868,693**	**547,395**	**298,425**	**12,601**	**9,716**	**556**	**100.0**	**63.0**	**34.4**
Murder and nonnegligent manslaughter	613	263	333	10	6	1	100.0	42.9	54.3
Rape[3]	2,065	1,316	709	21	18	1	100.0	63.7	34.3
Robbery	15,903	4,356	11,351	63	111	22	100.0	27.4	71.4
Aggravated assault	24,914	13,544	10,802	295	251	22	100.0	54.4	43.4
Burglary	34,610	19,948	13,913	331	385	33	100.0	57.6	40.2
Larceny-theft	150,213	90,606	54,725	2,368	2,431	83	100.0	60.3	36.4
Motor vehicle theft	9,428	5,090	4,111	135	81	11	100.0	54.0	43.6
Arson	2,928	2,157	694	43	32	2	100.0	73.7	23.7
Violent crime[4]	43,495	19,479	23,195	389	386	46	100.0	44.8	53.3
Property crime[4]	197,179	117,801	73,443	2,877	2,929	129	100.0	59.7	37.2
Other assaults	117,546	67,130	47,948	1,459	937	72	100.0	57.1	40.8
Forgery and counterfeiting	847	521	302	6	17	1	100.0	61.5	35.7
Fraud	3,517	2,045	1,352	71	49	0	100.0	58.1	38.4
Embezzlement	316	191	110	8	7	0	100.0	60.4	34.8
Stolen property; buying, receiving, possessing	8,349	4,222	3,952	81	85	9	100.0	50.6	47.3
Vandalism	37,364	27,564	8,968	511	304	17	100.0	73.8	24.0
Weapons; carrying, possessing, etc.	16,598	9,867	6,322	139	246	24	100.0	59.4	38.1

	Percentage Distribution[1]		Arrests Under 18 Total[2]	Ethnicity			Percentage Distribution[1]	
American Indian or Alaskan Native	Asian	Native Hawaiian or Other Pacific Islander	Total[2]	Hispanic or Latino	Not Hispanic or Latino	Total	Hispanic or Latino	Not Hispanic or Latino
1.5	**1.1**	**0.1**	**462,583**	**99,018**	**363,565**	**100.0**	**21.4**	**78.6**
1.6	1.0	0.2	274	89	185	100.0	32.5	67.5
1.0	0.9	*	1,775	255	1,520	100.0	14.4	85.6
0.4	0.7	0.1	8,444	1,830	6,614	100.0	21.7	78.3
1.2	1.0	0.1	13,862	3,531	10,331	100.0	25.5	74.5
1.0	1.1	0.1	19,303	5,139	14,164	100.0	26.6	73.4
1.6	1.6	0.1	77,411	14,425	62,986	100.0	18.6	81.4
1.4	0.9	0.1	4,869	1,418	3,451	100.0	29.1	70.9
1.5	1.1	0.1	1,499	295	1,204	100.0	19.7	80.3
0.9	0.9	0.1	24,355	5,705	18,650	100.0	23.4	76.6
1.5	1.5	0.1	103,082	21,277	81,805	100.0	20.6	79.4
1.2	0.8	0.1	61,697	11,478	50,219	100.0	18.6	81.4
0.7	2.0	0.1	444	66	378	100.0	14.9	85.1
2.0	1.4	0.0	1,798	266	1,532	100.0	14.8	85.2
2.5	2.2	0.0	175	22	153	100.0	12.6	87.4
1.0	1.0	0.1	4,782	1,318	3,464	100.0	27.6	72.4
1.4	0.8	*	21,695	5,450	16,245	100.0	25.1	74.9
0.8	1.5	0.1	9,694	3,401	6,293	100.0	35.1	64.9

(Continued)

(Continued)

| Offense Charged | Arrests Under 18 | | | | | | Percentage Distribution[1] | | |
| | Race | | | | | | | | |
	Total	White	Black or African American	American Indian or Alaska Native	Asian	Native Hawaiian or Other Pacific Islander	Total	White	Black or African American
Prostitution and commercialized vice	654	242	405	4	3	0	100.0	37.0	61.9
Sex offenses (except rape and prostitution)	8,298	5,925	2,202	65	102	4	100.0	71.4	26.5
Drug abuse violations	93,579	68,322	22,819	1,234	1,161	43	100.0	73.0	24.4
Gambling	622	59	556	0	7	0	100.0	9.5	89.4
Offenses against the family and children	2,210	1,462	648	88	12	0	100.0	66.2	29.3
Driving under the influence	5,908	5,395	313	112	85	3	100.0	91.3	5.3
Liquor laws	47,594	41,710	3,554	1,713	603	14	100.0	87.6	7.5
Drunkenness	5,863	5,081	549	141	81	11	100.0	86.7	9.4
Disorderly conduct	75,705	40,394	33,859	894	526	32	100.0	53.4	44.7
Vagrancy	729	509	214	2	3	1	100.0	69.8	29.4
All other offenses (except traffic)	154,523	104,323	46,334	2,197	1,543	126	100.0	67.5	30.0
Suspicion	175	146	29	0	0	0	100.0	83.4	16.6
Curfew and loitering law violations	47,622	25,007	21,351	610	630	24	100.0	52.5	44.8

Source: FBI (2014).

1. Because of rounding, the percentages may not add to 100.0.

2. The ethnicity totals are representative of those agencies that provided ethnicity breakdowns. Not all agencies provide ethnicity data; therefore, the race and ethnicity totals will not be equal.

3. The rape figures in this table are an aggregate total of the data submitted using both the revised and legacy Uniform Crime Reporting definitions.

4. Violent crimes in this table are offenses of murder and nonnegligent manslaughter, rape (revised and legacy definitions), robbery, and aggravated assault. Property crimes are offenses of burglary, larceny-theft, motor vehicle theft, and arson.

* Less than one-tenth of 1 percent.

	Percentage Distribution[1]			Arrests Under 18 Ethnicity			Percentage Distribution[1]	
American Indian or Alaskan Native	Asian	Native Hawaiian or Other Pacific Islander	Total[2]	Hispanic or Latino	Not Hispanic or Latino	Total	Hispanic or Latino	Not Hispanic or Latino
0.6	0.5	0.0	310	46	264	100.0	14.8	85.2
0.8	1.2	*	3,808	987	2,821	100.0	25.9	74.1
1.3	1.2	*	45,282	10,697	34,585	100.0	23.6	76.4
0.0	1.1	0.0	88	3	85	100.0	3.4	96.6
4.0	0.5	0.0	1,015	84	931	100.0	8.3	91.7
1.9	1.4	0.1	3,153	592	2,561	100.0	18.8	81.2
3.6	1.3	*	25,983	3,679	22,304	100.0	14.2	85.8
2.4	1.4	0.2	3,785	1,308	2,477	100.0	34.6	65.4
1.2	0.7	*	38,327	7,348	30,979	100.0	19.2	80.8
0.3	0.4	0.1	315	94	221	100.0	29.8	70.2
1.4	1.0	0.1	80,654	19,602	61,052	100.0	24.3	75.7
0.0	0.0	0.0	19	2	17	100.0	10.5	89.5
1.3	1.3	0.1	32,122	5,593	26,529	100.0	17.4	82.6

Table A.2

Arrests by Race, 2013—18 and Over

Uniform Crime Reports Table 43C

[11,951 agencies; 2013 estimated population 245,741,701]

Offense Charged	Arrests 18 and Over Race						Percentage Distribution[1]	
	Total	White	Black or African American	American Indian or Alaska Native	Asian	Native Hawaiian or Other Pacific Islander	Total	White
TOTAL	8,145,942	5,666,802	2,251,230	127,689	95,393	4,828	100.0	69.6
Murder and nonnegligent manslaughter	7,770	3,536	4,046	88	95	5	100.0	45.5
Rape[3]	11,450	7,630	3,520	139	155	6	100.0	66.6
Robbery	62,635	28,589	32,920	516	538	72	100.0	45.6
Aggravated assault	266,117	169,548	87,946	4,061	4,172	390	100.0	63.7
Burglary	168,479	117,042	47,796	1,635	1,811	195	100.0	69.5
Larceny-theft	840,723	586,567	229,633	14,034	10,174	315	100.0	69.8
Motor vehicle theft	42,879	29,774	11,849	550	644	62	100.0	69.4
Arson	5,436	4,041	1,231	87	75	2	100.0	74.3
Violent crime[4]	347,972	209,303	128,432	4,804	4,960	473	100.0	60.1
Property crime[4]	1,057,517	737,424	290,509	16,306	12,704	574	100.0	69.7
Other assaults	763,540	506,416	235,409	12,582	8,780	353	100.0	66.3
Forgery and counterfeiting	47,734	30,687	16,073	282	660	32	100.0	64.3
Fraud	109,403	72,637	34,606	1,074	1,045	41	100.0	66.4
Embezzlement	12,258	7,691	4,276	79	200	12	100.0	62.7
Stolen property; buying, receiving, possessing	66,192	46,015	18,735	603	777	62	100.0	69.5
Vandalism	123,714	86,278	33,598	2,440	1,334	64	100.0	69.7
Weapons; carrying, possessing, etc.	95,630	55,450	38,349	749	1,005	77	100.0	58.0

	Percentage Distribution[1]			Arrests 18 and Over	Ethnicity		Percentage Distribution[1]		
Black or African American	American Indian or Alaskan Native	Asian	Native Hawaiian or Other Pacific Islander	Total[2]	Hispanic or Latino	Not Hispanic or Latino	Total	Hispanic or Latino	Not Hispanic or Latino
27.6	**1.6**	**1.2**	**0.1**	**4,350,948**	**700,913**	**3,650,035**	**100.0**	**16.1**	**83.9**
52.1	1.1	1.2	0.1	4,576	963	3,613	100.0	21.0	79.0
30.7	1.2	1.4	0.1	7,896	1,751	6,145	100.0	22.2	77.8
52.6	0.8	0.9	0.1	35,031	6,651	28,380	100.0	19.0	81.0
33.0	1.5	1.6	0.1	164,955	40,073	124,882	100.0	24.3	75.7
28.4	1.0	1.1	0.1	101,364	18,896	82,468	100.0	18.6	81.4
27.3	1.7	1.2	*	417,750	48,529	369,221	100.0	11.6	88.4
27.6	1.3	1.5	0.1	26,586	6,785	19,801	100.0	25.5	74.5
22.6	1.6	1.4	*	2,632	366	2,266	100.0	13.9	86.1
36.9	1.4	1.4	0.1	212,458	49,438	163,020	100.0	23.3	76.7
27.5	1.5	1.2	0.1	548,332	74,576	473,756	100.0	13.6	86.4
30.8	1.6	1.1	*	392,048	54,461	337,587	100.0	13.9	86.1
33.7	0.6	1.4	0.1	25,556	3,798	21,758	100.0	14.9	85.1
31.6	1.0	1.0	*	56,557	5,057	51,500	100.0	8.9	91.1
34.9	0.6	1.6	0.1	7,205	699	6,506	100.0	9.7	90.3
28.3	0.9	1.2	0.1	38,730	8,672	30,058	100.0	22.4	77.6
27.2	2.0	1.1	0.1	61,414	9,723	51,691	100.0	15.8	84.2
40.1	0.8	1.1	0.1	49,893	11,881	38,012	100.0	23.8	76.2

(Continued)

(Continued)

Offense Charged	Arrests 18 and Over						Percentage Distribution[1]	
		Race						
	Total	White	Black or African American	American Indian or Alaska Native	Asian	Native Hawaiian or Other Pacific Islander	Total	White
Prostitution and commercialized vice	41,292	22,424	16,973	382	1,489	24	100.0	54.3
Sex offenses (except rape and prostitution)	38,255	27,770	9,260	557	642	26	100.0	72.6
Drug abuse violations	1,110,583	746,859	342,966	8,174	11,769	815	100.0	67.2
Gambling	4,433	1,374	2,806	27	219	7	100.0	31.0
Offenses against the family and children	76,255	49,555	24,871	1,326	499	4	100.0	65.0
Driving under the influence	904,562	761,045	113,615	12,463	16,746	693	100.0	84.1
Liquor laws	229,850	180,491	37,111	9,148	3,069	31	100.0	78.5
Drunkenness	350,564	283,065	56,336	7,258	3,469	436	100.0	80.7
Disorderly conduct	296,497	191,210	95,923	7,088	2,249	27	100.0	64.5
Vagrancy	20,625	13,223	6,588	579	219	16	100.0	64.1
All other offenses (except traffic)	2,448,416	1,637,532	744,520	41,756	23,547	1,061	100.0	66.9
Suspicion	650	353	274	12	11	0	100.0	54.3
Curfew and loitering law violations	-	-	-	-	-	-	-	-

Source: FBI (2014).

1. Because of rounding, the percentages may not add to 100.0.

2. The ethnicity totals are representative of those agencies that provided ethnicity breakdowns. Not all agencies provide ethnicity data; therefore, the race and ethnicity totals will not be equal.

3. The rape figures in this table are an aggregate total of the data submitted using both the revised and legacy Uniform Crime Reporting definitions.

4. Violent crimes in this table are offenses of murder and nonnegligent manslaughter, rape (revised and legacy definitions), robbery, and aggravated assault. Property crimes are offenses of burglary, larceny-theft, motor vehicle theft, and arson.

* Less than one-tenth of 1 percent.

	Percentage Distribution[1]			Arrests 18 and Over	Ethnicity			Percentage Distribution[1]	
Black or African American	American Indian or Alaskan Native	Asian	Native Hawaiian or Other Pacific Islander	Total[2]	Hispanic or Latino	Not Hispanic or Latino	Total	Hispanic or Latino	Not Hispanic or Latino
41.1	0.9	3.6	0.1	21,200	3,755	17,445	100.0	17.7	82.3
24.2	1.5	1.7	0.1	18,357	5,078	13,279	100.0	27.7	72.3
30.9	0.7	1.1	0.1	582,966	108,130	474,836	100.0	18.5	81.5
63.3	0.6	4.9	0.2	1,363	273	1,090	100.0	20.0	80.0
32.6	1.7	0.7	*	39,401	2,425	36,976	100.0	6.2	93.8
12.6	1.4	1.9	0.1	502,635	105,785	396,850	100.0	21.0	79.0
16.1	4.0	1.3	*	121,435	15,013	106,422	100.0	12.4	87.6
16.1	2.1	1.0	0.1	250,423	42,699	207,724	100.0	17.1	82.9
32.4	2.4	0.8	*	152,788	12,762	140,026	100.0	8.4	91.6
31.9	2.8	1.1	0.1	11,655	1,634	10,021	100.0	14.0	86.0
30.4	1.7	1.0	*	1,256,421	185,050	1,071,371	100.0	14.7	85.3
42.2	1.8	1.7	0.0	111	4	107	100.0	3.6	96.4
-	-	-	-	-	-	-	-	-	-

Glossary

Adjudication: The process of disposing of (or settling) a juvenile or criminal matter.

Arrest rates: Refers to the number of arrests per 100,000 persons for all persons 18 years or older. These arrest rates are reported by police agencies to the FBI and are reported annually in the *Uniform Crime Reports*.

Assimilation: The merging of cultural traits from previously distinct cultural groups.

Bail: Money, property, or other security offered in exchange for the release from custody of an arrested person and to guarantee the person's appearance at trial. Bail is forfeited if the accused does not appear in court.

Batson v. Kentucky: Batson, a Black man in Kentucky, was convicted by an all-White jury of second-degree burglary. The prosecutor used all of his peremptory challenges to exclude the few prospective Black jurors from the jury pool. In the 1986 landmark case, the U.S. Supreme Court decided that peremptory challenges could not be used for a racially discriminatory purpose. Thus, creating an all-White jury by deliberately eliminating all prospective Black candidates was discriminatory. The Supreme Court ruled in favor of Batson.

Best practices: A best practice is a technique, method, or process that is believed to be most effective at delivering a particular outcome given the same conditions or circumstances.

Black child savers: The child savers were civic actors who led social movements during the late 19th and 20th centuries to establish and develop the juvenile justice system and other child welfare reform in the United States and elsewhere. The Black child savers were those Black civic actors who were effective in reconfiguring prevailing color lines of juvenile social control, not by making race insignificant, but by pushing Black youth and community stakeholders into child welfare networks of juvenile social control—uplifting the deliberative radical democracy of American juvenile justice.

Black codes: Laws which were enacted shortly after the Civil War in the ex-confederate states to restrict the liberties of the newly freed slaves to ensure an ample supply of cheap agricultural labor and to maintain White economic prosperity in the South.

Bloody code: The name given to the English legal system from the late 17th century to the early 19th century. It was known as the *bloody code* because of the huge numbers of crimes for which the death penalty could be imposed. At that time, the attitudes of the wealthy men who made the law were unsympathetic. They felt that people who committed crimes were sinful, lazy, or greedy and deserved little mercy. Since the rich made the laws, they made laws that protected their interests. Any act that threatened their wealth, property, or sense of law and order was criminalized and made punishable by death.

Bracero Program: Created in 1942 by an executive order and lasting for more than 22 years, the program allowed Mexican nationals to take temporary agricultural work in the United States. More than 4.5 million Mexican nationals were legally contracted for work in the United States. Mexican peasants, desperate for cash work, were willing to take jobs at wages scorned by most Americans. The Braceros's presence had a significant effect on the business of farming and the culture of the United States.

Bureau of Justice Statistics (BJS): The branch of the Office of Justice Programs (OJP) within the U.S. Department of Justice that promotes the collection and analysis of crime data in the states and territories.

Bureau of Prisons: Established in 1930, the Bureau consists of 115 institutions, 6 regional offices, a Central Office (headquarters), 2 staff training centers, and 28 community corrections offices. The Bureau protects public safety by ensuring that Federal offenders serve their sentences of imprisonment in facilities that are safe, humane, cost-efficient, and appropriately secure. The Bureau helps reduce the potential for future criminal activity by encouraging inmates to participate in a range of programs that have proved to reduce recidivism.

Centers for Disease Control and Prevention: A research and funding arm of the Public Health Service, U.S. Department of Health and Human Services. The CDC, as it is known, oversees an ambitious research agenda on myriad health problems, including homicide, suicide, and intentional injuries. It is also the sponsor of the periodic *Youth Risk Behavior Survey,* a survey of U.S. high school students about their recent experiences with sexual activity and high-risk behaviors.

Cesare Lombroso: An Italian doctor, often referred to as the "father of criminology," who took a scientific approach to studying crime during the end of the 19th century. His influence spread not only throughout Europe, but to the United States and other countries as well. His theory was based on the idea of atavism, in which he deemed that criminals were an evolutionary throwback to an earlier stage in human evolution. His theory led to his classification of criminals in categories such as born criminals, criminaloids, and insane criminals, as well as to research on female offenders.

Child savers: Civic actors during the 19th and 20th centuries who led to the establishment and development of autonomous juvenile justice systems and other welfare reforms in the United States and elsewhere.

Chinese Exclusion Act of 1882: The first major and the only federal legislation that banned immigrants explicitly based on a specific nationality. The Act excluded Chinese laborers and those employed in mining from entering the country for 10 years under penalty of imprisonment and deportation.

Code of the streets: A theory developed by Yale University professor Elijah Anderson that presents an explanation for high rates of violence among African American adolescents. Anderson contends that economic disadvantage, separation from mainstream society, and racial discrimination encountered by some African American adolescents may lead to antisocial attitudes and to violent behavior.

Coker v. Georgia: Coker was convicted of raping a woman and was sentenced to death. In this 1977 landmark case, the United States Supreme Court overturned his death sentence, saying that death sentences are inappropriate punishments for rapes in which the life of the rape victim is not taken as well.

Collateral consequences: Unintended or unknown consequences certain offenders face for committing a crime, in addition to the penalties included in the criminal sentence. An example is the loss of voting rights for a convicted felon.

Collective efficacy: The tendency of members of a neighborhood or community to look out for one another's interests, including serving as surrogate parents.

Colonial model: A theory used to explain racial disparities in arrests and imprisonment. It builds upon the early writings of Frantz Fanon, who examined the relations between majority and minority groups in colonial settings. In an effort to explain high rates of crime and violence among Blacks, some criminologists have used the colonial model to analyze the psychological impact on those living in a society where the colonizer (often Whites) creates a race- and caste-based society based on racism. The colonial system, which devalues and discredits the culture and traditions of the colonized, leaves the colonized in a psychological state that results in self-hate and destructive behaviors such as crime (mostly intraracial).

Colonization: Occurs when one group forcibly takes over the country of another group. During this process, those who are colonized are then forced to adhere to the norms of the colonizer.

Community policing: A philosophy of policing that emphasizes identifying and solving a wide range of community problems that are thought to lead to crime and social disorder. In community-oriented policing, often simply termed *community policing,* the beat officer and community residents work together to exchange information, promote safety, and improve the overall quality of life in the neighborhood.

Community supervision: The spectrum of sentencing alternatives that permit the convicted offender to remain in the community as opposed to serving time in a remote correctional facility. Community supervision includes community-based correctional facilities, halfway houses, day reporting centers, probation, and parole.

Components of the policing industry: Refers to local police, state police, federal police, special jurisdiction police, and tribal police agencies that have law enforcement functions.

Conflict theory: A theoretical perspective in criminology that holds that opposing political, social, or other forces in society are responsible for a variety of social ills, including crime and delinquency.

Consent searches: Refers to permission an individual gives to a police officer to search his or her vehicle or property. Consent searches of vehicles during traffic stops become controversial if the driver believes he or she was racially profiled.

Convict-lease system: After the Civil War, Southern states leased prison inmates to private companies that used them as forced laborers. This system of enforced labor ran from 1865 to 1920.

Corrections: The component of the criminal justice system concerned with the imprisonment, control, and rehabilitation of convicted offenders. Corrections include the administration and study of prisons, community-based sanctions, parole, probation, and less intrusive alternatives.

Crime rates: A ratio of the number of crimes per number of residents in a population, standardized by multiplying by 100,000. Violent crime rates, property crime rates, and arrest rates are used to analyze patterns and trends.

Crime statistics: Statistical data compiled by the police and the courts and routinely published by governments as indices of the extent of crime.

Death penalty: Punishment for a crime that results in the execution of the defendant.

Department of Homeland Security: Created in 2002 to prevent terrorist attacks within the United States, to reduce vulnerability to terrorism, and to minimize the impact from and assist in the recovery from terrorist attacks.

Disposition: The conclusion of juvenile court proceedings, often with an adjudication in a juvenile case. A disposition is similar to the imposition of a sentence in a criminal case.

Disproportionate minority contact: The overrepresentation of minority youth in the various stages of the juvenile justice system.

Driving while Black/Brown: Coined in the 1990s, this is an expression used to describe the practice by law enforcement officers of targeting Black and other minority motorists for traffic stops when there is no violation of the law.

Dual-court system: Refers to the judicial branch of American government consisting of both state and federal courts.

Eighth Amendment: The Amendment to the United States Constitution, also a part of the Bill of Rights, which prohibits the federal government from imposing excessive bail, excessive fines, or cruel and unusual punishments.

Ethnicity: Refers to a group of people who identify with each other through a common heritage, consisting of a common language, a common culture (often including a shared religion), and a tradition of common ancestry.

Furman v. Georgia: In this landmark case, Furman, a Black man, was accused of murder. Despite evidence at his trial that he was mentally deficient, he was convicted of murder and sentenced to death. He appealed his sentence on the grounds that his Fourteenth Amendment rights were violated. At the time of this case, disproportionately more Black murderers were being given the death sentence than White murderers. In 1972, the United States Supreme Court set aside Furman's death penalty, saying that the death penalty was administered in a racially discriminatory way in Georgia. In addition, the Court stated this constituted cruel and unusual punishment. The case led to a moratorium on capital punishment in the United States until 1976.

Gender-specific programs: Programs for at-risk and delinquent girls that meet needs given their age and development. Gender-specific programs address such issues as teenage pregnancy, eating disorders, body self-image, and sexually transmitted diseases.

General strain theory: Robert Agnew's revision of the strain theory extended Robert Merton's anomie theory that was based on the general idea that economic strains are the primary contributor to crime. Agnew's theory also refers to the strains caused by the removal of positive stimuli (e.g., loss of a spouse, girlfriend/boyfriend) or the introduction of noxious stimuli (e.g., child abuse, criminal victimization), which can also contribute to criminal behavior.

Gregg v. Georgia: Gregg was convicted of robberies and murders in Atlanta, Georgia. This landmark case put an end to the moratorium set in *Furman v. Georgia* in 1972. The Supreme Court decision in *Gregg* rejected the legal argument that capital punishment, in and of itself, constituted "cruel and unusual punishment" and thus violated the Eighth Amendment of the U.S. Constitution. *Gregg* led to new death penalty statutes. Some state legislatures reformed their death penalty statutes to deal with the problem of undue jury discretion identified in *Furman* by mandating capital punishment for all persons convicted of first degree murder. In addition, the newly accepted provisions required two-stage trials in all death penalty cases, in which guilt or innocence would be determined in the first stage and the penalty would be assessed in the second stage.

Guided discretion: A term adopted from the landmark U.S. Supreme Court case *Gregg v. Georgia* that refers to the two-stage death penalty trial process. Under this approach, if a defendant was convicted of first degree murder or another death-eligible offense, the prosecutor could ask the court to conduct a second "penalty stage" of the trial. After this second proceeding, the jury could impose the death sentence only if it found that the prosecution had proved a statutorily specified "aggravating circumstance," such as that the murder was committed for financial gain.

Hate crime: A criminal offense motivated by hatred of a specific race, ethnicity, religion, or sexual orientation. In many states, hate crimes are codified as offenses distinguished from the core offenses, such as assault, vandalism, and intimidation. In addition, hate crimes newly qualify for enhanced sentencing.

Houses of refuge: Facilities for juveniles opened in the 1800s as the result of increased juvenile presence on the streets after an influx of immigrant families entering the United States in the late 1700s and early 1800s. Although houses of refuge existed presumably to protect potentially criminal youth from being easily influenced by the negative aspects of society, some critics argue that the use of houses of refuge was discriminatory, affecting only poor White immigrants while excluding Blacks.

Implicit Bias: An unconscious attitude toward or stereotype of an individual or group of individuals. Implicit biases can be either positive or negative.

Innocence Project: The Innocence Project uses DNA testing to establish the innocence of wrongfully convicted offenders. It was founded by civil rights attorneys Peter J. Neufeld and Barry C. Scheck in 1992 at the Benjamin N. Cardoza School of Law, located at Yeshiva University in New York City.

Intake: The point at which a youth formally becomes involved in the juvenile justice process.

Intensive probation: A form of probation that involves an extra measure of supervision and control by the probation officer, often used for chronic and other high-risk offenders who pose a great probability of reoffending.

IQ: An intelligence quotient (IQ) is a purported measure of an individual's general intellectual ability. Over the past century, there have been repeated attempts to link low intelligence with propensity to commit criminal acts and frequent claims that some supposed racial groups have lower intelligence than others. Critics have rejected such claims as racist pseudoscience.

Jury nullification: The disregard by a jury of the evidence presented and the rendering of its verdict based on other criteria.

Juvenile court: A court of law, sometimes a subdivision of a common pleas court or domestic relations court, that has jurisdiction over matters pertaining to the delinquency and unruliness of persons who have not yet attained adulthood.

Juvenile justice system: Refers to the agencies and processes designed to meet the needs of delinquent and dependent youth.

Lynching: The practice of illegally taking the life of another by hanging, generally accomplished by a mob and often motivated by racial or ethnic hatred. Now infrequent, lynching in the United States is associated with White supremacists and their targeting of Blacks.

Manumission: The formal act of freeing a slave from slavery.

Marshall hypotheses: A series of conjectures by Supreme Court Justice Thurgood Marshall in *Furman v. Georgia* regarding the value of opinion poll data on public sentiments about capital punishment. Because the results of such polls can be of great importance to the U.S. Supreme Court's assessment of the constitutionality of various statutes and policies and practices, the validity of these data is especially important. The Marshall hypotheses are as follows: (1) Americans know almost nothing about the death penalty, and (2) those citizens who were fully informed about the purposes of the penalty and its liabilities would find the penalty shocking, unjust, and unacceptable.

Mass incarceration: The punitive sentencing practices of the 1980s to 2000s that resulted in the hyperincarceration of offenders, especially Blacks and Hispanics.

McCleskey v. Kemp: McCleskey, a Black man, was convicted and sentenced to death for murdering a police officer during a grocery store robbery in 1978. Introducing into evidence that statistically more Black criminals receive the death penalty than White criminals and claiming that such disproportion is unconstitutional, McCleskey appealed. In 1987, the United States Supreme Court rejected the appeal, claiming Georgia's death penalty was not arbitrary and capricious, nor was it being applied in a discriminatory manner, regardless of the statistical evidence to the contrary.

Minority: Refers to a socially subordinate ethnic group (understood in terms of language, nationality, religion, and/or culture). Other minority groups include people with disabilities, "economic minorities" (working poor or unemployed), "age minorities" (who are younger or older than a typical working age), and sexual minorities. Members of minority groups are prone to differential treatment in the communities in which they live. This discrimination may be directly based on an individual's perceived membership in a minority group, without consideration of that individual's personal achievement. It may also occur indirectly, due to social structures that are not equally accessible to all.

Model minority: Used in social sciences to describe a racial minority group that has excelled in the United States despite prejudice and discrimination. This stereotype has become synonymous with the Asian American population.

National Crime Victimization Survey (NCVS): A survey of citizens 12 years of age and older conducted by the U.S. Bureau of the Census for the Bureau of Justice Statistics. The NCVS measures the respondents' experiences as victims of rape, robbery, assault, burglary, larceny, and motor vehicle theft.

National Incident-Based Reporting System (NIBRS): The crime reporting system intended to eventually replace the *Uniform Crime Report*. NIBRS collects detailed data on the offender, time, place, and other aspects of the incident for each criminal offense reported by police agencies in participating agencies.

Office of Juvenile Justice and Delinquency Prevention (OJJDP): A branch of the U.S. Department of Justice's Office of Justice Programs. OJJDP is charged with promoting a variety of programs to reduce juvenile delinquency and to improve the administration of juvenile justice. Authorized by the Juvenile Justice and Delinquency Prevention Act of 1974, the OJJDP administers discretionary and formula grant programs and provides technical assistance to state and local governments.

Opium dens: Establishments where opium was sold and smoked, prevalent in many parts of the world in the 19th century, most notably China, Southeast Asia, North America, and France. Opium smoking began in North America with the first migration of the Chinese laborers who were addicted from the British expansionist policy of trade in opium. The first opium dens in the United States were located in the Chinese community.

Parole: The conditional release under supervision of a convict prior to the expiration of the sentence. Parole is generally granted by a parole board. Upon release on parole, the offender reports to a parole officer, who ensures compliance with specified conditions.

People of color: A term primarily used in the United States to refer to non-Whites. The term has been used to replace the term *minority*.

Peremptory challenges: The right during voir dire to challenge the seating of jurors without citing a specific cause. (See also **Voir dire**.)

Plea bargaining: The process and result of an agreement between a prosecuting attorney and defense counsel to reduce the seriousness or number of charges in a criminal case in return for a guilty plea.

Police-community relations: Efforts to create a positive relationship between police and citizens that developed in the late 1960s and 1970s.

Police militarization: The utilization of military equipment by state and local police agencies. Initially approved for use during drug enforcement, military equipment is often used by Special Weapons and Tactics (SWAT) teams, Paramilitary Police Units (PPU), at border crossings, and during civil unrest.

Political prisoners: Prisoners who have been prosecuted and incarcerated because of their political beliefs.

Prejudice: When someone fosters a negative attitude toward a particular racial/ethnic group. This is usually in the form of acerbic stereotypes that often result in people making unfavorable generalizations about an entire group.

Pretrial release: The practice of conditionally releasing criminal defendants prior to trial without formal posting of bail. Those who participate in pretrial release generally must have stable residence and employment as well as other ties to the community that suggest they are likely to appear for trial.

Prisoner reentry: The return of offenders, probationers, parolees, and those released from jails to their community. Prisoner reentry involves the use of programs targeted at promoting the effective reintegration of offenders back to communities upon release from prison and jail. These programs are intended to assist offenders in acquiring the life skills needed to succeed in the community and become law-abiding citizens. These programs include prerelease programs, drug rehabilitation and vocational training, and work programs.

Prison-industrial complex: The industries that depend on the existence of prisons, including construction companies, food service companies, and other industries that are required to support the operation of prisons.

Private prisons: Correctional institutions that are either run or owned by private corporations.

Probation: The suspension of a sentence of a convicted offender and granting of freedom for a period of time under specified conditions. Probation is generally granted in lieu of confinement.

Profiling in airports: A term that became popular after the events of September 11, 2001. It refers to the targeting for a more intrusive inspection by airport security officials of Arabs, people of Middle Eastern descent, or those who appear to be Muslim. This practice has also been referred to as *flying while Arab*.

Public defender system: A federal, state, or local criminal justice agency that provides legal counsel for criminal defendants who have been accused or convicted of a crime or crimes and are too poor to hire a private attorney. Public defenders are attorneys paid as salaried government employees. The public defender system began in Los Angeles County in 1914 and has since become the most typical method of representing indigent defendants in court.

Public Law 280: A federal statute enacted by Congress in 1953 that enabled states to assume criminal, as well as civil, jurisdiction in matters involving American Indians as litigants on reservation land.

Race: Refers to the classification of humans into populations or groups based on various factors such as culture, language, social practice, or heritable characteristics.

Racial discrimination: The act of withholding or preventing someone from receiving social benefits, facilities, services, or opportunities on the basis of race, color, or national origin.

Racial profiling: Any police-initiated action that relies on the race, ethnicity, or national origin of an individual rather than the behavior of an individual or information that leads the police to a particular individual who has been identified as being, or having been engaged in, criminal activity.

Recidivism: Reoffending after an offender has been released from probation or corrections. The term includes re-arrest during terms of probation and arrest for technical violations/conditions of supervision.

Reentry courts: One of the problem-solving courts that have emerged since the 1990s. These courts are focused on ensuring that recently released offenders make a successful transition back to the community.

Reformatories: State correctional facilities intended to rehabilitate youthful or otherwise nonserious offenders. Reformatories were first used in the 1800s. Reformatories were originally intended to reform and educate young offenders rather than punish them.

Rehabilitation: A rationale for punishment that emphasizes correcting offender behavior through treatment. The goal of rehabilitation is to change behavior. Punishments that are in accordance with this theory are community service, probation orders, and any form of punishment that entails any form of guidance and aftercare toward the offender.

Relocation centers: Camps in the U.S. in which Japanese and Japanese Americans were interned during World War II. The U.S. internment camps were overcrowded and provided poor living conditions.

School punishment: Refers to the options available to school administrators to enforce school policies and regulate appropriate behavior. School punishment includes in-school and out-of-school suspensions and expulsions.

School-to-prison pipeline: The relationship between school punishment and an increased likelihood that students will eventually enter the juvenile justice or criminal justice system.

Sentencing disparities: Differences in sentences that include cases with similarly situated offenders. Sentencing disparities can be the result of legislative differences between jurisdictions or judicial or prosecutorial discretion.

Slave patrols: Organized groups that regularly patrolled both rural and urban areas of the Southern United States to enforce restrictions that White colonists placed upon enslaved African Americans during the 18th and 19th centuries. Slave patrols were responsible for apprehending runaways, breaking up unsanctioned gatherings and celebrations of enslaved people, as well as other functions.

Social buffers: A term used to refer to working class and middle class role models in areas where there are significant concentrations of poverty. These individuals provide examples of success and serve as social buffers until they abandon these communities. Without these social buffers, residents of these communities become socially isolated and lack exposure to mainstream individuals.

Social disorganization: Social disorganization theory argues that crime and delinquency rates are a direct result of heterogeneous, transitional, and poverty-stricken neighborhoods. Neighborhoods characterized by social disorganization also include some of the following factors: large numbers of families on welfare, large numbers of condemned buildings, large numbers of renters, and high truancy rates.

Statistical Briefing Book (SBB): An online tool that enables users to access information via OJJDP's website to learn more about juvenile crime and victimization and about youth involved in the juvenile justice system. Developed for OJJDP by the National Center for Juvenile Justice, SBB provides timely and reliable statistical answers to the most frequently asked questions from policy makers, the media, and the general public. In addition, the data analysis and dissemination tools available through the SBB give users quick and easy access to detailed statistics on a variety of juvenile justice topics.

Statutes: Laws formulated by a legislative body that governs a particular jurisdiction and that are aimed at requiring or prohibiting something.

Strain theory: A theoretical perspective in criminology that is often tied to Robert Merton. The theory proposes that in every society there are culturally prescribed goals (e.g., American Dream) and institutionally accepted means (e.g., education, work) to achieve them. When citizens aspire to the societal goals but are unable to achieve them through institutionally approved means, a strain occurs that can lead them to commit crime and to engage in other illicit and harmful behaviors (e.g., drug abuse, alcoholism).

Street stops: Occur when individuals are walking in their neighborhoods and elsewhere and are stopped by the police. They are usually asked to present proper identification and questioned.

Tasers: Electronic weapons that work by discharging high-voltage electrodes attached to long wires that, when they penetrate human flesh, render the individual temporarily immobile. Originally designed as a less-than-lethal weapon for police personnel.

Theory: A set of statements or principles devised to explain a group of facts or phenomena. A theory that has been repeatedly tested or is widely accepted can be used to make predictions about natural phenomena.

Truly disadvantaged: Refers to a segment of the American population often referred to as the *underclass* or the *ghetto underclass,* predominately Black, who often live in disorganized inner cities and urban areas characterized by poverty, family instability, unemployment, a poor educational system, and crime.

Uniform Crime Reporting program: A crime statistics program of the Federal Bureau of Investigation. The UCR has been the national reporting system since the 1930s. UCR collects summary-based information from law enforcement agencies on offenses reported and arrests made as well as more detailed data on homicides.

United States Sentencing Commission: An independent agency of the judicial branch of the federal government. It has the following three purposes: (1) to establish policy, procedure, and sentencing practices related to the punishment of federal crimes; (2) to advise Congress regarding the creation of crime policies; and (3) to research, analyze, and distribute information on federal crimes and sentencing issues.

Victimization data: Information collected from persons that provides their perceptions about their involvement in crime as a victim. The National Crime Victimization Survey (NCVS) is the primary source of victimization data. The data collected include type of crime; relationship between victim and offender; characteristics of the offender, including the use of weapons, drugs, and alcohol; type of property lost; whether the crime was reported to the police and reasons for reporting or not reporting. Basic demographic information, such as age, race, gender, and income, is also collected to enable analysis of crime by various subpopulations.

Victimization rates: A percentage calculated using victimization data obtained from the victims themselves to measure the existence of actual, rather than reported, crimes.

Voir dire: The process of selecting jurors prior to the commencement of a criminal trial. During the voir dire, prospective jurors are questioned by both the prosecutor and the defense attorney to learn about their backgrounds and possible biases.

Walnut Street Jail: An early prison in Philadelphia that emphasized solitary confinement.

War on Drugs: Term used to describe the attempt by the federal and state authorities to control the supply and distribution of illegal drugs. The War on Drugs has drawn criticism for its emphasis on supply reduction, likened by many to Prohibition, which failed in its efforts to stem the flow of alcohol.

W.E.B. Du Bois: Considered by some to be one of the first major sociological criminologists. William Edward Burghardt Du Bois was also an American civil rights activist, leader, Pan-Africanist, sociologist, educator, historian, writer, editor, poet, and scholar. Du Bois's life and work were an inseparable mixture of scholarship, protest activity, and polemics. All of his efforts were geared toward gaining equal treatment for Black people and toward marshaling and presenting evidence to refute the myths of racial inferiority. Du Bois was among the founders of the National Association for the Advancement of Colored People (NAACP) in 1910 and was founder and editor of the NAACP's journal *The Crisis*.

White ethnic: A term used in the United States to refer to Whites who are typically of European origin. The term *White ethnic* almost always carried the connotation of being blue-collar and referred to White immigrants and their descendants from southern and eastern Europe. In the early 20th century, many White ethnics claimed to have been placed in a low socioeconomic level due to discrimination and ethnic stereotypes by the White Anglo-Saxon Protestant, commonly referred to as WASP, elite.

White immigrants: Refers to British, German, Italian, Irish, French, Spanish, and other White ethnic groups that came to the United States as early as the 1500s. Most early White immigrants, including Jewish immigrants, came from European countries.

Wrongful convictions: A conviction in court of an accused person who, in fact, did not commit the alleged offense.

Zoot Suit Riots: A term used to describe a series of conflicts that occurred in Los Angeles, California, in the summer of 1943 between servicemen and Mexican American youths. Zoot suits were outfits popular among Mexican American youth at the time of the riots.

References

Abbott, E. (Ed.). (1931). *Crime and the foreign born* (National Commission on Law Observance and Enforcement, Report No. 10). Washington, DC: Government Printing Office.

ABC/*Washington Post* Poll. (2003). Retrieved March 2, 2003, from the Polling the Nations database at http://www.orspub.com/

About My Brother's Keeper. (2014). Retrieved from https://www.whitehouse.gov/my-brothers-keeper

Abraham, A. A. (1948). Juvenile delinquency in Buffalo and its prevention. *Journal of Negro Education, 17*(2), 124–133.

Adams, B., & Addie, S. (2010). *Delinquency cases waived to criminal court, 2007.* Retrieved on July 30, 2011, from https://www.ncjrs.gov/pdffiles1/ojjdp/230167.pdf

Adams, K. (1999). What we know about police use of force. In *Use of force by police: Overview of national and local data* (NCJ 176330, pp. 1–14). Washington, DC: U.S. Department of Justice, Office of Justice Programs.

Advancement Project (2010). *Test, punish, & push out: How "zero tolerance" and high stakes testing funnel youth into the school-to-prison pipeline.* Retrieved from http://www.advancementproject .org

Agnew, R. (1992). Foundation for a general strain theory of crime and delinquency. *Criminology, 30,* 47–87.

Agnew, R. (2004). *Why do criminals offend? A general theory of crime and delinquency.* Los Angeles: Roxbury.

Agnew, R. (2006). *Pressured into crime: An overview of general strain theory.* Los Angeles: Roxbury.

Agozino, B. (2003). *Counter-colonial criminology: A critique of imperialist reason.* London: Pluto Press.

Akers, R. L. (2000). *Criminological theories: Introduction, evaluation, and application.* Los Angeles: Roxbury.

Alexander, M. (2010). *The new Jim Crow: Mass incarceration in the age of colorblindness.* New York: The New Press.

Allen, H. E., Simonsen, C. E., & Latessa, E. J. (2004). *Corrections in America: An introduction.* Upper Saddle River, NJ: Prentice Hall.

Allen, L. (2015). Are tribal courts developed enough for VAWA? Pascua Yaqui proves it. *Indian Country Today Media Network.* Retrieved from http://indiancountrytodaymedianetwork.com/2015/05/20/ are-tribal-courts-developed-enough-vawa-pascua-yaqui-proves-it-160421

Allen, T. W. (1994). *The invention of the White race: Vol. 1. Racial oppression and social control.* New York: Verso.

Alliance for Justice. (2014). *The state of the judiciary: Judicial selections during the 113th Congress.* Retrieved from http://www.afj.org/wp-content/uploads/2013/10/Judicial-Selection-During- President-Obamas-Second-Term.pdf

American Bar Association and the National Bar Association. (2001). *Justice by gender.* Washington, DC: Author.

American Civil Liberties Union. (1999). *Driving while black: Racial profiling on our nation's highways.* New York: Author.

American Civil Liberties Union. (2012). *What's at stake: SB1070 at the Supreme Court.* Washington, DC: Author. Retrieved from https://www.aclu.org/infographic/infographic-whats-stake- sb-1070-supreme-court

American Civil Liberties Union. (2014). *War comes home: The excessive militarization of American policing.* New York: Author. Retrieved from https://www.aclu.org/sites/default/files/assets/jus14-warcomeshome-report-web-rel1.pdf

American Civil Liberties Union. (2015). *End juvenile life without parole.* Retrieved from https://www.aclu.org/end-juvenile-life-without-parole

Amnesty International. (2014). *Entombed: Isolated in the U.S. prison system.* Retrieved from http://www.amnestyusa.org/sites/default/files/amr510402014en.pdf

Anderson, C. (1994). *Black labor, white wealth.* Edgewood, MD: Duncan & Duncan.

Anderson, E. A. (1994, May). The code of the streets. *Atlantic Monthly,* pp. 81–94.

Anderson, E. A. (1999). *The code of the streets: Decency, violence, and the moral life of the inner city.* New York: Norton.

Anderson, J. (2001). What to do about "much ado" about drug courts? *International Journal of Drug Policy, 12,* 469–475.

Anderson, P. R., & Newman, D. J. (1998). *Introduction to criminal justice* (6th ed.). New York: McGraw-Hill.

Aptheker, B. (1971). The social functions of the prisons in the United States. In A. Y. Davis (Ed.), *If they come in the morning* (pp. 39–48). New Rochelle, NY: Third Press.

Aptheker, H. (1993). *American Negro slave revolts.* New York: International. (Original work published 1943)

Arab American Institute. (2011). *The AAI Foundation.* Retrieved from http://www.aaiusa.org

Archbold, C. A., Dahle, T. O., Fangman, M., Wentz, E., & Wood, M. (2013). Newspaper accounts of racial profiling: Accurate portrayal or perpetuation of myth? *Race and Justice, 3*(4), 300–320.

Argersinger v. Hamlin, 407 U.S. 25 (1972).

Arizona v. United States, 567 U.S. ___ (2012).

Arnold, T. K. (2014). Review of A Theory of African American Offending: Race, racism, and crime. *International Criminal Justice Review, 24,* 107–109.

Arthur, J. A. (1998). Proximate correlates of Blacks support for capital punishment. *Journal of Crime and Justice, 21,* 159–172.

Ashkenas, J., & Park, H. (2014). The race gap in America's police departments. *New York Times.* Retrieved from http://www.nytimes.com/interactive/2014/09/03/us/the-race-gap-in-americas-police-departments.html

Atkins v. Virginia, 536 U.S. 304 (2002).

Austin, J., & Irwin, J. (2001). *It's about time: America's imprisonment binge* (3rd ed.). Belmont, CA: Wadsworth.

Austin, R. (1983). The colonial model, subcultural theory, and intragroup violence. *Journal of Criminal Justice, 11,* 93–104.

Baadsager, P., Sims, B., Baer, J., & Chambliss, W. J. (2000). The overrepresentation of minorities in America's imprisonment binge. *Corrections Management Quarterly, 4,* 1–7.

Bachman, R. (1991). An analysis of American Indian homicide: A test of social disorganization and economic deprivation at the reservation county level. *Journal of Research in Crime and Delinquency, 28,* 456–471.

Badger, E., Keating, D., & Elliott, K. (2014). Where minority communities still have overwhelmingly White police. *Washington Post.* Retrieved from http://www.washingtonpost.com/blogs/wonkblog/wp/2014/08/14/where-minority-communities-still-have-overwhelmingly-white-police

Baker, D. V. (2003). The racist application of capital punishment to African Americans. In M. Free (Ed.), *Racial issues in criminal justice: The case of African Americans* (pp. 177–201). Westport, CT: Greenwood.

Baker, D. V. (2007). American Indian executions in historical context. *Criminal Justice Studies, 20,* 315–373.

Baker, D. V. (2008). Black female executions in historical context. *Criminal Justice Review, 33,* 64–88.

Baker, E. (2002). Flying while Arab: Racial profiling and air travel security. *Journal of Air Law and Commerce, 67,* 1375–1405.

Baldus, D. C., & Woodworth, G. (2003). Race discrimination and the death penalty: An empirical and legal overview. In J. Acker, R. Bohm, & C. S. Lanier (Eds.), *America's experiment with capital punishment* (2nd ed., pp. 501–551). Durham, NC: Carolina Academic Press.

Baldus, D. C., Woodworth, G., & Pulaski, C. A. (1990). *Equal justice and the death penalty: A legal and empirical analysis.* Boston: Northeastern University Press.

Banks, S., & Kyckelhahn, T. (2011). *Characteristics of suspected human trafficking incidents, 2008–2010*. Washington, DC: Bureau of Justice Statistics.

Banner, S. (2002). *The death penalty: An American history.* Cambridge, MA: Harvard University Press.

Barak, G., Leighton, P., & Cotton, A. (2014). *Class, race, gender, and crime* (4th ed.). New York: Rowman & Littlefield.

Barkan, S. F., & Cohn, S. F. (1994). Racial prejudice and support for the death penalty by Whites. *Journal of Research in Crime and Delinquency, 31,* 202–209.

Barker, T., & Carter, D. (1991). *Police deviance* (2nd ed.). Cincinnati, OH: Anderson.

Barlow, D. E., & Barlow, M. H. (2000). *Police in a multicultural society.* Prospect Heights, IL: Waveland Press.

Barlow, D. E., & Barlow, M. H. (2002). Racial profiling: A survey of African American police officers. *Police Quarterly, 5,* 334–358.

Barnes, J. C., & Boutwell, B. B. (2015). Biosocial criminology: The emergence of a new and diverse perspective. *Criminal Justice Studies, 28,* 1–5.

Barro, R. J. (1999, September 27). Does abortion lower the crime rate? *Business Week,* p. 30.

Bastian, L. (1990). *Hispanic victims.* Washington, DC: U.S. Department of Justice, Bureau of Justice Statistics.

Bastian, L. (1992). *Criminal victimization in the United States: 1973–1990 trends.* Washington, DC: U.S. Department of Justice, Office of Justice Programs.

Batson v. Kentucky, 476 U.S. 79, 108 (1986).

Battle v. Anderson, 376 F. Supp. 402 (1974).

Batton, C., & Kadleck, C. (2004). Theoretical and methodological issues in racial profiling research. *Police Quarterly, 7,1,* 30–64. Retrieved from http://www.sagepub.com

Baumer, E. (2013). Reassessing and redirecting research on race and sentencing. *Justice Quarterly, 30,* 231–261.

Baumer, E., Horney, J., Felson, R., & Lauritsen, J. (2003). Neighborhood disadvantage and the nature of violence. *Criminology, 41,* 39–71.

Baumer, E., Messner, S., & Rosenfeld, R. (2003). Explaining spatial variation in support for capital punishment: A multilevel analysis. *American Journal of Sociology, 108,* 844–875.

Bavon, A. (2001). The effect of the Tarrant County drug court project on recidivism. *Evaluation and Program Planning, 24,* 13–22.

Beard, A. (2007). *Judge finds Duke prosecutor in contempt.* Retrieved March 8, 2008, from http://www.abcnews.go.com/sports

Beaumont, G., & Tocqueville, A. (1964). *On the penitentiary system in the United States and its application in France.* Carbondale: Southern Illinois University Press. (Original work published 1833)

Beaver, K. M., DeLisi, M., Wright, J. P., Boutwell, B. B., Barnes, J. C., & Vaughn, M. G. (2013). No evidence of racial discrimination in criminal justice processing: Results from the National Longitudinal Study of Adolescent Health. *Personality and Individual Differences, 55,* 29–34.

Beck, E. M., & Tolnay, S. E. (1995). Violence toward African Americans in the era of the White lynch mob. In D. F. Hawkins (Ed.), *Ethnicity, race, and crime: Perspectives across time and place* (pp. 121–144). Albany: State University of New York Press.

Beckett, K., & Sasson, T. (2000). *The politics of injustice.* Thousand Oaks, CA: Pine Forge Press.

Bedau, H. A. (2009). Racism, wrongful convictions and the death penalty. *Tennessee Law Review, 76,* 615–624.

Bedau, H. A., & Radelet, M. L. (1987). Miscarriage of justice in potentially capital cases. *Stanford Law Review, 40,* 21–179.

Behrens, A., Uggen, C., & Manza, J. (2003). Ballot manipulation and the "menace of Negro domination": Racial threat and felon disenfranchisement in the United States, 1850–2002. *American Journal of Sociology, 109,* 559–605.

Belenko, S., Sprott, J. B., & Petersen, C. (2004). Drug and alcohol involvement among minority and female juvenile offenders: Treatment and policy issues. *Criminal Justice Policy Review, 15,* 3–36.

Belgrave, F. Z., Townsend, T. G., Cherry, V. R., & Cunningham, D. M. (1997). The influence of an Africentric worldview and demographic variables on drug knowledge, attitudes, and use among African American youth. *Journal of Community Psychology, 25,* 421–433.

Belknap, J., & Holsinger, K. (2006). The gendered nature of risk factors for delinquency. *Feminist Criminology, 1*(1), 48–71.

Belknap, J., & Holsinger, K. (2013). The gendered nature of risk factors for delinquency. In M. Chesney-Lind & L. Pasko (Eds.), *Girls, women, and crime: Selected readings* (pp. 101–118). Thousand Oaks, CA: Sage.

Bell, D. (1960). *The end of ideology.* Glencoe, IL: Free Press.

Bell, J. (2005). Solvable problem: Reducing the disproportionality of youths of color in juvenile detention facilities. *Corrections Today, 67,* 80–83.

Bendery, J. (2015, May). President Obama bans some military style equipment to local law enforcement. *The Huffington Post.* Retrieved from http://www.huffingtonpost.com/2015/05/18/obama-military-equipment-police_n_7304504.html

Benekos, P. J., & Merlo, A. V. (2008). Juvenile justice: The legacy of punitive policy. *Youth Violence and Juvenile Justice, 6*(1), 28–46.

Berk, R., Li, A., & Hickman, L. J. (2005) Statistical difficulties in determining the role of race in capital cases: A re-analysis of data from the state of Maryland. *Journal of Quantitative Criminology, 21,* 365–390.

Bernard, T. J., & Kurlycheck, M. C. (2010). *The cycle of juvenile justice* (2nd ed.). New York: Oxford University Press.

Bishop, D. M. (2005). The role of race and ethnicity in juvenile justice processing. In D. F. Hawkins & K. Kempf-Leonard (Eds.), *Our children, their children: Confronting racial and ethnic differences in American juvenile justice* (pp. 23–82). Chicago, IL: The University of Chicago Press.

Blakely v. Washington, 542 U.S. 296 (2004).

Blalock, H. M. (1967). *Toward a theory of minority group relations.* New York: Wiley.

Blauner, R. (1969). Internal colonialism and ghetto revolt. *Social Problems, 16,* 393–408.

Blauner, R. (1972). *Racial oppression in America.* New York: Harper & Row.

Bloom, B., Owen, B., Deschenes, E. P., & Rosenbaum, J. (2002). Moving toward justice for female juvenile offenders in the new millennium. *Journal of Contemporary Criminal Justice, 18,* 37–56.

Bloom, B., Owen, B., Deschenes, E. P., & Rosenbaum, J. (2013). Moving toward justice for female juvenile offenders in the new millennium: Modeling gender-specific policies and programs. In M. Chesney-Lind & L. Pasko (Eds.), *Girls, women, and crime: Selected readings.* Thousand Oaks, CA: Sage.

Blue, J. T. (1948). The relationship of juvenile delinquency, race, & economic status. *Journal of Negro Education, 17,* 469–477.

Blue, J. T. (1959). Concepts and methodology in the field of juvenile delinquency. *Journal of Human Relations, 17,* 473–482.

Blueprints Programs. (2015). *Blueprints for health: Youth development.* Retrieved from http://www.blueprintsprograms.com

Blumberg, A. S., & Niederhoffer, A. (1970). The social and historical setting. Chapter 1 in Niederhoffer & Blumberg, *The ambivalent force: Perspectives on the police,* pp. 1–39.

Blumer, M. (1984). *The Chicago school of sociology: Institutionalization, diversity, and the rise of sociological research.* Chicago: University of Chicago Press.

Blumstein, A. (1982). On the racial disproportionality of the United States' prison populations. *Journal of Criminal Law & Criminology, 73,* 1259–1281.

Blumstein, A. (1993). Racial disproportionality of U.S. prison populations revisited. *University of Colorado Law Review, 63.* Retrieved August 25, 2002, from Lexis-Nexis database.

Blumstein, A. (1996). *Youth violence, guns, and the illicit drug markets* (Research preview). Washington, DC: National Institute of Justice.

Blumstein, A. (2002). Prisons: A policy challenge. In J. Q. Wilson & J. Petersilia (Eds.), *Crime: Public policies for crime control* (pp. 451–483). Oakland, CA: Institute for Contemporary Studies.

Blumstein, A., & Wallman, J. (Eds.). (2005). *The crime drop in America* (2nd ed.). New York: Cambridge University Press.

Bobo, L. D., & Johnson, D. (2004). A taste for punishment: Black and White Americans' views on the death penalty and the war on drugs. *Du Bois Review, 1,* 151–180.

Bohm, R. M. (1991). American death penalty opinion, 1936–1986: A critical examination of Gallup polls. In R. M. Bohm (Ed.), *The death penalty in America: Current research* (pp. 113–145). Cincinnati, OH: Anderson.

Bohm, R. M. (1999). *Deathquest: An introduction to the theory and practice of capital punishment.* Cincinnati, OH: Anderson.

Bohm, R. M. (2001). *A primer on crime and delinquency theory* (2nd ed.). Belmont, CA: Wadsworth/Thomson Learning.

Bohm, R. M. (2007). *Death Quest III: An introduction to the theory and practice of capital punishment in the United States* (3rd ed.). Cincinnati, OH: Anderson.

Bohm, R. M., Clark, L., & Aveni, A. (1991). Knowledge and death penalty opinion: A test of the Marshall hypotheses. *Journal of Research in Crime and Delinquency, 28,* 360–387.

Bohm, R. M., & Vogel, B. L. (2010). *A primer on crime and delinquency theory.* Belmont, CA: Cengage/Wadsworth.

Bonger, W. A. (1943). *Race and crime.* New York: Columbia University Press.

Bonnet, F. (2012). Review of A Theory of African American Offending: Race, Racism, and Crime. *Contemporary Sociology, 41,* 242–243.

Borchard, E. M. (1932). *Convicting the innocent: Sixty-five actual errors of criminal justice.* Garden City, NY: Doubleday.

Bortner, M. A. (1984). *Inside a juvenile court: The tarnished ideal of individualized justice.* New York: New York University Press.

Bosworth, M., & Flavin, L. (Eds.). (2007). *Race, gender, & punishment: From colonialism to the war on terror.* New Brunswick, NJ: Rutgers University Press.

Bower, G. (2013). Maryland v. King: Possibly the most important criminal procedure case in decades. *Engage, 14,* 29–33.

Bowers, W. J., & Pierce, G. (1980). Arbitrariness and discrimination under post-Furman capital statutes. *Crime & Delinquency, 26,* 563–572.

Bowers, W. J., Sandys, M. R., & Steiner, B. D. (1998). Juror predispositions: Guilt-trial experience, and premature decision making. *Cornell Law Review, 83,* 1476–1556.

Bowers, W. J., Steiner, B. D., & Sandys, M. R. (2001). Death sentencing in Black and White: An empirical analysis of the role of jurors' race and jury composition. *The University of Pennsylvania Journal of Constitutional Law, 3,* 171–274.

Bradley, M. (1978). *The iceman inheritance: Prehistoric sources of Western man's racism, sexism, and aggression.* New York: Kayode.

Braga, A. A., Weisburd, D. L., Waring, E. J., Mazerolle, L. G., Spelman, W., & Gajewski, F. (1999). Problem-oriented policing in violent crime places: A randomized controlled experiment. *Criminology, 37,* 541–580.

Braman, D. (2002). Families and incarceration. In M. Mauer & M. Chesney-Lind (Eds.), *Invisible punishment: The collateral consequences of mass imprisonment* (pp. 117–135). New York: New Press.

Brandon, R., & Davies, C. (1973). *Wrongful imprisonment: Mistaken convictions and their consequences.* London: Archon Books.

Brennan, P. K. (2006). Sentencing female misdemeanants: An examination of the direct and indirect effects of race/ethnicity. *Justice Quarterly, 23,* 60–95.

Brennan, P. K., & Spohn, C. (2008). Race/ethnicity and sentencing outcomes among drug offenders in North Carolina. *Journal of Contemporary Criminal Justice, 24,* 371–398.

Brewer, T. W. (2004). Race and jurors' receptivity to mitigation in capital cases: The effect of jurors', defendants', and victims' race in combination. *Law and Human Behavior, 28,* 529–545.

Brezina, T., Agnew, R., Cullen, F. T., & Wright, J. P. (2004). The code of the street: A quantitative assessment of Elijah Anderson's subculture of violence thesis and its contribution to youth violence research. *Youth Violence and Juvenile Justice, 2,* 303–328.

Bridges, G. S., Conley, D., Engen, R. L., & Price-Spratlen, T. (1995). Social contexts of punishment: Effects of crime and community social structure on racial disparities in the administration of juvenile justice. In K. Kempf Leonard, C. Pope, & W. Feyerherm (Eds.), *Minorities in juvenile justice* (pp. 128–152). Thousand Oaks, CA: Sage.

Bridges, G., & Steen, S. (1998). Racial disparities in official assessments of juvenile offenders: Attributional stereotypes as mediating mechanisms. *American Sociological Review, 63,* 554–570.

Brodkin, K. (1999). *How Jews became White folks and what that says about race in America.* New Brunswick, NJ: Rutgers University Press.

Brodkin Sacks, K. (1997). How did Jews become White folks? In R. Delgado & J. Stefancic (Eds.), *Critical White studies: Looking behind the mirror* (pp. 395–401). Philadelphia: Temple University Press.

Brooks, W. M., Jr., & Willingham, T. Y. (2009). Juvenile waivers to adult court. In H. T. Greene & S. L. Gabbidon (Eds.), *Encyclopedia of race and crime* (pp. 424–427). Thousand Oaks, CA: Sage.

Brown v. Board of Education of Topeka et al., 347 US 483 (1954).

Brown, A., & Patten, E. (2013). *Hispanics of Cuban origin in the United States, 2011.* Pew Research Center. Retrieved from http://www.pewhispanic.org/2013/06/19/hispanics-of-cuban-origin-in-the-united-states-2011/

Brown, H., Guskin, E., & Mitchell, A. (2012). *Arab American population growth*. Retrieved from http://www.journalism.org/2012/11/28/arabamerican-population-growth/

Brown, L. M., Chesney-Lind, M., & Stein, N. (2007, 2013). Patriarchy matters: Toward a gendered theory of teen violence and victimization. In M. Chesney-Lind & L. Pasko (Eds.), *Girls, women, and crime: Selected readings* (pp. 21–38). Thousand Oaks, CA: Sage.

Brown, M. C., & Warner, B. D. (1992). Immigrants, urban politics and policing in 1900. *American Sociological Review, 57,* 293–305.

Brownstein, H. H. (1996). *The rise and fall of a violent crime wave: Crack cocaine and the social construction of a crime problem.* Guilderland, NY: Harrow & Heston.

Brunson, R. K. (2007). "Police don't like Black people": African-American young men's accumulated police experiences. *Criminology & Public Policy, 6,* 71–102.

Brunson, R. K., & Stewart, E. A. (2006). Young African American women, the street code, and violence: An exploratory analysis. *Journal of Crime & Justice, 29,* 1–19.

Brunson, R. K., & Weitzer, R. (2009). Police relations with black and white youths in different urban neighborhoods. *Urban Affairs Review, 44*(6), 858–885.

Bucerius, S. M., & Tonry, M. (2014). (eds.) *The Oxford handbook of ethnicity, crime, and immigration.* New York: Oxford University Press.

Bui, H. N. (2009). Parent-child conflicts, school troubles, and differences in delinquency across immigration generations. *Crime and Delinquency, 55,* 412–441.

Burch, A. (2011). *Arrest-related deaths, statistical tables.* Retrieved from http://www.bjs.gov/content/pub/pdf/ard0309st.pdf on 4/6/2015

Bureau of Indian Affairs. (1974). *The American Indians: Answers to 101 questions.* Washington, DC: U.S. Department of the Interior.

Bureau of Indian Affairs. (1976). *Law enforcement services annual report 1976.* Washington, DC: U.S. Department of the Interior.

Bureau of Justice Assistance. (2007). *2005 national gang threat assessment.* Retrieved February 22, 2008, from http://www.ojp.usdoj.gov/BJA/what/2005_threat_assesment.pdf

Bureau of Justice Statistics. (1992). *Criminal victimization in the United States: 1973–1990 trends.* Washington, DC: U.S. Department of Justice, Office of Justice Programs.

Bureau of Justice Statistics. (2001). *Hate crimes reported in NIBRS, 1997–99.* Washington, DC: U.S. Department of Justice, Office of Justice Programs.

Bureau of Justice Statistics. (2003). *Over half of the increase in state prison populations since 1995 is due to an increase in the prisoners convicted of violent offenses.* Washington, DC: Department of Justice. Retrieved March 22, 2004, from http://www.ojp.usdoj.gov/bjs/glance/corrtyp.htm

Bureau of Justice Statistics. (2006). *Compendium of federal justice statistics, 2004.* Washington, DC: Department of Justice.

Bureau of Justice Statistics. (2008). *Demographic trends in jail populations.* Retrieved July 21, 2008, from http://www.ojp.usdoj.gov/bjs/glancetables/jailracetab.htm.

Bureau of Justice Statistics. (2010). *Felony sentences in state courts, 2006: Statistical tables.* Washington, DC: Department of Justice.

Bureau of Justice Statistics. (2011a). *Key facts at a glance: Incarceration rate, 1980–2009.* Retrieved June 17, 2011, from http://bjs.ojp.usdoj.gov/content/glance/race.cfm

Bureau of Justice Statistics. (2011b). *Key facts at a glance: Violent crime rates by race of victim.* Retrieved June 17, 2011, from http://bjs.ojp.usdoj.gov/content/glance/race.cfm

Bureau of Labor Statistics. (2014). *Employed persons by detailed occupation, sex, race, and Hispanic or Latino ethnicity.* Retrieved from http://www.bls.gov/cps/cpsaat11.pdf

Burgess, E. W. (1925). The growth of the city: An introduction to a research project. In R. Park & E. W. Burgess (Eds.), *The city* (pp. 47–62). Chicago: University of Chicago Press.

Burns, S. (2011). *The Central Park Five: A chronicle of a city wilding.* New York: Knopf.

Burt, C. H., Simons, R. L., & Gibbons, R. X. (2012). Racial discrimination, ethnic-racial socialization, and crime: A micro-sociological model of risk and resilience. *American Sociological Review, 77,* 648–677.

Bush, W. S. (2010). *Who gets a childhood? Race and juvenile justice in twentieth-century Texas.* Athens: University of Georgia Press.

Bushway, S., Stoll, M., & Weiman, D. F. (Eds.). (2007). *Barriers to reentry? The labor market for released prisoners in post-industrial America.* New York: Russell Sage.

Butler, P. (1995). Racially based jury nullification: Black power in the criminal justice system. *The Yale Law Journal, 105,* 677–725.

Butler, P. (2009). *Let's get free: A hip-hop theory of justice.* New York: The New Press.

Cabaniss, E. R., Frabutt, J. M., Kendrick, M. H., & Arbuckle, M. B. (2007). Reducing disproportionate minority contact in the juvenile justice system: Promising practices. *Aggression and Violent Behavior: A Review Journal, 12,* 393–401.

Cahalan, M., & Parsons, L. (1986). *Historical corrections in the United States, 1850–1984.* Washington, DC: Bureau of Justice Statistics.

Camp, G. M., & Camp, C. G. (1985). *Prison gangs: Their extent, nature, and impact on prisons.* Washington, DC: U.S. Department of Justice.

The Campaign for the Fair Sentencing of Youth. (2009). *Human rights.* Retrieved July 2, 2011, from http://www.endjlwop.org

Cao, L., Adams, A. T., & Jensen, V. J. (2000). The empirical status of the Black subculture-of-violence thesis. In M. W. Markowitz & D. Jones Brown (Eds.), *The system in Black and White: Exploring the connections between race, crime, and justice* (pp. 47–61). Westport, CT: Praeger.

Carey, S. M., Finigan, M., Crumpton, D., & Waller, M. (2006). California drug courts: Outcomes, costs, and promising practices: An overview of Phase II in a statewide study. *Journal of Psychoactive Drugs, 3,* 345–356.

Carlson, P. M. (2001). Prison interventions: Evolving strategies to control security threat groups. *Corrections Management Quarterly, 5,* 10–22.

Carmichael, D., Booth, E., & Patnaik, A. (2010). *Addressing disproportionate minority contact in the Texas juvenile justice system: Causes and solutions from the community perspective.* Public Policy Research Institute, Texas A&M University. Retrieved from http://ppri.tamu.edu/PublicReports/100724_Final%20Report.pdf

Carmichael, D., Whitten, G., & Voloudakis, M. (2005). *Study of minority overrepresentation in the Texas juvenile justice system.* Submitted to the Office of the Governor, Criminal Justice Division. Public Policy Research Institute, Texas A&M University. Retrieved from http://dmcfinalreport.tamu.edu/DMRFinalReport.pdf

Carr, N. T., Hudson, K., Hanks, R. S., & Hunt, A. N. (2008). Gender effects along the juvenile justice system: Evidence of a gendered organization. *Feminist Criminology, 3,* 25–43.

Carrigan, W. D., & Webb, C. (2003). The lynchings of persons of Mexican origin or descent in the U.S., 1848–1929. *Journal of Social History, 37,* 411–438.

Carroll, C. (1900). *The Negro a beast.* St. Louis, MO: American Book and Bible House.

Carroll, L. (1974). *Hacks, Blacks, and cons: Race relations in a maximum security prison.* Prospect Heights, IL: Waveland Press.

Carson, E. A. (2014). *Prisoners in 2013.* Washington, DC: Bureau of Justice Statistics. NCJ 247282.

Carter, D. (1969). *Scottsboro: A tragedy of the American South.* Baton Rouge: Louisiana State University Press.

Carter, D. L. (1983). Hispanic interaction with the criminal justice system in Texas: Experiences, attitudes, and perceptions. *Journal of Criminal Justice, 11,* 213–227.

Castelle, G., & Loftus, E. F. (2002). Misinformation and wrongful convictions. In S. Westervelt & J. A. Humphrey (Eds.), *Wrongly convicted: Perspectives on failed justice* (pp. 17–35). New Brunswick, NJ: Rutgers University Press.

Catalano, S. (2013). *Intimate partner violence: Attributes of victimization, 1993–2011.* Washington, DC: Bureau of Justice Statistics. Retrieved from http://www.bjs.gov

Catalano, S. M. (2006). *Criminal victimization, 2005.* Washington, DC: U.S. Department of Justice, Office of Justice Programs, Bureau of Justice Statistics.

Catterall, H. (Ed.). (1968). *Judicial cases concerning American slavery and the Negro* (Vol. 1). New York: Negro University Press. (Original work published 1926)

Center for Constitutional Rights. (2014). *City of New York and Center for Constitutional Rights announce agreement in landmark stop and frisk case.* Retrieved from http://ccrjustice.org/newsroom/press-releases/city-of-new-york-and-center-constitutional-rights-announce-agreement-landmark-stop-and-frisk-case

Center for Prosecutorial Integrity. (2014). *Conviction integrity units: Vanguard of criminal justice reform.* Rockville, MD: Author.

Center for the Study and Prevention of Violence. (2011). *Selection criteria.* Retrieved on July 12, 2011, from http://www.colorado.edu/cspv/blueprints/criteria.html

Center for the Study and Prevention of Violence. (2015). *We know what works.* Retrieved from http://www.colorado.educ/cspv/blueprints

Cernkovich, S. A., Giordano, P. C., & Rudolph, J. L. (2000). Race, crime, and the American dream. *Journal of Research in Crime and Delinquency, 37,* 131–170.

Chabrán, R., & Chabrán, R. (1996). *The Latino encyclopedia.* Tarrytown, NY: Marshall Cavendish Corporation.

Chambliss, W. (1964). A sociological analysis of the law of vagrancy. *Social Problems, 12,* 67–77.

Chambliss, W. (Ed.). (1969). *Crime and the legal process.* New York: McGraw-Hill.

Chambliss, W. J. (1991). *Trading textbooks for prison cells.* Baltimore, MD: National Center for Institutions and Alternatives.

Chamlin, M. B., Myer, A. J., Sanders, B. A., & Cochran, J. K. (2008). Abortion as crime control: A cautionary tale. *Criminal Justice Policy Review, 19,* 135–152.

Chapin, B. (1983). *Criminal justice in colonial America, 1606–1660.* Athens: University of Georgia Press.

Chauhan, P., Fera, A. G., Welsh, M. B., Balazon, E., & Misshula, E. (2014). *Trends in misdemeanor arrests in New York.* New York: John Jay College of Criminal Justice.

Chavez-Garcia, M. (2012). *States of delinquency.* Oakland: University of California Press.

Chesney-Lind, M., & Pasko, L. (2013). *Girls, women, and crime: Selected readings.* Thousand Oaks, CA: Sage.

Chesney-Lind, M., & Shelden, R. G. (2004). *Girls, delinquency, and juvenile justice.* Belmont, CA: Wadsworth/Thomson Learning.

Chicago Commission on Race Relations. (1922). *The Negro in Chicago: A study of race relations and a race riot in 1919.* Chicago: Author.

Children's Defense Fund. (2013). *Dismantling the cradle to prison pipeline: Preventing pushouts in Mississippi schools.* Washington, DC: Children's Defense Fund. Retrieved from http://www.childrensdefense.org/library/data/dismantling-the-cpp.pdf

Chilton, B. (2004). Regional variations in lethal and nonlethal assaults. *Homicide Studies, 8,* 40–56.

Chiricos, T. G., & Crawford, C. (1995). Race and imprisonment: A contextual assessment of the evidence. In D. Hawkins (Ed.), *Ethnicity, race, and crime* (pp. 281–309). Albany: State University of New York Press.

Christianson, S. (1981). Our Black prisons. *Crime and Delinquency, 27,* 364–375.

Christianson, S. (1998). *With liberty for some: 500 years of imprisonment in America.* Boston: Northeastern University Press.

Christianson, S. (2004). *Innocent: Inside wrongful conviction cases.* New York: New York University Press.

Chu, L. (2014). *After decades of spending minority youth still overrepresented in system.* Retrieved from http://jjie.org/after-decades-of-spending-minority-youth-still-overrepresented-in-system/

Cintron, M. (2005). Latino delinquency: Defining and counting the problem. In E. Penn, H. Taylor Greene, & S. Gabbidon (Eds.), *Race and juvenile justice* (pp. 27–45). Durham, NC: Carolina Academic Press.

Clarke, H. J. (1992). *Christopher Columbus and the African holocaust.* Brooklyn, NY: A & B.

Clarke, J. W. (1998). "Without fear or shame": Lynching, capital punishment and the subculture of violence in the American South. *British Journal of Political Science, 28,* 269–289.

Clear, T. R. (2007). *Imprisoning communities: How mass incarceration makes disadvantaged neighborhoods worse.* New York: Oxford University Press.

Clear, T. R., & Cole, G. F. (2000). *American corrections* (5th ed.). Belmont, CA: Wadsworth.

Clear, T. R., & Cole, G. F. (2003). *American corrections* (6th ed.). Belmont, CA: Wadsworth.

Clear, T. R., & Dammer, H. R. (2003). *The offender in the community* (2nd ed.). Belmont, CA: Wadsworth.

Clear, T. R., Rose, D. R., & Ryder, J. A. (2001). Incarceration and the community: The problem of removing and returning offenders. *Crime & Delinquency, 47,* 335–351.

Clear, T. R., Rose, D. R., Waring, E., & Scully, K. (2003). Coercive mobility and crime: A preliminary examination of concentrated incarceration and social disorganization. *Justice Quarterly, 20,* 33–64.

Clement, P. T. (1993). The incorrigible child: Juvenile delinquency in the United States from the 17th through the 19th centuries. In A. G. Hess & P. F. Clement (Eds.), *History of juvenile delinquency:*

A collection of essays on crime committed by young offenders, in history and in selected countries (pp. 453–490). Aalen, Germany: Scientia Verlag.

Cloward, R. A., & Ohlin, L. E. (1960). *Delinquency and opportunity: A theory of delinquent gangs.* New York: The Free Press.

Coalition for Juvenile Justice. (2011). *Disproportionate minority contact (DMC): Facts and resources.* Retrieved from http://www.juvjustice.org/sites/default/files/ckfinder/files/DMC%20factsheet%20draft%20—%20Final%20for%20Print.pdf

Cochran, J. C. and Warren, P. Y. (2012). Racial, ethnic, and gender differences in perceptions of the police: The salience of officer race within the context of racial profiling. *Journal of Contemporary Criminal Justice 28*(2), 206–227.

Cochran, J. K., & Chamlin, M. B. (2005). Can information change public opinion? Another test of the Marshall hypotheses. *Journal of Criminal Justice, 33,* 573–584.

Cochran, J. K., & Chamlin, M. B. (2006). The enduring racial divide in death penalty support. *Journal of Criminal Justice, 34,* 84–99.

Cochran, J. K., Sanders, B., & Chamlin, M. B. (2006). Profiles in change: An alternative look at the Marshall hypotheses. *Journal of Criminal Justice Education, 17,* 205–226.

Cohen, A. K. (1955). *Delinquent boys: The culture of the gang.* New York: The Free Press.

Cohen, F. (1971). *Handbook of federal Indian law.* Albuquerque: University of New Mexico Press.

Cohen, S. (2003). *The wrong man: America's epidemic of wrongful death row convictions.* New York: Carroll & Graf.

Cohen, T. H. (2011). *Who's better at defending criminals? Does type of defense attorney matter in terms of producing favorable case outcomes?* Retrieved from http://ssrn.com/abstract=1876474

Cohen, T. H., & Reaves, B. A. (2007). *Pretrial release of felony defendants in state courts.* Washington, DC: Bureau of Justice Statistics. NCJ 214994

Coker v. Georgia, 429 U.S. 815 (1977).

Cole, D. (1999). *No equal justice.* New York: New Press.

Collins, C. F. (1997). *The imprisonment of African American women.* Jefferson, NC: McFarland.

Colvin, M. (1997). *Penitentiaries, reformatories, and chain gangs.* New York: St. Martin's Press.

Comey, J. B. (2015). *Hard truths for law enforcement and race.* Retrieved from http://www.fbi.gov/news/speeches/hard-truths-law-enforcement-and-race

Congressional Budget Office. (2010). *S. 678 Juvenile Justice and Delinquency Prevention Reauthorization Act of 2009.* Retrieved July 12, 2011, from http://www.cbo.gov/ftpdocs/110xx/doc11010/s678.pdf

Conley, D. J., & Debro, J. (2002). Black Muslims in California prisons: The beginning of a social movement for Black prisoners in the United States. In C. E. Reasons, D. C. Conley, & J. Debro (Eds.), *Race, class, gender, and justice in the United States* (pp. 278–291). Boston: Allyn & Bacon.

Cooper, A., & Smith, E. L. (2011). *Homicide trends in the United States, 1980–2008.* Washington, DC: Bureau of Justice Statistics.

Cooper, C. (2001/2002). Subjective states of mind & custodial arrest: Race-based policing. *The Journal of Intergroup Relations, 38,* 3–18.

Cooper, C. S. (2003). Drug courts: Current issues and future perspectives. *Substance Use & Misuse, 38,* 1671–1711.

Cooper, J. A., Walsh, A., & Ellis, L. (2010). Is criminology moving toward a paradigm shift? Evidence from a survey of the American Society of Criminology. *Journal of Criminal Justice Education, 21,* 332–347.

Coppa, F. J., & Curran, T. J. (1976). From the Rhine to the Mississippi: The German emigration to the United States. In F. J. Coppa & T. J. Curran (Eds.), *The immigrant experience in America* (pp. 44–62). Boston: Twayne.

The Council of State Governments Justice Center. (2015). *Federal interagency reentry council.* Retrieved from http://csgjusticecenter.org/nrrc/projects/firc

Courtwright, D. T. (2001). *Dark paradise.* Cambridge, MA: Harvard University Press.

Covington, J. (1995). Racial classification in criminology: The reproduction of racialized crime. *Sociological Forum, 10,* 547–568.

Covington, J. (2003). The violent Black male: Conceptions of race in criminological theories. In D. F. Hawkins (Ed.), *Violent crime: Assessing race & ethnic differences* (pp. 254–279). Cambridge, UK: Cambridge University Press.

Cox, A. K. (2013). Student death penalty attitudes: Does new information matter? *Journal of Criminal Justice Education, 24,* 443–460.

Cox, O. C. (1945). Lynching and the status quo. *Journal of Negro Education, 14,* 576–588.

Cox, R. (2014). Unethical intrusion: The disproportionate impact of law enforcement DNA sampling on minority populations. *American Criminal Law Review, 52,* 155–176.

Cresswell, L., & Deschenes, E. (2001). Minority and non-minority perceptions of drug court program severity and effectiveness. *Journal of Drug Issues, 31,* 259–292.

Crow, M. C., & Johnson, K. A. (2008). Race, ethnicity, and habitual-offender sentencing: A multilevel analysis of individual and contextual threat. *Criminal Justice Policy Review, 19,* 63–83.

Crutchfield, R. D. (2004). Warranted disparity? Questioning the justification of racial disparity in criminal justice processing. *Columbia Human Rights Law Review, 36,* 15–40.

Cuellar, J., & Curry, T. (2007). The prevalence and comorbidity between delinquency, drug abuse, suicide attempts, physical and sexual abuse, and self-mutilation among delinquent Hispanic females. *Hispanic Journal of Behavioral Sciences, 29*(1), 68–78.

Cullen, F. T. (2009). Preface. In A. Walsh & K. M. Beaver (Eds.), *Biosocial criminology: New directions in theory and research* (pp. xv–xvii). New York: Routledge.

Curran, D. J., & Renzetti, C. M. (2001). *Theories of crime.* Boston: Allyn & Bacon.

D'Addario, D. (2015). FBI investigating hate site linked to accused Charleston shooter. *Time.com.* Retrieved from http://time.com/3929352/dylann-roof-website-manifesto/

D'Alessio, S. J., Eitle, D., & Stolzenberg, L. (2005). The impact of serious crime, racial threat, and economic inequality on private police size. *Social Science Research, 34,* 267–282.

Daniels, R. (1988). *Asian America: Chinese and Japanese in the United States since 1850.* Seattle: University of Washington Press.

Darwin, C. (1859). *On the origin of species by means of natural selection, or the preservation of favoured races in the struggle for life.* London: John Murray.

Darwin, C. (1871). *The descent of man and selection in relation to sex.* London: John Murray.

Davidson, R. T. (1974). *Chicano prisoners: The keys to San Quentin.* Prospect Heights, IL: Waveland Press.

Davis, A. Y. (1981). *Women, race & class.* New York: Random House.

Davis, A. Y. (1997). Race and criminalization: Black Americans and the punishment industry. In W. Lubiano (Ed.), *The house that race built: Black Americans, U.S. terrain* (pp. 264–279). New York: Pantheon.

Davis, A. Y. (2000). From the convict lease system to the super-max prison. In J. James (Ed.), *States of confinement: Policing, detention, and prisons* (pp. 60–74). New York: St. Martin's Press.

Davis, A. Y. (2003). *Are prisons obsolete?* New York: Seven Stories Press.

Davis, C. (2007). At-risk girls and delinquency: Career pathways. *Crime and Delinquency, 53*(3), 408–435.

Davis, C. (2013). At-risk girls and delinquency: Career pathways. In M. Chesney-Lind, & L. Pasko (Eds.), *Girls, women, and crime: Selected readings* (pp. 69–85). Thousand Oaks, CA: Sage.

Davis, H. W. (2008). *Federal Advisory Committee on Juvenile Justice Annual Report, 2008.* Washington, DC: U.S. Department of Justice.

Davis, J., & Sorenson, J. (2010). Disproportionate minority confinement: An examination of Black-White disparity in placements, 1997–2006. *Crime and Delinquency, 30,* 1–25.

Davis, J., & Sorensen, J. R. (2013). Disproportionate juvenile minority confinement: A state-level assessment of racial threat. *Youth Violence and Juvenile Justice, 11, 4,* 296–312. Retrieved from http://yvj.sagepub.com

De Gruy, L. (2010). DNA testing may unfairly target people of color. *Los Angeles Wave.* Retrieved from http://www.wavenewspapers.com

De Las Casas, B. (1993). *The devastation of the Indies: A brief account.* Baltimore: Johns Hopkins University Press. (Original work published 1552)

Death Penalty Information Center. (2008). *Juveniles and the death penalty.* Retrieved March 26, 2008, from http://www.deathpenaltyinfo.org/article.php?did=205&scid=27.

Death Penalty Information Center. (2015). *States with and without the death penalty.* Retrieved from http://www.deathpenaltyinfo.org

DeFrances, C. J., & Litras, M. F. X. (2000). *Indigent defense services in large counties, 1999.* Washington, DC: Bureau of Justice Statistics.

Delgado, R. (2009). The law of the noose: A history of Latino lynching. *Harvard Civil Rights-Civil Liberties Law Review, 44,* 297–312.

Delgado, R., & Stefancic, J. (2001). *Critical race theory: An introduction*. New York: New York University Press.

DeLisi, M. (2011). Where is the evidence for racial profiling? *Journal of Criminal Justice, 39*, 461–462.

DeLisi, M., & Regoli, R. (1999). Race, conventional crime, and criminal justice: The declining importance of skin color. *Journal of Criminal Justice, 27*, 549–557.

Dempsey, J. S. (1999). *An introduction to policing*. Belmont, CA: Wadsworth.

Demuth, S., & Steffensmeier, D. (2004). The impact of gender and race-ethnicity in the pretrial release process. *Social Problems, 51*, 222–242.

Deschenes, E. P., & Esbensen, F. A. (1999). Violence among girls: Does gang membership make a difference? In M. Chesney-Lind & J. M. Hagedorn (Eds.), *Female gangs in America* (pp. 277–294). Chicago: Lakeview Press.

Desmond v. Blackwell, 235 F. Supp. 246 (1964).

Devine, P., Coolbaugh, K., & Jenkins, S. (1998). *Disproportionate minority confinement: Lessons from five states*. Washington, DC: Office of Juvenile Justice and Delinquency Prevention.

Dickey, G. (2004). *Downtown opium dens attracted many*. El Paso Community College Local History Project. Retrieved December 16, 2004, from http://www.epcc.edu/ftp/Homes/monicaw/borderlands/21_opium.htm

Dillon, R. R., Robbins, M. S., Szapocznik, J., & Pantin, H. (2008). Exploring the role of parental monitoring of peers on the relationship between family functioning and delinquency in the lives of African American and Hispanic adolescents. *Crime & Delinquency, 54*, 65–94.

DiLulio, J. J., Jr. (1995, November 27). The coming of the super-predators. *Weekly Standard*, p. 23.

DiLulio, J. (1996a). My Black crime problem, and ours. *City Journal, 6*, 14–28.

DiLulio, J. J., Jr. (1996b, Spring). They're coming: Florida's youth crime bomb. *Impact*, pp. 25–27.

Dinnerstein, L., & Reimers, D. M. (1982). *Ethnic Americans* (2nd ed.). New York: Harper & Row.

Dixon, T. L. (2015). Good guys are always still white: Positive change and continued misrepresentation of race and crime on local television news. *Communication Research*. doi: 0093650215579223

Donohue, J. J., & Levitt, S. D. (2001). The impact of legalized abortion on crime. *The Quarterly Journal of Economics, CXVI*, 379–420.

Donohue, J. J., & Levitt, S. D. (2004). Further evidence that legalized abortion lowered crime: A reply to Joyce. *Journal of Human Resources, 39*, 29–49.

Donohue, J. J., & Levitt, S. D. (2006). Measurement error, legalized abortion and the decline in crime: A response to Foote and Goetz (2005). *National Bureau of Economic Research Working Paper*, no. 11987.

Donzinger, S. R. (Ed.). (1996). *The real war on crime: The report of the national criminal justice commission*. New York: Harper Perennial.

D'Orso, M. (1996). *Like judgement day: The ruin and redemption of a town called Rosewood*. New York: Berkley.

Doucet, J. M., D'Antonio-Del Rio, J. M., & Chauvin, C. D. (2014). G.R.I.T.S.: The southern subculture of violence and homicide offenses by girls raised in the south. *Journal of Interpersonal Violence, 29*, 806–823.

Drug Policy Alliance. (2008). *Tulia, Texas*. Retrieved March 18, 2008, from http://www.drugpolicy.org/law/police/tulia/index.cfm

Du Bois, W. E. B. (1891). *Enforcement of the slave trade laws* (American Historical Association, Annual Report). Washington, DC: Government Printing Office.

Du Bois, W. E. B. (1899, May 18). The Negro and crime. *The Independent, 51*.

Du Bois, W. E. B. (1901). The spawn of slavery: The convict lease system in the South. *Missionary Review of the World, 14*, 737–745. Reprinted in S. L. Gabbidon, H. Taylor Greene, & V. Young. (2002). *African American classics in criminology and criminal justice* (pp. 83–88). Thousand Oaks, CA: Sage.

Du Bois, W. E. B. (1920). Crime. *The Crisis, 19*, 172–173.

Du Bois, W. E. B. (1996). *The Philadelphia Negro: A social study*. Philadelphia: The University of Pennsylvania Press. (Original work published 1899)

Dulaney, M. R. (1879). *The origin of races and color*. Philadelphia: Harper & Brothers.

Dulaney, W. M. (1996). *Black police in America*. Bloomington: Indiana University Press.

Dunlap, E., Golub, A., & Johnson, B. D. (2003). Girls' sexual development in the inner city: From compelled childhood sexual contacts to sex-for-things exchanges. *Journal of Child Sexual Abuse, 12*, 73–96.

Duran, R. J. (2012). Policing the Barrios: Exposing the shadows to the brightness of a new day. In M. Urbina (Ed.), *Hispanics in the U.S. criminal justice system: A new American demography* (pp. 42–62). Springfield, IL: Charles C Thomas.

Durose, M. R., Cooper, A. D., & Snyder, H. N. (2014). *Recidivism of prisoners released in 30 states in 2005: Patterns from 2005 to 2010.* NCJ 244205. Washington, DC: U.S. Department of Justice.

Durose, M. R., Smith, E. L., & Langan, P. A. (2007). *Contacts between police and the public, 2005.* Washington, DC: U.S. Department of Justice.

Dyer, J. (2000). *The perpetual prisoner machine: How America profits from crime.* Boulder, CO: Westview Press.

Dyson, M. E. (2006). *Come hell or high water: Hurricane Katrina and the color of disaster.* New York: Basic Civitas Books.

Eberheart v. Georgia, 433 U.S. 917 (1977).

Eddings v. Oklahoma, 455 U.S. 104 (1982).

Egley, A., & Howell, J. C. (2011). *Highlights of the 2009 national youth gang survey.* Retrieved October 26, 2011 from https://www.ncjrs.gov/pdffiles1/ojjdp/233581.pdf

Egley, A., Howell, J. C., & Harris, M. (2014). *Highlights of the 2012 National Youth Gang Survey.* Retrieved from http://www.ojjdp.gov/pubs/248025.pdf

Eith, C., & Durose, M. R. (2011). *Contacts between police and the public, 2008.* Retrieved October 21, 2011, from http://www.bjs.gov/content/pub/pdf/cpp08.pdf

Eitle, D., & Taylor, J. (2008). Are Hispanics the new "threat"? Minority group threat and fear of crime in Miami-Dade County. *Social Science Research, 37,* 1102–1115.

Eitle, D., & Turner, R. J. (2003). Stress exposure, race, and young male adult crime. *Sociological Quarterly, 44,* 243–269.

Ellis, L. (1997). Criminal behavior and *r/K* selection: An extension of gene-based evolutionary theory. *Deviant Behavior, 8,* 148–176.

Ellis, L., & Walsh, A. (1997). Gene-based evolutionary theories in criminology. *Criminology, 35,* 229–275.

Ellis, L., & Walsh, A. (1999). Criminologists' opinions about causes and theories of crime and delinquency. *The Criminologist, 24*(1), 4–6.

Ellis, L., & Walsh, A. (2000). *Criminology: A global perspective.* Needham Heights, MA: Allyn & Bacon.

Emsley, C. (1983). *Policing and its context, 1750–1870.* New York: Schocken Books.

Engel, R. S., & Calnon, J. M. (2004). Examining the influence of driver's characteristics during traffic stops with police: Results from a national survey. *Justice Quarterly, 21,* 49–90.

Engel, R. S., & Smith, M. R. (2009). Perceptual distortion and reasonableness during police shootings: Law, legitimacy, and future research. *Criminology & Public Policy, 8,* 141–152.

Engen, R. L., Gainey, R. R., Crutchfield, R. D., & Weis, J. G. (2003). Discretion and disparity under sentencing guidelines: The role of departures and structured sentencing alternatives. *Criminology, 41,* 99–130.

Ennis, R. S., Rios-Vargas, M., & Albert, N. G. (2011). *The Hispanic population: 2010.* Washington, DC: U.S. Census Bureau.

Ensor, M. O., & and Gozdziak, E. M. (2010). *Children and migration: At the crossroads of resiliency and vulnerability.* New York: Palgrave.

Epps, E. G. (1967). Socioeconomic status, race, level of aspiration and juvenile delinquency: A limited empirical test of Merton's conception of deviance. *Phylon, 28,* 16–27.

Equal Justice Initiative. (2007). *Cruel and unusual: Sentencing 13- and 14-year-old children to die in prison.* Retrieved from http://www.eji.org

Equal Justice Initiative. (2010). *Illegal racial discrimination in jury selection: A continuing legacy.* Montgomery, AL: Author.

Equal Justice Initiative. (2015a). *Florida Supreme Court unanimously decides Miller v. Alabama is retroactive.* Retrieved from http://www.eji.org

Equal Justice Initiative. (2015b). *Lynching in America: Confronting the legacy of racial terror.* Montgomery, AL: Author. Retrieved from http://www.eji.org

Escobar, E. J. (1999). *Race, police, and the making of a political identity: Mexican Americans and the Los Angeles Police Department, 1900–1945.* Berkeley: University of California Press.

Escobedo v. Illinois, 378 U.S. 478, 84 S. Ct. 1758 (1964).

Farole, D. J., & Langton, L. (2010). A national assessment of public defender office caseloads. *Judicature, 94,* 87–90.

Farrell, A., McDevitt, J., & Fahy, S. (2010). Where are all the victims? Understanding the determinants of official identification of human trafficking incidents. *Criminology & Public Policy, 9*(2), 201–233. Article first published at 8 APR 2010 DOI: 10.1111/j.1745-9133.2010.00621.x.

Faust, A. B. (1927). *The German element in the United States* (Vol. I). New York: The Steuben Society of America.

Feagin, R. F., & Booher Feagin, C. (2012). *Racial and ethnic relations* (9th ed.). New York: Pearson/Prentice-Hall.

Federal Advisory Committee on Juvenile Justice. (2013). *2013 recommendations to the president, congress, and OJJDP administrator.* Washington, DC: Office of Juvenile Justice and Delinquency Prevention. Retrieved from http://www.facjj.org

Federal Bureau of Investigation. (1930–2002). *Crime in the United States.* Washington, DC: Government Printing Office. Retrieved from http://www.fbi.gov/ucr/ucr.htm

Federal Bureau of Investigation. (1998). *National incident-based reporting system.* Washington, DC: Government Printing Office.

Federal Bureau of Investigation. (2001). *Crime in the United States, 2000.* Washington, DC: Government Printing Office.

Federal Bureau of Investigation. (2002). *Hate crime statistics, 1995–2001.* Washington, DC: Government Printing Office. Retrieved July 15, 2004, from http://www.fbi.gov/ucr/ucr.htm#hate

Federal Bureau of Investigation. (2003). *Crime in the United States, 2003 Section IV arrests.* Retrieved from http://www.fbi.gov/ucr/cius_03/pdf/03sec4.pdf

Federal Bureau of Investigation. (2004). *Crime in the United States, 2002.* Washington, DC: Government Printing Office. Retrieved from http://www.fbi.gov/ucr/cius_02/pdf/4section four.pdf

Federal Bureau of Investigation. (2005). *Crime in the United States, 2005 Section IV arrests.* Retrieved from http://www.fbi.gov/ucr/05cius/arrests/index.html

Federal Bureau of Investigation. (2006a). *Crime in the United States, 2006.* Retrieved from http://www.fbi.gov/ucr/cius2006/arrests/index.html

Federal Bureau of Investigation. (2006b). *Hate crime statistics, 2006.* Washington, DC: Government Printing Office. Retrieved February 2, 2008, from http://www.fbi.gov/ucr/hc2006/index.html

Federal Bureau of Investigation. (2006c). *Law enforcement officers feloniously killed and assaulted, 2006. Officers feloniously killed.* Retrieved March 18, 2008, from http://www.fbi.gov/ucr/killed/2006/feloniouslykilled.html

Federal Bureau of Investigation. (2007a). *Crime in the United States, 2006.* Washington, DC: Government Printing Office. Retrieved from http://www.fbi.gov/ucr/cius2006/index.html

Federal Bureau of Investigation. (2007b). *Hate crime statistics, 2006.* Washington, DC: Government Printing Office. Retrieved April 23, 2011, from http://www2.fbi.gov/ucr/hc2006/index.html

Federal Bureau of Investigation. (2008a). *Crime in the United States, 2007.* Washington, DC: Government Printing Office.

Federal Bureau of Investigation. (2008b). *Hate crime statistics, 2007.* Washington, DC: Government Printing Office. Retrieved April 23, 2011 from http://www2.fbi.gov/ucr/hc2007/index.html

Federal Bureau of Investigation. (2009a). *Crime in the United States, 2008.* Washington, DC: Government Printing Office. Retrieved from http://www.fbi.gov/about-us/cjis/ucr/crime-in-the-u.s/2010/crime-in-the-u.s.-2010/aboutucrmain

Federal Bureau of Investigation. (2009b). *Hate crime statistics, 2008.* Washington, DC: Government Printing Office. Retrieved April 23, 2011 from http://www2.fbi.gov/ucr/hc2008/index.html

Federal Bureau of Investigation. (2010a). *Crime in the United States, 2009.* Washington, DC: Government Printing Office.

Federal Bureau of Investigation. (2010b). *Hate crime statistics, 2009.* Washington, DC: Government Printing Office.

Federal Bureau of Investigation. (2010c). *Incidents, offenses, victims and known offenders, 2009: Table 1.* Retrieved from http://www.fbi.gov/stats-services/crimestats

Federal Bureau of Investigation. (2011a). *Arkansas men charged with federal hate crime related to the assault of five Hispanic men.* Retrieved from http://www.fbi.gov/littlerock/press-releases/2011/lr040811.htm

Federal Bureau of Investigation. (2011b). *Crime in the United States, 2010.* http://www.fbi.gov/about-us/cjis/ucr/crime-in-the-u.s/2010/crime-in-the-u.s.-2010

Federal Bureau of Investigation. (2011c). Crime in the United States by volume and rate per 100,000 inhabitants, 1991–2010. *Uniform Crime Reports.* Retrieved November 5, 2011, from http://www.fbi.gov/about-us/cjis/ucr/crime-in-the-u.s/2010/crime-in-the-u.s.-2010/tables/10tb101.xls

Federal Bureau of Investigation. (2011d). Crime in the United States Table 43. *Uniform Crime Reports.* Retrieved November 1, 2011, from http://www.fbi.gov/about-us/cjis/ucr/crime-in-the-u.s/2010/crime-in-the-u.s.-2010/tables/table-43

Federal Bureau of Investigation. (2011e). Estimated number of arrests: United States, 2010. *Uniform Crime Reports.* Retrieved November 5, 2011, from http://www.fbi.gov/about-us/cjis/ucr/crime-in-the-u.s/2010/crime-in-the-u.s.-2010/tables/10tb129.xls

Federal Bureau of Investigation. (2011f). *Hate crime statistics, 2010.* http://www.fbi.gov/about-us/cjis/ucr/hate-crime/2010/index

Federal Bureau of Investigation. (2011g). *Incidents, offenses, victims and known offenders, 2010: Table 1.* Retrieved from http://www.fbi.gov/stats-services/crimestats

Federal Bureau of Investigation. (2012a). *Crime in the United States, 2011: Table 43.* Retrieved from http://www.fbi.gov/stats-services/crimestats

Federal Bureau of Investigation. (2012b). *Incidents, offenses, victims and known offenders, 2011: Table 1.* Retrieved from http://www.fbi.gov/stats-services/crimestats

Federal Bureau of Investigation. (2013a). *Crime in the United States, 2012: Table 43.* Retrieved from http://www.fbi.gov/stats-services/crimestats

Federal Bureau of Investigation. (2013b). *Incidents, offenses, victims and known offenders, 2013: Table 1.* Retrieved from http://www.fbi.gov/stats-services/crimestats

Federal Bureau of Investigation. (2014a). *Crime in the United States, 2013: Table 43.* Retrieved from http://www.fbi.gov/stats-services/crimestats

Federal Bureau of Investigation. (2014b). *Incidents, offenses, victims and known offenders, 2009: Table 1.* Retrieved from http://www.fbi.gov/stats-services/crimestats

Federal Bureau of Investigation. (2014c). *National Incident Based Reporting System participation by state.* Retrieved from https://www.fbi.gov/about-us/cjis/ucr/nibrs/2013/resources/nibrs-participation-by-state

Federal Bureau of Investigation. (2014d). *Crime in the United States, 2013.* Retrieved from http://www.fbi.gov

Federal Bureau of Investigation. (2015). *CODIS-NDIS statistics.* Retrieved from http://www.fbi.gov/about-us/lab/biometric-analysis/codis/ndis-statistics

Federal Reserve Archival System for Economic Research. (n.d.). *Statistical abstract of the United States: 1929.* Retrieved from http://fraser.stlouisfed.org/publications/stat_abstract/issue/5354/

Feld, B. (1999). *Bad kids: Race and the transformation of the juvenile court.* New York: Oxford University Press.

Feldmeyer, B. (2009). Immigration and violence: The offsetting effects of immigrant concentration on Latino violence. *Social Science Research, 38,* 717–731.

Feldmeyer, B., & Ulmer, J. T. (2011). Racial/ethnic threat and federal sentencing. *Journal of Research in Crime and Delinquency, 48,* 238–270.

Fellner, J., & Mauer, M. (1998). *Losing the vote: The impact of felony disenfranchisement laws in the United States.* Washington, DC: Human Rights Watch and the Sentencing Project.

Fernandez, K. E., & Bowman, T. (2004). Race, political institutions, and criminal justice: An examination of the sentencing of Latino offenders. *Columbia Human Rights Law Review, 36,* 41–70.

Ferraro, V. (2015). Immigration and crime in the new destinations, 2000–2007: A test of the disorganizing effect of migration. *Journal of Quantitative Criminology.* doi: 10.1007/s10940–015–9252-y

Fielding, J., Tye, G., Ogawa, P., Imam, I., & Long, A. (2002). Los Angeles County drug court programs: Initial results. *Journal of Substance Abuse Treatment, 23,* 217–224.

Finger, B. (1959). *Concise world history.* New York: Philosophical Library.

Finkelhor, D., & Ormrod, R. (2004). *Prostitution of juveniles: Patterns from NIBRS.* Washington, DC: Office of Justice Programs, Office of Juvenile Justice and Delinquency Prevention.

Finkelstein, N. H. (2007). *American Jewish history.* Philadelphia: The Jewish Publication Society.

Fischer, B. (2003). Doing good with a vengeance: A critical assessment of the practices, effects and implications of drug treatment courts in North America. *Criminal Justice, 3,* 227–248.

Fixico, D. L. (2000). *The urban Indian experience in America*. Albuquerque: University of New Mexico Press.

Flanagan, T. J. (1996). Reform or punish: Americans' views of the correctional system. In T. J. Flanagan & D. R. Longmire (Eds.), *Americans view crime and justice: A national public opinion survey* (pp. 75–92). Thousand Oaks, CA: Sage.

Fleisher, M. S., & Decker, S. H. (2001). An overview of the challenge of prison gangs. *Corrections Management Quarterly, 5,* 1–9.

Fleury-Steiner, B. (2009). Capital jury project. In H. T. Greene & S. L. Gabbidon (Eds.), *Encyclopedia of race and crime* (pp. 91–93). Thousand Oaks, CA: Sage.

Fleury-Steiner, B., & Argothy, V. (2004). Lethal "borders": Elucidating jurors' racialized discipline to punish in Latino defendant death cases. *Punishment & Society, 6,* 67–84.

Flexon, J. L., Greenleaf, R. G., & Lurigio, A. J. (2010). The effects of self-control, gang membership, and parental attachment/identification on police contacts among Latino and African American youths. *International Journal of Offender Therapy and Comparative Criminology.* Retrieved on July 30, 2011. Published online before print December 27, 2010, doi: 10.1177/0306624X10394116

Flowers, R. B. (1988). *Minorities and criminality*. Westport, CT: Greenwood Press.

Floyd et al. v. City of New York et al., 959 F. Supp. 2d 540 (2008).

Fogelson, R. (1977). *Big-city police*. Cambridge, MA: Harvard University Press.

Foote, C. L., & Goetz, C. F. (2006). Testing economic hypotheses with state-level data: A comment on Donohue and Levitt (2001). *Federal Reserve Bank of Boston Working Paper,* no. 05–15.

Forst, B. (2003, July 28–30). *Managing errors in the new era of the policing*. Paper presented at the annual conference on Criminal Justice Research and Evaluation, Washington, DC.

Fowler, D., Lightsey, R., Monger, J., & Aseltine, E. (2010a). *Texas' School to Prison Pipeline School Expulsion*. Austin, TX: Texas Appleseed.

Fowler, D., Lightsey, R., Monger, J., & Aseltine, E. (2010b). *Texas' School to Prison Pipeline Ticketing, Arrest & Use of Force in Schools*. Austin, TX: Texas Appleseed.

Fox, C., & Huddleston, W. (2003). Drug courts in the U.S. *Issues of Democracy: The Changing Face of U.S. Courts, 8,* 13–19.

Fox, J. A., & Zawitz, M. W. (2007). *Homicide trends in the United States*. Retrieved June 18, 2011, from http://www.ojp.usdoj.gov/bjs/

Fox, L., & Cook, L. (2014). *Border war Pentagon program sends military war South*. Retrieved from http://www.usnews.com/news/articles/2014/09/17/pentagon-1033-program-sends-surplus-military-gear-to-us-borders

Franklin, J. H., & Moss, A. A. (2000). *From slavery to freedom: A history of African Americans* (8th ed.). New York: McGraw-Hill.

Franklin, T. (2013). Sentencing Native Americans in U.S. Federal courts: An examination of disparity. *Justice Quarterly, 30,* 310–339.

Frazier, E. F. (1939). Rebellious youth. In *The Negro family in the United States* (pp. 268–280). Chicago: University of Chicago Press.

Frazier, E. F. (1949). Crime and delinquency. In *The Negro in the United States* (pp. 638–653). New York: Macmillan.

Frederique, N. (2009). COINTELPRO and covert operations. In H. T. Greene & S. L. Gabbidon (Eds.), *Encyclopedia of race and crime* (pp. 133–135). Thousand Oaks, CA: Sage.

Fredrickson, D. D., & Siljander, R. P. (2002). *Racial profiling*. Springfield, IL: Charles C Thomas.

Free, M. D., & Ruesink, M. (2012). *Race and justice: Wrongful convictions of African-American men*. Boulder, CO: Lynne Rienner.

Freiburger, T. L., & Hilinski, C. M. (2010). The impact of race, gender, and age on the pretrial decision. *Criminal Justice Review, 35,* 318–334.

Frey, C. P. (1981). The house of refuge for colored children. *Journal of Negro History, 66,* 10–25.

Friedman, L. M. (1993). *Crime and punishment in American history*. New York: Basic Books.

Frontline (2004). *Four stories: Erma Faye Stewart and Regina Kelly*. Retrieved July 25, 2011, from http://www.pbs.org/wgbh/pages/frontline/shows/plea/four/stewart.html

Fulwood v. Clemmer, 206 F. Supp. 370 (1962).

Furman v. Georgia, 408 U.S. 238 (1972).

Fyfe, J. J. (1981). Race and extreme police-citizen violence. In J. F. Fyfe (Ed.), *Readings on police use of deadly force* (pp. 173–194). Washington, DC: Police Foundation.

Fyfe, J. J. (Ed.). (1982). *Readings on police use of deadly force*. Washington, DC: Police Foundation.

Gabbidon, S. L. (1999). W. E. B. DuBois on crime: American conflict theorist. *The Criminologist, 24,* 1, 3, 20.

Gabbidon, S. L. (2001). W. E. B. Du Bois: Pioneering American criminologist. *Journal of Black Studies, 31,* 581–599.

Gabbidon, S. L. (2003). Racial profiling by store clerks and security personnel in retail establishments: An exploration of "shopping while Black." *Journal of Contemporary Criminal Justice, 19,* 345–364.

Gabbidon, S. L. (2004). Crime prevention in the African American community: Lessons learned from the Nation of Islam. *Souls: A Critical Journal of Black Politics, Culture, and Society, 6,* 42–54.

Gabbidon, S. L. (2007). *W.E.B. Du Bois on crime and justice: Laying the foundations of sociological criminology.* Aldershot, UK: Ashgate.

Gabbidon, S. L. (2009). *Race, ethnicity, crime, & justice: An international dilemma.* Thousand Oaks, CA: Sage.

Gabbidon, S. L. (2015). *Criminological perspectives on race and crime* (3rd ed.). New York: Routledge.

Gabbidon, S. L., & Boisvert, D. (2012). Public opinion on crime causation: An exploratory study of Philadelphia area residents. *Journal of Criminal Justice, 40,* 50–59.

Gabbidon, S. L., Craig, R., Okafo, N., Marzette, L. N., & Peterson, S. A. (2008). The consumer racial profiling experiences of Black students at historically Black colleges and universities: An exploratory study. *Journal of Criminal Justice, 36,* 354–361.

Gabbidon, S. L., & Higgins, G. E. (2007). Consumer racial profiling and perceived victimization: A phone survey of Philadelphia area residents. *American Journal of Criminal Justice, 32,* 1–11.

Gabbidon, S. L., Higgins, G. E., and Nelson, M. (2011). Public support for racial profiling in airports: Results from a statewide poll. *Criminal Justice Policy Review:* 0887403411398305.

Gabbidon, S. L., & Jordan, K. (2013). Public opinion on the Trayvon Martin killing: A test of the racial gradient thesis. *Journal of Crime & Justice, 36,* 283–298.

Gabbidon, S. L., Kowal, L., Jordan, K. L., Roberts, J. L., & Vincenzi, N. (2008). Race-based peremptory challenges: An empirical analysis of litigation from the U.S. Court of Appeals, 2002–2006. *American Journal of Criminal Justice, 33,* 59–68.

Gabbidon, S. L., Penn, E. B., Jordan, K. L., & Higgins, G. E. (2009). The influence of race/ethnicity on the perceived prevalence and support for racial profiling at airports. *Criminal Justice Policy Review, 20*(3), 344–358.

Gabbidon, S. L., & Taylor Greene, H. (2001). The presence of African-American scholarship in early American criminology texts (1918–1960). *Journal of Criminal Justice Education, 12,* 301–310.

Gabbidon, S. L., & Taylor Greene, H. (Eds.). (2005). *Race, crime, and justice: A reader.* New York: Routledge.

Gabbidon, S. L., & Taylor Greene, H. (2013). *Race and crime: A text/reader.* Thousand Oaks, CA: Sage.

Gaes, G. G., Wallace, S., Gilman, E., Klein-Saffran, J., & Suppa, S. (2002). The influence of prison gang affiliation on violence and other prison misconduct. *The Prison Journal, 82,* 359–385.

Gallagher, C. A. (Ed.). (1997). *Rethinking the color line: Readings in race and ethnicity.* Mountain View, CA: Mayfield.

Gallegos-Castillo, A., & Patino, V. (2006). *Bridging community, research, and action: An emerging center on Latino youth development.* San Francisco, CA: National Center on Crime and Delinquency.

Galloway, A. L., & Drapella, L. A. (2006). Are effective drug courts an urban phenomenon? Considering their impact on recidivism among a nonmetropolitan adult sample in Washington State. *International Journal of Offender Therapy and Comparative Criminology, 50,* 280–293.

Gallup Organization. (2014). *Immigration historical trends.* Retrieved from http://www.gallup.com/poll/1660/immigration.aspx

Gans, H. J. (2005). Race as class. *Contexts, 4,* 17–21.

Gardell, R. (2010). *Federal Advisory Committee on Juvenile Justice Annual Report, 2010.* Washington, DC: U.S. Department of Justice.

Garfinkel, H. (1949). Research note on inter- and intra-racial homicides. *Social Forces, 27,* 369–381.

Gately, G. (2014). Foundations pledge nearly $200m to help boys, young men of color. *Juvenile Justice Information Exchange.* Retrieved from http://jjie.org/foundations-pledge-nearly-200m-to-help-boys-young-men-of-color/

Gau, J. M. (2013). Consent searches as a threat to procedural justice and police legitimacy: An analysis of consent requests during traffic stops. *Criminal Justice Policy Review, 24*(6), 759–777.

Gau, J. M., & Brunson, R. K. (2012). "One question before you get gone . . .": Consent search requests as a threat to perceived stop legitimacy. *Race and Justice, 2,* 250–273.

Geis, G. (1972). Statistics concerning race and crime. In C. E. Reasons & J. L. Kuykendall (Eds.), *Race, crime, and justice* (pp. 61–78). Palisades, CA: Goodyear.

Georges-Abeyie, D. (1989). Race, ethnicity, and the spatial dynamic. *Social Justice, 16,* 35–54.

Gerber, J., & Engelhardt-Greer, S. (1996). Just and painful: Attitudes toward sentencing criminals. In T. J. Flanagan & D. R. Longmire (Eds.), *Americans view crime and justice: A national public opinion survey* (pp. 62–74). Thousand Oaks, CA: Sage.

Gerstenfeld, P. B. (2010). Hate crimes. In Christopher J. Ferguson (Ed.), *Violent crime* (pp. 257–275). Thousand Oaks, CA: Sage.

Gerstenfeld, P. B. (2011). *Hate crimes.* Thousand Oaks, CA: Sage.

Ghandnoosh, N. (2014). *Race and punishment: Racial perceptions of crime and support for punitive policies.* Washington, DC: The Sentencing Project.

Gideon v. Wainwright, 372 U.S. 335 (1963).

Glaze, L. E., & Bonczar, T. P. (2010). *Probation and parole in the United States, 2009.* (NCJ 231674) Washington, D.C.: U.S. Department of Justice, Bureau of Justice Statistics.

Glaze, L. E., & Kaeble, D. (2014). *Correction populations in the United States, 2013.* Washington, DC: Bureau of Justice Statistics. NCJ 248479.

Glynn, M. (2013). *Black men, invisibility and crime: Towards a critical race theory of desistence.* London: Routledge.

Godinet, M. T. (2013). Testing a model of delinquency with Samoan adolescents. *Journal of Social Work, 13,* 54–74.

Goldkamp, J. S. (1982). Minorities as victims of police shootings: Interpretations of racial disproportionality and police use of deadly force. In J. Fyfe (Ed.), *Readings on police use of deadly force* (pp. 128–151). Washington, DC: Police Foundation.

Goldkamp, J. S., & Weiland, D. (1993). *Assessing the impact of Dade County's felony drug court.* Washington, DC: U.S. Department of Justice.

Goldstein, H. (1979). Improving policing: A problem oriented approach. *Crime and Delinquency, 25,* 236–258.

Golub, A., Johnson, B. D., & Dunlap, E. (2007). The race/ethnicity disparity in misdemeanor marijuana arrests in New York City. *Criminology & Public Policy, 6,* 131–164.

Gonzales-Day, K. (2006). *Lynching in the west: 1850–1935.* Durham, NC: Duke University Press.

Goodwin, R. (2008). *Crossing the continent, 1527–1540: The story of the first African American explorer of the American South.* New York: HarperCollins.

Goshe, S. (2015). Moving beyond the punitive legacy: Taking stock of persistent problems in juvenile justice. *Youth and Society, 15*(1), 42–56.

Gossett, T. (1963). *Race: The history of an idea in America.* Dallas: Southern Methodist University Press.

Gottfredson, D., Najaka, S., & Kearley, B. (2003). Effectiveness of drug treatment courts: Evidence from a randomized trial. *Criminology & Public Policy, 2,* 171–198.

Gould, J., & Leo, R. (2010). One hundred years later: Wrongful convictions after a century of research. *Journal of Criminal Law and Criminology, 100,* 825–868.

Gould, L. A. (2000). White male privilege and the construction of crime. In The Criminal Justice Collective of Northern Arizona University (Eds.), *Investigating difference: Human and cultural relations in criminal justice* (pp. 27–43). Boston: Allyn & Bacon.

Gould, S. J. (1996). *The mismeasure of man.* New York: Norton.

Gove, T. G. (2015). Implicit bias and law enforcement. *Police Chief.* Retrieved from http://www .policechiefmagazine.org

Graham, O. L., Jr. (2004). *Unguarded gates: A history of America's immigration crisis.* Lanham, MD: Rowman & Littlefield.

Graham v. Connor, 490 U. S. 386 (1989).

Graham v. Florida, 08–7412 (2010).

Gray, P. A. (ed.) (2014). *The disparate treatment of black youth in the juvenile justice system.* Dubuque, IA: Kendall Hunt Publishing.

Green, B. L., Furrer, C., Worcel, S., Burrus, S., & Finighan, M. W. (2007). How effective are family treatment drug courts? Outcomes from a four-site national study. *Child Maltreatment, 12,* 43–59.

Green, M. C. (2013). *DNA stops crime: The case for misdemeanor DNA collection.* Retrieved from http://victimsofcrime.org/docs/DNA%20Trainings/new-york-states-dna-databank-slides.pdf

Greenberg, D. (1976). *Crime and law enforcement in the colony of New York, 1691–1776.* Ithaca, NY: Cornell University Press.

Greene, E. & Evelo, A. J. (2013). Attitudes regarding life sentences for juvenile offenders. *Law and Human Behavior, 37*(4), 276–289.

Greene, H. T., Johnson, J., & Alexander, L. (2014) *An exploratory analysis of the school to prison pipeline and DMC in Texas.* A paper presented at the annual meeting of the Southwestern Association of Criminal Justice, Padre Island, TX, October 3, 2014.

Greene, J. R., Piquero, A. R., Collins, P., & Kane, R. (1999). Doing research in public housing: Implementation issues from Philadelphia's 11th Street Corridor Community Policing Program. *Justice Research and Policy, 1,* 67–95.

Greenfield, L. A., & Smith, S. K. (1999). *American Indians and crime.* Washington, DC: U.S. Department of Justice, Office of Justice Programs.

Greenleaf, R. G., Skogan, W. G., & Lurigio, A. J. (2008). Traffic stops in the Pacific Northeast: Competing hypotheses about racial disparity. *Journal of Ethnicity in Criminal Justice, 6,* 3–22.

Greenwald, F. (1993). Treatment of behavioral problems of children and youth by early indigenous Americans. In A. G. Hess & P. F. Clement (Eds.), *History of juvenile delinquency: A collection of essays on crime committed by young offenders, in history and in selected countries* (pp. 735–756). Aalen, Germany: Scientia Verlag.

Gregg v. Georgia, 428 U.S. 153 (1976).

Griffin, M. L., & Hepburn, J. R. (2006). The effect of gang affiliation on violent misconduct among inmates during the early years of confinement. *Criminal Justice and Behavior, 33,* 419–448.

Grimke, A. H. (1915). *The ultimate criminal.* Washington, DC: American Negro Academy.

Grimshaw, A. D. (Ed.). (1969). *Racial violence in the United States.* Chicago: Aldine.

Groves, R. M., & Cork, D. L. (Eds.). (2008). *Surveying victims: Options for conducting the National Crime Victimization Survey.* Washington DC: The National Academies Press. Retrieved from http://www.nap.edu/catalog/12090.html

Growette Bostaph, L. M. (2008). Repeat citizens in motor vehicle stops: A Black experience. *Journal of Ethnicity in Criminal Justice, 6,* 41–64.

Guerrero, A. P., Nishimura, S. T., Chang, J. Y., Ona, C., Cunanan, V. L., & Hishinuma, E. S. (2010). Low cultural identification, low parental involvement and adverse peer influences as risk factors for delinquent behaviour among Filipino youth in Hawaii. *International Journal of Social Psychiatry, 56,* 371–387.

Guevara, L., Herz, D., & Spohn, C. (2006). Gender and decision making: What role does race play? *Feminist Criminology, 1,* 258–282.

Guevara Urbina, M. (2012). *Hispanics in the United States criminal justice system: The new American demography.* Springfield, IL: Charles C Thomas.

Hagan, F. E. (2002). *Introduction to criminology: Theories, methods, and criminal behavior.* Belmont, CA: Wadsworth.

Hagan, J. (2010). *Who are the criminals? The politics of crime policy from the age of Roosevelt to the age of Reagan.* Princeton, NJ: Princeton University Press.

Hakins, S. (2004). *Too young to die.* Retrieved December 15, 2004, from http://www.fortunesociet.org/fa110205.htm

Hall, E. S., & Karanxha, Z. (2012). School today, jail tomorrow: The impact of zero tolerance on the over-representation of minority youth in the juvenile system. *PowerPlay: A Journal of Educational Justice, 4*(1), 1–30.

Hallett, M. A. (2006). *Private prisons in America: A critical race perspective.* Urbana: University of Illinois Press.

Hanson, R. A., & Ostrom, B. J. (1998). Indigent defenders get the job done and done well. In George F. Cole & Marc G. Gertz (Eds.), *The criminal justice system: Politics and policies* (7th ed). Belmont, CA: Wadsworth.

Harer, M. D., & Steffensmeier, D. J. (1996). Race and prison violence. *Criminology, 34,* 323–355.

Harjo, S. S. (2002). Redskins, savages, and other Indian enemies: A historical overview of American media coverage of Native peoples. In C. R. Mann & M. S. Zatz (Eds.), *Images of color, images of crime* (2nd ed., pp. 56–70). Los Angeles: Roxbury.

Harlow, C. W. (2005). *Hate crime reported by victims and police.* Washington, DC: U.S. Department of Justice, Office of Justice Programs.

Harmon, T. R. (2001). Guilty until proven innocent: An analysis of post-*Furman* capital errors. *Criminal Justice Policy Review, 12,* 113–139.

Harmon, T. R. (2004). Race for your life: An analysis of the role of race in erroneous capital convictions. *Criminal Justice Review, 29,* 76–96.

Harrell, A. (2003). Judging drug courts: Balancing the evidence. *Criminology & Public Policy, 2,* 207–212.

Harrell, E. (2007). *Black victims of violent crime.* Washington, DC: U.S. Department of Justice, Office of Justice Programs.

Harrell, E. (2009). *Asian, Native Hawaiian, and Pacific Islander victims of crime.* Washington, DC: U.S. Department of Justice, Office of Justice Programs.

Harrell, E., & Rand, M. R. (2010). *Crime against people with disabilities, 2008.* Washington, DC: U.S. Department of Justice, Office of Justice Programs.

Harris, D. A. (2002). *Profiles in injustice.* New York: New Press.

Hart, T. C., & Rennison, C. (2003). *Reporting crime to the police, 1992–2000.* Washington, DC: U.S. Department of Justice, Office of Justice Programs.

Hartley, R. D., Ventura Miller, H., & Spohn, C. (2010). Do you get what you pay for? Type of counsel and its effect on criminal court outcome. *Journal of Criminal Justice, 38,* 1063–1070.

Harvard Public Opinion Project. (2014). Low midterm turnout likely, conservatives more enthusiastic, Harvard Youth Poll finds [Press release]. Retrieved from http://www.iop.harvard.edu/sites/default/files_new/Harvard_PressReleaseSpring2014.pdf

Hassett-Walker, C. R. (2009). *Black middle-class delinquents.* El Paso, TX: LFB Scholarly.

Hassett-Walker, C. R. (2010). Delinquency and the Black middle-class: An exploratory study. *Journal of Ethnicity in Criminal Justice, 8,* 266–289.

Hatzenbuehler, M. L., Keyes, K., Hamilton, A., Uddin, M., & Galea, S. (2015). The collateral damage of mass incarceration: Risk of psychiatric morbidity among nonincarcerated residents of high-incarceration neighborhoods. *American Journal of Public Health, 105,* 138–143.

Hawkins, D. F. (1983). Black and White homicide differentials: Alternatives to an inadequate theory. *Criminal Justice and Behavior, 10,* 407–440.

Hawkins, D. F. (1986). Race, crime type, and imprisonment. *Justice Quarterly, 3,* 251–269.

Hawkins, D. F. (1987). Beyond anomalies: Rethinking the conflict perspective on race and capital punishment. *Social Forces, 65,* 719–745.

Hawkins, D. F. (2011). Things fall apart: Revisiting race and ethnic differences in criminal violence amidst a crime drop. *Race and Justice: An International Journal, 1,* 3–48.

Hawkins, D. F. (2014). Review of A Theory of African American Offending: Race, Racism, and Crime. *Race and Justice, 4,* 175–180.

Hawkins, D. F., & Hardy, K. A. (1989). Black-white imprisonment rates: A state-by-state analysis. *Social Justice, 16,* 75–94.

Hawkins, D. F., & Kempf-Leonard, K. (2005). *Our children, their children: Confronting racial and ethnic differences in American juvenile justice.* Chicago: The University of Chicago Press.

Hawkins, J. D., Herrenkohl, T. I., Farrington, D. P., Brewer, D., Catalano, R. F., Harachi, T. W., & Cothern, L. (2000). Predictors of youth violence. *Juvenile Justice Bulletin,* 1–10.

Hay, C., & Evans, M. M. (2006). Has Roe v. Wade reduced U.S. crime rates? Examining the link between mothers' pregnancy intentions and children's later involvement in law-violating behavior. *Journal of Research in Crime and Delinquency, 43,* 36–66.

Hayner, N. (1933). Delinquency areas in the Puget Sound region. *American Journal of Sociology, 39,* 314–328.

Hayner, N. (1938). Social factors in oriental crime. *American Journal of Sociology, 43,* 908–919.

Hayner, N. (1942). Variability in the criminal behavior of American Indians. *American Journal of Sociology, 47,* 602–613.

Healey, J. F. (2003). *Race, ethnicity, gender, and class: The sociology of group conflict and change* (3rd ed.). Thousand Oaks, CA: Pine Forge Press.

Healey, J. F. (2004). *Diversity and society: Race, ethnicity, and gender.* Thousand Oaks, CA: Pine Forge Press.

Healey, J. F. (2007). *Diversity and society: Race, ethnicity, and gender* (2nd ed.). Thousand Oaks, CA: Pine Forge Press.

Herberman, E., & Bonczar, T. P. (2014). *Probation and parole in the United States, 2013.* Washington, DC: Bureau of Justice Statistics. NCJ248029.

Herberman, E., & Kyckelhahn, T. (2014). *State government indigent defense expenditures, FY 2008–2012—updated.* Washington, DC: Bureau of Justice Statistics.

Hernandez v. New York, U.S. 352 (1991).

Herrnstein, R. J., & Murray, C. (1994). *The bell curve: Intelligence and class structure in American life.* New York: The Free Press.

Herz, D. C., & Walsh, J. E. (2004). Faith-based programs for reentry courts: A summary of issues and recommendations. *Juvenile and Family Court Journal, 55,* 15–25.

Hester, T., & Feeney, T. (2007). Assembly votes to abolish the death penalty. *Star-Ledger.* Retrieved from http://www.nj.com/news/index.ssf/2007/12/assembly_begins_debate_on_deat.html

Hickey, T. (1998). *Criminal procedure.* New York: McGraw-Hill.

Hickman, L. J., & Suttorp, M. J. (2008). Are deportable aliens a unique threat to public safety? Comparing the recidivism of deportable and nondeportable aliens. *Criminology & Public Policy, 7,* 59–82.

Hickman, M. J. (2003). *Tribal law enforcement, 2000.* Washington, DC: U.S. Department of Justice.

Hickman, M. J. (2006). *Citizen complaints about police use of force.* Washington, DC: U.S. Department of Justice.

Hickman, M. J., & Reaves, B. A. (2003). *Sheriffs' offices 2000.* Washington, DC: U.S. Department of Justice.

Higginbotham, A. L. (1978). *In the matter of color: Race and the American legal process: The colonial period.* Oxford, UK: Oxford University Press.

Higginbotham, A. L. (1996). *Shades of freedom: Racial politics and the presumptions of the American legal process.* Oxford, UK: Oxford University Press.

Higginbotham, A. L., & Jacobs, A. F. (1992). The law as an enemy: The legitimization of racial powerlessness through the Colonial and Antebellum criminal laws of Virginia. *North Carolina Law Review, 70,* 969–1070.

Higgins, G. E., & Gabbidon, S. L. (2008). Perceptions of consumer racial profiling and negative emotions: An exploratory study. *Criminal Justice and Behavior, 36,* 77–88.

Higgins, G. E., Gabbidon, S. L., & Jordan, K. (2008). Examining the generality of citizens' views on racial profiling in diverse situational contexts. *Criminal Justice and Behavior, 35,* 1527–1541.

Higgins, G. E., Gabbidon, S. L., & Martin, F. (2010). The influence of race/ethnicity and race relations on public opinion related to the immigration and crime link. *Journal of Criminal Justice 38,* 51–56.

Higgins, G., Gabbidon, S. L., & Vito, G. (2010). Exploring the influence of race relations and public safety concerns on public support for racial profiling during traffic stops. *International Journal of Police Science and Management, 12*(1), 12–22.

Higgins, G., Jennings, W., Jordan, K., & Gabbidon, S. (2011). Racial profiling in decisions to search: A preliminary analysis using propensity-score matching. *International Journal of Police Science and Management, 13,* 336–347.

Hinton, W. J., Sims, P. L., Adams, M. A., & West, C. (2007). Juvenile justice: A system divided. *Criminal Justice Policy Review, 18,* 466–483.

Hirsch, J. S. (2002). *Riot and remembrance: The Tulsa race riot and its legacy.* Boston: Houghton Mifflin.

Hirschi, T., & Hindelang, M. (1977). Intelligence and delinquency: A revisionist review. *American Sociological Review, 42,* 571–587.

Hockenberry, S. (2010). *Person offense cases in juvenile court, 2007*. Washington, DC: Department of Justice.

Hockenberry, S., & Puzzanchera, C. (2014). *Delinquency cases waived to criminal court, 2011*. Retrieved from http://www.ojjdp.gov/pubs/248410.pdf

Hockenberry, S., Sickmund, M., & Sladky, A. (2011). *Juvenile residential facility census, 2008: Selected findings*. Retrieved from https://www.ncjrs.gov/pdffiles1/ojjdp/231683.pdf

Hoffman, F. L. (1896). *Race traits and tendencies of the American Negro*. New York: Macmillan.

Hoffman, M. B., Rubin, P. H., & Shepherd, J. (2005). An empirical study of public defender effectiveness: Self-selection by the "marginally indigent." *Ohio State Journal of Criminal Law, 3*, 223–255.

Hogan, L. J. (1998). *The Osage Indian murders*. Frederick, MD: Amlex.

Holden-Smith, B. (1996). Inherently unequal justice: Interracial rape and the death penalty. *Journal of Criminal Law & Criminology, 86*, 1571–1583.

Holub, H. (2011). National Latino Peace Officers Association calls on secure communities task force. Retrieved July 18, 2011, from http://tucsoncitizen.com/view-from-baja-arizona/2011/07/12/national-latino-peace-officers-association-calls-on-secure-communities-task-force/

Hooton, E. A. (1939a). *Crime and the man*. Cambridge, MA: Harvard University Press.

Hooton, E. A. (1939b). *The American criminal: An anthropological study. Volume 1. The native white criminal of native parentage*. Cambridge, MA: Harvard University Press.

Houchins, D. E., Shippen, M. E., & Murphy, K. M. (2012). Evidence-based professional development considerations along the school-to-prison pipeline. *Teacher Education and Special Education: The Journal of Teacher Education Division of the Council for Exceptional Children, 35*(4), 271–283.

Housholder, D. J. (2005). Reconciling consent searches and Fourth Amendment jurisprudence: Incorporating privacy into the test for valid consent searches. *Vanderbilt Law Review*, 1280–1320.

Howard, D. (2014). Race, neighborhood, and drug court graduation. *Justice Quarterly*. doi: 10.1080/07418825.2014.908938

Howell, J. C. (2003). *Preventing and reducing juvenile delinquency: A comprehensive framework*. Thousand Oaks, CA: Sage.

Hsia, H. M., Bridges, G. S., & McHale, R. (2004). *Disproportionate minority confinement: Year 2002 update*. Washington, DC: U.S. Department of Justice, Office of Juvenile Justice and Delinquency Prevention.

Hsu, S. (2010). Senate Democrats' plan highlights nation's shift to the right on immigration. *The Washington Post*. Retrieved July 9, 2011, from http://www.washingtonpost.com/wp-dyn/content/article/2010/05/01/AR2010050100990.html

Hubbard, D. J., & Pratt, T. C. (2002). Meta-analysis of the predictors of delinquency among girls. *Journal of Offender Rehabilitation, 34*, 1–13.

Hudson v. McMillian, 503 U.S. 1 (1992).

Huebner, B. M. (2003). Administrative determinates of inmate violence. *Journal of Criminal Justice, 31*, 107–117.

Huff, C. R. (2002). Wrongful convictions and public policy: The American society of criminology 2001 presidential address. *Criminology, 40*, 1–18.

Huff, C. R. (2004). Wrongful convictions: The American experience. *Canadian Journal of Criminology and Criminal Justice, 46*, 107–120.

Huff, C. R., Rattner, A., & Sagarin, E. (1996). *Convicted but innocent: Wrongful conviction and public policy*. Thousand Oaks, CA: Sage.

Hughes, T. A., James Wilson, D., & Beck, A. J. (2001). *Trends in state parole, 1990–2000*. Washington, DC: Bureau of Justice Statistics.

Huling, T. (2002). Building a prison economy in rural America. In M. Mauer & M. Chesney-Lind (Eds.), *Invisible punishment: The collateral consequences of mass imprisonment* (pp. 197–213). New York: New Press.

Humes, K. R., Jones, N. A., & Ramirez, R. R. (2011). *Overview of race and Hispanic origin: 2010*. Washington, DC: U.S. Census Bureau.

Huntington, S. P. (2004). *Who are we? The challenges to America's national identity*. New York: Simon and Schuster.

Hurwitz, J., & Peffley, M. (2010). And justice for some: Race, crime, and punishment in the U.S. criminal justice system. *Canadian Journal of Political Science, 43*, 457–479.

Ignatiev, N. (1996). *How the Irish became White*. New York: Routledge.

Illinois suspends death penalty: Governor calls for review of "flawed" system. (2000). Retrieved March 5, 2003, from http://www.CNN.com

In re Gault, 387 U.S. 387 (1967).

In re Winship, 397 U.S. 358 (1970).

Institute of Texan Cultures. (1998). *The El Paso Chinese colony.* Retrieved December 16, 2004, from http://www.texancultures.utsa.edu/txtext/chinese/chineseelpaso.htm

Institute on Race and Poverty. (2003). *Minnesota statewide racial profiling report: All participating jurisdictions.* Minneapolis, MN: Institute on Race and Poverty.

International Association of Chiefs of Police. (2003). *Police use of force in America 2001.* Retrieved December 16, 2004, from http://www.theiacp.org

Ioimo, R., Tears, R. S., Meadows, L. A., Becton, J. B., & Charles, M. T. (2007). The police view of biased-based policing. *Police Quarterly, 10,* 270–287.

Iorizzo, L. J., & Mondello, S. (2006). *The Italian Americans* (3rd ed.). Youngstown, NY: Cambria Press.

Jackson, G. (1970). *Soledad brother: The prison letters of George Jackson.* Chicago: Lawrence Hill Books.

Jackson, J., Sr., & Jackson, J., Jr. (1996). *Legal lynching: Racism, injustice, and the death penalty.* New York: Marlowe.

Jackson, P. I. (1989). *Minority group threat, crime, and policing.* New York: Praeger.

Jamal, A., & Naber, N. (Eds.). (2008). *Race and Arab Americans before and after 9/11: From invisible citizens to visible subjects.* Syracuse, NY: Syracuse University Press.

Jang, S. J., & Johnson, B. R. (2003). Strain, negative emotions, and deviant coping among African Americans: A test of general strain theory. *Journal of Quantitative Criminology, 19,* 79–105.

Jang, S. J., & Johnson, B. R. (2005). Gender, religiosity, and reactions to strain among African Americans. *The Sociological Quarterly, 46,* 323–357.

Jang, S. J., & Lyons, J. A. (2006). Strain, social support, and retreatism among African Americans. *Journal of Black Studies, 37,* 251–274.

Jenkins, P. (1994). The ice age: The social construction of a drug panic. *Justice Quarterly, 11,* 7–31.

Johnson, B. D. (2003). Racial and ethnic disparities in sentencing departures across modes of conviction. *Criminology, 41,* 449–489.

Johnson, B. D., & Betsinger, S. (2009). Punishing the "model minority": Asian American sentencing outcomes in federal district courts. *Criminology, 47,* 1043–1090.

Johnson, D. R. (1981). *American law enforcement: A history.* St. Louis, MO: Forum Press.

Johnson, G. B. (1941). The Negro and crime. *Annals of the American Academy of Political and Social Sciences, 217,* 93–104.

Johnson, S. L. (1996). *Subcultural backlash: A new variable in the explanation of the over-representation of African-Americans in the criminal justice system.* Unpublished doctoral dissertation, The Pennsylvania State University.

Johnson Listwan, S., Sundt, J., Holsinger, A., & Latessa, E. (2003). The effect of drug court programming on recidivism: The Cincinnati experience. *Crime and Delinquency, 49,* 389–411.

Johnson v. California, 543 U.S. 499 (2005).

Johnston, L. D., O'Malley, P. M., Bachman, J. G., & Schulenberg, J. E. (2007). *Monitoring the future national survey results on drug use, 1975–2006. Volume I: Secondary school students* (NIH Publication No. 07–6205). Bethesda, MD: National Institute on Drug Abuse.

Johnston, L. D., O'Malley, P. M., Bachman, J. G., & Schulenberg, J. E. (2011a). *Monitoring the future national results on adolescent drug use: Overview of key findings, 2010.* Ann Arbor: Institute for Social Research, The University of Michigan. Retrieved July 4, 2011, from http://monitoringthe future.org/pubs/monographs/mtf-overview2010.pdf

Johnston, L. D., O'Malley, P. M., Bachman, J. G., & Schulenberg, J. E. (2011b). *Monitoring the future national survey results on drug use, 1975–2010: Volume I, Secondary school students.* Ann Arbor: Institute for Social Research, The University of Michigan. Retrieved on August 2, 2011, from http://monitor ingthefuture.org/pubs/monographs/mtf-v011_2010.pdf

Jones, C. A., & Greene, H. T. (2014). *An exploratory analysis of disproportionate minority contact in predominantly minority populated counties.* Unpublished manuscript.

Jones, N. (2010). *Between good and ghetto.* New Brunswick, NJ: Rutgers University Press.

Jones, T. (1977). The police in America: A Black viewpoint. *The Black Scholar,* pp. 22–39.

Jones v. Willingham, 248 F. Supp. 791 (1965).

Jones-Brown, D. (2007). Forever the symbolic assailant: The more things change, the more they stay the same. *Criminology & Public Policy, 6,* 103–122.

Jones-Brown, D., Stoudt, B. G., Johnston, B., & Moran, K. (2013). *Stop, question and frisk policing practices in New York City: A primer (Revised).* New York: John Jay College of Criminal Justice.

Jordan, K., Gabbidon, S. L., & Higgins, G. E. (2009). Exploring the perceived extent of and citizens' support for consumer racial profiling: Results from a national poll. *Journal of Criminal Justice, 37,* 353–359.

Jordan, K., & Myers, D. (2007). The decertification of transferred youth: Examining the determinants of reverse waiver. *Youth Violence & Juvenile Justice: An Interdisciplinary Journal, 5,* 188–206.

Joyce, T. (2004a). Did legalized abortion lower crime? *Journal of Human Resources, 39,* 1–38.

Joyce, T. (2004b). *Further tests of abortion and crime.* National Bureau of Economic Research Working Paper, no. 10564.

Juvenile Justice Information Exchange. (2014). *After decades of spending, minority youth still overrepresented in system.* Retrieved from http://jjie.org/after-decades-of-spending-minority-youth-still-overrepresented-in-system/

Kahane, L. H., Paton, D., & Simmons, R. (2008). The abortion-crime link: Evidence from England and Wales. *Economica, 75,* 1–21.

Kanellos, N. (1977). *The Hispanic-American almanac.* Detroit, MI: Gale Research.

Kastellec, J. (2013). Racial diversity and judicial influence on appellate courts. *American Journal of Political Science, 57,* 167–183.

Katz, W. L. (1986). *The invisible empire: The Ku Klux Klan impact on history.* Seattle, WA: Open Hand.

Kaufman, J. M., Rebellon, C. J., Thaxton, S., & Agnew, R. (2008). A general strain theory of racial differences in criminal offending. *The Australian and New Zealand Journal of Criminology, 41,* 421–437.

Kavanaugh-Earl, J., Cochran, J. K., Smith, D. M., Fogel, S. J., & Bjerregaard, B. (2008). Racial bias and the death penalty. In M. J. Lynch, E. B. Patterson, & K. K. Childs (Eds.), *Racial divide* (pp. 147–196). Monsey, NY: Criminal Justice Press.

Kayyali, R. A. (2006). *The Arab Americans.* Westport, CT: Greenwood Press.

Kazemian, L., Pease, K., & Farrington, D. P. (2011). DNA retention policies: The potential contribution of criminal career research. *European Journal of Criminology, 8,* 48–64.

Keith, M. (1996). Criminalization and racialization. In J. Muncie, E. McLaughlin, & M. Langan (Eds.), *Criminological perspectives: A reader* (pp. 271–283). London, UK: Sage.

Kelling, L., & Moore, M. H. (1988). *The evolving strategy of policing.* Washington, DC: National Institute of Justice.

Kempf-Leonard, K. (2007). Minority youths and juvenile justice: Disproportionate minority contact after nearly 20 years of reform efforts. *Youth Violence and Juvenile Justice, 5,* 71–87.

Kennedy, M. (2014). The end of mandatory juvenile life without parole. *Criminal Justice Policy Review, 25, 5,* 553–578. Retrieved from http://cjp.sagepub.com on November 3, 2014.

Kennedy, R. (1997). *Race, crime, and the law.* New York: Pantheon Books.

Kent v. United States, 383 U.S. 541 (1966).

Kim, C. Y., Losen, D. J., & Hewitt, D. T. (2010). *The School-To-Prison Pipeline.* New York: New York University Press.

Kim, H. (2001). The Filipino Americans. *Journal of American Ethnic History, 20,* 135–137.

Kim, H. C. (1999). *Koreans in the hood: Conflict with African Americans.* Baltimore, MD: Johns Hopkins University Press.

Kimbrough v. United States, 128 S. Ct. 558 (2007).

Kindermann, C., Lynch, J., & Cantor, D. (1997). *Effects of the redesign on victimization estimates.* Washington, DC: U.S. Department of Justice, Office of Justice Programs.

Kindle, P. A. (2012). Review of A Theory of African American Offending: Race, racism, and crime. *Journal of Forensic Social Work, 2:* 186–188.

King, M. (2006). *Guide to the States' Juvenile Justice Programs.* Retrieved from: http://www.ncjj.org/PDF/taspecialbulletinstateprofiles.pdf on April 15, 2015.

King, R. D. (2007). The context of minority group threat: Race, institutions, and complying with hate crime law. *Law & Society Review, 41,* 189–224.

Kirk, D. S., Papachristos, A. V., Fagan, J., & Tyler, T. R. (2012). The paradox of law enforcement in immigrant communities: Does tough immigration enforcement undermine public safety? *The Annals of the American Academy of Political and Social Science, 64, 1,* 79–68. Retrieved from http://ann.sagepub.com on April 21, 2015.

Kirwan Institute (2014). *Racial disproportionality in school discipline: Implicit bias is heavily implicated.* Retrieved from: http://kirwaninstitute.osu.edu/racial-disproportionality-in-school-discipline-implicit-bias-is-heavily-implicated/ on April 23, 2015.

Klaus, P., & Maston, C. (2000). *Criminal victimization in the United States, 1995.* Washington, DC: U.S. Department of Justice.

Klein, R. (2014). States are prioritizing prisons over education, budgets show. *The Huffington Post.* Retrieved from http://www.huffingtonpost.com/2014/10/30/state-spending-prison-and-education_n_6072318.html

Klinger, D. A., & Brunson, R. K. (2009). Police officers' perceptual distortions during lethal force situations: Informing the reasonableness standard. *Criminology & Public Policy, 8*(1), 153–162.

Klinger, D. A., & Grossman, D. (2002). Who should deal with foreign terrorists on U.S. soil? Socio-legal consequences of September 11 and ongoing threat of terrorist attacks in America. *Harvard Journal of Law and Public Policy, 25,* 815–835.

Klofas, J. M., Hipple, N. K., & McGarrell, E. F. (2010) *The new criminal justice.* New York: Routledge Taylor & Francis.

Knepper, P. (2001). *Explaining criminal conduct: Theories and systems in criminology.* Durham, NC: Carolina Academic Press.

Knepper, P. E. (1996). Race, racism, and crime statistics. *Southern University Law Review, 24,* 71–112.

Knepper, P. E., & Potter, D. M. (1998). Crime, politics, and minority populations: Use of official statistics in the United States and Japan. *International Journal of Comparative and Applied Criminal Justice, 22,* 145–155.

Kraska, P. B. (2007). Militarization and policing—its relevance to 21st century police. *Policing, 1,4,* 1–13.

Krauss, E., & Schulman, M. (1997). The myth of Black jury nullification: Racism dressed up in jurisprudential clothing. *Cornell Journal of Law and Public Policy, 7,* 57–76.

Krisberg, B. (1975). *Crime and privilege: Toward a new criminology.* Englewood Cliffs, NJ: Prentice Hall.

Krivo, L. J., & Peterson, R. D. (1996). Extremely disadvantaged neighborhoods and urban crime. *Social Forces, 75,* 619–650.

Krivo, L. J., & Peterson, R. D. (2000). The structural context of homicide: Accounting for racial differences in process. *American Sociological Review, 65,* 547–559.

Kroeger, B. (2004, March 20). *When a dissertation makes a difference.* Retrieved March 22, 2004, from http://www.nytimes.com/

Krogstad, J. M. (2014). *Latino confidence in local police lower than among whites.* Washington, DC: Pew Research Center. Retrieved from: http://www.pewresearch.org/fact-tank/2014/08/28/latino-confidence-in-local-police-lower-than-among-whites/ on April 3, 2015.

Kubiak, S. P., & Allen, T. (2011). Public opinion regarding life without parole in consecutive statewide surveys. *Crime & Delinquency, 57,* 495–515.

Kubrin, C. E. (2005). Gangstas, thugs, and hustlas: Identity and the code of the streets in rap music. *Social Problems, 52,* 360–378.

Kupckik, A. (2009). Things are tough all over. *Punishment and Society, 11*(3), 291–317.

Kupchik, A. & Catlaw, T. J. (2014). Discipline and participation: The long-term effects of suspension and school security on the political and civic engagement of youth. *Youth & Society, 47, 1,* 95–124. Retrieved from http://yas.sagepub.com on April 11, 2015.

Kusow, A., Wilson, L. C., & Martin, D. E. (1997). Determinants of citizen satisfaction with the police: The effects of residential location. *Policing, 20,* 655–664.

Kutateladze, B. L., Andiloro, N. R., & Johnson, B. D. (2014). Opening Pandora's box: How does defendant race influence plea bargaining. *Justice Quarterly.* Doi: doi.org/10.1080/07418825.2014.915340.

Kutateladze, B. L., Andiloro, N. R., Johnson, B. D., & Spohn, C. (2014). Cumulative disadvantage: Examining racial and ethnic disparity in prosecution and sentencing. *Criminology, 52,* 514–551.

Kuykendall, M. A., & Burns, D. E. (1980). The Black police officer: An historical perspective. *Journal of Contemporary Criminal Justice, 1,* 4–12.

La Mala, M. (2011). *Illinois is on a roll: Drops secure communities.* Retrieved July 26, 2011, from http://vivirlatino.com/2011/05/05/illinois-is-on-a-roll-drops-secure-communities.php

LaChappelle, L. (2014). Capital punishment in the era of globalization: A partial test of the Marshall hypothesis among college students. *American Journal of Criminal Justice, 39,* 839–854.

LaFree, G. (1995). Race and crime trends in the United States, 1946–1990. In D. F. Hawkins (Ed.), *Ethnicity, race, and crime* (pp. 169–193). Albany: State University of New York Press.

LaFree, G., Baumer, G. P., & O'Brien, R. (2010). Still separate and unequal? A city-level analysis of the black-white gap in homicide arrests since 1960. *American Sociological Review, 75*(1), 75–100. Retrieved from http://www.jstor.org/stable27801512

LaFree, G., O'Brien, R., & Baumer, E. P. (2006). Is the gap between black and white arrest rates narrowing? In Ruth D. Peterson, Lauren J. Krivo, and John Hagan (Eds). *The many colors of crime: Inequalities of race, ethnicity, and crime in America.* New York: New York University Press.

LaFree, G., & Russell, K. (1993). The argument for studying race and crime. *Journal of Criminal Justice Education, 4,* 273–289.

Lambert, E., & Clarke, A. (2001). The impact of information on an individual's support of the death penalty: A partial test of the Marshall hypothesis among college students. *Criminal Justice Policy Review, 12,* 215–234.

Lambert, E. G., Camp, S. D., Clarke, A., & Jiang, S. (2011). The impact of information on death penalty support, revisited. *Crime & Delinquency, 57,* 572–599.

Lane, R. (1967). *Policing the city: Boston, 1822–1885.* Cambridge, MA: Harvard University Press.

Langbein, J. H. (1976). The historical origins of the sanction of imprisonment for serious crimes. *Journal of Legal Studies, 5,* 35–60.

Lange, J. E., Johnson, M. B., & Voas, R. B. (2005). Testing the racial profiling hypothesis for seemingly disparate traffic stops on the New Jersey Turnpike. *Justice Quarterly, 22, 2,* 194–222.

Langton, L., (2010). *Women in law enforcement, 1987–2008.* Retrieved on July 13, 2011, from http://bjs.ojp.usdoj.gov/content/pub/pdf/wle8708.pdf

Langton, L,. & Durose, M. (2013). *Police behavior during traffic and street stops, 2011.* Washington, DC: US Department of Justice. Retrieved from http://www.bjs.gov/index.cfm?ty=pbdetail&iid=4779 on April 2, 2015.

Langton, L., & Farole, D. J. (2009). *Public defender offices, 2007: Statistical tables.* Washington, DC: Bureau of Justice Statistics. (NCJ 228538)

Langton, L., & Farole, D. (2010). *State public defender programs, 2007.* Washington, DC: Bureau of Justice Statistics. (NCJ228229)

Langton, L., & Planty, M. (2011). *Hate crime, 2003–2009.* Washington, DC: Bureau of Justice Statistics.

Lanier, C., & Huff-Corzine, L. (2006). American Indian homicide: A county level analysis utilizing social disorganization theory. *Homicide Studies, 10,* 181–194.

Lanier, M. M., & Henry, S. (1998). *Essential criminology.* Boulder, CO: Westview.

Lattimore, P. K. (2007). The challenge of reentry. *Corrections Today, 69,* 88–91.

Lau, A. S., McCabe, K. M., Yeh, M., Garland, A. F., Hough, R. L., & Landsverk, J. (2003). Race/ethnicity and rates of self-reported maltreatment among high-risk youth in public sectors of care. *Child Maltreatment, 8,* 183–194.

Lawrence, R., & Hemmens, C. (2008). Section I: History and development of the juvenile court and justice process. In Lawrence & Hemmens (Eds), *Juvenile justice a text reader.* pp. 19–38.

Le, T. N., Monfared, G., & Stockdale, G. D. (2005). The relationship of school, parent, and peer contextual factors with self-reported delinquency for Chinese, Cambodian, Laotian or Mien, and Vietnamese youth. *Crime and Delinquency, 51,* 192–219.

Lee, C. (2007). Hispanics and the death penalty: Discriminatory charging practices in San Joaquin County, California. *Journal of Criminal Justice, 35,* 17–27.

Lee, G. M., Bohm, R. M., & Pazzani, L. M. (2014). Knowledge and death penalty opinion: The Marshall hypotheses revisited. *American Journal of Criminal Justice, 39,* 642–659.

Lee, J. (2012). Review of A Theory of African American Offending: Race, racism, and crime. *Criminal Justice Review, 37,* 408–410.

Lee, M. T., & Martinez, R. (2002). Social disorganization revisited: Mapping the recent immigration and black homicide relationship in northern Miami. *Sociological Focus, 35,* 363–380.

Lee, N. (1995). Culture conflict and crime in Alaskan native villages. *Journal of Criminal Justice, 23,* 177–189.

LeFlouria, T. (2011). The hand that rocks the cradle cuts cordwood: Exploring Black women's lives and labor in Georgia's convict camps, 1865–1917. *Labor: Studies in Working Class History of the Americas, 8,* 47–63.

Lehrer, E. (2007). Crime's up: An old issue is about to resurface. *The Weekly Standard, 12,* 23–26.

Leiber, M. J. (2002). Disproportionate minority confinement (DMC) of youth: An analysis of state and federal efforts to address the issue. *Crime & Delinquency, 48,* 3–45.

Leiber, M. J., & Blowers, A. N. (2003). Race and misdemeanor sentencing. *Criminal Justice Policy Review, 14,* 464–485.

Leiber, M. J., & Mack, K. Y. (2003). The individual and joint effects of race, gender, and family status on juvenile justice decision-making. *Journal of Research in Crime and Delinquency, 40,* 34–70.

Leiber, M., & Rodriguez, N. (2011). The implementation of the disproportionate minority confinement/contact (DMC) mandate: A failure or success? *Race and Justice, 1,* 103–124.

Leo, R. A. (2002). False confessions: Causes, consequences, and solutions. In S. Westervelt & J. A. Humphrey (Eds.), *Wrongly convicted: Perspectives on failed justice* (pp. 36–54). New Brunswick, NJ: Rutgers University Press.

Leonard, K. K., Pope, C., & Feyerherm, W. H. (1995). *Minorities in juvenile justice.* Thousand Oaks, CA: Sage.

Lesane-Brown, C. (2006). A review of racial socialization within black families. *Developmental Review, 26,* 400–426.

Levitt, S. D., & Dubner, S. J. (2005). *Freakonomics: A rogue economist explores the hidden side of everything.* New York: William Morrow.

Light, I. (1977). The ethnic vice industry, 1880–1944. *American Sociological Review, 42,* 464–479.

Lilley, S. (2013). *How U.S. Latinos feel about undocumented immigration.* Retrieved from http://nbclatino.com/2013/10/04/how-u-s-latinos-feel-about-undocumented-immigration/

Lilly, R. J., Cullen, F. T., & Ball, R. A. (2001). *Criminological theory: Context and consequences.* Thousand Oaks, CA: Sage.

Lilly, R. J., Cullen, F. T., & Ball, R. A. (2011). *Criminological theory: Context and consequences* (5th ed.). Thousand Oaks, CA: Sage.

Lindquist, C., Ayoub, L. H., Dawes, D., Harrison, P. M., Malsch, A. M., Walters, J. H., Rempel, M., & Carey, S. M. (2014). *The National Institute of Justice's Evaluation of Second Chance Act Adult Reentry Courts: Staff and client perspectives on reentry courts from year 2.* Retrieved from http://www.courtinnovation.org/sites/default/files/documents/NIJ_Second_Chance_Act_Year_2_summary_report_0814.pdf

Lipsey, M. W., Howell, J. C., Kelly, M. R., Chapman, G., & Carver, D. (2010). *Improving the effectiveness of juvenile justice programs. A new perspective on evidence-based practice.* Washington, DC: Georgetown Public Policy Institute, Center for Juvenile Justice Reform.

Liptak, A. (2015). U.S. justices may review capital cases in which judges overrode juries. *New York Times.* Retrieved from http://www.nytimes.com/2015/03/10/us/justices-may-weigh-cases-of-alabama-judges-overriding-juries.html

Listenbee, R., Torre, J., Boyle, G., Cooper, S., Deer, S., Durfee, D., . . . Taguba, A. (2012). *Report of the Attorney General's National Task Force on Children Exposed to Violence.* Washington, DC: U.S. Department of Justice.

Liu, G., Johnson, C., & Vidmar, N. (2014). *Do racial disparities exist during pretrial decision making? Evidence from North Carolina.* Retrieved from http://dx.doi.org/10.2139/ssrn.2470182

Lombroso, C. (1911). *Criminal man.* New York: Putnam. (Original work published 1876)

Longazel, J. G., Parker, L. S., & Sun, I. Y. (2011). Experiencing court, experiencing race: Perceived procedural injustice among court users. *Race and Justice, 1,* 202–227.

Longmire, D. R. (1996). Americans' attitudes about the ultimate weapon: Capital punishment. In T. J. Flanagan & D. R. Longmire (Eds.), *Americans view crime and justice: A national public opinion survey* (pp. 93–108). Thousand Oaks, CA: Sage.

Lopez, R., Roosa, M. W., Tein, J. T., & Dinh, K. T. (2004). Accounting for Anglo-Hispanic differences in school misbehavior. *Journal of Ethnicity in Criminal Justice, 2,* 27–46.

Lotke, E. (1996). *The prison-industrial complex.* Baltimore, MD: National Center on Institutions and Alternatives.

Lotke, E. (1998). Hobbling a generation: Young African American men in Washington, D.C.'s criminal justice system: Five years later. *Crime and Delinquency, 44,* 355–366.

Lott, J. R., & Whitley, J. (2007). Abortion and crime: Unwanted children and out-of-wedlock births. *Economic Inquiry, 45,* 304–324.

Loury, G. C. (Ed.). (2008). *Race, incarceration, and American values.* Cambridge, MA: MIT Press.

Luna-Firebaugh, E. M. (2003, July 28–30). *Tribal law enforcement in P.L. 280 states.* Paper presented at the annual conference on Criminal Justice Research and Evaluation, Washington, DC.

Lynn, R. (2002). Skin color and intelligence in African Americans. *Population and Environment, 23,* 365–375.

MacDonald, H. (2003). *Are cops racist? How the war against the police harms Black Americans.* Chicago: Ivan R. Dee.

MacDonald, H. (2004). The immigrant gang plague. *City Journal,* Summer, 30–43.

MacDonald, H. (2008). Is the criminal-justice system racist? *City Journal.* Retrieved May 6, 2008, from www.city-journal.org/

MacDonald, J., Hipp, J. R., & Gill, C. (2013). The effects of immigrant concentration on changes in neighborhood crime rates. *Journal of Quantitative Criminology, 29,* 191–215.

Maguire, C. N., McCallum, L. A., Storey, C., & Whitaker, J. P. (2014). Familial searching: A specialist forensic DNA profiling service utilizing the National DNA Database to identify unknown offenders via their relatives—The UK experience. *Forensic Science International: Genetics, 8,* 1: 1–9.

Maguire, K. (Ed.). (2011a). *Sourcebook of criminal justice statistics.* Table 2.12.2011. Washington, DC: Author.

Maguire, K. (Ed). (2011b). *Sourcebook of criminal justice statistics.* (Table 1.82.2010). Washington, DC: Author.

Maguire, K. (Ed). (2011c). *Sourcebook of criminal justice statistics.* (Table 1.81.2010). Washington, DC: Author.

Maguire, K., & Pastore, A. L. (Eds.). (2003). *Sourcebook of criminal justice statistics.* Retrieved from http://www.albany.edu/source book/pdf/t213.pdf

Maltz, M. (1977). Crime statistics: A historical perspective. *Crime & Delinquency, 23,* 32–40.

Mandak, J. (2003, June 12). *The Patriot-News* (AP), p. B7.

Mann, C. R. (1990a). Black female homicide in the United States. *Journal of Interpersonal Violence, 5,* 176–201.

Mann, C. R. (1990b). Random thoughts on the ongoing Wilbanks-Mann discourse. In B. D. Maclean & D. Milovanovic (Eds.), *Racism, empiricism, and criminal justice* (pp. 15–19). Vancouver, Canada: Collective Press.

Mann, C. R. (1993). *Unequal justice: A question of color.* Bloomington: Indiana University Press.

Manza, J., Brooks, C., & Uggen, C. (2004). Civil death or civil rights? Public attitudes towards felon disenfranchisement in the United States. *Public Opinion Quarterly, 68,* 276–287.

Manza, J., & Uggen, C. (2006). *Locked out: Felon disenfranchisement and democracy in America.* New York: Oxford University Press.

Mapp v. Ohio, 367 U.S. 1081, 81 S.CT (1961).

Marger, M. (Ed.). (1997). *Race and ethnic relations: American and global perspectives* (4th ed.). Belmont, CA: Wadsworth.

Marion, N. E., & Oliver, W. M. (2006). *The public policy of crime and criminal justice.* Upper Saddle River, NJ: Pearson/Prentice Hall.

Marlowe, D. B. (2011). The verdict on drug courts and other problem-solving courts. *Chapman Journal of Criminal Justice, 2,* 57–96.

Martin, D. L. (2002). The police role in wrongful convictions: An international comparative study. In S. Westervelt & J. A. Humphrey (Eds.), *Wrongly convicted: Perspectives on failed justice* (pp. 77–95). New Brunswick, NJ: Rutgers University Press.

Martin, S. A., Harris, K., & Jack, B. W. (2015). The health of young African American men. *JAMA,* DOI: 10.1001/jama.2015.2258

Martinez, R. (2002). *Latino homicide.* New York: Routledge.

Martinez, R. (2003). Moving beyond black and white violence: African American, Haitian, and Latino homicides in Miami. In D. F. Hawkins (Ed.), *Violent crime: Assessing race and ethnic differences* (pp. 22–43). New York: Cambridge University Press.

Martinez, R. (2006). Coming to America: The impact of the new immigration on crime. In R. Martinez & A. Valenzuela (Eds.), *Immigration and crime: Race, ethnicity, and violence* (pp. 1–19). New York: New York University Press.

Martinez, R., Lee, M. T., & Nielsen, A. L. (2001). Revisiting the Scarface legacy: The victim/offender relationship and Mariel homicides in Miami. *Hispanic Journal of Behavioral Sciences, 23,* 37–56.

Martinez, R., Stowell, J. I., & Lee, M. T. (2010). Immigration and crime in an era of transformation: A longitudinal analysis of homicides in San Diego neighborhoods, 1980–2000. *Criminology, 48*(3), 797–830.

Martinez, R., & Valenzuela, A. (Eds.). (2006). *Immigration and crime: Race, ethnicity, and violence.* New York: New York University Press.

Martinson, R. (1974). What works? Questions and answers about prison reform. *Public Interest, 24,* 22–54.

Maryland v. King, 133 S. Ct. 1958 (2013).

Massey, D. S., & Denton, N. A. (1993). *American apartheid.* Cambridge, MA: Harvard University Press.

Mauer, M. (1990). *Young African American men and the criminal justice system: A growing national problem.* Washington, DC: The Sentencing Project.

Mauer, M. (1999). *Race to incarcerate.* New York: New Press.

Mauer, M. (2004). Extended view: Racial disparity and the criminal justice system: An assessment of causes and responses. *SAGE Race Relations Abstracts, 29,* 34–56.

Mauer, M. (2006). *Race to incarcerate* (Rev. ed.). New York: New Press.

Mauer, M. (2011). Voting behind bars: An argument for voting by prisoners. *Howard Law Journal, 54,* 549–566.

Mauer, M., & Cole, D. (2011). Five myths about incarceration. *The Washington Post.* Retrieved from http://www.washingtonpost.com/opinions/five-myths-about-incarceration/2011/06/13/AGfIWvYH_story.html

Mauer, M., & Huling, T. (1995). *Young African Americans and the criminal justice system: Five years later.* Washington, DC: The Sentencing Project.

Maupin, J. R., & Maupin, J. R. (1998). Juvenile justice decision making in a rural Hispanic community. *Journal of Criminal Justice, 26,* 373–384.

Mazerolle, L. G., & Terrill, W. (1997). Problem-oriented policing in public housing: Identifying the distribution of problem places. *Policing, 20,* 235–255.

McCamey, W. P., Scaramella, G. L., & Cox, S. M. (2003). *Contemporary municipal policing.* Boston: Allyn & Bacon.

McCleskey v. Kemp, 481 U.S. 279 (1987).

McCluskey, C. P. (2002). *Understanding Latino delinquency.* New York: LFB Scholarly.

McCluskey, C. P., Krohn, M. D., Lizotte, A. J., & Rodriguez, M. L. (2002). Early substance use and school achievement: An examination of Latino, White, and African-American youth. *Journal of Drug Issues, 32,* 921–944.

McCluskey, C. P., & Tovar, S. (2003). Family processes and delinquency: The consistency of relationships by ethnicity and gender. *Journal of Ethnicity in Criminal Justice, 1,* 37–61.

McGee, Z. T. (1999). Patterns of violent behavior and victimization among African American youth. *Journal of Offender Rehabilitation, 30,* 47–64.

McGee, Z. T. (2003). Community violence and adolescent development: An examination of risk and protective factors among African American youth. *Journal of Contemporary Criminal Justice, 19,* 293–314.

McGee, Z. T., & Baker, S. R. (2002). Impact of violence on problem behavior among adolescents. *Journal of Contemporary Criminal Justice, 18,* 74–93.

McGee, Z. T., Barber, A., Joseph, E., Dudley, J., & Howell, R. (2005). Delinquent behavior, violent victimization, and coping strategies among Latino adolescents. *Journal of Offender Rehabilitation, 42*(3), 41–56.

McGuffee, K., Garland, T. S., & Eigenberg, H. (2007). Is jury selection fair? Perceptions of race and the jury selection process. *Criminal Justice Studies, 20,* 445–468.

McIntosh, P. (2002). White privilege, color, and crime: A personal account. In C. R. Mann & M. S. Zatz (Eds.), *Images of color, images of crime* (2nd ed., pp. 45–53). Los Angeles: Roxbury.

McIntyre, C. C. L. (1992). *Criminalizing a race: Free Blacks during slavery.* New York: Kayode.

McKeiver v. Pennsylvania 1971 403 U.S. 528.

McMahon, J., Garner, J., Davis, R., & Kraus, A. (2002). *How to correctly collect and analyze racial profiling data: Your reputation depends on it.* Washington, DC: U.S. Department of Justice, Office of Community-Oriented Policing Services.

Meagher, T. J. (2005). *The Columbia guide to Irish American history.* New York: Columbia University Press.

Mears, D. (2002). Sentencing guidelines and the transformation of juvenile justice in the 21st century. *Journal of Contemporary Criminal Justice, 18,* 6–19.

Mears, D. P., & Watson, J. (2006). Towards a fair and balanced assessment of supermax prisons. *Justice Quarterly, 23,* 232–270.

Meehan, A. J., & Ponder, M. C. (2002). Race and place: The ecology of racial profiling African American motorists. *Justice Quarterly, 19*(3), 399–430.

Meier, A., & Rudwick, E. (1970). *From plantation to ghetto* (Rev. ed.). New York: Hill & Wang.

Mennel, R. M. (1973). *Thorns and thistles.* Hanover: University of New Hampshire Press.

Menninger, K. (1966). *The crime of punishment.* New York: Viking Press.

Menon, R. (1997). Juvenile justice in Texas: Factors correlated with processing decisions. Retrieved from: http://www.ojjdp.gov/dmc/pdf/texasojjdpmainreport.pdf

Merton, R. K. (1938). Social structure and anomie. *American Sociological Review, 3,* 672–682.

Merton, R. K., & Ashley-Montagu, M. F. (1940). Crime and the anthropologist. *American Anthropologist, 42,* 384–408.

Messner, S. F., Krohn, M. D., & Liska, A. E. (Eds.). (1989). *Theoretical integration in the study of deviance and crime: Problems and prospects.* Albany: State University of New York Press.

Miller, E. J. (2007). The therapeutic effects of managerial reentry courts. *Federal Sentencing Reporter, 20,* 127–135.

Miller, H. V., Barnes, J. C., & Hartley, R. (2011). Reconsidering Hispanic gang membership and acculturation in a multivariate framework. *Crime and Delinquency, 5,* 331–355.

Miller, J. (2001). Bringing the individual back in: A commentary on Wacquant and Anderson. *Punishment & Society, 3,* 153–160.

Miller, J. (2008). *Getting Played.* New York: New York University Press.

Miller, J. G. (1992a). *Hobbling a generation: Young African American males in Washington, D.C.'s, criminal justice system.* Baltimore, MD: National Center for Institutions and Alternatives.

Miller, J. G. (1992b). *Hobbling a generation: Young African American males in the criminal justice system of America's cities.* Baltimore, MD: National Center for Institutions and Alternatives.

Miller, J. G. (1996). *Search and destroy: African American males in the criminal justice system.* New York: Cambridge University Press.

Miller, K. (1969). *Out of the house of bondage.* New York: Arno Press and *The New York Times.* (Original work published 1908)

Miller, L. L. (2013). Power to the people: Violent victimization, inequality and democratic politics. *Theoretical Criminology, 17, 3,* 283–313.

Miller, W. (1958). Lower class culture as a generating milieu of gang delinquency. *Journal of Social Issues, 14,* 5–19.

"Minnesota advocates for human rights express concern about immigration crackdown." (2008, January 14). *Minnesota Lawyer.* Gale document no. A173409283.

Minnesota Sentencing Guidelines Commission. (2010). *Sentencing practices: Annual summary statistics for felony offenders sentenced in 2009.* St. Paul, MN: Author.

Minton, T. D. (2014). *Jails in Indian country, 2013.* Washington, DC: Bureau of Justice Statistics. NCJ247017.

Minton, T. D., & Golinelli, D. (2014). *Jail inmates at midyear 2013 statistical tables.* Washington, DC: Bureau of Justice Statistics. NCJ 245350.

Miranda v. Arizona, 384 U.S. 436,86 S.Ct. 1602 (1966).

Mirande, A. (1987). *Gringo justice.* Notre Dame, IN: Notre Dame University Press.

Mitchell, A. D. (2006). The effect of the Marshall hypothesis on attitudes towards the death penalty. *Race, Gender & Class, 13,* 221–239.

Mitchell, O. (2005). A meta-analysis of race and sentencing research: Examining the inconsistencies. *Journal of Quantitative Criminology, 21,* 439–466.

Mitchell, O. (2009). Is the war on drugs racially biased? *Journal of Crime & Justice, 32,* 49–75.

Mitchell, O., Wilson, D. B., Eggers, A., & MacKenzie, D. L. (2012). Assessing the effectiveness of drug courts on recidivism: A meta-analytic review of traditional and non-traditional drug courts. *Journal of Criminal Justice, 40*, 60–71.

Mizell, J. (2014). *An overview of public opinion and discourse on criminal justice issues.* New York: Opportunity Agenda. Retrieved from http://opportunityagenda.org/files/field_file/2014.08.23-CriminalJusticeReport-FINAL_0.pdf

Mmari, K., Blum, R. W., & Teufel-Shone, N. (2010). What increases risk and protection for delinquent behaviors among American Indian youth? Findings from three tribal communities. *Youth & Society, 41*(3), 382–413.

Models for Change. (2011). *Racial and ethnic fairness/DMC.* Retrieved June 28, 2011, from http://www.modelsforchange.net/about/Issues-for-change/Racial-fairness.html

Monkkonen, E. H. (1981). *Police in urban America, 1860–1920.* Cambridge, NY: Cambridge University Press.

Moore, J. W., & Hagedorn, J. M. (2001). *Female gangs: A focus on research* (Bulletin. Youth Gang Series). Washington, DC: U.S. Department of Justice, Office of Juvenile Justice and Delinquency Prevention.

Moore, N. M. (2015). *The political roots of racial tracking in American criminal justice.* New York: Cambridge University Press.

Morgan, K. D., & Smith, B. (2008). The role of race on parole decision-making. *Justice Quarterly, 25*, 411–435.

Morin, J. L. (2005). *Latino/a rights and justice in the United States: Perspectives and approaches.* Durham, NC: Carolina Academic Press.

Morrison Institute for Public Policy. (2010, May). *Illegal immigration: Perceptions and realities, Part I.* Phoenix: Arizona State University.

Moses, E. R. (1933). Delinquency in the Negro community. *Opportunity, 2*, 304–307.

Moses, E. R. (1936). Community factors in Negro delinquency. *Journal of Negro Education, 5, 2*, 220–227.

Mosher, C. J., Miethe, T. D., & Hart, T. C. (2011). *The mismeasure of crime* (2nd ed.). Thousand Oaks, CA: Sage.

Mosher, C. J., Miethe, T. D., & Phillips, D. M. (2002). *The mismeasure of crime.* Thousand Oaks, CA: Sage.

Motivans, M. (2015). *Federal justice statistics, 2012-statistical tables.* Washington, DC: Bureau of Justice Statistics. NCJ 248470.

MSNBC (2011). *Police fear "war on cops."* Retrieved on November 18, 2011, from http://www.msnbc.msn.com/id/41235743/ns/us_news-crime_and_courts/

Mudde, C. (2012). *The relationship between immigration and nativism in Europe and North America.* Washington, DC: Migration Policy Institute.

Muhammad, K. G. (2010). *The Condemnation of Blackness.* Cambridge, MA: Harvard University Press.

Muhlhausen, D. B. (2004). *The determinants of sentencing in Pennsylvania: Do the characteristics of judges matter?* Washington, DC: The Heritage Foundation.

Mumola, C. J. (2007). *Arrest-related deaths in the United States, 2003–2005.* Washington, DC: U.S. Department of Justice, Office of Justice Programs.

Munoz, E. A., & Freng, A. B. (2008). Age, racial/ethnic minority status, gender and misdemeanor sentencing. *Journal of Ethnicity in Criminal Justice, 5*, 29–57.

Munoz, E. A., & McMorris, B. J. (2002). Misdemeanor sentencing decisions: The cost of being Native American. *The Justice Professional, 15*, 239–259.

Munoz, E. A., McMorris, B. J., & DeLisi, M. J. (2005). Misdemeanor criminal justice: Contextualizing effects of Latino ethnicity, gender, and immigration status. *Race, Gender & Class, 11*, 112–134.

Myers, M. A. (1998). *Race, labor, & punishment in the New South.* Columbus: Ohio State University Press.

Myrdal, G. (1944). *An American dilemma: The Negro problem and modern democracy.* New York: Harper & Brothers.

Nasser, H. E., & Overberg, P. (2012). Census continues to undercount Blacks, Hispanics and kids. *USA Today.* Retrieved from http://usatoday30.usatoday.com/news/nation/story/2012-05-22/census-hispanic-black/55140150/1

Nation, D. (2011). *Citizens' preferences about police work: An argument for racial variations.* El Paso, TX: LFB Scholarly.

National Advisory Commission on Civil Disorders. (1968). *Report of the National Advisory Commission on Civil Disorders*. Washington, DC: Government Printing Office.

National Association for the Advancement of Colored People. (2011). *Misplaced priorities: Over incarcerate, under educate*. Baltimore, MD: Author.

National Center for Injury Prevention and Control. (2010). *Youth violence facts at a glance*. Retrieved October 24, 2011, from http://www.cdc.gov/Violence Prevention/pdf/YV-DataSheet-a.pdf

National Center for Juvenile Justice. (2004). *State juvenile justice profiles*. Retrieved July 15, 2004, from http://www.ncjj.org/stateprofiles/

National Center for State Courts. (2015). *Drug courts, substance abuse, and mental health*. Retrieved from http://www.ncsc.org/Services-and-Experts/Government-Relations/Appropriations/Drug-Courts-Substance-Abuse-and-Mental-Health.aspx

National Coalition to Abolish the Death Penalty. (2004). *America's shame: Killing kids*. Retrieved December 15, 2004, from http://www.ncadp.org/fact_sheet1.html

National Commission on Law Observance and Enforcement. (1931a). *Crime and the foreign born* (Report No. 10). Washington, DC: Government Printing Office.

National Commission on Law Observance and Enforcement. (1931b). *Report on lawlessness in law enforcement*. Washington, DC: U.S. Government Printing Office.

National Conference of State Legislatures. (2010). *U.S. Supreme Court rules juvenile life without parole sentences for non-homicide unconstitutional*. Retrieved July 9, 2011, from www.ncsl.org/default.aspx?tabid=20419

The National Domestic Violence Hotline. (2015). *Emily's story*. Retrieved from http://www.thehotline.org/portfolio-item/emilys-story

National Drug Control Strategy. (2014). Retrieved from https://www.whitehouse.gov/sites/default/files/ndcs_2014.pdf

National Indian Gaming Commission. (n.d.). *Gaming revenue reports*. Retrieved from http://www.nigc.gov/Gaming_Revenue_Reports.aspx

National Institute of Justice. (2015). *Drug courts*. Retrieved from http://www.nij.gov/topics/courts/drug-courts/Pages/welcome.aspx

National Law Enforcement Officers Memorial Fund (2013). *Law enforcement officer deaths: 2013*. Washington, DC: Author.

National Law Enforcement Officers Memorial Fund (2014). *Preliminary 2014 law enforcement officer fatalities report*. Washington, DC: Author.

National Law Enforcement Officers Memorial Fund. (2015). *Officer deaths by year*. Retrieved from http://www.nleomf.org/facts/officer-fatalities-data/year.html

National Minority Advisory Council on Criminal Justice. (1979). *Racism in the criminal courts* (draft). Washington, DC: U.S. Department of Justice.

National Organization of Black Law Enforcement Executives. (2001). *A NOBLE perspective: Racial profiling: A symptom of biased-based policing*. Retrieved July 31, 2004, from http://www.noblenational.org/pdf/RacialProfiling901.pdf

National Urban League Poll. (2001). Retrieved March 17, 2004, from Polling the Nations database at http://www.orspub.com/

National Youth Gang Center. (2008). *Frequently asked questions regarding gangs*. Retrieved March 20, 2008, from http://www.iir.com/nygc/faq.htm#q3

National Youth Gang Center (2015). *National youth gang survey analysis*. Retrieved from https://www.nationalgangcenter.gov/Survey-Analysis

Neisser, U., et al. (1996). Intelligence: Knowns and unknowns. *American Psychologist, 51*, 77–101.

Nelson, M., Gabbidon, S. L., & Boisvert, D. (2015). Philadelphia area residents' views on the disproportionate representation of blacks and Hispanics in the criminal justice system. *Journal of Crime & Justice, 38*, 270–290.

Neubauer, D., & Fradella, H. (2014). *America's courts & the criminal justice system* (11th ed.). Belmont, CA: Wadsworth.

Neverdon-Morton, C. (1989). *Afro-American women of the South and the advancement of the race, 1895–1925*. Knoxville: University of Tennessee Press.

New York State Special Commission on Attica. (1972). *Attica: The official report of the New York State Special Commission on Attica*. New York: Praeger.

Newsome, M. (2007). A new DNA test can ID a suspect's race, but police won't touch it. *Wired, 16*(1). Retrieved from http://www.wired.com/politics/law/magazine/16–01/ps_dna

Newport, F., & Ludwig, J. (2000). *Protests by Blacks over Amadou Diallo verdict not surprising given long-standing perceptions among Blacks that they are discriminated against in most areas of their daily lives.* Retrieved from http://www.gallup.com/poll/fromtheed/ed003.asp

Nolan, J. J., III, Akiyama, Y., & Berhanu, S. (2002). The Hate Crime Statistics Act of 1990: Developing a method for measuring the occurrence of hate violence. *American Behavioral Scientist, 46,* 136–153.

Norris, R. J. (2011). Assessing compensation statutes for the wrongfully convicted. *Criminal Justice Policy Review.* DOI: 10.1177/0887403411409916.

Northern v. Nelson, 315 F. Supp. 687 (1970).

Norton, H. K. (2004). Virtual museum of the City of San Francisco. *The Chinese.* Retrieved from http://www.sfmusuem.org

Novak, K. J. (2009). Policy essay: Reasonable officers, public perceptions, and policy challenges. *Criminology & Public Policy, 8*(1), 117–140.

O'Brien, R. M., Shichor, D., & Decker, D. L. (1980). An empirical comparison of the validity of the UCR and NCS crime rates. *The Sociological Quarterly, 21*(3), 391–401. Retrieved from http://www.jstor.org

Office of the Governor, Criminal Justice Division. (2014). *2013–2014 biennial report to the 84th Texas legislature.* Retrieved from http://gov.texas.gov/files/cjd/CJD_2013-2014_Biennial_Report.pdf

Office of Juvenile Justice and Delinquency Prevention. (2004). *Disproportionate minority contact. About DMC: Core requirement of JJDP Act.* Retrieved July 15, 2004, from http://www.ojjdp.ncjrs.org/dmc/about/core.html

Office of Juvenile Justice and Delinquency Prevention. (2008). *Statistical briefing book.* Retrieved March 20, 2008, from http://ojjdp.ncjrs.gov/ojstatbb/crime/qa05101.asp?qaDate=2006.

Office of Juvenile Justice and Delinquency Prevention. (2015). *Statistical briefing book.* Retrieved from http://ojjdp.ncjrs.gov

Office of the Missouri Attorney General. (2014). *Racial profiling data 2013.* Ferguson, MO: Author.

Office of National Drug Control Policy. (n.d.). Retrieved from http://www.whitehousedrugpolicy.gov/about/index.html

Ogletree, C. (2012). *The presumption of guilt.* New York: Palgrave Macmillan.

Ogletree, C. J., & Sarat, A. (Eds.). (2006). *From lynch mobs to the killing state: Race and the death penalty in America.* New York: New York University.

Oliver, W. (1984). Black males and the tough guy image: A dysfunctional compensatory adaptation. *The Western Journal of Black Studies, 8,* 199–203.

Oliver, W. (1989a). Black males and social problems: Prevention through Afrocentric socialization. *Journal of Black Studies, 20,* 15–39.

Oliver, W. (1989b). Sexual conquest and patterns of Black-on-Black violence: A structural-cultural perspective. *Violence and Victims, 4,* 257–273.

Oliver, W. (1994). *The violent social world of Black men.* New York: Lexington Books.

Oliver, W. (2000). The third generation of community policing: Moving through innovation, diffusion, and institutionalization. *Police Quarterly, 3, 4,* 367–388. Retrieved from pqx.sagepub.com on March 17, 2015.

Oliver, W. (2003). The structural-cultural perspective: A theory of Black male violence. In D. F. Hawkins (Ed.), *Violent crime: Assessing race and ethnic differences* (pp. 280–318). Cambridge, UK: Cambridge University Press.

Oliver, W. (2006). "The streets": An alternative Black male socialization institution. *Journal of Black Studies, 36,* 918–937.

Oliver, W. (2007). *Homeland Security for policing.* Upper Saddle River, NJ: Prentice Hall.

Oliver, W. (2009). Policing for homeland security: Policy & research. *Criminal Justice Policy Review, 20, 3,* 253–260. Retrieved from cjp.sagepub.com on August 24, 2014.

O'Neill Shermer, L., & Johnson, B. D. (2010). Criminal prosecutions: Examining prosecutorial discretion and charge reductions in the U.S. Federal District Courts. *Justice Quarterly, 27,* 394–430.

The Opportunity Agenda. (2006). *The opportunity survey: Understanding the roots of attitudes on inequality.* New York: Author. Retrieved from http://opportunityagenda.org/opportunity-survey

Orfalea, G. (2006). *The Arab Americans: A history.* Northampton, MA: Olive Branch Press.

Oshinsky, D. M. (1996). *"Worse than slavery": Parchman farm and the ordeal of Jim Crow justice.* New York: The Free Press.

Packer, H. (1968). *The limits of the criminal sanction.* Palo Alto, CA: Stanford University Press.

Pager, D. I. (2007a). *Marked: Race, crime, and finding work in an era of mass incarceration.* Chicago: University of Chicago Press.

Pager, D. I. (2007b). Two strikes and you're out: The intensification of racial and criminal stigma. In D. Weiman, S. Bushway, & M. Stoll (Eds.), *Barriers to reentry? The labor market for released prisoners in post-industrial America* (pp. 151–173). New York: Russell Sage.

Palmer, J. W. (2010). *Constitutional rights of prisoners* (9th ed.). New Providence, NJ: Lexis/Nexis Anderson.

Paoline III, E. A., & Terrill, W. (2005). The impact of police culture on traffic stop searches: An analysis of attitudes and behavior. *Policing: An International Journal of Police Strategies & Management, 28*(3), 455–472.

Parenti, C. (1999). *Lockdown America: Police and prisons in the age of crisis.* New York: Verso.

Parker, K. F., Dewees, M. A., & Radelet, M. L. (2002). Racial bias and the conviction of the innocent. In S. Westervelt & J. A. Humphrey (Eds.), *Wrongly convicted: Perspectives on failed justice* (pp. 114–131). New Brunswick, NJ: Rutgers University Press.

Parsons-Pollard, N. Y. (2011). *Disproportionate minority contact: Current issues and policies.* Durham, NC: Carolina Academic Press.

Paternoster, R. (1983). Race of the victim and location of crime: The decision to seek the death penalty in South Carolina. *Journal of Criminal Law and Criminology, 74,* 701–731.

Paternoster, R., & Brame, R. (2003). *An empirical analysis of Maryland's death sentencing system with respect to the influence of race and legal jurisdiction.* Retrieved from http://www.newsdesk.umd.edu/pdf/finalrep.pdf

Paternoster, R., & Brame, R. (2008). Reassessing race disparities in Maryland capital cases. *Criminology, 46,* 971–1008.

Patterson, B., Andrews, B., & Barber, G. (2015). The recent, hateful history of attacks on black churches. *Mother Jones.* Retrieved from http://www.motherjones.com/mojo/2015/06/attacks-black-churches-since-1995

Patterson, W. L. (Ed.). (1970). *We charge genocide: The historic petition to the United Nations for relief from a crime of the United States government against the Negro people.* New York: International Publishers. (Original work published 1951)

Pattillo, M. E. (1998). Sweet mothers and gangbangers: Managing crime in a Black middle-class neighborhood. *Social Forces, 76,* 747–774.

Payne, A. A., & Welch, K. (2010). Modeling the effects of racial threat on punitive and restorative school discipline practices. *Criminology, 48,* 1019–1062.

Payne, B. K., & Button, D. M. (2009). Developing a citywide youth violence prevention plan. *International Journal of Offender Therapy and Comparative Criminology, 53*(5), 517–534.

Pazmino, G. (2015). *De Blasio signs background check, car wash bills.* Retrieved from http://www.capitalnewyork.com/article/city-hall/2015/06/8571198/de-blasio-signs-background-check-car-wash-bills

Peguero, A. A., & Shekarkhar, Z. (2011). Latino/a student misbehavior and school punishment. *Journal of Behavioral Sciences, 33,* 54–70.

Penn, E., Taylor Greene, H., & Gabbidon, S. L. (Eds.). (2006). *Race and juvenile justice.* Durham, NC: Carolina Academic Press.

Pennsylvania panel advises death penalty moratorium. (2003). Retrieved March 5, 2003, from http://www.CNN.com

Pennsylvania Supreme Court. (2003). *Pennsylvania Supreme Court Committee on Racial and Gender Bias in the Justice System* (Final report). Retrieved from http://www.courts.state.pa.us

Perez, D. M., Jennings, W. D., & Giver, A. R. (2008). Specifying general strain theory: An ethnically relevant approach. *Deviant Behavior, 29,* 544–578.

Perez, E. (2015). Attorney General Eric Holder sees success in fewer drug prosecutions. *CNN.com.* Retrieved from http://www.cnn.com/2015/02/17/politics/attorney-general-eric-holder-drug-sentencing-prosecutions

Perloff, R. M. (2000). The press and lynchings of African Americans. *Journal of Black Studies, 30,* 315–330.

Perry, B. (2000). Perpetual outsiders: Criminal justice and the Asian American experience. In The Criminal Justice Collective of Northern Arizona University (Eds.), *Investigating difference: Human and cultural relations in criminal justice* (pp. 99–110). Boston: Allyn & Bacon.

Perry, B. (2002). Defending the color line: Racially and ethnically motivated hate crime. *American Behavioral Scientist, 46,* 72–92.

Perry, B. (2009). *Policing race and place in Indian Country: Over- and underenforcement.* Lanham, MD: Lexington Books.

Perry, S. W. (2004). *Census of tribal justice agencies in Indian Country, 2002.* Washington, DC: U.S. Department of Justice.

Perry, S. W. (2005). *Census of tribal justice agencies in Indian Country, 2002.* Washington, DC: U.S. Department of Justice, Bureau of Justice Statistics. NCJ 205332. Retrieved July 13, 2011, from http://bjs.ojp.usdoj.gov/content/pub/pdf/ctjaic02.pdf

Petersilia, J. (1983). *Racial disparities in the criminal justice system.* Santa Monica, CA: RAND.

Petersilia, J. (2002). Community corrections. In J. Q. Wilson & J. Petersilia (Eds.), *Crime: Public policies for crime control* (pp. 483–508). Oakland, CA: Institute for Contemporary Studies.

Petersilia, J. (2003). *When prisoners come home: Parole and prisoner reentry.* New York: Oxford University Press.

Peterson, D., Taylor, T. J., & Esbensen, F. (2004). Gang membership and violent victimization. *Justice Quarterly, 21*(4), 794–815.

Peterson, R. D., & Krivo, L. J. (1993). Racial segregation and Black urban homicide. *Social Forces, 71,* 1001–1026.

Peterson, R. D., & Krivo, L. J. (2005). Macrostructural analyses of race, ethnicity, and violent crime: Recent lessons and new directions for research. *Annual Review of Sociology, 31,* 331–356.

Peterson, R., & Krivo, L. (2010). *Divergent social worlds.* New York: Russell Sage.

Petrie, M. A., & Coverdill, J. E. (2010). Who lives and dies on death row? Race, ethnicity, and post-sentence outcomes in Texas. *Social Problems, 57,* 630–652.

The Pew Center on the States. (2008). *One in 100: Behind bars in America 2008.* Retrieved at http://www.pewcenteronthestates.org/report_detail.aspx?id=35904

The Pew Center on the States. (2011). *State of recidivism: The revolving door of America's prisons.* Washington, DC: The Pew Charitable Trusts.

The Pew Research Center. (2014a). *Sharp racial divisions in reactions to Brown, Garner decisions.* Washington, DC: Pew Research Center/*USA Today* Survey.

The Pew Research Center. (2014b). *America's new drug policy landscape.* Retrieved from http://www.people-press.org/2014/04/02/section-2-views-of-marijuana-legalization-decriminalization-concerns/

The Pew Research Center. (2014c). *U.S. deportations of immigrants reach record high in 2013.* Retrieved from http://pewresearch.org

Phillips, S. (2012). Continued racial disparities in the capital of capital punishment? The Rosenthal era. Houston Law Review, Vol. 50, No. 1, 2012; U Denver Legal Studies Research Paper No. 12-05. Available at http://ssrn.com/abstract=2033905

Phillips, U. B. (1915). Slave crime in Virginia. *American Historical Review, 20,* 336–340.

Pickerill, J. M., Mosher, C., & Pratt, T. (2009). Search and seizure, racial profiling, and traffic stops: A disparate impact framework. *Law & Policy, 31*(1), 1–30.

Pierce, G. L., & Radelet, M. L. (2011). Death sentencing in East Baton Rouge Parish, 1990–2008. *Louisiana Law Review, 71,* 647–673.

Piquero, A. (2008). Disproportionate minority contact. *Future of Children, 18*(2), 59–79.

Piquero, N. L., & Piquero, A. R. (2001). Problem-oriented policing. In R. G. Dunham & G. P. Alpert (Eds.), *Critical issues in policing* (4th ed., pp. 531–540). Prospect Heights, IL: Waveland Press.

Piquero, N., & Sealock, M. (2010). Race, crime, and general strain theory. *Youth Violence and Juvenile Justice, 6,* 170–186.

Pisciotta, A. W. (1983). Race, sex, and rehabilitation: A study of differential treatment in the juvenile reformatory, 1825–1900. *Crime and Delinquency 29*(2), 254–269.

Pittman, G. (2011). Black men survive longer in prison than out. *Reuters Online.* Retrieved from http://www.reuters.com/article/2011/07/14/us-prison-blacks-idUSTRE76D71920110714

Platt, A. (1969). *The child savers: The invention of delinquency.* Chicago: University of Chicago Press.

Platt, A. (1977). *The child savers: The invention of delinquency* (2nd ed.). Chicago: University of Chicago Press.

Platt, A. (2009). *The child savers: The invention of delinquency* (expanded 40th anniversary edition). Piscataway, NJ: Rutgers University Press.

Plessy v. Ferguson, 163 U.S. 537 (1896).

Polizzi, D. (2013). Review of A Theory of African American Offending: Race, Racism, and Crime. *Journal of Theoretical and Philosophical Criminology, 5,* 96–98.

Polk, W. R. (2006). *The birth of America: From Columbus to the revolution.* New York: HarperCollins.

Pope, C. E., & Feyerherm, W. H. (1990, June/September). Minority status and juvenile justice processing: An assessment of the research literature, Parts I & II. *Criminal Justice Abstracts, 22,* 327–336 (Part I); *22,* 527–542 (Part II).

Pope, C. E., Lovell, R., & Hsia, H. M. (2002). *Disproportionate minority confinement: A review of the research literature from 1989 through 2001.* Washington, DC: Office of Juvenile Justice and Delinquency Prevention.

Porter, N. D. (2010). *Expanding the vote: State felony disenfranchisement reform, 1997–2010.* Washington, DC: The Sentencing Project.

Porter, N. D. (2011). *On the chopping block: State prison closings.* Washington, DC: The Sentencing Project.

Posadas, C. E., & Medina, C. A. (2012) Immigration lockdown: The exclusion of Mexican immigrants through legislation. In M. Urbina (Ed.), *Hispanics in the U.S. criminal justice system: The new American demography* (pp. 80–93). Springfield, IL: Charles C Thomas.

Potter, H. (Ed.). (2007). *Racing the storm: Racial implications and lessons learned from Hurricane Katrina.* Lanham, MD: Lexington Books.

Powell v. Alabama, 287 U.S. 45 (1932).

Pratt, T. C. (1998). Race and sentencing: A meta-analysis of conflicting empirical research results. *Journal of Criminal Justice, 26,* 513–523.

President's Commission on Law Enforcement and the Administration of Justice. (1967). *Task force report on the police.* Washington, DC: U.S. Government Printing Office.

Preuhs, R. R. (2001). State felon disenfranchisement policy. *Social Science Quarterly, 82,* 733–748.

Price, B. E. (2006). *Merchandizing prisoners: Who really pays for prison privatization?* Westport, CT: Praeger.

Pridemore, W. A., & Freilich, J. D. (2006). A test of recent subcultural explanations of white violence in the United States. *Journal of Criminal Justice, 34,* 1–16.

Public Policy Institute of California. (2008). *Poll data.* Retrieved March 24, 2008, from Polling the Nations database.

Public Report of the Forgotten Victims of Attica. (2003). Retrieved June 4, 2004, from http://newyorkv .homestead.com/files/fvoareportfinal.htm

Puzzanchera, C., Adams, B., & Sickmund, M. (2010). *Juvenile court statistics 2006–2007.* Pittsburgh, PA: National Center for Juvenile Justice. Retrieved August 1, 2011, from http://www.ncjjservehttp .org/ncjjwebsite/pdf/jcsreports/jcs2007.pdf

Puzzanchera, C., Sladky, A., & Kang, W. (2014). *Easy access to juvenile populations: 1990–2013.* Retrieved from http://www.ojjdp.govojstabb/ezapop

Puzzanchera, C., Stahl, A., Finnegan, T. A., Tierney, N., & Snyder, H. (2003a). *Juvenile court statistics, 1998.* Washington, DC: Office of Juvenile Justice and Delinquency Prevention.

Puzzanchera, C., Stahl, A. Finnegan, T. A., Tierney, N., & Snyder, H. (2003b). *Juvenile court statistics, 1999.* Washington, DC: Office of Juvenile Justice and Delinquency Prevention.

Pyrooz, D. C., Decker, S. H., & Fleisher, M. (2011). From the street to prison, from the prison to the street: Understanding and responding to prison gangs. *Journal of Aggression, Conflict and Peace Research, 3,* 12–24.

Quetelet, A. Q. (1984). *Research on the propensity for crime at different ages.* Cincinnati, OH: Anderson. (Original work published 1833)

Quinney, R. (1970). *The social reality of crime.* Boston: Little, Brown.

Racial Profiling Data Collection Resource Center at Northeastern University. (2003). Retrieved from http://www.racialprofilinganalysis.neu.edu

Racial Profiling Data Collection Resource Center at Northeastern University. (2008). Retrieved February 23, 2008, from http://www.racialprofilinganalysis.neu.edu

Radelet, M. L. (1989). Executions of Whites for crimes against Blacks: Exceptions to the rule? *The Sociological Quarterly, 30,* 529–544.

Radelet, M. L., Bedau, H. A., & Putnam, C. E. (1992). *In spite of innocence: The ordeal of 400 Americans wrongly convicted of crimes punishable by death.* Boston: Northeastern University Press.

Radosh, P. F. (2008). War on drugs: Gender and race inequities in crime control strategies. *Criminal Justice Studies, 21,* 167–178.

Rand, M., & Catalano, S. (2007). *Criminal victimizations, 2006.* Washington, DC: U.S. Department of Justice, Office of Justice Programs.

Rantala, R. R., & Edwards, T. J. (2000). *Effects of NIBRS on crime statistics.* Washington, DC: U.S. Department of Justice, Office of Justice Programs.

Raper, A. (1933). *The tragedy of lynching.* Chapel Hill: University of North Carolina Press.

Rasmussen Reports. (2009). Retrieved July 1, 2011, from the Polling the Nations database at http://www.orspub.com/

Ray, M. C., & Smith, E. (1991). Black women and homicide: An analysis of the subculture of violence thesis. *The Western Journal of Black Studies, 15,* 144–153.

Reasons, C. E., Conley, D. C., & Debro, J. (Eds.). (2002). *Race, class, gender, and justice in the United States.* Boston: Allyn & Bacon.

Reaves, B. A. (2001). *Felony defendants in large urban counties, 1998.* Washington, DC: Bureau of Justice Statistics.

Reaves, B. (2006). *Federal law enforcement officers, 2004.* Washington, DC: U.S. Department of Justice. Retrieved from www.ojp.usdoj.gov/bjs/welcome.html

Reaves, B. (2007). *Census of state and local law enforcement agencies, 2004.* Washington, DC: U.S. Department of Justice.

Reaves, B. (2010). *Local police departments, 2007.* Retrieved from http://bjs.ojp.usdoj.gov/content/pub/pdf/lpd07.pdf

Reaves, B. A. (2011). *Tribal law enforcement, 2008.* NCJ 234217. Retrieved from http://bjs.ojp.usdoj.gov/content/pub/pdf/tle08.pdf

Reaves, B. A. (2012). *Federal law enforcement officers, 2008.* Washington, DC: Bureau of Justice Statistics. Retrieved from http://www.bjs.gov/content/pub/pdf/fle008.pdf

Reaves, B. A. (2013). *Felony defendants in large urban counties, 2009—Statistical Tables.* Washington, DC: Bureau of Justice Statistics.

Reaves, B., & Bauer, L. (2003). *Federal law enforcement officers, 2002.* Washington, DC: U.S. Department of Justice.

Reaves, B., & Hickman, M. (2002a). *Census of state and local law enforcement agencies, 2000.* Washington, DC: U.S. Department of Justice.

Reaves, B., & Hickman, M. (2002b). *Police departments in large cities, 1990–2000.* Washington, DC: U.S. Department of Justice.

Reaves, B., & Hickman, M. (2003). *Local police departments, 2000.* Washington, DC: U.S. Department of Justice.

Regan, S. (2014). *5 ways the government keeps Native Americans in poverty.* Retrieved from http://www.forbes.com/sites/realspin/2014/03/13/5-ways-the-government-keeps-native-americans-in-poverty/2/

Reid, I. De A. (1957). Race and crime. *Friends Journal, 3,* 772–774.

Reiman, J. (2004). *The rich get richer, and the poor get prison: Ideology, class, and criminal justice* (7th ed.). Boston: Allyn & Bacon.

Reiman, J. (2007). *The rich get richer and the poor get prison: Ideology, class, and criminal justice* (8th ed.). Boston: Allyn & Bacon.

Reisig, M. D., & Parks, R. B. (2001). *Satisfaction with police—What matters?* Washington, DC: U.S. Department of Justice.

Rennison, C. M. (2001a). *Criminal victimization 2000: Changes 1999–2000 with trends 1992–2000.* Washington, DC: U.S. Department of Justice, Office of Justice Programs.

Rennison, C. M. (2001b). *Violent victimization and race, 1992–1998.* Washington, DC: U.S. Department of Justice, Office of Justice Programs.

Rennison, C. M. (2002). *Hispanic victims of violent crime, 1993–2000* (NCJ 191208). Washington, DC: U.S. Department of Justice, Office of Justice Programs.

Rennison, C. M., & Rand, M. R. (2003). *Criminal victimization, 2002.* Washington, DC: U.S. Department of Justice, Office of Justice Programs.

Renowned criminologist eschews alarmist theories. (1999, September 13). *The Patriot News,* p. B5.

Rice, S. K., & White, M. D. (Eds.). (2010). *Race, ethnicity, and policing: New and essential readings.* New York: NYU Press.

Richardson, J. F. (1970). *The New York police.* New York: Oxford University Press.

Richie, B. (2002). The social impact of mass incarceration on women. In M. Mauer & M. Chesney-Lind (Eds.), *Invisible punishment: The collateral consequences of mass imprisonment* (pp. 136–149). New York: New Press.

Riley, J. L. (2014). Family secret: What the left won't tell you about black crime. *The Washington Times.* Retrieved from http://www.washingtontimes.com/news/2014/jul/21/family-secret-what-the-left-wont-tell-you-about-bl/

Rios, V. (2011). *Punished: Policing the lives of Black and Latino youth.* New York: NYU Press.

Rippley, L. J. (1976). *The German-Americans.* Boston: Twayne.

Roane, K. R. (2001, April 30). Policing the police is a dicey business. *U.S. News & World Report,* p. 28.

Robinson, L. N. (1911). *History and organization of criminal statistics in the United States.* Boston: Houghton Mifflin.

Rocque, M. (2008). Strain, coping mechanisms, and slavery: A general strain theory application. *Crime, Law, and Social Change, 49,* 245–269.

Rocque, M., Posick, C., & Felix, S. (2015). The role of the brain in urban violent offending: Integrating biology with structural theories of "the streets." *Criminal Justice Studies.* doi: dx.doi.org/10.108 0/1478601X.2014.1000006

Rodriguez, N. (2007). Juvenile court context and detention decisions: Reconsidering the role of race, ethnicity, and community characteristics in juvenile court processes. *Justice Quarterly, 24,* 629–656.

Rodriguez, N. (2013). Concentrated disadvantage and the incarceration of youth: Examining how context affects juvenile justice. *Journal of Research in Crime and Delinquency, 50*(2), 189–215. Retrieved from http://jrc.sagepub.com

Roe v. Wade, 410 U.S. 113 (1973).

Rojek, J., Rosenfeld, R., & Decker, S. (2004). The influence of driver's race on traffic stops in Missouri. *Police Quarterly, 7*(1), 126–147.

Rojek, J., Rosenfeld, R., & Decker, S. (2012). Policing race: the racial stratification of searches in police traffic stops. *Criminology, 50*(4), 993–1024.

Romero, N., & Sanchez, G. (2012). Critical issues facing Hispanic defendants: From detection to arrest. In M. G. Urbina (Ed.), *Hispanics in the U.S. criminal justice system* (pp. 63–79). Springfield, IL: Charles C Thomas.

Roper v. Simmons, 543 U.S. 551 (2005).

Rose, D. R., & Clear, T. R. (1998). Incarceration, social capital, and crime: Implications for social disorganization theory. *Criminology, 36,* 441–479.

Rosenfeld, R., Edberg, M., Fang, X., & Florence, C. S. (2013). *Economics and youth violence: Crime, disadvantage, and community.* New York: New York University Press.

Rosenmerkel, S., Durose, M., & Farole, D. (2009). *Felony sentences in state courts, 2006—statistical tables.* Washington, DC: Bureau of Justice Statistics. NCJ 226846.

Ross, L. E. (1992). Blacks, self-esteem, and delinquency: It's time for a new approach. *Justice Quarterly, 9,* 609–624.

Ross, L. E. (2010). A vision of race, crime, and justice through the lens of critical race theory. In E. McLaurin & T. Newburn (Eds.), *The Sage handbook of criminological theory* (pp. 391–409). London: Sage.

Rossman, S. B., Roman, J. K., Zweig, J. M., Rempel, M., & Lindquist, C. H. (2011). *The multi-site adult court evaluation: Executive summary.* Washington, DC: Urban Institute.

Rudwick, E. M. (1960). The Negro policeman in the South. *Journal of Criminal Law, Criminology, and Police Science, 51,* 273–276.

Rushton, J. P. (1995). Race and crime: International data for 1989–1990. *Psychological Reports, 76,* 307–312.

Rushton, J. P. (1999). *Race, evolution, and behavior* (special abridged ed.). New Brunswick, NJ: Transaction.

Rushton, J. P., & Templer, D. I. (2012). Do pigmentation and the melanocortin system modulate aggression and sexuality in humans as they do in other animals? *Personality and Individual Differences, 53,* 4–8.

Rushton, J. P., & Whitney, G. (2002). Cross-national variation in violent crime rates: Race, *r-K* theory, and income. *Population and Environment, 23,* 501–511.

Russell, K. K. (1998). *The color of crime: Racial hoaxes, white fear, black protectionism, police harassment, and other macroaggressions.* New York: New York University Press.

Russell, K. K. (1999). Critical race theory and social justice. In B. A. Arrigo (Ed.), *Social justice/ criminal justice: The maturation of critical theory in law, crime, and deviance* (pp. 178–188). Belmont, CA: West/Wadsworth.

Russell, K. K. (2002). "Driving while black": Corollary phenomena and collateral consequences. In C. E. Reasons, D. J. Conley, & J. Debro (Eds.), *Race, class, gender, and justice in the United States* (pp. 191–200). Boston: Allyn & Bacon.

Russell-Brown, K. (2004). *Underground codes: Race, crime, and related fires.* New York: New York University Press.

Russell-Brown, K. (2006). While visions of deviance danced in their heads. In D. D. Trout (Ed.), *After the storm: Black intellectuals explore the meaning of Hurricane Katrina* (pp. 111–123). New York: New Press.

Sachar, H. M. (1993). *A history of Jews in America.* New York: Vintage.

Sacks, M. (2012). Arizona immigration law ruling: Supreme Court delivers split decision. *The Huffington Post.* Retrieved from http://www.huffingtonpost.com/2012/06/25/arizona-immigration-law-ruling_n_1614067.html

Sale, K. (1990). *The conquest of paradise: Christopher Columbus and the Columbian legacy.* New York: Knopf.

Saleh-Hanna, V. (Ed.). (2008). *Colonial systems of control: Criminal justice in Nigeria.* Ottawa: University of Ottawa Press.

Sampson, R. J. (1985). Race and criminal violence: A demographically disaggregated analysis of urban homicide. *Crime and Delinquency, 31,* 47–82.

Sampson, R. J. (1987). Urban Black violence: The effects of male joblessness and family disruption. *American Journal of Sociology, 93,* 348–382.

Sampson, R. J. (2012). *Great American city: Chicago and the enduring neighborhood effect.* Chicago: University of Chicago Press.

Sampson, R. J., & Bean, L. (2006). Cultural mechanisms and killing fields: A revised theory of community-level racial inequality. In J. Hagan, R. Peterson, & L. Krivo (Eds.), *The many colors of crime: Inequalities of race, ethnicity, and crime in America* (pp. 8–36). New York: New York University Press.

Sampson, R. J., & Groves, W. B. (1989). Community structure and crime: Testing social-disorganization theory. *American Journal of Sociology, 94,* 774–802.

Sampson, R. J., Raudenbush, S. W., & Earls, F. (1997). Neighborhoods and violent crime: A multilevel study of collective efficacy. *Science, 277,* 918–924.

Sampson, R. J., & Wilson, W. J. (1995). Toward a theory of race, crime, and urban inequality. In J. Hagan & R. D. Peterson (Eds.), *Crime and inequality* (pp. 37–54). Stanford, CA: Stanford University Press.

Sandholtz, N., Langton, L., & Planty, M. (2013). *Hate crime victimization, 2003–2011.* Washington, DC: Bureau of Justice Statistics.

Schaefer, R. T. (2011). *Racial and ethnic groups* (12th ed.). New York: Pearson/Prentice-Hall.

Schafer, J. A., Carter, D. L., Katz-Bannister, A. J., & Wells, W. M. (2006). Decision making in traffic stop encounters: A multivariate analysis of police behavior. *Police Quarterly, 9*(2), 184–209.

Schafer, J. A., Huebner, B. M., & Bynum, T. S. (2003). Citizen perceptions of police services: Race, neighborhood context, and community policing. *Police Quarterly, 6,* 440–468.

Schall v. Martin, 467 U.S. 253 (1984).

Scheb, J. M., Lyons, W., & Wagers, K. A. (2008). Race, prosecutors, and juries: The death penalty in Tennessee. *Justice System Journal, 29,* 338–347.

Scheingold, S. A. (1984). *The politics of law and order: Street crime and public policy.* New York: Longman.

Schildkraut, D. J. (2009). The dynamics of public opinion on ethnic profiling after 9/11. *American Behavioral Scientist, 53,* 61–79.

Schlesinger, T. (2005). Racial and ethnic disparity in pretrial case processing. *Justice Quarterly, 22,* 170–192.

Schwartz, A. (2011). *DNA familial testing: Civil liberties and civil rights concerns.* Chicago: American Civil Liberties Union.

Schwartz, J. (2010). Murder in comparative context. In Christopher J. Ferguson (Ed.), *Violent crime* (pp. 276–299). Thousand Oaks, CA: Sage.

Scott, G. (2001). Broken windows behind bars: Eradicating prison gangs through ecological hardening and symbol cleansing. *Corrections Management Quarterly, 5,* 23–36.

Sellin, T. (1928). The Negro criminal: A statistical note. *The American Academy of Political and Social Sciences, 130,* 52–64.

Sellin, T. (1935). Race prejudice in the administration of justice. *The American Journal of Sociology, 41,* 212–217.

Sellin, T. (1938). *Culture conflict and crime.* New York: Social Science Research Council.

Sellin, T. J. (1976). *Slavery and the penal system.* New York: Elsevier.

The Sentencing Project. (2011a). *Felon disenfranchisement laws in the United States.* Washington, DC: Author.

The Sentencing Project. (2011b). *On the chopping block: State prison closings.* Washington, DC: Author.

Serwer, A. (2011). *Judicial override in death penalty cases: Another reason why electing judges is a bad idea.* Retrieved from http://prospect.org

Sesardic, N. (2010). Race: A social construction of a biological concept. *Biological Philosophy, 25,* 143–162.

Severson, K. (2013). North Carolina repeals law allowing racial bias claim in death penalty challenges. *New York Times.* Retrieved from http://www.nytimes.com/2013/06/06/us/racial-justice-act-repealed-in-north-carolina.html

Shane, S. (1999, April 4). Genetic research increasingly finds "race" a null concept. *The Baltimore Sun,* pp. 1A, 6A.

Shapiro, A. L. (1997). The disenfranchised. *American Prospect, 35,* 60–62.

Sharp, E. B. (2006). Policing urban America: A new look at the politics of agency size. *Social Science Quarterly, 87,* 291–307.

Shaw, C., & McKay, H. D. (1969). *Juvenile delinquency in urban areas.* Chicago: University of Chicago Press. (Original work published 1942)

Shedd, C. (2015). The legacy effect: Charting the next iteration of the carceral state. *Du Bois Review, 12,* 213–219.

Sheehan, R., & Cordner, G. W. (1995). *Police administration* (3rd ed.). Cincinnati, OH: Anderson.

Shekarkhar, Z., & Gibson, C. (2011). Gender, self-control, and offending behaviors among Latino youth. *Journal of Contemporary Criminal Justice, 72,* 63.

Shelden, R. G. (2001). *Controlling the dangerous classes.* Needham Heights, MA: Allyn & Bacon.

Shelden, R. G., & Brown, W. (2003). *Criminal justice in America: A critical view.* Needham Heights, MA: Allyn & Bacon.

Shelden, R. G., & Osborne, L. T. (1989). "For their own good": Class interests and the child saving movement in Memphis, Tennessee, 1900–1917. *Criminology, 27,* 747–767.

Sherman, L. W. (1974). *Police corruption: A sociological perspective.* Garden City, NY: Anchor Books.

Sherman, L. W. (1980). Execution without trial: Police homicide and the Constitution. *Vanderbilt Law Review, 33,* 71–100. (Reprinted in J. F. Fyfe, Ed., 1982, *Readings on police use of deadly force,* pp. 88–89.)

Sherman, L. (1997). Introduction: The congressional mandate to evaluate. In L. W. Sherman, D. Gottfredson, D. MacKenzie, J. P. Eck, P. Reuter, & S. Bushway (Eds.), *Preventing crime: What works, what doesn't, what's promising.* Washington, DC: National Institute of Justice.

Sherman, L. (2002). *Trust and confidence in criminal justice.* NIJ Journal No. 2 48.

Sherman, L. W., Gottfredson, D., MacKenzie, D., Eck, J. P., Reuter, P., & Bushway, S. (Eds.). (1997). *Preventing crime: What works, what doesn't, what's promising.* Washington, DC: National Institute of Justice.

Short, J., & Sharp, C. (2005). *Disproportionate minority contact in the juvenile justice system.* Washington, DC: Child Welfare League of America.

Sickmund, M., & Puzzanchera, C. (Eds.). (2014). *Juvenile offenders and victims: 2014 national report.* Washington, DC: Office of Juvenile Justice and Delinquency Prevention.

Sickmund, M., Sladky, T. J., & Kang, W. (2011). *Census of juveniles in residential placement databook.* Retrieved from http://www.ojjdp.gov/ojstatbb/ezacjrp

Siegel, L. J. (2002). *Juvenile delinquency: The core.* Belmont, CA: Wadsworth/Thomson Learning.

Sigelman, L., Welch, S., Bledsoe, T., & Combs, M. (1997). Police brutality and public perceptions of racial discrimination: A tale of two beatings. *Political Research Quarterly, 50,* 777–791.

Sigler, M. (2010). Private prisons, public functions, and the meaning of punishment. *Florida State University Law Review, 38,* 149–178.

Simanski, J. F. (2014). *Immigration enforcement actions: 2013.* Washington, DC: Department of Homeland Security Office of Immigration Statistics.

Simerman, J. (2015, January). *George Toca, La. inmate at center of debate on juvenile life sentences, to go free.* Retrieved from http://www.theneworleansadvocate.com

Simmons v. Roper, S.C. 84454 (2003).

Simons, D. H. (2003, June 23). Genetic tests can reveal ancestry, giving police a new source of clues. *U.S. News & World Report, 134,* p. 50.

Simons, R. L., Chen, Y. F., Stewart, E. A., & Brody, G. H. (2003). Incidents of discrimination and risk for delinquency: A longitudinal test of strain theory with an African American sample. *Justice Quarterly, 20,* 827–854.

Simons, R. L., Gordon Simons, L., Burt, C., Brody, G. H., & Cutrona, C. (2005). Collective efficacy, authoritative parenting and delinquency: A longitudinal test of a model integrating community- and family-level processes. *Criminology, 43,* 989–1029.

Sinozich, S., & Langton, L. (2014). *Rape and sexual assault victimization among college-age females, 1995–2013.* Washington, DC: Bureau of Justice Statistics.

Skiba, R. J., Michael, R. S., Nardo, A. C., & Peterson, R. L. (2002). The color of discipline: Sources of racial and gender disproportionality in school punishment. *Urban Review, 34,* 317–342.

Skogan, W. G. (1981). *Issues in the measurement of victimization.* Washington, DC: Bureau of Justice Statistics.

Skogan, W. G. (2005). Citizen satisfaction with police encounters. *Police Quarterly, 8,* 298–321.

Skogan, W. G., Steiner, L., DuBois, J., Gudell, J. E., & Fagan, A. (2002). *Community policing and "the new immigrants": Latinos in Chicago.* Chicago: Northwestern University Press.

Smith, E., & Hattery, A. J. (2011). Race, wrongful conviction & exoneration. *Journal of African American Studies, 15,* 74–94.

Smith, E. L., & Cooper, A. (2013). *Homicide in the U.S. known to law enforcement, 2011.* Washington, DC: Bureau of Justice Statistics.

Smith, J. (2009). Native American courts. In H. T. Greene & S. L. Gabbidon (Eds.), *Encyclopedia of race and crime.* Thousand Oaks, CA: Sage.

Smith, M. R., & Alpert, G. P. (2007). Explaining police bias: A theory of social conditioning and illusory correlation. *Criminal Justice and Behavior 34*(10), 1262–1283.

Smith, S. K., Steadman, G. W., Minton, T. D., & Townsend, M. (1999). *Criminal victimization and perceptions of community safety in 12 cities, 1998.* Washington, DC: U.S. Department of Justice.

Snell, T. (2014). *Capital punishment, 2013: Statistical tables.* Washington, DC: Bureau of Justice Statictics. NCJ 248448.

Snyder, H. N. (1997). *Juvenile arrests 1995.* Washington, DC: Office of Juvenile Justice and Delinquency Prevention.

Snyder, H. N. (2000). *Juvenile arrests 1999.* Washington, DC: Office of Juvenile Justice and Delinquency Prevention.

Snyder, H. N. (2003). *Juvenile arrests 2001.* Washington, DC: Office of Juvenile Justice and Delinquency Prevention.

Snyder, H. N. (2011). *Arrests in the United States, 1980–2009.* Washington, DC: U.S. Department of Justice, Office of Justice Programs.

Snyder, M., & Sickmund, M. (1999). *Juvenile offenders and victims: 1999 national report.* Washington, DC: Office of Juvenile Justice and Delinquency Prevention.

Snyder, M., & Sickmund, M. (2008). *Juvenile offenders and victims: 2006 national report.* Washington, DC: Office of Juvenile Justice and Delinquency Prevention.

Solis, C., Portillos, E., & Brunson, R. (2009). Latino/a youths' experiences and perceptions of negative police encounters. *The Annals of the American Academy of Political and Social Science, 623,* 39–51.

Sommers, S. R., & Norton, M. I. (2007). Race-based judgments, race-neutral justifications: Experimental examination of peremptory use and the *Batson* challenge procedure. *Law and Human Behavior, 31,* 261–273.

Sorenson, J., Hope, R., & Stemen, D. (2003). Racial disproportionality in state prison admissions: Can regional variation be explained by differential arrest rates? *Journal of Criminal Justice, 31,* 73–84.

Sorenson, J. R., Cunningham, M. D., Vigen, M. P., & Woods, S. O. (2011). Serious assaults on prison staff: A descriptive analysis. *Journal of Criminal Justice, 39,* 143–150.

Sowell, T. (1981). *Ethnic America: A history.* New York: Basic Books.

Spohn, C. S. (2000). Thirty years of sentencing reform: The quest for a racially neutral sentencing process. In J. Horney (Ed.), *Policies, processes and decisions of the criminal justice system* (pp. 427–501). Washington, DC: National Institute of Justice.

Spohn, C. (2009). *How do judges decide? The search for fairness and justice in punishment* (2nd ed.). Thousand Oaks, CA: Sage.

Spohn, C. (2014). *Racial disparities in prosecution, sentencing, and punishment.* In S. Bucerius & M. Tonry (Eds.), *Oxford handbook on race, ethnicity, immigration and crime* (pp. 166–193). New York: Oxford University Press.

Spohn, C., & Brennan, P. K. (2011). The joint effects of offender race/ethnicity and gender on substantial assistance departures in federal courts. *Race and Justice: An International Journal, 1,* 49–78.

Spohn, C., & Holleran, D. (2000). The imprisonment penalty paid by young, unemployed black and Hispanic male offenders. *Criminology, 38,* 281–306.

Staff, J., & Kreager, D. A. (2008). Too cool for school? Violence, peer status and high school dropout. *Social Forces, 87,* 445–471.

Stahl, A. L. (2008a). *Delinquency cases in juvenile court, 2004* (OJDP Fact Sheet no. 01). Washington, DC: Office of Juvenile Justice and Delinquency Prevention.

Stahl, A. L. (2008b). *Petitioned status offense cases in juvenile court, 2004* (OJDP Fact Sheet no. 02). Washington, DC: Office of Juvenile Justice and Delinquency Prevention.

Stanford v. Kentucky, 492 U.S. 361 (1989).

Staples, R. (1975). White racism, Black crime, and American justice: An application of the colonial model to explain crime and race. *Phylon, 36,* 14–22.

State v. Soto, 324 N.J. Super 66, 734 A.2d 35 (1996).

Stauffer, A. R., Smith, M. D., Cochran, J. K., Fogel, S. J., & Bjerregaard, B. (2006). The interaction between victim race and gender on sentencing outcomes in capital murder trials: A further exploration. *Homicide Studies, 10,* 98–117.

Steffensmeier, D., & Britt, C. L. (2001). Judges' race and judicial decision making: Do black judges sentence differently? *Social Science Quarterly, 82,* 749–764.

Steffensmeier, D., & Demuth, S. (2000). Ethnicity and sentencing outcomes in U.S. federal courts: Who is punished more harshly? *American Sociological Review, 65,* 705–729.

Steffensmeier, D., & Demuth, S. (2001). Ethnicity and judges' sentencing decisions: Hispanic-black-white comparisons. *Criminology, 39,* 145–178.

Steffensmeier, D., Feldmeyer, B., Harris, C. T., & Ulmer, J. T. (2011). Reassessing trends in black violent crime, 1980–2008: Sorting out the "Hispanic effect" in Uniform Crime Reports arrests, National Crime Victimization Survey offender estimates, and U.S. prisoner counts. *Criminology, 49*(1), 197–251.

Stevenson, B. (2010). *Illegal racial discrimination in jury selection: A continuing legacy.* Montgomery, AL: Equal Justice Initiative.

Stevenson, B. (2011). *The death penalty in Alabama: Judicial override.* Montgomery, AL: Equal Justice Initiative.

Stewart, E. A. (2007). Either they don't know or they don't care: Black males and negative police experiences. *Criminology & Public Policy, 6,* 123–130.

Stewart, E. A., Martinez, R., Baumer, E. P., & Gertz, M. (2015). The social context of Latino threat and punitive Latino sentiment. *Social Problems.* doi: 10.1093/socpro/spu002

Stewart, E. A., Schreck, C. J., & Brunson, R. K. (2008). Lessons of the street code: Policy implications for reducing violent victimization among disadvantaged citizens. *Journal of Contemporary Criminal Justice, 24,* 137–147.

Stewart, E. A., Schreck, C. J., & Simons, R. L. (2006). I ain't gonna let no one disrespect me: Does the code of the street reduce or increase violent victimization among African American adolescents? *The Journal of Research in Crime and Delinquency, 43,* 427–457.

Stewart, E. A., & Simons, R. L. (2006). Structure and culture in African-American adolescent violence: A partial test of the code of the street thesis. *Justice Quarterly, 23,* 1–33.

Stewart, E. A., Simons, R. L., & Conger, R. D. (2002). Assessing neighborhood and social psychological influences on childhood violence in an African American sample. *Criminology, 40,* 801–829.

Stinson, P. (2014). A criminal record may no longer be a stumbling block to employment in some places. *The Huffington Post.* Retrieved from http://www.huffingtonpost.com/2014/05/22/criminal-record-employment_n_5372837.html

Stolz, B. A. (2010). Human trafficking: Policy. *Criminology & Public Policy, 9*(2), 267–274.

Stowell, J. I. (2007). *Immigration and crime: Considering the direct and indirect effects of immigration on violent criminal behavior.* New York: LFB Scholarly Press.

Stowell, J. I., Messner, S. F., McGeever, K. F., & Raffalovich, L. E. (2009). Immigration and the recent violent crime drop in the U.S.: A pooled, cross-sectional time-series analysis of metropolitan areas. *Criminology, 47,* 889–928.

Streib, V. (2004). *The juvenile death penalty today: Death sentences and executions for juvenile crimes.* Retrieved April 30, 2004, from http://www.law.onu.edu/faculty/streib/JuvDeathApr302004.pdf

Strom, K. (2001). *Hate crimes reported in the NIBRS, 1997–1999.* Washington, DC: USDOJ, OJP, BJS.

Suavecito Apparel Co. (2004). *Zoot suit riots.* Retrieved December 16, 2004, from http://www.suavecito.com/history.htm

Subcommittee on Civil and Constitutional Rights. (1994). *Racial disparities in federal death penalty prosecutions: 1988–1994* (Staff report). Washington, DC: 103rd Congress, Second Session.

Sudbury, J. (Ed.). (2005). *Global lockdown: Race, gender and the prison industrial complex.* New York: Routledge.

Sullivan, C., & McGloin, J. M. (2014). Looking back to move forward: Some thoughts on measuring crime and delinquency over the past 50 years. *Journal of Research in Crime and Delinquency, 51,* 445–466.

Sutherland, E. H. (1947). *Principles of criminology* (4th ed.). Philadelphia: Lippincott.

Swain v. Alabama, 380 U.S. 202 (1965).

Swan, A. L. (1977). *Families of black prisoners: Survival and progress.* Boston: G. K. Hall.

Sweeney, M. A. (2014). Shadow immigration enforcement and its constitutional dangers. *Journal of Criminal Law and Criminology, 104, 2,* 227–282.

Swift, A. (2014). *Americans: "Eye for an eye" top reason for death penalty.* Retrieved from http://www.gallup.com/poll/178799/americans-eye-eye-top-reason-death-penalty.aspx

Takagi, P. (1974). A garrison state in a "democratic" society. *Crime and Social Justice: A Journal of Radical Criminology, 5,* 27–33. (Reprinted in J. F. Fyfe, Ed., 1982, *Readings on police use of deadly force,* pp. 195–213.)

Takaki, R. (1989). *Strangers from a different shore: A history of Asian Americans.* Boston: Little, Brown.

Tapia, M. (2012). *Juvenile arrest in America: Race, social class, and gang membership.* New York: LFB Scholarly.

Tapia, M., & Harris, P. M. (2012). The dynamics of arresting Latinas and Latinos: Current barriers and prospects for future research. In M. G. Urbina (Ed.), *Hispanics in the U.S. criminal justice system: The new American demography* (pp. 94–109). Springfield, IL: Charles C Thomas.

Tarlow, M., & Nelson, M. (2007). The time is now: Immediate work for people coming home from prison as a strategy to reduce their reincarceration and restore their place in the community. *Federal Sentencing Reporter, 20,* 138–140.

Tarver, M., Walker, S., & Wallace, H. (2002). *Multicultural issues in the criminal justice system.* Boston: Allyn & Bacon.

Tatum, B. L. (1994). The colonial model as a theoretical explanation of crime and delinquency. In A. Sulton (Ed.), *African-American perspectives on crime causation, criminal justice administration, and crime prevention* (pp. 33–52). Englewood, CO: Sulton Books.

Tatum, B. L. (2000). Deconstructing the association of race and crime: The salience of skin color. In M. W. Markowitz & D. Jones-Brown (Eds.), *The system in black and white: Exploring the connections between race, crime, and justice* (pp. 31–46). Westport, CT: Praeger.

Taylor, B. M. (1989). *New directions for the National Crime Survey*. Washington, DC: U.S. Department of Justice, Office of Justice Programs.

Taylor, D. L., Biafora, F. A., Warheit, G., & Gil, A. (1997). Family factors, theft, vandalism, and major deviance among a multiracial/multiethnic sample of adolescent girls. *Journal of Social Distress and the Homeless, 6,* 71–87.

Taylor, K. (2011). *System overload: The costs of under-resourcing public defense*. Washington, DC: Justice Policy Institute. Retrieved from http://www.justicepolicy.org/research/2756

Taylor, P. (1931). The problem of the Mexican. In *Crime and the foreign born*. National Commission on Law Observance and Enforcement Report No. 10 (pp. 199–243). Washington, DC: U.S. Government Printing Office.

Taylor Greene, H. (2004). Do African American police make a difference? In M. D. Free, Jr. (Ed.), *Racial issues in criminal justice: The case of African Americans* (pp. 207–220). Monsey, NY: Criminal Justice Press.

Taylor Greene, H., & Gabbidon, S. (2000). *African American criminological thought*. Albany: State University of New York Press.

Taylor Greene, H., Gabbidon, S. L., & Ebersole, M. (2001). A multi-faceted analysis of the African American presence in juvenile delinquency textbooks published between 1997 and 2000. *Journal of Crime and Justice, 24,* 87–101.

Taylor Greene, H., & Penn, E. (2005). Reducing juvenile delinquency: Lessons learned. In E. Penn, H. Taylor Greene, & S. L. Gabbidon (Eds.), *Race and juvenile justice* (pp. 223–241). Durham, NC: Carolina Academic Press.

Tennessee v. Garner, 471 U.S. 1 (1985).

Terrill, W. (2009). The elusive nature of reasonableness. *Criminology & Public Policy, 8,* 163–172.

Terry v. Ohio, 392 U.S. 1 (1968).

Texeira, E. (2005, August 28). Should the term "minority" be dropped? Word confuses, insults people some critics say. *Patriot-News,* p. A15.

Thompson v. Oklahoma, 487 U.S. 815 (1988).

Thornberry, T. P. (1998). Membership in youth gangs and involvement in serious and violent offending. In R. Loeber & D. P. Farrington (Eds.), *Serious and violent juvenile offenders: Risk factors and successful interventions* (pp. 147–166). Thousand Oaks, CA: Sage.

Thornberry, T. P., Huizinga, D., & Loeber, R. (2004). The causes and correlates studies: Findings and policy implications. *Juvenile Justice, 10*(1), 3–19.

Thurman, Q., Zhao, J., & Giacomazzi, A. (2001). *Community policing in a community era*. Los Angeles: Roxbury.

Tillyer, R., & Klahm, C. (2011). Searching for contraband: Assessing the use of discretion by police officers. *Police Quarterly, 14*(2), 166–185.

Tillyer, R., Klahm, C. F., & Engel, R. S. (2012). The discretion to search a multilevel examination of driver demographics and officer characteristics. *Journal of Contemporary Criminal Justice, 28*(2), 184–205.

Tita, G., & Abrahamse, A. (2004, February). *Gang homicide in LA, 1981–2001*. Sacramento, CA: California Attorney General's Office.

Tolnay, S., & Beck, E. (1995). *A festival of violence: An analysis of southern lynchings, 1882–1930*. Urbana: University of Illinois Press.

Tonry, M. (1995). *Malign neglect: Race, crime, and punishment in America*. New York: Oxford University Press.

Tonry, M. (2011). *Punishing race: A continuing American dilemma*. New York: Oxford University Press.

Tonry, M. H., & Melewski, M. (2008). The malign neglects of drug and crime control policies in black America. In M. H. Tonry (Ed.), *Crime and justice: A review of research* (Vol. 37). Chicago: University of Chicago Press.

Tracy, P. E. (2005). Race, ethnicity, and juvenile justice: Is there bias in post-arrest decision making? In D. Hawkins & K. Kempf-Leonard (Eds.), *Our children, their children: Confronting racial and ethnic differences in American juvenile justice* (pp. 300–349). Chicago: University of Chicago Press.

Travis, J. (2005). *But they all come back: Facing the challenges of prisoner reentry*. Washington, DC: Urban Institute Press.

Travis, J. (2007). Reflection on the reentry movement. *Federal Sentencing Reporter, 20,* 84–87.

Trujillo, L. (1995). La evolucion del "bandido" al "pachuco": A critical examination and evaluation of criminological literature on Chicanos. In A. S. Lopes (Ed.), *Criminal justice and Latino communities* (pp. 21–45). New York: Garland. (Reprinted from *Issues in Criminology, 74*[9], 44–67, 1974.)

Trulson, C. R., Marquart, J. W., & Kawuncha, S. K. (2006). Gang suppression and institutional control. *Corrections Today, 68,* 26–31.

Truman, J. L., & Langton, L. (2014). *Criminal victimization, 2013.* Retrieved from http://www.bjs .gov/index.cfm

Truman, J. L., & Morgan, R. E. (2014). *Special report: Nonfatal domestic violence, 2003–2012.* Washington, DC: U.S. Department of Justice.

Truman, J. L., & Rand, M. R. (2010). *Criminal victimization, 2009.* NCJ 231327. Washington, DC: Bureau of Justice Statistics.

Tseloni, A., & Pease, K. (2011). DNA retention after arrest: Balancing privacy interests and public protection. *European Journal of Criminology, 8,* 32–47.

Tso, T. (1996). The process of decision making in tribal courts. In M. O. Nielson & R. A. Silverman (Eds.), *Native Americans, crime, and justice* (pp. 170–180). Boulder, CO: Westview Press.

Tulchin, S. H. (1939). *Intelligence and crime.* Chicago: University of Chicago Press.

Turk, A. T. (1969). *Criminality and legal order.* Chicago: Rand McNally & Company.

Turner, K. B., & Johnson, J. B. (2005). A comparison of bail amounts for Hispanics, Whites, and African Americans: A single county analysis. *American Journal of Criminal Justice, 30,* 35–53.

Tyler, S. L. (1973). *A history of Indian policy.* Washington, DC: U.S. Department of Interior.

Uchida, C. (1997). The development of American police. In R. G. Dunham & G. P. Alpert (Eds.), *Critical issues in policing* (pp. 18–35). Prospect Heights, IL: Waveland Press.

Uggen, C., & Manza, J. (2002). Democratic contraction? Political consequences of felon disenfranchisement in the United States. *American Sociological Review, 67,* 777–803.

Uggen, C., Manza, J., & Behrens, A. (2003). Felon voting rights and the disenfranchisement of African Americans. *Souls: A Critical Journal of Black Politics, Culture & Society, 5,* 47–55.

Ulmer, J. T., & Johnson, B. (2004). Sentencing in context: A multilevel analysis. *Criminology, 42,* 137–177.

United States. (2014). *National drug control strategy.* Washington, DC: Office of National Drug Control Policy, Executive Office of the President. Retrieved from https://www.whitehouse.gov/sites/ default/files/ndcs_2014.pdf

United States v. Barry, 938 F.2d, 1327, 1329 (D.C. Cir. 1991).

United States v. Booker, 543 U.S. 220 (2005).

University at Albany, School of Criminal Justice. (2011). *Capital jury project.* Retrieved from http:// www.albany.edu/scj/capital_jury_project.php

Unnever, J. D. (2008). Two worlds far apart: Black-white differences in beliefs about why African-American men are disproportionately imprisoned. *Criminology, 46,* 511–538.

Unnever, J. D. (2014). A theory of African offending: A test of core propositions. *Race and Justice, 4,* 98–123.

Unnever, J. D. (2015). Causes of African-American juvenile delinquency. In M. D. Krohn & J. Lane (Eds.), *The handbook of juvenile delinquency and juvenile justice* (pp. 121–138). New York: John Wiley & Sons.

Unnever, J. D., & Cullen, F. T. (2007). Reassessing the racial divide in support for capital punishment: The continuing significance of race. *Journal of Research in Crime and Delinquency, 44,* 124–158.

Unnever, J. D., & Gabbidon, S. L. (2011). *A theory of African American offending: Race, racism, and crime.* New York: Routledge.

Unnever, J., & Gabbidon, S. (2015). Do blacks speak with one voice? Immigrants, public opinions, and perceptions of criminal injustices. *Justice Quarterly, 32*(4), 680–704.

Urban, L. S., St. Cyr, J. L., & Decker, S. H. (2003). Goal conflict in the juvenile court: The evolution of sentencing practices in the United States. *Journal of Contemporary Criminal Justice, 19,* 454–479.

Urbina, M. G. (2011). *Capital punishment and Latino offenders: Racial and ethnic differences in death sentences.* El Paso, TX: LFB Scholarly.

Urbina, M. G. (2012). *Hispanics in the U.S. criminal justice system.* Springfield, IL: Charles C Thomas.

U.S. Bureau of Justice Statistics. (2006). *Compendium of federal justice statistics, 2004.* Washington, DC: U.S. Department of Justice.

U.S. Bureau of Labor Statistics. (2010). *Labor force statistics from the Current Population Survey.* Retrieved from http://www.bls.gov/cps/cpsaat11.pdf

U.S. Census Bureau. (1995). *Top 25 American Indian tribes for the United States: 1990 and 1980.* Retrieved December 12, 2003, from http://www.census.gov/population/socdemo/race/indian/ailant1.txt

U.S. Census Bureau. (2000). *State & County QuickFacts.* Retrieved from http://www.census.gov/main/www/cen2000.html

U.S. Census Bureau. (2003). *Statistical abstracts of the United States.* Washington, DC: Author.

U.S. Census Bureau. (2004). *U.S. interim projections by age, race, and Hispanic origin.* Retrieved January 18, 2008, from http://www.census.gov

U.S. Census Bureau. (2007). *Minority population tops 100 million.* Retrieved January 17, 2008, from http://www.census.gov

U.S. Census Bureau. (2008). *Statistical abstract of the U.S.* Retrieved from http://www.census.gov/compendia/statab/

U. S. Census Bureau. (2009–2013). *5-Year American community survey.* Retrieved from http://factfinder.census.gov/faces/tableservices/jsf/pages/productview.xhtml?src=bkmk

U.S. Census Bureau. (2010). *2010 Census data.* Retrieved from http://2010.census.gov/2010census/data/

U.S. Census Bureau. (2011a). *2010 Census redistricting data (Public Law 24–171) summary file.* Retrieved from http://2010.census.gov/2010census

U.S. Census Bureau. (2011b). *Census 2000 redistricting data (Public Law 24–171) summary file.* Retrieved from http://www.census.gov/rdo/data/redistricting _data.html

U.S. Census Bureau. (2011c). *Statistical abstract of the United States: 2011.* Retrieved from http://www.census.gov/compendia/statab/2011/tables/11s0225.pdf

U.S. Census Bureau. (2011d). *Statistical abstract of the United States: 2012.* Retrieved from http://www.census.gov/compendia/statab/2012edition.html

U.S. Census Bureau. (2015). *EEO state and local government job groups by sex, and race/ethnicity for worksite geography, total population universe—Civilians employed at work 16 years and over 2006–2010.* Retrieved from http://factfinder.census.gov

U.S. Department of Education. (2013). *Civil rights data collection.* Retrieved from http://ocrdata.ed.gov

U.S. Department of Homeland Security. (2009). *Secure communities.* Retrieved July 12, 2011, from http://www.ice.gov/doclib/foia/secure_communities/securecommunitiesstrategicplan09.pdf

U.S. Department of Homeland Security. (2011). *Immigration enforcement actions: 2010.* Washington, DC: Office of Immigration Statistics.

U.S. Department of Justice. (2000). *The federal death penalty system: A statistical survey (1988–2000).* Washington, DC: Author.

U.S. Department of Justice. (2010). Assistant attorney General Thomas E. Perez speaks at the national association for civilian oversight of law enforcement. *Justice News.* Retrieved from http://www.justice.gov/crt/opa/pr/speeches/2010/crt-speech-100920.html

U.S. Department of Justice. (2011a, May 16). Arkansas man pleads guilty to federal hate crime related to the assault of five Hispanic men [Press release]. Retrieved from http://www.justice.gov/opa/pr/2011/May/11-crt-626.html

U.S. Department of Justice. (2011b, December 15). Assistant Attorney General Thomas E. Perez speaks at the Maricopa County Sheriff's Office investigative findings announcement [Press release]. Retrieved from http://www.justice.gov/crt/opa/pr/speeches/2011/crt-speech-111215.html

U.S. Department of Justice. (2011c, December 19). *Investigation of the East Haven Police Department.* Retrieved from http://www.justice.gov/crt/about/spl/documents/easthaven_findletter_12-19-11.pdf

U.S. Department of Justice. (2011d, June 23). Justice Department files lawsuit against the Alamance County, North Carolina, Sheriff's Office [Press release]. Retrieved from http://www.justice.gov/opa/pr/justice-department-files-lawsuit-against-alamance-county-north-carolina-sheriff-s-office

U.S. Department of Justice. (2015). *Justice department announces findings of two civil rights investigations in Ferguson, MO.* Retrieved from http://www.justice.gov/opa/pr/justice-department-announces-findings-two-civil-rights-investigations-ferguson-missouri

U.S. Department of Justice, Community Oriented Policing Services. (2014). President's Task Force on 21st Century Policing. Retrieved from http://www.cops.usdoj.gov/policingtaskforce

U.S. Department of Justice & Equal Employment Opportunity Commission. (2015). *Diversity in law enforcement: A literature review.* Washington, DC: US DOJ Civil Rights Division. Retrieved from http://www.cops.usdoj.gov/pdf/taskforce/Diversity_in_Law_Enforcement_Literature_Review.pdf

U.S. Department of State. (2014). *Trafficking in persons report.* Retrieved from http://www.state.gov/j/tip/rls/tiprpt/

U.S. General Accounting Office. (1990). *Death penalty sentencing: Research indicates pattern of racial disparities.* Washington, DC: Author.

U.S. General Accounting Office. (1997). *Drug courts: Overview of growth, characteristics, and results.* Washington, DC: Author.

U.S. Government Accountability Office. (2011). *Criminal alien statistics.* Washington, DC: Author. Retrieved from http://www.gao.gov/new.items/d11187.pdf

U.S. Senate. (2002). *Senate hearing before the subcommittee on crime and drugs of the committee on the judiciary, United States (107–911).* Washington, DC: U.S. Government Printing Office.

U.S. Sentencing Commission. (2002). *Cocaine and federal sentencing policy.* Retrieved from www.ussc.gov/r_congress/02crach/2002crackrpt.pdf

U.S. Sentencing Commission. (2007). *Cocaine and federal sentencing policy.* Retrieved March 19, 2008, from http://www.ussc.gov/r_congress/cocaine2007.pdf

U.S. Sentencing Commission. (2014). *Overview of federal criminal cases: Fiscal year 2013.* Washington, DC: Author.

van den Haag, E. (1975). *Punishing criminals: Concerning a very old and painful question.* New York: Basic Books.

Van Sertima, I. (1976). *They came before Columbus: The African presence in ancient Americas.* New York: Random House.

Van Stelle, K. R., Allen, G. A., & Moberg, D. P. (1998). Alcohol and drug prevention among American Indian families: The family circles program. In J. Valentine, J. A. De Jong, & N. J. Kennedy (Eds.), *Substance abuse prevention in multicultural communities* (pp. 53–60). Binghamton, NY: Haworth Press.

Vandiver, M. (2006). *Lethal punishment: Lynchings and legal executions in the South.* New Brunswick, NJ: Rutgers University Press.

Varano, S. P., Huebner, B. M., & Bynum, T. S. (2011). Correlates and consequences of pre-incarceration gang involvement among incarcerated youthful felons. *Journal of Criminal Justice, 39,* 30–38.

Vaske, J., Beaver, K. M., Wright, J. P., Boisvert, D., & Schnupp, R. (2009). An interaction between DAT1 and having an alcoholic father predicts serious alcohol problems in a sample of males. *Drug and Alcohol Dependence, 104,* 17–22.

Vaske, J., Makarios, M., Boisvert, D., Beaver, K. M., & Wright, J. P. (2009). The interaction of DRD2 and violent victimization on depression: An analysis by gender and race. *Journal of Affective Disorders, 112*(1), 120–125.

Vaughn, M. G., Wallace, J. M., Davis, L. E., Fernandes, G. T., & Howard, M. O. (2008). Variations in mental health problems, substance use, and delinquency between African American and Caucasian juvenile offenders: Implications for reentry services. *International Journal of Offender Therapy and Comparative Criminology, 52*(3), 311–329.

Vega, T. (2014). School's discipline for girls differs by race and hue. *New York Times.* Retrieved from www.nytimes.com/2014/12/11/us/school-discipline-to-girls-differs-between-and-within-race

Vega, W. A., & Gil, A. G. (1998). Different worlds: Drug use and ethnicity in early adolescence. In W. A. Vega & A. G. Gil (Eds.), *Drug use and ethnicity in early adolescence* (pp. 1–12). New York: Plenum Press.

Velez, M. B. (2006). Toward an understanding of the lower rates of homicide in Latino versus Black neighborhoods: A look at Chicago. In J. Hagan, R. Peterson, & L. Krivo (Eds.), *The many colors of crime: Inequalities of race, ethnicity, and crime in America* (pp. 91–107). New York: New York University Press.

Velez, M. B. (2009). Contextualizing the immigration and crime effect: An analysis of homicide in Chicago neighborhoods. *Homicide Studies, 13,* 325–335.

Venkatesh, S. A. (2006). *Off the books: The underground economy of the urban poor.* Cambridge, MA: Harvard University Press.

Venkatesh, S. (2008). *Gang leader for a day: A rogue sociologist takes to the streets.* New York: The Penguin Press.

Violent history: Attacks on black churches. (2015). *New York Times.* Retrieved from http://www.nytimes.com/interactive/2015/06/18/us/19blackchurch.html

Visher, C. A. (2007). Returning home: Emerging findings and policy lessons about prisoner reentry. *Federal Sentencing Reporter, 20,* 93–102.

Vold, G. B., Bernard, T. J., & Snipes, J. B. (1998). *Theoretical criminology* (4th ed.). Oxford, UK: Oxford University Press.

Wacquant, L. (2000). The new "peculiar institution": On the prison as surrogate ghetto. *Theoretical Criminology, 4,* 377–389.

Wacquant, L. (2001). Deadly symbiosis: When ghetto and prison meet and mesh. *Punishment & Society, 3,* 95–134.

Wacquant, L. (2002). Scrutinizing the street: Poverty, morality, and the pitfalls of urban ethnography. *American Journal of Sociology, 107,* 1468–1532.

Wacquant, L. (2011). From slavery to mass incarceration: Rethinking the race question in the United States. In M. Tonry (Ed.), *Why punish? How much?* (pp. 382–402). New York: Oxford University Press.

Wagner, M. (2015). 51 officers killed in the line of duty last year, nearly double 2013's historic low: FBI. *New York Daily News.* Retrieved from http://www.nydailynews.com/news/national/51-officers-killed-line-duty-year-fbi-article-1.2217901

Wakeling, S., Jorgensen, M., Michaelson, S., Begay, M., Hartmann, F., & Wiener, M. (2001). *Policing on Indian reservations.* Washington, DC: U.S. Department of Justice.

Walker, M. (2015). Finding a home after prison tough for released felons. *USA Today.* Retrieved from http://www.usatoday.com/story/news/nation/2015/02/28/another-barrier-prison-finding-home/24197429/

Walker, S. (1989). *Sense and nonsense about crime: A policy guide* (2nd ed.). Pacific Grove, CA: Brooks/Cole.

Walker, S. (2001). *Police accountability: The role of citizen oversight.* Belmont, CA: Wadsworth/Thomson Learning.

Walker, S., & Katz, S. M. (2002). *Police in America.* New York: McGraw-Hill.

Walker, S., Spohn, C., & DeLone, M. (1996). *The color of justice: Race, ethnicity, and crime in America.* Belmont, CA: Wadsworth.

Walker, S., Spohn, C., & DeLone, M. (2007). *The color of justice: Race, ethnicity, and crime in America* (4th ed.). Belmont, CA: Thomson Learning.

Walker, S., Spohn, C., & DeLone, M. (2012). *The color of justice: Race, ethnicity, and crime in America* (5th ed.). Belmont, CA: Cengage/Wadsworth.

Walker-Barnes, C. J., Arrue, R. M., & Mason, C. A. (1998). *Girls and gangs: Identifying risk factors for female gang involvement.* Retrieved from http://www.unc.edu/~cwalkerb/present1/pdf

Walsh, A. (2004). *Race and crime: A biosocial analysis.* New York: Nova Science.

Walsh, A., & Beaver, K. M. (Eds.). (2009). *Biosocial criminology: New directions in theory and research.* New York: Routledge.

Walsh, A., & Ellis, L. (Eds.). (2003). *Biosocial criminology: Challenging environmentalism's supremacy.* New York: Nova Science.

Ward, G. (2001). *Color lines of social control: Juvenile justice administration in a racialized social system, 1825–2000.* Unpublished doctoral dissertation, University of Michigan, Ann Arbor.

Ward, G. K. (2012). *The black child savers: Racial democracy and juvenile justice.* Chicago: University of Chicago Press.

Ward, G. (2014). The slow violence of state organized race crime. *Theoretical Criminology, 19*(3), 299–314.

Ward, G., & Kupchik, A. (2009). Accountable to what? Professional orientations toward accountability-based juvenile justice. *Punishment & Society, 11*(1), 85–109.

Warner, S. B. (1929). *Survey of criminal statistics in the United States for National Commission on Law Observance and Enforcement.* Washington, DC: Government Printing Office.

Warner, S. B. (1931). Crimes known to the police: An index of crime? *Harvard Law Review, 45,* 307.

Warnshuis, P. L. (1931). Crime and criminal justice among the Mexicans of Illinois. In *Crime and the foreign born* (National Commission on Law Observance and Enforcement, Report No. 10, pp. 265–329). Washington, DC: Government Printing Office.

Warren, P. Y., Tomaskovic-Devey, D., Smith, W. R., Zingraff, M., & Mason, M. (2006). Driving while Black: Bias processes and racial disparity in stops. *Criminology, 44,* 709–736.

Washington, L. (1994). *Black judges on justice: Perspectives from the bench.* New York: New Press.

Watts, F. P. (1941). A comparative clinical study of delinquent and nondelinquent boys. *Journal of Negro Education, 10*(2), 190–207.

Websdale, N. (2001). *Policing the poor: From slave plantation to public housing.* Boston: Northeastern University Press.

Wegman, J. (2014). Supreme Court revisits sentences for juveniles. *New York Times.* Retrieved from http://takingnote.blogs.nytimes.com/2014/12/13/supreme-court-revisits-life-sentences-for-juveniles

Weisburd, D., Greenspan, R., Hamilton, E., Williams, H., & Bryand, K. (2000). *Police attitudes toward abuse of authority: Findings from a national study.* Washington, DC: U.S. Department of Justice.

Weisheit, R. A., & Wells, L. E. (2004). Youth gangs in rural America. *NIJ Journal, 251,* 2–6.

Weitzer, R. (1999). Citizens' perceptions of police misconduct: Race and neighborhood context. *Justice Quarterly, 16,* 819–846.

Weitzer, R., & Tuch, S. (2002). Perceptions of racial profiling: Race, class, and personal experience. *Criminology, 40,* 435–456.

Weitzer, R., & Tuch, S. (2006). *Race and police in America: Conflict and reform.* New York: Cambridge University Press.

Weitzer, R., Tuch, S. A., & Skogan, W. G. (2008). Police-community relations in a majority-black city. *Journal of Research in Crime and Delinquency, 45,* 398–428.

Welch, K., & Payne, A. A. (2012). Exclusionary school punishment: The effect of racial threat on expulsion. *Youth Violence & Juvenile Justice, 10*(2), 155–171. Retrieved from http://yvj .sagepub.com

Wenzel, S., Longshore, D., Turner, S., & Ridgely, M. S. (2001). Drug courts: A bridge between criminal justice and health services. *Journal of Criminal Justice, 29,* 241–253.

Western, B. (2006). *Punishment and inequality in America.* New York: Russell Sage.

Western, B., & Wildeman, C. (2009). The Black family and mass incarceration. *Annals of the American Academy of Political and Social Sciences, 621,* 221–242.

Whitaker, C. (1990). *Black victims.* Washington, DC: U.S. Department of Justice.

The White House. (2014, February 27). Presidential memorandum: Creating and expanding ladders of opportunity for boys and young men of color [Press release]. Retrieved from https://www .whitehouse.gov

Whren v. United States, 517 U.S. 806 (1996).

Wilbanks, W. (1987). *The myth of a racist criminal justice system.* Pacific Grove, CA: Brooks/Cole.

Wildeman, C., & Wakefield, S. (2014). The long arm of the law: The concentration of incarceration in families in the era of mass incarceration. *Journal of Gender, Race, and Justice, 17,* 367–389.

Wilder, K. (2003). *Assessing residents' satisfaction with community policing: A look into quality of life and interaction with police.* Unpublished master's thesis, Old Dominion University, Norfolk, VA.

Wilkins v. Maryland State Police, Civ. No. MJG-93-468 at 7 (D.MD. 1994).

Wilkins v. Missouri (1989). See Stanford v. Kentucky.

Williams, E. (1944). *Capitalism and slavery.* London: Andre Deutsch.

Williams, F. P., and M. D. McShane. (2010). *Criminological theory* (5th ed.). Upper Saddle River, NJ: Prentice Hall.

Williams, H., & Murphy, P. (1990). *The evolving strategy of police: A minority view.* Washington, DC: National Institute of Justice.

Williams, M. (2002). A comparison of sentencing outcomes for defendants with public defenders versus retained counsel in a Florida circuit court. *Justice Systems Journal, 23,* 249–257.

Williams, M. R., & Holcomb, J. E. (2004). The interactive effects of victim race and gender on death sentence disparity findings. *Homicide Studies, 8,* 350–376.

Williams, S. (2007, October 8). Police urged not to check legal status: Activists want immigration standing off-limits in stops; some chiefs agree. *The Milwaukee Journal Sentinel.* Retrieved March 7, 2008, from http://find.galegroup.com/ips/retrieve.do

Wilson, J. Q., & Herrnstein, R. (1985). *Crime and human nature.* New York: Simon & Schuster.

Wilson, W. J. (1987). *The truly disadvantaged.* Chicago: University of Chicago Press.

Wilson, W. J. (1996). *When work disappears: The world of the new urban poor.* New York: A. A. Knopf.

Wilson, W. J., & Chaddha, A. (2009). The role of theory in ethnographic theory. *Ethnography, 10,* 549–564.

Wilson, S., Johnson, J. & Greene, H. T. (2015). *An exploratory of school punishment and DMC in Texas.* Paper presented at the annual meeting of the Academy of Criminal Justice Sciences, Orlando, Florida, March 6, 2015.

Winterdyk, J., & Ruddell, R. (2010). Managing prison gangs: Results from a survey of U.S. prison systems. *Journal of Criminal Justice, 38,* 730–736.

Withrow, B. L. (2006). *Racial profiling: From rhetoric to reason.* Upper Saddle River, NJ: Prentice Hall.

Wolf, A. M., & Hartney, C. (2005). A portrait of detained youth in the state of Hawaii. *Crime & Delinquency, 51,* 180–191.

Wolf, A. M., Graziano, J., & Hartney, C. (2009). The provision and completion of gender-specific services for girls on probation variations by race and ethnicity. *Crime & Delinquency, 55, 2,* 294–312.

Wolfgang, M. (1963). Uniform crime reports: A critical appraisal. *University of Pennsylvania Law Review, 111,* 708–738.

Wolfgang, M. E. (1958). *Patterns in criminal homicide.* Philadelphia: University of Pennsylvania Press.

Wolfgang, M. E., & Ferracuti, F. (1967). *The subculture of violence: Towards an integrated theory in criminology.* London: Tavistock.

Wolfgang, M. E., & Riedel, M. (1973). Race, judicial discretion, and the death penalty. *The Annals of the American Academy of Political and Social Sciences, 407,* 119–133.

Woodward, C. (1971). *The origins of the New South, 1877–1913.* Baton Rouge: Louisiana University Press.

Wooldredge, J. (2012). Distinguishing race effects on pre-trial release and sentencing decisions. *Justice Quarterly. 29,* 41–75.

Wordes, M., Bynum, T. S., & Corley, C. J. (1994). Locking up youth: The impact of race on detention decisions. *Journal of Research in Crime and Delinquency, 31,* 149–165.

Work, M. (1900). Crime among the Negroes of Chicago. *American Journal of Sociology, 6,* 204–223.

Work, M. (1913). Negro criminality in the South. *Annals of the American Academy of Political and Social Sciences, 49,* 74–80.

Work, M. (1939). Negro criminality in the South. *Annals of the American Academy of Political and Social Sciences, 49,* 74–80.

Wright, B. (1987). *Black robes, White justice.* New York: Carol.

Wright, J. P. (2009). Inconvenient truths: Science, race, and crime. In A. Walsh & K. M. Beaver (Eds.). *Biosocial criminology: New directions in theory and research* (pp. 137–153). New York: Routledge.

Wright, J. P., & Boisvert, D. (2009). What biosocial criminology offers criminology. *Criminal Justice and Behavior, 36,* 1228–1240.

Wright, R. R. (1969). *The Negro in Pennsylvania: A study in economic history.* New York: Arno Press and *The New York Times.* (Original work published 1912)

Wu, F. H. (2002). *Yellow: Race in America beyond black and white.* New York: Basic Books.

Xu, Y., Fiedler, M. L., & Flaming, K. H. (2005). Discovering the impact of community policing: The broken windows thesis, collective efficacy, and citizens' judgment. *The Journal of Research in Crime and Delinquency, 42,* 147–186.

Young, V. (1993). Punishment and social conditions: The control of Black juveniles in the 1800s in Maryland. In A. G. Hess & P. F. Clement (Eds.), *History of juvenile delinquency: A collection of essays on crime committed by young offenders, in history and in selected countries* (pp. 557–575). Aalen, Germany: Scientia Verlag.

Young, V. (1994). Race and gender in the establishment of juvenile institutions: The case of the South. *Prison Journal, 74,* 244–265.

Young, V. (2007, October 25). Immigration crackdown feasts on motorists. *St. Louis Post-Dispatch.* Retrieved March 7, 2008, from General Reference Center Gold, Gale, Texas Southern University.

Young, V., & Reviere, R. (2006). *Women behind bars: Gender and race in U.S. prisons.* Boulder, CO: Lynne Rienner.

Young v. Robinson, 29 Cr. L. 2587 (1981).

Zalman, M. (2011). *Qualitatively estimating the incidence of wrongful convictions—a postscript.* Retrieved from http://works.bepress.com/marvin_zalman/1

Zane, N., Aoki, B., Ho, T., Huang, L., & Jang, M. (1998). Dosage-related changes in a culturally responsive prevention program for Asian American youth. In J. Valentine, J. A. De Jong, & N. J. Kennedy (Eds.), *Substance abuse prevention in multicultural communities* (pp. 105–125). Binghamton, NY: Haworth Press.

Zangrando, R. L. (1980). *The NAACP crusade against lynching, 1900–1950.* Philadelphia: Temple University Press.

Zatz, M. S. (1987). The changing form of racial/ethnic biases in sentencing. *Journal of Research in Crime and Delinquency, 24,* 69–92.

Zimmerman, C. S. (2002). From the jailhouse to the courthouse: The role of informants in wrongful convictions. In S. Westervelt & J. A. Humphrey (Eds.), *Wrongly convicted: Perspectives on failed justice* (pp. 55–76). New Brunswick, NJ: Rutgers University Press.

Zimring, F. (2003). *The contradictions of American capital punishment.* New York: Oxford University Press.

Index

About the Authors

Shaun L. Gabbidon, PhD, is distinguished professor of criminal justice at Penn State Harrisburg. Professor Gabbidon has served as a fellow at Harvard University's W. E. B. Du Bois Institute for Afro-American Research and has taught at the Center for Africana Studies at the University of Pennsylvania. The author of more than 100 scholarly publications, including more than 60 peer-reviewed articles and 11 books, his most recent books include *Criminological Perspectives on Race and Crime*, 3rd ed. (2015, Routledge); and the co-authored book *A Theory of African American Offending* (2011, Routledge). Dr. Gabbidon can be contacted at slg13@psu.edu.

Helen Taylor Greene, PhD, is a professor in the Department of Administration of Justice in the Barbara Jordan–Mickey Leland School of Public Affairs at Texas Southern University. She is an author, co-author, and co-editor of numerous articles, book chapters, and books. She co-edited the *Encyclopedia of Race and Crime* (2009, Sage Publications) and *Race and Crime: A Text/Reader* (2011, Sage Publications) with Dr. Gabbidon. In 2014, she received the W. E. B. Du Bois Award from the Western Society of Criminology for contributions to the study of race and crime. Dr. Taylor Greene can be contacted at greeneht@tsu.edu.